T0320184

Regenerative Agriculture

This book aims to focus on the current state of knowledge and scientific advances about the complex and intertwined issues of regenerative farming as a transformative solution for offsetting the disastrous climate effects of burning fossil fuels and impairments of natural resource bases. Regenerative agriculture advocates no-till practices, planting cover crops, integrating livestock and crop production, improving animal welfare practices, improving the social and economic well-being of communities, sequestering carbon, improving soil health, and increasing yields and profit with a positive impact on food access or food safety regardless of farm size.

This book examines the innovations that will equip agriculture to cope with the competing challenges of addressing food and nutrition security, improving livelihoods, combating climate change, and sustainably managing natural resources. The scope of this book extends to agricultural scientists, students, consultants, site owners, industrial stakeholders, regulators, and policymakers.

Regenerative Agriculture
Translating Science to Action

Edited by
Amitava Rakshit, Manoj Parihar, Vijay Singh Meena,
Prakash Kumar Jha, Deepranjan Sarkar, and
Purushothaman Chirakkuzhyil Abhilash

CRC Press
Taylor & Francis Group
Boca Raton London New York

CRC Press is an imprint of the
Taylor & Francis Group, an **informa** business

Designed cover image: Amitava Rakshit

First edition published 2024
By CRC Press
2385 NW Executive Center Drive, Suite 320, Boca Raton, FL 33431

and by CRC Press
4 Park Square, Milton Park, Abingdon, Oxon, OX14 4RN

CRC Press is an imprint of Taylor & Francis Group, LLC

© 2024 selection and editorial matter, Amitava Rakshit, Manoj Parihar, Vijay Singh Meena, Prakash Kumar Jha, Deepranjan Sarkar, and Purushothaman Chirakkuzhyil Abhilash; individual chapters, the contributors

Reasonable efforts have been made to publish reliable data and information, but the author and publisher cannot assume responsibility for the validity of all materials or the consequences of their use. The authors and publishers have attempted to trace the copyright holders of all material reproduced in this publication and apologize to copyright holders if permission to publish in this form has not been obtained. If any copyright material has not been acknowledged please write and let us know so we may rectify in any future reprint.

Except as permitted under U.S. Copyright Law, no part of this book may be reprinted, reproduced, transmitted, or utilized in any form by any electronic, mechanical, or other means, now known or hereafter invented, including photocopying, microfilming, and recording, or in any information storage or retrieval system, without written permission from the publishers.

For permission to photocopy or use material electronically from this work, access www.copyright.com or contact the Copyright Clearance Center, Inc. (CCC), 222 Rosewood Drive, Danvers, MA 01923, 978-750-8400. For works that are not available on CCC please contact mpkbookspermissions@tandf.co.uk

Trademark notice: Product or corporate names may be trademarks or registered trademarks and are used only for identification and explanation without intent to infringe.

Library of Congress Cataloging-in-Publication Data
Names: Rakshit, Amitava, editor. | Parihar, Manoj, editor. | Meena, Vijay Singh, editor. |
Jha, Prakash Kumar, editor. | Sarkar, Deepranjan, editor. | Abhilash, P. C. (Purushothaman Chirakkuzhyil)
Title: Regenerative agriculture : translating science to action / edited by
Amitava Rakshit, Manoj Parihar, Vijay Singh Meena, Prakash Jha,
Deepranjan Sarkar and Purushothaman Chirakkuzhyil Abhilash
Description: First edition | Boca Raton, FL : CRC Press, 2024 |
Includes bibliographical references and index.
Identifiers: LCCN 2023053220 (print) | LCCN 2023053221 (ebook) |
ISBN 9781032314051 (hardback) | ISBN 9781032314068 (paperback) |
ISBN 9781003309581 (ebook)
Subjects: LCSH: Organic farming. | Sustainable agriculture. | Agricultural innovations. |
Agriculture--Environmental aspects. | Crops and climate.
Classification: LCC S605.5 .R384 2024 (print) | LCC S605.5 (ebook) |
DDC 631.5/84–dc23/eng/20240207
LC record available at https://lccn.loc.gov/2023053220
LC ebook record available at https://lccn.loc.gov/2023053221

ISBN: 9781032314051 (hbk)
ISBN: 9781032314068 (pbk)
ISBN: 9781003309581 (ebk)

DOI: 10.1201/9781003309581

Typeset in Times
by codeMantra

Dedication

Dedicated to our parents for their endless love, support, and encouragement to go on every adventure

Contents

SECTION I   Ideas and Basic Principles of Regenerative Agriculture

SECTION II   Strategies and Platform Regenerative Agriculture: Research and Development

SECTION III Converging Science to Action in Different Continents: Practice and Performance

Preface

Agriculture faces unprecedented and devastating challenges. As a result of intensive farming and indiscriminate use of natural and introduced resources, soil capacity is dramatically declining, with some experts predicting fewer harvests remaining and the additional agony of losing soil faster than it's replenished. Ownership of large-scale farms—where most of the food and agricultural pollution comes from—is increasingly concentrated in the hands of industrial or those who tend to value immediate gains and profits over the long-term health of our land and people.

Regenerative farming, however, presents solutions to transform farmers into environmental and societal heroes. It promotes the health of degraded soils by restoring their organic carbon. Regenerative agriculture sequesters atmospheric carbon dioxide, reversing industrial agriculture's contributions to climate change. By reducing erosion and water pollution, regenerative practices are producing healthier soils. Reversing climate change by rebuilding soil organic matter and restoring degraded soil biodiversity can reverse climate change, resulting in both carbon drawdown and improving the water cycle. Specifically, regenerative agriculture is a holistic land management practice that leverages the power of photosynthesis in plants to close the carbon cycle and build soil health, crop resilience, and nutrient density. Regenerative agriculture reverses this paradigm to build for the future.

We have looked into greater detail at these issues, with a particular focus on how regenerative agriculture could save soil, water, and the climate. We will present a holistic overview of the shifting emphasis from yield toward the management of a functioning ecosystem, which is not well documented will specifically be highlighted. Renowned scientists from all over the world who are working on the above-mentioned have contributed to this book. The scope of this ebook extends to agricultural and social scientists, students, consultants, agrarian stakeholders, regulators, and policymakers. This book focuses on the current state of knowledge and scientific advances about the complex and intertwined issues of regenerative farming as a transformative solution for offsetting the disastrous climate effects of burning fossil fuels and impairments of natural resource bases.

Acknowledgments

We extend our thanks to all the valued contributors who produced updated ideas from no-till practices, planting cover crops, integrating livestock and crop production, improving animal welfare practices, and improving the social and economic well-being of communities from the unique perspective of being involved in both basic and applied research.

We also wish to acknowledge the help rendered by IOE Cell, Banaras Hindu University, and the Council of Science and Technology, Uttar Pradesh, in preparing this handbook. We gratefully acknowledge the support of the production team led by Renu Upadhaya and Joytsna Jangra.

Last but not least, we would like to express our deepest gratitude to our caring, loving, and supportive family members for their generous support and encouragement during the preparation of this manuscript.

Editor Biographies

Dr. Amitava Rakshit, an IIT-Kharagpur alumnus, is the faculty member in the Department of Soil Science and Agricultural Chemistry at the Institute of Agricultural Sciences, Banaras Hindu University (BHU), Varanasi, UP, India. His research areas include: Nutrient use efficiency, simulations modeling, organic farming, integrated nutrient management, and bioremediation. His consulting capabilities are: Composting techniques, soil health management, and input quality control. He was involved in "Participatory Research" and "Lab to Land" Programmes of ICAR; Department of Agricultural Cooperation, Government of India; Department of Agriculture, Government of West Bengal; NHB, New Delhi; and NHM for on-farm demonstrations of agro-technologies in cereals/pulses/oilseeds/cash crops/vegetables/fruits. He was actively involved in imparting training and dissemination of technical knowledge and information to diversified end users. He has supervised approximately seven research projects, many in partnership with industry. He is widely acknowledged for his skills in linking research with the broader community in regional languages. Currently, he has been working closely with undergraduate and post-graduate students in BHU. He has visited Norway, Finland, Denmark, France, Austria, Russia, Thailand, Egypt, Turkey, UAE, and Bangladesh on a number of occasions pertaining to his research work and presentation. Dr. Rakshit has previously worked at the Department of Agriculture, Government of West Bengal, in research extension and implementation roles. He is a fellow of TWAS Nxt (Italy), Biovision Nxt (France), Society of Earth Scientists, and Crop and Weed Science Society. Currently, he is presently the Chief Editor of the International Journal of Agriculture Environment and Biotechnology (NAAS: 4.55). He has been serving as a review college member of the British Ecological Society, London, since 2011--2012. He was awarded with Best Teacher's Award by BHU (ICAR, New Delhi) both at both undergraduate and postgraduate layer in 2012 and 2014. He is a member of the Global Forum on Food Security and Nutrition of FAO, Rome, and the Commission on Ecosystem Management of the International Union for Conservation of Nature. He is the author of twenty-two (22) books (Springer, CRC, Elsevier, CBS, ATINER, ICFAI, Kalyani, Jain Publishers, IBDC, Scientific Publishers, and DPS). He has published 100 research papers, 40 book chapters, 28 popular articles, and 3 manuals.

Dr. Manoj Parihar is currently working at ICAR-Vivekananda Parvatiya Krishi Anusandhan Sansthan, Almora, India, as a Soil Scientist in the Crop Production Division. He did his graduation from SKRAU, Bikaner, and was selected as an ICAR-JRF fellow for post-graduation at Banaras Hindu University (BHU), Varanasi. He has been awarded his doctorate from the same university in the year 2018. He has received various recognitions such as ICAR-SRF, UGC-BSR, and UGC-RGNF, etc. His research works extend to arbuscular mycorrhizal fungal diversity, ecological functions, and inoculum production aspects for improving soil health and sustainable agricultural production. He has edited two books and has published more than 10 book chapters and more than 25 peer-reviewed journal papers.

Dr. Vijay Singh Meena is working as a Project Coordinator at the International Maize and Wheat Improvement Center (CIMMYT)-Borlaug Institute for South Asia (BISA). He worked as a scientist at ICAR-Vivekananda Parvatiya Krishi Anusandhan Sansthan, Almora, India. His research areas include various aspects of soil aggregation, carbon management index, and carbon and nitrogen sequestration potential under different land types and cropping systems of the north-western Indian Himalayas. He identified the carbon management index as the key indicator to measure soil degradation in different agroecosystems. His research revealed that the application of FYM and vermicompost along with vegetative barriers across the slope are highly effective in sustaining the soil quality. He reported that potassium solubilizing rhizobacteria (KSR) enhances 25-40% potassium (K) availability and helps plants to uptake K from the soils. Dr. Meena identified that the combined application of organic and inorganic sources is important in sustaining the productivity of Himalayan soils and preventing soil erosion. Combined use of FYM and inorganic fertilizers on an equal N basis (50+50FYM) resulted in higher productivity of maize and wheat crops than an individual source. However, in-situ green manuring and inorganic fertilizers on an equal N basis (50+50GM) resulted in the reduction of runoff and soil loss, and maintained system productivity, leading to the conservation of natural resources in soils of the maize-wheat cropping system. He is instrumental in the preparation and distribution of >4,000 soil health cards to different hill farmers at the current institute. He recently reported the carbon and nitrogen sequestration potential of different land use and cropping systems in the Indian Himalayas. He also edited seven Springer books on microbes and agricultural sustainability. He has received several scholarships and awards during his academic and professional career. In a nutshell, Dr. Meena is working in the field of natural resources management for sustainable agricultural production. He has an h-index of 55, and i10-index of 112 with more than 9,300 citations in international literature.

Dr. Prakash Kumar Jha is currently working as an Assistant Professor of Agricultural Climatology in the Department of Plant and Soil Sciences at Mississippi State University (MSU), USA. Before joining MSU, he served as an associate scientist and postdoctoral fellow at Feed the Future Innovation Lab for Collaborative Research on Sustainable Intensification, Kansas State University, USA. He holds a Ph.D. in Crop and Soil Sciences from Michigan State University, USA; an M.Sc. degree in Environmental Sciences from Indian Agricultural Research Institute, India; and a B.Sc. degree in Agricultural Sciences from Banaras Hindu University, India. He has published over 35 research articles in highly respected journals, seven book chapters, and has edited two books. He is a crop and climate modeler with interest in sustainable agricultural systems. His specific research interests focus on investigating the influence of agronomic management on crop growth and development from field to ecological scale. He investigates complexities in agricultural systems, integrating crop simulation models, remote sensing, and climate forecast to formulate decision support systems for better management strategies at multiple scales of agroecosystems. He is passionate about teaching and the opportunity to mentor students interested in sustainable agricultural landscapes and fundamentals of digital agroecosystems.

 **Dr. Deepranjan Sarkar** is working as an Assistant Professor (Soil Science) in the Agriculture Department of Integral Institute of Agricultural Science and Technology, Integral University, Lucknow, India. He received his M.Sc. (Ag.) degree in Soil Science and Agricultural Chemistry from Uttar Banga Krishi Viswavidyalaya and his Ph.D. from Banaras Hindu University, India. His research interests include soil fertility, plant nutrition, plant-microbe interactions, carbon sequestration, and UNSDGs. During his Ph.D. program, he performed a comprehensive assessment of bio-priming technology in the Middle Gangetic Plains of India and presented his works at numerous national and international seminars or conferences. Additionally, he is involved in developing new technologies for the sustainable management of soil health and crop production. Dr. Sarkar is involved in teaching soil science subjects at UG and PG levels. He has received prestigious awards from BHU, IIT-KGP, TWAS, and the Soil Science Society of America. He is a Life Member/Member of AMI-India, ISCA-Kolkata, IUCN, etc. He has authored more than 30 peer-reviewed publications. Currently, he is serving as a Guest Editor in Sustainability (MDPI), an Early Career Editorial Board Member of Resource, Environment and Sustainability (Elsevier), and a Review Editor in Frontiers Journals. He is also acting as a Reviewer of Peer-Reviewed Journals of Springer, Elsevier, PLoS, Wiley, etc.

 **Dr. Purushothaman Chirakkuzhyil Abhilash** is a senior Assistant Professor of Sustainability Science at the Institute of Environment and Sustainable Development (IESD) at Banaras Hindu University, in Varanasi, India. He is also the Lead of the Agroecosystem Specialist Group of the IUCN-Commission on Ecosystem Management. He is a fellow of the National Academy of Agricultural Sciences, India. His research interests include sustainable biomass production from marginal and degraded lands for supporting a bio-based economy, restoring degraded lands for regaining ecosystem services, land system management, sustainable utilization of agrobiodiversity, nature-based solutions and ecosystem-based adaptations for climate-resilient and planet-healthy food production, and sustainable agri-scape management for food and nutritional security. He is particularly interested in sustainability analysis, system sustainability, sustainability indicators, circular economy principles, policy realignment, and the localization of UN-SDGs for sustainable development. He is sitting on the editorial board of prestigious journals in Ecology/Environment/Sustainability from leading international publishers, and is also serving as a subject expert for UN-IPBES, IRP-UNEP, UNDP-BES Network, IPCC, UNCCD, APN, GLP, and IUCN Commissions (CEM, CEC, CEESP, and SSC) for fostering global sustainability.

Contributors

Mert Acar
Department of Soil Science and Plant Nutrition
Cukurova University
Adana, Turkey

Becky Nancy Aloo
University of Eldoret
Eldoret, Kenya

Mariya Ansari
Department of Mycology and Plant Pathology
Banaras Hindu University
Varanasi, India

Raghupathi Balasani
Jawaharlal Nehru Technological University
Hyderabad, India

Arijit Barman
ICAR-National Bureau of Soil Survey and
    Land Use Planning, Regional Centre
Jorhat, India

Prabhakar Prasad Barnwal
Division of Soil Science and Agricultural
    Chemistry
Indian Agricultural Research Institute
New Delhi, India

Ankita Begam
ICAR-Agricultural Technology Application
    Research Institute Kolkata
Kolkata, West Bengal

Shiwani Bhadwal
Department of Agricultural Economics,
    Institute of Agricultural Sciences
Banaras Hindu University
Varanasi, India

Manju Bhargavi
Agriculture Polytechnic
PJTSAU
Nizamabad, India

Sayantan Bhattacharjee
Department of Aquatic Environment
    Management, Faculty of Fishery Sciences
West Bengal University of Animal and Fishery
    Sciences
Kolkata, India

Malay K. Bhowmick
International Rice Research Institute (IRRI)
South Asia Regional Centre (ISARC)
Varanasi, India

Serdar Bilen
Department of Soil Science and Plant
    Nutrition
Ataturk University
Erzurum, Turkey

Melis Cercioglu
Department of Forest Engineering, Faculty of
    Forestry
Izmir Katip Celebi University
Izmir, Turkey

Chingtham Chanbisana
College of Horticulture
Imphal, India

Anirudha Chattopadhyay
Pulses Research Station
S.D. Agricultural University
Sardarkushinagar, India

Bayram Cagdas Demirel
Department of Plant and Animal Production,
    Vocational School of Technical Sciences
Akdeniz University
Antalya, Turkey

Anwesha Dey
Department of Agricultural Economics,
    Institute of Agricultural Sciences
Banaras Hindu University
Varanasi, India

Bodiga Divya
Sam Higginbottom University of Agricultural,
    Technology and Sciences
Prayagraj, India

Gopal Dutta
Department of Agricultural Meteorology
Bidhan Chandra Krishi Viswavidyalaya
Nadia, India

Susanta Dutta
Agronomy Division, School of Agriculture
Lovely Professional University
Phagwara, India

BisweswarGorain
ICAR-CSSRI
RRS Bharuch
Gujarat, India

Gafur Gozukara
Department of Soil Science and Plant
    Nutrition
Eskisehir Osmangazi University
Eskişehir, Turkey

Surabhi Hota
ICAR-National Bureau of Soil Survey and
    Land Use Planning, Regional Centre
Jorhat, India

Sofia Houida
Mohammed V University
Rabat, Morocco

Saritha JD
Agricultural College
PJTSAU
Nagarkurnool, India

Kapil Jindal
Department of Mycology and Plant Pathology,
    Institute of Agricultural Sciences
Banaras Hindu University
Varanasi, India

Sonali Katoch
Department of Agricultural Economics,
    Institute of Agricultural Sciences
Banaras Hindu University
Varanasi, India

Arun Kumar
AICRP on Sorghum Regional Agricultural
    Research Station
Nandyal, India

Ashok Kumar
ICAR-National Bureau of Soil Survey and
    Land Use Planning, Regional Centre
New Delhi, India

Rahul Kumar
Department of Mycology and Plant Pathology,
    Institute of Agricultural Sciences
Banaras Hindu University
Varanasi, India

Lalhmingsanga
Multi-technology Testing Centre & Vocational
    Training Centre
Imphal, India

Benicha, M.
National Institute of Agricultural Research
    (INRA)
Rabat, Morocco

R. S. Meena
ICAR-National Bureau of Soil Survey and
    Land Use Planning, Regional Centre
Jorhat, India

Aalok Mishra
Department of Mycology and Plant Pathology
Banaras Hindu University
Varanasi, India

Ajay Kumar Mishra
International Rice Research Institute (IRRI)
South Asia Regional Centre (ISARC)
Varanasi, India

K.K. Mourya
ICAR-National Bureau of Soil Survey and
    Land Use Planning, Regional Centre
Jorhat, India

Arpan Mukherjee
Institute of Environment and Sustainable
    Development
Banaras Hindu University
Varanasi, India

Kishore Nalabolu
College of Engineering, Madakasira
Acharya N G Ranga Agricultural University
Hyderabad, India

Benson Nyongesa Ouma
University of Eldoret
Eldoret, Kenya

Ekrem Ozlu
Great Lakes Bioenergy Research Center
W.K. Kellogg Biological Station
and
Department of Plant, Soil and Microbial
   Sciences
Michigan State University
Hickory Corners, Michigan

Bappa Paramanik
Dakshin Dinajpur Krishi Vigyan Kendra
Uttar Banga Krishi Viswavidyalaya
Dinajpur, India

Srijita Paul
SAMETI
Ramakrishna Mission Ashrama
Kolkata, India

Subhadip Paul
Division of Soil Science and Agricultural
   Chemistry
Indian Agricultural Research Institute
New Delhi, India

Panneerselvam Peramaiyan
International Rice Research Institute (IRRI)
South Asia Regional Centre (ISARC)
Varanasi, India

Jogarao Poiba
Regional Agricultural Research Station
Chintapalle, India

Aboutayeb, R.
National Institute of Agricultural Research
   (INRA)
Rabat, Morocco

Moussadek, R.
ICARDA Rabat
Rabat, Morocco

Mrabet, R.
National Institute of Agricultural Research
   (INRA)
Rabat, Morocco

Sana Rafi
Jamia Millia Islamia
New Delhi, India

Dewali Roy
Indian Agricultural Research Institute
New Delhi, India

Dinesha S
Dr. Rajendra Prasad Central Agricultural
   University
Pusa, India

Rakesh S
Uttar Banga Krishi Viswavidyalaya
CoochBehar, India

Rahul Sadhukhan
Multi-technology Testing Centre & Vocational
   Training Centre
Imphal, India

Himadri Saha
Bidhan Chandra Krishi Viswavidyalaya
Nadia, India

Sayantan Sahu
Department of Chemistry and Biochemistry
University of Maryland
College Park, Maryland

U.S. Saikia
ICAR-National Bureau of Soil Survey and
   Land Use Planning, Regional Centre
Jorhat, India

Ankita Sarkar
Department of Mycology and Plant Pathology
Banaras Hindu University
Varanasi, India

Ajay Satpute
ICAR-National Bureau of Soil Survey and
   Land Use Planning, Regional Centre
Jorhat, India

L. Devarishi Sharma
Multi-technology Testing Centre & Vocational
    Training Centre
Imphal, India

Sheetal Sharma
International Rice Research Institute (IRRI)
South Asia Regional Centre (ISARC)
Varanasi, India

Anirban Sil
Division of Agricultural Chemicals
Indian Agricultural Research Institute
New Delhi, India

Ashu Singh
Department of Soil Science and Agricultural
    Chemistry, Institute of Agricultural Sciences
Banaras Hindu University
Varanasi, India

H. P. Singh
Department of Agricultural Economics,
    Institute of Agricultural Sciences
Banaras Hindu University
Varanasi, India

J. P. Singh
Department of Plant Pathology
S.M.M.T.D. College
Ballia, India

Jayesh Singh
Department of Soil Science and Agricultural
    Chemistry, Institute of Agricultural Sciences
Banaras Hindu University
Varanasi, India

Rakesh Singh
Department of Agricultural Economics,
    Institute of Agricultural Sciences
Banaras Hindu University
Varanasi, India

Satyendra Pratap Singh
Department of Mycology and Plant Pathology,
    Institute of Agricultural Sciences
Banaras Hindu University
Varanasi, India

Sudhanshu Singh
International Rice Research Institute (IRRI)
South Asia Regional Centre (ISARC)
Varanasi, India

Rojeet Thangjam
College of Horticulture
Imphal, India

Gopal Tiwari
ICAR-National Bureau of Soil Survey and
    Land Use Planning
Nagpur, India

John Baptist Tumuhairwe
Makerere University
Kampala, Uganda

Gokhan Ucar
Western Mediterranean Agricultural Research
    Institute
Antalya, Turkey

Shilpi Verma
ICAR-National Bureau of Soil Survey and
    Land Use Planning, Regional Centre
New Delhi, India

Beatrice Angiyo Were
University of Eldoret
Eldoret, Kenya

Section I

Ideas and Basic Principles of Regenerative Agriculture

1 Inorganic C Dynamics in Soil
Implications on C Sequestration and Soil Quality

Bisweswar Gorain and Srijita Paul

1.1 INTRODUCTION

Soil carbon, comprising soil inorganic carbon (SIC) and organic carbon (SOC), is the largest carbon pool in the terrestrial ecosystem and thus plays an important role in the global carbon cycle and climate change (Lal, 2004; Lorenz and Lal 2010). The estimated global SOC storage ranges from 1,220 to 1,576 Pg, and that of the SIC storage is 700 to 1,700 Pg in the top $100\,cm^3$ soil (Lal, 2010). Most of the studies related to climate change and crop production revolve around SOC dynamics, paying very little attention to SIC, despite it being a crucial component of carbon sequestration and climate change mitigation (Lal and Kimble, 2000). Soil inorganic carbon, primarily calcium and magnesium carbonate, is formed mainly through the following two reactions:

$$CO_2 + H_2O = HCO_3^- + H^+ \qquad (1.1)$$

$$Ca^{2+} + 2HCO_3^- = CaCO_3 + H_2O + CO_2 \qquad (1.2)$$

Thus, the formation of calcium carbonate is affected by the concentration of carbon dioxide (CO_2) in soil air, soil reaction (pH), Ca^{2+} content and soil moisture regime. An increase in soil pH (i.e., a decrease in H^+) would drive the reaction (1.1) to the right, resulting in enhanced production of HCO_3^-. And until the point where there is no limitation of soluble Ca^{2+}/Mg^{2+} in soil, precipitation of calcium/magnesium carbonate would occur in soil. On the other hand, an increase in soil CO_2 or a decrease in soil pH would drive the reaction (1.2) to the left. In that scenario, prevailing acidic soil conditions could lead to the dissolution of soil carbonate, resulting in a decrease in the inherent SIC stock; the reverse is true in alkaline soil conditions (Wang, 2015). However, there are limited studies to date to assess the impact of environmental conditions on SIC dynamics (Zhang, 2011).

1.2 RELATIONSHIP OF SIC AND SOC

Generally, SIC and SOC show a see-saw relationship with respect to soil quality. SIC increases soil pH and exchangeable sodium percentage (ESP) and decreases the soil hydraulic conductivity, whereas SOC behaves in the reverse manner (Figure 1.1). Thus, unlike SOC, the prevalence of SIC is known to deteriorate soil quality.

1.3 RELATIVE DISTRIBUTION OF C STOCKS ON EARTH AND IN INDIA

The total stock of SIC (including limestones and fixed carbonates) accounts for 1.8×10^{22} g C (Table 1.1), which is nearly 41.81% of the total soil C stock. In India, the total carbon stock is 63.9 Pg out of which total organic carbon is 29.92 Pg, and inorganic carbon is 32.98 Pg. The major contribution of inorganic carbon is carbonate in arid soils. Globally, soils are the largest

DOI: 10.1201/9781003309581-2

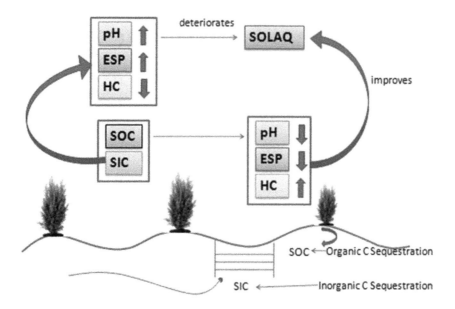

FIGURE 1.1   Model depicting the relationship between soil parameters and soil and land quality.

TABLE 1.1
Sources and Relative Proportion of Different Carbon Sources

Carbon Sources	Carbon Stocks (g C)	Percentage
Atmospheric CO_2	6.4×10^{17}	0.001
Living biomass	8.3×10^{17}	0.002
Dissolved organics	1.5×10^{18}	0.003
Organic carbon in soils and sediments	3.5×10^{18}	0.008
Dissolved CO_2	3.8×10^{19}	0.088
Limestone and fixed carbonates	1.8×10^{22}	41.817
Trapped organic carbon	2.5×10^{22}	58.079

terrestrial pool of carbon (C) and therefore contribute significantly to net atmospheric CO_2 fluxes (Eswaran et al., 2000; Mielnick et al., 2005). In order to assess total C stock and fluxes in terrestrial environments, both organic and inorganic pools need to be considered. Soil organic carbon (SOC) amounts to 1,200–1,600 Pg in the top 1 m of depth (Post et al., 1982; Eswaran et al., 1993, 2000; Sombroek et al., 1993; Batjes, 1996; Jobbágy and Jackson, 2000). Soil inorganic carbon (SIC) stock in the same depth accounts for 940 Pg at the global scale (Eswaran et al., 2000), making it the most dominant form of carbon in arid and semiarid regions (Lal and Kimble, 2000). There exists a dynamic equilibrium between soil inorganic carbon and atmospheric carbon, i.e. CO_2. The magnitude of SIC exchange with the atmosphere is about 0.023 PgCyr[-1], with a turnover time of about 85,000 years (Lal and Kimble, 2000). Soils are more likely to have greater SIC exchange in humid regions with forest vegetation and where grassland is replaced by forest. Due to its long turnover time in arid and non-forest areas, the formation of secondary carbonate in the soil can be an effective C sequestration mechanism in these regions (Lal and Kimble, 2000). Inorganic carbon in the soil occurs primarily as carbonate minerals, *viz.*, calcite ($CaCO_3$) and dolomite ($MgCO_3$) (Batjes, 1996), and based on their mode of origin, they may be classified into: lithogenic inorganic carbon (LIC) and pedogenic inorganic carbon (PIC) (West et al., 1988). While the LIC is inherited from the parent material, the latter (PIC) results from the precipitation of carbonate ions derived from the root as well as microbial respiration and calcium and magnesium ions yielded by weathering reactions, primarily hydrolysis (Lal and Kimble, 2000). The optimum soil moisture, a higher partial pressure of carbon dioxide (pCO_2) and an increase in soluble Ca/Mg concentrations can lead to a favorable soil environment, leading to the precipitation of PIC (Wilding et al., 1990). Pedogenic inorganic carbonate accumulation in semiarid or arid soils occurs because of a dearth of soil moisture due to high evapotranspiration and less precipitation, which constrains significant leaching (Nordt et al., 2000). Secondary carbonates have the ability not only to sequester atmospheric carbon dioxide on a large scale but also to sequester organic matter (organic carbon) in the form of humified compounds that are precipitated without transformation or polymerization (Duchaufour, 1976; Scharpenseel et al., 2000). For instance, in the Rego Black Chernozem soils, bonding of organic matter to precipitated carbonates has been observed, leading to large deposits of organic matter as well as $CaCO_3$ in the surface horizons (Landi et al., 2003a, b, 2004), enabling these soils to sequester organic matter, including humified compounds that are precipitated without transformation or polymerization (Duchaufour, 1976; Scharpenseel et al., 2000). A significantly positive correlation (r = 0.88, P < 0.001) between the abundance of SOC and SIC was also observed in 31 profiles in the cropland of the upper Yellow River Delta, China (Guo, 2016).

1.4 PROCESSES OF CARBONATE FORMATION IN SOIL

There are four important processes for carbonate formation in soil. They are pedogenic carbonate formation, weathering of silicate minerals, microbial carbonates and management practices-induced carbonates in soil.

1.4.1 PEDOGENIC CARBONATE FORMATION

Pedogenic carbonate is formed from lithogenic carbonate sources (*viz.*, rocks and minerals) by a process called calcification. The reaction of calcium with carbonic acid is responsible for this phenomenon.

$$CO_2 + H_2O = H_2CO_3$$

$$H_2CO_3 + Ca = Ca(HCO_3)_2$$

$$Ca(HCO_3)_2 = CaCO_3 + H_2O + CO_2$$

Pedogenic carbonate formation is dependent upon the native soil Ca content, pH and partial pressure of CO_2. As the concentration of CO_2 increases, more calcite is produced in the non-limiting conditions of Ca and Mg. A part of the SIC remains in dissolved form in soil, known as dissolved soil inorganic carbon (DSIC). Both in saline and alkaline soils, dissolved inorganic C is usually much less as compared to the total SIC. The mean residence time of DSIC was less as compared to total SIC, but the reverse trend was observed in case of accumulation rate (Wang et al., 2013).

1.4.2 WEATHERING OF SILICATE MINERALS

During the weathering of the calcium silicate mineral, 2 moles of CO_2 react with 1 mole of the mineral in the presence of water to form bicarbonates. Later, they react with Ca to form calcium carbonate. In this way, SIC is formed in soils. The reaction involved in the process is as follows:

$$CaSiO_3 + 3H_2O + 2CO_2 = H_4SiO_4 + 2HCO_3 + Ca$$

1.4.3 BIOLOGICALLY INDUCED CARBONATE FORMATION

There are four important mechanisms by which microbes help in the formation of carbonate (Sanderman, 2012). These are:

1.4.3.1 Acidic Polysaccharides-Mediated Carbonate Precipitation

Calcite is adsorbed on the polysaccharides secreted by microbes, thereby favoring their accumulation (Kawano and Hwang, 2011). The process can be illustrated by the following flowchart:

Bacterial cells secrete several polysaccharides
↓
Polysaccharides having functional carboxyl groups
↓
Having more surface-charged sites
↓
Adsorption of $CaCO_3$

1.4.3.2 Role of Anoxygenic Phototropic Bacteria (APB)

Anoxygenic phototropic bacteria plays significant role in carbonate formation (Bundeleva et al., 2011). The mechanism is illustrated below:

Metabolic intracellular incorporation during growth
↓
Reversible adsorption at the cell surface
↓
Calcium precipitation in the form of $CaCO_3$

1.4.3.3 Extracellular Microbial Carbonate Precipitation

Microbes, e.g., *Proteus vulgaris*, *Bacillus mycoides*, *B. salinus* and *Bacillus polymyxa* (Table 1.2) facilitate extracellular carbonate precipitation. This microbe-mediated aerobic or anaerobic oxidation of carbonaceous compounds such as carbohydrates, organic acids and hydrocarbons in neutral to alkaline soils leads to the formation of carbonates (Rivadeneyra et al., 2006). The mechanism is illustrated as follows:

$$CO_2 + H_2O = H_2CO_3$$

$$H_2CO_3 + OH = HCO_3 + H_2O$$

$$HCO_3 + OH = CO_3 + H_2O$$

TABLE 1.2

Production of Carbonates of Different Metals and Associated Microbes

Carbonates	Microbes
Magnesium carbonate ($MgCO_3$)	*Streptomyces* sp.
Manganese carbonate ($MnCO_3$)	*Bacillus polymyxa*
Ferrous carbonate ($FeCO_3$)	*Bacillus pasteurii*
Strontium carbonate ($SrCO_3$)	*Pseudomonas* sp.
Sodium carbonate (Na_2CO_3)	*Bacillus circulans*

1.4.3.4 Intracellular $CaCO_3$ Precipitation

Calcareous alga forms $CaCO_3$ by ATP-driven H/Ca exchange in this process. For each unit of calcium entry in the algal body, two units of H are released in the surrounding area to maintain the ionic balance. The CO_2 regenerated is used for photosynthesis by algae. The microorganisms involved are *Characorallina* and *Hymenomonus* sp. The following reactions occur in this type of calcite precipitation:

$$Ca + CO_3 + H_2O = CaCO_3 + 2H$$

$$HCO_3 + H = CO_2 + H_2O$$

1.5 MANAGEMENT PRACTICES-INDUCED CARBONATES IN SOIL

The different management practices that lead to carbonate precipitation in soil are as follows:

1.5.1 Aerobic or Anaerobic Hydrolysis of Added Organic Nitrogen Compounds in Soil

The aerobic or anaerobic hydrolysis of organic nitrogen compounds releases NH_3, which reacts with CO_2 in soil air to form ammonium carbonate, and thus SIC is sequestered in soil. The process may be represented as follows:

$$R\text{-}NH_2 + HOH = NH_3 + R\text{-}OH + Energy$$

$$NH_3 + H_2O = NH_4 + OH$$

$$2NH_3 + H_2CO_3 = (NH_4)_2CO_3$$

The involved microorganisms are *Micrococcus* sp. and *Bacillus pasteurii*.

1.5.2 Reduction of Calcium Sulfate (Amendment in Sodic Soils) by Sulfate-Reducing Bacteria

Sulfate-reducing bacteria reduce gypsum to CO_2, which later forms calcite. The involved microbes are *Desulfovibrio* sp., *Desulfotomaculatum* sp., etc. The reactions involved in the process are as follows:

$$CaSO_4 + 2(CH_2O) = CaS + 2CO_2 + 2H_2O$$

$$CaS + 2H_2O = Ca(OH)_2 + H_2S$$

$$CO_2 + H_2O = H_2CO_3$$

$$Ca(OH)_2 + H_2CO_3 = CaCO_3 + 2H_2O$$

1.5.3 Hydrolysis of Urea Added as Fertilizer

The hydrolysis of urea (Estiu and Merz, 2004) leads to the formation of carbonate in soil by the following mechanism:

$$NH_2(CO)NH_2 + H_2O = (NH_4)_2CO_3$$

$$(NH_4)_2CO_3 + Ca(OH)_2 = CaCO_3 + NH_4OH$$

The involved microbes are *Pseudomonas* sp. and *Variovorax* sp.

Like calcium carbonate production, carbonates of Na, Mg and Sr may also be produced by some specialized microbes. A list of these microbes, along with the synthesized carbonate compounds, is tabulated as follows:

1.6   FACTORS AFFECTING $CaCO_3$ PRECIPITATION IN SOIL

The different factors that help with calcite precipitation in soil are as follows:

- pH
- Temperature
- CO_2 concentration
- Management practices such as liming and irrigation water

1.6.1   DISTRIBUTION OF CARBONATE SPECIES ACCORDING TO SOLUTION pH

Carbonic acid is dominant at pHs below 6, and between 6 and 10.3, bicarbonate species are dominant. At pH levels above 10.3, carbonate is dominant, and in this stage, carbonate precipitation occurs.

1.6.2   TEMPERATURE

In regions with high soil temperatures, soils are usually deficient in moisture due to high evapotranspiration, preventing the formation of carbonic acid. This preserves the precipitated carbonate minerals, as their dissolution does not occur. However, in humid regions with low temperatures, soil CO_2 and water form carbonic acid, which reacts with hydroxides and oxides of Ca and/or Mg and causes the precipitation of Ca and Mg carbonates.

1.6.3   EFFECT OF CO_2 ON $CaCO_3$ PRODUCTION IN SOIL

In soils with no moisture limitation, an increase in CO_2 leads to carbonic acid synthesis, which reacts with oxides and hydroxides of alkaline earth metals (Ca and Mg), causing the formation and precipitation of carbonates in soil. Calcite production increases proportionately with soil CO_2 concentration until a critical point.

1.6.4   MANAGEMENT PRACTICES SUCH AS LIMING AND IRRIGATION WATER

Excess liming of acid soils for amelioration may lead to calcification. Irrigation with poor-quality (calcium-laden) irrigation water in saline soils may also lead to calcification, resulting in calcite precipitation.

1.7   BIODEGRADATION OF CARBONATES: A BIOCHEMICAL BASIS

The carbonate thus formed by the above processes is subjected to loss by several means. The reactions involved in the microbial degradation of calcite are presented as follows:

$$CaCO_3 + H = Ca + HCO_3$$

$$HCO_3 + H = H_2CO_3$$

$$H_2CO_3 = H_2O + CO_2$$

$$CO_2 + H_2O = H_2CO_3 (CO_2 \text{ from root and microbial respiration})$$

$$H_2CO_3 + CaCO_3 = Ca + 2HCO_3$$

The microbes involved are as follows: *B. mycoides* and *B. megaterium.*

The different modes of microbial degradation of carbonate in soil are as follows:

- Attack by mineral acids (carbonic acids) and hydrolysis of mineral
- Attack by organic acids such as acetic, oxalic and hydrolysis of mineral
- Production of noxious compounds such as H_2S and production of oxidants and metal sulfide
- Effect of biofilms and exoenzymes on the corrosion of cells (*Micrococcus halobius*)
- Production of chelating compounds and increased solubility of insoluble compounds

1.8 IMPACT OF SIC ON CARBON SEQUESTRATION (PASSIVE CARBON SEQUESTRATION)

The precipitation of Ca and Mg carbonates in soils abundant in silicate minerals is a promising method of passive mineral carbonation, alternatively called passive carbon sequestration. The proportion of different carbon pools within the artificial soils formed by incorporating composts with dolerite and basalt quarry fines changed with time, synthesizing new carbonate minerals. The annual rate of accumulation of SIC as carbonate minerals is estimated to be 4.8 t C ha^{-1} upto a depth of 0.3 m, similar to urban soils containing demolition wastes from construction (annually 3.0 t C ha^{-1} to 0.3 m) (Manning et al., 2013). In their study, substantial potential was observed for artificial soils for the purpose of carbon capture, which will reduce atmospheric greenhouse gases, *viz.*, CO_2, and reverse climate change.

1.8.1 SIC Sequestration Varies with Precipitation in Different Climatic Regions

The SIC pool is mainly concentrated in the soils of arid and semiarid ecoregions with a mean annual precipitation (MAP) of 500 mm (Batjes, 1998; Lal and Kimble, 2000). Around 84% of the total SIC pool in China exists in areas with that precipitation level. However, about 4.19 Pg of SIC are stored in areas with a higher MAP ranging 500–800 mm. The overall decrease in SOC contents in the topsoil and increase in the subsoil layers are expected in the Mediterranean agricultural soils in short- (2030), medium- (2050) and long-term (2100) climate change scenarios. However, the intensity of these fluctuations will depend on the land use systems and management practices. The agricultural systems with unscientific irrigation will be particularly vulnerable to losses of SOC stocks.

1.8.2 SIC Content in Different Land Cover Types

The magnitude of SIC content for different land covers is in the following order: desert>grassland> cropland>marsh>shrub land>meadow>forest. Land cover type has a strong influence on the vertical distribution of roots and SOC (Jobbágy and Jackson, 2000; Lal and Kimble, 2000), and these imprints are likely to affect SIC distribution.

1.8.3 Long-Term Effects of Manuring and Fertilization on SIC Sequestration

The addition of lime improves the SIC stock in soil due to calcite precipitation, whereas the addition of FYM increases SOC and reduces SIC due to the calcite degradation by carbonic acid, thereby improving soil quality and yields. In Alfisol (acidic soil) under the rice-rice cropping system in Pattambi, Kerala, this trend was observed. In a long-term (17-year) experiment, the effect of manuring and fertilization on TSC, SOC and SIC in calcareous Vertisol under a ground-nut-wheat cropping system in Junagadh, Gujarat, was studied, and it was found that the addition of FYM reduced the SIC content due to the action of carbonic acid on soil carbonate (Miriyala et al., 2017).

1.9   IMPACT OF SIC ON SOIL QUALITY

1.9.1   Relationship of Soil Physical Indicators with Carbonate Content

Bulk density was found to reduce with an increase in carbonate content, as Ca might have improved soil aggregation and increased porosity (Chaudhari et al., 2013).

1.9.2   Relationship of Soil Chemical Indicators with Carbonate Concentration in Calcareous Soils

It was found that EC increased proportionately with calcite. OC also increased with SIC in this case. Fe was negatively correlated with carbonate as it induces a higher pH (Chaudhari et al., 2013).

1.9.3   Relationship of Soil Biological Indicators with Electrical Conductivity in Salt-Affected Arid Soils (0–15 cm)

Correlation analysis revealed a strong and significant depressive (non-linear) relationship between soil salinity and all microbial indices analyzed. Microbial biomass C, the percentage of organic C present as microbial biomass C, microbial biomass N, biomass N to total N ratio, basal respiration, potentially mineralizable N, arginine ammonification rate and FDA hydrolysis rate were all negatively correlated with EC, and the relationship between these biological parameters and EC was exponential. On the other hand, the metabolic quotient was positively correlated with EC, and aquadratic relationship between qCO_2 and EC was observed.

The effect of urea-N and broiler litter-N (at 100,200 and 300 kg N/ha) on the biological proper-ties of calcareous soil was studied, and it was observed that in calcareous soil, the application of broiler N was much more effective in increasing microbial proliferation as compared to urea. This signifies that in degraded calcareous soils, manuring may improve the soil quality.

1.10   CONCLUSIONS

The dynamics of SIC are largely controlled by pH, CO_2 concentration in the soil atmosphere, rainfall, temperature and cropping systems, which could therefore help in evolving appropri-ate management strategies to preserve the SIC pool for long-term C sequestration. Treatment of dolerite and basalt with compost is one such approach to enhancing passive C sequestration in soil, thereby reducing CO_2 emissions to the atmosphere and thus mitigating global warming and climate change. An increase in soil carbonate may improve soil physical properties (BD), but it adversely affects chemical indicators, mainly EC, which in turn affects biological indicators (*viz.*, MBC, MBN, PMN and enzyme activities) and thus deteriorates the soil quality (Chaudhari et al., 2013). Thus, suitable management practices (*viz.*, manuring, crop residue retention, crop rotation, etc.) that improve SOC pools and retain SIC stocks are to be evolved and practiced to make the best use of the carbonate-rich soils both in terms of C sequestration and soil quality to feed the world. For this, the cumulative effect of the soil-root-microbe continuum on SIC dynamics needs to be explored further.

REFERENCES

Batjes, N.H. 1996. Total carbon and nitrogen in the soils of the world. *European Journal of Soil Science* 47: 151–163.

Batjes, N.H. 1998. Mitigation of atmospheric CO_2 concentrations by increased carbon sequestration in the soil. *Biology and Fertility of Soils* 27: 230–235.

Bundeleva, I.A., Shirokova, L.S., Bénézeth, P., Pokrovsky, O.S., Kompantseva, E.I., and Balor, S. (2012). Calcium carbonate precipitation by anoxygenic phototrophic bacteria. *Chemical Geology* 291: 116–131. https://doi.org/10.1016/j.chemgeo.2011.10.003

Chaudhari, P.R., Ahire, D.V., Ahire, V.D., Chakravarty, M., and Maity, S. 2013. Soil bulk density as related to soil texture, organic matter content and available total nutrients of Coimbatore soil. *International Journal of Scientific and Research Publications* 3:2.

Duchaufour, P. 1976. Dynamics of organic matter in soils of temperate regions: its action on pedogenesis. *Geoderma* 15: 31–40.

Estiu, G., & Merz, K. M. (2004). The hydrolysis of urea and the proficiency of urease. *Journal of the American Chemical Society* 126(22): 6932–6944. https://doi.org/10.1021/ja049327g

Eswaran, H., Reich, P.F., and Kimble, J.M. 2000. Global carbon stocks. In *Global Climate Change Pedogenic Carbonates*, ed. R. Lal, J.M. Kimble, H. Eswaran, and B.A. Stewart, 15–25. CRC Press, Boca Raton, FL.

Eswaran, H., Vandenberg, E., and Reich, P. 1993. Organic-carbon in soils of the world. *Soil Science Society of America Journal* 57:192–194.

Guo, Y. 2016. Dynamics of soil organic and inorganic carbon in the cropland of upper Yellow River Delta, China. *Scientific Reports* 6: 36105. doi: 10.1038/srep36105.

Jobbágy, E.G. and Jackson, R.B. 2000. The vertical distribution of soil organic carbon and its relation to climate and vegetation. *Ecological Application* 10: 423–436.

Kawano, M., & Hwang, J. (2011). Roles of microbial acidic polysaccharides in precipitation rate and polymorph of calcium carbonate minerals. *Applied Clay Science*, 51(4): 484–490. https://doi.org/10.1016/j.clay.2011.01.013

Lal, R. (2004). Agricultural activities and the global carbon cycle. Nutrient Cycling in Agroecosystems 70: 103–116. https://doi.org/10.1023/B:FRES.0000048480.24274.0f

Lal, R. (2010). Terrestrial sequestration of carbon dioxide (CO_2). In *Developments and Innovation in Carbon Dioxide (CO_2) Capture and Storage Technology* (Vol. 2, pp. 271–303). Woodhead Publishing Series in Energy. https://doi.org/10.1533/9781845699581.3.271

Lal, R. and Kimble, J.M. 2000. Pedogenic carbonate and the global carbon cycle. In *Global Climate Change and Pedogenic Carbonates*, ed. R. Lal, J.M. Kimble, H. Eswaran, B.A. Stewart, 1–14. CRC Press, Boca Raton, FL.

Landi, A., Anderson, D.W., and Mermut, A.R. 2003a. Organic carbon storage and stable isotope composition of soils along a grassland to forest environmental gradient in Saskatchewan. *Canadian Journal of Soil Science* 83: 405–414.

Landi, A., Mermut, A.R., and Anderson, D.W. 2003b. Origin and rate of pedogenic carbonate accumulation in Saskatchewan soils, Canada. *Geoderma* 117: 143–156.

Landi, A., Mermut, A.R., and Anderson, D.W. 2004. Carbon distribution in a hummocky landscape from Saskatchewan, Canada. *Soil Science Society of America Journal* 68: 175–184.

Lorenz, K., and Lal, R. (2010). Carbon dynamics and pools in major forest biomes of the world. In *Carbon Sequestration in Forest Ecosystems*. Springer, Dordrecht. https://doi.org/10.1007/978-90-481-3266-9_4

Manning, D.A.C., Renforth, P., Lopez-Capela, E., Robertsonc, S., and Ghazirehd, N. 2013. Carbonate precipitation in artificial soils produced from basaltic quarry fines and composts: an opportunity for passive carbon sequestration. *International Journal of Greenhouse Gas Contamination* 17: 309–317.

Mielnick, P., Dugas, W.A., Mitchell, K., and Havstad, K. 2005. Long-term measurements of CO_2 flux and evapotranspiration in a Chihuahuan desert grassland. *Journal of Arid Environments* 60: 423–436.

Miriyala, P., Sukumaran, N.P., Nath, B.N., Ramamurty, P.B., Sijinkumar, A.V., Vijayagopal, B., Ramaswamy, V., & Sebastian, T. 2017. Increased chemical weathering during the deglacial to mid-Holocene summer monsoon intensification. *Scientific Reports*, 7, Article number: 44310. https://doi.org/10.1038/srep44310

Nordt, C., Wilding, L.P., and Drees, L.R. 2000. Pedogenic carbonate transformations in leaching soil system: implications for the global C cycle. In: *Global Climate Change and Pedogenic Carbonates*, ed. R. Lal, J.M. Kimble, H. Eswaran, and B.A. Stewart, 43–64. CRC Press, Boca Raton, FL.

Post, W.M., Emmanuel, W.R., Zinke, P.J., and Stangenberger, G. 1982. Soil carbon pools and world life zones. *Nature* 298: 1586–1589.

Rivadeneyra, M.A., Delgado, R., P00E1rraga, J., and Ramos-Cormenzana, A. 2006. Precipitation of minerals by 22 species of moderately halophilic bacteria in artificial marine salts media: influence of salt concentration. *Folia Microbiologica* 51(5): 445–453.

Sanderman, J. 2012. Can management induced changes in the carbonate system drive soil carbon sequestration? A review with particular focus on Australia. *Agriculture, Ecosystems and Environment* 155: 70–77.

Scharpenseel, H.W., Mtimet, A., and Freytag, J. 2000. Soil inorganic carbon and global change. In *Global Climate Change and Pedogenic Carbonates*, ed. R. Lal, J.M. Kimble, H. Eswaran, and B.A. Stewart, 27–42. CRC Press, Boca Raton, FL.

Sombroek, W.G., Nachtergale, F.O., and Hebel, A. 1993. Amounts, dynamics, and sequestration of carbon in tropical and subtropical soils. *AMBIO* 22: 417–426.

Wang, X., Wang, J., Xu, M., Zhang, W., Fan, T., & Zhang, J. 2015. Carbon accumulation in arid croplands of northwest China: pedogenic carbonate exceeding organic carbon. *Scientific Reports*, 5, Article number: 11439. https://doi.org/10.1038/srep11439

Wang, Y., Wang, Z., and Li, Y. 2013. Storage/turnover rate of inorganic carbon and its dissolvable part in the profile of saline/alkaline soils. PL*o*S *One* 8(10): e82029.

West, L.T., Drees, L.R., Wilding, L.P., and Rabenhorst, M.C. 1988. Differentiation of pedogenic and lithogenic carbonate forms in Texas. *Geoderma* 43: 271–287.

Wilding, L.P., West, L.T., and Drees, L.R. 1990. Field and laboratory identification of calcic and petrocalcic horizons. In *Proceedings of the Fourth International Soil Correlation Meeting (ISCOM IV) Characterization, Classification, and Utilization of Aridisols. Part A: Papers*, ed. J.M. Kimble and W.D. Nettleton, 79–92. US Department of Agriculture-Soil Conservation Service, Lincoln, NE.

Zhang, J. 2011. Perspectives on studies on soil carbon stocks and the carbon sequestration potential of China. *Chinese Science Bulletin* 56: 3748–3758.

2 Unravelling the Dynamic Role of Beneficial Microbes in Regenerative Agriculture

Rahul Kumar, Kapil Jindal, J. P. Singh, and Satyendra Pratap Singh

2.1 INTRODUCTION

The term "regenerative organic agriculture" was coined by the late Robert Rodale(of the Rodale Institute), who defined regenerative farming as "a long-term, holistic design that attempts to grow as much food using as few resources as possible in a way that revitalizes the soil rather than depleting it while offering a solution to carbon sequestration". Regenerative agriculture rejuvenates our agricultural lands. It is a system approach where farming is done in favour of nature, not against it. This is a biological model working on the principles of ecology and is also our best criteria for a quick drawdown of atmospheric carbon dioxide (Lal, 2004). Rhodes (2015) argues that if a solution is not inherently regenerative, it cannot be sustainable over the long run. Hence, regenerative agriculture needed to be embraced. According to soil microbiologists, soil microorganisms can be categorized as "useful" or "damaging" depending on how they affect the quality of the soil, crop growth, and production. The activities of micro- and microorganisms largely affect the stability of ecosystems. The microbes can ensure increased fertilizer use efficiency in a sustainable and eco-friendly manner, thus leading to elevated crop yield. Microbes can regulate crucial functional processes in soil, *viz.*, nutrient recycling, nitrogen fixation, neutralization of fixed nutrients, generation of plant growth regulators, management of plant pathogenic microbes (Figure 2.1), soil structure enhancement, activation of resistance, decomposition of residues, and positive and negative plant–microbe interactions, improving soil health and productivity (Harris, 2009; Gupta, 2012). Soil sickness occurs due to unwarranted erosion of soil, the leaching of agrochemicals into ground water, and improper handling of human and animal waste, which results in serious environmental threats. It is imperative to reduce the injudicious use of chemical pesticides and fertilizers while simultaneously increasing agricultural production, which is the need of the hour to feed the global population. This chapter focuses on the diverse roles of beneficial microbes and various processes helping in the regeneration of agriculture, as discussed in the following sections.

2.1.1 Biological Nitrogen Fixation

Beijerink discovered biological nitrogen fixation in 1901, which is carried out by a specialized group of prokaryotes. During the fixation process, N_2 gets converted into ammonia, which is further metabolized by nitrogen-fixing microbes. Biological nitrogen fixation is a key function in nutrient recycling, where atmospheric dinitrogen (N_2) is reduced to ammonia with the aid of the nitrogenase enzyme. This enzyme is extremely sensitive to oxygen; hence, it requires an anoxic environment for activity. Nitrogen fixation is an energy-intensive process that uses 16 moles of ATP for every mole of nitrogen fixed. Since nitrogen is a vital part of amino acids, nucleic acids, and chlorophyll, it becomes a very relevant element for plant growth and development. Beneficial nitrogen fixation (BNF) is carried out by beneficial microbes, which can be exploited to decrease

DOI: 10.1201/9781003309581-3

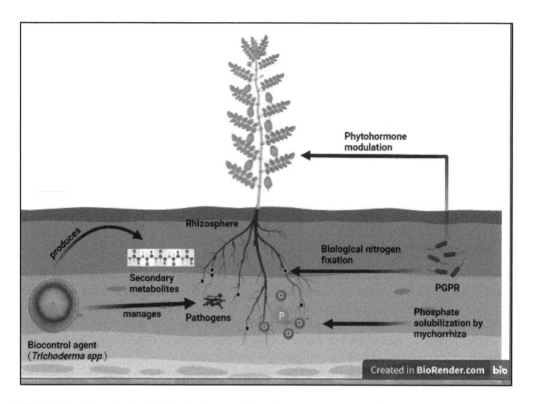

FIGURE 2.1   Strategies by which microbes contribute themselves to regenerative agriculture.

the nitrogen dependency on synthetic nitrogen products. Some of the BNF microbes fix nitrogen independently, while others associate with plants as endophytes and symbiotes, forming nodules (Unkovich et al., 2008). There are economic, agronomic and environmental benefits to using BNF in cropping systems (Anglade et al., 2015). Various *Rhizobium* species get associated with legume crops, forming a nodule-like structure where they enzymatically convert N_2 into NH_3, which is further converted into different nitrogenous molecules used by plants for the synthesis of organic compounds. Apart from symbiotic nitrogen fixers, there are non-symbiotic nitrogen-fixing bacterial genera, *viz., Clostridium, Beijerinkia, Azotobacter, Azospirillum*, etc. (Kennedy et al., 2004; Malik et al., 2002). The oxidation of ammonia to nitrite is facilitated by bacteria such as *Nitrosomonas* and *Nitrosphaera* in soils, whereas the oxidation of nitrite to nitrate is mediated by *Nitrobacter* (Aislabie and Deslippe, 2013). Symbiotic nitrogen fixation is carried out by cyanobacteria, also known as blue green algae (BGA) or cyanophyta, where plants provide bacteria with carbohydrates and other organic compounds and bacteria supply them with fixed nitrogen (Sulieman and Tran, 2014).

2.1.2   MYCORRHIZA AND PHOSPHATE SOLUBILIZATION

Under most soil conditions, phosphorus is the least mobile and readily available to plants compared to the other major nutrients. Plant species, the nutritional status of the soil, and ambient soil conditions all influence the bioavailability of inorganic phosphorus in the rhizosphere. Phosphate-solubilizing microbes (PSM) could play a crucial role in supplying phosphate to plants in a more eco-friendly and sustainable manner to dodge phosphorus deficiency. Phosphate-mobilizing microorganisms are soil fungi that help in the mobilization of immobile or unavailable forms of phosphorous to mobile or available forms through their hyphal structures in the soil. Except for the Brassicaceae family, these soil microorganisms have a mutualistic relationship with all crop plants. This fungus mobilizes zinc and sulphur, in addition to phosphorus. Mycorrhizae literally means "fungus root," and it refers to the

TABLE 2.1
Role of Beneficial Microbes in Different Agro-Ecological Conditions

Agro Ecological Condition	Soil-Beneficial Microbes	Role of Microbes in Soil	References
Tropical	*Ralstonia taiwanensis* and *Burkholderia* spp.	Legume nodulation	Moulin et al. (2001)
	AMF	Cultivation of cassava	Umukoro (2020)
	Phosphate-solubilizing microorganisms(PSM) *viz. Pseudomonas, Bacillus* and *Rhizobium*	Provide phosphorus to plants already precipitated with iron, aluminium and calcium	Gyaneshwar et al. (2002)
Sub-tropical	*Gluconacetobacter diazotrophicus*	Improves growth of sugarcane	Suman et al. (2005)
	Trichoderma spp.	Red rot suppression caused by *Colletotrichum falcatum* in sugarcane	Joshi et al. (2019)
	Arthrobacter spp. (CC-BC03), *S. marcescens* (CC-BC14)	Phosphate solubilization	Chen et al. (2006)
	Trichoderma viride	Used for trash management in sugarcane	Yadav et al. (2009)
Temperate	*T. harzianum*	*Dematophora necatrix, Fusarium oxysporum*, and *Pythium aphanidermatum* were significantly inhibited by chitinase production	Mohiddin et al. (2021)
	T. afroharzianum strains BT4 and AT5	Biocontrol of wilt disease of chilli	Mohiddin et al. (2021)

non-pathogenic association between certain soil fungi and plant roots. In general, mycorrhizal fungi, categorized into three types, ectomycorrhiza, endomycorrhiza, and ectendomycorrhiza, are found in association with plant roots. Microbial biomass also plays an important role in the phosphorus cycle in the soil, so its subsequent release is critical for maintaining phosphorus pathways and movement in the soil-plant system. PSM can also protect orthophosphate by forming a complex with other soil nutrients (Oberson and Joner, 2005). The synergistic role and mechanisms of PSB and AMF in the solubilization of phosphorus from various organic and inorganic sources are unknown. Plants absorb P as primary orthophosphate or secondary orthophosphate from the soil solution. If the orthophosphate in the soil solution is insufficient to meet the plant's needs, it is replenished from other soil P pools (Bieleski, 1973). Under greenhouse and field conditions, most PSMs have different effects. This is due to a number of factors, including a complex soil environment, a lack of knowledge about soil microbes and their mechanisms, the interaction of microbes in the soil community, and the lack of a specific partner for association (Richardson, 2001). The PSB provides P to plants in an environmentally friendly and sustainable manner. Plants provide PSB with habitat, food, energy, shelter, and biological diversity. PSB solubilizes P and delivers it to plants through a variety of mechanisms, including the production of phenolic compounds (Patel et al., 2008). Soil-beneficial microbes perform crucial roles in different agro-ecological regions of the world (Table 2.1).

2.1.3 PLANT GROWTH-PROMOTING RHIZOBACTERIA (PGPR)

PGPR provides a variety of services and benefits to the plant in exchange for reduced carbon and other metabolites from the plant. Due to the importance of the rhizomicrobiome in agriculture, a diverse range of root exudates and plant cell debris attract a variety of unique patterns of microbial colonization. Rhizomicrobiome microbes play key roles in improved soil texture, nutrient acquisition and assimilation, and secreting and modulating secondary metabolites, antibiotics, hormones, and various signal compounds, all of which contribute to increased plant growth (Rachel et al., 2018). Seed biopriming methods involving PGPR have been formulated to enhance the crop defence system against salt stress, resulting in increased crop productivity to meet future human food demand. The close connection that develops between soil, plant, and microbes throughout the plant's life cycle promotes plant development, induces systemic resistance in the host plant against phytopathogens, and alleviates salinity stress (Tabassum et al., 2017). Some of the bacteria are the result of plant-microbe co-evolution, transforming into facultative intracellular endophytes. PGPR is one of these free-living bacteria that have a positive impact on plants both directly and indirectly (Bulgarelli et al., 2013). Some of the bacteria are the result of plant-microbe co-evolution transforming into facultative intracellular endophytes. Plant growth-promoting rhizobacteria (PGPR) is one of these free-living bacteria that have a positive impact on plants both directly and indirectly. Rhizobacteria that are helpful have been used to increase nutrient and water uptake and abiotic and biotic stress tolerance. By offering effective ways to investigate how plants adapt to different stresses and the suitable tolerance mechanisms, the potential role of PGPR can support their employment in sustainable agriculture. These mechanisms can then be used to develop genetically engineered plants that can withstand any climatic fluctuations. Typically, dynamic microbial ecologies and soils with high organic matter require less fertilizer than soils that are managed conventionally (Bender et al., 2016). The importance of beneficial microorganisms in stress management and the creation of climate change-resilient agriculture are rising. Recent research has employed molecular methods to elucidate the intricate dynamics of plant–microbe interactions, particularly those leading to induced stress tolerance in crops. The application of these advanced techniques provides effective means to explore how plants adapt to diverse stressors and the underlying tolerance mechanisms. The potential role of Plant Growth-Promoting Rhizobacteria (PGPR) in this context underscores their significance in promoting sustainable agriculture practices. Understanding these mechanisms not only supports the judicious utilization of PGPR but also opens avenues for the development of genetically engineered plants capable of withstanding a spectrum of climatic fluctuations (Nagpal et al., 2022).

2.1.4 BIOCONTROL AGENTS

Biocontrol agents encompass genetically modified crops, insects, nematodes, and microbesor natural products derived from living organisms capable of suppressing phytopathogens. The biological control of plant diseases is the eradication of plant pathogen populations by living organisms (Heimpel and Mills, 2017). The most eco-friendly method for eradicating diseases without endangering the environment is biological control. Rhizosphere microorganisms are crucial in the management of plant diseases. Numerous antagonistic microorganisms have recently been used as efficient biocontrol agents to suppress a variety of plant diseases. Due to the negative effects of chemical fungicides on other non-target organisms, biological control mechanisms are thought to be crucial measures for disease management (Köhl et al., 2019). Some of them interact with plants by triggering resistance or priming plants without interacting directly with the pathogen of interest. Other microbial biological control agents (MBCAs) modulate pathogen growth conditions through nutrient competition or other mechanisms. Bacteria, fungi, actinomycetes, protozoa, or viruses that are gram-positive or gram-negative can act as biocontrol agents. Biocontrol agents work through either direct antagonism (hyperparasitism and antibiosis) or indirect interaction (induced resistance, competition, etc.). The development of stable formulations can be planned with the aid of an understanding of the organism. Different bacterial genera have different levels of difficulty in their formulation. Typically, bacteria that produce spores outlive those that don't (McQuilken et al., 1998). Numerous microorganisms that are found in soil and in contact with plants exhibit entomopathogenic behaviour and can be utilized as efficient biocontrol agents, also known as biopesticides, against various agricultural pest insects (Sindhu et al., 2017). It is known that some biocontrol strains can produce a variety of antibiotics that can repress one or more pathogens, thereby increasing the biocontrol effectiveness of the BCA. Zwittermicin and kanosamine are both produced by the *Bacillus cereus* strain UW85 (Pal and Gardener, 2006). The abundance of fluorescent pseudomonads in natural soils and plant roots, as well as their capacity to use a variety of plant exudates as nutrients, makes them suitable for use as biological control agents. The bacterial population with biocontrol and plant growth-promoting activities includes *Azospirillum*, *Arthrobacter*, *Azotobacter*, *Bacillus*, *Pseudomonas*, *Rhizobium*, *Rhodococcus*, *Serratia*, *Streptomyces*, and other fungal bioagents including *Beauveria*, *Metarhizium*, *Trichoderma*, and *Verticillium* species, which are also important pathogen and insect antagonists in the rhizosphere (Ahmad et al., 2008; Björkman et al., 1998; Tariqet al., 2017).

2.1.5 Secondary Metabolite Production

Secondary metabolites are substances that play a protective role for plants but do not directly contribute to their growth. Bioactive substances with antimicrobial and herbicidal properties are produced by about 80% of fungal endophytes. However, under certain circumstances, they play significant roles in the establishment of interactions with other organisms, development, and signalling processes, which highlights the significance of studying them in the context of biocontrol. They are also an abundant source of many other secondary metabolites, including antifungal, anticancer, and antiparasitic substances. The expression of these clusters would help in the exploitation of the chemical diversity of microbes because the secondary metabolites (bioactive compounds) are primarily produced when cryptic gene clusters are activated, which are obsolete under normal conditions (Xu et al., 2019). Actinomycetes exhibit an astounding array of diverse biological effects in addition to antimicrobial properties and secondary metabolite production. More than 10,000 antimicrobial agents used in pharmaceutical production are produced by the order Actinomycetales (Sharma et al., 2014). In addition to siderophores and cell wall-degrading enzymes, fluorescent *Pseudomonas* spp. also produces a wide range of secondary metabolites (SMs) that are crucial to their diverse lifestyles, functioning in nutrient acquisition, virulence, and defence against rivals and predators encountered in natural habitats (Mishra and Arora, 2018). Dialkylresorcinols, phloroglucinols, pyrrolnitrin, pyoluteorine, lipopeptides, and hydrogen cyanide are the SMs that are best known. Different bacterial strains produce the brightly coloured tricyclic compounds known as phenazines, which have potent antibacterial and antifungal properties (Guttenberger et al., 2017). It is necessary to take advantage of fluorescent pseudomonads in order to make use of their variety of secondary metabolites in regulating phytopathogens. Fluorescent pseudomonads produce varying amounts of HCN in the rhizosphere, depending on environmental factors (Schippers et al., 1990). In addition to secondary metabolites like phytoalexin elicitor, *Mucor ramosissimus* species also produce extracellular enzymes such as lipase and endopolygalacturonase (Elkhateeb and Daba, 2022). In addition to pyrones, terpenoids, steroids, and polyketides, *Trichoderma* spp. also produces a wide range of nonpolar, low-molecular-weight compounds known as secondary metabolites. The siderophores and numerous peptaibiotics known as peptaiboles, which frequently contain non-standard amino acids, are also produced by *Trichoderma* species (Degenkolb et al., 2006).

2.1.6 Improvement of Soil Structure

Soil microbes play a vital role in maintaining soil structure. The development and stability of aggregates are significantly influenced by soil microorganisms. By using the more easily accessible carbon substrates from fresh leftovers and roots, bacteria and fungi make a variety of mucilaginous polysaccharides. These substances work as glue to enable bacteria and fungi to adhere to sands, clays, and organic materials, which leads to the production of new aggregates. The core of microaggregates (20–250 μm) is made up of decaying microbial waste and plant residues that are encrusted with soil particles by mucilages (Six et al., 2004). Networks of fungal hyphae stimulate the production of macroaggregates (250 to –2,000 μm) by the enmeshment of soil particles with organic debris (Gupta and Germida, 1988). Fungi that are saprophytic and mycorrhizal both aid in the creation and stability of aggregates. At scales of less than 50 mm, mucigels' effects on aggregates can be most clearly observed. Microbial metabolites penetrate the mineral crust in the area more and more as organic matter decomposes, strengthening interparticle bonds and enhancing aggregate stability. A healthy soil structure offers a variety of niches that can support various microbial populations in terms of redox potential and substrate availability. In different aggregate size classes, diverse bacterial and fungal communities are distributed differently and serve different purposes (Gupta and Germida, 1988). Bacteria frequently live in aggregate pores as microcolonies with 2–16 bacteria apiece, and substantial colonization is limited to microsites with higher carbon availability, such as the rhizosphere and outer surfaces of recently formed macroaggregates (Foster, 1988). The location of various phenotypic and functional categories of bacteria differs in various areas of aggregates; for example, diazotrophs and denitrifying bacteria are typically found in the interior parts of aggregates (Hattori, 1988; Mummy et al., 2006). The positioning of aggregates with respect to roots, organic residues, and macropores is more crucial for figuring out the makeup and activity of the microbial community. Protozoan predators protect bacteria found inside smaller micro-aggregates, aggregates, and micropores from desiccation and grazing. When compared to organisms found in macropores, the turnover of these species is often modest. Disturbance alters the variety and activity of soil microorganisms by affecting the aggregation, aeration, and accessibility of substrates.

2.1.7 SIDEROPHORE PRODUCTION

Siderophores are low-molecular-weight (<10 kDa) high-affinity ferric iron chelators produced by microbes such as bacteria, fungi, and some plants when there is an iron deficiency. The word siderophore comes from the Greek words *sidero*, which means iron, and *phore*, which means carrier. Siderophore is produced by plant growth-promoting microorganisms (PGPM) and bioagents; these elements promote plant development and suppress diseases (Ghosh et al., 2015). Outside the cell, the insoluble ferric iron ion (Fe^{3+}) forms a strong bond with a siderophore. The Fe^{3+}-siderophore combination is recognized by siderophore receptors or siderophore-binding proteins that are present on the outer membrane. The complexes are then moved to the cytosol by passing through the membrane via the siderophore-mediated iron transport system. Inside the cell, Fe^{3+} is transformed into soluble ferrous iron form (Fe^{2+}), and after the release of iron ion siderophore, this ferrous iron form (Fe^{2+}) is accessible to microbes(Ahmed and Holmström, 2014; Hider and Kong, 2010; Saha et al., 2016). Although scavenging iron is the main function of siderophore in the environment, siderophore also creates complexes and aids microbial organisms in accessing them. Over the past two decades, siderophore-producing bacteria have drawn more interest because of their potential contribution to plant growth and defence. It has been demonstrated that these microbes secrete antibiotics to stop the growth of other microorganisms in order to enhance iron nutrition. By lowering the iron concentration, they have also been found to slow down the growth of infections, particularly fungi (Ilyas and Bano, 2012). Siderophores helps kill phytopathogens by strongly attaching to the iron and reducing the amount of iron those pathogens can absorb (Beneduzi et al., 2012; Ahmed and Holmström, 2014). With the recent development of medical knowledge, the use of siderophore is becoming more and more significant for cancer treatment, antimalarial drugs, antibiotics, MRIs, etc.

2.1.8 PHYTOHORMONE MODULATION

Phytohormones are some of the most crucial growth regulators well-known for having a significant influence on plant metabolism and also play a pivotal role in the activation of plant defence response mechanisms against stresses. The effect of gibberellic acids on plant responses was identified prior to the isolation and structural characterization of the active compounds (Keswani et al., 2022). Recent studies have demonstrated that phytohormones produced by microorganisms associated with roots prove to be significant metabolic engineering targets for promoting host tolerance to abiotic stresses. Rhizobacteria that promote plant growth produce phytohormones such as auxins, cytokinins, gibberellins, and ethylene that can impact cell proliferation in the root architecture by overproducing lateral roots and root hairs, which then results in an increase in nutrition and water uptake by plants (Arora et al., 2013).

Indole acetic acid (IAA): IAA is the most prevalent natural auxin present in plants and is a plant growth regulator that has a favourable impact on root development (Miransari and Smith, 2014). IAA, produced by up to 80% of rhizobacteria, is thought to work in tandem with endogenous IAA in plants to promote cell growth and improve mineral and nutrient uptake from the soil. It is a byproduct of L-tryptophan metabolism produced by a variety of microorganisms, including PGPR (Keswani et al., 2020). Rhizobacteria are typically found on seed or root surfaces (Vessey, 2003). IAA influences plant cell division, extension, and differentiation; promotes seed and tuber germination; speeds up the xylem and root development; regulates vegetative growth processes; starts the formation of lateral and adventitious roots; mediates responses to light, gravity, and fluorescence; and influences photosynthesis, pigment formation, and various biosynthesis of metabolites and stress resistance (Spaepen and Vanderleyden, 2011).

Cytokinins and gibberellins: various rhizobacteria such as *Azotobacter* spp., *Pantoea agglomerans*, *Rhizobium* spp., *Pseudomonas fluorescens*, *Rhodospirillum rubrum*, *Bacillus subtilis*, and *Paenibacillus polymyxa* can produce cytokinins, gibberellins, or both for the promotion of plant growth (Kang et al., 2010). Cytokinins can also be produced by some strains of phytopathogens. However, it appears that rhizobacteria produce lower quantities of cytokinin than phytopathogens, indicating their stimulatory effects rather than inhibitory effects on plant development.

Ethylene: A major phytohormone with a variety of biological effects is ethylene. Activities may induce root initiation, suppress root elongation, promote fruit ripening, encourage lower wilting, stimulate seed germination, encourage leaf abscission, or activate the synthesis of other plant hormones, to name just a few ways that they may influence plant growth and development (Glick et al., 2007). Iqbal et al. (2012) reported enhanced nodule number, nodule dry weight, fresh biomass, grain yield, straw yield, and nitrogen content in lentil grains as a result of reduced ethylene production through inoculation with strains of *Pseudomonas* spp. that promote plant growth coupled with *R. leguminosarum*, *Acetobacter*, *Achromobacter*, *Agrobacterium*, *Alcaligenes*, *Azospirillum*, *Bacillus*, *Burkholderia*, *Enterobacter*, *Pseudomonas*, *Ralstonia*, *Serratia*, and *Rhizobium* are only a few of the many genera in which bacterial strains demonstrating ACC deaminase activity have been discovered recently.

2.2 CONCLUSIONS AND FUTURE PROSPECTS

Utilizing advantageous microbes to boost crop productivity and output is becoming increasingly popular because synthetic chemicals have detrimental effects on human and environmental health. Research in this area has improved our comprehension of microbial physiology and procedures in plant–microbe interactions. In order to develop eco-sustainable agriculture, modern agricultural techniques that use the synthesis of organic or microbial-based products as the best substitute for chemical fertilizers and pesticides can increase agricultural productivity. These techniques also use microbial resources to improve agriculture in a sustainable way. The use of microbial mechanisms and activities in agricultural production is also now wellknown. Moreover, technological advancements have made it possible for us to fully comprehend how microbes influence plant growth and development in regenerative agriculture. The significance of microbial communities in accomplishing agricultural and environmental sustainability has gained attention in recent years, and their use in agroecosystems and the resolution of important environmental problems have actually produced outstanding results. It is plausible that systematic and logical investigation and analysis of beneficial microbes for their ecological functions will disclose novel mechanisms governing various biological processes essential to plant health and provide viable, concrete solutions to agricultural and environmental problems.

REFERENCES

Ahmad, F., Ahmad, I., & Khan, M. S. (2008). Screening of free-living rhizospheric bacteria for their multiple plant growth promoting activities. *Microbiological Research*, 163(2), 173–181.

Ahmed, E., & Holmström, S. J. (2014). Siderophores in environmental research: roles and applications. *Microbial Biotechnology*, 7(3), 196–208.

Aislabie, J., & Deslippe, J. R. (2013). Soil microbes and their contribution to soil services. In John R. Dymond (ed.) Ecosystem *Services in New Zealand: Conditions and Trends* (pp. 143–161). Manaaki Whenua Press, Lincoln, New Zealand.

Anglade, J., Billen, G., & Garnier, J. (2015). Relationships for estimating N_2 fixation in legumes: incidence for N balance of legume-based cropping systems in Europe. *Ecosphere*, 6(3), 1–24.

Arora, N. K., Tewari, S., & Singh, R. (2013). Multifaceted plant-associated microbes and their mechanisms diminish the concept of direct and indirect PGPRs. In Naveen Kumar Arora (ed.). *Plant Microbe Symbiosis: Fundamentals and Advances* (pp. 411–449). Springer, New Delhi.

Bender, S. F., Wagg, C., & van der Heijden, M. G. (2016). An underground revolution: biodiversity and soil ecological engineering for agricultural sustainability. *Trends in Ecology & Evolution*, 31(6), 440–452.

Beneduzi, A., Ambrosini, A., & Passaglia, L. M. (2012). Plant growth-promoting rhizobacteria (PGPR): their potential as antagonists and biocontrol agents. *Genetics and Molecular Biology*, 35, 1044–1051.

Bieleski, R. L. (1973). Phosphate pools, phosphate transport, and phosphate availability. Annual Review of Plant Physiology, 24, 225–252.

Björkman, T., Blanchard, L. M., & Harman, G. E. (1998). Growth enhancement of *shrunken-2 (sh2)* sweet corn by *Trichoderma harzianum* 1295-22: effect of environmental stress. *Journal of the American Society for Horticultural Science*, 123(1), 35–40.

Bulgarelli, D., Schlaeppi, K., Spaepen, S., Van Themaat, E. V. L., & Schulze-Lefert, P. (2013). Structure and functions of the bacterial microbiota of plants. Annual Review of Plant Biology, 64, 807–838.

Chen, Y. P., Rekha, P. D., Arun, A. B., Shen, F. T., Lai, W. A., & Young, C. C. (2006). Phosphate solubilizing bacteria from subtropical soil and their tricalcium phosphate solubilizing abilities. *Applied Soil Ecology*, 34(1), 33–41.

Degenkolb, T., Gräfenhan, T., Berg, A., Nirenberg, H. I., Gams, W., & Brückner, H. (2006). Peptaibiomics: screening for polypeptide antibiotics (peptaibiotics) from plant-protective *Trichoderma* species. *Chemistry & Biodiversity*, 3(6), 593–610.

Elkhateeb, W. A., & Daba, G. M. (2022). Insight into secondary metabolites of *Circinella*, *Mucor* and *Rhizopus* the three musketeers of order *Mucorales*. *Biomedical Journal of Scientific & Technical Research*, 41(2), 32534–32540.

Foster, R. C. (1988). Microenvironments of soil microorganisms. *Biology and Fertility of Soils*, 6(3), 189–203.

Ghosh, S. K., Pal, S., & Chakraborty, N. (2015). The qualitative and quantitative assay of siderophore production by some microorganisms and effect of different media on its production. *International Journal of Chemical Sciences*, 13(4), 1621–1629.

Glick, B. R., Todorovic, B., Czarny, J., Cheng, Z., Duan, J., & McConkey, B. (2007). Promotion of plant growth by bacterial ACC deaminase. *Critical Reviews in Plant Sciences*, 26(5–6), 227–242.

Gupta, V. V. (2012). Beneficial microorganisms for sustainable agriculture. *Microbiology Australia*, 33(3), 113–115.

Gupta, V. V. S. R., & Germida, J. J. (1988). Distribution of microbial biomass and its activity in different soil aggregate size classes as affected by cultivation. *Soil Biology and Biochemistry*, 20(6), 777–786.

Guttenberger, N., Blankenfeldt, W., & Breinbauer, R. (2017). Recent developments in the isolation, biological function, biosynthesis, and synthesis of phenazine natural products. *Bioorganic & Medicinal Chemistry*, 25(22), 6149–6166.

Gyaneshwar, P., Naresh Kumar, G., Parekh, L. J., & Poole, P. S. (2002). Role of soil microorganisms in improving P nutrition of plants. *Plant and Soil*, 245(1), 83–93.

Harris, J. (2009). Soil microbial communities and restoration ecology: facilitators or followers? *Science*, 325(5940), 573–574.

Hattori, T. (1988). Soil aggregates as microhabitats for microorganisms. *Report of the Institute of Agricultural Research*, Tohoku University, 37, 23–36.

Heimpel, G. E., & Mills, N. J. (2017). Biological *Control*. Cambridge University Press, Cambridge.

Hider, R. C., & Kong, X. (2010). Chemistry and biology of siderophores. *Natural Product Reports*, 27(5), 637–657.

Ilyas, N., & Bano, A. (2012). Potential use of soil microbial community in agriculture. In Dinesh K. Maheshwari (ed.). *Bacteria in Agrobiology: Plant Probiotics* (pp. 45–64). Springer, Berlin, Heidelberg.

Iqbal, M. A., Khalid, M., Shahzad, S. M., Ahmad, M., Soleman, N., & Akhtar, N. (2012). Integrated use of *Rhizobium leguminosarum*, plant growth promoting rhizobacteria and enriched compost for improving growth, nodulation and yield of lentil (*Lens culinaris* Medik.). *Chilean Journal of Agricultural Research*, 72(1), 104–110.

Joshi, D., Singh, P., Holkar, S. K., & Kumar, S. (2019). *Trichoderma*-mediated suppression of red rot of sugarcane under field conditions in subtropical India. *Sugar Tech*, 21(3), 496–504.

Kang, B. G., Kim, W. T., Yun, H. S., & Chang, S. C. (2010). Use of plant growth-promoting rhizobacteria to control stress responses of plant roots. *Plant Biotechnology Reports*, 4(3), 179–183.

Kennedy, I. R., Choudhury, A. T. M. A., & Kecskés, M. L. (2004). Non-symbiotic bacterial diazotrophs in crop-farming systems: can their potential for plant growth promotion be better exploited? *Soil Biology and Biochemistry*, 36(8), 1229–1244.

Keswani, C., Singh, S. P., Cueto, L., García-Estrada, C., Mezaache-Aichour, S., Glare, T. R., & Sansinenea, E. (2020). Auxins of microbial origin and their use in agriculture. *Applied Microbiology and Biotechnology*, 104(20), 8549–8565.

Keswani, C., Singh, S. P., García-Estrada, C., Mezaache-Aichour, S., Glare, T. R., Borriss, R., … Sansinenea, E. (2022). Biosynthesis and beneficial effects of microbial gibberellins on crops for sustainable agriculture. *Journal of Applied Microbiology*, 132(3), 1597–1615.

Köhl, J., Kolnaar, R., & Ravensberg, W. J. (2019). Mode of action of microbial biological control agents against plant diseases: relevance beyond efficacy. *Frontiers in Plant Science*, 10, 845.

Lal, R. (2004). Soil carbon sequestration to mitigate climate change. *Geoderma*, 123(1–2), 1–22.

Malik, K.A., Mirza, M.S., Hassan, U., Mehnaz, S., Rasul, G., Haurat, J., & Normand, P. (2002). The role of plant associated beneficial bacteria in rice-wheat cropping system. In Ivan R Kennedy and Abu T M A Choudhury (eds.). *Biofertilizers in Action* (pp. 73–83). Rural Industries Research and Development Corporation, Canberra.

McQuilken, M. P., Halmer, P., & Rhodes, D. J. (1998). Application of microorganisms to seeds. In H. D. Burges (ed.). *Formulation of Microbial Biopesticides* (pp. 255–285). Springer, Dordrecht.

Miransari, M., & Smith, D. L. (2014). Plant hormones and seed germination. *Environmental and Experimental Botany*, 99, 110–121.

Mishra, J., & Arora, N. K. (2018). Secondary metabolites of fluorescent pseudomonads in biocontrol of phytopathogens for sustainable agriculture. *Applied Soil Ecology*, 125, 35–45.

Mohiddin, F. A., Padder, S. A., Bhat, A. H., Ahanger, M. A., Shikari, A. B., Wani, S. H., … Abdel Latef, A. A. H. (2021). Phylogeny and optimization of *Trichoderma harzianum* for chitinase production: evaluation of their antifungal behaviour against the prominent soil borne phyto-pathogens of temperate India. *Microorganisms*, 9(9), 1962.

Moulin, L., Munive, A., Dreyfus, B., & Boivin-Masson, C. (2001). Nodulation of legumes by members of the β-subclass of Proteobacteria. *Nature*, 411(6840), 948–950.

Mummy, D., Holben, W., Six, J., & Stahl, P. (2006). Spatial stratification of soil bacterial populations in aggregates of diverse soils. *Microbial Ecology*, 51, 404–411.

Nagpal, S., Mandahal, K. S., Kumawat, K. C., & Sharma, P. (2022). Beneficial rhizobacteria unveiling plant fitness under climate change. In Anukool Vaishnav, S.S Arya, and D K Choudhary (eds.). *Plant Stress Mitigators* (pp. 281–321). Springer, Singapore.

Oberson, A., & Joner, E. J. (2005). Microbial turnover of phosphorus in soil. In B. L. Turner, E. Frossard, and D. S. Baldwin (eds.). Organic Phosphorus in the Environment (pp. 133–164).

Pal, K. K., & Gardener, B. M. (2006). Biological control of plant pathogens. *The Plant Health Instructor*, 2, 1117–1142.

Patel, D. K., Archana, G., & Kumar, G. N. (2008). Variation in the nature of organic acid secretion and mineral phosphate solubilization by *Citrobacter* sp. DHRSS in the presence of different sugars. Current Microbiology, 56(2), 168–174.

Rachel, M. G., Mondal, M. M. A., Pramanik, M. H. R., & Awal, M. A. (2018). Mulches enhanced growth and yield of onion. *Bangladesh Journal of Scientific and Industrial Research*, 53(4), 305–310. http://dx.doi.org/10.3329/bjsir.v53i4.39195

Rhodes, C. J. (2015). Permaculture: regenerative-not merely sustainable. *Science Progress*, 98(4), 403–412.

Richardson, A. E. (2001). Prospects for using soil microorganisms to improve the acquisition of phosphorus by plants. *Functional Plant Biology*, 28(9), 897–906.

Saha, M., Sarkar, S., Sarkar, B., Sharma, B. K., Bhattacharjee, S., & Tribedi, P. (2016). Microbial siderophores and their potential applications: a review. *Environmental Science and Pollution Research*, 23(5), 3984–3999.

Schippers, B., Bakker, A. W., Bakker, P. A. H. M., & Van Peer, R. (1990). Beneficial and deleterious effects of HCN-producing pseudomonads on rhizosphere interactions. *Plant and Soil*, 129(1), 75–83.

Sharma, M., Dangi, P., & Choudhary, M. (2014). Actinomycetes: source, identification, and their applications. *International Journal of Current Microbiology and Applied Sciences*, 3(2), 801–832.

Sindhu, S. S., Sehrawat, A., Sharma, R., & Khandelwal, A. (2017). Biological control of insect pests for sustainable agriculture. In Tapan Kumar Adhya, Banwari Lal, Balaram Mohapatra, Dhiraj Paul, and Subhasis Das (eds.). *Advances in Soil Microbiology: Recent Trends and Future Prospects* (pp. 189–218). Springer, Singapore.

Six, J., Bossuyt, H., Degryze, S., & Denef, K. (2004). A history of research on the link between (micro) aggregates, soil biota, and soil organic matter dynamics. *Soil and Tillage Research*, 79(1), 7–31.

Spaepen, S., & Vanderleyden, J. (2011). Auxin and plant-microbe interactions. *Cold Spring Harbor Perspectives in Biology*, 3(4), a001438.

Sulieman, S., & Tran, L. S. P. (2014). Symbiotic nitrogen fixation in legume nodules: metabolism and regulatory mechanisms. *International Journal of Molecular Sciences*, 15(11), 19389–19393.

Suman, A., Gaur, A., Shrivastava, A. K., & Yadav, R. L. (2005). Improving sugarcane growth and nutrient uptake by inoculating *Gluconacetobacter diazotrophicus*. *Plant Growth Regulation*, 47(2), 155–162.

Tabassum, B., Khan, A., Tariq, M., Ramzan, M., Khan, M. S. I., Shahid, N., & Aaliya, K. (2017). Bottlenecks in commercialisation and future prospects of PGPR. *Applied Soil Ecology*, 121, 102–117.

Tariq, M., Noman, M., Ahmed, T., Hameed, A., Manzoor, N., & Zafar, M. (2017). Antagonistic features displayed by plant growth promoting rhizobacteria (PGPR): a review. *Journal of Plant Science and Phytopathology*, 1(1), 38–43.

Umukoro, B. O. J. (2020). Tropical crops and microbes. In M. Blumenberg, M. Shaaban, and A. Elgaml (eds.), *Microorganisms*. IntechOpen. DOI: 10.5772/intechopen.82960.

Unkovich, M., Herridge, D., Peoples, M., Cadisch, G., Boddey, B., Giller, K., & Chalk, P. (2008). *Measuring Plant-Associated Nitrogen Fixation* in *Agricultural Systems*. Australian Centre for International Agricultural Research (ACIAR), Canberra, Australia.

Vessey, J. K. (2003). Plant growth promoting rhizobacteria as biofertilizers. *Plant and Soil*, 255(2), 571–586.

Xu, F., Wu, Y., Zhang, C., Davis, K. M., Moon, K., Bushin, L. B., & Seyedsayamdost, M. R. (2019). A genetics-free method for high-throughput discovery of cryptic microbial metabolites. *Nature Chemical Biology*, 15(2), 161–168.

Yadav, R. L., Shukla, S. K., Suman, A., & Singh, P. N. (2009). *Trichoderma* inoculation and trash management effects on soil microbial biomass, soil respiration, nutrient uptake and yield of ratoon sugarcane under subtropical conditions. *Biology and Fertility of Soils*, 45(5), 461–468.

3 Plant Defence Regulation
Role Play of Mycorrhizal Fungi

*Mariya Ansari, Aalok Mishra, Anirudha Chattopadhyay,
Arpan Mukherjee, and Ankita Sarkar*

3.1 INTRODUCTION

The earth is in crisis, be it a 'biodiversity crisis', 'soil crisis', 'food crisis' or 'ecological crisis'. Sustainability and ecological balance are at a tripping point due to the exploitation of natural resources, exhaustive agricultural practices, urbanization and the resultant climate change. Several concepts were brought forward to deal with and fix the earth's failing system. One such concept that rose to the limelight in the recent decade due to its promising outcome was 'Regenerative Agriculture', which encompassed the solution to the abovementioned crisis. The foremost principles of regenerating agriculture are the rehabilitation of ecological systems and cycles, biodiversity and revitalizing soil and nutrients for regenerating the agricultural and earth systems as a whole. Regenerative agriculture, in a broader sense, mainly focuses on the reversal of biodiversity loss and the reclamation of soil, which is the mediator of almost all systems. Several regenerative practices and methodologies were adopted and incorporated over the decade in contemporary agriculture to address this issue, and the probable solution lied just below the soil in the form of a symbiotic relationship between plant roots and a fungus called mycorrhiza.

The term 'Mycorrhiza' came from the Greek words '*mykes*' and '*rhiza*' meaning fungi-root. The term was first used by Professor A.B. Frank in the 1880s as 'mykorhiza', and he first described the widespread symbiotic association between plant roots and fungi (Pandey et al., 2019). Mycorrhiza, being cosmopolitan in distribution, is found in almost all the ecosystems, from evergreen and boreal forests to desert land. The soil microbial world is dominated by mycorrhizal association, which is reported to colonize 90% of plant species and is without a doubt a potential candidate in regenerative agriculture owing to its multi-dimensional regenerating and reclamation properties. Mycorrhiza has the potential to maintain soil biodiversity, soil health and fertility through nutrient cycling, nutrient re-allocation and C-sequestration, which fits the basic criteria of regenerative agriculture. Mycorrhizal association is a two-way beneficial interaction system where the plant system provides shelter and photosynthates to fungi, whereas the fungal partner benefits the plant by improving soil health and fertility, nutrient uptake, enhancing soil microbial activity, and inducing resistance under stressful conditions. The DNA-based phylogenetic analysis and fossil record suggest that mycorrhiza evolved around 450–500 million years ago between the Ordovician and Devonian periods as an endomycorrhizal association (AM) with first-land plants (Brundrett, 2002). Fossil evidence further revealed that the first ectomycorrhizal association took place about 200–150 million years ago in the Jurassic period in the Pinaceae family. It is evident that mycorrhizal association played a key role in the evolutionary process of terrestrial plants showing co-evolutionary behaviour. Apparently, both partners evolved parallelly and became dependent on each other for sharing the limited resources in response to the environmental extremities prevailing in that era. AMF, being the most common mycorrhizal association, forms symbiosis with 74% of flowering plants (Brundrett, 2009). About 80% of the present-day terrestrial plants, including liverworts, ferns, grasses, gymnosperms and angiosperms, has symbiotic relationship with Arbuscular Mycorrhiza. This widespread association has become the footstep of exploring the diversified role of mycorrhiza in regenerative agriculture.

DOI: 10.1201/9781003309581-4

3.2 MYCORRHIZAL FUNGI: BIODIVERSITY, FUNCTIONALITY

In the evolutionary phase, mycorrhiza formed associations with the majority of plant species residing in diverse ecological niches. Mycorrhizas have been reported from major ecosystems around the world, showing a high degree of adaptation to both different environmental conditions and host ranges. AM has been reported from the dessets of the Arabic peninsula (Al-Yahya'ei et al., 2011) to the Himalayan ranges (Lin et al., 2011), from arctic regions (Varga et al., 2015) to tropical forests (Lovelock et al., 2003). While some of the AM isolates have been reported to be confined to natural communities, most of them are reported to be cosmopolitan (Rosendahl et al., 2009). Mycorrhizal association is present in 83% Dicots, 79% Monocots and 100% Gymnosperms (Dad et al., 2023). Some lower groups of land plants (species of hornworts and liverworts) associate with AM, EM or ericoid mycorrhizal fungi (Read et al., 2000; Schussler, 2000; Ligrone et al., 2007; Pressel et al., 2010). The composition of AM fungal communities and their richness depend on host plants, climate and soil conditions (Opik et al., 2006). Based on environmental ribosomal DNA sequences, it is estimated that global AM fungal richness ranges from 341 (Opik et al., 2013) to 1,600 operational taxonomic units (OTUs) (Koljalg et al., 2013) or even higher (Kivlin et al., 2011). It is reported that most plant species host between 1 and 75 AM fungal OTUs, which indicates that the local species richness of AM fungi is higher than the global species richness. AM fungal sporulation and proliferation are also highly dependent on plant host identity. Colonization of the root system for nutritional exchange of Carbon, Nitrogen and Phosphorus is found on the surface of roots, around the epidermal cells of the roots or inside the plant root cortex. On the basis of the location of fungal hyphae in the plant root tissue, mycorrhizal fungi can be divided into two major groups: Ectomycorrhiza (outside root) and Endomycorrhiza (inside root). Both of these groups penetrate the epidermis of the host cell, but endomycorrhiza can be further divided into arbuscular mycorrhiza (AM), ericoid mycorrhiza (ErM) and orchid mycorrhiza (OrM), which form structures such as arbuscles, vesicles and spores, whereas in ectomycorrhiza, hartig nets and thick mantles are found (Figure 3.1).

Certain mycorrhizal fungi show characteristics of both ecto and endomycorrhiza, which are called ecto-endomycorrhiza and are strictly restricted to certain plant genera and subfamilies like pine, spruce, Ericaceae and Arbutoidae, respectively. These mycorrhiza types have different distribution, colonization habit and associations with different groups of plants (Table 3.1).

3.3 MYCORRHIZAL FUNGI AND ENVIRONMENTAL STRESS

The conventional agricultural practices and human activities have created an imbalance in the ecosystem. Degradation of soil with organic and inorganic pollutants/chemicals, heavy metals, and biotic and abiotic stress has intensified in the past decade. A shift in the pattern of the crop production system is imperative if ecological balance and sustenance have to be achieved. Regenerative agriculture revitalizes land, but the major challenge frequently linked is the restoration of soil health and biodiversity. This being the major constraint around the world, it requires a thorough and strict approach to mitigate the problem. The abundance of mycorrhiza even in polluted/degraded soil areas and its reclamation and ameliorating properties make it an important component in tackling such a challenge. The potential of mycorrhiza in ameliorating biotic and abiotic stress is discussed below.

3.3.1 INORGANIC CHEMICALS, ORGANIC CHEMICALS

The recent explosion of advanced agricultural practices and overexploitation of natural resources has resulted in unprecedented effects on the soil system and ecological balance. The increase in levels of heavy metals (arsenic, lead, chromium, tin, mercury, etc), pesticides, insecticides and herbicides contribute significantly to soil pollution. It enters the soil system, the food chain and the animal system, posing a high risk to soil and animal health. In the last few decades, the focus has shifted from traditional remediation approaches to bioremediation, wherein mycorrhiza can

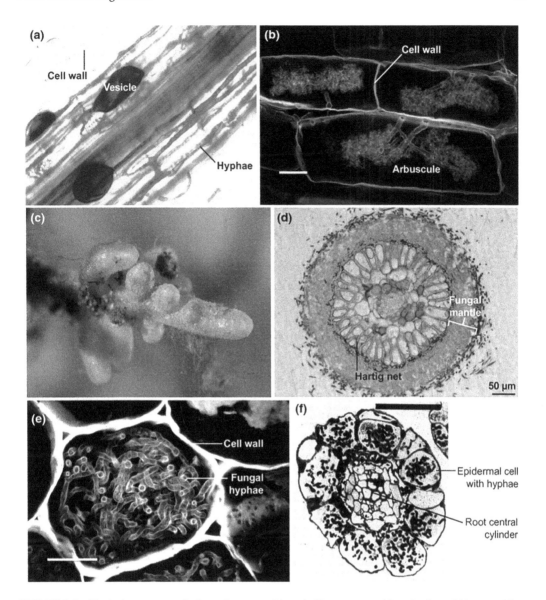

FIGURE 3.1 Typical structures of arbuscular mycorrhizas (a, b), ectomycorrhizas (c, d), orchid mycorrhizas (e), and ericoid mycorrhizas (f) (van der Heijden et al., 2015).

reportedly play a key role. Micro-bioremediation, phytoremediation and rhizoremediation are the concepts of bioremediation, which explores the potential of microbes and plants and the synergistic interaction of plant-microbe in ameliorating polluted soil sustainably.

3.3.1.1 Mycorrhiza in Reclamation of Soil Polluted with Inorganic Chemicals

Inorganic chemical pollutants, basically heavy metals (arsenic, lead, chromium, tin, and mercury) exert stress in the plant metabolic system by reducing the uptake of macro- and micronutrients and thereby decreasing plant growth (Zhao et al., 2019; Wu et al., 2019; Turan, 2020). Several studies suggest that metal toxicity affects numerous cellular mechanisms, such as lipid peroxidation of membranes, inhibition of root growth, accumulation of reactive oxygen species, disturbance of regulatory mechanisms and uptake of essential nutrients, and even death of plant in severe cases (Berni et al., 2019; Seneviratne et al., 2019; Saleem et al., 2020). In mycorrhizal-associated plants,

TABLE 3.1

Mycorrhizal Type, Their Distribution and Colonization

Mycorrhizal Type	Distribution	Fungal Identity	Colonization Percentage
Arbuscular mycorrhiza	Found in terrestrial ecosystem, Association with 80% of terrestrial plants (excluding brassicaceae, chenopodiaceae, polygonaceae, junaceae), hornworts and liverworts	Glomeromycota	71%
Ectomycorrhiza	Common in temperate forest. Mostly in gymnosperms (Pinaceae), Angiosperms (Rosaseae, Myrtaceae, juglandaceae)	Basidiomycota and Ascomycota and some zygomycota	2%
Orchid mycorrhiza	Orchidaceae family	Basidiomycota	10%
Ericoid mycorrhiza	Common in temperate regions, colonizes families like Ericaceae, Empetraceae and Epacridaceae and some liverworts	Mainly Ascomycota and some Basidiomycota	1.4%
Non-mycorrhizal	Found mostly in arid, alpine and degraded habitat	–	8%

the mycorrhizal partner acts as a barrier and shield for plant (Ma et al., 2019) and neutralizes the effect of metal stress by immobilizing heavy metals in roots (Luo et al., 2014; Wu et al., 2016; Miransari, 2011). Several strategies are exhibited by mycorrhiza to eliminate heavy metals from the ecosystem, with phytoremediation (phytoextraction and phytostabilization) and bioremediation being the most significant. Several mechanisms for the alleviation of heavy metals through AMF include the following:

3.3.1.1.1 Activation of Enzymatic and Non-Enzymatic Defence System

Heavy metals cause oxidative stress in plants, and as such, ROS are produced in high quantities. AM symbiosis promotes the antioxidant defence system (enzymatic and non-enzymatic defence systems), increases antioxidant enzyme activities and hence increases plant tolerance to stress (Riaz et al., 2018, 2019; Yan et al., 2019). Several reports have documented that AMF activates defence mechanisms in plant hosts (Debiane et al., 2009; Lenoir et al., 2017; Sharma et al., 2017; Devi et al., 2019). Activation of defence system (catalase, peroxidase and superoxide dismutase) and decreased membrane lipid peroxidation induced by *Glomus mossae* were reported under Cu stress in *Dysosma versipellis* (Luo et al., 2014). In mungbean, AMF alleviated Ar stress by reducing oxidative stress (Alam et al., 2019). In *Solanum nigrum*, the colonization of *Funneliformis mosseae* helped alleviate oxidative damage due to Cd stress and also increased glutathione reductase activities from 17% to 99% in the plant, which scavenges H_2O_2 (Jiang et al., 2016). In Pd-contaminated soil, amendment of the brinjal plant with AMF showed increased antioxidation defence response against heavy metal stress (Chaturvedi et al., 2018)

3.3.1.1.2 AMF Induced Increase in Nutrient Uptake and Plant Biomass

Metal toxicity affects the mineral nutrient content in soil and also the nutrient uptake capacity of plants from such soil. Mycorrhiza improves nutrient and water uptake by plants and reduces metal uptake by plants. AMF improves shoot biomass and restricts the translocation of metal to the aerial parts by retaining metal in mycorrhizal plant roots (Huang et al., 2018; Janeeshma and Puthur, 2020). As per a report by Cui et al. (2019), AMF could alleviate Cd toxicity in soybeans by facilitating the partitioning of minerals in the shoots and roots of soybeans. AMF (*Claroideoglomus etunicatum*) improved plant biomass and nutrient status (N, P and K uptake by 20.1%–76.8%) in maize plants grown in Cd and Lanthanum stress pot experiments; it decreased uptake of heavy metals into plant organs, hence alleviating the toxicity (Chang et al., 2018).

3.3.1.1.3   Retention of Heavy Metals by Fungal Structure

The fungus, being much finer than roots, has a great ability to absorb trace elements and minerals. The fungi act as biosorbants for a wide range of heavy metals, such as Cd, Zn, Ni, Cu and Pb, and effectively cause their immobalization (Gadd, 2010). Mycorrhizal fungi exhibit an important mechanism wherein they immobilize heavy metals in fungal biomass. In a recent report, high Cd accumulation was documented in fungal arbuscules and intercellular hyphae using SR-μXRF imaging. Cd accumulation was predominantly found in arbuscules, which restricted its delivery into plant cells (Chen et al., 2018). In another report, Zn was found sequestrated by fungal structure in the roots of mycorrhizal-associated maize grown in Zn/Pb-polluted soil (Tian et al., 2018).

3.3.1.1.4   AMF Assisted Sequestration, Chelation of Heavy Metals

Certain mycorrhizal ecotypes are highly resistant to heavy metals and better adapted to metal toxicity than others by storing metal ions in arbuscules, vacuoles and vesicles, thereby preventing translocation to the plants. AMF is associated with plants secreting glomalin, which is reported to reduce the bioavailability of heavy metals (Cornejo et al., 2008). Glomalin-related soil proteins chelate heavy metals and decrease their bioavailability in the rhizosphere through metal speciation (González-Chávez et al., 2004; Huang et al., 2005; Subramanian et al., 2009; Malekzadeh et al., 2016; Wang et al., 2017a,b). Inoculation of plants with *Glomus aggregatum* showed a decrease in concentrations of Cd, Pd, Zn and Cu in shoots by the release of glomalin, which chelates metals in soil (Nafady and Elgharably, 2018). In Cd-contaminated soil, AMF was reported to increase the concentration of glomalin in the rhizosphere, thus limiting Cd content in plant tissue by reducing the translocation of Cd in sorghum roots (Babadi et al., 2019). Metallothione, a metal-binding protein produced by fungi upon exposure to high concentrations of heavy metals (Folli-Pereira et al., 2012), is involved in the sequestration and regulation of heavy metal ion concentration in the fungal cytosol. The formation of complexes between heavy metals and metallothione or phytochelatins within mycorrhiza has been reported (Merlos et al., 2016).

3.3.1.2   Mycorrhiza in Reclamation of Soil Polluted with Organic Chemicals

Agrochemicals such as insecticides, fungicides, herbicides and other organic chemicals [polyaromatic hydrocarbons (PAHs), polychlorinated biphenyls (PCBs) and phthalates (PAESs)] and petroleum hydrocarbons have contaminated agricultural soil due to their uncontrolled use. These organic pollutants have a toxic effect on cell ultrastructure, membrane stability and cell biosynthesis (photosynthesis, synthesis of lipids, proteins and hormones), which ultimately interferes with plant growth and development. AMF can be found in soil polluted with petroleum hydrocarbons and pesticides (Xu et al., 2012). AMF reduces organic contaminants in soil and crops through the following mechanisms:

3.3.1.2.1   AMF-Induced Alleviation of Oxidative Stress

Organic contaminants cause the accumulation of reactive oxygen species (ROS) and oxidative stress in plants (Fan et al., 2018; Lenoir et al., 2017; Wang et al., 2017c,d), which damages lipids, proteins and nucleic acids, thereby altering the normal structure and function of cells. AMF is reported to alleviate oxidative stress by mediating the plant's antioxidation system. The accumulation of MDA (maaondualdehyde, an indicator of lipid peroxidation) and 8-hydroxy-2-deoxyguanosine (an indicator of DNA alteration) in AM plants was recorded to be lower in concentration than in non-mycorrhizal plants, confirming the protective nature of AMF against oxidative damage (Debiane et al., 2008, 2009; Tang et al., 2009; Wu et al., 2014; Dong et al., 2017). In mycorrhizal alfalfa, accumulation of more plastoglobules and granal stacks in the chloroplast was documented which possibly alleviates oxidative damage induced by atrazine (Fan et al., 2018).

3.3.1.2.2   AMF-Induced Increased Biomass

Organic contaminants decrease the water availability and solubility of soil minerals and nutrients due to their hydrophilic and lyophilic nature. AMF improves water stress by enhancing osmotic adjustment, water use efficiency, gas exchange direct absorption (Lenoir et al., 2016), or by regulating the expression of drought-inducible genes (Kim et al., 2012).

3.3.1.2.3 Alleviation of Contaminants through Enzymes

AMF produces certain enzymes that hydrolyse and degrade organic pollutants. Its inoculation accelerated the degradation of the organophosphorus pesticide phoxim and decreased its residue in vegetables and soil by decreasing the activity of soil phosphatases (Wang et al., 2011a, b). In the atrazine stress condition, the transcriptome analysis of alfalfa colonized by *F. mosseae* showed increased expression of the five laccase gene, confirming the AMF involvement in the degradation of atrazine (Song et al., 2016). In another study, a tomato plant inoculated with AMF and grown in methamidophos-polluted soil showed enhanced activity of methylamine dehydrogenase in the soil rhizosphere, which promotes methamidophos degradation (Xu et al., 2016).

3.3.1.2.4 Accumulation of Contaminants by AMF Structures and Glomalin

Bioimmobalization by AMF structure and extraradical bioimmobilization diminishes and reduces the contaminant concentration around the root and in the soil. *Rhizophagus custos* is reported to accumulate PHE in extraradical mycelia and spores, preventing its entry into roots (Aranda et al., 2013). In another report, immobalization of PAHs in cortical cells of mycorrhiza supressed their translocation to the shoots (Rajtor and Piotrowska-Seget, 2016). Yang et al. (2017) reported that the total glomalin-related soil protein (GRSP) content of alfalfa grown in PAH-polluted soil was positively correlated with the removal rates of PAHs in the soil and AMF hyphal density.

3.3.2 HARNESSING THE POTENTIAL OF MYCORRHIZA IN AMELIORATING ABIOTIC STRESS

Abiotic stress is a common phenomenon around the globe due to climate change and global warming. Drought, salinity, temperature and ozone stress are major abiotic stresses that influence various metabolic processes and the functioning of plants. It disturbs stomatal opening, osmotic and ionic balance, reduction/inhibition of photosynthetic activity, protein and gene expression, thereby effecting overall growth and productivity (Lenoir et al., 2016). The amelioration of several abiotic stresses by mycorrhiza using different mechanisms is discussed as follows:

3.3.2.1 Drought

Drought stress reduces photosynthetic rate, stomatal conductance and water-use efficiency in plants (Abbaspour et al., 2012) and also results in the closure of stomata, leading to decreased CO_2 intake and impaired photosynthesis (Mathur et al., 2019). Several studies have shown the positive effect of AMF symbiosis on plants under abiotic stress conditions. AMF is reported to improve/influence leaf water potential, gas exchange and the upregulation of photosynthetic rate by increasing the hydraulic conductivity of root. It also alters water regulation in plant partner by stimulating osmolytes or by regulating hormonal signalling (Fan and Liu, 2011). Cheng et al. (2021) reported that under drought stress, AMF trifoliate orange documented higher root volume and diameter as compared to non-AMF plants and exhibited better stomatal conductance, transpiration rate, photosynthetic activity and intercellular CO_2 concentration. Chaperon production has been reported in AMF under drought stress, which prevents the missfolding or aggregation of proteins. In *R. irregularis*, two genes encoding for 14-3-3 and luminal binding protein have been reported. In another study, enhanced drought tolerance in an AMF-inoculated tomato plant was reported, in which AMF regulated 14-3-2 genes (TFT1-TFT12) in the ABA signalling pathway (a non-nutritional mechanism utilized by AM symbiosis to regulate stomatal conductance and other physiological traits), thus improving plant water relations (Bahadur et al., 2019).

3.3.2.2 Salinity Stress

Salinity stress inhibits electron transfer from PSII to PSI and reduces photosynthetic efficacy by reducing PSII active sites. It also enhances ROS, thereby disturbing the ionic homeostatic in plants, which effects nutrient uptake, the cell membrane and its ultrastructures, leading to ionic and osmotic stress (Arif et al., 2020). Reports of increased proline and glycine content in AMF-inoculated plants against ROS in the thylakoid membrane were observed, which improved photosynthesis under salinity conditions. In AMF-inoculated plants, an augmentation in photosynthetic efficiency was observed in saline stress conditions (Klinsukon et al., 2021). Also, inoculation with AMF significantly increased the quantum efficiency under salt stress, showing the ameliorating effect of AMF in preventing photodamage to PSII. AMF-inoculated plants documented increased content of salicylic acid (SA), jasmonic acid (JA), other inorganic nutrients and acids, which play a crucial role in plants under saline stress (Fahad et al., 2015). C4 plants inoculated with AMF showed better salinity stress amelioration for electron transport rates, quantum yield and photosynthetic rate than C3 plants (Wang et al., 2019a,b).

3.3.2.3 Temperature Stress

3.3.2.3.1 High Temperature

Heat stress has a significant impact on plant growth and development; it retards growth rate, causes loss of plant vigour, abscission and senescence of leaves, inhibits seed germination, growth rate and biomass, enhances oxidative stress, causes cell injury and eventually causes a reduction in yield. Gavito et al. (2005) reported that under heat stress, AMF-inoculated plants showed better growth than non-AMF plants. AM colonization brings about morphological changes in root length and biomass, and increases the uptake of water and nutrient from the soil. Colonization with AM protected the photosynthetic apparatus by assisting in photoprotection of cellular structure and lipid phase stabilization of thylakoid membranes (Zhu et al., 2017). In maize plants inoculated with AM, AMF increased the active alpha centres, whereas in non-inoculated maize, inactive beta and gamma centres were activated. Thus, the protection of the inoculated maize plant from heat stress was bestowed on the manipulation of photosystem II heterogeneity (Mathur and Jajoo, 2020).

3.3.2.3.2 Low Temperature

Cold stress causes poor seed germination and seedling growth, wilting, low tillering, decreased photosynthesis, poor reproduction and grain yield (Suzuki et al., 2008; Ganugi et al., 2019). AMF increases plant tolerance to cold stress in various ways. AMF aids the host plant in retaining moisture and increases the protein and secondary metabolite content of the plant under cold stress (Abdel Latef and Chaoxing, 2011). In a report, AM-inoculated maize plants recorded higher proline and sugar content compared to non-inoculated ones (Chen et al., 2014; Charest et al., 1993), owing to the probability that soluble sugars play a crucial role as osmoprotectants under cold stress (Zhu et al., 2017).

3.3.2.4 Ozone Stress

Ozone (O_3) is highly phytotoxic when present in the troposphere and has a detrimental effect on plant species. An increase in ozone level is reported to cause significant leave injury, early senescence and a decrease in photosynthetic rate (Ismail et al., 2014; Wang et al., 2015). AMF being an obligate biotroph, the effect of ozone stress on host plants also affects the colonization of AMF either directly or indirectly. Since ozone is a strong oxidant that affects the photosynthetic machinery of the host plant, it impairs the food supply chain to AMF (McCool and Menge, 1984; Morgan et al., 2003; Feng et al., 2008; Parniske, 2008; Wanget al., 2011a,c). Reports suggest that the colonization rate of AMF in crops affected by ozone stress is variable; it either decreases (McCool and Menge, 1984; Wang et al., 2015), increases (Brewer and Heagle, 1983) or remains unaffected (Duckmanton and Widden, 1994; Wang et al., 2011b). Although the susceptibility of AMF to ozone stress is irrefutable, certain reports suggest its positive effect on plant growth. A 68% and 131% increase in shoot and root biomass was observed in AMF-colonized plants, respectively, under ozone concentrations above 80ppb (Wang et al., 2017a,d). AMF has the capacity to improve plant growth under ozone stress.

3.3.3 Mycorrhiza and Its Role in Ameliorating Biotic Stress

Plant systems come across various microorganisms, pathogens, nematodes and insects, and some of them have deleterious interactions with the plant system. Plants colonized with AMF show increased resistance, survival rate and growth under pathogen attack, and thus it offers an eco-friendly approach to biotic stress management by minimizing the use of agrochemicals, which is one of the major goals of regenerative agriculture. Although AMF imparts tolerance against various phytopathogens, some reports also conclude that it has a neutral and negative impact on the host under attack. Nevertheless, AM fungi provide protection to the plants through various actions, such as competition for colonization at the infection site or photosynthetic pathways, improvement of plant nutrition, root damage competition, exhibition of morphological and anatomical changes in the roots, change in the mycorrhizosphere microbial population and activation of plant defence mechanisms.

3.3.3.1 Competition for Host Photosynthates and Colonization Site

AMF and pathogen both colonize the root cell, and there might be direct competition for photosynthates, space and infection sites. AMF colonization in the cortex of the root hinders pathogens capacity to colonize the same. It is reported that AMF mycelium blocks the molecular crosstalk necessary for host-pathogen interaction. Penetration of *Phytophthora parasitica* was blocked by the mycorrhizal roots of tomatoes (Cordier et al., 1998). Both AMF and root pathogens depend on host photosynthates and Linderman in 1994 reported that they compete for C-compounds in the root system. The higher carbon demand exerts a negative impact on pathogens when AMF have primary access to photosynthates (Poveda et al., 2020). However, there is no solid proof to support such a mechanism for pathogen control by AMF. Cordier et al. (1996) reported that the pathogen – *Phytophthora* did not penetrate arbuscule-containing cells, its development occurred in the AM fungal-colonized and adjacent-uncolonized regions of AM root systems.

3.3.3.2 Competition for Nutrient Uptake and Damage Compensation

AMF colonization can increase the root surface area of plants by 100 folds compared to non-colonized plants (Smith and Read, 2008). The increase in nutrient uptake by AMF-associated plants from the rhizosphere exerts intense competition for nutrient uptake with soil pathogens. AMF not only competes for nutrients with soil-borne phytopathogens but also enhances the host tolerance against pathogen attack by compensating for the root damage caused by the pathogen (Linderman, 1994). It has been reported that AMF compensates for loss/damage to root biomass by pathogen attack (Linderman, 1994), nematodes and fungi (Cordier et al., 1996).

3.3.3.3 Anatomical and Morphological Changes in the Root System and Altered Rhizosphere Interactions

AMF induces changes in the meristematic and nuclear activities of root cells and also alters root morphology, which could affect pathogen infection development. However, a thorough study is required to determine the relationship between AM-induced resistance due to anatomical and morphological changes in roots and pathogen attack. Numerous metabolites, lipids, proteins, polysaccharide and root exudates are secreted into the rhizosphere, which functions as a signal molecule and takes part in interaction. Some compounds in the root exudate favour microbial growth, while others have inhibitory action on pathogens, creating a pathogen-free environment. Previous studies reported that AMF alters the quality and quantity of root exudates (Bansal and Mukerji, 1994) and reduces the pathogen population by influencing the rhizosphere microbiota (Citernesi et al., 1996; Larsen et al., 2003). Henkes et al. (2018) reported that AM-associated wheat plants resulted in a shift in the microbial PLFA (phospholipid fatty acids) pattern in comparison to the control, showing altered rhizospheric interaction.

3.3.3.4 Activation of Host Plant Defence System

AM symbiosis elicits various defence reactions in plants, which aid in an early defence response to attacks by root pathogens. The compounds produced by plants in defence response to mycorrhizal association are phytoalexins, callose, hydroxyprolin-rich glycoproteins, PR proteins, chitinases, β-1,3-glucanases, phenolic compounds and enzymes of the phenypropanoid pathway (Ahuja et al., 2012; Azcon-Aguilar and Barea, 1996). AM fungi have microbe-associated molecular patterns (MAMP) and effector proteins on their surface, which are recognized by plant receptor proteins and activate MAMP-triggered immunity (MTI) and effector-triggered immunity (ETI). MAMP triggers the production of reactive oxygen species, the release of antimicrobial compounds and ethylene biosynthesis (Tsuda and Katagiri, 2010), and programmed cell death in certain cases (Thomma et al., 2011). ETI results in a hypersensitive response (HR), which is localized necrosis at the point of pathogen entry. AMF also activates induced systemic resistance (ISR) to reduce the impact of plant pathogens (Pozo and Azcón-Aguilar, 2007). ISR results in the accumulation of PR-1a proteins, callose-rich coat formation around fungal hyphae and cell wall thickening in the leaves, stems or roots of mycorrhiza-colonized plants. AM symbiosis also enables protection against aboveground pathogens through mycorrhiza-induced resistance (MIR), which occurs through the jasmonic acid (JA)-dependent defence pathway (Pozo and Azcón-Aguilar, 2007). Jaiti et al. (2008) reported that MIR-mediated accumulation of phenolics resulted in protection of date palm against *Fusarium oxysporum*. In another study, tomato plants colonized with *Funneliformis mosseae* showed increased activities of β-1,3-glucanase, phenylalamine ammonialyase (PAL) and lipoxygenase enzyme in their leaves upon *Alternaria solani* infection (Song et al.,2015) (Figure 3.2, Table 3.2).

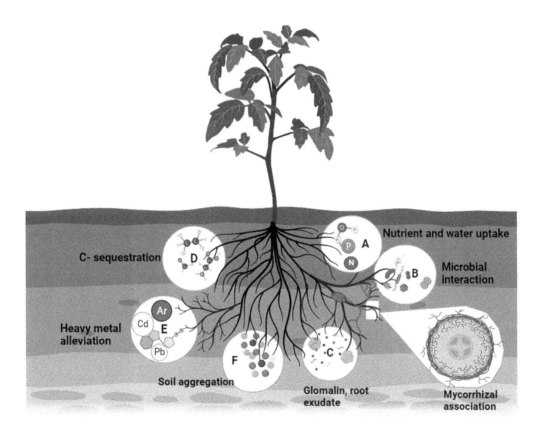

FIGURE 3.2 Mycorrhiza in regenerative agriculture.

TABLE 3.2

Mechanism and Effect of Mycorrhiza in Plant Stress Tolerance

S. No	Nature of Stress	Plant Partner	Mycorrhizal Partner	Mechanism/Effect on Host Plant	References
1.	**Heavy metal**				
	Arsenic toxicity	*Triticum aestivum*	*Rhizoglomus intraradicles, Glomus etunicatum*	Strengthening antioxidant defence system by increasing antioxidation enzymes (superoxide dismutase, catalases and guaiacol peroxidase), antioxidant molecules (carotenoids, proline and α-tocopherol) and thiol metabolism	Sharma et al. (2017)
	Cadmium toxicity	*Zea mays*	*Glomus intraradices*	Higher activities of superoxide dismutase, peroxide, catalase and lower Cd concentration in roots, stem and leaves	Liu et al. (2018)
	Fe	*Glycine max*	*Gigaspora rosea*	Improved shoot Zn and systematically modulated Mn and Fe in host plant ionome, micronutrient balancing strategy	Ibiang et al. (2017)
	Cd, Cr, Ni, Pb	*Zea mays*	*Rhizophagus fasciculatus, R. intraradices, Funneliformis mosseae, Glomus aggregatum*	Phytoextraction, modulation of direct translocation of heavy metals, accumulation of proline, increased chlorophyll content of leaves and phosphorus content of roots and shoots, improvement in soil enzyme activity like dehydrogenase, β-glucosidase, acid and alkaline phosphatase	Singh et al. (2019)
	Cadmium	*Trigonella foenumgraecum*	*Glomus monosporum, G. clarum, Gigaspora nigra*	Stimulation and activation of antioxidant systems, increase in antioxidant enzyme activity (catalase, superoxide dismutase), decrease in translocation factor, MDA content (malonialdehyde) in inoculated *Trigonella* plant (Phyto-stabilization)	Abdelhameed and Metwally (2019)
2.	**Abiotic Stress**				
a.	Drought	*Solanum lycopersicum*	*Funneliformis mosseae, F. geosporum, Claroideoglomus etunicatum, C. claroideum, Glomus microaggregatum, Rhizophagus irregularis*	Modulated the physiological status of plant, improved water use efficiency, better stomatal conductance, efficient PSII and higher water potential of leaves	Bakr et al. (2018)
	Drought	Tobacco	AMF	Improved glomalin-related soil proteins (GRSP), accumulation of phenols and flavonoids and osmolytes content. Upregulation of lipoxygenase (LOX) and phenylalanine ammonia-lyases (PAL) enzymes. AMF reduced MDA content, improved APX (ascorbate peroxidase), catalase, peroxidase (POD), Superoxide dismutase (SOD), glutathione (GSH) and ascorbate (AsA) activities	Begum et al. (2021)

(Continued)

TABLE 3.2 (Continued)
Mechanism and Effect of Mycorrhiza in Plant Stress Tolerance

S. No	Nature of Stress	Plant Partner	Mycorrhizal Partner	Mechanism/Effect on Host Plant	References
	Drought	*Triticum aestivum*	*Mixed culture of R. intraradices, G. mosseae*	Drought stress-induced damage to the structure and function of PSI and PSII alleviated by AMF colonization, enhance photosynthesis and maximum quantum yield of PSII photochemistry in inoculated plants, enhanced uptake and translocation of water and carbon sink stimulation	Mathur et al. (2019)
	Drought	*Triticum aestivum*	AMF	AMF reduced the ROS and improved the activities of Catalase, APX (ascorbate peroxidase), GR (glutathione reductase) and SOD (Superoxide dismutase)	Tereucan et al. (2022)
	Drought + Heat stress	*Solanum lycopersicum*	*Septoglomus deserticola, S. constrictum*	Moderation of oxidative stress by decreasing lipid peroxidation, hydrogen peroxide level, improving leaf and root antioxidation enzyme activities, increased leaf water potential, enhanced stomatal conductance, biomass production	Duc et al. (2018)
b.	High temperature	Pearl millet	*Rhizophagus aggregatus, Funneliformis mosseae*	Increased chlorophyll concentration, root and shoot dry weight	Ndeko et al. (2022)
	High temperature	*Triticum aestivum*	*Rhizophagus irregularis, Funneliformis mosseae, F. geosporum, Claroideoglomus claroideum*	Nutrient allocation and composition altered by AM symbiosis, increased C availability	Cabral et al. (2016)
c.	Cold temperature	*Hordeum vulgare*	*Glomus versiforme, R. irregularis*	Maintains membrane integrity, biomass production, improved antioxidant activities, osmotic and water homeostasis	Hajiboland et al. (2019)
	Cold temperature	*Solanum melongena*	*Rhizophagus irregularis, Funneliformis mosseae, Claroideoglomus etunicatum, Diversispora versiformis*	Improved photochemical reactions and activation of antioxidant defence mechanisms, accumulation of protecting molecules and reduction of membrane damages	Pasbani et al. (2020)
d.	Salinity	*Cucumis sativus*	*Glomus mosseae, G. etunicatum, G. intraradices*	Increased biomass, photosynthetic pigment synthesis and enhanced antioxidant enzymes	Hashem et al. (2018)
	Salinity	*Lactuca sativa*	*Claroideoglomus claroideum*	Reduction of oxidation damage, enhanced growth, development	Santander et al. (2019)
	Salinity	*Pisum sativum*	*Rhizoglomus intraradices, Funneliformis mosseae*	Enhanced nutrient uptake, synthesis of chlorophyll, compatible osmolyte accumulation, lower cellular leakage of electrolyte, increased biomass, higher growth attributes and yield	Parihar et al. (2020)

(Continued)

TABLE 3.2 (Continued)
Mechanism and Effect of Mycorrhiza in Plant Stress Tolerance

S. No	Nature of Stress	Plant Partner	Mycorrhizal Partner	Mechanism/Effect on Host Plant	References
3.	**Biotic Stress**				
a.	*Fungus*				
	Macrophomina phaseolina	*Glycine max*	*Rhizophagus irregularis*	Transcriptional reprogramming, Upregulation of genes involved in secondary metabolites (metabolites involved in phenylpropanoid pathway), hormone metabolism (GA, auxin), stress and signalling, upregulation of genes encoding PR proteins (such as PR1, PR5), dirigent-like protein (DLP), disease resistance-responsive plant basic secretory proteins (BSP), Upregulation of protein serine proteases and down regulation of cysteine proteases.	Marquez et al. (2018)
	Fusarium oxysporum	*Solanum lycopersicum*	*Rhizophagus irregularis*	Decreased disease index due to induced expression of JA synthesis genes including allene oxide cyclase gene (AOC) and lipoxygenase D gene (LOXD) and increased activities of polyphenol oxidase (PPO) and phenylalanine ammonia lyase (PAL) in wild type Castlemart tomato.	Wang et al. (2022)
	Rhizoctonia solani	watermelon	AMF	Decreased disease incidence, reduced *R. solani* induced oxidative stress by improving antioxidant defence. Reduced the relative electrolyte leakage, H_2O_2 accumulation, and lipid peroxidation, and increased the root activity and antioxidant enzymes activities and their transcripts in roots, suggesting mitigation of oxidative stress caused by *R. solani*.	Wu et al. (2021)
b.	**Bacteria**				
	Xanthomonas translucens	*Triticum aestivum*	*Funneliformis mosseae*	AM-induced bioprotective effect, activation of defence-responsive genes (PR proteins, RPM1, MLO) as well as genes and proteins (e.g., RS, GLP, PAL) involved in plant immunity. Activation of broad spectrum defence (BSD) leading to activation of MIR.	Fiorilli et al. (2018)
	Candidatus liberobacter solanacearum	*Solanum lycopersicum*	*Rhizophagus irregularis*	Delayed and reduced the incidence of pathogen symptoms, improvements in plant vigor and MIR-mediated effects on disease progress, psyllid fitness (reduced oviposition), or both.	Tiénébo et al. (2019)

(Continued)

TABLE 3.2 (Continued)
Mechanism and Effect of Mycorrhiza in Plant Stress Tolerance

S. No	Nature of Stress	Plant Partner	Mycorrhizal Partner	Mechanism/Effect on Host Plant	References
c.	*Virus*				
	Tomato bushy stunt virus	*Solanum lycopersicum*	*Rhizoglomus irregulare*	Regulation of PR proteins in tomato plants, lower level of virus accumulation and a higher expression of PR genes in plants inoculated with MZ before virus inoculation	Khoshkhatti et al. (2020)
	Cucumber mosaic virus	*Cucumis sativum*	*Funneliformis mosseae*	Exerts a priming effect by increasing salicylic acid level and a modulation of reactive oxygen species (ROS)-related genes, toward a limitation of ROS accumulation	Miozzi et al. (2020)
d.	*Plant Pathogenic Nematodes*				
	Nacobbus aberrans	*Solanum lycopersicum*	*Glomus intraradices*	AMF-induced physiological change in roots, Increase in aerial and root biomass of tomato, reduction in the number of galls and nematode population induced by *N. aberrans*	Marro et al. (2014)
	Meloidogyne incognita	*Coffea arabica*	*Glomus* spp., *Gigaspora* spp., *Acaulospora* spp.	Competition for common resources such as host photosynthate, nutrition, infection-site and space within the plant root for their survival and multiplication and ultimately decreased nematode densities	Pham et al. (2020)
e.	*Insects*				
	Lissorhoptrus oryzophilus	*Oryza sativum*	*Rhizophagus irregularis, Glomus aggregatum, Funeliformis mosseae, Claroideoglomus etunicatum*	Increased rice tolerance to insect pests by influencing plant biomass and yields	Bernaola and Stout (2021)
	Spodoptera litura	*Brassica juncea*	*Gomus mosseae, Gigaspora* sp. *Scutellospora* sp.	VAM-supplemented plants showed an active systemic response against herbivores with an increase in antioxidant enzymes (SOD, CAT, POD, APX, GR and monodehydroascorbate reductase	Sharma and Mathur (2020)

3.4   MYCORRHIZA FUNGI IN PLANT DEFENCE REGULATION

Mycorrhizal association plays a significant role in modulating plant defence responses against soil-borne disease and pests (Sanchez-Bel et al., 2016). Plants develop an enhanced defensive strategy called mycorrhiza-induced resistance in response to AMF colonization (Cameron et al., 2013). MIR shows similarity to pathogen-induced SAR and non-pathogenic rhizobacterium-ISR. Mycorrhiza-induced systemic resistance is the result of ethylene and jasmonic acid (JA)-dependent defence exerted by mycorrhizosphere bacteria. AMF-based priming involves transcriptional regulation of NPR1 and PR1, an epitome of the SA pathway (Cameron et al., 2013).

MIR is systemically present from root to shoot and is effective against various soil and foliar pathogens. The first case of primed MIR was reported in symbiotic Ri-T-DNA-transformed carrot root, where an increased defence response was observed in the colonized root compared to the non-colonized root against *Fusarium oxysporum*. AMF is reported to suppress plant diseases and pests through ISR (Jung et al., 2012; Song et al., 2015). Several mechanisms have been proposed to ascertain the induction and regulation of defence responses, such as the accumulation of defence-related regulatory molecules (transcription factors or MAP kinases) and chromatin modification. Cameron et al. (2013) proposed the mechanism involved in mycorrhizal association and MIR in four phases:

a. The first phase comprises the release of plant root exudates (amino acids, sugars, phenolic compounds and secondary metabolites), which attract soil microbes to the roots and strigolactone, a root exudate, recruits AMF to plant roots (Akiyama et al., 2005).
b. The second phase includes the induction of an immune response against AMF by the recognition of AMF's MAMPs by PRRs of plants, which triggers an immune response by stimulating SA accumulation.
c. In the third phase, mycorrhiza suppresses plant immunity through calcium/calmodulin kinase DMI3, which represses early-acting defence genes (Siciliano et al.,2007) and induces the production of abscisic acid for its colonization by suppressing the SA-dependent defence response (Ton et al., 2009).
d. The last phase is ISR and mycorrhizosphere development.

When a symbiotic relationship is formed with its host, AMF enhances gene-encoded products displaying anitimicrobial activity. For example, in the root colonized with *Glomus intraradices*, induction of genes TC104515, TC101060 and TC98064 was observed (Liu et al., 2007), which encoded a cysteine-rich protein that showed antifungal activity (Terras et al., 1995) by eliciting a hypersensitive response with a matching resistance gene (de Wit, 1992).

The mutualistic association with mycorrhiza results in reprogramming of the primary and secondary metabolic pathways of the host plant. AMF-mediated modulation in root metabolites also impacts the aboveground metabolites by signalling or transportation (Wang et al., 2018; Schweiger and Muller, 2015). After colonization, primary metabolites (carbohydrates, proteins and lipids) responsible for growth and development increase in plants. Sugar is an important regulator in plant-AMF association (Keymer et al., 2017; Shachar-Hill et al., 1995), and AMF also has the potential to reprogram sugar metabolism (Pedone-Bonfim et al., 2012) and also impacts tricarboxylic acid (Rivero et al., 2015). AMF assimilates hexoses and transforms them into trehalose and glycogen; the concentration of trehalose increases with mycorrhizal colonization and instills protection against abiotic stress. AMF has the potential to upregulate or downregulate plant metabolism based on plant growth conditions. However, total sugar, organic acids and amino acids are differentially regulated by different AMF species in various plants. Under abiotic stress (drought, cold stress, salinity, heavy metals and nutrient deficiencies), the accumulation of sugar in AMF-colonized plants has been reported (Giasson et al., 2008; Wang et al., 2019a,b). Upregulation of sugar and lipids has been observed under water-stressed conditions, which is consistent with an increase in plant biomass

(Bernardo et al., 2019). Several reports suggest that AMF colonization has a positive, negative or no effect on the amino acid content of the host plant (Fester et al., 2011; De Souza et al., 2014).

The first secondary metabolite synthesized in AMF-colonized plants is strigolactones, which acts as a germination signal for mycorrhizal spores. Secondary metabolites provide protection against biotic and abiotic stress (Pagare et al., 2015; Hussein and El-Anssary, 2018). AMF activates several secondary metabolite pathways (carotenoid, phenylpropanoid and antioxidant pathways) (Hill et al., 2018; Chen et al., 2013). Terpenoids, alkaloids and phenolics (major classes of secondary metabolites) are altered in response to AMF colonization (Andrade et al., 2013; Pandey et al., 2018). AMF induces changes in the composition and abundance of secondary metabolites. Carotenoids and phenylpopanoids act as signalling compounds and are important for indirect defence priming in host plants. The increase in phenolic content in mycorrhizal-associated plants is due to upregulation of signalling pathways such as the nitrogen oxide pathway, salicylic acid pathway and hydrogen peroxide pathway (Zhang et al., 2013). Under AMF colonization, significant reprogramming in the phenylpropanoid pathway was observed, and flavonoids are reported to inhibit the production of ROS due to biotic/abiotic stress and regulate the plant-plant-symbiotic association (Mierziak et al., 2014). In trifoliate orange, AMF was reported to modulate the polyamine metabolic pathway to increase the accumulation of pustrescine and cadaverine, which scavenged ROS and maintained ionic homeostasis and cell function under drought stress (Zhang et al., 2020).

Phytohormones such as jasmonic acid (JA), abscisic acid (ABA), salicylic acid (SA) and ethylene (ET) are involved in host plant defence (Pieterse et al., 2012). The SA (attenuates SA level), JA (improves JA-dependent response leading to priming of defence mechanisms) and ET signalling pathways are involved in priming host defence and regulating plant defence (Pozo et al., 2009; Song et al., 2011; Pozo and Azcon-Aguilar, 2007). AM alters hormones in host plants, thereby increasing the absorption of phosphorous, calcium and magnesium and inducing better photosynthesis and resistance against pathogens (Ntengna et al., 2019). Mycorrhiza is reported to induce the SA signalling pathway (Song et al., 2015) and genes expressing JA to increase resistance against pathogen attack (De Vos et al., 2005). 'Immune response' and 'Regulation of phytohormones' predominantly consist of transcription factors such as JAZ1 (orthologs of JAR1 and JAR8) and MYBs (orthologs of MYB4, MYB5, MYB14 and MYB108), which are key regulators of the JA response. AMF also primes the JA pathway as an alert signal against leaf-chewing insects and necrotropic pathogens (Pozo and Azcón-Aguilar, 2007; Jung et al., 2012) by transcriptional regulation of MYBs (induced by JA), lipoxygenase (LOX), coronatine-insensitive (COI), allene-oxide cyclase (AOC), 12-oxophytodienoate reductase (OPR), alleneoxide synthase (AOS), etc.

3.5 FUTURE ASPECTS

The practical aspects of regenerative agriculture and its adoptability are still in their initial stages. The major methodologies adopted are mainly limited to some altered agronomic practices. The focus should be diverted towards alternative concepts such as the utilization of soil microbes for addressing regenerative agriculture principles. The interaction of rhizosphere microorganisms such as plant growth-promoting rhizobacteria (PGPR), mycorrhiza helper bacteria (MHB) and mycorrhiza can determine the structure of the plant community. The triple symbiosis between plant-bacteria-fungi could emerge as an amendment against various stresses and special attention should be given to the belowground microbial interaction to explore the different facets and functional guilds of such associations for cleaner crop production. As the world is gradually shifting towards eco-friendly approaches for a sustainable ecosystem, harnessing the full potential of mycorrhiza in various fields will be the paradigm for such a goal. Various studies have explored the key role of mycorrhiza in bioremediation, bioprotection and biodegradation. Although various experiments have been conducted to test the remediation efficiency of mycorrhiza in alleviating heavy metals and abiotic or biotic stress, limited studies have been done under field conditions or in contaminated soil areas. Further experiments and research at the ground level are required to understand the mechanisms involved in mycorrhizal-mediated amelioration. Recent studies imply that certain organic and inorganic amendments could facilitate the efficacy of arbuscular mycorrhizal fungi (AMF) in alleviating heavy metal toxicity; such dimensions should be explored to harness the maximum mycorrhizal potential in alleviating contaminants. More focus should be given to the genomics, proteomics, transcriptomics, and metabolomics aspects of mycorrhiza-plant association to decode and utilize the mechanisms involved in the induction of defense responses against various stresses.

3.6 MYCORRHIZA EMERGED AS AN INEVITABLE OPTION IN REGENERATIVE AGRICULTURE

The last few decades witnessed an increase in the use of chemical fertilizers, pesticides and herbicides for intensification of agricultural crop production to meet the booming demand. This threatened the global biodiversity, ecological and nutrient balance, and sustenance of natural resources. The concepts of organic farming, sustainable agriculture and regenerative agriculture came into view as remedial measures to sustain the resources for the present and the future. Several approaches, methods and techniques have been devised to achieve the goal of healthier crop production. Mycorrhiza, with its diversified potential in crop production, has emerged as an inevitable and promising candidate for regenerative agriculture. Mycorrhizal association improves crop yield and quality, soil health and fertility, nutrient and water uptake by plants, enhances soil microbial activity, stimulates plant metabolism and protects the plant from biotic and abiotic stress through various mechanisms. The beneficial impact of mycorrhiza is not limited to the above-mentioned features; various studies have proved its potential in the remediation of soil polluted with organic, inorganic and heavy metals. It can reclaim degraded, unproductive soil into agriculturally productive soil. Utilization of the full potential of mycorrhiza in crop production could help in tackling multi-dimensional problems at once.

3.7 CONCLUSION

The horizon of mycorrhizal use in different areas is expanding as more research and techniques are undertaken and developed. AMF are truly referred to as 'agro-ecosystem engineers' and their role in regenerative agriculture becomes imperative due to their widespread contribution in reclamation and remediation. They are significant contributors to maintaining soil health, fertility, ecological balance and biodiversity, which is the basic goal of regenerative agriculture. Exploration and utilization of belowground associations for the adoption of regenerative agriculture is a possibility in the near future. Mycorrhiza, which evolved parallelly in association with terrestrial plants, is a paradigm of such association. Undoubtedly, the exploitation of mycorrhizal as a potential biofertilizer, biodegrader and bioprotector could decrease the dependency on agrochemicals and the consequent environmental damage as a result of it.

REFERENCES

Abbaspour H, Saeidi-Sar S, Afshari H, Abdel-Wahhab MA. 2012. "Tolerance of mycorrhiza infected Pistachio (*Pistacia vera* L.) seedling to drought stress under glasshouse conditions". *Journal of Plant Physiology* 169:704–709.

Abdel Latef AA, Chaoxing H. 2011. "Arbuscular mycorrhizal influence on growth, photosynthetic pigments, osmotic adjustment and oxidative stress in tomato plants subjected to low temperature stress". *Acta Physiologiae Plantarum* 33:1217–1225.

Abdelhameed RE, Metwally RA. 2019. "Alleviation of cadmium stress by arbuscular mycorrhizal symbiosis". *International Journal of Phytoremediation* 21:663–671.

Ahuja I, Kissen R, Bones AM. 2012. "Phytoalexins in defense against pathogens". *Trends in Plant Science* 17:73–90.

Akiyama K, Matsuzaki K, Hayashi H. 2005 "Plant sesquiterpenes induce hyphal branching in arbuscular mycorrhizal fungi". *Nature* 435, 824–827. https://doi.org/10.1038/nature03608

Alam MZ, Anamul Hoque M, Ahammed GJ, Carpenter-Boggs L. 2019. "Arbuscular mycorrhizal fungi reduce arsenic uptake and improve plant growth in Lens culinaris". PLoS One 14(5):e0211441. https://doi.org/10.1371/journal.pone.0211441

Al-Yahya'ei M, Oehl F, Vallino M, Lumini E, Redecker D, Wiemken A, Bonfante P. 2011. "Unique arbuscular mycorrhizal fungal communities uncovered in date palm plantations and surrounding desert habitats of Southern Arabia". *Mycorrhiza* 21:195–209.

Andrade SAL, Malik S, Sawaya ACHF, Bottcher A, Mazzafera P. 2013. "Association with arbuscular mycorrhizal fungi influences alkaloid synthesis and accumulation in *Catharanthus roseus* and *Nicotiana tabacum* plants". *Acta Physiologiae Plantarum* 35:867–880.

Aranda E, Scervino JM., Godoy P, Reina R, Ocampo JA, Wittich RM, García-Romera I. 2013. "Role of arbuscular mycorrhizal fungus *Rhizophagus custos* in the dissipation of PAHs under root-organ culture conditions". *Environmental Pollution* 181:182–189. https://doi.org/10.1016/j.envpol.2013.06.034

Azcon-Aguilar C, Barea JM. 1996. "Arbuscular mycorrhizas and biological control of soil-borne plant pathogens– an overview of the mechanisms involved". *Mycorrhiza* 6:457–464.

Babadi M, Zalaghi R, Taghavi M. 2019. "A non-toxic polymer enhances sorghum-mycorrhiza symbiosis for bioremediation of Cd". *Mycorrhiza* 29:375–387.

Bahadur A, Batool A, Nasir F, Jiang S, Mingsen Q, Zhang Q, Pan J, Liu Y, Feng H. 2019. "Mechanistic insights into arbuscular mycorrhizal fungi-mediated drought stress tolerance in plants". *International Journal of Molecular Science* 20:4199.

Bakr J, Pék Z, Helyes L, Posta K. 2018. "Mycorrhizal inoculation alleviates water deficit impact on field-grown processing tomato". *Polish Journal of Environmental Studies* 27(5):1949–1958.

Bansal M, Mukerji KG. 1994. "Positive correlation between VAM-induced changes in root exudation and mycorrhizosphere mycoflora". *Mycorrhiza* 5:39–44.

Begum N, Akhtar K, Ahanger MA, Iqbal M, Wang P, Mustafa NS, Zhang L. 2021. "Arbuscular mycorrhizal fungi improve growth, essential oil, secondary metabolism, and yield of tobacco (*Nicotiana tabacum* L.) under drought stress condition". *Environmental Science Pollution Research* 28:45276–45295. https://doi.org/10.1007/s11356-021-13755

Bernaola L, Stout MJ. 2021. "The effect of mycorrhizal seed treatments on rice growth, yield, and tolerance to insect herbivores". *Journal of Pest Science* 94:375–392.

Bernardo L, Carletti P, Badeck FW, Rizza F, Morcia C, Ghizzoni R, Rouphael Y, Colla G, Terzi V, Lucini L. 2019. "Metabolomic responses triggered by arbuscular mycorrhiza enhance tolerance to water stress in wheat cultivars". *Plant Physiology and Biochemistry* 137:203–212.

Berni R, Luyckx M, Xu X, Legay S, Sergeant K, Hausman JF, Lutts S, Cai G, Guerriero G. 2019. "Reactive oxygen species and heavy metal stress in plants: impact on the cell wall and secondary metabolism". *Environmental and Experimental Botany* 161:98–106.

Brewer PF, Heagle AS. 1983. "Interactions between *Glomus geosporum* and exposure of soybeans to ozone or simulated acid rain in the field". *Phytopathology* 73:1035–1040.

Brundrett MC. 2002. "Coevolution of roots and mycorrhizas of land plants". *New Phytologist* 154(2):275–304.

Brundrett MC. 2009. "Mycorrhizal associations and other means of nutrition of vascular plants: understanding the global diversity of host plants by resolving conflicting information and developing reliable means of diagnosis". *Plant Soil* 320:37–77.

Cabral C, Ravnskov S, Tringovska I, Wollenweber B. 2016. "Arbuscular mycorrhizal fungi modify nutrient allocation and composition in wheat (*Triticum aestivum* L.) subjected to heat-stress". *Plant and Soil* 408:385–399.

Cameron DD, Neal AL, van Wees SCM, Ton J. 2013. "Mycorrhiza-induced resistance: more than the sum of its parts?" *Trends in Plant Science* 18:539–545.

Chang Q, Diao FW, Wang QF, Pan L, Dang ZH, Guo W. 2018. "Effects of arbuscular mycorrhizal symbiosis on growth, nutrient and metal uptake by maize seedlings (*Zea mays* L.) grown in soils spiked with Lanthanum and Cadmium". *Environmental Pollution* 241:607–615.

Charest C, Dalpé Y, Brown A. 1993. "The effect of vesicular-arbuscular mycorrhizae and chilling on two hybrids of *Zea mays* L." *Mycorrhiza* 4:89–92.

Chaturvedi R, Favas P, Pratas J, Varun M, Paul MS. 2018. "Assessment of edibility and effect of arbuscular mycorrhizal fungi on *Solanum melongena* L. grown under heavy metal (loid) contaminated soil". *Ecotoxicology and Environmental Safety* 148:318–326.

Chen H, Yang X, Wang P, Wang Z, Li M, Zhao FJ. 2018. "Dietary cadmium intake from rice and vegetables and potential health risk: a case study in Xiangtan, southern China". *Science of the Total Environment* 639:271–277.

Chen S, Jin W, Liu A, Zhang S, Liu D, Wang F, Lin X, He C. 2013. "Arbuscular mycorrhizal fungi (AMF) increase growth and secondary metabolism in cucumber subjected to low temperature stress". *Scientia Horticulturae* 160:222–229.

Chen XY, Song FB, Liu FL, Tian C, Liu S, Xu H, Zhu X. 2014. "Effect of different arbuscular mycorrhizal fungi on growth and physiology of maize at ambient and low temperature regimes". *The Scientific World Journal* 2014:956141.

Cheng H-Q, Zou Y-N, Wu Q-S, Kuca K. 2021. "Arbuscular mycorrhizal fungi alleviate drought stress in trifoliate orange by regulating H+-ATPase activity and gene expression". *Frontiers in Plant Science* 12:659694.

Citernesi AS, Fortuna P, Filippi C, Bagnoli G, Giovannetti M. 1996. "The occurrence of antagonistic bacteria in *Glomus mosseae* pot cultures". *Agronomie* 16:671–677.

Cordier C, Gianinazzi S, Gianinazzi-Pearson V. 1996. "Colonisation patterns of root tissues by *Phytophthora nicotianae* var. *parasitica* related to reduced disease in mycorrhizal tomato". *Plant and Soil* 185:223–232.

Cordier C, Pozo MJ, Barea JM, Gianinazzi S, Gianinazzi-Pearson V. 1998. "Cell defense responses associated with localized and systemic resistance to *Phytophthora parasitica* induced in tomato by an arbuscular mycorrhizal fungus". *Molecular Plant-Microbe Interactions* 11:1017–1028.

Cornejo P, Meier S, Borie G, Rillig MC, Borie F. 2008. "Glomalin-related soil protein in a Mediterranean ecosystem affected by a copper smelter and its contribution to Cu and Zn sequestration". *Science of the Total Environment* 406:154–160.

Cui G, Ai S, Chen K, Wang X. 2019. "Arbuscular mycorrhiza augments cadmium tolerance in soybean by altering accumulation and partitioning of nutrient elements, and related gene expression". *Ecotoxicology and Environmental Safety* 171:231–239.

Dad JM, Rashid I, Chen A. 2023. "Is climate change pushing gymnosperms against the wall in the northwestern Himalayas?" *Reg Environ Change* 23:51. https://doi.org/10.1007/s10113-023-02050-1

De Souza LA, Camargos LS, Schiavinato MA, De Andrade SAL. 2014. "Mycorrhization alters foliar soluble amino acid composition and influences tolerance to Pb in *Calopogonium mucunoides*". *Theoretical and Experimental Plant Physiology* 26:211–216.

De Vos M, Van Oosten VR, Van Poecke RMP, Van Pelt JA, Pozo MJ, Mueller MJ, Buchala AJ, Metraux JP, Van Loon LC, Dicke M, Pieterse CMJ. 2005. "Signal signature and transcriptome changes of *Arabidopsis* during pathogen and insect attack". *Molecular Plant-Microbe Interactions* 18:923–937.

de Wit PJ. 1992. "Molecular characterization of gene-for-gene systems in plant-fungus interactions and the application of avirulence genes in control of plant pathogens". *Annual Review of Phytopathology* 30:391–418.

Debiane D, Garcon G, Verdin A, Fontaine J, Durand R, Grandmougin-Ferjani A, Shirali P, Sahraoui ALH. 2008. "In vitro evaluation of the oxidative stress and genotoxic potentials of anthracene on mycorrhizal chicory roots". *Environmental and Experimental Botany* 64(2):120–127.

Debiane D, Garcon G, Verdin A, Fontaine J, Durand R, Shirali P, Grandmougin-Ferjani A, Lounes-Hadj Sahraoui A. 2009. "Mycorrhization alleviates benzo[a]pyrene-induced oxidative stress in an in vitro chicory root model". *Phytochemistry* 70(11–12):1421–1427.

Devi TS, Gupta S, Kapoor R. 2019. "Arbuscular mycorrhizal fungi in alleviation of cold stress in plants". In: Satyanarayana T, Deshmukh S, Deshpande M. (eds) Advancing Frontiers in Mycology and Mycotechnology, 435–455. Springer, Singapore.

Dong J, Wang L, Ma F, Yang J, Zhang X, Zhao T, Qi S. 2017. "Effects of *Funnelliformis mosseae* inoculation on alleviating atrazine damage in *Canna indica* L. var. flava Roxb."*International Journal of Phytoremediation* 19(1):46–55.

Duc NH, Csintalan Z, Posta K. 2018. "Arbuscular mycorrhizal fungi mitigate negative effects of combined drought and heat stress on tomato plants". *Plant Physiology and Biochemistry* 132:297–307.

Duckmanton L, Widden P. 1994. "Effect of ozone on the development of vesicular-arbuscular mycorrhizae in sugar maple saplings". *Mycologia* 86:181–186.

Fahad S, Nie L, Chen Y, Wu C, Xiong D, Saud S, Hongyan L, Cui K, Huang J. 2015. "Crop plant hormones and environmental stress". In: Lichtfouse E (ed) Sustainable *Agriculture Reviews*, Springer Cham, 371–400.

Fan QJ, Liu JH. 2011. "Colonization with arbuscular mycorrhizal fungus affects growth, drought tolerance and expression of stress-responsive genes in *Poncirus trifoliata*". *Acta Physiologiae Plantarum* 33:1533–1542.

Fan X, Chang W, Feng F, Song F. 2018. "Responses of photosynthesis-related parameters and chloroplast ultrastructure to atrazine in alfalfa (*Medicago sativa* L.) inoculated with arbuscular mycorrhizal fungi". *Ecotoxicology and Environmental Safety* 166:102–108

Feng ZZ, Kobayashi K, Ainsworth EA. 2008. "Impact of elevated ozone concentration on growth, physiology, and yield of wheat (*Triticum aestivum* L.): a meta-analysis". *Global Change Biology* 14:2696–2708.

Fester T, Fetzer I, Buchert S, Lucas R, Rillig MC, Härtig C. 2011. "Towards a systemic metabolic signature of the arbuscular mycorrhizal interaction". *Oecologia* 167:913–924.

Fiorilli V, Vannini C, Ortolani F, Garcia-Seco D, Chiapello M, Novero M, Domingo G, Terzi V, Morcia C, Bagnaresi P, Moulin L, Bracale M, Bonfante P. 2018. "Omics approaches revealed how arbuscular mycorrhizal symbiosis enhances yield and resistance to leaf pathogen in wheat". *Scientific Reports* 8:9625.

Folli-Pereira MDS, Meira-Haddad LSA, Bazzolli DMS, Kasuya MCM. 2012. "Arbuscular mycorrhiza and plant tolerance to stress". *Revista Brasileira De Ciencia Do Solo* 36:1663–1679.

Gadd GM. 2010. "Metals, minerals and microbes: geomicrobiology and bioremediation". *Microbiology*, 156(3):609–643. https://doi.org/10.1099/mic.0.037143-0

Gavito ME, Olsson PA, Rouhier H, Medinapeñafiel A, Jakobsen I, Bago A, Azcon-Aguilar C. 2005. "Temperature constraints on the growth and functioning of root organ cultures with arbuscular mycorrhizal fungi". *New Phytologist* 168:179–188.

Giasson P, Karam A, Jaouich A. 2008. "Arbuscular mycorrhizae and alleviation of soil stresses on plant growth". In Zaki Anwar Siddiqui, Mohd. Sayeed Akhtar, and Kazuyoshi Futai (eds.). *Mycorrhizae: Sustainable Agriculture and Forestry*, 99–134. Springer Science and Business Media, Berlin, Germany.

González-Chávez MC, Carrillo-González R, Wright SF, Nichols KA. 2004. "The role of glomalin, a protein produced by arbuscular mycorrhizal fungi, in sequestering potentially toxic elements". *Environmental Pollution* 130:317–323.

Hajiboland R, Joudmand A, Aliasgharzad N, Tolrá R, Poschenrieder C. 2019. "Arbuscular mycorrhizal fungi alleviate low-temperature stress and increase freezing resistance as a substitute for acclimation treatment in barley". *Crop and Pasture Science* 70:218–233.

Hashem A, Alqarawi AA, Radhakrishnan R, Al-Arjani AF, Aldehaish HA, Egamberdieva D, Abd_Allah EF. 2018. "Arbuscular mycorrhizal fungi regulate the oxidative system, hormones and ionic equilibrium to trigger salt stress tolerance in *Cucumis sativus* L." *Saudi Journal of Biological Sciences* 25(6):1102–1114.

Henkes GJ, Kandeler E, Marhan S, Scheu S, Bonkowski M. 2018. "Interactions of mycorrhiza and protists in the rhizosphere systemically alter microbial community composition, plant shoot-to-root ratio and within-root system nitrogen allocation". *Frontiers in Environmental Science* 6:117.

Hill EM, Robinson LA, Abdul-Sada A, Vanbergen AJ, Hodge A, Hartley SE. 2018. "Arbuscular mycorrhizal fungi and plant chemical defence: effects of colonisation on aboveground and belowground metabolomes". *Journal of Chemical Ecology* 44:198–208.

Huang X, Wang L, Zhu S, Ho SH, Wu J, Kalita PK, Ma F. 2018. "Unraveling the effects of arbuscular mycorrhizal fungus on uptake, translocation, and distribution of cadmium in *Phragmites australis* (Cav.) Trin. ex Steud". *Ecotoxicology and Environmental Safety* 149:43–50.

Huang Y, Tao S, Chen YJ. 2005. "The role of arbuscular mycorrhiza on change of heavy metal speciation in rhizosphere of maize in wastewater irrigated agriculture soil". *Journal of Environmental Science* 17:276–280.

Hussein, R. A. & El-Anssary, A. A. 2018. *Plants Secondary Metabolites: The Key Drivers of the Pharmacological Actions of Medicinal Plants*. InTechOpen. DOI: 10.5772/intechopen.76139

Ibiang YB, Mitsumoto H, Sakamoto K. 2017. "Bradyrhizobia and arbuscular mycorrhizal fungi modulate manganese, iron, phosphorus, and polyphenols in soybean (*Glycine max* (L.) Merr.) under excess zinc". *Environmental and Experimental Botany* 137:1–13.

Ismail IM, Basahi JM, Hassan IA. 2014. "Gas exchange and chlorophyll fluorescence of pea (*Pisum sativum* L.) plants in response to ambient ozone at a rural site in Egypt". *Science of the Total Environment* 497:585–593.

Jaiti F, Kassami M, Meddich A, El Hadrami I. 2008. "Effect of arbuscular mycorrhization on the accumulation of hydroxycinnamic acid derivatives in date palm seedlings challenged with *Fusarium oxysporum* f. sp. *albedinis*". *Journal of Phytopathology* 156:641–646.

Janeeshma E, Puthur JT. 2020. "Direct and indirect influence of arbuscular mycorrhizae on enhancing metal tolerance of plants". *Archives of Microbiology* 202:1–16.

Jiang QY, Zhuo F, Long SH, Di Zhao H, Yang DJ, Ye ZH, Li SS, Jing YX. 2016. "Can arbuscular mycorrhizal fungi reduce Cd uptake and alleviate Cd toxicity of *Lonicera japonica* grown in Cd-added soils?" *Scientific Reports* 6:21805.

Jung SC, Martinez-Medina A, Lopez-Raez JA, Pozo MJ. 2012. "Mycorrhiza-induced resistance and priming of plant defenses". *Journal of Chemical Ecology* 38:651–664.

Keymer A, Pimprikar P, Wewer V, Huber C, Brands M, Bucerius SL, Delaux PM, Klingl V, Von Röpenack-Lahaye E, Wang TL, Eisenreich W, Dormann P, Parniske M, Gutjahr C. 2017. "Lipid transfer from plants to arbuscular mycorrhiza fungi". eLife 6:e29107.

Khoshkhatti N, Eini O, Koolivand D, Pogiatzis A, Klironomos JN, Pakpour S. 2020. "Differential response of mycorrhizal plants to *Tomato bushy stunt virus* and *Tomato mosaic virus* infection". Microorganisms 8:E2038. https://doi.org/10.3390/microorganisms8122038

Kim YC, Glick BR, Bashan Y, Ryu CM. 2012. Enhancement of plant drought tolerance by microbes. In: Aroca, R. (ed). *Plant Responses to Drought Stress*. Springer, Berlin, Heidelberg. https://doi.org/10.1007/978-3-642-32653-0_15

Kivlin SN, Hawkes CV, Treseder KK. 2011. "Global diversity and distribution of arbuscular mycorrhizal fungi". *Soil Biology & Biochemistry* 43:2294–2303.

Klinsukon C, Lumyong S, Kuyper TW, Boonlue S. 2021. "Colonization by arbuscular mycorrhizal fungi improves salinity tolerance of eucalyptus (*Eucalyptus camaldulensis*) seedlings". *Scientific Reports* 11:4362.

Koljalg U, Nilsson RH, Abarenkov K, Tedersoo L, Taylor AFS, Bahram M, Bates ST, Bruns TD, Bengtsson-Palme J, Callaghan TM, et al. 2013. "Towards a unified paradigm for sequence-based identification of fungi". *Molecular Ecology* 22:5271–5277.

Larsen J, Ravnskov S, Jakobsen I. 2003. "Combined effect of an arbuscular mycorrhizal fungus and a biocontrol bacterium against *Pythium ultimum* in soil". *Folia Geobotanica* 38:145–154.

Lenoir I, Fontaine J, Sahraoui ALH. 2016. "Arbuscular mycorrhizal fungal responses to abiotic stresses: a review". *Phytochemistry* 123:4–15.

Lenoir I, Fontaine J, Tisserant B, Laruelle F, Sahraoui ALH. 2017. "Beneficial contribution of the arbuscular mycorrhizal fungus, *Rhizophagus irregularis*, in the protection of *Medicago truncatula* roots against benzo[a]pyrene toxicity". *Mycorrhiza* 27:465–476.

Ligrone R, Carafa A, Lumini E, Bianciotto V, Bonfante P, Duckett JG. 2007. "Glomeromycotean associations in liverworts: a molecular, cellular, and taxonomic analysis". *American Journal of Botany* 94:1756–1777.

Lin FR, Metter EJ, O'Brien RJ, Resnick SM, Zonderman AB, & Ferrucci L. 2011. "Hearing loss and incident dementia". *Archives of Neurology* 68(2):214–220. doi:10.1001/archneurol.2010.362.

Linderman RG. 1994. "Role of VAM fungi in biocontrol". In: Pfeger FL, Linderman RG (eds) *Mycorrhizae and Plant Health*, 1–26. APS Press, St. Paul, MN.

Liu J, Maldonado-Mendoza I, Lopez Meyer M, Cheung F, Town CD, Harrison MJ. 2007. "Arbuscular mycorrhizal symbiosis is accompanied by local and systemic alterations in gene expression and an increase in disease resistance in the shoots". *The Plant Journal* 50:529–544.

Liu L, Li J, Yue F, Yan X, Wang F, Bloszies S, Wang Y. 2018. "Effects of arbuscular mycorrhizal inoculation and biochar amendment on maize growth, cadmium uptake and soil cadmium speciation in Cd-contaminated soil". *Chemosphere* 194:495–503.

Lovelock CE, Andersen K, Morton JB. 2003. "Arbuscular mycorrhizal communities in tropical forests are affected by host tree species and environment". *Oecologia* 135:268–279.

Luo ZB, Wu C, Zhang C, Li H, Lipka U, Polle A. 2014. "The role of ectomycorrhizas in heavy metal stress tolerance of host plants". *Environmental and Experimental Botany*, 108, 47–62. https://doi.org/10.1016/j.envexpbot.2013.10.018

Ma Y, Rajkumar M, Oliveira RS, Zhang C, Freitas H. 2019. "Potential of plant beneficial bacteria and arbuscular mycorrhizal fungi in phytoremediation of metal-contaminated saline soils". *Journal of Hazardous Materials* 379:120813.

Malekzadeh E, Aliasgharzad N, Majidi J, Abdolalizadeh J, Aghebati-Maleki L. 2016. "Contribution of glomalin to Pb sequestration by arbuscular mycorrhizal fungus in a sand culture system with clover plant". *European Journal of Soil Biology* 74:45–51.

Marquez N, Giachero ML, Gallou A, Debat HJ, Cranenbrouck S, Di Rienzo JA, Pozo MJ, Ducasse DA, Declerck S. 2018. "Transcriptional changes in mycorrhizal and nonmycorrhizal soybean plants upon infection with the fungal pathogen *Macrophomina phaseolina*". *Molecular Plant-Microbe Interactions* 31(8):842–855.

Marro N, Lax P, Cabello M, Doucet ME, Becerra AG. 2014. "Use of the arbuscular mycorrhizal fungus *Glomus intraradices* as biological control agent of the nematode *Nacobbus aberrans* parasitizing tomato". *Brazilian Archives of Biology and Technology* 57:668–674. https://doi.org/10.1590/S1516-8913201402200

Mathur, S., Tomar, R. S., & Jajoo, A. 2019. Arbuscular Mycorrhizal fungi (AMF) protect the photosynthetic apparatus of wheat under drought stress. *Photosynthesis Research* 139: 227–238. https://doi.org/10.1007/s11120-018-0538-4

Mathur S, Jajoo A. 2020. "Arbuscular mycorrhizal fungi protects maize plants from high temperature stress by regulating photosystem II heterogeneity". *Industrial Crops and Products* 143:111934.

McCool PM, Menge JA. 1984. "Interaction of ozone and mycorrhizal fungi on tomato as influenced by fungal species and host variety". *Soil Biology and Biochemistry* 16:425–427.

Merlos MA, Zitka O, Vojtech A, Azco´n-Aguilar C, Ferrol N. 2016. "The arbuscular mycorrhizal fungus *Rhizophagus irregularis* differentially regulates the copper response of two maize cultivars differing in copper tolerance". *Plant Science* 253:68–76.

Mierziak J, Kostyn K, Kulma A. 2014. "Flavonoids as important molecules of plant interactions with the environment". *Molecules* 19:16240–16265.

Miozzi L, Vaira AM, Brilli F, Casarin V, Berti M, Ferrandino A, Nerva L, Accotto GP, Lanfranco L. 2020. "Arbuscular mycorrhizal symbiosis primes tolerance to cucumber mosaic virus in tomato". *Viruses* 12:675. https://doi.org/10.3390/v12060675

Miransari M. 2011. "Hyperaccumulators, arbuscular mycorrhizal fungi and stress of heavy metals". *Biotechnology Advances* 29:645–653.

Morgan PB, Ainsworth EA, Long SP. 2003. "How does elevated ozone impact soybean? A meta-analysis of photosynthesis, growth and yield." Plant, Cell & Environment 26:1317–1328.

Nafady NA, Elgharably A. 2018. "Mycorrhizal symbiosis and phosphorus fertilization effects on *Zea mays* growth and heavy metals uptake". *International Journal of Phytoremediation* 20:869–875.

Ndeko AB, Founoune-Mboup H, Kane A, Cournac L. 2022. "Arbuscular mycorrhizal fungi alleviate the negative effect of temperature stress in millet lines with contrasting oil aggregation potential". *Gesunde Pflanzen* 74(1):53–67.

Ntengna YF, Tchameni NS, Fokom R, Sameza ML, Minyaka E, Ngonkeu MEL, Nana Wakam L, Etoa FX, Nwaga D. 2019. "Effects of arbuscular mycorrhiza fungi on stimulation of nutrient content and induction of biochemical defense response in *Xanthosoma sagittifolium* plants against root rot disease caused by *Pythium myriotylum*". *International Journal of Advance Agricultural Research* 7:98–107.

Öpik M, Moora M, Liira J, Zobel M. 2006. "Composition of root-colonizing arbuscular mycorrhizal fungal communities in different ecosystems around the globe". *Journal of Ecology*, 94(4):778–790. https://doi.org/10.1111/j.1365-2745.2006.01136.x

Opik M, Zobel M, Cantero JJ, Davison J, Facelli JM, Hiiesalu I, Jairus T, Kalwij JM, Koorem K, Leal ME, et al. 2013. "Global sampling of plant roots expands the described molecular diversity of arbuscular mycorrhizal fungi". *Mycorrhiza* 23:411–430.

Pagare S, Bhatia M, Tripathi N, Pagare S, Bansal YK. 2015. "Secondary metabolites of plants and their role: overview". *Current Trends in Biotechnology and Pharmacy* 9:293–304.

Pandey, D., Kehri, H.K., Zoomi, I., Akhtar, O., & Singh, A.K. 2019. Mycorrhizal fungi: Biodiversity, ecological significance, and industrial applications. In A. Yadav, S. Mishra, S. Singh, and A. Gupta (eds.), *Recent Advancement in White Biotechnology Through Fungi*. Fungal Biology. Springer, Cham. https://doi.org/10.1007/978-3-030-10480-1_5

Pandey DK, Kaur P, Dey A. 2018. "Arbuscular mycorrhizal fungi: effects on secondary metabolite production in medicinal plants". In: Ajar Nath Yadav, Sangram Singh, Shashank Mishra, and Arti Gupta (eds) *Fungi and Their Role in Sustainable Development: Current Perspectives*, 507–538.

Parihar M, Rakshit A, Rana K, Tiwari G, Jatav SS. 2020. "The effect of arbuscular mycorrhizal fungi inoculation in mitigating salt stress of pea (*Pisum sativum* L.)" *Communications in Soil Science and Plant Analysis* 51:1545–1559.

Parniske M. 2008. "Arbuscular mycorrhiza: the mother of plant root endosymbiosis". *Nature Reviews Microbiology* 6:763–775.

Pasbani B, Salimi A, Aliasgharzad N, Hajiboland R. 2020. "Colonization with arbuscular mycorrhizal fungi mitigates cold stress through improvement of antioxidant defense and accumulation of protecting molecules in eggplants". *Scientia Horticulturae* 272:109575.

Pham TT, Giang BL, Nguyen NH, Yen PND, Hoang VDM, Ha BTL, Le NTT. 2020. "Combination of mycorrhizal symbiosis and root grafting effectively controls nematode in replanted coffee soil". *Plants* 9:555. https://doi.org/10.3390/plants9050555

Pieterse CM, Van der Does D, Zamioudis C, Leon-Reyes A, Van Wees SCM. 2012. "Hormonal modulation of plant immunity". *Annual Review of Cell and Developmental Biology* 28(1):489–521.

Poveda J, Abril-Urias P, Escobar C. 2020. "Biological control of plant-parasitic nematodes by filamentous fungi inducers of resistance: *Trichoderma*, mycorrhizal and endophytic fungi". *Frontiers in Microbiology* 11:992.

Pozo MJ, Azcon-Aguilar C. 2007. "Unraveling mycorrhiza-induced resistance". Current *Opinion* in *Plant Biology* 10(4):393–398.

Pozo MJ, Verhage A, García-Andrade J, García JM, Azcon-Aguilar C. 2009. "Priming plant defence against pathogens by arbuscular mycorrhizal fungi". In Concepción Azcón-Aguilar, Jose Miguel Barea, Silvio Gianinazzi, and Vivienne Gianinazzi-Pearson (eds.): *Mycorrhizas– Functional Processes and Ecological Impact*, 123–135. Springer, Berlin, Heidelberg.

Pressel S, Bidartondo MI, Ligrone R, Duckett JG. 2010. "Fungal symbioses in bryophytes: new insights in the twenty first century". *Phytotaxa* 9:238–253.

Rajtor M, Piotrowska-Seget Z. 2016. "Prospects for arbuscular mycorrhizal fungi (AMF) to assist in phytoremediation of soil hydrocarbon contaminants". *Chemosphere* 162:105–116.

Read DJ, Duckett JG, Francis R, Ligrone R, Russell A. 2000. "Symbiotic fungal associations in 'lower' land plants". *Philosophical Transactions of the Royal Society of London Series B-Biological Sciences* 355:815–830.

Riaz M, Yan L, Wu X, Hussain S, Aziz O, Jiang C. 2019. "Boron supply maintains efficient antioxidant system, cell wall components and reduces aluminium concentration in roots of trifoliate orange". *Plant Physiology and Biochemistry* 137:93–101.

Riaz M, Yan L, Wu X, Hussain S, Aziz O, Wang Y, Imran M, Jiang C. 2018. "Boron alleviates the aluminium toxicity in trifoliate orange by regulating antioxidant defense system and reducing root cell injury". *Journal of Environmental Management* 208:149–158.

Rivero J, Gamir J, Aroca R, Pozo MJ, Flors V. 2015. "Metabolic transition in mycorrhizal tomato roots". *Frontiers in Microbiology* 6:598.

Rosendahl S, McGee P, Morton JB. 2009. "Lack of global population genetic differentiation in the arbuscular mycorrhizal fungus *Glomus mosseae* suggests a recent range expansion which may have coincided with the spread of agriculture". *Molecular Ecology* 18:4316–4329.

Saleem MH, Ali S, Rehman M, Rana MS, Rizwan M, Kamran M, Imran M, Riaz M, Soliman MH, Elkelish A, Liu L. 2020. "Influence of phosphorus on copper phytoextraction via modulating cellular organelles in two jute (*Corchorus capsularis* L.)varieties grown in a copper mining soil of Hubei Province, China". *Chemosphere* 248:126032.

Sanchez-Bel P, Troncho P, Gamir J, Pozo MJ, Camañes G, Cerezo M, Flors V. 2016. "The nitrogen availability interferes with mycorrhiza-induced resistance against *Botrytis cinerea* in tomato". *Frontiers in Microbiology* 7:1598.

Santander C, Ruiz A, Garcia S, Aroca R, Cumming J, Cornejo P. 2019. "Efficiency of two arbuscular mycorrhizal fungi inocula to improve saline stress tolerance in lettuce plants by changes of antioxidant defense mechanisms". *Journal of the Science of Food and Agriculture* 100:1577–1587.

Schussler A. 2000. "*Glomus claroideum* forms an arbuscular mycorrhiza-like symbiosis with the hornwort *Anthoceros punctatus*". *Mycorrhiza* 10:15–21.

Schweiger R, Müller C. 2015. "Leaf metabolome in arbuscular mycorrhizal symbiosis". *Current Opinion in Plant Biology* 26:120–126.

Seneviratne M, Rajakaruna N, Rizwan M, Madawala HMSP, Ok YS, Vithanage M. 2019. "Heavy metal-induced oxidative stress on seed germination and seedling development: a critical review". *Environmental Geochemistry and Health* 41:1813–1831.

Shachar-Hill Y, Pfeffer PE, Douds D, Osman SF, Doner LW, Ratcliffe RG. 1995. "Partitioning of intermediary carbon metabolism in vesicular-arbuscular mycorrhizal leek". *Plant Physiology* 108:7–15.

Sharma G, Mathur V. 2020. "Modulation of insect-induced oxidative stress responses by microbial fertilizers in *Brassica juncea*". *FEMS Microbiology Ecology* 96:fiaa040. https://doi.org/10.1093/femsec/fiaa040

Sharma S, Anand G, Singh N, Kapoor R. 2017. "Arbuscular mycorrhiza augments arsenic tolerance in wheat (*Triticum aestivum* L.) by strengthening antioxidant defense system and thiol metabolism". *Frontiers in Microbiology* 8:906.

Siani NG, Fallah S, Pokhrel LR, Rostamnejadi A. 2017. "Natural amelioration of Zinc oxide nanoparticle toxicity in fenugreek (*Trigonella foenum-gracum*) by arbuscular mycorrhizal (*Glomus intraradices*) secretion of glomalin". *Plant Physiology and Biochemistry* 112:227–238.

Siciliano V, Genre A, Balestrini R, Cappellazzo G, deWit PJGM, Bonfante P. 2007. "Transcriptome analysis of arbuscular mycorrhizal roots during development of the prepenetration apparatus". *Plant Physiology* 144(3):1455–1466. https://doi.org/10.1104/pp.107.097980

Singh G, Pankaj U, Chand S, Verma RK. 2019. "Arbuscular mycorrhizal fungi-assisted phytoextraction of toxic metals by *Zea mays* L. from tannery sludge". *Soil and Sediment Contamination: An International Journal* 28:729–746.

Smith SE, Read DJ. 2008. "Mycorrhizal symbiosis". *The Quarterly Review of Biology* 3:273–281.

Song F, Li J, Fan X, Zhang Q, Chang W, Yang F, Geng G. 2016. "Transcriptome analysis of *Glomus mosseae/ Medicago sativa* mycorrhiza on atrazine stress". *Scientific Reports* 6:20245.

Song F, Song G, Dong A, Kong X. 2011. "Regulatory mechanisms of host plant defense responses to arbuscular mycorrhiza". *Acta Ecologica Sinica* 31(6):322–327.

Song Y, Chen D, Lu K, Sun Z, Zeng R. 2015. "Enhanced tomato disease resistance primed by arbuscular mycorrhizal fungus". *Frontiers in Plant Science* 6:786.

Subramanian KS, Tenshia V, Jayalakshmi K, Ramachandran V. 2009."Biochemical changes and zinc fractions in arbuscular mycorrhizal fungus (*Glomus intraradices*) inoculated and uninoculated soils under differential zinc fertilization". *Applied Soil Ecology* 43:32–39.

Suzuki K, Nagasuga K, Okada M. 2008. "The chilling injury induced by high root temperature in the leaves of rice seedlings". *Plant and Cell Physiology* 49:433–442.

Tang M, Chen H, Huang JC, Tian ZQ. 2009. "AM fungi effects on the growth and physiology of *Zea mays* seedlings under diesel stress". *Soil Biology and Biochemistry* 41(5):936–940.

Tereucán, G., Ruiz, A., Nahuelcura, J., Oyarzún, P., Santander, C., Winterhalter, P., Ferreira, P. A. A., & Cornejo, P. 2022. Shifts in biochemical and physiological responses by the inoculation of arbuscular mycorrhizal fungi in Triticum aestivum growing under drought conditions. *Journal of the Science of Food and Agriculture* 102(5): 1927–1938. https://doi.org/10.1002/jsfa.11530

Terras FR, Eggermont K, Kovaleva V, Raikhel NV, Osborn RW, Kester A, Rees SB, Torrekens S, Leuven FV, Vanderleyden J. 1995. "Small cysteine-rich antifungal proteins from radish: their role in host defense". *The Plant Cell* 7:573–588.

Thomma BPHJ, Nurnberger T, Joosten MHAJ. 2011. "Of PAMPs and effectors: the blurred PTI-ETI dichotomy". The Plant Cell 23:4–15.

Tian H, Fang L, Duan C, Wang Y, Wu H. 2018. "Dominant factor affecting Pb speciation and the leaching risk among land-use types around Pb-Zn mine". *Geoderma*, 326:123–132. https://doi.org/10.1016/j.geoderma.2018.04.016

Tiénébo EO, Harrison K, Abo K, Brou YC, Pierson LS 3rd, Tamborindeguy C, Pierson EA, Levy JG. 2019. "Mycorrhization mitigates disease caused by "Candidatus Liberobacter solanacearum" in tomato". Plants 8:507. https://doi.org/10.3390/plants8110507

Tsuda K, Katagiri F. 2010. "Comparing signaling mechanisms engaged in pattern-triggered and effector-triggered immunity". *Current Opinion in Plant Biology*, 13(4):459–465. https://doi.org/10.1016/j.pbi.2010.04.006

Turan V. 2020. "Potential of pistachio shell biochar and dicalcium phosphate combination to reduce Pb speciation in spinach, improved soil enzymatic activities, plant nutritional quality, and antioxidant defense system". *Chemosphere* 245:125611.

van der Heijden MGA, Martin FM, Selosse M-A, Sanders IR. 2015. "Mycorrhizal ecology and evolution: the past, the present, and the future". *New Phytologist*. https://doi.org/10.1111/nph.13288

Varga S, Finozzi C, Vestberg M, Kytoviita MM. 2015. "Arctic arbuscular mycorrhizal spore community and viability after storage in cold conditions". *Mycorrhiza* 25:335–343.

Wang F, Sun Y, Shi ZY. 2019a. "Arbuscular mycorrhiza enhances biomass production and salt tolerance of sweet sorghum". *Microorganisms* 7:289.

Wang FY, Shi ZY, Tong RJ, Xu XF. 2011a. "Dynamics of phoxim residues in green onion and soil as influenced by arbuscular mycorrhizal fungi". *Journal of Hazardous Materials* 185(1):112–116.

Wang FY, Tong RJ, Shi ZY, Xu XF, He XH. 2011b. "Inoculations with arbuscular mycorrhizal fungi increase vegetable yields and decrease phoxim concentrations in carrot and green onion and their soils". *PLoS One* 6(2):e16949.

Wang H, Hao Z, Zhang X, Xie W, Chen B. 2022. "Arbuscular mycorrhizal fungi induced plant resistance against Fusarium wilt in jasmonate biosynthesis defective mutant and wild type of tomato". *Journal of Fungi*8(5):422. https://doi.org/10.3390/jof8050422.

Wang L, Ji B, Hu Y, Liu R, Sun W. 2017a. "A review on in situ phytoremediation of mine tailings". *Chemosphere* 184:594–600.

Wang M, Schäfer M, Li D, Halitschke R, Dong C, McGale E, Paetz C, Song Y, Li S, Dong J, Heiling S, et al. 2018. "Blumenols as shoot markers of root symbiosis with arbuscular mycorrhizal fungi". *Elife* 7:e37093.

Wang S, Augé RM, Toler HD. 2017b. "Arbuscular mycorrhiza formation and its function under elevated atmospheric O3: a meta-analysis". *Environmental Pollution* 226:104–117.

Wang SG, Diao XJ, Li YW, Ma LM. 2015. "Effect of *Glomus aggregatum* on photosynthetic function of snap bean in response to elevated ozone". *The Journal of Agricultural Science* 153:837–852.

Wang SG, Feng ZZ, Wang XK, Gong WL. 2011c. "Arbuscular mycorrhizal fungi alter the response of growth and nutrient uptake of snap bean (*Phaseolus vulgaris* L.) to O3". *Journal of Environmental Sciences* 23:968–974.

Wang W, Shi J, Xie Q, Jiang Y, Yu N, Wang E. 2017c. "Nutrient exchange and regulation in arbuscular mycorrhizal symbiosis". *Molecular Plant* 10:1147–1158.

Wang X, Teng Y, Zhang N, Christie P, Li Z, Luo Y, Wang J. 2017d. "Rhizobial symbiosis alleviates polychlorinated biphenyls-induced systematic oxidative stress via brassinosteroids signaling in alfalfa". *Science of the Total Environment* 592:68–77.

Wang Y, Wang J, Yan X, Sun S, Lin J. 2019b. "The effect of arbuscular mycorrhizal fungi on photosystem II of the host plant under salt stress: a meta-analysis". *Agronomy* 9:806.

Wu F, Yu X, Wu S, Wong M. 2014. "Effects of inoculation of PAH-degrading bacteria and arbuscular mycorrhizal fungi on responses of ryegrass to phenanthrene and pyrene". *International Journal of Phytoremediation* 16(2):109–122.

Wu M, Yan Y, Wang Y, Mao Q, Fu Y, Peng X, Yang Z, Ren J, Liu A, Chen S, Ahammed GJ. 2021. "Arbuscular mycorrhizal fungi for vegetable (VT) enhance resistance to *Rhizoctonia solani* in watermelon by alleviating oxidative stress". *Biological Control* 152:104433.

Wu S, Zhang X, Chen B, Wu Z, Li T, Hu Y, Sun Y, Wang Y. 2016. "Chromium immobilization by extraradical mycelium of arbuscular mycorrhiza contributes to plant chromium tolerance". *Environmental and Experimental Botany* 122:10–18.

Wu S, Zhang X, Huang L, Chen B. 2019. "Arbuscular mycorrhiza and plant chromium tolerance". *Soil Ecology Letter* 1:94–104.

Xu L, Zhang J, Yuan Y, Liu R, Li M. 2016. "Effects of arbuscular mycorrhizal fungi and plant growth-promoting rhizobacteria on remediation of soil polluted with methamidophos". *Acta Pedologica Sinica* 53:919–929.

Xu ZL, Deng H, Deng XF, Yang JY, Jiang YM, Zeng DP, Huang F, Shen YD, Lei HT, Wang H, Sun YM. 2012. "Monitoring of organophosphorus pesticides in vegetables using monoclonal antibody-based direct competitive ELISA followed by HPLC–MS/MS". *Food Chemistry* 131(4), 1569–1576. https://doi.org/10.1016/j.foodchem.2011.10.020

Yan L, Du C, Riaz M, Jiang C. 2019. "Boron mitigates citrus root injuries by regulating intracellular pH and reactive oxygen species to resist H+-toxicity". *Environmental Pollution* 255:113254.

Yang Y, He C, Huang L, Ban Y, Tang M. 2017. "The effects of arbuscular mycorrhizal fungi on glomalin-related soil protein distribution, aggregate stability and their relationships with soil properties at different soil depths in lead-zinc contaminated area". *PLOS ONE* 12(8), e0182264. https://doi.org/10.1371/journal.pone.0182264

Zhang F, Zou YN, Wu Q, Ku˘ca K. 2020. "Arbuscular mycorrhizas modulate root polyamine metabolism to enhance drought tolerance of trifoliate orange". *Environmental and Experimental Botany* 171:103926.

Zhang RQ, Zhu H, Zhao HQ, Yao Q. 2013. "Arbuscular mycorrhizal fungal inoculation increases phenolic synthesis in clover roots via hydrogen peroxide, salicylic acid and nitric oxide signalling pathways". *Journal of Plant Physiology* 170:74–79.

Zhao H, Wei Y, Wang J, Chai T. 2019. "Isolation and expression analysis of cadmium-induced genes from Cd/Mn hyperaccumulator *Phytolacca americana* in response to high Cd exposure". *Plant Biology* 21:15–24.

Zhu X, Song F, Liu F. 2017. "Arbuscular mycorrhizal fungi and tolerance of temperature stress in plants". In: WuQS (ed) *Arbuscular Mycorrhizas and Stress Tolerance of Plants*, 163–194. Springer Nature, Singapore.

4 Phosphate-Solubilizing Rhizobacteria

Diversity, Mechanisms, and Prospects for Regenerative Agriculture

*Becky Nancy Aloo, Benson Nyongesa Ouma,
Beatrice Angiyo Were, and John Baptist Tumuhairwe*

4.1 INTRODUCTION

The world population has increased multifold in the past decades, and so has food production to equal the demand for food. According to FAO (2017), the demand for food and other agricultural products is expected to increase by 50% between 2012 and 2050. This requires that more and more food be produced using appropriate strategies. Some of the approaches to increasing food production involve intensive and extensive agriculture. While extensive agriculture involves increasing the land under production, intensive agriculture entails producing more food on the existing farmlands. The former is no longer feasible under shrinking land sizes occasioned by population and industrialization pressures. As such, agricultural intensification is largely pursued and facilitated by several chemical inputs to boost crop production and control crop diseases. While agrochemicals are significant in this regard, their continued and indiscriminate use has been a source of debate for environmentalists and researchers the world over owing to their adverse environmental effects. In attempts to find suitable solutions, scientists worldwide have shifted their attention to alternative and more sustainable agricultural practices.

Regenerative agriculture is a relatively new approach that is quickly gaining attention among sustainability researchers as a solution to sustainable food systems. Different scholars have described regenerative agriculture differently (Table 4.1), and a consensus on the definition seems to be lacking at the moment. However, all existing definitions so far tend to point towards crop production mechanisms that employ sustainable mechanisms for healthier people and a healthy planet. A recent meta-analysis of literature by Schreefel et al. (2020) concludes that soil health and biodiversity conservation are the bases of regenerative agriculture. In this chapter, we adopt the definition fronted by Rhodes (2017) that regenerative agriculture denotes 'alternative ways of producing food with lower or net positive environmental impacts'. In this context, alternative mechanisms of plant nutrition and fertilization are critical components of regenerative agriculture. Some scholars have argued that the use of external inputs such as fertilizers is inevitable to increase crop yields and sustain soils degraded through agricultural intensification (Vanlauwe et al., 2014). Here, we argue that the use of synthetic inputs may not support regenerative agriculture in its entirety and that alternative crop fertilization mechanisms are both urgent and necessary, considering the negative environmental effects of synthetic agro-inputs. We borrow from White (2020) that 'the first step in the regenerative transition is to stop using the synthetic chemicals, which are also killing beneficial insects and important soil microbes and fungi'.

DOI: 10.1201/9781003309581-5

TABLE 4.1

Various Definitions of Regenerative Agriculture

Definition	Source
A suite of practices that restores and maintains soil health and fertility, supports biodiversity, protects watersheds, and improves ecological and economic resilience	White (2020)
Improving soil functionality, soil quality, or soil health	Sanyal and Wolthuizen (2021)
Farming designed to minimize external inputs and off-site impacts	Al-Kaisi and Lal (2020)
A semi-closed agricultural system designed to minimize external inputs or external impacts of agronomy	Pearson (2007)
Agriculture in which inputs of energy, in the form of fertilizers and fuels, are minimized because these key agricultural elements are recycled as far as possible	Rhodes (2012)
Alternative ways of producing food with lower or net positive environmental impacts	Rhodes (2017)
An approach to farming that uses soil conservation as the entry point to regenerate and contribute to multiple ecosystem services	Schreefel et al. (2020)
Producing adequate and nutritious food while restoring and sustainably managing soil health	Lal (2020)
Development of healthy soil that can produce high-quality nutrient-rich food while improving, rather than degrading land, ultimately leading to productive farms, healthy communities, and economies	Diwan et al. (2021)
A broad suite of principles and practices aimed at regenerating soils and ecosystems through an array of considered agricultural activities	Lunn-Rockliffe et al. (2020)
It is the synonym of sustainable agriculture or precision farming where high food production occurs with accurate use of agricultural resources	Goswami (2021)

Phosphorus, being one of the most essential plant nutrients whose availability in soil is largely limited due to rapid fixation and immobilization and largely supplied as artificial fertilizers, alternative P fertilization mechanisms can contribute to the overall goals of regenerative and sustainable agriculture.

For decades, agricultural research has investigated the use of plant growth-promoting rhizobacteria (PGPR) as an alternate method of plant fertilization (Agami et al., 2016; Ahad et al., 2014; Aloo et al., 2021a; Bechtaoui et al., 2019). Among the PGPR are phosphate-solubilizing bacteria (PSB) that dissolve complex P forms, converting them to plant-accessible forms (Ahmad et al., 2019; Karpagam and Nagalakshmi, 2014; Naik et al., 2008). Although a lot of literature exists on different PSBs and their potential in agricultural fields, their methods of action and projections in regenerative agriculture are still poorly comprehended. In this chapter, we try to link the PSB and regenerative agriculture. Based on current and prospective application situations, this chapter evaluates the variety, modes of action, and opportunities of PSB in regenerative agriculture. Such data is important in gauging their potential and assessing their chances of creating sustainable agriculture systems.

4.2 PHOSPHORUS LIMITATION IN SOIL AND CONVENTIONAL MITIGATION MECHANISMS

Phosphorus (P), after nitrogen, is the second-most crucial nutrient in plant growth and development. Although the element is abundant in most soils, its availability to plants is scarce because it exists in complex and insoluble forms, with just approximately 0.1% accessible for plant usage (Sanchez, 2016). According to Mahidi et al. (2011), P anions are highly reactive and frequently become immobilized in soil through ionic interactions with different cations such as Mg^{2+}, Al^{3+}, Ca^{2+}, and Fe^{3+}, especially at low pH, resulting in a very low fraction available to plants. As a result, P is frequently a main limiting nutrient in most soils.

Conventional agriculture is heavily reliant on artificial P fertilizers, which have long been used to compensate for P shortfalls in crop fields. According to FAO (2017), annually, roughly 52.3 billion tons of P-based fertilizers are used on agricultural fields. It is estimated that a total of 25.9 kg/ha of P was consumed to produce cereals in 2000 (FAO, 2013). A significant upsurge in the use of the same fertilizers was observed in 2014 at 33.2 kg/ha, and the current total world demand for P fertilizers is 48,264 thousand tonnes (FAO, 2022). According to Khan (2018), the application of P fertilizers is further expected to increase by >150% by the year 2050 to support intensive crop production.

Contrary to popular opinion, continual P fertilizer application has been demonstrated to add to the persistent disruption of natural and plant-beneficial microbes in agricultural ecosystems, as discussed extensively in Aloo et al. (2021b). Phosphate fertilizers have also been implicated in increased soil acidity (Sarkar et al., 2012). Due to quick fixing in soil via precipitation into metal-cation complexes, the efficacy of applied chemical P fertilizers is questioned and is estimated to hardly surpass 30% (Alori et al., 2017). Furthermore, P is a limited resource, and owing to its high demand, it is anticipated that the world's known supplies might be consumed in the current century (Leghari et al., 2016).

Among the mechanisms that are quickly gathering attention for mitigating P deficiency in plants are the PSB in plant rhizospheres. These are seen as viable, environmentally friendly alternatives to crop P fertilization. Concerning regenerative agriculture, PSB can also be viable alternatives for increasing P availability and uptake by plants with net positive environmental impacts, unlike their synthetic counterparts. This chapter, therefore, focuses on PSB as an alternative crop fertilization tool and assesses its potential in regenerative agriculture. We begin our focus on PSB by presenting their diversity in Section 4.3.

4.3 THE DIVERSITY OF P SOLUBILIZING RHIZOBACTERIA

Several rhizobacterial strains have been investigated for their P solubilizing capabilities in liquid or solid tricalcium phosphate (TCP) or rock phosphate (RP) (Table 4.2). Although these bacteria can be isolated from plant rhizospheres (Alam et al., 2002; Oliveira et al., 2009), rhizoplanes (Islam et al., 2007; Sarkar et al., 2012), and non-rhizosphere soils (Ekundayo, 2010; Srinivasan et al., 2012), PSB from the rhizosphere tend to be more active metabolically and better P solubilizers (Ejikeme and Uzoma, 2013). Similarly, endophytic PSB tends to be better P solubilizers relative to their external counterparts. The ecological advantages that make this possible have been articulated in Aloo et al. (2021c) and are largely advanced to be as a result of the intimate relations between endophytes and plant root tissues, which make their plant growth-promoting (PGP) effects, feel more strongly.

Most PSB belong to the *Pseudomonas* and *Bacillus* genera. Several enterobacteria, such as *Erwinia*, *Enterobacter*, *Klebsiella*, and *Serratia*, have also been implicated in P solubilization (Borgi et al., 2020; Guo et al., 2021; Gupta et al., 2021; Lee et al., 2019; Ribaudo et al., 2020; Sagar et al., 2018). Other PSBs include *Rhodococcus*, *Arthrobacter*, *Chryseobacterium*, *Gordonia*, *Phyllobacterium*, *Delftia*, *Pantoea*, *Micrococcus*, *Flavobacterium*, *Xanthobacter*, *Acinetobacter*, *Burkholderia*, and *Achromobacter*.

Although symbiotic nitrogenous rhizobia, which are known to be widely associated with the root nodules of various leguminous plants, can also solubilize P (Bechtaoui et al., 2019; Harshitha et al., 2020; Jindal and Chakraborty, 2018; Singh and Gera, 2018; Verma et al., 2020), Similar results have been established for *Mesorhizobium* (Muleta et al., 2021; Peix et al., 2001). Studies have shown that these species produce various organic acids, which are commonly associated with P solubilization, as further discussed in Section 4.4 of this chapter. Rare PSBs, including *Acetobacter*, *Gluconacetobacter*, and *Ralstonia*, have also been associated with P solubilization and the subsequent increase in plant growth and yield (Aydogan and Algur, 2014; Song et al., 2001). Some PSB may also double up as halophiles, which can increase their usability in regenerative agriculture, particularly concerning plant stress tolerance in degraded and saline soils. *Kushneria sinocarnis*,

TABLE 4.2

The P Solubilization Potential of Various Rhizobacteria Through In Vitro Solubilization of Solid and Liquid TCP or Rock Phosphate

Host Plant	Rhizobacteria	Solubilization Index (mm in Solid TCP/RP)	Solubilization Potential in Liquid TCP/RP (µg/mL)	Reference
Apple (*Malus domestica*)	*Pseudomonas aeruginosa*	46	76	Sharma et al. (2017)
Chilli (*Capsicum annum* L.)	*B. megaterium, P. putida, P. fluorescens*	2–6	22.3–46.0	Baliah et al. (2016)
Cotton (*Gossypium* sp.)	*B. megaterium, P. putida, P. fluorescens*	2–6	22.3–46.0	Baliah et al. (2016)
Faba bean (*Vicia faba* L.)	*Serratia plymuthica*	–	100–450	Borgi et al. (2020)
Lentil (*Lens culinaris*)	*Enterobacter, Bacillus, Pseudomonas* spp.	–	52–674	Midekssa et al. (2015)
Maize (*Zea mays*)	*B. subtilis*	–	330.7	Wang et al. (2020)
	Burkholderia cenocepacia	1.6–1.9	–	You et al. (2020)
	Pseudomonas plecoglossicida, Achromobacter insolitus, Enterobacter hormaechei	2.1–5.67	–	Oo et al. (2020)
	Burkholderia cepacia	–	>3,000	Zhao et al. (2014)
	P. fluorescens, Azospirillum brasilense		22.6	Kadmiri et al. (2018)
	Alcaligenes aquaticus, Burkholderia cepacia	3.82–4.88	277.72–305.49	Pande et al. (2017)
Sorghum (Sorghum bicolor)	*Pseudomonas, Bacillus, Rhizobium, Pantoea*, and *Stenotrophomonas* spp.	0.5–4.83	–	Teshome et al. (2019)
Mushroom (*Agaricus bisporus*)	*Acinetobacter baumannii, B. megaterium, Paenibacillus taichungensis*	–	19.45–60.87	Zhang et al. (2017)
Oil palm tree (*Elaeis guineensis*)	*P. fluorescens*	–	15.29–103.41 mg/L	Fankem et al. (2006)
Okra (*Abelmoschus esculentus*)	*B. megaterium, P. putida, P. fluorescens*	2–6	22.3–46.0	Baliah et al. (2016)
Rice (*Oryza sativa*)	*Bacillus* spp., *Burkholderia* spp., *Paenibacillus*			
	Paenibacillus sp.	–	73.84–99.66	Qu et al. (2020)
Giant Miscanthus (*Miscanthus giganteus*)	*P. fluorescens*	–	400–1300	Otieno et al. (2015)
Potato (*Solanum tuberosum* L.)	*Klebsiella* sp., *Citrobacter* sp., *Serratia* sp.	1.00–5.56	66.2–160.74	Aloo et al. (2021a)
	Non-identified	1.00–2.2	–	Jadoon et al. (2019)
Runner bean (*Phaseolus coccineus*)	*B. mycoides, P. lini, B. pumilus*	1.33–3.19	17.51–19.84	Mihalache et al. (2018)
	Paenibacillus cineris, P. graminis, B. acidiceler, B. simplex, P. plecoglossicida	0.1–3.5	–	Astriani et al. (2020)
Sugarcane (*Saccharum officinarum*)	*K. pneumoniae, B. cepacia, C. freundii, A. lwoffii, P. fluorescens, Proteus vulgaris, F. aerogenes*	1.52–2.23	–	Sadiq et al. (2013)

(Continued)

TABLE 4.2 (*Continued*)
The P Solubilization Potential of Various Rhizobacteria Through In Vitro Solubilization of Solid and Liquid TCP or Rock Phosphate

Host Plant	Rhizobacteria	Solubilization Index (mm in Solid TCP/RP)	Solubilization Potential in Liquid TCP/RP (µg/mL)	Reference
Taro (*Colocasia esculenta*)	*Aquabacterium commune, Bacillus* sp.	1.25–3.84	–	Thiruvengadam et al. (2020)
Tomato (*Solanum lycopersicum*)	*B. megaterium, P. putida, P. fluorescens*	2–6	22.3–46.0	Baliah et al. (2016)
Different legumes	*Bacillus* sp., *Proteus* sp., *Pseudomonas* sp., *Azospirillum* sp.	–	18.15–61.96	Selvi et al. (2017)
Wheat (*Triticum aestivum*)	Not specified	4–7	30–246	Batool and Iqbal (2019)
	Pantoea, Pseudomonas, Serratia, Enterobacter	2.3–2.7	59.1–90.2	Rfaki et al. (2020)
	Streptomyces sp		1,916	Jog et al. (2014)
	P. fluorescens, B. megaterium, Serratia marcenes, B. subtilis	–	0.22–80.8	El-Deen et al. (2020)
Populus nigra	Not identified	–	454.6	Samavat and Rahimifard (2021)
Cabbage	*Pseudomonas* spp.	1.11–4.33	247.9–440.9	Woo et al. (2010)
Castor (*Ricinus communis*)	*Bacillus firmus*	–	14.47–50.18	Sandilya et al. (2018)

a halophilic bacteria identified from the silt of Daqiao saltern on China's eastern coast, is one such bacterium (Sharma et al., 2014).

Phosphorus solubilization is often induced under low-soluble P conditions and similarly inhibited under reverse conditions (Buch et al., 2008; Liu et al., 2020; Ludueña et al., 2017). This is to say that the associated genes are unregulated under low P conditions and vice versa (Liu et al., 2020; Zeng et al., 2016). The PSB diversity is quite diverse across ecological niches, and there is a great opportunity in the next few years to uncover several additional powerful isolates from diverse settings. Phosphate-solubilizing bacteria are numerous, and probably more than 99% of them have not been identified. In this regard, culture-independent methods that are more precise, reproducible, and non-dependent on culture conditions could be more helpful in understanding their functions and ecology (Alaylar et al., 2020). However, such methods cannot exhaustively indicate the quantity of P solubilizers in soils, and much of this bacteria remains unexplored. A lot of these rhizobacteria have already been explored in planta for increased P uptake and overall PGP in many plants, e.g. *Pseudomonas* sp. And *Arthrobacter nicotinovorans* (Pereira and Castro, 2014), *Sinorhizobium meliloti, B. flexus,* and *B. megaterium* (Ibarra-Galeana et al., 2017)*, P. fluorescens, Enterobacter* sp., and *Pantoea agglomerans* (Sarikhani et al., 2020). Still, many of these have already been formulated and marketed for practical applications in crop production to promote regenerative agriculture. These are further discussed in Section 4.5 of this chapter.

4.4 MECHANISMS AND GENETICS OF P SOLUBILIZATION

As shown in Figure 4.1, the methods of P solubilization are dependent on the P forms in the soil. While inorganic P forms appear in soil as insoluble mineral complexes, most of which are formed following the application of chemical fertilizers, organic P is usually found in organic matter.

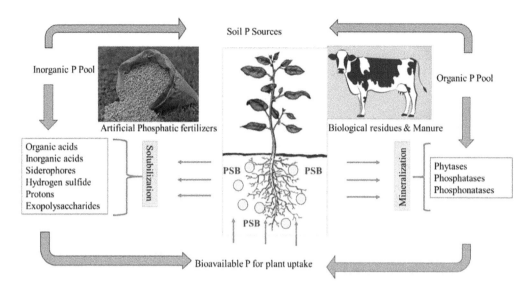

FIGURE 4.1   Forms of P in soil and mechanisms of rhizobacterial solubilization.

Alori et al. (2017) established that organic P can account for up to 50% of total P in soil. The most frequent type of organic P is phytate/inositol P, which is mainly inaccessible to plants due to phytase deficiency. Phosphomonoesters, phosphodiesters, phospholipids, nucleic acids, and phosphotriesters are some other organic P compounds that have been discovered.

Many rhizobacteria can mineralize both organic and inorganic complex P molecules. Several rhizobacterial taxa have been shown in the literature to be capable of solubilizing inorganic P compounds such as rock phosphate and tri- and di-calcium phosphate. Experiments show that the main process of P solubilization is the formation of mineral-dissolving molecules such as organic acids, protons, siderophores, hydroxyl ions, and CO_2.

Organic acids, therefore, solubilize bound P by competing for adsorption sites with metal cations and/or generating soluble complexes with metal ions linked to P. Citric, oxalic, gluconic, 2-ketogluconic, lactic, malonic, butyric, succinic, fumaric, tartaric, propionic, acetic, glutaric, malic, adipic, and glyoxalic acids are the most common organic acids that solubilize P (Table 4.3). Gluconic acid is by far the most researched organic acid for P solubilization. It is formed when glucose dehydrogenase (GDH) and its cofactor, pyrroloquinoline quinone (PQQ), directly oxidize glucose (Goldstein et al., 2003).

The functions of gluconic acid in P solubilization have been demonstrated through genetic manipulation in various bacteria (Kim et al., 2003; Krishnaraj and Goldstein, 2001; Merfort et al., 2006). Recently, Bharwad et al. (2021) revealed that mineral phosphate solubilization mutants of *Acinetobacter* sp. SK2 isolated from the *Vigna radiata* rhizosphere with a deficiency in glucose dehydrogenase encoding gene *gdhA* failed to release phosphate from the growth medium.

Organic acids are byproducts of microbial metabolism, such as oxidative respiration or organic source fermentation; thus, the type of carbon critically influences the type of organic acid produced by rhizobacteria (Chen et al., 2016; Marra et al., 2019; Patel et al., 2008; Rasul et al., 2021). As a result, the efficacy of P solubilization by rhizobacteria varies greatly. According to Delfim et al. (2018), the efficiency of P solubilization is greatly dependent on the type of organic acid produced and its concentration. However, the quality rather than the quantity of acids could be more important for P solubilization because the efficiency of solubilization is dependent upon the strength and nature of acids (Marra et al., 2019). In the same light, tri- and dicarboxylic acids are more effective as compared to monobasic and aromatic acids, and aliphatic acids are also found to be more effective in phosphate solubilization compared to phenolic, citric, and fumaric acids (Mahidi et al., 2011).

TABLE 4.3

Diversity of Phosphate-Solubilizing Rhizobacteria Isolated from Various Host Plants and Their Plant Growth Promoting Activities

Host/Test Plant	Bacteria	Organic Acid(s)	Reference
Apple (*Malus pumila*)	*P. aeruginosa*	Succinic, malonic, citric, malic, schimic, quinic, tartaric, fumaric, lactic	Sharma et al. (2017)
Faba bean (*Vicia faba*)	*Serratia plymuthica*	Gluconic, lactic	Borgi et al. (2020)
Runner bean (*Phaseolus coccineus*)	*B. mycoides, P. lini, B. pumilus*	Oxalic, tartaric, isocitric, lactic, acetic, succinic	Mihalache et al. (2018)
Oil palm tree (*Elaeis guineensis*)	*P. aeruginosa, P. fluorescens*	Citric, malic, tartaric, gluconic	Fankem et al. (2006)
Sunflower (*Helianthus annuus*)	*Enterobacter* sp.	Malic acid, gluconic	Shahid et al. (2012)
Several legumes	*Bacillus* sp., *Proteus* sp., *Pseudomonas* sp., *Azospirillum* sp.	Citric, malic, succinic, fumaric, tartaric, gluconic, succinic, ketobutyric, glyoxalic, glutaric	Selvi et al. (2017)
Coffee (*Coffea arabica*)	*Pseudomonas chlorophis, Erwinia rhapontici, Bacillus* sp., *Serratia marcescens*	2-Ketogluconic, gluconic, acetic, propionic	Muleta et al. (2013)
Miscanthus giganteus	*Pseudomonads*	Gluconic	Otieno et al. (2015)
Mangrove	*Serratia* sp.	Lactic, malic, acetic	Behera et al. (2016, 2017)
	B. amyloliquefaciens, B. licheniformis, B. atrophaeus, Paenibacillus	Lactic, isovaleric, isobutyric, acetic	Vazquez et al. (2000)
Lentil (*Lens culinaris*)	*Enterobacter, Bacillus, Pseudomonas* spp.	Not identified	Midekssa et al. (2015)
Maize (*Zea mays*)	*Burkholderia cepacia, Alcaligenes aquatilis*	Gluconic, formic, citric	Pande et al. (2017)
	Not determined	Malic	Fitriatin et al. (2020a)
	Several	Oxalic, tartaric, acetic, lactic, maleic	Khumairah et al. (2019)
Rice (*Oryza sativa*)	*Enterobacter* sp.	Citric, lactic, tartaric	Dash and Dangar (2019)
	Bacillus, Burkholderia, Paenibacillus sp.	Gluconic, oxalic, citric, tartaric, succinic, formic, acetic	Chawngthu et al. (2020)
Araucaria	*Pantoea agglomerans*	Gluconic, oxalic, tartaric, malic, acetic, citric, succinic	Li et al. (2020)
Wheat (*Triticum aestivum*)	*Pantoea, Pseudomonas, Serratia, Enterobacter*	Oxalic, citric, gluconic, succinic, fumaric, acetic	Rfaki et al. (2020)
	Streptomyces spp.	Malic	Jog et al. (2014)
Azospirillum sp., *Azotobacter* sp., *Pseudomonas* sp., *Entobactor* sp., *Bacillus* sp.		Oxalic, citric, gluconic	Saleemi et al. (2017)
Populus nigra	Not identified	Aspartic, fumaric, citric, maleic	Samavat and Rahimifard (2021)
Not mentioned	*Klebsiella pneumoniae, Pseudomonas aeruginosa, Enterobacter aerogenes*	Gluconic	Stella and Halimi (2015)
	Rhizobium sp., *Herbaspirillum* sp.	Gluconic, oxalic, lactic	Santos-Torres et al. (2021)

Because of this, the simultaneous production of different organic acids may enhance the P solubilization potential of rhizobacteria (Marra et al., 2019).

The presence of genes that act as P-solubilizers, such as *pqq*, *gdh*, *gcd*, and *gabY*, in rhizospheric PSB is well documented (Table 4.4). The *gcd* and *pqq* genes have also recently been used to detect PSB using modern sequencing technologies such as metagenomics (Liang et al., 2020; Wu et al., 2022).

Bacterial genes associated with *pqq* biosynthesis are clustered in the *pqqABCDEF* operon (Xu et al., 2022). The *pqqC* gene catalyzes the final step of the *pqq* biosynthesis, namely cyclization

TABLE 4.4

Genes, Gene Products, and Gene Functions of Phosphorus Solubilizing Bacteria

Gene	Product	Function	Rhizobacteria	Reference
gcd	Glucose dehydrogenase	Oxidizes glucose to ketogluconic acid	*Chrobactrum* sp., *Pantoea* sp.	Rasul et al. (2021)
			Pseudomonas spp, *Bacillus* sp.	Rasul et al. (2019)
			Pseudomonas putida	An and Moe (2016)
			Rhizobium sp., *Herbaspirillum* sp.	Santos-Torres et al. (2021)
			P. plecoglossicida	Wang et al. (2018)
			Pantoea agglomerans	Shariati et al. (2017)
			R. aceris	Xu et al. (2022)
gdh	Glucose dehydrogenase	Oxidizes glucose to ketogluconic acid	*P. agglomerans*	Shariati et al. (2017)
			Acinetobacter sp.	Bharwad et al. (2021)
gltA	Citrate synthase	Cofactor for quinoprotein glucose dehydrogenase	*Pantoea agglomerans*	Shariati et al. (2017)
phn	Lyases	Organophosphate solubilization	*Pantoea agglomerans*	Shariati et al. (2017)
			Rahnella aceris	Xu et al. (2022)
			Pantoea agglomerans	Shariati et al. (2017)
pho	Phosphatases	Organic P solubilization	*Ochrobactrum* sp., *Pantoea* sp.	Rasul et al. (2021)
			Burkholderia multivorans	Liu et al. (2020)
			Burkholderia multivorans	Zeng et al. (2017)
			Pseudomonas mendocina	Hegyi et al. (2021)
			Pantoea agglomerans	Li et al. (2020)
phy	Phytase	Phytic acid solubilization	*Ochrobactrum* sp., *Pantoea* sp.	Rasul et al. (2021)
pqq	Pyrroloquinoline quinone	Cofactor for glucose dehydrogenase	*Rhizobium* sp., *Herbaspirillum* sp.	Santos-Torres et al. (2021)
			P. putida	An and Moe (2016)
			Rhizobium tropici	Cho et al. (2003)
			Erwinia herbicola	Rodríguez et al. (2000)
			B. cenocepacia	You et al. (2020)
			Herbaspirillum seropedicae	Wagh et al. (2014)
			Enterobacter intermedium	Kim et al. (2003)
			Pantoea ananatis	Andreeva et al. (2011)
			R. aceris	Xu et al. (2022)
			K. pneumoniae, Enterobacter aerogenes, P. aeruginosa	Stella and Halimi (2015)
			Serratia marcescens	Mohamed and Farag (2020)
pst	Pi transporter	P ion transportation	*Burkholderia multivorans*	Zeng et al. (2017)
			B. cenocepacia	You et al. (2020)
			Rahnella aceris	Xu et al. (2022)

and oxidation of the intermediate 3a-(2-amino-2-carboxy-ethyl)-4,5-dioxo-4,5,6,7,8,9 hexahydro-quinoline-7,9-dicarboxylic acid to *pqq* (Magnusson et al., 2004). *PqqD* is involved in the formation of a ternary complex with the radical *S*-adenosylmethionine protein *pqqE* in the *pqq* biosynthetic pathway (Latham et al., 2015). *pqqE* catalyzes the cleavage of *S*-adenosyl-L-methionine in a reductive manner to form methionine as well as a 5′-deoxyadenosyl radical during the initial steps in the production of *pqq* (Wecksler et al., 2009). *pqqF* is a coenzyme that cleaves peptide bonds in a small peptide gene *pqqA*, providing glutamate and tyrosine, which are necessary for *pqq* synthesis (Wecksler et al., 2009).

The P solubilization activity is induced by high levels of P-ion and depressed by high levels of P-ion. For instance, insufficient P-ion leads to a glucose shift towards the direct oxidative pathway of glucose catabolism (Buch et al., 2008). The P-ion regulates the transcription of the *gcd* gene and triggers the secretion of gluconic acid and the gluconic acid-mediated PS ability (Liu et al., 2020; Zeng et al., 2016). These results suggest a genetic manipulation strategy for reducing the P-ion sensitivity of PSB by modifying the glucose oxidative pathway, which would improve the PS activity of PSB.

Gram-negative bacteria are reportedly more effective P solubilizers than Gram-positive bacteria owing to the release of diverse organic acids (Girmay et al., 2019), but this needs further validation. Apart from organic acids, PSB can also employ alternative chelating substances and inorganic acids such as sulphiridic, sulfuric, carbonic, and nitric acids, but their contribution and effectiveness in this regard are limited. Nevertheless, this may explain why rhizobacterial P solubilization may occur without the production of organic acid.

Organic matter, which comprises organic P forms, is a second and substantial component of soil P, accounting for 15%–85% of total P in most soils. The most common organophosphates are phytin or phytic acid and pothers such as phospholipids and nucleic acids. Mineralization by several PSB enzymes results in the solubilization of organic P forms. These enzymes include phosphatases, phytases, lyases, and phosphatases. Phytases are PSB enzymes that mediate the degradation of phytate or phytic acid, which is the primary constituent of organic P in soil. Phosphatases, which can be acidic or alkaline depending on their optimal pH, are nonspecific enzymes released by bacteria and function by dephosphorylating phospho-ester or phospho-anhydride bonds inorganic matter (Alori et al., 2017). The enzymes have been quantified and studied in PSBs such as *Bacillus*, *Citrobacter*, *Enterobacter*, *Klebsiella*, *Proteus*, *Pseudomonas*, *Rhizobium*, and *Serratia* (Fitriatin et al., 2020b; Haran and Thaher, 2019; Singh and Banik, 2019). There is some evidence that acid phosphatases may mediate better P solubilization than their alkaline counterparts (Haran and Thaher, 2019; Sarkar et al., 2021), but this needs further verification. The expression of phosphatases is regulated by the *pho* operon (Table 4.4) and is mostly enhanced during P-ion starvation.

Numerous different bacterial processes for P solubilization have been proposed, apart from inorganic P solubilization by acidification and bacterial enzymes. The sink theory is one of the most significant theories of organic solubilization P. In the presence of labile C, microorganisms quickly immobilize P, acting as a sink for it and then becoming its source for plants when it is released from their cells. As a result, the release of P trapped by PSB happens predominantly when cells die as a result of changes in environmental circumstances, hunger, or predation. Bacterial siderophores, complexing agents with a high iron affinity, may also play a role in P solubilization (Ghosh et al., 2015). However, this method of P solubilization has received little attention, and the generation of siderophores by PSB has yet to be explicitly connected to P solubilization. Given the dominance of mineral dissolution over ligand exchange via organic acid anions, the possible function of siderophore in P solubilization should be investigated further.

Phosphorus solubilization by PSB has been studied for a while now, although it still appears to be in its infancy. It happens through several methods, with a wide variety amongst creatures in this regard. PSB strains can utilize multiple pathways for mineral P solubilization, and the solubilization processes of different P types may be interrelated and independent. This implies that any organism can cause P solubilization in one or more ways. Though a single process is difficult to pinpoint, the production of organic acids and the subsequent pH drop seem critical. All in all, screening for rhizosphere-competent strains with *gcd*, *pho*, and *phy* genes may help to identify new microbial taxa that solubilize and mineralize inorganic and organic P for more efficient applications in crop production.

4.5 PROSPECTS OF P SOLUBILIZING RHIZOBACTERIA IN REGENERATIVE AGRICULTURE

It is undeniable that synthetic P fertilizers may enhance plant mineral P nutrition; nevertheless, the resources needed to manufacture these fertilizers are limited and diminishing. Furthermore, due to fixation, P accessibility to plants is still restricted, even in chemically supplied soils. Around 75%–90% of the additional chemical P fertilizer is formed by complexes of metals and cations that quickly become permanent in soils, with long-term environmental effects such as soil fertility loss, eutrophication, and carbon footprint (Sharma et al., 2013).

Researchers across the world have been investigating different plant fertilization strategies to support regenerative agriculture for decades. This has created an opportunity for the identification of effective PGP rhizobacteria and their formulation into biofertilizers by their incorporation into various carrier materials. The utilization of such organisms is strongly promoted in this area since they are less harmful to the environment and less expensive than their manufactured equivalents. This special group of rhizobacteria can also be active antagonists of phytopathogens (e.g., Astriani et al., 2020; Bektas and Kusek, 2021; Zhao et al., 2014). Their production is also relatively inexpensive, as it makes use of readily available and inexpensive agribusiness waste material. The utilization of waste products in biofertilizer formulations particularly contributes to environmental sustainability, not only by offering an eco-friendly plant fertilization method but also by lowering environmental waste.

The use of PSB as biofertilizers for agriculture enhancement has been a subject of study for several years now. The potential advantages of their inoculation have been demonstrated in a variety of plants such as soybean (Bononi et al., 2020), maize (Patil et al., 2012; Pereira and Castro, 2014), rice (Fitriatin et al., 2021; Gomez-Ramirez and Uribe-Velez, 2021), wheat (Emami et al., 2020), mung bean (Hassan et al., 2017), cabbage (Woo et al., 2010), and many more. A number of these organisms are already being used as efficient inoculants in agronomic methods to boost crop yield in various regions worldwide (Table 4.5). PSB technology can increase soil fertility and aid in the realization of sustainable agriculture by reducing the use of chemical fertilizers. PSB inoculation can also improve P use efficiency in agricultural fields.

The first commercial biofertilizer, "*Phosphobacterin*," was developed in the former Soviet Union utilizing *Bacillus megaterium* var. *phosphaticum* and was later widely used in East European nations and India. Although certain Gram-negative PSBs, such as *Pseudomonas*, are competent P solubilizers, their incorporation into biofertilizers is difficult since they do not contain spores and hence have limited shelf lives, limiting their applicability.

4.6 FUTURE TRENDS AND RESEARCH FOCUS

Microbial-mediated P control is an environmentally friendly and cost-effective strategy for crop sustainability (Sharma et al., 2013). The involvement of rhizobacteria in P solubilization is well documented, as already discussed in Section 4.3 of this chapter. However, most of the studies have focused on the separation of these microbes from the rhizospheric soil and their *in vitro* assessment of P solubilization activities, with limited investigations under field conditions. Since the present and future goal is regenerative agriculture that relies less on synthetic fertilizers, it is both urgent and necessary to test and confirm their abilities at plant P nutrition under field conditions to facilitate their applicability.

TABLE 4.5

Examples of Commercially Available Phosphate Solubilizing Rhizobacterial Biofertilizers in Different Countries

Product	Bacteria	Company	Crop	Country	Reference
Bac up*	*B. subtilis*	Biological control	Not specified	South Africa	Mohammadi and Sohrabi (2012)
Bio Gold*	*P. fluorescens, Azotobacter chroococcum*	Bio Power Lanka	Cardamom, potato, vegetables, fruits, cereals	Sri Lanka	Mehnaz (2016)
Bio Phos®	*B. megaterium*	Bio Power Lanka	Not mentioned	Sri Lanka	Mehnaz (2016)
Bioativo*	PGPR consortia	Embrafos Ltd	Bean, maize, sugarcane, rice, carrot, cotton, maize, citrus, tomatoes, soybean	Brazil	Kenneth et al. (2019)
Biomix, Gmax PGPR	*Azotobacter, P. fluorescens,* phosphobacteria	GreenMax Agrotech	Several plants and field crops	India	Kenneth et al. (2019)
Biophos	Non-identified PSB	Ajay Bio-Tech Ltd	Various crops	India	https://www.indiamart.com/proddetail/biophos-2275660562.html
Biophos, Get-Phos, Reap P, Phosphonive	*B. megaterium* var.*phosphaticum*	Not mentioned	All crops	India	Thomas and Singh (2019)
Bio-phos, Humi-phos	Non-identified PSB	Auriga Group of companies	Not specified	Pakistan	Mehnaz (2016)
B-RUS, Extrasol*	*B. subtilis*	Ag-Chem Africa (Pty) Ltd	Not specified	South Africa	Mohammadi and Sohrabi (2012)
Calphorous	Non-identified PSB	Camson BioTechnologiesLimited	Legumes, cereals, vegetables	India	http://wwwcamsonbiotechologies.com/products/bio_fertilizers_and_stimulants.htm
Composter*	*Bacillus* sp.	BioControl Products SA (Pty) Ltd	Not specified	South Africa	Mohammadi and Sohrabi (2012)
Ferti-Bio*	PGPR consortia	Microbial Biotechnologies	Rice, wheat, corn, cotton, sugarcane, vegetables	Pakistan	Kenneth et al. (2019)
Fosforina®	*P. fluorescens*	National Program Project Agricultural Biotechnology of Cuba	Tomato	Cuba	Mishra and Arora (2016)
FZB 23®	*B. amyloliquefaciens*	AbiTEP GmbH	Vegetables	Germany	Kenneth et al. (2019)
Gmax FYTON, Ashtha PF	*P. fluorescens, Azotobacter,* Phosphobacteria	GreenMax AgroTech	Tomatoes, chilli, orchards, vineyards, ornamentals, potato, cucumbers, eggplant	India	Chandra and Sharma (2017)

(Continued)

TABLE 4.5 (Continued)
Examples of Commercially Available Phosphate Solubilizing Rhizobacterial Biofertilizers in Different Countries

Product	Bacteria	Company	Crop	Country	Reference
Gmax, Phosphomax, Astha	B. megaterium, P. striata	Varsha Bioscience and Technology	All crops	India	Chandra and Sharma (2017)
Inomix	B. subtilis, P. fluorescens	LAB (Labbiotech)	Cereals	Spain	https://en.iabiotec.com/products/microbial-inoculants/
LifeForce*, Biostart*, Landbac*, Waterbac*	Bacillus sp.	Microbial solution (Pty) Ltd	Not specified	South Africa	Mohammadi and Sohrabi (2012)
Likuiq Semia*	Bradyrhizobium elkanii	Microbial solution (Pty) Ltd	Not specified	South Africa	Tairo and Ndakidemi (2014)
NAT-P	P. fluorescens	BioControl Products SA (Pty) Ltd	Not specified	South Africa	Parani and Saha (2012)
Organo/Organico*	Bacillus, Enterobacter, Pseudomonas, Stenotromonas, Rhizobium	Amka Products (Pty) Ltd	Not specified	South Africa	Mohammadi and Sohrabi (2012)
P Sol B® - BM	B. megaterium, Pseudomonas striate	AgriLife	Not specified	South Africa	Mishra and Arora (2016)
Phosphatika	Not mentioned	TNAU Agritech Portal	Not specified	India	http://agritech.tnau.ac.in
Phosphobacteria	Not mentioned	Monarch Bio-Fertilizers and Research Centre	Not specified	India	http://www.monarchbio.co.in/bio_fertilizers.html
Phosphobacteria	B. megaterium var. phosphaticum	Agro bio tech Research Centre LTD	Not specified	India	http://www.abtecbiofert.com/products.html
Phosphobacterium	Not mentioned	SAFS Organic Enterprises	Not specified	India	https://www.indiamart.com/safsorganicenterprises/bio-fertilizer.html#bio-fertilizer-phosphobacterium
Phylazonit	Azotobacter chroococcum, B. megaterium	Ministry of Agriculture	Not specified	Hungary	Dash et al. (2017)
Rhizosum® P	B. megaterium	Biosym Technologies	Not specified	India	Mehnaz (2016)
Sardar Biofertilizer	Azotobacter, Azospirillum, non-identified PSB	Gujarat State Fertilizers and Chemicals	All types of crops	India	http://www.gsfclimited.com/bio_fertilizers.asp?mnuid=3&fid=32
Signum	Rhizobacter; Bradyrhizobium	Rhizobacter S. A.	Legumes and cereals	Argentina	http://www.rhizobacter.com/argentian/productos/
Symbion-P	B. megaterium var. Phosphaticum	T. Stanes &Company Limited	Cereals, legumes, vegetables	India	http://www.tstanes.com/products-symbion-p.html
Vault NP	Bradyrhizobium japonicum	Becker Underwood	Legumes	USA	Tairo and Ndakidemi (2014)

PSBs are common in soils; however, their density and P solubilizing ability vary from soil to soil depending on the prevailing environmental conditions (Jha et al., 2013; Wei et al., 2014). This warrants the investigation of P solubilization and mobilization patterns, especially concerning the impacts of climate change and changing environmental conditions on P solubilization efficiency as we pursue regenerative agriculture. Still, in the context of climate change, important strides can be made if efficient PSBs that are tolerant to various abiotic stressors in the environment can be identified, since these can help to drive the concept of regenerative agriculture even in changing climates that present various abiotic stresses. More on this potential can be found in the recent review by Kour et al. (2019) on the biodiversity and biotechnological applications of drought-tolerant PSB for the mitigation of drought strain in plants. Similar results have also been established by Abdelmoteleb and Gonzalez-Mendoza (2020) for the P-solubilization potential of *Bacillus* sp. under salinity stress. Apart from P solubilization, various rhizobacterial PSBs possess other PGP traits such as nitrogen fixation, the production of PGP hormones and siderophores, and the solubilization of other plant-required nutrients such as zinc and potassium. Such PSBs can be more advantageous to plants as opposed to those that possess only the P solubilization function. For instance, PSBs that produce PGP hormones, apart from increasing P availability in the rhizosphere, can also increase root development to enhance the uptake of more P (You et al., 2020). Alternatively to using PSB as microbial inoculants, mixed cultures or co-inoculation with other microorganisms with specialized capabilities may be used.

A number of the already identified PSB also possess antagonistic activities against several plant pathogens (Astriani et al., 2020; Awais et al., 2019; Saleemi et al., 2017; Woo et al., 2010; Zhao et al., 2014). Such potential should be explored and exploited with the mission and vision of reducing the use of chemical pesticides and promoting regenerative agriculture, owing to the negative effects of synthetic pesticides on non-target soil microbes.

Molecular research has identified and characterized many genes involved in the solubilization of minerals and organ P. Nevertheless, studies on P solubilization and PSB at the genetic level are still inconclusive and largely unexplored. The genetic engineering and expression of these genes in chosen rhizobacterial strains pave the way for the development of PSB with enhanced P-solubilizing capacities as agricultural inoculants. Indeed, such advancements may be advantageous since a single, designed inoculant can be used to inoculate many crops. Molecular-based approaches provide us with a new window for quantifying target gene expression with high potential in plant rhizosphere soils (Alaylar et al., 2020). Microarrays may also be used to estimate the diversity around certain features or functional groupings of microbes, such as PSB. Combined, these technologies provide prospects for studying the ecology of microbial communities and allow for the assessment of individual inoculants' survival and persistence under a variety of environmental circumstances. Molecular techniques can bring new perspectives to the understanding of biosynthetic pathways and their regulation related to microbial phosphate-solubilization. These approaches can thus develop more knowledge about PSB mechanisms of action and pave the way for the development of more successful potential in them.

In field experiments, the establishment and performance of PSB generated in the laboratory are affected significantly by environmental factors such as salt, pH, moisture, temperature, and the soil's climatic conditions. Additionally, inocula generated from a given soil do not perform as well in soils with varying qualities (Sharma et al., 2013). Hence, it isnecessary to study the activities of PSB in association with these factors before using of PSB as a biofertilizer. The growing need for the discovery of new strains of PSB necessitates the replacement of the time-consuming and less sensitive conventional methods with alternative approaches that are more accurate, reliable, less time-consuming, and show reproducible results (Alaylar et al., 2020). The present methodologies and improvements in our knowledge of the functional diversity, rhizosphere colonization capacity, and mode of operations of PSB are anticipated to enable their deployment as dependable choices in the maintenance of sustainable agriculture systems.

4.7   CONCLUDING REMARKS

Phosphorus is a key limiting element in agricultural lands. Considering the cost and the harmful impacts of chemical fertilizers, efforts should be centered on PSB technology, which offers an excellent opportunity to reduce chemical-based agriculture. While such inoculants have the potential to be developed, their broad use is now constrained by a lack of knowledge of their variety, ecology, and population dynamics in soil, as well as by uneven performance across a range of settings. Current and future developments in understanding them fully will allow their employment as dependable components in regenerative agriculture systems. Furthermore, researchers need to address issues such as efficacy, delivery systems, and nutritional aspects to reap maximum benefits from their application.

REFERENCES

Abdelmoteleb, A., & Gonzalez-Mendoza, D. (2020). Isolation and identification of phosphate solubilizing *Bacillus* spp. from *Tamarix ramosissima* rhizosphere and their effect on growth of *Phaseolus vulgaris* under salinity stress. *Geomicrobiology Journal*, *37*(10), 901–908.

Agami, R., Medani, R., Abd El-Mola, I., & Taha, R. (2016). Exogenous application with plant growth promoting rhizobacteria (PGPR) or proline induces stress tolerance in basil plants (*Ocimum basilicum* L.) exposed to water stress. *International Journal of Agricultural and Environmental Research*, *2*(5), 78–92.

Ahad, A., Akhtar, N., Vasmatkar, P., & Baral, P. (2014). Biochemical characterization and molecular fingerprinting of plant growth promoting rhizobacteria. *International Journal of Agriculture, Environment and Biotechnology*, *7*(3), 491–498.

Ahmad, M., Adil, Z., Hussain, A., Mumtaz, M. Z., Nafees, M., Ahmad, I., & Jamil, M. (2019). Potential of phosphate solubilizing *Bacillus* strains for improving growth and nutrient uptake in mungbean and maize crops. *Pakistan Journal of Agricultural Sciences*, *56*(2), 283–289.

Alam, S., Khalil, S., Ayub, N., & Rashid, M. (2002). In vitro solubilization of inorganic phosphate by phosphate solubilizing microorganisms (PSM) from maize rhizosphere. *International Journal of Agricultural Biology*, *4*(4), 454–458.

Alaylar, B., Egamberdieva, D., Gulluce, M., Karadayi, M., & Arora, N. K. (2020). Integration of molecular tools in microbial phosphate solubilization research in agriculture perspective. *World Journal of Microbiology and Biotechnology*, *36*(7), 1–12.

Al-Kaisi, M. M., & Lal, R. (2020). Aligning science and policy of regenerative agriculture. *Soil Science Society of America Journal*, *84*(6), 1808–1820.

Aloo, B. N., Mbega, E. R., Makumba, B. A., Hertel, R., & Daniel, R. (2021a). Molecular identification and in vitro plant growth-promoting activities of culturable potato (*Solanum tuberosum* L.) rhizobacteria in Tanzania. *Potato Research*, *64*(1), 67–95.

Aloo, B. N., Mbega, E. R., Makumba, B. A., & Tumuhairwe, J. B. (2021b). Effects of agrochemicals on the beneficial plant rhizobacteria in agricultural systems. *Environmental Science and Pollution Research*, *28*(43), 60406–60424.

Aloo, B. N., Tripathi, V., Mbega, E. R., & Makumba, B. A. (2021c). Endophytic rhizobacteria for mineral nutrients acquisition in plants: Possible functions and ecological advantages. In D. K. Maheshwari & S. Dheeman (Eds.), *Endophytes: Mineral Nutrient Management* (Vol. 3, pp. 267–291). Sustainable Development and Biodiversity, vol 26. Springer, Cham. https://doi.org/10.1007/978-3-030-65447-4_12

Alori, E. T., Glick, B. R., & Babalola, O. O. (2017). Microbial phosphorus solubilization and its potential for use in sustainable agriculture. *Frontiers in Microbiology*, *8*, 971.

An, R., & Moe, L. A. (2016). Regulation of pyrroloquinoline quinone-dependent glucose dehydrogenase activity in the model rhizosphere-dwelling bacterium *Pseudomonas putida* KT2440. *Applied and Environmental Microbiology*, *82*(16), 4955–4964.

Andreeva, I. G., Golubeva, L. I., Kuvaeva, T. M., Gak, E. R., Katashkina, J. I., & Mashko, S. V. (2011). Identification of *Pantoea ananatis* gene encoding membrane pyrroloquinoline quinone (PQQ)-dependent glucose dehydrogenase and pqqABCDEF operon essential for PQQ biosynthesis. *FEMS Microbiology Letters*, *318*(1), 55–60.

Astriani, M., Zubaidah, S., Abadi, A. L., & Suarsini, E. (2020). *Pseudomonas plecoglossicida* as a novel bacterium for phosphate solubilizing and indole-3-acetic acid-producing from soybean rhizospheric soils of East Java, Indonesia. *Biodiversitas Journal of Biological Diversity*, *21*(2), 578–586.

Awais, M., Tariq, M., Ali, Q., Khan, A., Ali, A., Nasir, I. A., & Husnain, T. (2019). Isolation, characterization and association among phosphate solubilizing bacteria from sugarcane rhizosphere. *Cytology and Genetics*, *53*(1), 86–95. doi: 10.3103/S0095452719010031

Aydogan, M. N., & Algur, O. F. (2014). Solubilization of Mazidagi rock phosphate by locally isolated *Aeromonas hydrophila* MFB-25. *Journal of Pure and Applied Microbiology*, *8*(1), 413–420.

Baliah, N. T., Pandiarajan, G., & Kumar, B. M. (2016). Isolation, identification and characterization of phosphate solubilizing bacteria from different crop soils of Srivilliputtur Taluk, Virudhunagar District, Tamil Nadu. *Tropical Ecology*, *57*(3), 465–474.

Batool, S., & Iqbal, A. (2019). Phosphate solubilizing rhizobacteria as alternative of chemical fertilizer for growth and yield of *Triticum aestivum* (Var. Galaxy 2013). *Saudi Journal of Biological Sciences*, *26*(7), 1400–1410.

Bechtaoui, N., Raklami, A., Tahiri, A.-I., Benidire, L., El Alaoui, A., Meddich, A., Göttfert, M., & Oufdou, K. (2019). Characterization of plant growth promoting rhizobacteria and their benefits on growth and phosphate nutrition of faba bean and wheat. *Biology Open*, *8*(7), bio043968. doi:10.1242/bio.043968

Behera, B., Singdevsachan, S., Mishra, R., Sethi, B., Dutta, S., & Thatoi, H. (2016). Phosphate solubilising bacteria from mangrove soils of Mahanadi river delta, Odisha, India. *World Journal of Agricultural Research*, *4*(1), 18–23.

Behera, B., Yadav, H., Singh, S., Mishra, R., Sethi, B., Dutta, S., & Thatoi, H. (2017). Phosphate solubilization and acid phosphatase activity of *Serratia* sp. isolated from mangrove soil of Mahanadi river delta, Odisha, India. *Journal of Genetic Engineering and Biotechnology*, *15*(1), 169–178.

Bektas, I., & Kusek, M. (2021). Biological control of onion basal rot disease using phosphate solubilising rhizobacteria. *Biocontrol Science and Technology*, *31*(2), 190–205.

Bharwad, K., Ghoghari, N., & Rajkumar, S. (2021). Crc regulates succinate-mediated repression of mineral phosphate solubilization in *Acinetobacter* sp. SK2 by modulating membrane glucose dehydrogenase. *Frontiers in Microbiology*, *12*, 1307.

Bononi, L., Chiaramonte, J. B., Pansa, C. C., Moitinho, M. A., & Melo, I. S. (2020). Phosphorus-solubilizing *Trichoderma* spp. From Amazon soils improve soybean plant growth. *Scientific Reports*, *10*(1), 1–13.

Borgi, M. A., Saidi, I., Moula, A., Rhimi, S., & Rhimi, M. (2020). The attractive *Serratia plymuthica* BMA1 strain with high rock phosphate-solubilizing activity and its effect on the growth and phosphorus uptake by *Vicia faba* L. plants. *Geomicrobiology Journal*, *37*(5), 437–445. doi:10.1080/01490451.2020.1716892

Buch, A., Archana, G., & Kumar, G. N. (2008). Metabolic channeling of glucose towards gluconate in phosphate-solubilizing *Pseudomonas aeruginosa* P4 under phosphorus deficiency. *Research in Microbiology*, *159*(9-10), 635–642.

Chandra, D., & Sharma, A. (2017). Commercial microbial products: Exploiting beneficial plant–microbe interaction. In D. Singh, H. Singh, & R. Prabha (Eds.), *Plant–Microbe Interactions in Agro-Ecological Perspectives* (pp. 607–626). Springer.

Chawngthu, L., Hnamte, R., & Lalfakzuala, R. (2020). Isolation and characterization of rhizospheric phosphate solubilizing bacteria from wetland paddy field of Mizoram, India. *Geomicrobiology Journal*, *37*(4), 366–375. doi:10.1080/01490451.2019.1709108

Chen, W., Yang, F., Zhang, L., & Wang, J. (2016). Organic acid secretion and phosphate solubilizing efficiency of *Pseudomonas* sp. PSB12: Effects of phosphorus forms and carbon sources. *Geomicrobiology Journal*, *33*(10), 870–877.

Cho, Y.-S., Park, R.-D., Kim, Y.-W., Hwangbo, H., Jung, W.-J., Suh, J.-S., Koo, B.-S., Krishnan, H.-B., & Kim, K.-Y. (2003). PQQ-dependent organic acid production and effect on common bean growth by *Rhizobium tropici* CIAT 899. *Journal of Microbiology and Biotechnology*, *13*(6), 955–959.

Dash, N., & Dangar, T. K. (2019). Phosphate mineralization by a rice (*Oryza sativa* L.) rhizoplanic *Enterobacter* sp. *American-Eurasian Journal of Sustainable Agriculture*, *13*(4), 1–18.

Dash, N., Pahari, A., & Dangar, T. K. (2017). Functionalities of phosphate-solubilizing bacteria of rice rhizosphere: Techniques and perspectives. In P. Shukla (Ed.), *Recent Advances in Applied Microbiology* (pp. 151–163). Springer.

Delfim, J., Schoebitz, M., Paulino, L., Hirzel, J., & Zagal, E. (2018). Phosphorus availability in wheat, in volcanic soils inoculated with phosphate-solubilizing *Bacillus thuringiensis*. *Sustainability*, *10*(1), 144.

Diwan, A., Harke, S., Pande, B., & Panche, A. (2021). Regenerative agriculture farming. *Indian Farming*, *71*(12), 3–8.

Ejikeme, C., & Uzoma, C. (2013). Comparative study on solubilization of tri-calcium phosphate (TCP) by phosphate solubilizing fungi (PSF) isolated from Nsukka pepper plant rhizosphere and root free soil. *Journal of Yeast and Fungal Research*, *4*(5), 52–57.

Ekundayo, F. O. (2010). Comparative influence of benomyl on rhizosphere and non-rhizosphere bacteria of cowpea and their ability to solubilise phosphate. *Journal of Soil Science and Environmental Management*, *1*(9), 234–242.

El-Deen, S. R. O., El-Azeem, A., Samy, A., Abd Elwahab, A. F., & Mabrouk, S. S. (2020). Effects of phosphate solubilizing microorganisms on wheat yield and phosphatase activity. *Egyptian Journal of Microbiology*, 55 (The 14th Conference of Applied Microbiology), 71–86.

Emami, S., Alikhani, H. A., Pourbabaee, A. A., Etesami, H., Motasharezadeh, B., & Sarmadian, F. (2020). Consortium of endophyte and rhizosphere phosphate solubilizing bacteria improves phosphorous use efficiency in wheat cultivars in phosphorus deficient soils. *Rhizosphere*, *14*, 100196.

Fankem, H., Nwaga, D., Deubel, A., Dieng, L., Merbach, W., & Etoa, F. X. (2006). Occurrence and functioning of phosphate solubilizing microorganisms from oil palm tree (*Elaeis guineensis*) rhizosphere in Cameroon. *African Journal of Biotechnology*, *5*(24), 2450–2460.

FAO (2013). Statistical Yearbook 2013 (pp. 1–307). Food and Agriculture Organization of the United Nations. https://reliefweb.int/sites/reliefweb.int/files/resources/FAO_2013_stats_yrbook.pdf

FAO (2017). The Future of Food and Agriculture – Trends and Challenges (pp. 1–180). Food and Agriculture Organization of the United Nations. https://www.fao.org/3/i6583e/i6583e.pdf

FAO (2022). Fertilizer Indicators. Food and Agriculture Organization of the United Nations. https://www.fao.org/faostat/en/#data/EF/visualize

Fitriatin, B. N., Fauziah, D., Fitriani, F. N., Ningtyas, D. N., Suryatmana, P., Hindersah, R., Setiawati, M. R., & Simarmata, T. (2020a). Biochemical activity and bioassay on maize seedling of selected indigenous phosphate-solubilizing bacteria isolated from the acid soil ecosystem. *Open Agriculture*, *5*(1), 300–304.

Fitriatin, B. N., Manurung, D. F., Sofyan, E. T., & Setiawati, M. R. (2020b). Compatibility, phosphate solubility and phosphatase activity by phosphate solubilizing bacteria. *Haya Saudi Journal of Life Science*, *5*(12), 281–284.

Fitriatin, B. N., Sofyan, E. T., & Turmuktini, T. (2021). Increasing soil P and yield of upland rice through application phosphate solubilizing microbes. *Haya Saudi Journal of Life Science*, *6*, 163–167.

Ghosh, P., Rathinasabapathi, B., & Ma, L. Q. (2015). Phosphorus solubilization and plant growth enhancement by arsenic-resistant bacteria. *Chemosphere*, *134*, 1–6.

Girmay, K. (2019). Phosphate solubilizing microorganisms: promising approach as biofertilizers. *International Journal of Agronomy*, Article ID 4917256, 7 pages. https://doi.org/10.1155/2019/4917256.

Goldstein, A., Lester, T., & Brown, J. (2003). Research on the metabolic engineering of the direct oxidation pathway for extraction of phosphate from ore has generated preliminary evidence for PQQ biosynthesis in *Escherichia coli* as well as a possible role for the highly conserved region of quinoprotein dehydrogenases. Biochimica et Biophysica Acta (BBA)-Proteins and Proteomics, 1647(1–2), 266–271.

Gomez-Ramirez, L. F., & Uribe-Velez, D. (2021). Phosphorus solubilizing and mineralizing *Bacillus* spp. Contribute to rice growth promotion using soil amended with rice straw. *Current Microbiology*, *78*(3), 932–943.

Goswami, S. (2021). Regenerative agriculture is new tomorrow. *International Journal of Agriculture Sciences*, *12*, 10988–10999.

Guo, S., Feng, B., Xiao, C., Wang, Q., Zhou, Y., & Chi, R. (2021). Effective solubilization of rock phosphate by a phosphate-tolerant bacterium *Serratia* sp. *Geomicrobiology Journal*, *38*(7), 561–569. doi:10.1080/01490451.2021.1903623

Gupta, P., Trivedi, M., & Soni, H. (2021). Isolation, identification and evaluation of indigenous plant growth promoting bacterium *Klebsiella pneumoniae* PNE1. *International Journal for Research in Applied Sciences and Biotechnology*, *8*(6), 47–56. doi:10.31033/ijrasb.8.6.9

Haran, M. S., & Thaher, A. T. (2019). Efficiency of phosphate solubilizing bacteria isolated from different regions in dissolving of the insoluble phosphate and the activity of phosphatase enzyme. *International Journal of Botany Studies*, *4*(4), 122–127.

Harshitha, A., Goudar, G., Krishnaraj, P. U., & Koti, R. V. (2020). Characterization of plant growth promoting rhizobial isolates for pigeon pea (*Cajanus cajan* [L.] Mill sp). *International Journal of Current Microbiology and Applied Sciences*, *9*(7), 3776–3788.

Hassan, W., Bashir, S., Hanif, S., Sher, A., Sattar, A., Wasaya, A., Atif, H., & Hussain, M. (2017). Phosphorus solubilizing bacteria and growth and productivity of mung bean (*Vigna radiata*). *Pakistan Journal of Botany*, *49*(3), 331–336.

Hegyi, A., Nguyen, T. B. K., & Posta, K. (2021). Metagenomic analysis of bacterial communities in agricultural soils from Vietnam with special attention to phosphate solubilizing bacteria. Microorganisms, 9(9), 1796.

Ibarra-Galeana, J. A., Castro-Martínez, C., Fierro-Coronado, R. A., Armenta-Bojórquez, A. D., & Maldonado-Mendoza, I. E. (2017). Characterization of phosphate-solubilizing bacteria exhibiting the potential for growth promotion and phosphorus nutrition improvement in maize (*Zea mays* L.) in calcareous soils of Sinaloa, Mexico. *Annals of Microbiology*, *67*(12), 801–811.

Islam, M. T., Deora, A., Hashidoko, Y., Rahman, A., Ito, T., & Tahara, S. (2007). Isolation and identification of potential phosphate solubilizing bacteria from the rhizoplane of *Oryza sativa* L. cv. BR29 of Bangladesh. *Zeitschrift Für Naturforschung C*, *62*(1–2), 103–110. doi:10.1515/znc-2007-1-218

Jadoon, S., Afzal, A., Asad, S., Sultan, T., Tabassam, T., Umer, M., & Asif, M. (2019). Plant growth promoting traits of rhizobacteria isolated from potato (*Solanum tuberosum* L.) and their antifungal activity against *Fusarium oxysporum*. *Journal of Animal & Plant Sciences*, *29*(4), 1026–1036.

Jha, A., Saxena, J., & Sharma, V. (2013). Investigation on phosphate solubilization potential of agricultural soil bacteria as affected by different phosphorus sources, temperature, salt, and pH. *Communications in Soil Science and Plant Analysis*, *44*(16), 2443–2458.

Jindal, R., & Chakraborty, D. (2018). Phosphate solubilizing activity of *Rhizobium* sp. isolated from *Vigna mungo* grown in semi-arid region. *Asian Journal of Microbiology and Biotechnology*, *3*(1), 34–39.

Jog, R., Pandya, M., Nareshkumar, G., & Rajkumar, S. (2014). Mechanism of phosphate solubilization and antifungal activity of *Streptomyces* spp. isolated from wheat roots and rhizosphere and their application in improving plant growth. *Microbiology*, *160*(4), 778–788.

Kadmiri, I. M., Chaouqui, L., Azaroual, S. E., Sijilmassi, B., Yaakoubi, K., & Wahby, I. (2018). Phosphate-solubilizing and auxin-producing rhizobacteria promote plant growth under saline conditions. *Arabian Journal for Science and Engineering*, *43*(7), 3403–3415.

Karpagam, T., & Nagalakshmi, P. (2014). Isolation and characterization of phosphate solubilizing microbes from agricultural soil. *International Journal of Current Microbiology and Applied Sciences*, *3*(3), 601–614.

Kenneth, O. C., Nwadibe, E. C., Kalu, A. U., & Unah, U. V. (2019). Plant growth promoting rhizobacteria (PGPR): A novel agent for sustainable food production. *American Journal of Agricultural and Biological Sciences*, *14*, 35–54.

Khan, H. I. (2018). Appraisal of biofertilizers in rice: To supplement inorganic chemical fertilizer. *Rice Science*, *25*(6), 357–362.

Khumairah, F., Nurbaity, A., Setiawati, M., Fitriatin, B., & Simarmata, T. (2019). The ability of phosphorhizobacteria isolates to produce organic acid and promote phosphatase activity to increase the growth of maize (Zea mays *L.*) in selected medium. *IOP Conference Series: Earth and Environmental Science*, *334*(1), 012023.

Kim, C. H., Han, S. H., Kim, K. Y., Cho, B. H., Kim, Y. H., Koo, B. S., & Kim, Y. C. (2003). Cloning and expression of pyrroloquinoline quinone (PQQ) genes from a phosphate-solubilizing bacterium *Enterobacter intermedium*. *Current Microbiology*, *47*(6), 457–461.

Kour, D., Rana, K. L., Yadav, A. N., Yadav, N., Kumar, V., Kumar, A., Sayyed, R., Hesham, A. E.-L., Dhaliwal, H. S., & Saxena, A. K. (2019). Drought-tolerant phosphorus-solubilizing microbes: Biodiversity and biotechnological applications for alleviation of drought stress in plants. In R. Sayyed, N. Arora, & M. Reddy (Eds.), *Plant Growth Promoting Rhizobacteria for Sustainable Stress Management* (pp. 255–308). Springer.

Krishnaraj, P., & Goldstein, A. (2001). Cloning of a *Serratia marcescens* DNA fragment that induces quinoprotein glucose dehydrogenase-mediated gluconic acid production in *Escherichia coli* in the presence of stationary phase *Serratia marcescens*. *FEMS Microbiology Letters*, *205*(2), 215–220.

Lal, R. (2020). Regenerative agriculture for food and climate. *Journal of Soil and Water Conservation*, *75*(5), 123–124.

Latham, J. A., Iavarone, A. T., Barr, I., Juthani, P. V., & Klinman, J. P. (2015). PqqD is a novel peptide chaperone that forms a ternary complex with the radical S-adenosylmethionine protein PqqE in the pyrroloquinoline quinone biosynthetic pathway. *Journal of Biological Chemistry*, *290*(20), 12908–12918.

Lee, K.-E., Adhikari, A., Kang, S.-M., You, Y.-H., Joo, G.-J., Kim, J.-H., Kim, S.-J., & Lee, I.-J. (2019). Isolation and characterization of the high silicate and phosphate solubilizing novel strain *Enterobacter ludwigii* GAK2 that promotes growth in rice plants. *Agronomy*, *9*(3), 144. doi:10.3390/agronomy9030144

Leghari, S. J., Buriro, M., Jogi, Q., Kandhro, M. N., & Leghari, A. J. (2016). Depletion of phosphorus reserves, a big threat to agriculture: Challenges and opportunities. *Science International*, *28*(3), 2697–2702.

Li, L., Chen, R., Zuo, Z., Lv, Z., Yang, Z., Mao, W., Liu, Y., Zhou, Y., Huang, J., & Song, Z. (2020). Evaluation and improvement of phosphate solubilization by an isolated bacterium *Pantoea agglomerans* ZB. *World Journal of Microbiology and Biotechnology*, *36*(2), 27. doi:10.1007/s11274-019-2744-4

Liang, J.-L., Liu, J., Jia, P., Yang, T., Zeng, Q., Zhang, S., Liao, B., Shu, W., & Li, J. (2020). Novel phosphate-solubilizing bacteria enhance soil phosphorus cycling following ecological restoration of land degraded by mining. *The ISME Journal, 14*(6), 1600–1613.

Liu, Y.-Q., Wang, Y.-H., Kong, W.-L., Liu, W.-H., Xie, X.-L., & Wu, X.-Q. (2020). Identification, cloning and expression patterns of the genes related to phosphate solubilization in *Burkholderia multivorans* WS-FJ9 under different soluble phosphate levels. *AMB Express, 10*(1), 108. doi:10.1186/s13568-020-01032-4

Ludueña, L. M., Anzuay, M. S., Magallanes-Noguera, C., Tonelli, M. L., Ibañez, F. J., Angelini, J. G., Fabra, A., McIntosh, M., & Taurian, T. (2017). Effects of P limitation and molecules from peanut root exudates on pqqE gene expression and pqq promoter activity in the phosphate-solubilizing strain Serratia sp. S119. Research in Microbiology, 168(8), 710–721.

Lunn-Rockliffe, S., Davies, M., Moore, H., Wilman, A., McGlade, J., & Bent, D. (2020). Farmer Led Regenerative Agriculture for Africa (pp. 1–63). Institute for Global Prosperity. https://discovery.ucl.ac.uk/id/eprint/10106717/1/Lunn-Rockliffe%2C%20Davies%20et%20al.%202020%20RA%20report.pdf

Magnusson, O. T., Toyama, H., Saeki, M., Rojas, A., Reed, J. C., Liddington, R. C., Klinman, J. P., & Schwarzenbacher, R. (2004). Quinone biogenesis: Structure and mechanism of PqqC, the final catalyst in the production of pyrroloquinoline quinone. *Proceedings of the National Academy of Sciences, 101*(21), 7913–7918.

Mahidi, S., Hassan, G., Hussain, A., & Rasool, F. (2011). Phosphorus availability issue– Its fixation and role of phosphate solubilizing bacteria in phosphate solubilization– Case study. *Agricultural Science Research Journal, 2*, 174–179.

Marra, L. M., de Oliveira-Longatti, S. M., Soares, C. R. F. S., Olivares, F. L., & Moreira, F. M. de S. (2019). The amount of phosphate solubilization depends on the strain, C-source, organic acids and type of phosphate. *Geomicrobiology Journal, 36*(3), 232–242.

Mehnaz, S. (2016). An overview of globally available bioformulations. In N. Arora, S. Mehnaz, & R. Balestrini (Eds.), *Bioformulations: For Sustainable Agriculture* (pp. 267–281). Springer.

Merfort, M., Herrmann, U., Ha, S., Elfari, M., Bringer-Meyer, S., Görisch, H., & Sahm, H. (2006). Modification of the membrane-bound glucose oxidation system in *Gluconobacter oxydans* significantly increases gluconate and 5-keto-d-gluconic acid accumulation. *Biotechnology Journal: Healthcare Nutrition Technology, 1*(5), 556–563.

Midekssa, M. J., Loscher, C. R., Schmitz, R. A., & Assefa, F. (2015). Characterization of phosphate solubilizing rhizobacteria isolated from lentil growing areas of Ethiopia. *African Journal of Microbiology Research, 9*(25), 1637–1648.

Mihalache, G., Mihasan, M., Zamfirache, M. M., Stefan, M., & Raus, L. (2018). Phosphate solubilizing bacteria from runner bean rhizosphere and their mechanism of action. *Romanian Biotechnological Letters, 23*(4), 13853–13861.

Mishra, J., & Arora, N. K. (2016). Bioformulations for plant growth promotion and combating phytopathogens: A sustainable approach. In N. Arora, S. Mehnaz, & R. Balestrini (Eds.), *Bioformulations: For Sustainable Agriculture* (pp. 3–33). Springer.

Mohamed, E., & Farag, A. G. (2020). Effect of physicochemical parameters on inorganic phosphate solubilisation by Serratia marcescens PH1 and organic acids production. *Egyptian Journal of Microbiology, 55*(The 14th Conference of Applied Microbiology), 47–56.

Mohammadi, K., & Sohrabi, Y. (2012). Bacterial biofertilizers for sustainable crop production: A review. *ARPN Journal of Agricultural and Biological Science, 7*(5), 307–316.

Muleta, A., Tesfaye, K., Haile Selassie, T. H., Cook, D. R., & Assefa, F. (2021). Phosphate solubilization and multiple plant growth promoting properties of *Mesorhizobium* species nodulating chickpea from acidic soils of Ethiopia. *Archives of Microbiology, 203*(5), 2129–2137. doi: 10.1007/s00203-021-02189-7

Muleta, D., Assefa, F., Börjesson, E., & Granhall, U. (2013). Phosphate-solubilising rhizobacteria associated with *Coffea arabica* L. in natural coffee forests of southwestern Ethiopia. *Journal of the Saudi Society of Agricultural Sciences, 12*(1), 73–84.

Naik, P. R., Raman, G., Narayanan, K. B., & Sakthivel, N. (2008). Assessment of genetic and functional diversity of phosphate solubilizing fluorescent pseudomonads isolated from rhizospheric soil. *BMC Microbiology, 8*(1), 1–14.

Oliveira, C. A., Alves, V. M. C., Marriel, I. E., Gomes, E. A., Scotti, M. R., Carneiro, N. P., Guimarães, C. T., Schaffert, R. E., & Sá, N. M. H. (2009). Phosphate solubilizing microorganisms isolated from rhizosphere of maize cultivated in an oxisol of the Brazilian Cerrado Biome. *Soil Biology and Biochemistry, 41*(9), 1782–1787. doi:10.1016/j.soilbio.2008.01.012

Oo, K. T., Win, T. T., Khai, A. A., & Fu, P. (2020). Isolation, screening and molecular characterization of multi-functional plant growth promoting rhizobacteria for a sustainable agriculture. *American Journal of Plant Sciences*, *11*(6), 773–792.

Otieno, N., Lally, R. D., Kiwanuka, S., Lloyd, A., Ryan, D., Germaine, K. J., & Dowling, D. N. (2015). Plant growth promotion induced by phosphate solubilizing endophytic *Pseudomonas* isolates. *Frontiers in Microbiology*, *6*, 745.

Pande, A., Pandey, P., Mehra, S., Singh, M., & Kaushik, S. (2017). Phenotypic and genotypic characterization of phosphate solubilizing bacteria and their efficiency on the growth of maize. *Journal of Genetic Engineering and Biotechnology*, *15*(2), 379–391.

Parani, K., & Saha, B. (2012). Prospects of using phosphate solubilizing *Pseudomonas* as bio fertilizer. *European Journal of Biological Sciences*, *4*(2), 40–44.

Patel, D. K., Archana, G., & Kumar, G. N. (2008). Variation in the nature of organic acid secretion and mineral phosphate solubilization by Citrobacter sp. DHRSS in the presence of different sugars. Current Microbiology, *56*(2), 168–174. doi:10.1007/s00284-007-9053-0

Patil, P. M., Kuligod, V., Hebsur, N., Patil, C., & Kulkarni, G. (2012). Effect of phosphate solubilizing fungi and phosphorus levels on growth, yield and nutrient content in maize (*Zea mays*). *Karnataka Journal of Agricultural Sciences*, *25*(1), 58–62.

Pearson, C. J. (2007). Regenerative, semiclosed systems: A priority for twenty-first-century agriculture. *Bioscience*, *57*(5), 409–418.

Peix, A., Rivas-Boyero, A. A., Mateos, P. F., Rodriguez-Barrueco, C., Martínez-Molina, E., & V elazquez, E. (2001). Growth promotion of chickpea and barley by a phosphate solubilizing strain of *Mesorhizobium mediterraneum* under growth chamber conditions. *Soil Biology and Biochemistry*, *33*(1), 103–110. doi:10.1016/S0038-0717(00)00120-6

Pereira, S. I., & Castro, P. M. (2014). Phosphate-solubilizing rhizobacteria enhance *Zea mays* growth in agricultural P-deficient soils. *Ecological Engineering*, *73*, 526–535.

Qu, L.-L., Peng, C.-L., & Li, S.-B. (2020). Isolation and screening of a phytate phosphate-solubilizing *Paenibacillus* sp. and its growth-promoting effect on rice seeding. *The Journal of Applied Ecology*, *31*(1), 326–332.

Rasul, M., Yasmin, S., Yahya, M., Breitkreuz, C., Tarkka, M., & Reitz, T. (2021). The wheat growth-promoting traits of *Ochrobactrum* and *Pantoea* species, responsible for solubilization of different P sources, are ensured by genes encoding enzymes of multiple P-releasing pathways. *Microbiological Research*, *246*, 126703. doi:10.1016/j.micres.2021.126703

Rasul, M., Yasmin, S., Zubair, M., Mahreen, N., Yousaf, S., Arif, M., Sajid, Z. I., & Mirza, M. S. (2019). Phosphate solubilizers as antagonists for bacterial leaf blight with improved rice growth in phosphorus deficit soil. *Biological Control*, *136*, 103997.

Rfaki, A., Zennouhi, O., Aliyat, F. Z., Nassiri, L., & Ibijbijen, J. (2020). Isolation, selection and characterization of root-associated rock phosphate solubilizing bacteria in Moroccan wheat (*Triticum aestivum* L.). *Geomicrobiology Journal*, *37*(3), 230–241.

Rhodes, C. J. (2012). Feeding and healing the world: Through regenerative agriculture and permaculture. *Science Progress*, *95*(4), 345–446.

Rhodes, C. J. (2017). The imperative for regenerative agriculture. *Science Progress*, *100*(1), 80–129.

Ribaudo, C., Zaballa, J. I., & Golluscio, R. (2020). Effect of the phosphorus-solubilizing bacterium *Enterobacter ludwigii* on barley growth promotion. *American Scientific Research Journal for Engineering, Technology, and Sciences*, *63*(1), 144–157.

Rodríguez, H., Gonzalez, T., & Selman, G. (2000). Expression of a mineral phosphate solubilizing gene from *Erwinia herbicola* in two rhizobacterial strains. *Journal of Biotechnology*, *84*(2), 155–161. doi:10.1016/S0168-1656(00)00347-3

Sadiq, H. M., Jahangir, G. Z., Nasir, I. A., Iqtidar, M., & Iqbal, M. (2013). Isolation and characterization of phosphate-solubilizing bacteria from rhizosphere soil. *Biotechnology & Biotechnological Equipment*, *27*(6), 4248–4255.

Sagar, A., Thomas, G., Rai, S., Mishra, R. K., & Ramteke, P. W. (2018). Enhancement of growth and yield parameters of wheat variety AAI-W6 by an organic farm isolate of plant growth promoting *Erwinia* species (KP226572). *International Journal of Agriculture, Environment and Biotechnology*, *11*(1), 159–171.

Saleemi, M., Kiani, M. Z., Sultan, T., Khalid, A., & Mahmood, S. (2017). Integrated effect of plant growth-promoting rhizobacteria and phosphate-solubilizing microorganisms on growth of wheat (*Triticum aestivum* L.) under rainfed condition. *Agriculture & Food Security*, *6*(1), 1–8.

Samavat, S., & Rahimifard, M. (2021). Phosphate solubilization and organic acids production by fluorescent pseudomonads associated with *Populus nigra* rhizosphere. *Journal of Applied Biological Sciences*, *15*(2), 196–205.

Sanchez, C. A. (2016). Phosphorus. In A. V. Barker & D. J. Pilbeam (Eds.), *Handbook of Plant Nutrition* (pp. 67–106). CRC Press.

Sandilya, S. P., Bhuyan, P. M., Gogoi, D. K., & Kardong, D. (2018). Phosphorus solubilization and plant growth promotion ability of rhizobacteria of R. communis L growing in Assam, India. Proceedings of the National Academy of Sciences, India Section B: Biological Sciences, *88*(3), 959–966.

Santos-Torres, M., Romero-Perdomo, F., Mendoza-Labrador, J., Gutiérrez, A. Y., Vargas, C., Castro-Rincon, E., Caro-Quintero, A., Uribe-Velez, D., & Estrada-Bonilla, G. A. (2021). Genomic and phenotypic analysis of rock phosphate-solubilizing rhizobacteria. *Rhizosphere*, *17*, 100290.

Sanyal, D., & Wolthuizen, J. (2021). Regenerative agriculture: Beyond sustainability. *International Journal on Agriculture Research and Environmental Sciences*, *2*(1), 17–18.

Sarikhani, M. R., Aliasgharzad, N., & Khoshru, B. (2020). P solubilizing potential of some plant growth promoting bacteria used as ingredient in phosphatic biofertilizers with emphasis on growth promotion of *Zea mays* L. *Geomicrobiology Journal*, *37*(4), 327–335.

Sarkar, A., Islam, T., Biswas, G., Alam, S., Hossain, M., & Talukder, N. (2012). Screening for phosphate solubilizing bacteria inhabiting the rhizoplane of rice grown in acidic soil in Bangladesh. *Acta Microbiologica et Immunologica Hungarica*, *59*(2), 199–213. doi:10.1556/amicr.59.2012.2.5

Sarkar, D., Rakesh, S., Sinha, A., Mukhopadhyay, P., & Singh, Y. (2021). Effect of phosphate solubilizing bacteria on phosphatase activities, yield and phosphorus nutrition of wheat in an acidic Entisol. *Journal of the Indian Society of Soil Science*, *69*(4), 429–439.

Schreefel, L., Schulte, R. P. O., de Boer, I. J. M., Schrijver, A. P., & van Zanten, H. H. E. (2020). Regenerative agriculture – The soil is the base. *Global Food Security*, *26*, 100404. doi:10.1016/j.gfs.2020.100404

Selvi, K., Paul, J., Vijaya, V., & Saraswathi, K. (2017). Analyzing the efficacy of phosphate solubilizing microorganisms by enrichment culture techniques. *Biochemistry and Molecular Biology Journal*, *3*(1), 1–7.

Shahid, M., Hameed, S., Imran, A., Ali, S., & van Elsas, J. D. (2012). Root colonization and growth promotion of sunflower (*Helianthus annuus* L.) by phosphate solubilizing *Enterobacter* sp. Fs-11. *World Journal of Microbiology and Biotechnology*, *28*(8), 2749–2758.

Shariati, V., Malboobi, M. A., Tabrizi, Z., Tavakol, E., Owlia, P., & Safari, M. (2017). Comprehensive genomic analysis of a plant growth-promoting rhizobacterium *Pantoea agglomerans* strain P5. *Scientific Reports*, *7*(1), 1–12.

Sharma, R., Pal, J., & Kaur, M. (2017). Isolation of phosphate solubilizing Pseudomonas strains from apple rhizosphere in the Trans Himalayan region of Himachal Pradesh, India. BioRxiv. doi: 10.1101/193672

Sharma, S., Sayyed, R. Z., Trivedi, M. H., & Gobi, T. A. (2013). Phosphate solubilizing microbes: Sustainable approach for managing phosphorus deficiency in agricultural soils. *SpringerPlus*, *2*(1), 587. doi:10.1186/2193-1801-2-587

Sharma, S., Trivedi, M., Sayyed, R., & Thivakaran, G. (2014). Status of soil phosphorus in context with phosphate solubilizing microorganisms in different agricultural amendments in Kachchh, Gujarat, Western India. *Annual Research & Review in Biology*, *4*(18), 2901–2909.

Singh, K., & Gera, R. (2018). Assessing phosphate solubilization ability of *Sesbania grandiflora* rhizobia isolated from root nodules using diverse agroecological zones of Indian soils for biofertilizer production. *International Journal of Chemical Studies*, *6*(4), 398–402.

Singh, P., & Banik, R. M. (2019). Effect of purified alkaline phosphatase from *Bacillus licheniformis* on growth of *Zea mays* L. *Plant Science Today*, *6*(1), 583–589.

Song, O. R., Lee, S. J., Lee, M. W., Choi, S. L., Chung, S. Y., Lee, Y. G., & Choi, Y. L. (2001). Isolation and phosphate-solubilizing characteristics of PSM, Aeromonas hydrophila DA33. *Journal of Life Science*, *11*(2), 63–69.

Srinivasan, R., Alagawadi, A. R., Yandigeri, M. S., Meena, K. K., & Saxena, A. K. (2012). Characterization of phosphate-solubilizing microorganisms from salt-affected soils of India and their effect on growth of sorghum plants [*Sorghum bicolor* (L.) Moench]. *Annals of Microbiology*, *62*(1), 93–105. doi:10.1007/s13213-011-0233-6

Stella, M., & Halimi, M. (2015). Gluconic acid production by bacteria to liberate phosphorus from insoluble phosphate complexes. *Journal of Tropical Agriculture and Food Science*, *43*(1), 41–53.

Tairo, E. V., & Ndakidemi, P. A. (2014). Macronutrients uptake in soybean as affected by *Bradyrhizobium japonicum* inoculation and phosphorus (P) supplements. *American Journal of Plant Sciences*, *5*(4), 43263.

Teshome, B., Abatneh, E., & Ayinalem, E. (2019). In vitro screening and identification of P-solubilizing rhizobacteria associated with *Sorghum bicolor* L. *Agricultural Research and Technology*, *20*(2), 556122.

Thiruvengadam, S., Ramki, R., Rohini, S., Vanitha, R., & Romauld, I. (2020). Isolation, screening and evaluation of multifunctional strains of high efficient phosphate solubilizing microbes from rhizosphere soil. *Research Journal of Pharmacy and Technology*, *4*, 1825–1828.

Thomas, L., & Singh, I. (2019). Microbial biofertilizers: Types and applications. In B. Giri, R. Prasad, Q. S. Wu, & A. Varma (Eds.), *Biofertilizers for Sustainable Agriculture and Environment* (Vol. 55, pp. 1–19). Springer.

Vanlauwe, B., Wendt, J., Giller, K. E., Corbeels, M., Gerard, B., & Nolte, C. (2014). A fourth principle is required to define conservation agriculture in sub-Saharan Africa: The appropriate use of fertilizer to enhance crop productivity. *Field Crops Research*, *155*, 10–13.

Vazquez, P., Holguin, G., Puente, M., Lopez-Cortes, A., & Bashan, Y. (2000). Phosphate-solubilizing microorganisms associated with the rhizosphere of mangroves in a semiarid coastal lagoon. *Biology and Fertility of Soils*, *30*(5), 460–468.

Verma, M., Singh, A., Dwivedi, D. H., & Arora, N. K. (2020). Zinc and phosphate solubilizing *Rhizobium radiobacter* (LB2) for enhancing quality and yield of loose leaf lettuce in saline soil. *Environmental Sustainability*, *3*(2), 209–218. doi:10.1007/s42398-020-00110-4

Wagh, J., Shah, S., Bhandari, P., Archana, G., & Kumar, G. N. (2014). Heterologous expression of pyrroloquinoline quinone (pqq) gene cluster confers mineral phosphate solubilization ability to *Herbaspirillum seropedicae* Z67. *Applied Microbiology and Biotechnology*, *98*(11), 5117–5129.

Wang, D. M., Sun, L., Sun, W.-J., Cui, F.-J., Gong, J.-S., Zhang, X.-M., Shi, J.-S., & Xu, Z.-H. (2018). Purification, characterization and gene identification of a membrane-bound glucose dehydrogenase from 2-keto-d-gluconic acid industrial producing strain *Pseudomonas plecoglossicida* JUIM01. *International Journal of Biological Macromolecules*, *118*, 534–541. doi: 10.1016/j.ijbiomac.2018.06.097

Wang, Y. Y., Li, P. S., Zhang, B. X., Wang, Y. P., Meng, J., Gao, Y. F., He, X. M., & Hu, X. M. (2020). Identification of phosphate-solubilizing microorganisms and determination of their phosphate-solubilizing activity and growth-promoting capability. *BioResources*, *15*(2), 2560–2578.

Wecksler, S. R., Stoll, S., Tran, H., Magnusson, O. T., Wu, S., King, D., Britt, R. D., & Klinman, J. P. (2009). Pyrroloquinoline quinone biogenesis: Demonstration that PqqE from *Klebsiella pneumoniae* is a radical *S*-adenosyl-l-methionine enzyme. *Biochemistry*, *48*(42), 10151–10161.

Wei, C. Y., Lin, L., Luo, L. J., Xing, Y. X., Hu, C. J., Yang, L. T., Li, Y. R., & An, Q. (2014). Endophytic nitrogen-fixing *Klebsiella variicola* strain DX120E promotes sugarcane growth. *Biology and Fertility of Soils*, *50*(4), 657–666.

White, C. (2020). Why regenerative agriculture? *American Journal of Economics and Sociology*, *79*(3), 799–812.

Woo, S.-M., Lee, M., Hong, I., Poonguzhali, S., & Sa, T. (2010). Isolation and characterization of phosphate solubilizing bacteria from Chinese cabbage. In *19th World Congress of Soil Science, Soil Solutions for a Changing World*, 56–59. Brisbane, Australia.

Wu, X., Cui, Z., Peng, J., Zhang, F., & Liesack, W. (2022). Genome-resolved metagenomics identifies the particular genetic traits of phosphate-solubilizing bacteria in agricultural soil. *ISME Communications*, *2*(1), 1–4.

Xu, S., Zhao, Y., Peng, Y., Shi, Y., Xie, X., Chai, A., Li, B., & Li, L. (2022). Comparative genomics assisted functional characterization of *Rahnella aceris* ZF458 as a novel plant growth promoting rhizobacterium. *Frontiers in Microbiology*, *13*, 850084.

You, M., Fang, S., MacDonald, J., Xu, J., & Yuan, Z.-C. (2020). Isolation and characterization of Burkholderia cenocepacia CR318, a phosphate solubilizing bacterium promoting corn growth. Microbiological Research, *233*, 126395.

Zeng, Q., Wu, X., Wang, J., & Ding, X. (2017). Phosphate solubilization and gene expression of phosphate-solubilizing bacterium *Burkholderia multivorans* WS-FJ9 under different levels of soluble phosphate. *Journal of Microbiology and Biotechnology*, *27*(4), 844–855.

Zeng, Q., Wu, X., & Wen, X. (2016). Effects of soluble phosphate on phosphate-solubilizing characteristics and expression of gcd gene in *Pseudomonas frederiksbergensis* JW-SD2. *Current Microbiology*, *72*(2), 198–206.

Zhang, J., Wang, P., Fang, L., Zhang, Q.-A., Yan, C., & Chen, J. (2017). Isolation and characterization of phosphate-solubilizing bacteria from mushroom residues and their effect on tomato plant growth promotion. *Polish Journal of Microbiology*, *66*(1), 57–65.

Zhao, K., Penttinen, P., Zhang, X., Ao, X., Liu, M., Yu, X., & Chen, Q. (2014). Maize rhizosphere in Sichuan, China, hosts plant growth promoting *Burkholderia cepacia* with phosphate solubilizing and antifungal abilities. *Microbiological Research*, *169*(1), 76–82.

Section II

Strategies and Platform
Regenerative Agriculture
Research and Development

5 Land Degradation Neutrality
Concept and Approaches

K.K. Mourya, Arijit Barman, Surabhi Hota,
Gopal Tiwari, Shilpi Verma, Ashok Kumar,
R.S. Meena, Prakash Kumar Jha, and U.S. Saikia

5.1 INTRODUCTION

Land degradation is a complex process, which is evident from the reduced biological productivity of terrestrial ecosystems and its adverse impact on human and animal life (Lal et al., 2012). Land is a broad term that includes soil, vegetation, and water resources in a landscape. Among the land components, deterioration in soil quality and health directly affects agricultural productivity, food security, and environmental quality as soil acts as a sink of atmospheric carbon dioxide through carbon sequestration (German Federal Environment Agency, 2011). Land degradation is estimated to affect 1.5 billion people worldwide (Gnacadja, 2012). Intensive agriculture practices and land use changes coupled with climate change have impacted the natural balance between soil loss and formation, leading to land degradation (Foley et al., 2005). Degraded lands have poor soil quality, which supports less vegetation growth, and the loss of native vegetation in the region adversely affects the range of ecosystem services (Gisladottir and Stocking, 2005). Identification of the drivers of land degradation is important for devising restorative measures. Drivers of land degradation are classified as natural factors, human activities, or a combination of both (Gisladottir and Stocking, 2005). Soil erosion and desertification are the two important land degradation processes that negatively impact the soil's physical, chemical, and biological properties (Kosmas et al., 2006; Lal et al., 2012; López-Garrido et al., 2014; Hota et al., 2022a, b). Unscientific land use changes and deforestation hastened soil erosion and the loss of productive top soils, limiting soil productivity and causing flooding in low-lying areas and siltation of water bodies (Gobin et al., 2004; Kirkby et al., 2008). Land desertification is common in the semi-arid and arid regions where scarcity of water limits the productive potential of soils (Kosmas et al., 2003). Dryland is the most vulnerable to desertification, supporting about 38% of the global human population and about 50% of the global livestock population (Gnacadja, 2012). Africa is the most vulnerable region to desertification, and it could lose 25% of its arable land by 2025 if restorative measures are not taken (UNCCD, 2011a). The global demand for food, water, and energy is continuously increasing with the exponential growth of the human population, which ultimately exerts pressure on land resources (Conacher, 2009).

To meet the increasing global food demand, different models have projected an increase in food demand of 35%–56% between 2010 and 2050 (van Dijk et al., 2021). Therefore, extraordinary measures are required to halt land degradation to meet the global food demand. The concept of land degradation neutrality (LDN) or zero net land degradation (ZNLD) was first discussed in the United Nations Convention to Combat Desertification (UNCCD) in 2011. Since then, efforts have been made to raise global awareness of the need to work toward achieving a land degradation neutral world (UNCCD, 2011b; Gilbey et al., 2019). LDN is documented as a sustainable development goal (SDG-15.3) by UNCCD. The UNCCD 12th Conference of the Parties (COP12) in 2015 defined the concept of LDN as "a state whereby the amount and quality of land resources necessary to support ecosystem functions and services and enhance food security remain stable or increase within specified temporal and spatial scales and ecosystems" (Orr et al., 2017). The aim of LDN is to "combat desertification, restore degraded land and soil, including land affected by desertification, drought, and floods, and strive to achieve a land degradation-neutral world" by 2030 (UNCCD, 2015). The LDN framework widely uses three indicators to monitor land degradation: (i) change in land cover, (ii) change in productivity of land, and (iii) change in carbon storage (Cowie et al., 2018). The development of sustainable land management (SLM) practices and technologies for restoring affected land is needed for producing food commodities and reducing poverty in developing countries, and it could result in benefits of USD 1.4 trillion (Gnacadja and Wiese, 2016). The LDN target can be achieved through collaborative efforts from all stakeholders, including institutional support, financial assistance, and land governance (Allen et al., 2020). In this chapter, we have discussed in detail the status of land degradation, the effect of crop productivity, management strategies in different ecosystems to halt land degradation, and efforts taken to achieve a land degradation-neutral world.

5.2 LAND DEGRADATION CURRENT STATUS: IMPACTS ON FOOD SECURITY

Land degradation is a slow and unnoticeable process. These processes are visible in the form of barren hillsides, cracked and parched plains, water and wind-eroded sites, nutrient-deficient deserted land, and vast garbage dumps. Globally, degraded land is estimated between 1 to 6 billion hectares (Gibbs and Salmon, 2015) and is having a serious impact on ecosystem services such as resources, habitat, healthy soils, and clean water and air (Montanarella et al., 2018). Among the degraded lands, over 20% of cultivated areas, 30% of forests, and 10% of grasslands are suffering from varying degrees of degradation, which remains a cause for serious concern due to its adverse impact on food production, the environment, and livelihood security (Bai et al., 2008). According to the Space Application Centre (SAC) 2016 in India, within a period of 8 years (from 2003–2005 to 2011–2013), there has been an increase of 1.87 million hectares of land under degradation. According to Costanza et al. (2008), 35% of the world's arable land has already been degraded, and intensive agriculture alone is causing accelerated soil erosion, salinization, or waterlogging of possibly 6 million hectares per year. According to estimates from the World Wildlife Fund (2016), half of the topsoil on the planet has been lost in the last 150 years (WWF Soil Erosion and Degradation, 2018). Globally, 52% of agricultural land is moderately or severely degraded (Food and Agriculture Organization, 2018). Drought, flooding, excessive use of chemicals, loss of nutrients, intensive and unsustainable agriculture, deforestation, urbanization, overgrazing, water pollution, increasing amount of solid waste, and the disposal of non-biodegradable waste are considered the most important causes of land degradation that lead to a temporary or permanent decline in the actual or potential productivity of land.

Land degradation processes are the combined result of numerous factors, including human-induced (unsustainable cultivation practices, overgrazing, deforestation) and natural hazards (climatic variations, erosion by wind and water) (Bai et al., 2008, ISRIC, 2016) (Figure 5.1). These factors are complex and often interwoven, triggering a chain reaction (Figure 5.2). According to the World Commission on Environment and Development (WCED) report (1987), almost every continent is dealing with varying degrees of land degradation issues, such as soil erosion in North America; soil acidification in Europe; deforestation and desertification in Asia, Africa, and Latin America; and waste and water pollution almost everywhere. The most widespread and studied soil degradation processes are water and wind erosion.

5.2.1 Types of Land Degradation

5.2.1.1 Land Degradation due to Water Erosion

It is the removal of soil particles by the action of water, usually seen as sheet erosion (the uniform removal of a thin layer of topsoil), rill erosion (small channels in the field), or gully erosion (large channels, similar to incised rivers). One important feature of soil erosion by water is the selective

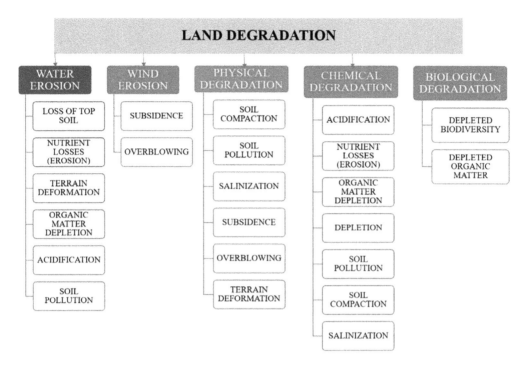

FIGURE 5.1   Land degradation types and their causes.

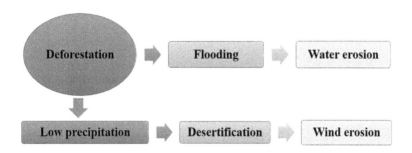

FIGURE 5.2   Interwoven land degradation processes.

removal of the finer and more fertile fraction of the soil. Water erosion is the most significant land degradation process in India, accounting for 10.98% of total land degradation in 2011–2013 (SAC, 2016). Water erosion can cause frequent natural disasters like flooding and landslides, and approximately 24 billion tonnes of topsoil is lost annually (Bakker, 1990). In erosional processes, coastal erosion represents a strong link to climate change due to the melting of glaciers caused by global warming (Mentaschi et al., 2018). Development of gully networks, transport and deposition of soil, and siltation of natural and artificial water bodies are among the large-scale land degradation processes (Poesen and Hooke, 1997; Ravi et al., 2010).

5.2.1.2   Land Degradation due to Wind Erosion

It is the process by which soil particles are removed by the action of the wind. Wind erosion has been reported to degrade 5.55% of the land in India from 2011 to 2013 (SAC, 2016). Usually, this is sheet erosion, where soil is removed in thin layers, but sometimes the effect of the wind can carve out hollows and other features. Wind erosion most easily occurs with fine to medium-sized sand particles. Sedimentation or soil burial may occur through flooding, where fertile soil is buried under less fertile sediments; or wind-blown sands inundate grazing lands; or catastrophic events such as volcanic eruptions. Extreme levels of soil erosion result in the exhumation of stones and rocks, and finer soil particles have been removed by wind or water action, resulting in increased stoniness and rock cover on the land. Soil organic matter, carbonates, oxides of iron, and aluminium are the binding agents between soil particles to form stable soil aggregates. One well-accepted indicator of increased erodibility of soil is the level of organic matter in the soil. Where the organic matter content of a soil falls below 2%, the soil is more prone to erosion because soil aggregates are less strong and individual particles are more likely to be dislodged.

5.2.1.3   Degradation of Soil Physical Properties

Physical degradation is a process that does not involve material detachment or transport. It is a degradation of soil's physical properties because of reduced organic matter, resulting in poor soil structure, aeration, and water-holding capacity. Soil compaction, hardening, sealing, ground subsidence, waterlogging, and any other mechanism leading to the loss of pore volume are examples of physical degradation. Soil compaction is a worldwide problem, especially with the adoption of mechanized agriculture. In some regions of Europe and North America, compaction is the cause of yield reductions of 25%–50% (Ericksson et al., 1974). Ground subsidence is typically caused by the depletion of groundwater or oil reserves. Subsidence involves a sustained collapse of the ground surface, which can lead to other degradation processes such as salinization and permanent flooding. Waterlogging is caused by a rise in groundwater close to the soil surface or inadequate drainage of surface water, often resulting from poor irrigation management. Because of waterlogging, water saturates the root zone, leading to an oxygen deficiency.

5.2.1.4   Degradation of Soil Chemical Properties

Chemical land degradation processes include nutrient depletion, nutrient imbalance, acidification, salt imbalance, and increased metal toxicity. Excessive N fertilization and, to a lesser extent, cation depletion through harvesting exports lead to acidification in croplands (Guo et al., 2010). Localized contamination and diffuse contamination of heavy metals due to acidification are other important causes of soil degradation. Depletion of the organic matter pool in soil is one of the most significant chemical degradation processes in the context of climate change. Depletion of soil organic carbon (SOC) pools is caused by increased microbial respiration under the effects of global warming and tillage operations, as well as reductions in below-ground plant biomass inputs (Bellamy et al., 2005; Bond-Lamberty et al., 2018; Yadav et al., 2021; Mourya et al., 2021).

Soil salinization is characterized by an increase in the salt concentration in the soil solution. An increase in sodium cations (Na^+) on the exchange sites of the soil clay minerals adversely affects the soil structure and cationic nutrient balance. Salinization often occurs in conjunction with poor irrigation water management. Mostly, sodicity tends to occur naturally in semi-arid environments. Areas where the water table fluctuates may be prone to sodicity. Salinization, although perceived and reported in soils, is typically triggered by the rise of the water table, which drives salts to the surface in dry to sub-humid climates (Schofield and Kirkby, 2003). While salty soils and ecosystems occur naturally in dry to sub-humid climates (primary salinity), human interventions have expanded their distribution (secondary salinity). Irrigation without proper drainage has been the predominant cause of salinization. Changes in evapotranspiration and precipitation patterns can aggravate this process by building salts in the root zone through capillary action in longer dry period (Schofield and Kirkby, 2003).

5.2.1.5   Degradation of Soil Biological Properties

Degradation of a land's biotic components can contribute to biological degradation. For example, indiscriminate destruction of forests and woodlands and vegetation clearing associated with land use changes can cause deforestation, barren land, and net carbon losses from soil pools and vegetation. In natural or semi-natural ecosystems, a change in plant composition without a significant change in vegetation structure can degrade rangelands and forests. In India, 8.91% of the area was degraded by vegetation degradation in 2011–2013 (SAC, 2016).

According to the WWF, the conversion of forests and natural grasslands to farm fields for cultivation and the transition from natural vegetation to intensive commercial crops such as coffee, cotton, palm oil, soybeans, and wheat have resulted in increased soil erosion beyond the soil's ability to adapt and maintain it. Selective grazing in rangelands and selective logging in forests are the persistent causes of degradation. This can lead to long-term impoverishment and, in extreme cases, a full loss of the forest cover through its interaction with other agents such as fires or progressive intensification of land use (Illius and O'Connor, 1999; Sasaki et al., 2008; Foley et al., 2007).

Invasive alien species are another source of biological degradation. Their arrival into cultivated systems is constantly reshaping crop production strategies, making agriculture unviable on occasion. In natural and semi-natural systems such as rangelands, invasive plant species not only threaten livestock production through diminished forage quality, poisoning, and other deleterious effects but also have cascading effects on other processes such as altered fire regimes and water cycling (Brooks et al., 2004).

Other biotic components of ecosystems, for example, invertebrate invasions in continental waters, can exacerbate other degradation processes such as eutrophication (Walsh et al., 2016). Shifts in soil microbial and meso-faunal composition, which can be caused by pollution with pesticides (Hota et al., 2021) or nitrogen deposition, alter many soil functions, including microbial respiration rates and C release to the atmosphere (Hussain et al., 2009; Crowther et al., 2015). In natural, dry ecosystems, biological soil crusts composed of a broad range of organisms, including mosses, are a particularly sensitive "entry point" for degradation (Field et al., 2010), with evidence of sensitivity to climate change (Reed et al., 2012).

5.2.1.6 Desertification

Desertification is defined as the "land degradation in dryland areas due to various factors, including climatic variations and/or human activity" (UNCCD, 1995). Areas affected by desertification are found in North and South America, Africa, southern Europe, Asia, and Australia. In Africa, over one billion hectares are affected by desertification (D'Odorico et al., 2013). In the desertification process, a fertile land loses its fertility and becomes desert. Drastic change in global climate, frequent drought, and extreme weather conditions are the natural causes of desertification. Aridity index is studied to identify the desertification process. Long-term data on precipitation and temperate climate are required to estimate the aridity index, and the availability of long-term data is the main limitation in desertification assessments (Farjalla et al., 2014). Man-made factors of desertification include overgrazing, cultivation on high slopes and marginal lands, faulty land use, and management practices that disturb the natural balance of ecosystem. Adoption of sustainable land management practices depends upon socio-economic conditions of the local population, which also contribute to the land degradation/desertification process (Reddy et al., 2018).

5.2.2 Impact of Land Degradation on Crop Productivity

FAO describes land degradation as "a change in the soil health status resulting in a diminished capacity of the ecosystem to provide goods and services for its beneficiaries" (FAO, 2014). Food is a basic human need, and agriculture is the primary source of our food; nearly 97% of our food comes from land (Costanza et al., 1997). In 2016, the global population was estimated at 7.4 billion (Population Reference Bureau, 2016). The United Nations estimates that the global population will further increase to a minimum of 9.1 billion by 2050 and 11.2 billion by 2100 (UN Population Division, 2015). Fast-growing global populations have put unprecedented demand on agriculture, coupled with losses of soil organic carbon and nitrogen that reduce the ability of the agricultural sector to produce enough food (GLASOD). There are serious productivity losses of up to 20% caused by soil erosion in Asia, especially in India, China, Iran, Israel, Jordan, Lebanon,

Nepal, and Pakistan (Dregne, 1992). Marginally degraded land reduces crop yield by 10%, moderately degraded land reduces crop yield by 10%–50%, and severely degraded soil reduces crop yield by more than 50%.

Thus, agriculture in the 21st century faces multiple challenges. These challenges are indeed massive, particularly when arable land is shrinking and soil degradation is increasing every passing day. According to FAO, crop yields would continue to grow but at a slower rate than in the past. On average, the annual crop yield growth rate during the current decade is likely to be about half (0.8%) of its historical growth rate of 1.7% and then decline further (FAO, 2009). Food crops in China may experience a 9% loss in productivity by 2030 if land degradation continues at the current rate. Productivity losses are expected to reach 30% by 2050, with soil degradation occurring at twice the current rate. The loss of cropland is likely to cause a 13%–18% decline in China's food production capacity by 2030–2050 compared to 2005, when the production was 482 Mt. Thus, food supply may deteriorate significantly from an 18% surplus in 2005 to a 22%–32% deficit by 2050 (Ye and Van Ranst, 2009). With the advancement of technology, land degradation will be mitigated in a more efficient way to support sustainable crop production. Sustainable land management technologies must be used for soil conservation, reduction of waterlogging and salinization, and judicious use of fertilizers and pesticides. An increased awareness towards environmental ethics, including the conservation of forests, reduction in non-biodegradable waste, preservation of water bodies, and optimal use of water resources, is essential if we wish to avoid a reduction in crop productivity in the decades ahead.

5.3   ASSESSMENT OF LAND DEGRADATION

In achieving the goals of LDN, accurate and real-time information about land resources is a prerequisite before developing any sustainable land management strategies (Liniger et al., 2019). The fundamental techniques for gathering information about natural resources are soil surveying and land evaluation. However, traditional methods of soil survey are very time-consuming and labour intensive. Advancements in geospatial techniques, including remote sensing and geographic information systems (GIS), and the availability of high-resolution satellite images and digital elevation models (DEM) have greatly aided in generating real-time information about land resources (Reddy et al., 2008; Nagaraju et al., 2014). These geospatial technologies, along with conventional soil survey methods, are capable of generating information in several aspects, such as landforms, soils, land use/land cover, and erosion, which helps in developing soil water conservation measures and land use plans at the watershed level (Reddy et al., 2008; Surya et al., 2020). However, classification and mapping of degraded land remain a challenge because of non-uniform criteria and guidelines for degraded lands (Safriel, 2017).

5.4   ACHIEVING LAND DEGRADATION NEUTRALITY

After the identification and mapping of different types of land degradation mechanisms operating in an ecosystem development and adoption of sustainable land management practices are necessary to be implemented at place. Monitoring of changes in soil organic carbon is considered as the most sensitive indicator for land degradation, especially in managed ecosystems. Soil organic carbon not only improves soil health but also has a significant impact on the mitigation of global climate change through carbon sequestration. In this section, some of the sustainable land management practices are discussed, which will help to achieve land degradation neutrality.

5.4.1   Modification of the Crop with Respect to Degraded Soil

The intergenic differences between crop genotype and salinity tolerance can be exploited for screening purposes based on satisfactory higher yield under given levels of root zone salinity

(Minhas and Gupta, 1992; Koyama et al., 2001). Less water-demanding crops like oilseed crops can tolerate higher levels of irrigation water salinity over salinity-sensitive pulses and vegetables. Mono cropping is recommended in arid and semi-arid zones (rainfall<400 mm) for maintaining salt balance. Minhas et al. (2004) recommended the growing of semi-tolerant and tolerant (mustards, wheat, cotton) crops for the successful use of saline waters, whereas crops like rice, sugarcane, and forages, which require liberal water use, should be avoided. Tolerance limits to the use of saline waters and salt accumulation in the soil can be modified by soil texture (mainly), annual rainfall, and ionic constituents of salinity. Water with electrical conductivity (EC) of more than 12 dS/m can be used for growing tolerant and semi-tolerant crops in coarse-textured soils, whereas EC of more than 2 dS/m can often create salinity problems in fine-textured soils (Sharma and Minhas, 2005). Other factors such as ageing, crop cultivars, and the presence of other toxic constituents along with salinity also can change in tolerance of crops to osmotic stress (Minhas, 1996; Katerji et al., 2000).

There is a wide inherent salt tolerance variation among crop cultivars, besides intergenic variations of crops to salinity tolerance. For developing salt-tolerant rice cultivars, breeders are interested in quantitative trait loci (QTL) mapping and marker-assisted breeding. Cultivars with desired traits can be developed by introgression of markers tightly linked to the submergence tolerance gene (SUB1) and QTL for salinity tolerance at the seedling stage (qSALTOL) in the background of high-yielding cultivars (Singh et al., 2010). Usually, there is a negative correlation between tolerance of varieties and their potential yields. A list of all salt-tolerant varieties developed in India along with their level of tolerance to soil salinity is given in Table 5.1.

Physico-chemical properties such as organic carbon, nutrient contents, water permeability, and microbial activity are improved, whereas soluble salts and exchangeable Na^+ content are decreased after a few years in saline soil under salt-tolerant trees and shrubs (Mishra et al., 2003).

Crops differ in their tolerance to soil sodicity (Abrol and Bhumbla, 1979). Suitable alkali-tolerant crop (Table 5.2) and cropping sequence (Table 5.3) can manage the soil sodicity. Rice-based cropping pattern can be followed to reclaim the sodicity. The introduction of one green manuring crop such as glyricidia/sesbania in the cropping sequence is most profitable.

TABLE 5.1
Recommended Salt Tolerant Varieties

Crop	Tolerant Varieties	Sodic pH$_2$	Saline EC$_e$ (dS/m)	Coastal Saline EC$_e$ (dS/m)
Rice	CSR 10, CSR 11, CSR 12, CSR 13	9.8–10.2	6–11	—
	CSR 19, CSR 23, CSR 27, CSR 30, CSR 36	9.4–9.8	6.11	—
	CSR 1–3, CSR 4, CST7-1, SR26B, Sumati	—	6–9	4
Wheat	KRL 1–4, WH157	<9.3	6–10	—
	Raj3077, KRL19	<9.3	6–10	
Barley	DL200, Ratna, BH97, DL348	8.8–9.3		
Indian mustard (Raya)	Pusa Bold, Varuna	8.8–9.2	6–8	—
	Kranti, CS52, CSTR330-1,	8.8–9.3	6–9	—
	CST609-B 10, CS54	8.8–9.3	6–9	
Gram	Karnal Chana 1	<9.0	<6.0	—
Sugarbeet	Ramonskaaya 06, Maribo Resistapoly	9.5–10	<6.5	—
Sugarcane	Co453, Co1341	<9.0	EC$_e$–10	—

TABLE 5.2
Relative Tolerance to Soil Sodicity of Different Crops

Range of ESP	Crops
10–15	Safflower, Mash, Peas, Lentil, Pigeon pea, Urd bean
15–20	Bengal gram, Soybean, Maize
20–25	Ground nut, Cow pea, Onion, Pearl millet
25–30	Linseed, Garlic, Guar, Lemon grass, Pamarosa, Sugarcane, Cotton
30–50	Wheat, Raya, Sorghum, Sunflower, Berseem, Senji, Blue panic
50–60	Barley, sesbania, Para grass, Rhodes grass, Matricaria
60–70	Rice, Sugarbeet, Karnal grass

Source: Singh and Sharma (2004).

TABLE 5.3
Selected Cropping Sequence for Alkali Soils

	Year of Reclamation		
Season	First	Second	Third
Summer (April–May)	Leaching/Sesbania or green manuring	Sesbania for green manuring	Sesbania green manuring/Fallow/ Cowpea (Fodder)/Maize (Fodder)/Rice
Kharif	Rice/Sesbania	Rice/Wheat/Barley/	Rice/Wheat/Barley/Raya/Berseem/
Rabi	Barley/Wheat	Shaftal/Senji/Sugarbeet	Shaftal/Senji/Sugarbeet

5.4.2 Sub-Surface Drainage Techniques in Waterlogged Saline Lands

Waterlogging and salinity build-up have caused massive land degradation in irrigated lands of northwestern India. Sub-surface drainage helps to maintain the water table at the requisite depth and also leaches away the harmful salts (Datta et al., 2000; Manjunatha et al., 2004). About 60,000 ha waterlogged saline areas have been reclaimed using this technology (CSSRI, 2018). The use of groundwater by crops is related to water table depth and salinity of sub-surface water (Shannon and Grieve, 2000). The provision of sub-surface drainage allows the removal of salt accumulated in the field up to 1 m soil depth (Minhas, 1993; Sharma et al., 1994). Yield reductions were much smaller in fields having a sub-surface drainage system than in fields with a deep water table, and the differences were larger at applied water salinities of more than 10 dS/m (Table 5.4).

TABLE 5.4
Relative Yield of Wheat with Saline Irrigation Under Conditions of a Deep Water Table and a High Water Table but Provided with Sub-Surface Drainage

	Relative Yield (%)	
Irrigation Water Salinity (dS/m)	Deep Water Table	Shallow Water Table
0.6	95	100
4.0	90	94
8.0	83	86
12.0	60	78
16.0	42	74

Sub-surface drainage helped in maintaining a more favourable moisture regime in the root zone, which leads to higher productivity, higher incomes to the adopters, and generation of farm employment and exhibits improvements in soil properties.

5.4.3 Soil Erosion Control Techniques

Tolerance to soil loss (T) is defined as the upper threshold limit of soil erosion that can be allowed without degrading the long-term productivity of a particular soil. It is projected that ~59% of land within the hilly region requires some form of erosion management to achieve T (Mandal et al., 2010). Soil conservation measures, such as contour ploughing, bunding, and use of strips and terraces, can decrease erosion and slow runoff water. Mechanical measures, *e.g.*, physical barriers such as embankments and windbreaks, vegetation cover (and use of vegetative buffer strips and geotextiles), and soil husbandry are important measures to control soil erosion (Srinivasarao et al., 2014). In addition, conservation agriculture (CA), agro-forestry, integrated nutrient management (INM), and diversified cropping also conserve soil and water (Soni et al., 2020). In vertisols (of central India), runoff and soil loss were lower from broad bed and furrow land surface management practices than from a flat-on-grade system (Table 5.5). The broad bed and furrow system decreased soil loss to a greater extent (31%–55%) than its effect on runoff volume (24%–32%) compared with that of the flat-on-grade system.

5.4.4 Agronomic Management Techniques

Agronomical practices like the use of cover crops, mixed/inter/strip cropping, crop rotation, green manuring, and mulch farming are vital practices associated with integrated nutrient management, *i.e.*, the application of NPK mineral fertilizers along with organic manure, which increases crop productivity, improves SOC content, and decreases soil loss. Growing soybean (*Glycine max*)/groundnut (*Arachis hypogoea*)/cowpea (*Vigna radiata*) with maize (*Zea mays*)/jowar (*Sorghum bicolor*)/bajra (*Pennisetum glaucum*) is a common example of intercropping in the drylands (Srinivasarao et al., 2014). With green manuring, wheat had greater water use (289 mm) than wheat in a wheat-fallow system (273 mm) or wheat (270 mm) rotated with maize (Sharda et al., 1999). Strip cropping is a combination of contouring and crop rotation in which alternate strips of row crops and soil-conserving crops are grown on the same slope, perpendicular to the wind or water flow in drylands and hilly regions, respectively. The practice of line sowing of wheat and mustard (*Brassica juncea* L.) crops and maintaining a row ratio of 8:1 ensured optimum use of space and soil moisture, and increased wheat equivalent yield by 14% and net returns by 30% compared to mixed sowing (Table 5.6) (Singh et al., 1992; Sharma et al., 2013).

TABLE 5.5
Seasonal Rainfall, Runoff and Soil Loss from Different Land Configuration, Broad-Bed and Furrow (BBF) and Flat on Grade (FOG)

Year	Rainfall (mm)	Runoff (mm)		Soil Loss (ton/ha)	
		BBF	FOG	BBF	FOG
2003	1,058	163.0 (15.4%)	214.9 (20.3%)	2.0	2.9
2004	798.2	124.0 (15.5%)	183.3 (23.0%)	0.7	1.5
2005	946.0	177 (18.7%)	246 (26.1%)	1.4	3.1
2006	1,513.0	502 (33.2%)	873 (57.7%)	3.5	6.4

Source: Mandal et al. (2013).

TABLE 5.6

Water Use Efficiency, Yield and Net Return as Affected by Different Technologies and Crop Rotation in Farmers' Fields of Uttarakhand, Jammu and Kashmir and Himachal Pradesh

Inter Cropping	Crops	Water Use Efficiency (kg/ha/mm)			Yield (t/ha)			Net Return (INR/ha)		
		C	T	Increase%	C	T	Increase%	C	T	Increase%
Maize + cowpea	Maize	3.19	5.60	76	2.21[a]	3.67[a]	66	4,448	11,690	163
(1:2) – wheat	Wheat	5.30	8.31	57	1.13	1.64	46	3,176	6,149	88
Maize – wheat +	Maize	3.00	4.34	45	1.94	2.75	42	3,248	8,658	163
mustard (9:1)	Wheat	6.33	9.66	50	1.31[a]	1.93[b]	47	4,455	9,041	105
Maize – potato –	Maize	3.09	4.52	46	1.95	2.86	46	3,361	9,135	172
onion (irrigated)	Potato	53.70	76.50	42	17.10	23.50	33	9,775	19,250	97
	Onion	18.87	25.45	35	12.05	15.10	25	38,700	51,050	32

Source: Ghosh et al. (2011).

60 INR (Indian Rupees) ~ 1 USD (2014).

[a] Maize equivalent yield.

[b] Wheat equivalent yield.

C, Conventional; T, Intercropping/crop rotation.

TABLE 5.7

Soil and Water Conservation Measures to be Taken Up Based on Seasonal Rainfall in the Peninsular India

Seasonal Rainfall (mm)	Soil and Water Conservation Measures	
<500	Contour cultivation with conservation furrows,	Tied ridges, contour bunds
500–750	ridging, sowing across slope, mulching, scoops, off season tillage, inter row water harvesting system, small basins, field bunds, Khadin	Zingg terrace modified contour bunds and broad bed furrow
750–1,000	Broad bed furrow (Vertisols), field bunds, vegetative bunds and graded bunds	Conservation furrows, sowing across slope, conservation tillage, lock and spill drains, small basins, NadiZingg terrace
>1,000		Level terrace and Zingg terrace (conservation bench terrace)

When crops like maize, sorghum, and castor (*Ricinus communis* L.) are cultivated along with legumes such as groundnut, green gram (*Vigna radiata* L.), black gram (*Vigna mungo* L.), soybean, and cowpea in inter-row spaces, sufficient cover on the ground is ensured and erosion hazards are decreased (Rao and Khan, 2003). Pathak et al. (2009) reported several soil conservation measures based on rainfall in a particular area (Table 5.7).

In the drylands, Srinivasarao et al. (2009) found that integrated nutrient management could improve C accumulation rates up to 0.45 ton/ha/year in a groundnut-based cropping system (Table 5.8).

5.4.5 Amelioration Techniques

Excess exchangeable Na^+ in sodic soils is replaced by the application of chemicals rich in Ca^{2+} followed by leaching with good-quality water. The efficiency of an amendment vis-à-vis other available options, effects on soil properties and crop growth, and the likely expenditure are the major

TABLE 5.8

Carbon Accumulation Rate in Soil (0–20 cm) and Potential Carbon Emission Reduction (CER) Under Different INM Practices

Production Systems	Suggested INM Practice	C Accumulation (ton/ha/year)		Potential CER from the Suggested Practice	
		Farmers' Practice	Suggested Practice	ton/ha	Value (US $)
Groundnut-based (in Alfisols)	50% RDF + 4 ton groundnut shell per hectare	0.080	0.45	0.370	1.85
Groundnut–finger millet (in Alfisols)	FYM 10 ton +10%RDF (NPK)	−0.138	0.241	0.379	1.90
Finger millet–finger millet (in Alfisols)	FYM 10 ton + 100% RDF (NPK)	0.046	0.378	0.332	1.66
Sorghum-based (in Vertisols)	25 kg N/ha (through FYM) + 25 kg N/ha (through urea)	0.101	0.288	0.187	0.94
Soybean based (in Vertisols)	6 ton FYM/ha+20 kg N + 13 kg P	−0.219	0.338	0.557	2.79
Rice-based (in Inceptisols)	100% organic (FYM)	0.014	0.128	0.142	0.71
Pearl millet-based (in Aridisols)	50% N (inorganic fertilizer) + 50% N (FYM)	−0.252	−0.110	0.142	0.71

CER at US$ 5/ton C (prevailing market price of CER for agroforestry and other related practices).
RDF, Recommended dose of fertilizer; FYM, Farmyard manure.

guiding principles in sodic soil reclamation programmes (Abrol et al., 1988). Depending on the soil chemical properties, either direct (*e.g.*, gypsum) or indirect (sulphuric acid, elemental sulphur, etc.) sources of calcium may be applied to reduce the effect of soil sodicity (Horney et al., 2005). In India, gypsum is the most widely used amendment in sodic soils. It is, however, becoming evident that gypsum may not be available in desired quantity and quality in the future. This state of affairs has enhanced the interest in organic inputs, alternative amendments, and nano-scale materials in sodic soil reclamation.

It has been shown that the use of easily available and cheap organic amendments such as green manure, farmyard manure, poultry manure, municipal solid waste compost, and rice straw increases the productivity of salt-affected lands as organic matter input often accelerates salt leaching and improves aggregate stability, water flux, and water-holding capacity (Walker and Bernal, 2008). Press-mud application and wheat residue incorporation gave the highest rice and wheat yields in soils irrigated with high residual sodium carbonate (RSC:8.5 me/L) water (Yaduvanshi and Sharma, 2007). Similarly, the combined use of press-mud (10 Mg/ha), FYM (10 Mg/ha), and gypsum (5 Mg/ha) significantly enhanced rice and wheat yields under continuous sodic irrigation (Yaduvanshi and Swarup, 2005). Application of 50% distillery effluent along with bio-amendments was best in improving the properties of sodic soil and in improving germination and seedling growth of pearl millet (Kaushik et al., 2005). These results show that alternative amendments could partially replace gypsum in reclamation programmes.

Biodegradable municipal solid waste has huge potential for enhancing crop productivity in saline soils. In a field experiment conducted for three consecutive years in mustard-pearl millet cropping system in saline soil, integrated use of organic amendments *viz.* municipal solid waste compost (MSWC), rice straw compost, and gypsum-enriched compost (GEC) along with 25% recommended dose of fertilizers (RDF) resulted in significant increase (32% higher over 100% RDF) in microbial biomass carbon, decrease in soil salinity (one unit over control), and increase in crop yields (25% higher over 100% RDF) in both mustard and pearl-millet than the use of organic amendments and mineral fertilizers alone (CSSRI, 2017). A number of polymer-based soil conditioners have also given encouraging results in degraded soils. They enhance soil aggregate stability and water permeability, leading to a reduction in surface runoff and soil displacement, particularly in sodic soils, presumably attributed to diminished clay dispersion. Ultimately, this contributes to an improvement in soil aggregation and a subsequent increase in soil hydraulic conductivity (Liu and Lal, 2012).

Liming is the most desirable practice for amelioration of acid soils. Lime raises soil pH, thereby increasing the availability of plant nutrients and reducing the toxicity of Fe and Al (Sharma and Sarkar, 2005; Fageria and Baligar, 2008; Bhat et al., 2007). Sharma and Sarkar (2005) and Bhat et al. (2007) recommended a low dose of lime (*i.e.*, one-tenth to one-fifth of the lime requirement) applied along with fertilizers in furrows at the time of sowing. Bhat et al. (2010) also tested low-cost locally available basic slag, a by-product of a steel factory as an ameliorant for acidic red and lateritic soils of West Bengal under mustard-rice.

Reclaiming acid sulphate soils may follow approaches like: (i) pyrite and soil acidity can be removed by leaching after drying and aeration; (ii) pyrite oxidation can be limited or stopped and existing acidity inactivated by maintaining a high water table, with or without (iii) additional liming and fertilization with phosphorus, though liming may often be uneconomical in practical use. For coastal acid sulphate soils of Sundarbans, the application of lime, superphosphate, and rock phosphate has been found useful (Bandyopadhyay, 1989).

5.4.6 ALTERNATIVE LAND USE SYSTEMS

Best land use on degraded land is to retire to permanent vegetation, because the use of highly saline waters for crop production in such an area is neither feasible nor economical. Conventional planting methods result in poor survival percentage under saline environments. That's why Tomar et al. (2002) devised "SPFIM"(sub-surface planting and furrow irrigation method) system of planting to establish good plantations and to improve biomass production from such lands. In this method, saplings are planted in furrows, and raised beds act as micro-catchments. This improved method not only saves irrigation time and labour but also leads to lesser salts in the soil profile. Irrigation is added only to sapling-planted furrows covering one-fifth to one-tenth of the total area. Quantities equating 10% of open pan evaporation sufficed for the optimal growth of several tree species in arid and semi-arid areas (Minhas et al., 1997). In addition to creating favourable water regimes in the rooting zone during irrigations to furrow-planted saplings, this method had an added advantage as a consequence of salt movement towards the inter-row areas caused by infiltration of rainfall during the monsoon season. Preferred choices for tree species are: *Tamarix articulate, Prosopis juliflora, Acacia nilotica, Acacia tortilis, Fironia limonia, Acacia farnesiana,* and *Melia azadirach* (Tomar et al., 2002). Halophytic species like Salvadora, Sueda, *etc.*, have been identified for bio-saline agriculture. Fruit tree-based agri-horti systems like *Aegle marmelos, Emblica officinalis,* and *Carissa congesta* as main components and cluster bean and barley as subsidiary components have been identified for areas having marginal quality water (EC_{iw}6–10 dS/m) (Dagar et al., 2008).

In India, many tolerant species for saline soils have been tried for a long (Table 5.9): *Prosopis juliflora, Salvadorapersica, S. oleoides, Tamarixericoides, T. troupii, Salsolabaryosma,* successful on sites with $EC_e > 35$ dS/m; *Tamarix articulata, Acacia farnesiana, Parkinsonia aculeate* on sites with moderate salinity (EC_e 25–35 dS/m); *Casuarina (glauca, obesa, equiselifolia), Acacia tortilis, A. nilotica, Callistemon lanceolata, Pongamia pinnata, Eucalyptus camaldulensis, Albizia lebbeck* on sites with moderate salinity (EC_e 15–25 dS/m); trees like *Casuarina cunninghamiana, Eucalyptus tereticornis, Acacia catcechu, A. ampliceps, A. eburnea, A. leucocephala, Dalbergia sissoo* on sites with lower salinity (EC_e 10–15 dS/m).

In alkaline wastelands, mechanical impedance is a major cause of poor root proliferation. This problem could be overcome by planting *Prosopis juliflora*, which has roots to vertically penetrate a hard pan (Singh, 1996). Mishra et al. (2004) opined that soil erosion can be decreased in alkaline soils with *Prosopis juliflora* and *Casuarina equisetifolia* due to the formation of stable soil aggregates in

TABLE 5.9

Ameliorative Effects of Tree Plantation on Salt Affected Soils of India

Region	Tree Species	Soil Depth (cm)	Original pH	Original EC (dS/m)	After pH	After EC (dS/m)	References
Karnataka	*Acacia nilotica* (age 10 years)	0–15	9.20	3.73	7.90	2.05	Basavaraja et al. (2010)
Karnal	*Eucalyptus tereticornis* (age 9 years)	0–10	10.06	1.90	8.02	0.63	Mishraet al. (2003)
Luknow and Bahraich in north India	*Terminaliaarjuna* *Prosopisjuliflora* *Tectonagrandis*	0–15	9.60 ± 0.42	1.47 ± 0.45	8.40 ± 0.27 8.70 ± 0.33 6.15 ± 0.23	0.31 ± 0.07 0.42 ± 0.06 0.06 ± 0.006	Singh and Kaur (2012)

TABLE 5.10

Ameliorating Effects of Tree Plantation on Alkali Soils

Species	Original pH	Original OC (%)	After 20 years pH	After 20 years OC (%)
Eucalyptus tereticornis	10.3	0.12	9.18	0.33
Acacia nilotica	10.3	0.12	9.03	0.55
Albizia lebbeck	10.3	0.12	8.67	0.47
Terminalia arjuna	10.3	0.12	8.15	0.58
Prosopis juliflora	10.3	0.12	8.03	0.58

the surface layers. Kaur et al. (2000) analysed the role of agroforestry systems (*Acacia*, *Eucalyptus* and *Populus* along with rice–berseem (*Trifolium alexandrinum* L.)) to improve soil organic matter, microbial activity, and N availability and observed that (i) microbial biomass C and N were greater by 42% and 13%, respectively, in tree-based systems than mono-cropping; and (ii) soil organic C increased by 11%–52% due to integration of trees along with crops after 6–7 years. Comparative effect of different tree species on soil properties is given in Table 5.10.

Moreover, the degraded lands in arid and semi-arid regions are traditionally left for pastures but their forage productivity is low, unstable, and un-remunerative. Usually, there are acute shortages of fodder during winters/post-monsoon periods. When the limited saline ground water resources were utilized to supplement rainwater supplies, the forage grasses like *Panicum laevifolium* followed by *P. maximum* (both local wild and cultivated) out-performed other grasses (Tomar et al., 2003). Saline irrigation not only improved their productivity by three to four fold but fodder (about 30%) could also be made available during scarce periods of April–June, when the most pastoral nomads are forced to move towards the adjoining irrigated areas in search of fodder. These brackish water-based agro-forestry systems have also emerged as eco-friendly phytoremediation crops for degraded soils (Qadir and Oster, 2002). Besides this, a number of medicinal and aromatic crops have been screened for salinity and sodicity tolerance in India. Crops like Isabgol (*Plantago ovata*) and Matricaria can be successfully cultivated in soils having pH of 9.5 and EC between 8 and 10 dS/m (Dagar et al., 2004, 2006). Similarly, dill (*A. graveolens*), a spice crop, and Salvadora, a non-edible oil tree, can be grown in salt-affected vertisols very successfully. Tomar and Minhas (2004) reported that *Aloe barbadensis* and *Andrographis paniculata* perform and yield well under saline irrigation. Industrial species like *Euphorbia* and *mulathi* (*Glycyrrhiza glabra*) also have good scope for cultivation in salty environments. Fruit crops also showed greater potential for salinity tolerance. Experiments conducted under shallow saline water-table conditions have shown the possibility of commercial cultivation of guava (cv. *Allahabad Safeda*) and bael (*Aegle marmelos*, cv. NB-5) in saline soils irrigated with saline water (3.0–4.0 dS/m) (CSSRI, 2017).

5.5 SCIENCE-POLICY INTERFACE IN LAND DEGRADATION NEUTRALITY

The international community recognized the seriousness of the consequences of land degradation, and as a result of the perceived need, member states of the United Nations Sustainable Development Conference (Rio 20+) in 2012 agreed to strive for a degradation-neutral world by 2030 (Akhtar-Schuster et al., 2017). However, it may not be possible to achieve this gigantic task without an effective science-policy interface. Therefore, it is imperative that the international community, *viz.*, scientists, researchers, policy planners, government agencies, and ministries, formulate an effective and achievable policy framework based on scientific interventions. Some of the important policy dimensions to achieve the land degradation neutrality state are as follows:

5.5.1 POLICY FRAMEWORK TOWARDS SOCIAL INCLUSIVENESS

In order to achieve the LDN world, the policy documents must take into account the inventory of major global socio-economic drivers, their analysis in terms of cause-effect relationships in the context of land degradations so as to ensure full involvement of the international community in achieving the target set for 2030. Studies available on LDN also stressed upon investigation on socio-economic drivers of success (Salvati and Carlucci, 2014), local perceptions of communities about restoration measures and beneficiaries (Crossland et al., 2018), the leap forward for LDN target setting and implementation (Allen et al., 2020; Aynekulu et al., 2017) or an assessment of the resilience needed to achieve the LDN (Cowie et al., 2019).

5.5.2 POLICIES FOCUSING ON SUSTAINABLE LAND USE PLANNING

Land use planning as a holistic approach needs to be considered, while policies are framed for LDN. This may not only help to avoid land use conflict and unjustifiable claims on land resources, which are being seen increasingly in many parts of the world (Schulze et al., 2021). Moreover, sustainable land management policies rely on best management practices such as maintaining adequate soil organic carbon stock (SOC) level that helps in preventing land degradation. However, the effects of land use on SOC are not well known and also depend on the land use land cover of the preceding years (Cha et al., 2020; Mayer et al., 2020). Thus, sustainable (environmentally) land use planning advocating for organic matter addition to improve the soil health, increase energy use efficiency, and reduce carbon footprint in agriculture need to be popularized amongst the stakeholders for its adoption at large scale (Kumar et al., 2022). The organic matter addition helps in binding the soil surfaces (improving soil structure and aggregation), thereby reducing the topsoil losses due to wind erosion. Chappell et al. (2019) reported that wind erosion depleted the SOC stocks of land systems such as intensive grazing systems with a large portion as bared soil surface. Moreover, studies also stress upon integrated land-use planning principle with respect to a "no net loss" target (Orr et al., 2017) and on participatory planning processes with a focus on gender sensitivityand imbalances in power and information access (Orr et al., 2017).

5.5.3 POLICIES ORIENTED TOWARDS FOOD AND LIVELIHOOD SECURITY IN LIGHT OF LDN

Food and livelihood security should be kept at the centre stage while formulating the policies particularly targeting the issues associated with the LDN. Land degradation has been reported to affect the food security, economic and social well-being, and livelihoods of 1.5 billion people (Stavi and Lal, 2015; van der Esch et al., 2017). The problem may further be aggravated on account of increasing pressure on land resources due to the rising global population and deteriorating health and productivity of the land (Montanarella et al., 2016).

5.5.4 POLICIES TO ADDRESS THE CLIMATE CHANGE ISSUES

The policies developed for achieving LDN target must focus on the climatically sensitive areas which are hotspots of land degradation. Global expanse of degraded land includes 73% of the world's dryland rangelands and 47% of marginal rainfed croplands (Gisladottir and Stocking, 2005). In the absence of urgent actions, climate change impacts, such as droughts and floods, will further exacerbate the extent of land degradation (Conacher, 2009; Stavi and Lal, 2015). According to the FAO, restoring currently degraded soils could remove up to 63 billion tonnes of carbon from the atmosphere, which would offset a small but important share of global greenhouse gas emissions (Neely et al., 2009). Proven approaches to halting and reversing land degradation that mitigate climate change include green infrastructure development, reducing soil loss, remediation of contaminated land, and conservation agriculture (Lal, 2012; Kust et al., 2017). A study finds that restoration of over 26 million hectares of degraded land can create a carbon sink of 2.5–3 billion tonnes (Dhyani et al., 2022). One of the three indicators for assessing LDN is soil organic carbon (Chappell et al., 2019).

Given the importance of soil's carbon absorption and storage functions, the avoidance, reduction, and reversal of land degradation are considered to be the third most important greenhouse gas mitigation options needed by 2030 to keep global warming under the 2°C threshold targeted in the Paris Agreement on climate change (Hilmi et al., 2021). Moreover, management of degraded land reported to have positive impacts on climate change mitigation and adaptation, biodiversity conservation, food security, and sustainable livelihoods and therefore should be considered as the need of the hour (Cowie et al., 2007).

5.5.5 POLICIES ON ADOPTION AND IMPLEMENTATION OF TECHNOLOGICAL INTERVENTIONS

Effective policies need to be formulated for the adoption and implementation of appropriate technological interventions meant to achieve zero net loss soil degradation. In this context, LDN is recognized as a novel approach the world over to address the issues of land degradation. Strict provisions need to be laid down in policy documents to adopt the ways and means to implement the response hierarchy, viz., Avoid > Reduce > Reverse land degradation, while devising interventions for LDN (Cowie et al., 2018). Further, policy framework also needs to emphasize on participatory process involving local communities, particularly the land users in designing, implementing, and monitoring interventions to achieve LDN. In this context, land resources inventory (LRI)-based land use planning (LUP) at micro-scales up to cadastral level needs to be advocated in the degraded areas so that land constraints-based best management practices can be suggested to arrest various kinds of land resources degradation. Research endeavour should mandatorily be directed towards employing the latest technologies such as remote sensing and geographical information systems (RS&GIS) in monitoring and recording the spatio-temporal variations in the three UNCCD land-based global indicators, i.e., land cover, land productivity in terms of net primary productivity (NPP), and carbon stocks as soil organic carbon (SOC) (UNCCD, 2013). In this end, policies should clearly state that scientific research endeavours should strictly follow the "one-out, all-out" approach (Orr et al., 2017) for the research outputs of these three global indicators to achieve the visible differences in the hitherto degraded areas to currently reclaimed one through this approach. Furthermore, while formulating the research policies on LDN, the government and scientific community must lay emphasis on the inclusion of local communities' knowledge, wisdom, and experiences at the time of data validation and interpretation of monitoring data on the three land-based global indicators. Scientific policy documents oriented to achieve the targets of LDN within the timeframe need to be reviewed regularly adopting a continuous learning approach in the following order: anticipate, plan, track, interpret, review, adjust, and create the next plan (Cowie et al., 2018).

5.5.6 GOVERNMENT SUPPORT TO THE ABOVE POLICY ISSUES

Government policies must consider the land for the benefit of all, with emphasis on vulnerable and marginalized people. Agroforestry practices should sufficiently garner the government support in degraded areas to ensure improved productivity of land and increased resilience to climate change, which in turn maintain the sustainable delivery of ecosystem services from both natural and managed ecosystems. Government of the day should focus on synergy between socio-economic and environmental goals so that socially just and inclusive development may be achieved on a sustainable basis. Moreover, the national government should also set special local LDN targets based on national priorities that are achievable and can be monitored after a set duration but should conform to the international targets of the year 2030 set for land degradation neutrality (Akhtar-Schuster et al., 2017). Accordingly, every government is required to formulate, revise, and implement land use policies for nations.

5.6 CONCLUSION

In this chapter, we have discussed the concept of land degradation neutrality and ways to achieve it. LDN is a very broad term that indicates a holistic approach towards utilizing the land resources to extract optimum productivity as well as return to the land equal to or more than whatever is extracted. Presently, our land utilization system is running on a negative balance of soil nutrients and soil C and other soil resources, utilized for cropping, due to faulty management practices. The concept of LDN is still more of a theory in the present context, which demands accelerating the efforts of research and extension to the farmers' field. This needs constant assessment and monitoring of the land degradation processes and the real-time quantification of losses occurring from present land use. Understanding the real-time situations leading to land degradation, such as environmental and anthropogenic factors, and providing real-time solutions to address them is very much necessary in the present scenario. Geospatial techniques can play a meaningful role in supporting to achieve LDN target through the qualitative and quantitative assessment of land resources which are necessary to the ecosystem functions and services and enhance food security and production by the reclamation and restoration processes. For rapid assessment and monitoring, artificial intelligence and machine learning techniques have to be explored more to develop new models and algorithms. The LDN approach should be a global goal rather than a local one, and to achieve it, a global collaborative approach is the need of the hour. In 2015, UNCCD developed Land Degradation Neutrality programme in collaboration with over 120 countries and committed to setting LDN targets, following which 80 countries have already set their target. The LDN target follows the Sustainable Development Goal (SDG) target in 15.3 states to achieve a land degradation-neutral world by combating desertification and restoration of degraded land and soil by 2030. This seems to be a huge task for the researchers as well as the policy makers. However, a well-planned, integrated, and prompt action towards research as well as implementation may help realize the dream of achieving LDN globally.

REFERENCES

Abrol, I.P., & Bhumbla, D.R. (1979). Crop responses to differential gypsum applications in a highly sodic soil and the tolerance of several crops to exchangeable sodium under field conditions. *Soil Science*, 127(2), 79–85.

Abrol, I.P., Yadav, J.S.P., & Massoud, F.I. (1988). Salt-affected soils and their management. FAO Soils Bulletin No. 39. Food and Agriculture Organization of the United Nations, Rome, Italy.

Akhtar-Schuster, M., Stringer, L.C., Erlewein, A., Metternicht, G., Minelli, S., Safriel, U., & Sommer, S. (2017). Unpacking the concept of land degradation neutrality and addressing its operation through the Rio Conventions. *Journal of Environmental Management*, 195(Pt 1), 4–15.

Allen, C., Metternicht, G., Verburg, P., Akhtar-Schuster, M., da Cunha, M. I., & Santiváñez, M. S. (2020). Delivering an enabling environment and multiple benefits for land degradation neutrality: Stakeholder perceptions and progress. *Environmental Science & Policy*, 114, 109–118.

Aynekulu, E., Lohbeck, M., Nijbroek, R., Ordonez, J.C., Turner, K.G., Vågen, T., & Winowiecki, L. (2017). Review of methodologies for land degradation neutrality baselines: Sub-national case studies from Costa Rica and Namibia. International Center for Tropical Agriculture (CIAT) and World Agroforestry Center (ICRAF), Nairobi, Kenya. https://hdl.handle.net/10568/80563.

Bai, Z.G., Dent, D.L., Olsson, L., & Schaepman, M.E. (2008). Global assessment of land degradation and improvement. 1. Identification by remote sensing. Report 2008/01. ISRIC -World Soil Information, Wageningen.

Bakker, H. J. I. (ed.) (1990). *The World Food Crisis: Food Security in Comparative Perspective*. Canadian Scholars Press, Toronto, 530pp.

Bandyopadhyay, A.K. (1989). Effect of lime, superphosphate, powdered oystershell, rock phosphate and submergence on soil properties and crop growth in coastal saline acid sulphate soils of Sundarbans. In: *Proceedings of the International Symposium on Rice Production on Acid Soil of the Tropics*, 26–30 June, Kandy, Sri Lanka.

Basavaraja, P.K., Sharma, S.D., Dhananjaya, B.N.,& Badrinath, M.S. (2010). Acacia nilotica: A tree species for amelioration of sodic soils in Central dry zone of Karnataka, India. In: *Proceedings of the 19th World Congress of Soil Science, Soil Solutions for a Changing World*, 1–6 August, Brisbane, Australia, pp. 73–76.

Bellamy, P. H., Loveland, P. J., Bradley, R. I., Lark, R. M., & Kirk, G. J. (2005). Carbon losses from all soils across England and Wales 1978–2003. *Nature*, 437(7056), 245–248.

Bhat, J.A., Kundu, M.C., Hazra, G.C., Santra, G.H., & Mandal, B. (2010). Rehabilitating acid soils for increasing crop productivity through low-cost liming material. *Science of the Total Environment*, 408, 4346–4353.

Bhat, J.A., Mandal, B., & Hazra, G.C. (2007). Basic slag as a liming material to ameliorate soil acidity in Alfisols of sub-tropical India. *American-Eurasian Journal of Agricultural & Environmental Sciences*, 2, 321–327.

Bond-Lamberty, B., Bailey, V. L., Chen, M., Gough, C. M., & Vargas, R. (2018). Globally rising soil heterotrophic respiration over recent decades. *Nature*, 560(7716), 80–83.

Brooks, M. L., D'antonio, C. M., Richardson, D. M., Grace, J. B., Keeley, J. E., DiTomaso, J. M., Hobbs, R. J., Pellant, M., & Pyke, D. (2004). Effects of invasive alien plants on fire regimes. *BioScience*, 54(7), 677–688.

Cha, S., Kim, C. B., Kim, J., Lee, A. L., Park, K. H., Koo, N., & Kim, Y. S. (2020). Land-use changes and practical application of the land degradation neutrality (LDN) indicators: A case study in the subalpine forest ecosystems, Republic of Korea. *Forest Science and Technology*, 16(1), 8–17.

Chappell, A., Webb, N. P., Leys, J. F., Waters, C. M., Orgill, S., & Eyres, M. J. (2019). Minimising soil organic carbon erosion by wind is critical for land degradation neutrality. *Environmental Science & Policy*, 93, 43–52.

Conacher, A. (2009). Land degradation: A global perspective. *New Zealand Geographer*, 65(2), 91–94.

Costanza, R., d'Arge, R., De Groot, R., Farber, S., Grasso, M., Hannon, B., Limburg, K., Naeem, S., O'Neill, R. V., Paruelo, J., Raskin, R. G., Sutton, P. & Van Den Belt, M. (1997). The value of the world's ecosystem services and natural capital. *Nature*, 387(6630), 253–260.

Costanza, R., Pérez-Maqueo, O., Martinez, M. L., Sutton, P., Anderson, S. J., & Mulder, K. (2008). The value of coastal wetlands for hurricane protection. *Ambio*, 37, 241–248.

Cowie, A. L., Orr, B. J., Sanchez, V. M. C., Chasek, P., Crossman, N. D., Erlewein, A., Louwagie, G., Maron, M., Metternicht, G. I., Minelli, S., Tengberg, A. E., Walter, S., & Welton, S. (2018). Land in balance: The scientific conceptual framework for land degradation neutrality. *Environmental Science & Policy*, 79, 25–35. doi: 10.1016/j.envsci.2017.10.011

Cowie, A. L., Schneider, U. A., & Montanarella, L. (2007). Potential synergies between existing multilateral environmental agreements in the implementation of land use, land-use change and forestry activities. *Environmental Science & Policy*, 10(4), 335–352.

Cowie, A. L., Waters, C. M., Garland, F., Orgill, S. E., Baumber, A., Cross, R., O'Connell, D., & Metternicht, G. (2019). Assessing resilience to underpin implementation of land degradation neutrality: A case study in the rangelands of western New South Wales, Australia. *Environmental Science & Policy*, 100, 37–46.

Crossland, M., Winowiecki, L. A., Pagella, T., Hadgu, K., & Sinclair, F. (2018). Implications of variation in local perception of degradation and restoration processes for implementing land degradation neutrality. *Environmental Development*, 28, 42–54.

Crowther, T. W., Thomas, S. M., Maynard, D. S., Baldrian, P., Covey, K., Frey, S. D., van Diepen, L. T. A., & Bradford, M. A. (2015). Biotic interactions mediate soil microbial feedbacks to climate change. *Proceedings of the National Academy of Sciences*, 112(22), 7033–7038.

CSSRI (2017). Annual report 2016–17. Central Soil Salinity Research Institute, Karnal, India.

CSSRI (2018). Area reclaimed by SSD technology. https://www.cssri.org/index.php?option=com_content&view=article&id=49&Itemid=49. Accessed 7 July 2018.

D'Odorico, P., Bhattachan, A., Davis, K. F., Ravi, S., & Runyan, C. W. (2013). Global desertification: Drivers and feedbacks. *Advances in Water Resources*, 51, 326–344.

Dagar, J.C., Tomar, O.S., & Kumar, Y. (2006). Cultivation of medicinal isabgol (*Plantago ovata*) in different alkali soils in semi-arid regions of northern India. *Land Degradation and Development*, 17, 275–283.

Dagar, J.C., Tomar, O.S., Kumar, Y., & Yadav, R.K. (2004). Growing three aromatic grasses in different alkali soils in semi-arid regions of northern India. *Land Degradation & Development*, 15, 143–151.

Dagar, J.C., Tomar, O.S., Minhas, P.S., Singh, G., & Jeet, R. (2008). Dryland biosaline agriculture– Hisar experience. Technical Bulletin No. 6/2008. Central Soil Salinity Research Institute, Karnal, 28p.

Datta, K.K., de Long, C., & Singh, O.P. (2000). Reclaiming salt affected land through drainage in Haryana, India: A financial analysis. *Agricultural Water Management*, 46, 55–71.

Dhyani, S., Santhanam, H., Dasgupta, R., Bhaskar, D., Murthy, I. K., & Singh, K. (2022). Exploring synergies between India's climate change and land degradation targets: Lessons from the Glasgow Climate COP. *Land Degradation & Development*, 34, 196–206.

Dregne, H.E. (1992). *Degradation and Restoration of Arid Lands*. Texas Technical University, Lubbock.

Ericksson, J., Hakansson, I., & Danfors, B. (1974). The effect of soil compaction on soil structure and crop yields. Bulletin 354. Swedish Institute of Agricultural Engineering, Uppsala.

Fageria, N.K., & Baligar, V.C. (2008). Ameliorating soil acidity of tropical Oxisols by liming for sustainable crop production. *Advances in Agronomy*, 99, 345–399.

Farjalla, N., Haddad, E.A., Camargo, M., Lopes, R., & Vieira, F. (2014). Climate change in Lebanon: Higher-order regional impacts from agriculture. *REGION*, 1, 9–24.

Field, J.P., Belnap, J., Breshears, D.D., Neff, J.C., Okin, G.S., Whicker, J.J., Painter, T.H., Ravi, S., Reheis, M.C., & Reynolds, R.L. (2010). The ecology of dust. *Frontiers in Ecology and the Environment*, 8(8), 423–430.

Foley, J.A., Asner, G.P., Costa, M.H., Coe, M.T., DeFries, R., Gibbs, H.K., Howard, E.A., Olson, S., Patz, J., Ramankutty, N., & Snyder, P. (2007). Amazonia revealed: Forest degradation and loss of ecosystem goods and services in the Amazon Basin. *Frontiers in Ecology and the Environment*, 5(1), 25–32.

Foley, J. A., DeFries, R., Asner, G. P., Barford, C., Bonan, G., Carpenter, S. R., …Snyder, P. K. (2005). Global consequences of land use. *Science*, 309(5734), 570–574.

Food and Agriculture Organization (2009). Global agriculture towards 2050. How to feed the world 2050. https://www.fao.org/fileadmin/templates/wsfs/docs/Issues_papers/HLEF2050_Global_Agriculture.pdf

Food and Agriculture Organization (2014). Land degradation assessment in dryland. https://www.fao.org/

Food and Agriculture Organization (2018). Land and water. https://www.fao.org/land-water/land/httpwwwfaoorgsoils-portalen/en/

German Federal Environment Agency (2011). Common statement: Protecting soils for our common future, a call for action. Berlin. https://www.umweltbundesamt.de/boden-undaltlasten/boden/downloads/statement_protecting_soils_for_our_common_future_september_2011.pdf.

Ghosh, B.N., Sharma, N.K., & Dadhwal, K.S. (2011). Integrated nutrient management and intercropping/cropping system impact on yield, water productivity and net return in valley soils of north-west Himalayas. *Indian Journal of Soil Conservation*, 39, 236–242.

Gibbs, H.K., & Salmon, J.M. (2015). Mapping the world's degraded lands. *Applied Geography*, 57, 12–21.

Gilbey, B., Davies, J., Metternicht, G., & Magero, C. (2019). Taking Land Degradation Neutrality from concept to practice: Early reflections on LDN target setting and planning. *Environmental Science & Policy*, 100, 230–237. https://doi.org/10.1016/j.envsci.2019.04.007

Gisladottir, G., & Stocking, M. (2005). Land degradation control and its global environmental benefits. *Land Degradation & Development*, 16(2), 99–112.

Gnacadja, L. (2012). Moving to zero-net rate of land degradation. Statement by Executive Secretary. UN Convention to Combat Desertification, Rio de Janeiro.

Gnacadja, L., & Wiese, L. (2016). Land degradation neutrality: Will Africa achieve it? Institutional solutions to land degradation and restoration in Africa. In: R. Lal, D. Kraybill, D. Hansen, B. Singh, T. Mosogoya, & L. Eik (eds) *Climate Change and Multi-Dimensional Sustainability in African Agriculture: Climate Change and Sustainability in Agriculture*, pp. 61–95.

Gobin, A., Jones, R., Kirkby, M., Campling, P., Govers, G., Kosmas, C., & Gentile, A. R. (2004). Indicators for pan-European assessment and monitoring of soil erosion by water. *Environmental Science & Policy*, 7(1), 25–38.

Guo, J. H., Liu, X. J., Zhang, Y., Shen, J. L., Han, W. X., Zhang, W. F., Christie, P., Goulding, K. W. T., Vitousek, P. M., & Zhang, F. S. (2010). Significant acidification in major Chinese croplands. *Science*, 327(5968), 1008–1010.

Hilmi, N., Chami, R., Sutherland, M. D., Hall-Spencer, J. M., Lebleu, L., Benitez, M. B., & Levin, L. A. (2021). The role of blue carbon in climate change mitigation and carbon stock conservation. *Frontiers in Climate*, 3, 710546. doi: 10.3389/fclim.2021.710546.

Horney, R.D., Taylor, B., Munk, D.S., Roberts, B.A., Lesch, S.M., & Plant, R.E. (2005). Development of practical site-specific management methods for reclaiming salt-affected soil. *Computers and Electronics in Agriculture*, 46, 379–397.

Hota, S., Mishra, V., Mourya, K. K., Saikia, U. S., & Ray, S. K. (2022a). Fertility capability classification (FCC) of soils of a lower Brahmaputra valley area of Assam, India. *Environment Conservation Journal*, 23(3), 192–201. doi:10.36953/ECJ.10462244

Hota, S., Mishra, V., Mourya, K.K., Giri, K., Kumar, D., Jha, P.K., Saikia, U.S., Prasad, P.V.V., & Ray, S.K. (2022b). Land use, landform, and soil management as determinants of soil physicochemical properties and microbial abundance of lower Brahmaputra valley, India. *Sustainability*, 14, 2241. doi:10.3390/su140422

Hota, S., Sharma, G. K., Subrahmanyam, G., Kumar, A., Shabnam, A. A., Baruah, P., Kaur, T., & Yadav, A. N. (2021). Fungal communities for bioremediation of contaminated soil for sustainable environments. In: A. N. Yadav (ed.) *Recent Trends in Mycological Research. Fungal Biology*, pp. 27–42. Springer, Cham. doi:10.1007/978-3-030-68260-6_2

Hussain, S., Siddique, T., Saleem, M., Arshad, M., & Khalid, A. (2009). Impact of pesticides on soil microbial diversity, enzymes, and biochemical reactions. *Advances in Agronomy*, 102, 159–200.

Illius, A. W., & O'Connor, T. G. (1999). On the relevance of nonequilibrium concepts to arid and semiarid grazing systems. *Ecological Applications*, 9(3), 798–813.

ISRIC. (2016). Data and software policy. https://www.isric.org/sites/default/files/ISRIC_Data_Policy_2016jun21.pdf. Accessed 15 May 2019.

Katerji, N., van Hoorn, J.W., Hamdy, A., & Mastrorilli, M. (2000). Salt tolerance classification of crops according to soil salinity and to water stress day index. *Agricultural Water Management*, 43, 99–109.

Kaur, B., Gupta, S.R., & Singh, G. (2000). Soil carbon, microbial activity and nitrogen availability in agroforestry systems on moderately alkaline soils in Northern India. *Applied Soil Ecology*, 15, 283–294.

Kaushik, A., Nisha, R., Jagjeeta, K., & Kaushik, C.P. (2005). Impact of long and short-term irrigation of a sodic soil with distillery effluent in combination with bio-amendments. Bio-Resource Technology, 96, 1860–1866.

Kirkby, M. J., Irvine, B. J., Jones, R. J., Govers, G., & Pesera Team. (2008). The PESERA coarse scale erosion model for Europe. I.– Model rationale and implementation. *European Journal of Soil Science*, 59(6), 1293–1306.

Kosmas, C., Tsara, M., Moustakas, N., & Karavitis, C. (2003). Identification of indicators for desertification. *Annals of Arid Zone*, 42, 393–416.

Kosmas, C., Tsara, M., Moustakas, N., Kosma, D., & Yassoglou, N. (2006). Environmentally sensitive areas and indicators of desertification. In: W. G. Kepner, J. L. Rubio, D. A. Mouat & F. Pedrazzini (eds.) *Desertification in the Mediterranean Region. A Security Issue*. NATO Security through Science Series. Springer, Dordrecht, pp. 525–547.

Koyama, M.L., Levesley, A., Koebner, R.M.A., Flowers, T.J., & Yeo, A.R. (2001). Quantitative trait loci for component physiological traits determining salt tolerance in rice. *Plant Physiology*, 125, 406–422.

Kumar, A., Singh, D., & Mahapatra, S. K. (2022). Energy and carbon budgeting of the pearl millet-wheat cropping system for environmentally sustainable agricultural land use planning in the rainfed semi-arid agro-ecosystem of Aravalli foothills. *Energy*, 246, 123389. doi:10.1016/j.energy.2022.123389

Kust, G., Andreeva, O., & Cowie, A. (2017). Land degradation neutrality: Concept development, practical applications and assessment. *Journal of Environmental Management*, 195, 16–24.

Lal, R. (2012). Climate change and soil degradation mitigation by sustainable management of soils and other natural resources. *Agricultural Research*, 1, 199–212.

Lal, R., Safriel, U., & Boer, B. (2012, May). Zero net land degradation: A new sustainable development goal for Rio+ 20. United Nations Convention to Combat Desertification (UNCCD), Rio de Janeiro.

Liniger, H., Harari, N., van Lynden, G., Fleiner, R., de Leeuw, J., Bai, Z., & Critchley, W. (2019). Achieving land degradation neutrality: The role of SLM knowledge in evidence-based decision-making. *Environmental Science & Policy*, 94, 123–134.

Liu, R., & Lal, R. (2012). Nano-enhanced materials for reclamation of mine lands and other degraded soils: A review. *Journal of Nanotechnology*. doi:10.1155/2012/461468.

López-Garrido, R., Madejón, E., León-Camacho, M., Girón, I., Moreno, F., & Murillo, J. M. (2014). Reduced tillage as an alternative to no-tillage under Mediterranean conditions: A case study. *Soil and Tillage Research*, 140, 40–47.

Mandal, D., Sharda, V.N., & Tripathi, K.P. (2010). Relative efficacy of two biophysical approaches to assess soil loss tolerance for Doon Valley soils of India. *Journal of Soil and Water Conservation* 65, 42–49.

Mandal, D., Srivastava, P., Giri, N., Kaushal, R., Cerda, A., & Alam, N. M. (2017). Reversing land degradation through grasses: a systematic meta-analysis in the Indian tropics. *Solid Earth*, 8(1), 217–235. https://doi.org/10.5194/se-8-217-2017.

Manjunatha, M.V., Oosterbaan, R.J., Gupta, S.K., Rajkumar, H., & Jansen, H. (2004). Performance of subsurface drains for reclaiming waterlogged saline lands under rolling topography in Tungabadra irrigation project in India. *Agricultural Water Management*, 69, 69–82.

Mayer, M., Prescott, C.E., Abaker, W.E., Augusto, L., Cécillon, L., Ferreira, G.W., James, J., Jandl, R., Katzensteiner, K., Laclau, J.-P., Laganiére, J., Nouvellon, Y., Paré, D., Stanturf, J.A., Vanguelova, E.I., & Vesterdal, L. (2020). Tamm Review: Influence of forest management activities on soil organic carbon stocks: A knowledge synthesis. *Forest Ecology Management*, 466, 118127.

Mentaschi, L., Vousdoukas, M. I., Pekel, J. F., Voukouvalas, E., & Feyen, L. (2018). Global long-term observations of coastal erosion and accretion. *Scientific Reports*, 8(1), 12876.

Minhas, P.S. (1993). Modelling crop response to water and salinity stresses. In: N. K. Tyagi, S. K. Kamra, P. S. Minhas & N. T. Singh (eds.) *Sustainable Irrigation in Saline Environment*. CSSRI, Karnal, India, pp. 96–109.

Minhas, P.S. (1996). Saline water management for irrigation in India. *Agricultural Water Management*, 30, 1–24.

Minhas, P.S., & Gupta, R.K. (1992). *Quality of Irrigation Water Assessment and Management*. ICAR Pub., New Delhi, India, p. 123.

Minhas, P.S., Sharma, D.R., & Chauhan, C.P.S. (2004). Management of saline and alkali waters for irrigation. In: *Advances in Sodic Land Reclamation, International conference on "Sustainable Management of Sodic Lands"*, 9–14 February, Lucknow, India, pp. 121–162.

Minhas, P.S., Singh, Y.P., Tomar, O.S., Gupta, R.K., & Gupta, R. K. (1997). Effect of saline irrigation and its schedules on survival, growth, biomass production and water use by *Acacia nilotica* and *Dalbergia sissoo* in a highly calcareous soil. *Journal of Arid Environments*, 36, 181–192.

Mishra, A., Sharma, S.D., & Khan, G.H. (2003). Improvement in physical and chemical properties of sodic soil by 3, 6, and 9 years old plantation of *Eucalyptus tereticornis*: Bio-rejuvenation of sodic soil. *Forest Ecology and Management*, 184, 115–124.

Mishra, A., Sharma, S.D., & Pandey, R. (2004). Amelioration of degraded sodic soil by afforestation. *Arid Land Research and Management*, 18, 13–23.

Montanarella, L., Pennock, D. J., McKenzie, N., Badraoui, M., Chude, V., Baptista, I., …Vargas, R. (2016). World's soils are under threat. *Soil*, 2(1), 79–82.

Montanarella, L., Scholes, R., Brainich, A. (eds.) (2018). The IPBES assessment report on land degradation and restoration. Secretariat of the Intergovernmental Science Policy Platform on Biodiversity and Ecosystem Services, Bonn, Germany.

Mourya, K. K., Jena, R. K., Ray, P., Ramachandran, S., Sharma, G. K., Hota, S., & Ray, S. K. (2021). Profile distribution of soil organic carbon fractions under different landforms in the Meghalaya plateau of India. *Environment Conservation Journal*, 22(3), 9–16.

Nagaraju, M. S. S., Kumar, N., Srivastava, R., & Das, S. N. (2014). Cadastral-level soil mapping in basaltic terrain using Cartosat-1-derived products. *International Journal of Remote Sensing*, 35(10), 3764–3781.

Neely, C., Bunning, S., & Wilkes, A. (2009). *Review of Evidence on Drylands Pastoral Systems and Climate Change*. FAO, Rome.

Orr, B.J., Cowie, A. L., Castillo Sanchez, V.M., Chasek, P., Crossman, N. D., Erlewein, A., Louwagie, G., Maron, M., Metternicht, G. I., Minelli, S., Tengberg, A.E., Walter, S., & Welton, S. (2017). Scientific conceptual framework for land degradation neutrality. A report of the science-policy interface. United Nations Convention to Combat Desertification (UNCCD), Bonn, Germany.

Pathak, P., Mishra, P.K., Rao, K.V., Wani, S.P., & Sudi, R. (2009). Best opt-options on soil and water conservation. In: S. P. Wani, B. Venkateshwarlu, K. L. Sahrawat, K. V. Rao & Y. S. Ramakrishna (eds.) *Best Bet Options for Integrated Watershed Management, Proceedings of the Comprehensive Assessment of Watershed Programs in India*, 23–27 July, Andhra Pradesh, India, pp. 75–94.

Poesen, J. W., & Hooke, J. M. (1997). Erosion, flooding and channel management in Mediterranean environments of southern Europe. *Progress in Physical Geography*, 21(2), 157–199.

Population Reference Bureau (2016). World population data sheet. https://www.prb.org/Publications/Datasheets/2016/2016-world-population-data-sheet.aspx

Qadir, M., & Oster, J.D. (2002). Vegetative bioremediation of calcareous sodic soils: History, mechanism, and evaluation. *Irrigation Science*, 21, 91–101.

Rao, J.V., & Khan, I.A. (2003). Research gaps in intercropping systems under rainfed conditions in India, an on farm survey. CRIDA, Hyderabad, India.

Ravi, S., Breshears, D. D., Huxman, T. E., & D'Odorico, P. (2010). Land degradation in drylands: Interactions among hydrologic-aeolian erosion and vegetation dynamics. *Geomorphology*, 116(3–4), 236–245.

Reddy, G. O., Kumar, N., & Singh, S. K. (2018). Remote sensing and GIS in mapping and monitoring of land degradation. In: G. Reddy & S. Singh (eds.) *Geospatial Technologies in Land Resources Mapping, Monitoring and Management*. Springer, Cham, pp. 401–424.

Reddy, G. P. O., Maji, A. K., Nagaraju, M. S. S., Thayalan, S., & Ramamurthy, V. (2008). *Ecological Evaluation of Land Resources and Land Use Systems for Sustainable Development at Watershed Level in Different Agro-Ecological Zones of Vidarbha Region, Maharashtra Using Remote Sensing and GIS Techniques*. NBSS Publication, Nagpur, India.

Reed, S. C., Coe, K. K., Sparks, J. P., Housman, D. C., Zelikova, T. J., & Belnap, J. (2012). Changes to dryland rainfall result in rapid moss mortality and altered soil fertility. *Nature Climate Change*, 2(10), 752–755.

Safriel, U. (2017). Land degradation neutrality (LDN) in drylands and beyond– Where has it come from and where does it go. *Silva Fennica*, 51(1B), article id 1650. https://doi.org/10.14214/sf.1650.

Salvati, L., & Carlucci, M. (2014). Zero net land degradation in Italy: The role of socioeconomic and agroforest factors. *Journal of Environmental Management*, 145, 299–306.

Sasaki, T., Okayasu, T., Jamsran, U., & Takeuchi, K. (2008). Threshold changes in vegetation along a grazing gradient in Mongolian rangelands. *Journal of Ecology*, 96(1), 145–154.

Schofield, R. V., & Kirkby, M. J. (2003). Application of salinization indicators and initial development of potential global soil salinization scenario under climatic change. *Global Biogeochemical Cycles*, 17(3), 1078. doi:10.1029/2002GB001935, pages 1–13.

Schulze, K., Malek, Ž., & Verburg, P. H. (2021). How will land degradation neutrality change future land system patterns? A scenario simulation study. *Environmental Science & Policy*, 124, 254–266. doi: 10.1016/j.envsci.2021.06.024

Shannon, M.C., & Grieve, C.M. (2000). Options for using low-quality water for vegetable crops. *HortScience*, 35, 1058–1062.

Sharda, V.N., Sharma, N.K., Mohan, S.C., & Khybry, M.L. (1999). Green manuring for conservation and production in western Himalayas: 2. Effect on moisture conservation, weed control and crop yields. *Indian Journal of Soil Conservation*, 27, 31–35.

Sharma, B.R., & Minhas, P.S. (2005). Strategies for managing saline/alkali waters for sustainable agricultural production in South Asia. *Agricultural Water Management*, 78, 136–151.

Sharma, D.P., Singh, K.N., Rao, K.V.G.K., Kumbhare, P.S., & Oosterban, R.J. (1994). Conjunctive use of saline and non-saline irrigation waters in semi-arid regions. *Irrigation Science*, 15, 25–33.

Sharma, N.K., Ghosh, B.N., Khola, O.P.S., & Dubey, R.K. (2013). Residue and tillage management for soil moisture conservation in post maize harvesting period under rainfed conditions of north-west Himalayas. *Indian Journal of Soil Conservation*, 42, 120–125.

Sharma, P.D., & Sarkar, A.K. (2005). Managing acid soils for enchancing productivity. Technical Bulletin. Indian Council of Agricultural Research, New Delhi, India, p. 23.

Singh, A., & Kaur, J. (2012). Impact of conservation tillage on soil properties in rice wheat cropping system. *Agricultural Science Research Journal*, 2, 30–41.

Singh, G. (1996). The role of Prosopis in reclaiming high-pH soils and in meeting firewood and forage needs of small farmers. In: P. Felker & J. Moss (eds.), *Prosopis: Semiarid Fuelwood and Forage Tree Building Consensus for the Disenfranchised*, pp. 4.21–4.34. Center for Semi-Arid Forest Resources, Kingsville.

Singh, G., Ram, B., Narain, P., Bhushan, L.S., & Abrol, I.P. (1992). Soil erosion rates in India. *Indian Journal of Soil Conservation*, 47, 97–99.

Singh, K.N., & Sharma, D. P. (2004). Crops and sequential cropping for sodic soils. *Indian Farming*, 53, 26–30.

Singh, R.K., Redoña, E., & Refuerzo, L. (2010). Varietal improvement for abiotic stress tolerance in crop plants: Special reference to salinity in rice. In: A. Pareek, S. Sopory & H. Bohnert (eds) *Abiotic Stress Adaptation in Plants: Physiological, Molecular and Genomic Foundation*. Springer Science+Business Media B.V., pp. 387–415.

Soni, J. K., Choudhary, V. K., Singh, P. K., & Hota, S. (2020). Weed management in conservation agriculture, its issues and adoption: A review. *Journal of Crop and Weed*, 16(1), 9–19.

Space Application Centre (2016). Desertification and land degradation atlas of India. https://www.sac.gov.in/SACSITE/Desertification_Atlas _2016_SAC_ ISRO.pdf

Srinivasarao, C.H., Ravindra Chary, G. Venkateswarlu, B. Vittal, K.P.R., Prasad, J.V.N.S., Singh, S.R.S.K., Gajanan, G.N., Sharma, R.A., Deshpande, A.N., Patel, J.J., & Balaguravaiah, G. (2009). *Carbon Sequestration Strategies in Rainfed Production Systems of India*. Central Research Institute for Dryland Agriculture, Hyderabad, India, p. 102.

Srinivasarao, C.H., Venkateswarlu, B., & Lal, R. (2014). Long-term manuring and fertilizer effects on depletion of soil organic stocks under pearl millet-cluster bean-castor rotation in western India. *Land Degradation & Development*, 25, 173–183.

Stavi, I., & Lal, R. (2015). Achieving zero net land degradation: Challenges and opportunities. *Journal of Arid Environments*, 112, 44–51.

Surya, J. N., Walia, C. S., Singh, H., Yadav, R. P., & Singh, S. K. (2020). Soil suitability evaluation using remotely sensed data and GIS: A case study from Kumaon Himalayas. *Journal of the Indian Society of Remote Sensing*, 48(10), 1355–1371.

Tomar, O.S., & Minhas, P.S. (2004). Performance of medicinal plant species under saline irrigation. *Indian Journal of Agronomy*, 49, 209–211.

Tomar, O.S., Minhas, P.S., Sharma, V.K., Singh, Y.P., & Gupta, R. K. (2002). Performance of 32 tree species and soil conditions in a plantation established with saline irrigation. *Forest Ecology and Management*, 177(1–3), 333–346.

Tomar, O.S., Minhas, P.S., Sharma, V.K., Singh, Y.P., & Gupta, R. K. (2003). Response of 9 grasses to saline irrigation and its schedules in a semi-arid climate of north-west India. *Journal of Arid Environments*, 55(3), 533–544.

United Nations Convention to Combat Desertification. (1995). Down to earth: A simplified guide to the Convention to Combat Desertification, why it is necessary and what is important and different about it. Secretariat for the United Nations Convention to Combat Desertification, Bonn, Germany.

United Nations Convention to Combat Desertification. (2011a). Towards a land degradation neutral world. The submission of the UNCCD Secretariat to the preparatory process for the Rio +20 conference.

United Nations Convention to Combat Desertification. (2011b). Submission by the United Nations Convention to Combat Desertification on Decision 6/CP.17.

United Nations Convention to Combat Desertification. (2013). Report of the Conference of the Parties on its eleventh session, held in Windhoek from 16 to 27 September 2013. Part two: Action taken by the Conference of the Parties at its eleventh session. ICCD/COP (11)/23/Add.1. United Nations Convention to Combat Desertification (UNCCD), Bonn.

United Nations Convention to Combat Desertification. (2015). Integration of the sustainable development goals and targets into the implementation of the United Nations convention to combat desertification and the intergovernmental working group report on land degradation neutrality. Decision 3/COP.12. Report of the Conference of the Parties on its twelfth session. ICCD/COP(12)/20/Add.1.unccd.int/sites/default/files/ sessions/documents/ICCD_COP12_20_Add.1/20add1eng.pdf

UN Population Division (2015). *World Urbanization Prospects: The 2014 Revision*. Department of Economic and Social Affairs, New York. https://esa.un.org/unpd/wup/ publications/files/wup

van der Esch, S., Brink, B. T., Stehfest, E., Bakkenes, M., Sewell, A., Bouwman, A., Meijer, J., Westhoek, H., & van den Berg, M. (2017). Exploring future changes in land use and land condition and the impacts on food, water, climate change and biodiversity: Scenarios for the UNCCD Global Land Outlook 2076. Netherlands Environmental Assessment Agency (PBL), The Hague, Netherlands. https://www.pbl.nl/sites/default/files/cms/publicaties/pbl-2017-exploring-future-changes-in-land-use-and-land-condition-2076b.pdf.

van Dijk, M., Morley, T., Rau, M. L., & Saghai, Y. (2021). A meta-analysis of projected global food demand and population at risk of hunger for the period 2010-2050. *Nature Food*, 2(7), 494–501.

Walker, D.J., & Bernal, M.P. (2008). The effects of olive mill waste compost and poultry manure on the availability and plant uptake of nutrients in a highly saline soil. Bioresource Technology, 99(2), 396–403.

Walsh, J. R., Carpenter, S. R., & Vander Zanden, M. J. (2016). Invasive species triggers a massive loss of ecosystem services through a trophic cascade. *Proceedings of the National Academy of Sciences*, 113(15), 4081–4085.

World Commission on Environment and Development. (1987). *Our Common Future*. Oxford University Press, Oxford.

World Wildlife Fund. (2016). Soil erosion and degradation. https://www.worldwildlife.org/threats/soil-erosion-and-degradation

WWF Soil Erosion and Degradation (2018). Global Symposium on Soil Organic Carbon. Retrieved from http://www.fao.org/about/meetings/soil-organic-carbon-symposium/en/

Yadav, R.K., Purakayastha, T.J., Ahmed, N., Das, R., Chakrabarty, B., Biswas, S., Sharma, V.K., Singh, P., Talukdar, D., Mourya, K.K., Walia, S.S., Singh, R., Shukla, V. K., Yadava, M. S., Ravisankar, N., & Yadav, B. D. (2021). Long-term effect of fertilization and manuring on soil aggregate carbon mineralization. *The Indian Journal of Agricultural Sciences*, 91(2), 254–257.

Yaduvanshi, N.P.S., & Sharma, D.R. (2007). Use of wheat residue and manures to enhance nutrient availability and rice-wheat yields in sodic soil under sodic water irrigation. *Journal of the Indian Society of Soil Science*, 55, 330–334.

Yaduvanshi, N.P.S., & Swarup, A. (2005). Effect of continuous use of sodic irrigation water with and without gypsum, farmyard manure, pressmud and fertilizer on soil properties and yields of rice and wheat in a long term experiment. *Nutrient Cycling in Agroecosystems*, 73, 111–118.

Ye, L., & Van Ranst, E. (2009). Production scenarios and the effect of soil degradation on long-term food security in China. *Global Environmental Change*, 19(4), 464–481.

6 Assessment and Restoration of Organic Carbon
Making a Solid Ground for Regenerative Agriculture in India

Jayesh Singh and Ashu Singh

6.1 INTRODUCTION

Degradation of Indian soil health and the environment due to oxidation of soil organic carbon has become a pressing reality. Carbon dioxide (CO_2) is one of the major or key contributors to climate change as it is the only carbon among all the major sources of pollutant gases that share the highest proportion of greenhouse gas emission. In order to feed the increasing population and to achieve food security, increased, intensified agricultural practices are now being followed augmenting the oxidation of sequestered soil organic carbon in the form of CO_2 emission to the atmosphere contributing to climate change and vanishing soil organic carbon (SOC) from the agricultural soil pervasively affecting the fertility and the productivity. In the oxidation process that occurred along a spectrum through which SOC is shifted to "available" (labile) state from a "protected" (recalcitrant) state, i.e., to the cells of microbes where it might be mineralized implying that the primary mechanism of loss of carbon from the soil is via microbial decomposition but in the formation of aggregates and organic minerals, microbes play a critical role (Shovik et al., 2015; Lal, 2003). Hence, it can be understood that it's the carbon use efficiency of microbes which maintains the equilibrium between SC stabilization and losses via respiratory emission or in the form of any soluble microbial product. In an agricultural system, a large portion of biomass is produced, it may be a portion not used as food, fuel, or fodder is cycled via decomposer. Thus, the amount of CO_2 utilized by plants through photosynthesis for their biomass production enters in soil residue of the plant which is nearly the same as the amount of emitted CO_2 during the decomposition process. In order to reduce the losses, checking oxidation is the only key that can be beneficial even when the soil cannot sequester carbon further as if it reached its equilibrium. This will definitely not be going to further increase the current stock of carbon in the soil but will surely stop further losses from the agricultural soil and will be proved a helping hand in mitigating the CO_2 concentration in the atmosphere (Dattaand Meena, 2021). The physical and chemical environment of soil (how much the soil is under oxygen starvation, pore space of very soil, moisture holding capacity, pH, temperature) and nature of organic matter (i.e., that at what extent organic matter is susceptible or resistant to microbial decomposition) contribute to consider the rate of SOC decomposition but simultaneously all the above-mentioned properties also influence agricultural management practices (Goh, 2004). In conclusion, it is suggested that the decomposition of soil organic carbon (SOC) can be effectively controlled through the strategic management of soil properties mentioned earlier. The implementation of prudent agricultural practices, varying in combination and intensity based on specific locations, is crucial for achieving this goal (Lal, 2004a).

However, the sequestration process of carbon into the soil is significantly affected by management factors, soil factors, and environmental factors. Management factors include the changes in land use pattern, fallowing pattern and period, crop rotation, types of plant cover, crop residue

DOI: 10.1201/9781003309581-8

retention, irrigation, biomass burning, wetland drainage, blind use of fertilizer, conventional tillage, conservation farming, and precision farming (Memon et al., 2018). Besides, soil factor relates to the texture and structure of the soil, moisture content, porosity, soil erosion, reclamation of problematic soil, aeration, and soil biota, whereas, environmental factor consists of climate, region, and rainfall. Therefore, adopting better agricultural techniques (BATs) has a huge potential to reduce carbon dioxide emissions and the effects of climate change while also increasing the sequestration of carbon (Datta and Meena, 2021; Lal, 2004b).

6.2 METHODOLOGY

An exhaustive review of the literature was done with the help of the academic search engine scholar. google.com. Hardcopy of research papers, review papers, book chapters, and annual project reports were also used to obtain the maximum possible required database over the matter Regenerative approaches and practices, soil organic carbon stock, carbon emission, factors effecting sequestration, checking oxidation, stabilization, impact of soil organic carbon onto soil health and agricultural production, productivity, and climate change mitigation. The below sections of this chapterdiscussed all these aspects in detail.

6.2.1 CURRENT STATUS OF ORGANIC CARBON IN INDIAN SOIL

The total carbon stock of India including SIC and SOC has been calculated at 35.55 ± 1.87 Pg out of which the maximum of the carbon stock is present in the northern part of India in which the contribution of organic carbon is mainly to the eastern portion, whereas the inorganic carbon contributes to western portion. In recent assessments, the content of SOC in Indian soils has been found very low which is because of India having approx. 60% of its area under tropical climate which restricts the agglomeration of SOC. Further evaluation of SOC based on long-term fertilizer experiments and new site data concluded that the two most fertile and major food-growing plains of India i.e., black soil region and Indo-Gangetic plains are depicting an increase in the OC content.

The content of carbon in various soil orders and types was estimated by Bhattacharya et al. (2000b) which concludes that vertisols, Inceptisols, and Alfisols have a major contribution of SOC stocks in the uppermost 30 cm depth of very soil and within similar depth the soil of order Aridisols depicts low SOC stock but SIC stock was very high approx. 33%. Maximum organic carbon storage is found in the red soils of order Alfisols and Ultisols, alluvial soils of order Entisols and Inceptisols and black soil of Vertisol order. Carbon concentration and the areal extent of the soil are the two factors that greatly control the carbon stock in soil, this is the rationale behind soils having lower carbon stock while having high carbon content in soil, both areal extent and carbon concentration should be high to have high carbon stock. That's why the brown soils of forest, which are mainly depicted by Mollisols, even having high carbon content, show a lower stock of carbon in it (Table 6.1).

6.2.1.1 Carbon Stock under Different Bioclimates of India

The storage value of carbon for various bioclimatic systemsis shown in Figure 6.1. The bioclimatic system receiving low annual rainfall, <500 mm, is considered as *arid bioclimatic system,* this system covers approx.15.8% of the TGA with a contribution of about 10% of the total stock of the SOC. The soils of these areas have a lesser amount of organic carbon as the area of this bioclimatic system doesn't suitdense vegetation. On the basis of the temperature of the atmosphere, the arid bioclimatic system is further categorized into cold arid and hot arid; 29% of the total arid ecosystem of the country is composed of cold arid bioclimate, which accounts for 60%of the SOC stock of arid bioclimate. The Ladakh plateau and the north Kashmir Himalayas come under the arid bioclimate system. At subzero level, the atmospheric temperature remains very low, which causes hyper-aridity and restricts the growth of vegetations; it may be the rationale behind higher SOC content in the soils of cold arid bioclimatic zone. It is interesting to note that out of the total arid bioclimate area,

TABLE 6.1

Stock of Soil Carbon in Different Soil Orders of India at Various Depth Range

Soil Order	Soil Depth (cm)	Carbon Stock (Pg) 1 Pg = 10^{15} g		
		SOC	SIC	Total Carbon
Entisols	0–30	0.62 (6)[a]	0.89 (21)	1.51 (11)
	0–150	2.56 (8)	2.86 (8)	5.42 (8)
Vertisol	0–30	2.59 (27)	1.07 (26)	3.66 (27)
	0–150	8.77 (29)	6.14 (18)	14.90 (23)
Inceptisol	0–30	2.17 (23)	0.62 (15)	2.79 (20)
	0–150	5.81 (19)	7.04 (21)	12.85 (20)
Aridisol	0–30	0.74 (8)	1.40 (34)	2.14 (16)
	0–150	2.02 (7)	13.40 (39)	15.42 (24)
Mollisols	0–30	0.09 (1)	0.00	0.09 (1)
	0–150	0.49 (2)	0.07 (0.2)	0.56 (1)
Alfisols	0–30	3.14 (33)	0.16 (4)	3.30 (24)
	0–150	9.72 (32)	4.48 (13)	14.20 (22)
Ultisols	0–30	0.20 (2)	0.00	0.20 (1)
	0–150	0.55 (2)	0.00	0.55 (1)
Total	0–30	9.55	4.14	13.69
	0–150	29.92	33.98	63.90

Source: Modified from Bhattacharya et al. (2000b, 2011), Pal et al. (2015) and Meena et al. (2021).

[a] Values in parenthesis depicts the SOC, SIC and total carbon percentage.

71% of the area comes under hot arid bioclimate system but the share of SOC is only 40% of the total SOC stock to the arid ecosystem.

Semi-arid bioclimate: This bioclimate system has a temperature range of 25°C–27°C, and the mean annual rainfall ranges between 500 and 700 mm. The vegetation of this bioclimate varies from bushy thorns and grasses to deciduous forest. In this bioclimate, total SOC stock is reported to be 2.9 Pg and is about 30% of the whole SOC stock of India.

Subhumid bioclimate: The bioclimate is constituted by 14 AESRs and 5 ACZs. The mean annual temperature of this system ranges between 22°C and 29°C and receives an average annual rainfall of 900–1,700 mm. The major part of Indo-Gangetic plains and parts of the southern peninsula come under this bioclimate. The soils of these areashave higher SOC content as these areas are rich in vegetation in comparison with semi-arid and arid bioclimate. This bioclimate has 2.5 Pg of SOC stock of the uppermost 30 cm of the soil, and it is 26% of the total SOC stock.

Humid to per humid bioclimate: This bioclimate acquires 34.9 M ha area, which is 11% of the TGA. The estimation of SOC has been done in the uppermost 30 cm of the soil and recorded at 2.1 Pg. This bioclimate consists of Arunachal Pradesh, Meghalaya, Mizoram, Manipur, and the hills of Tripura as these areas receive higher rainfall and have cool winter months. That's why it has higher SOC stock (Bhattacharyya et al., 2000a).

Coastal bioclimate: This bioclimate covers an area of 20.4 M ha which is 62% of the TGA. It is the epitome of 10 AESRs and ACZs. This bioclimate shares 1.3 Pg SOC which is 13% of the total SOC stock (Velayutham et al., 1999, 2019) (Figure 6.2).

6.2.1.2 Soil Carbon Stock of Various Indian Agroclimatic Zones

6.2.1.2.1 The Himalaya Zones (ACZs 1 and 2)

Owing to the thick vegetation cover, it encompasses 19% area and contributes 33% of the SOC reserve of the country. Barring the central and western India, the Northern mountains of the country

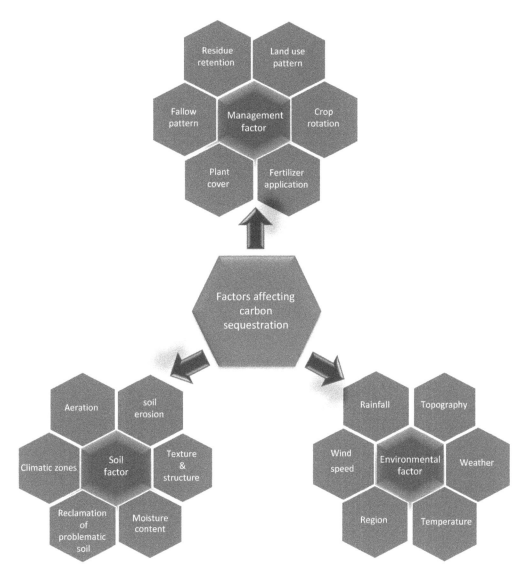

FIGURE 6.1   Factors affecting the soil carbon sequestration process. Source: Lal (2003).

have the maximum concentration of forest ecosystem except parts of central and western India. The study of Eswaran et al. (1993) tells that about 40%of the total SOC stock of the global soils resides in forest ecosystems. When the forest is used for agriculture or converted to pasture for ranching, the upper layer of soils having stored carbon in it is most sensitive to change, and the estimate of SOC in any ecosystem shows a valuable baseline for evaluating the original status of SOC. Hence, the SOC stock of ACZ 1 and 2 can be harnessed as a baseline data set to evaluate the effects of land use changes in the Himalayan Range of India (Bhattacharyya et al., 2008).

6.2.1.2.2   The Gangetic Plains

Lower Gangetic Plains (ACZ 3): (i) The Barind Plains, (ii) central alluvial plains, (iii) alluvial coastal saline plains, and (iv) Rarh plains (Planning Commission, 1989) are found in these plains. It also encloses 3% of the total geographical area TGA. The major soil contribution is 3%, 1%, and 2% of the SOC, SIC, and TC stocks of the country, respectively.

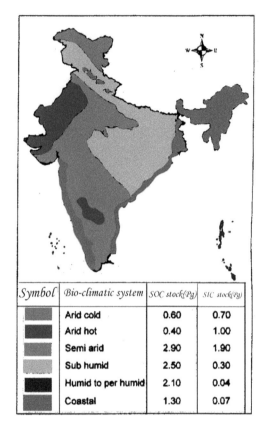

Symbol	Bio-climatic system	SOC stock(Pg)	SIC stock(Pg)
	Arid cold	0.60	0.70
	Arid hot	0.40	1.00
	Semi arid	2.90	1.90
	Sub humid	2.50	0.30
	Humid to per humid	2.10	0.04
	Coastal	1.30	0.07

FIGURE 6.2 Carbon stock in major bioclimatic systems in India (soil depth 0–0.3). Modified from Bhattacharyya et al. (2008).

Middle Gangetic Plains (ACZ 4): Twelve districts of eastern UP and 27 districts of Bihar Plains constitute this zone. North-west alluvial plains and north-east alluvial (Tarai) plains are the two sub-zones of this region (Bhattacharyya et al., 2011) covering 5% of the TGA (total geographical area) of the country. Major soils contribute 2%, 3%, and 3% of the SOC, SIC, and TC stocks of the country.

Upper Gangetic Plains (ACZ 5): Comprising 32 districts of Uttar Pradesh, it occupies 4% of the TGA of the country. Central plains (alluvial), north-western plains (alluvial – Tarai), and south-western plains (alluvial) form the threesub-zone of these plains. The dominant soil contributes 3%, 2%, and 3% of the SOC, SIC, and TC stocks of the country, respectively.

Trans-Gangetic Plains (ACZ 6): Covering 4% area of the country, it comprises the states of Punjab, Haryana, Delhi, and part of Rajasthan (Shriganganagar district). There are three sub-zones: (i) foothills of Shivalik and Himalayas, (ii) semi-arid plains, and (iii) arid zone b ordering the Thar desert. The dominant soil contributes 2%, 4%, and 3% of the SOC, SIC, and TC stocks ofthe country, respectively (Bhattacharyya et al., 2011).

6.2.1.2.3 Plateau and Hills

Eastern plateau and hills (ACZ7): This zone is constituted by five sub-zones:(i) Wainganga, Madhya Pradesh Eastern Hills and Orissa Island, (ii) Northern Orissa, (iii) Madhya Pradesh Eastern Hills and Plateau, (iv) South Chota Nagpur and Eastern Hills and Plateau, and (v) Chhattisgarh and South-Western Orissa Hills (Planning Commission, 1989); 13% of the total geographical area is occupied by this zone. The major soil contributes 9%, 1%, and 7% of the SOC, SIC, and TC stocks of the country, respectively.

Central plateau and hills regions (ACZ8): It spans around 46 districts of UP, MP, and Rajasthan and has 14 sub-zones, which are as follows:

    I. Flood-prone eastern plains
    II. Semiarid eastern plains
    III. Southern plains and Aravalli hills
    IV. Transitional plains
    V. Southern plains
    VI. South-eastern plains
    VII. Gird
    VIII. Central Narmada valley
    IX. Satpura plateau
    X. Vindhya plateau
    XI. Kymorde plateau and Satpura hills
    XII. Borth hills
    XIII. Bundelkhand (Madhya Pradesh)
    XIV. Bundelkhand (Uttar Pradesh)
        Western and eastern parts of it have dry and sub-humid climate, respectively. SOC, SIC, and TC have their 9%, 6%, and 8% portions in these soils, respectively. Valleys, ravines, mounds, and low hills show different physiography of these 14 sub-zones.

Western plateau and hills region (ACZ9): It comprises the prominent portion of Maharashtra and some parts of Madhya Pradesh and Jhalawar, a district of Rajasthan. Hills, scarcity, plateau north, and plateau south are the foursub-zones found in this area. SOC, SIC, and TIC receive 9%, 18%, and 11% of the nation's stock from the main soil.

    Southern plateau and hills region (ACZ 10): Besides covering 12% area of thecountry, it contains 35 districts of Tamil Nadu, Karnataka, and Andhra Pradesh. This region has been separated into six sub-zones. The share of principal soils is 10%, 18%, and 13% of the SOC, SIC, and TC stocks of the country.

6.2.1.2.4 Coastal Plain

With a narrow west coast except the Gulf of Cambay and the Gulf of Kutch, it shows a wider size in the south, contrary to the former. The eastern coastal plains are broader owing to the depositional activities of Mahanadi, Godavari, Krishna, and Kaveri, which are east-flowing rivers; 10% area comes in the gamut of these plains.

    East coast plains and hills (ACZ 11): With six sub-zones such as (i) north Orissa, (ii) north coastal Andhra Pradesh, (iii) South coastal Tamil Nadu, (iv) Thanjavur, (v) south coastal Tamil Nadu, and (vi) south coastal Andhra Pradesh, this occupies 6% area of the country. One can find a principal soil contribution of 6%, 4%, and 5% of the SOC, SIC, and TC stocks of the country, respectively.

    West coastal plains and Ghats region (ACZ 12): Coastal areas of Tamil Nadu, Kerala, Karnataka, Maharashtra, and Goa with several flora and aromatics crops and condiments come in this zone covering 4% area of the country; it is divided into four sub-zones, such as (i) hilly, (ii) midland, (iii) coastal midland, and (iv) coastal hill. SOC, SIC, and TC stocks of the country receive 8%, 2%, and 6%, respectively, from prominent soil.

    Gujarat plains and hills (ACZ 13): This is the epitome of 19 districts of Gujarat, with six sub-zones, such as (i) south Gujarat, (ii) middle Gujarat, (iii) north Gujarat, (iv) North-west arid, (v) North Saurashtra, and (vi) South Saurashtra, and occupies 6% of the total geographical area of the country. The principal soil contribution is 4%, 9%, and 6% of the SOC, SIC, and TC stocks of the country, respectively.

    Western dry (ACZ 14): This is the epitome of nine districts of Rajasthan attributed to hot sandy desert, variable rainfall, and very low flora representation. Thar, Shobhasar, and Kolu being chief soil of this region donate 1%, 11%, and 6% of the SOC, SIC, and TC stocks of the country, respectively.

The islands (ACZ 15): This is the epitome of island territories of the Andaman and Nicobar Islands and Lakshadweep, which are tropical with a mean annual rainfall of 3,000 mm. The chief soils contribute 1%, 0.34%, and 1% of the SOC, SIC, and TC stocks of the country, respectively (Pal et al., 2015; Bhattacharyya et al., 2011) (Figure 6.3).

6.2.2 GREENHOUSE GAS EMISSION FROM DIFFERENT INDIAN AGRICULTURAL SYSTEM

6.2.2.1 Crop Residue Burning

Huge amount of crop residueis produced during and after crop harvest, both on and off the farm. Crop residue production is reported to be 500 Mt per year by the Ministry of New and Renewable Energy. The highest crop residue is generated by Uttar Pradesh with the amount of 60 Mt, Punjab 51 Mt, and Maharashtra 46 Mt. It is estimated that among all the crops, cereals' residue contributes the highest, which is 352 Mt, followed by fibres (66 Mt), oilseeds (29 Mt), pulses (13 Mt), and sugarcane (12 Mt). Among all the cereal crops' residue, rice accounts for 34% of the total. The top and leaves of sugarcane produce 12 Mt of agricultural residues in India, or 2% of all crop residues. However, crop residues are basically used for animal feed, biogas production, as mulch, and as raw fuel in rural houses. But, after all these utilizations, a huge amount of crop residue remains in the farmer's field, and hence, for the next crop sowing, residues are burnt on the farm (https://agricoop. nic.in/sites/default/files/NPMCR; Meena et al., 2021). In the recent past year, the 'on farm' residue burning has intensified due to the use of combined harvester [about 75% of the cropped area in the northern part of the Indo-Gangetic plain (Punjab, Haryana, and Western Uttar Pradesh) is harvested with combine harvesters resulting crop residue generation at huge scale]https://agricoop.nic.in/sites/ default/files/NPMCR, exorbitant labour cost to clear the field. However, in the case of rice, it is reported that burning of crop residue emits carbon in the form of carbon dioxide, which is 70% of the total carbon present in rice residue; carbon monoxide, which is 7% of total carbon; and methane, which is 0.66% of total carbon present in rice residue (Batra, 2022).

6.2.2.2 Livestock and Carbon Emission

As of now in the Indian agriculture sector, livestock has become an integral part and a concerning source of GHG emission. In terms of CO_2 equivalent, the total greenhouse produced from Indian livestock has been calculated to be 247.2 Mt, out of which the total amount of methane emission thatincludes the enteric fermentation and manure management of livestock was calculated as 11.75 Tg/year (Chhabra et al., 2013). CO_2 has the highest direct warming impact as its concentration and quantities emitted are much higher in comparison to other greenhouse gases; in this sequence, methane (CH_4) comes as the second most concerning and nocuous greenhouse gas. If methane is emitted into the atmosphere, then it may sustain there for about 9–15 years. Huge amount of CO_2, CH_4, and nitrous oxide is emitted by various livestock activities. Respiratory process of all animals directly releases carbon dioxide (Table 6.2).

Moreover, methane is released by ruminants and also by monogastric animals to some extent as the product of their digestion process. The manures of animals depending upon the way how they are produced and how they are managed (way of storage, collection, or how they are spread) also emit gases like carbon dioxide, methane, ammonia, and nitrous oxide.

The carbon balance of pastoral land or land of feed crops is affected greatly by livestock, hence contributing to the emission of huge amount of carbon into the atmosphere. Even the fossil fuel that is used for the production process, feed production for livestock, and processing-marketing of the product of livestock emits greenhouse gases at large scale. There are many indirect impacts thatare not easy to calculate as emissions concerned with land use differ pervasively, based on factors like soil, climate, vegetation, and human activities as well.

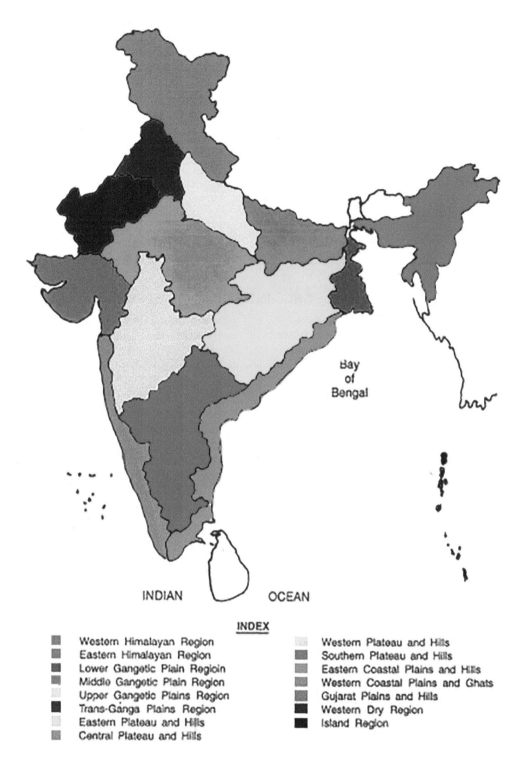

FIGURE 6.3 Agro-climatic zones of India.: Modified from Planning Commission (1989); Ahmad et al. (2017).

TABLE 6.2

Estimated Livestock's Count and Respirational Carbon Dioxide Release

Species	World Total (Billion)	Carbon Dioxide Emissions (Billion Tons CO$_2$)
Cattle and buffaloes	1.496	1.906
Camels	0.019	0.018
Small ruminants	1.784	0.514
Pigs	0.933	0.59
Poultry (chicken, ducks, turkey and geese)	17.437	0.061
Horses	0.055	0.071
Total	–	3.161

Source: Modified from Steinfeld et al. (2006a, b).

TABLE 6.3

Concentration of Major Concerning GHGs during Pre-Industrial Period and Present Status

Gas	Pre-Industrial Concentration (1750)	Current Tropospheric Concentration	Global Warming Potential
Carbon dioxide (CO$_2$)	277 ppm	414 ppm	1
Methane	600 ppb	1,800 ppb	23
Nitrous oxide (N$_2$O)	270 ppb	318 ppb	296

Source: United States Environmental Protection Agency (2022), UNFCCC (2007).

However, carbon (C) is the element that is the basis for all the existing life on the earth planet. The two major sinks for its storage as we know are the soil and the ocean. Here we are dividing the global carbon cycle into two categories; the first is the geological global carbon cycle thatoperates for a long duration of time, i.e., millions of years, and the other is the biological or physical global carbon cycle, and it operates for a short duration of time, i.e., days to thousands of years. Besides, it is estimated that the addition of carbon in the atmosphere is something around 4.5 and 6.5 billion tons per year. The destruction of organic carbon in the soil is mostly because of the burning of fossil fuels and changes in land use. The emission of carbon from livestock respiration contributes a very small portion to the net release of carbon which can be ascribed to the livestock sector. There are many other channels that contribute greatly to carbon emission, which include the burning of fossil fuel for the production of mineral fertilizer that is used in feed production, release of methane due tothe breakdown of animals' manure and fertilizers, pervasive use of fossil-based fuel for the production and transportation of refrigerated and processed animal products, and use of fossil fuel for the production of animals feed (major contributor) (Steinfeld et al., 2006a) (Table 6.3).

6.2.2.2.1   GHGs Emitted by Livestock Enterprise

As one of the most essential elements for plants and animals is Nitrogen but only by two process it becomes available to plants or animals either via lightning or via fixation by rhizobia as it gets converted into reactive form. This limitation of availability of fixed nitrogen limits the production of food to feed increasing population. Hence by the Haber Bosch process we are producing 100 million tonnes of artificial nitrogenous fertilizer per year (Bakker et al., 2012; Smith, 2002). The considerable amount of worlds crop production is fed to animals, either via agro-based industry or direct feeding. In the case of crops having high energy requirement like maize which is used

TABLE 6.4

Nitrogenous Chemical Fertilizer Used for Feed and Pastures in Some Developed and Developing Countries

S. No.	Country	Total N Consumption (%)	Absolute Amount (1,000 tons/year)
1.	USA	51	4,697
2.	China	16	2,998
3.	Germany	62	1,247
4.	France	52	1,317
5.	Canada	55	897
6.	UK	70	887
7.	Brazil	40	678
8.	Spain	42	491
9.	Mexico	20	263
10.	Turkey	17	262

Source: Harrison (2002), FAO (2002).

in the concentrate feed production, mineral N fertilizer is applied. Therefore, animal food chain should be considered responsible for the gaseous emission during the fertilizers manufacturing.

Considering the economic and environmental safety, nowadays natural gas has become desirable fuel for the fertilizers manufacturing process. It was expected that natural gas would account for approximately one third of global energy use in 2020. In mid of the 1990s, 5% of the natural gas was consumed by ammonia industry, while there are many other sources of energy which can be used for ammonia production. According to current production level of coal it is clear that coal reserve is sufficient enough for more than 200 years so, coal can be used as now the supplies of oil and gas has diminished. In current scenario China's 60% of nitrogen fertilizer production is based on coal. It is necessary to know the quantity of uses of fertilizer in the animal's food chain. Combining the requirement of fertilizer by crops for the 1997 (FAO, 2002) with amount or portion of these crops which are used as feed in countries where N fertilizers consumption is more (Kshatriya et al., 2002; Bruinsma, 2003) conveys that animal production attribute a very biggish share of this consumption. However, USA has largest share of total nitrogen consumption about 51%for feed and pastures and China stands second in total nitrogen consumption of 16% of its total consumption for the same it is mentioned in below table for some developed and developing countries (Table 6.4).

Other than the western European countries, above mentioned countries are having large production units and consumption rate of chemical fertilizer. The larger portion of the N-fertilizer going in animals feed has main contribution of maize, in temperate and tropical climates the huge area is covered by maize and thus requires high doses of nitrogenous fertilizer. It is estimated that more than half of the total yield of the maize is utilized as feed. Not only maize but also the other grains like sorghum and barley are the huge consumers of the N-fertilizer.

Opposite to the fact that oilseed crops have N fixing microbes, when intensively grown becomes the good consumers of chemical N fertilizer like rapeseed, soybean, and sunflower these are pervasively used for animal's feed. Additionally, energy is also used for packaging of fertilizers, their transport and application of fertilizers. It has been estimated that annual emission of CO_2 is even more than 40 million tons.

6.2.2.2.2 *Carbon Emitted by Fossil Fuel Uses on Farm for Feed Production*

According to Sainz (2003) , the intensity of production of livestock decides the consumption of energy at different stages of livestock production. In present scenario the major amount of energy is spent for feed production irrespective of whose feed is it, it may be forage for ruminants, it may be feed for poultry i.e., concentrate feed or for pigs. Along with fertilizers, considerable amount of energy is used for seed, herbicides/pesticides manufacturing, the machinery used for land preparation, harvesting, transportation uses diesel and electricity is used for operating pumps for irrigation water extraction from ground, drying and heating etc. It has been estimated that globally, the use of fossil fuels in the production of fertilizer for animal feed production and emissions related to fertilizer application, together with indirect emissions, produce around 240 Tg CO_2-eq./year. Therefore, it has been proved through several researches reports that fossil fuel used for all above purpose emits CO_2 more than sequestration rate (Steinfeld et al., 2006a).

6.2.2.2.3 CO₂ Emission from Soil

Carbon in the form of CO_2 is released into the atmosphere through the soil as a result of biological and chemical processes, for instance, microbial respiration and root respiration as well as faunal respiration which occurs at the surface of soil or upper layer of soil having high concentration of plant residue and chemical oxidation, respectively (Lal, 1999). Many factors are responsible for the carbon dioxide emission from the soil, for instance, pH, texture, available fractions of carbon (labile or recalcitrant), and temperature. However, the most concerning factor is the exposure of the inner soil to highertemperature through intensive tillage practice (Lal, 2004c, d), which significantly contributes to organic carbon losses from the soil. It is estimated that around 20%–30% of soil organic carbon is oxidized and released in the form of CO_2 into the atmosphere (Lal, 1999) (Figure 6.4).

6.2.2.2.4 GHG Emission due to Land Use Changes

Changes in land usage are a very complicated process. It happens as a result of the interaction of various factors, some of which are direct and others are indirect. There can be many transitions, including clearing, grazing, cultivation, abandonment, and secondary forest regrowth. Deforestation is the land-use change process that produces the majority of greenhouse gas emissions from the

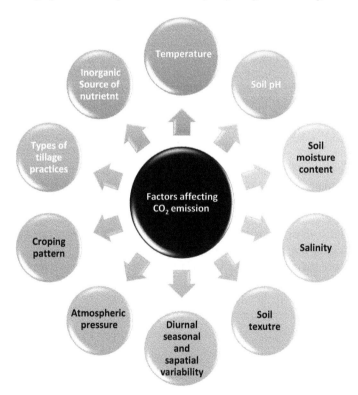

FIGURE 6.4 Key factors affecting soil carbon losses from cultivated land.

perspective of climate change (IPCC, 2007; https://www.ipcc.ch). A nation's ability to produce enough food and grow economically depends on its agricultural sector (Funk and Brown, 2009). Prudentland management has a mitigatingimpact on the amount of nitrous oxide (N_2O) and methane (CH_4) gases released into the atmosphere by agricultural activities (Duxbury, 1994; Paustian et al., 1998; Johnson and Marshall, 2007).

Both the identification of the primary causes of deforestation and the connection between these causes and GHG emissions are still up for debate. However, it has been calculated that land use changes pertaining to livestock have the potential to emit 2.4 billion tons of carbon dioxide equivalent per year. It consists of respirational emission and enteric fermentation emission of GHGs. Furthermore, when forests are harvested or burned, vegetations and soils emit huge amount of carbon into the atmosphere, and now it is known that forest land or soil has more carbon content than that of annual crops and pasture. The intricate pattern of net flux can be produced when forests are cleared, which changes the direction of net CO_2 flux over time (Tubiello et al., 2015). Estimation of CO_2 emission from changes in land use is not a direct process as those of fossil fuel combustion for different processes for feed production and all.

6.2.2.2.5 Emission of CO_2 from Cultivated Soils Related to Livestock

It has been estimated that the release of carbon dioxide from cultivated soil related to livestock may total up to 28 million tonnes CO_2 per year. The total amount of carbon sequestered in the soil acts as a balance between the input of dead vegetation and releases CO_2 via decomposition and mineralization processes. When the soil is in an aerobic state, carbon that enters the soil is unstable and hence rapidly respires into the atmosphere. In a similar way, it has been reported that on North American Great Plains, nearly half of the total sequestered soil organic carbon has been released within the last 50–100 years via burning, erosion, volatilization, harvesting, and grazing (Bolin et al., 1982). Mostly, the losses of SOC take place where the natural cover is being converted to managed land. Thus, we can conclude that minimal human disturbance can check the decomposition and mineralization process (Figure 6.5).

6.2.3 POSSIBLE MITIGATION OPTIONS

The agriculture sector has a crucial role in mitigating climate change and in restoring soil health through adopting various regenerative practices. Several researches and studies have proved that crop rotation, zero tillage, crop residue retention and mulching with crop residues, judicious use of ground water for irrigation through drip irrigation system, agroforestry system, maximum utilization of organic inputs and integrated farming system can exponentially enhance the soil health by enhancing the soil organic carbon content. Moreover, we are emphasizing those mitigation techniques and practices that have great potential to reduce the major current source of GHG emission augmenting to achieve net zero emission. Therefore, there is an urgent need to adopt alternative agricultural methods (van der Werf et al., 2020; Di Bene et al., 2022) that includeagroecological approaches, permaculture (Mollison, 1988; Holmgren, 2020), carbon farming (Baumber et al., 2019, 2020; Toensmeier, 2016; Ridinger, 2016), natural farming (Fukuoka, 1978), keyline farming (Yeomans and Yeomans, 1993), organic agriculture (Howard, 2006; Leu, 2020), and biodynamic agriculture (Steiner and Creeger, 1993). These methods of production have pounded conventional agriculture since the 1970s and 1980s in response to the apparent conflict between sustaining our expanding human population through agricultural production and maintaining the ecosystem functions that humanity and production depend upon. Although the origin of some of these practices goes back to the early 20th century, the idea of sustainability, which was brought into sharp focus on a worldwide scale in the middle of the 1980s, plays a significant role in their promotion as alternatives. In this context, "conventional agriculture" refers to the predominant production system in a region, and "conventional agriculture alternatives" refer to all other systems (Figure 6.6).

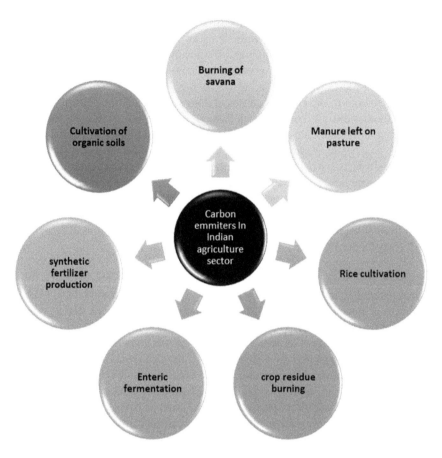

FIGURE 6.5 Key carbon-emitting practices of the Indian agriculture sector.

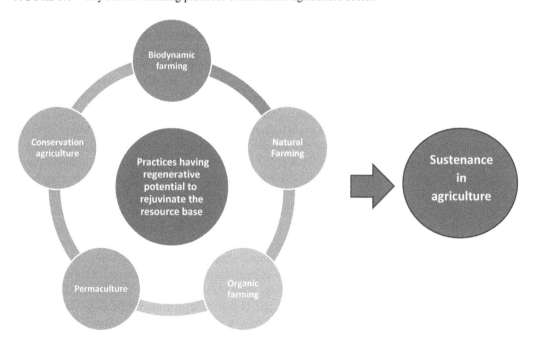

FIGURE 6.6 Integration of various regenerative farming approaches towards sustainability in agriculture.

6.2.3.1 Agricultural Intensification and Promoting Afforestation

It becomes challenging while working for land use change as reduction in deforestation and enhancement in afforestation is its primary and significant exigent. Deforestation in Amazon for the pervasive extension of livestock has now become an example that contributes largely to global CO_2 emission. If proper development strategies were executed for the regulation of frontier expansion and for making economic alternatives, then surely, we must impose restrictions to the prophesy enhancement of the emissions (Carvalho et al., 2004). The aim for sequestration cannot be achieved with the same rate or with the same intensity by following intensification (Steinfeld et al., 2006b). Areas where deforestation is being done should be managed, or quickly, the practice promoting sustainable agriculture should be adopted like the deliberate growing of woody perennials along with pasture system and livestock; intensive silvopastoral system (ISPS) is the advanced form of silvopastoral system in which fodder shrubs are grown with high density of upto 4,000–40,000 plants/hectare with grasses and palm trees are 100–600 trees/hectare. This system can protect the soil from immutable damage. ISPS is a major player in the addition of extra biodegradable plant material and thus has the potential to enhance the carbon content of the soil along with improving the entire soil health (Campanhola and Pandey, 2018).

6.2.3.2 Sequestering SOC under Different Cropping Systems

In comparison to arable soil, cultivated soil has an unparalleled ability for the net sequestration of carbon. The world's agricultural and degraded soil's carbon sink capacity has been estimated to be 50%–66% of historic losses of carbon from soils of 42–78 gigatonnes of carbon (Lal, 2004a, d).

Photosynthesis and respiration create the dynamic equilibrium of input and output. It characterizes the soil processes regarding carbon. Moreover, the adoption of conventional practices for cultivation leads to the transformation of natural systems into cultivated agriculture; thus, the soil of top 1 m depth loses its organic carbon (OC) content on the order of 20%–50% as compared to its pre cultivation stock (Paustian et al., 1997; Lal and Bruce, 1999).

Soil health is majorly benefited by growing cover crops as it improves or enhances the quality of soil; because it largely contributes to biomass addition resulting in the increment of soil organic carbon, it promotes the formation of soil aggregates, and the canopy of the crops acts as shelter and prevents the splash erosion along with preventing the surface runoff and hence improves the soil organic carbon.

We can't calculate the saturation point of terrestrial soil carbon sequestration because still we are not well versed in SOC dynamics at every level together with landscape, molecular, global, and regional scales (Metting et al., 1999; Smith et al., 2005). It has been reported that in most cases, improved practices lead to an increment of soil carbon of nearly 0.3 tonnes of carbon content per hectare every year (Watson et al., 2000); these practices have the potential to sequester approx. 270 million tonnes of carbon annually in the coming few decades if adopted on 60% of the arable land of the globe (Lal, 1997). The rate of carbon sequestration by these practices might be higher initially for about 20–25 years but then little paucity occurs (Kimble et al., 1998).

6.2.3.3 Reciprocating Organic Carbon Losses from Pastures

It was reported that two-thirds of the world's grasslands were degraded in the 1990s era (Dregne et al., 1991) because of the repercussion of salinization, acidification, excessive grazing, alkalinization, and other processes. Improvement in grassland management has huge potential to reciprocate soil carbon losses resulting in net sequestration via adopting the regenerative way of utilization of trees, improved species, fertilization, and other plantation measures. Carbon sequestration potential is much higher in improved pastures as compared to any other anthropogenic land use practice (Watson et al., 2000; Steinfeld et al., 2006a). It is not merely helpful for the sequestration of carbon but also leads to biodiversity restoration. Soils of dryland pasture are susceptible to/tend to deterioration repercussion of which there is drastic paucity in soil organic carbon pool (Dregne, 2002). However, the soil of dry land has more potential to hold or retain the sequestered carbon than wet soil because the limitation of water checks the soil mineralization and hence the carbon flux to the atmosphere, as well as enables dryland soil to hold carbon for longer duration in comparison with forest soil (FAO, 2004). As the dry land soil has a large area coverage on the globe, about 41% of the earth's surface (CGIAR, 2011) exhibits good scope for carbon sequestration. These soils are far away from reaching their carbon saturation point, and these soils have undergone substantial carbon loss since the ancient period.

Controlling or having improved management for desertification and soil health restoration can sequester 12–18 billion tonnes of carbon over a 50-year duration (Lal, 2001, 2004b, c). According to Lal's estimation (2004b), there is a huge potential in a dryland ecosystem, which can sequester around 1 billion tonnes of soil carbon per year; to achieve the benefit of this very potential, he emphasizes on the requirement of:

> coordinated soulful efforts at global level to check desertification, reversing degraded ecosystem to its natural health and pervasive adaption of those management practices on cropping and grazing land which has been proved as milestone for the minimal carbon losses and having potential to sequester more atmospheric carbon to these very soil.

There are several methods for mitigating soil carbon losses that include all the soil erosion protective measures, increasing the production of grassland, rehabilitating badly degraded land by landscaping, or developing gardening patches. These techniques are found very effective in the Australian research report (CSIRO, 2009).

6.2.3.4 Checking SOC Oxidation through Management of Physical and Chemical Environment of the Soil

The physical and chemical features (like temperature, moisture, aeration, pH, and availability of the nutrient in the soil) of the soil have a huge contribution to the mineralization/oxidation process of SOC. Not merely these very features but also the physical and chemical properties of the organic matter and even the availability of the organic matter for microbes and microbial decaying play crucial roles. All chemical and physical features can be managed by judicious agricultural practices. Two possible ways have great potential for mitigating the SOC losses from agricultural soil through mineralization: (i) *minimal or zero* soil tillage and (ii) *agroforestry system*.

1. **Minimal or zero soil tillage:** Types of tillage differ in accordance with climate, nature of the soil, type of climate, objective of cultivation, types of crops to be grown, availability of machineries, farmer's own desire as per the tradition or culture. These factors playa crucial role in the selection of tillage types. It becomes essential to reckon the impact of tilth and tillage frequency on soil's organic matter content, as OM content is directly proportional to the SOC content. Conventional tillage practices are the most intensive form of tillage (uses of soil inverting mould board plough) (Paustian et al., 2019) and cause maximum soil disturbance resulting in exposure of inner soil to the air and then leading to oxidation of sequestered organic carbon content (Nath and Lal, 2017).

   Therefore, there is a need to emphasize the adoption of zero tillage or no tillage as it has the prime focus on minimal or least soil disturbance, and improving soil aggregates, it is pervasive acceptance that soil having more aggregates has great potential to protect certain fraction of SOM, and hence, it increases residential time of SOM in the soil (Adu and Oades, 1978; Beare et al., 1994a; Golchin et al., 1994a, b; Jastrow, 1996). Intensive tillage practices are often deleterious to soil structure. As tillage practices expose the new soil to the outer atmosphere augmenting the wet-dry and freeze-thaw cycle at the earth's surface (Rovira and Greacen, 1957; Beare et al., 1994b), and due to this exposure of new soil to the outer surface, soil aggregates become more prone to detriment. Moreover, shifting from conventional tillage towards no or zero tillage has huge potential for more aggregation of soil as well as can increase the stability of soil aggregates. (Cambardella and Elliott, 1993;

Beare et al., 1994a, b; Franzluebbers and Arshad, 1996). When the soil aggregates get stabilized, it complements the stabilization of soil organic matter mainly in organic soils (Lutzow et al., 2006). If soil aggregate contains soil organic matter in it, then SOM is physically protected against biological degradation through aggregate formation. As a repercussion of aggregate formation, the sequestration process of SOC and soil structural stability get long-term support (Six et al., 2000). The main mechanism for the stabilization of SOC is the physical protection against SOC decomposition in soil aggregates (Six et al., 2002; Chaplot and Cooper, 2015). It indicates the crucial role of soil aggregate for the stabilization of SOC, so in this sequence, it becomes important to adopt those methodologies for agricultural operations that causethe least disturbance to the soil aggregates; there is an urgent need to shifting the conventional intensive tillage practices towards the no-tillage or zero-tillage practices.

2. **Agroforestry system:** There is huge potential for SOC sequestration through multispecies agroforestry system as tree species in this system have good interaction with roots and deep below the soil, but experimental evidences are not limpid (Ong et al., 2004; Rao et al., 2004). Emphasis should be given to the selection of those tree species that penetrate deep into the soil and have extensive/broad rhizosphere augmenting the addition of more carbon input into the soil and can lead to increased sequestration of SOC in agroforestry system (Kell, 2012; Lorenz and Lal, 2010). Instead of coniferous tree species, the selection of such tree species having broadleaf would complement to generate more SOC inputs as the roots of every tree have more root biomass and well-adhered root system (Laganiere et al., 2010). The adoption of conservation-effective strategies that minimize water and nutrient losses contributes to retard the decomposition rate of biomass and enhance the rate of biomass carbon input into the soil of agroforestry system, as well as increase the chemical, biological, and physical stabilization mechanisms for the protection of soil organic carbon losses (Lal and Follet, 2009).

It has been reported that to achieve a higher SOC pool in an agroforestry system, demands for higher biomass carbon return to soil must be fulfilled; also, there is a need to strengthening the stabilization of organic matter or reducing the biomass decomposition (Lal, 2005; Sollins et al., 2007). Agroforestry system is more capable of utilizing the available resources for biomass production (in compare to Monoculture), and thus, more biomass production leads towards higher carbon return into the soil. There are some agroforestry practices through which we can directly add carbon to the soil. They are:

- Leaving the pruned-off parts or material of the woody species at the site's soil, so that it can act as mulch and insitu decomposition of tree litter.
  - Promoting livestock grazing and addition of dung to the soil.
  - Let woody species grow and contribute litters at the surface and beneath the ground during the fallow phases of crops.
  - For the animal production system, integrate trees and their litter.
  - Let the litter of shade-tolerant species be added into the soil that grows under the canopy shade of the tree.
  - Deliberate growing of agricultural crops during the establishment period of forestry plantation so that the soil can benefit from soil carbon input by agricultural crops (Lorenz and Lal, 2005).

Moreover, instead of litter quality, the amount of litter input as well as its interaction with the soil matrix is more crucial to regulate SOC formation and stabilization (Gentile et al., 2011a, b).

In a well-managed agroforestry system, there are huge possibilities for increasing the SOC pool through reduced tillage practices, and saying NO to burning, controlled erosion (Soto-Pinto et al., 2010). Hedgerow intercropping system and deliberate growing of trees along with perennial crops grown for alley cropping may play a crucial role in the prevention of soil erosion (Albrecht and Kandji, 2003). There is a need to focus on minimizing the erosional SOC losses because a large proportion of clay and humus are removed via the eroding action of water and wind leaving less productive gravel, coarse sand, and stones behind (Troeh et al., 2004). In this regard, agroforestry system is a milestone practice that has the potential to reduce erosional SOC losses significantly. The basic principle of these practices is that soil is never left un-vegetated (improved fallow and Taungya system of cultivation). Riparian buffer strip, windbreak, and shelter belts are some of the most efficient agroforestry practices to check the erosional SOC losses (Lorenz and Lal, 2014).

6.2.3.5 Checking SOC through (Fe) Mineral

In the present scenario of climate change and aiming to net zero emission of carbon from terrestrial carbon sink, the interaction of organic carbon with soil minerals has been found to playa crucial role in the stabilization of organic carbon in the soil (Lalonde et al., 2012; Riedel et al., 2013). Greater stability of organic carbon has been noted particularly in association with Fe minerals through co-precipitation and sorption in comparison to organic carbon which is not bonded with Fe mineral (Eusterhues et al., 2003; Feng et al., 2014; Kalbitz et al., 2005; Porras et al., 2018; Quideau et al., 2001).

Moreover, recent researches and studies demonstrated that under anoxic condition, the reduction of Fe and reductive emission of soil organic carbon (Adhikari and Hartemink, 2016; Adhikari and Yang, 2015; Hall and Silver, 2013; Thompson et al., 2006; Zhao et al., 2017) showed the release of SOC around 4%–10% to solution, and simultaneously, reduction of Fe oxide in soil has been calculated to be 13%–38% during an 8-day anoxic incubation (Chadwick and Chorover, 2001; Chorover et al., 2007). Re-exposing the reduced soil to oxic conditions can result in rapid oxidation of Fe(II) according to Fe(II) speciation, its sorption to soil particles, and its interaction with organic carbon and minerals (Chen and Thompson, 2018). Hence, this very re-oxidation of Fe might firmly influence the destiny of SOC (Chen et al., 2018). Instead of associating with Fe(II), DOC associates more preferentially with newly precipitated Fe(III). Therefore, the availability of organic carbon is altered for abiotic and biotic degradation (Gregory and Duan, 2001).

6.2.3.6 Soil Carbon Stabilization through Mycorrhiza

Glomalin is basically a glycoprotein synthesized particularly by arbuscular mycorrhizal fungi's hyphae and spores to some extent. The very fungi survive on most of the plants' roots and utilize the plant's carbon for the synthesis of glomalin to seal and form a coating layer to the outer lining of its hyphae to carry water and nutrient (Holatko et al., 2021; Comis and Wright, 2003). Experimental findings of researches found glomalin in those samples only where, plant roots were colonized with AMF (Smith and Read, 2010). Glomalin is hydrophobic, insoluble, recalcitrant, and sticky in nature, hence called super glue for the soil particles augmenting the soil aggregate formation. As glomalin is extremely rich in such glycoprotein which is insoluble and hydrophobic in nature, it enablesto check the decomposition of SOM. Along with aggregate formation, glomalin contributes to good soil structure and porosity, improves the resistance against wind and water erosion (Wuest et al., 2005), positively affects the sequestration of carbon, and improves stabilization (Nie et al., 2018). It nixes the pollutant's toxicity (Vodnik et al., 2008). Glomalin protein has its unique and miraculous role in the stabilization process of soil aggregate and its impact over the stabilization of soil organic carbon (Wilson et al., 2009). SOC can be retained and protected by stable soil aggregates until it is broken down (Hossain, 2021); that's why in the above section, we were emphasizing towards zero or minimal tillage practices as stabilization of soil aggregate is one of the most concerning factors. The major components for soil aggregate formation are organic matter which can be easily decomposed, clay particle and microstructure, woody debris and litters, hyphae of fungi, root residues, and glomalin. The amalgamation of these very components leads to the formation of larger microaggregates, and then, they are converted to macroaggregates through adhesive agents of OM and hyphae of AMF (Miller and Jastrow, 2000). Within the soil aggregate, SOC remains physically

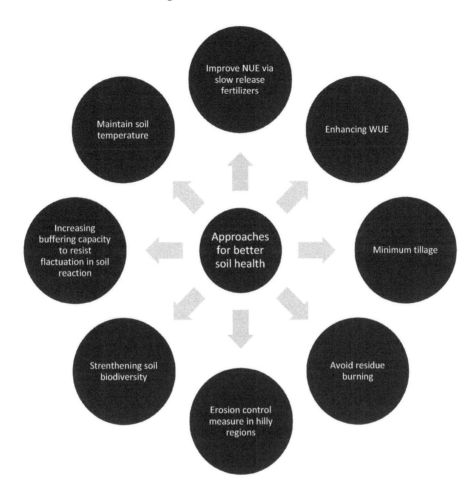

FIGURE 6.7   Promising approaches to be adopted for improving the health of Indian soils.

protected through soil aggregation to check the activity of microbes over SOC (Amado et al., 2006). When the soil aggregates become stable, it checks the microbial activity, and ultimately SOC storage is enhanced (Rillig, 2004; Rillig et al., 2007). The quantity of glomalin in soil has a correlation with the length of AMF's hyphae and soil aggregate's stability (Wright and Upadhyaya, 1996) indicating that indirect stabilization of soil aggregate can enable glomalin for soil carbon storage. The formation of a netted bag-like structure with the AMF's hyphae which is sticky in nature thus adhering the soil particles together and leadingto aggregate formation is the initial way of SOC stabilization (Johnson et al., 2002) (Figure 6.7).

6.3   CONCLUSION

The assessment and restoration of organic carbon in Indian agricultural soils are pivotal for fostering regenerative agriculture, addressing climate change, and ensuring sustainable food production. The significant role of soil organic carbon (SOC) in maintaining soil health, fertility, and productivity underscores the importance of implementing regenerative farming practices. The pressing reality of soil degradation due to increased agricultural intensification leading to SOC oxidation has contributed to environmental concerns, including the release of carbon dioxide (CO_2) into the atmosphere. Mitigating this issue requires a comprehensive approach, considering the equilibrium between SOC stabilization and losses through microbial decomposition.

Strategic management of soil properties, encompassing physical, chemical, and environmental factors, is crucial for controlling SOC decomposition. Prudent agricultural practices tailored to specific locations can play a pivotal role in achieving this goal. Moreover, the evaluation of SOC distribution across different soil orders highlights the need for region-specific strategies. While challenges persist, such as the low SOC content in tropical climates, promising signs emerge from assessments indicating an increase in organic carbon content in major food-growing regions. This underscores the potential impact of sustainable agricultural practices on SOC restoration. In summary, promoting regenerative agriculture, understanding the dynamics of SOC in diverse soil types, and implementing location-specific strategies are vital steps toward enhancing carbon sequestration, soil health, and overall environmental sustainability in the Indian agricultural landscape.

REFERENCES

Adhikari, D., & Yang, Y. (2015). Selective stabilization of aliphatic organic carbon by iron oxide. *Scientific Reports*, *5*(1), 1–7.

Adhikari, K., & Hartemink, A. E. (2016). Linking soils to ecosystem services– A global review. *Geoderma*, *262*, 101–111.

Adu, J. K., & Oades, J. M. (1978). Physical factors influencing decomposition of organic materials in soil aggregates. *Soil Biology and Biochemistry*, *10*(2), 109–115.

Ahmad, L., Habib Kanth, R., Parvaze, S., & Sheraz Mahdi, S. (2017). Agro-climatic and agro-ecological zones of India. In Latief Ahmad , Raihana Habib Kanth , Sabah Parvaze, and Syed Sheraz Mahdi (eds.). *Experimental Agrometeorology: A Practical Manual* (pp. 99–118). Springer, Cham.

Albrecht, A., & Kandji, S. T. (2003). Carbon sequestration in tropical agroforestry systems. *Agriculture, Ecosystems & Environment*, *99*(1–3), 15–27.

Amado, A. M., Farjalla, V. F., Esteves, F. D. A., Bozelli, R. L., Roland, F., & Enrich-Prast, A. (2006). Complementary pathways of dissolved organic carbon removal pathways in clear-water Amazonian ecosystems: photochemical degradation and bacterial uptake. *FEMS Microbiology Ecology*, *56*(1), 8–17.

Bakker, R. H., Pedersen, E., van den Berg, G. P., Stewart, R. E., Lok, W., & Bouma, J. (2012). Impact of wind turbine sound on annoyance, self-reported sleep disturbance and psychological distress. *Science of the Total Environment*, *425*, 42–51.

Batra, P. (2022). Crop residue burningin India: Policy changes and potential solution [blog]. Available at: https://krishijagran.com/blog/crop-residue-burning-in-india-policy-challenges-and-potential-solutions/

Baumber, A., Metternicht, G., Cross, R., Ruoso, L. E., Cowie, A. L., & Waters, C. (2019). Promoting co-benefits of carbon farming in Oceania: applying and adapting approaches and metrics from existing market-based schemes. *Ecosystem Services*, *39*, 100982.

Baumber, A., Waters, C., Cross, R., Metternicht, G., & Simpson, M. (2020). Carbon farming for resilient rangelands: people, paddocks and policy. *The Rangeland Journal*, *42*(5), 293–307.

Beare, M. H., Hendrix, P. F., Cabrera, M. L., & Coleman, D. C. (1994b). Aggregate-protected and unprotected organic matter pools in conventional-and no-tillage soils. *Soil Science Society of America Journal*, *58*(3), 787–795.

Beare, M. H., Hendrix, P. F., & Coleman, D. C. (1994a). Water-stable aggregates and organic matter fractions in conventional-and no-tillage soils. *Soil Science Society of America Journal*, *58*(3), 777–786.

Bhattacharyya, T., Pal, D. K., Chandran, P., Ray, S. K., Mandal, C., & Telpande, B. (2008). Soil carbon storage capacity as a tool to prioritize areas for carbon sequestration. Current *Science*, *95*, 482–494.

Bhattacharyya, T., Pal, D. K., Chandran, P., Ray, S. K., Mandal, C., Wani, S. P., & Sahrawat, K. L. (2011). Carbon status of Indian soils: an overview. In: Srinivasa Rao, Ch., Venkateswarlu, B., Srinivas, K., Kundu, S.,& Singh, A. K. (eds.) *Soil Carbon Sequestration for Climate Change Mitigation and Food Security* (pp. 11–30). Central Research Institute for Dryland Agriculture, Hyderabad.

Bhattacharyya, T., Pal, D. K., Mandal, C., & Velayutham, M. (2000a). Organic carbon stock in Indian soils and their geographical distribution. *Current Science*, *79*, 655–660.

Bhattacharyya, T., Pal, D. K., Velayutham, M., Chandran, P., & Mandal, C. (2000b). Total carbon stock in Indian soils: issues, priorities and management. In: *Proceedings of the Land Resource Management for Food and Environment Security Conference*. Soil Conservation Society of India, New Delhi.

Bhattacharyya, T., Pal, D. K., Chandran, P., Ray, S. K., Mandal, C., Wani, S. P., & Sahrawat, K. L. (2011). Carbon status of Indian soils: an overview. In *Soil Carbon Sequestration for Climate Change Mitigation and Food Security* (pp. 11–30). Central Research Institute for Dryland Agriculture, Hyderabad. ISBN 978-93-80883-08-3.

Bolin, B., Crutzen, P. J., Vitousek, P. M., Woodmansee, R. G., Goldberg, E. D., & Cook, R. B. (1982). *SCOPE 21– The Major Biogeochemical Cycles and Their Interactions*. Scientific Committee on Problems of the Environment (SCOPE), United States.

Bruinsma, J. (ed.) (2003) World Agriculture: Towards 2015/2030. An FAO Perspective. Earthscan Publications Ltd., London. Available at: https://www.fao.org/3/y4252e/y4252e.pdf

Cambardella, C. A., & Elliott, E. T. (1993). Carbon and nitrogen distribution in aggregates from cultivated and native grassland soils. *Soil Science Society of America Journal, 57*(4), 1071–1076.

Campanhola, C., & Pandey, S. (eds.) (2018). *Sustainable Food and Agriculture: An Integrated Approach*. The Food and Agriculture organization of the United Nations (FAO). Published by Elsevier Inc. All rights reserved.

Carvalho, G., Moutinho, P., Nepstad, D., Mattos, L., & Santilli, M. (2004). An amazon perspective on the forest-climate connection: opportunity for climate mitigation, conservation and development? *Environment, Development and Sustainability, 6*(1), 163–174.

CGIAR (2011) CGIAR research program on dryland systems. Available at: https://cac-program.org/crpds

Chadwick, O. A., & Chorover, J. (2001). The chemistry of pedogenic thresholds. *Geoderma, 100*(3–4), 321–353.

Chaplot, V., & Cooper, M. (2015). Soil aggregate stability to predict organic carbon outputs from soils. *Geoderma, 243*, 205–213.

Chen, C., & Thompson, A. (2018). Ferrous iron oxidation under varying pO_2 levels: the effect of Fe(III)/Al(III) oxide minerals and organic matter. *Environmental Science & Technology, 52*(2), 597–606.

Chen, C., Meile, C., Wilmoth, J., Barcellos, D., & Thompson, A. (2018). Influence of pO_2 on iron redox cycling and anaerobic organic carbon mineralization in a humid tropical forest soil. *Environmental Science & Technology, 52*(14), 7709–7719.

Chhabra, A., Manjunath, K. R., Panigrahy, S., & Parihar, J. S. (2013). Greenhouse gas emissions from Indian livestock. *Climatic Change, 117*(1), 329–344.

Chorover, J., Kretzschmar, R., Garcia-Pichel, F., & Sparks, D. L. (2007). Soil biogeochemical processes within the critical zone. *Elements, 3*(5), 321–326.

Comis, D., & Wright, S. F. (2003). Glomalin: the real soil builder. ARS Sustainable Agricultural Systems Laboratory in Beltsville, MD. Retrieved from https://www.ars.usda.gov/news-events/news/research-news/2003/glomalin-the-real-soil-builder/

CSIRO (2009). An analysis of greenhouse gas mitigation and carbon biosequestration opportunities from rural land use. Available at: https://publications.csiro.au/rpr/download?pid=changeme:822&dsid=DS1

Datta, R., & Meena, R. S. (eds.)(2021). *Soil Carbon Stabilization to Mitigate Climate Change*. Springer, Singapore.

Di Bene, C., Diacono, M., Montemurro, F., Testani, E., & Farina, R. (2022). EPIC model simulation to assess effective agro-ecological practices for climate change mitigation and adaptation in organic vegetable system. *Agronomy for Sustainable Development, 42*(1), 1–17.

Dregne, H. E. (2002). Land degradation in the drylands. *Arid Land Research and Management, 16*(2), 99–132.

Dregne, H., Kassas, M., & Rozanov, B. (1991). A new assessment of the world status of desertification. *Desertification Control Bulletin, 20*(1), 7–18.

Duxbury, J. M. (1994). The significance of agricultural sources of greenhouse gases. *Fertilizer Research, 38*(2), 151–163.

Eswaran, H., Van den Berg, E., & Reich, P. (1993). Organic carbon in soils of the world. *Soil Science Society of America Journal, 57*, 192–194.

Eusterhues, K., Rumpel, C., Kleber, M., & Kögel-Knabner, I. (2003). Stabilisation of soil organic matter by interactions with minerals as revealed by mineral dissolution and oxidative degradation. *Organic Geochemistry, 34*(12), 1591–1600.

FAO (2002). Fertilizer use by crop. FAO Fertilizer and Plant Nutrition Bulletin. FAO, Rome. Available at: https://www.researchgate.net/profile/Anoop_Srivastava7/post/Where_can_I_find_data_on_how_much_of_certain_types_of_fertilizers_Nitrogen_Solutions_Urea_etc_specific_states_use/attachment/59e05cd9b53d2fe117b57970/AS%3A548886122110976%401507876057345/download/fpnb17.pdf

FAO (2004). Carbon sequestration in dryland soils. FAO, Rome. Available at: https://www.fao.org/publications/card/en/c/99d4ed39-672d-57db-889a-3416a8a5638d/

Feng, W., Plante, A. F., Aufdenkampe, A. K., & Six, J. (2014). Soil organic matter stability in organo-mineral complexes as a function of increasing C loading. *Soil Biology and Biochemistry, 69*, 398–405.

Franzluebbers, A. J., & Arshad, M. A. (1996). Water-stable aggregation and organic matter in four soils under conventional and zero tillage. *Canadian Journal of Soil Science, 76*(3), 387–393.

Fukuoka, M. (1978). *The One-Straw Revolution: An Introduction to Natural Farming*. Translated from the Japanese by Chris Pearce, Tsune Kurosawa and Larry Korn Originally published in Japan as Shizen Noho Wara Ippon No Kakumei, Other India Press Mapusa 403 507, Goa, India.

Funk, C. C., & Brown, M. E. (2009). Declining global per capita agricultural production and warming oceans threaten food security. *Food Security*, *1*(3), 271–289.

Gentile, R., Vanlauwe, B., Kavoo, A., Chivenge, P., & Six, J. (2011b). Residue quality and N fertilizer do not influence aggregate stabilization of C and N in two tropical soils with contrasting texture. In: Bationo, A., Waswa, B., Okeyo, J., Maina, F., & Kihara, J. (eds.) *Innovations as Key to the Green Revolution in Africa* (pp. 795–805). Springer, Dordrecht.

Gentile, R., Vanlauwe, B., & Six, J. (2011a). Litter quality impacts short-but not long-term soil carbon dynamics in soil aggregate fractions. *Ecological Applications*, *21*(3), 695–703.

Goh, K. M. (2004). Carbon sequestration and stabilization in soils: implications for soil productivity and climate change. *Soil Science and Plant Nutrition*, *50*(4), 467–476.

Golchin, A., Oades, J. M., Skjemstad, J. O., & Clarke, P. (1994a). Study of free and occluded particulate organic matter in soils by solid state 13C Cp/MAS NMR spectroscopy and scanning electron microscopy. *Soil Research*, *32*(2), 285–309.

Golchin, A., Oades, J. M., Skjemstad, J. O., & Clarke, P. (1994b). Soil structure and carbon cycling. *Soil Research*, *32*(5), 1043–1068.

Gregory, J., Duan, J. (2001). Hydrolyzing metal salts as coagulants. *Pure and Applied Chemistry*, *73*, 2017–2026.

Hall, S. J., & Silver, W. L. (2013). Iron oxidation stimulates organic matter decomposition in humid tropical forest soils. *Global Change Biology*, *19*(9), 2804–2813.

Harrison, P. (2002). World agriculture: towards 2015/2030. Summary report. FAO, Rome.

Holatko, J., Prichystalova, J., Hammerschmiedt, T., Datta, R., Meena, R. S., Sudoma, M., ...Brtnicky, M. (2021). Glomalin: akey indicator for soil carbon stabilization. In: Datta, R.,& Meena, R. S. (eds.) *Soil Carbon Stabilization to Mitigate Climate Change* (pp. 47–81). Springer, Singapore.

Holmgren, D. (2020). *Essence of Permaculture*. Melliodora Publishing. Retrieved from https://holmgren.com.au/essence-of-permaculture-free/

Hossain, M. B. (2021). Glomalin and contribution of glomalin to carbon sequestration in soil: a review. *Turkish Journal of Agriculture-Food Science and Technology*, *9*(1), 191–196.

Howard, A. (2006). *The Soil and Health: A Study of Organic Agriculture*. University Press of Kentucky, Devin-Adair.

IPCC (2007) Climate change 2007: impacts, adaptation and vulnerability. Contribution of Working Group II to the Fourth Assessment Report of the IPCC. Cambridge University Press, New York. Available at: https://www.ipcc.ch/site/assets/uploads/2018/03/ar4_wg2_full_report.pdf

Jastrow, J. D. (1996). Soil aggregate formation and the accrual of particulate and mineral-associated organic matter. *Soil Biology and Biochemistry*, *28*(4–5), 665–676.

Johnson, D., Leake, J. R., Ostle, N., Ineson, P., & Read, D. J. (2002). In situ 13CO2 pulse-labelling of upland grassland demonstrates a rapid pathway of carbon flux from arbuscular mycorrhizal mycelia to the soil. *New Phytologist*, *153*(2), 327–334.

Johnson, J. E., & Marshall, P. A. (2007). The Great Barrier Reef and climate change: vulnerability and management implications. In Climate Change and the Great Barrier Reef: A Vulnerability Assessment, http://hdl.handle.net/11017/139, ISBN: 9781876945619.

Kalbitz, K., Schwesig, D., Rethemeyer, J., & Matzner, E. (2005). Stabilization of dissolved organic matter by sorption to the mineral soil. *Soil Biology and Biochemistry*, *37*(7), 1319–1331.

Kell, D. B. (2012). Large-scale sequestration of atmospheric carbon via plant roots in natural and agricultural ecosystems: why and how. *Philosophical Transactions of the Royal Society B: Biological Sciences*, *367*(1595), 1589–1597.

Kimble, J. M., Follett, R. F., & Cole, C. V. (1998). *The Potential of US Cropland to Sequester Carbon and Mitigate the Greenhouse Effect*. CRC Press, USA.

Kshatriya, M., Kifugo, S., Msoffe, F., Neselle, M., & Said, M. Y. (2002). Novel forms of livestock and wildlife integration adjacent to protected areas in Africa-Tanzania: mapping land cover changes in Simanjiro and Monduli districts. FAO Report on GEF Tanzania project. FAO, Rome, Italy.

Laganiere, J., Angers, D. A., & Pare, D. (2010). Carbon accumulation in agricultural soils after afforestation: a meta-analysis. *GlobalChange Biology*, *16*(1), 439–453.

Lal, R. (1997). Residue management, conservation tillage and soil restoration for mitigating greenhouse effect by CO2-enrichment. *Soil and Tillage Research*, *43*(1–2), 81–107.

Lal, R. (1999). Soil management and restoration for C sequestration to mitigate the accelerated greenhouse effect. *Progress in Environmental Science*, *1*(4), 307–326.

Lal, R. (2001). Potential of desertification control to sequester carbon and mitigate the greenhouse effect. *Climatic Change*, *51*(1), 35–72.

Lal, R. (2003). Global potential of soil carbon sequestration to mitigate the greenhouse effect. *Critical Reviews in Plant Sciences*, *22*(2), 151–184.

Lal, R. (2004a). Carbon emission from farm operations. *Environment International*, *30*(7), 981–990.

Lal, R. (2004b). Carbon sequestration in dryland ecosystems. *Environmental Management*, *33*(4), 528–544.

Lal, R. (2004c). Soil carbon sequestration impacts on global climate change and food security. *Science*, *304*(5677), 1623–1627.

Lal, R. (2004d). Soil carbon sequestration in India. *Climatic Change*, *65*(3), 277–296.

Lal, R. (2005). Forest soils and carbon sequestration. *Forest Ecology and Management*, 220(1–3), 242–258.

Lal, R., & Bruce, J. P. (1999). The potential of world cropland soils to sequester C and mitigate the greenhouse effect. *Environmental Science & Policy*, *2*(2), 177–185.

Lal, R., & Follett, R. F. (2009). *Soil Carbon Sequestration and the Greenhouse Effect*. Available at: https://cals.arizona.edu/research/archer/publications/books_chapters_proceedings/Boutton-et-al_2009_Soil-Carbon-Sequestration.pdf

Lalonde, K., Mucci, A., Ouellet, A., & Gélinas, Y. (2012). Preservation of organic matter in sediments promoted by iron. *Nature*, *483*(7388), 198–200.

Leu, A. (2020). An overview of global organic and regenerative agriculture movements. In: Auerbach, R. (ed.) *Organic Food Systems: Meeting the Needs of Southern Africa* (pp. 21–31). CABI, CAB International.

Lorenz, K., & Lal, R. (2005). The depth distribution of soil organic carbon in relation to land use and management and the potential of carbon sequestration in subsoil horizons. *Advances in Agronomy*, *88*, 35–66.

Lorenz, K., & Lal, R. (2010). *Carbon Sequestration in Forest Ecosystems* (1st ed.). Springer Science & Business Media. https://doi.org/10.1007/978-90-481-3266-9

Lorenz, K., & Lal, R. (2014). Soil organic carbon sequestration in agroforestry systems. A review. *Agronomy for Sustainable Development*, *34*(2), 443–454.

Lützow, M. V., Kögel-Knabner, I., Ekschmitt, K., Matzner, E., Guggenberger, G., Marschner, B., & Flessa, H. (2006). Stabilization of organic matter in temperate soils: mechanisms and their relevance under different soil conditions– a review. *European Journal of Soil Science*, *57*(4), 426–445.

Meena, R. S., Kumar, S., Sheoran, S., Jhariya, M. K., Bhatt, R., Yadav, G. S., …Lal, R. (2021). Soil organic carbon restoration in India: programs, policies, and thrust areas. In: *Soil Organic Matter and Feeding the Future* (pp. 305–338). CRC Press, Boca Raton.

Memon, M. S., Guo, J., Tagar, A. A., Perveen, N., Ji, C., Memon, S. A., & Memon, N. (2018). The effects of tillage and straw incorporation on soil organic carbon status, rice crop productivity, and sustainability in the rice-wheat cropping system of eastern China. *Sustainability*, *10*(4), 961.

Metting, F. B., Smith, J. L., & Amthor, J. S. (1999). Science needs and new technology for soil carbon sequestration. In: Rosenberg, N.J., Izaurralde, C.R., & Malone, E.L. (eds.), *Carbon Sequestration in Soils. Science Monitoring and Beyond* (pp. 1–34). Batelle Press, Ohio.

Miller, R. M., & Jastrow, J. D. (2000). Mycorrhizal fungi influence soil structure. In: Kapulnik, Y., & Douds, D. D. (eds.) *Arbuscular Mycorrhizas: Physiology and Function* (pp. 3–18). Springer, Dordrecht.

Mollison, B. (1988). *Permaculture: A Designer's Manual*. Tagari Publications, Tyalgum.

Nath, A. J., & Rattan, L. A. L. (2017). Effects of tillage practices and land use management on soil aggregates and soil organic carbon in the north Appalachian region, USA. *Pedosphere*, *27*(1), 172–176.

Nie, X., Li, Z., Huang, J., Liu, L., Xiao, H., Liu, C., & Zeng, G. (2018). Thermal stability of organic carbon in soil aggregates as affected by soil erosion and deposition. *Soil and Tillage Research*, *175*, 82–90.

Ong, C. K., Kho, R. M., & Radersma, S. (2004). Ecological interactions in multispecies agroecosystems: concepts and rules. In: van Noordwijk, M., Cadisch, G., & Ong, C. K. (eds.) *Below-Ground Interactions in Tropical Agroecosystems: Concepts and Models with Multiple Plant Components* (pp. 1–15). CABI, CAB International.

Pal, D. K., Wani, S. P., & Sahrawat, K. L. (2015). Carbon sequestration in Indian soils: present status and the potential. *Proceedings of the National Academy of Sciences, India Section B: Biological Sciences*, *85*(2), 337–358.

Paustian, K., Andren, O., Janzen, H. H., Lal, R., Smith, P., Tian, G., …Woomer, P. L. (1997). Agricultural soils as a sink to mitigate CO2 emissions. *Soil Use and Management*, *13*, 230–244.

Paustian, K., Cole, C. V., Sauerbeck, D., & Sampson, N. (1998). CO2 mitigation by agriculture: an overview. *Climatic Change*, *40*(1), 135–162.

Paustian, K., Collins, H. P., & Paul, E. A. (2019). Management controls on soil carbon. In Eldor A. Paul, Keith H. Paustian, E. T. Elliott, C. Vernon Cole (eds.). *Soil Organic Matter in Temperate Agroecosystems* (pp. 15–49). CRC Press.

Planning Commission (1989). Agro-climatic regional planning: an overview.144pp.

Porras, R. C., Pries, C. H., Torn, M. S., & Nico, P. S. (2018). Synthetic iron (hydr)oxide-glucose associations in subsurface soil: effects on decomposability of mineral associated carbon. *Science of the Total Environment, 613*, 342–351.

Quideau, S. A., Chadwick, O. A., Benesi, A., Graham, R. C., & Anderson, M. A. (2001). A direct link between forest vegetation type and soil organic matter composition. *Geoderma, 104*(1–2), 41–60.

Ridinger, R. B. (2016). Review of the carbon farming solution: a global toolkit of perennial crops and regenerative agriculture practices for climate change mitigation and food security, by Eric Toensmeier. *Journal of Agricultural & Food Information*, 17(2–3), 200.

Riedel, T., Zak, D., Biester, H., & Dittmar, T. (2013). Iron traps terrestrially derived dissolved organic matter at redox interfaces. *Proceedings of the National Academy of Sciences, 110*(25), 10101–10105.

Rillig, M. C. (2004). Arbuscular mycorrhizae, glomalin, and soil aggregation. *Canadian Journal of Soil Science, 84*(4), 355–363.

Rillig, M. C., Caldwell, B. A., Wösten, H. A. B., et al. (2007). Role of proteins in soil carbon and nitrogen storage: controls on persistence. *Biogeochemistry*, 85, 25–44. https://doi.org/10.1007/s10533-007-9102-6.

Rovira, A. D., & Greacen, E. L. (1957). The effect of aggregate disruption on the activity of microorganisms in the soil. *Australian Journal of Agricultural Research, 8*(6), 659–673.

Sainz, R. D. (2003). Framework for calculating Fossil Fuel Use in Livestock Systems. A study commissioned under FAO Livestock, Environment and Development Initiative. Food and Agriculture Organization of the United Nations, Rome. Available at: https://www.fao.org/3/an913e/an913e.pdf

Shovik, D., Bhadoria, P. B. S., Mandal, B., Rakshit, A., & Singh, H. B. (2015). Soil organic carbon: Towards better soil health, productivity, and climate change mitigation. *Climate Change and Environmental Sustainability, 3*(1), 26–34. DOI: 10.5958/2320-642X.2015.00003.4

Six, J., Conant, R. T., Paul, E. A., & Paustian, K. (2002). Stabilization mechanisms of soil organic matter: implications for C-saturation of soils. *Plant and Soil, 241*(2), 155–176.

Six, J., Elliott, E. T., & Paustian, K. (2000). Soil macroaggregate turnover and microaggregate formation: a mechanism for C sequestration under no-tillage agriculture. *Soil Biology and Biochemistry, 32*(14), 2099–2103.

Smith, B. E. (2002). Nitrogenase reveals its inner secrets. *Science, 297*(5587), 1654–1655.

Smith, P., Andrén, O., Karlsson, T., Perälä, P., Regina, K., Rounsevell, M., & Van Wesemael, B. (2005). Carbon sequestration potential in European croplands has been overestimated. *Global Change Biology, 11*(12), 2153–2163.

Smith, S. E., & Read, D. J. (2010). *Mycorrhizal Symbiosis*. Academic Press. https://doi.org/10.1016/B978-0-12-370526-6.X5000-9

Sollins, P., Swanston, C., & Kramer, M. (2007). Stabilization and destabilization of soil organic matter– a new focus. *Biogeochemistry, 85*(1), 1–7

Soto-Pinto, L., Anzueto, M., Mendoza, J., Ferrer, G. J., & de Jong, B. (2010). Carbon sequestration through agroforestry in indigenous communities of Chiapas, Mexico. *Agroforestry Systems, 78*(1), 39–51.

Steiner, R., & Creeger, C. E. (1993). *Agriculture*. SteinerBooks, Anthroposophic Press Inc.

Steinfeld, H., Gerber, P., Wassenaar, T. D., Castel, V., Rosales, M., & de Haan, C. (2006a). *Livestock's Long Shadow: Environmental Issues and Options*. FAO, Rome.

Steinfeld, H., Gerber, P., Wassenaar, T. D., Castel, V., Rosales, M., & de Haan, C. (2006b). Chapter 3: Livestock's role in climate change and air pollution. In: *Livestock's Long Shadow: Environmental Issues and Options*. FAO, Rome. Available at: https://www.fao.org/3/a0701e/a0701e03.pdf

Thompson, L. G., Mosley-Thompson, E., Brecher, H., Davis, M., León, B., Les, D., …Mountain, K. (2006). Abrupt tropical climate change: past and present. *Proceedings of the National Academy of Sciences, 103*(28), 10536–10543.

Toensmeier, E. (2016). *The Carbon Farming Solution: A Global Toolkit of Perennial Crops and Regenerative Agriculture Practices for Climate Change Mitigation and Food Security*. Chelsea Green Publishing, White River Junction, VT.

Troeh, F. R., Hobbs, J. A., & Roy, L. D. (2004). *Soil and Water Conservation and Environment Protection* (3rd ed.). Pearson, New Jersey. Available at: https://www.osti.gov/biblio/364112

Tubiello, F. N., Salvatore, M., Ferrara, A. F., House, J., Federici, S., Rossi, S., …Smith, P. (2015). The contribution of agriculture, forestry and other land use activities to global warming, 1990–2012. *GlobalChange Biology, 21*(7), 2655–2660.

UNFCCC (2007) Global warming potentials (IPCC Second Assessment Report). Available at: https://unfccc.int/process/transparency-and-reporting/greenhouse-gas-data/greenhouse-gas-data-unfccc/global-warming-potentials

United States Environmental Protection Agency (2022) Climate change indicators: atmospheric concentrations of greenhouse gases. Available at: https://www.epa.gov/climate-indicators/climate-change-indicators-atmospheric-concentrations-greenhouse-gases

van der Werf, H. M., Knudsen, M. T., & Cederberg, C. (2020). Towards better representation of organic agriculture in life cycle assessment. *Nature Sustainability*, *3*(6), 419–425.

Velayutham, M., Pal, D. K., & Bhattacharyya, T. (1999). Organic carbon stock in soils of India. In *Global Climate Change and Tropical Ecosystems* (1st ed., pp. 25). CRC Press. DOI: 10.4324/9780203753187

Velayutham, M., Pal, D. K., & Bhattacharyya, T. (2019). Organic carbon stock in soils of India. In John M. Kimble, B. A. Stewart (eds.). *Global Climate Change and Tropical Ecosystems* (pp. 71–95). CRC Press, Boca Raton.

Vodnik, D., Grčman, H., Maček, I., Van Elteren, J. T., & Kovačevič, M. (2008). The contribution of glomalin-related soil protein to Pb and Zn sequestration in polluted soil. *Science of the Total Environment*, *392*(1), 130–136.

Watson, R. T., Noble, I. R., Bolin, B., Ravindranath, N. H., Verardo, D. J., & Dokken, D. J. (2000). *Land Use, Land-Use Change and Forestry: A Special Report of the Intergovernmental Panel on Climate Change*. Cambridge University Press, Cambridge.

Wilson, G. W., Rice, C. W., Rillig, M. C., Springer, A., & Hartnett, D. C. (2009). Soil aggregation and carbon sequestration are tightly correlated with the abundance of arbuscular mycorrhizal fungi: results from long-term field experiments. *Ecology Letters*, *12*(5), 452–461.

Wright, S. F., & Upadhyaya, A. (1996). Extraction of an abundant and unusual protein from soil and comparison with hyphal protein of arbuscular mycorrhizal fungi. *Soil Science*, *161*(9), 575–586.

Wuest, S. B., Caesar-TonThat, T. C., Wright, S. F., & Williams, J. D. (2005). Organic matter addition, N, and residue burning effects on infiltration, biological, and physical properties of an intensively tilled silt-loam soil. *Soil and Tillage Research*, *84*(2), 154–167.

Yeomans, K. B., & Yeomans, P. A. (1993). *Water for Every Farm*. Keyline Designs, Australia.

Zhao, Q., Adhikari, D., Huang, R., Patel, A., Wang, X., Tang, Y., ...Yang, Y. (2017). Coupled dynamics of iron and iron-bound organic carbon in forest soils during anaerobic reduction. *Chemical Geology*, *464*, 118–126.

7 The Application of Organic Manure for Better Soil Health and Higher Crop Production

Melis Cercioglu, Ekrem Ozlu, Gafur Gozukara,
Mert Acar, Gokhan Ucar, Bayram Cagdas Demirel,
Sofia Houida, and Serdar Bilen

7.1 INTRODUCTION

As an organic amendment, manure is used in agriculture to benefit soil health and crop production. Organic fertilizers, such as manure, compost, and others, are one of the most important inputs for macro-and micronutrients that are essential to maintaining high crop yields and quality in modern agricultural production. There were about 1.9 billion livestock units in the world in 2018, mostly comprised of cattle, that produced an estimated 125 million megagram N (FAOSTAT, 2020).

Increases in the adoption and application rates of manure have resulted in considerable improvements in soil quality indicators (Ozlu, 2016). However, application of manure using best management practices is imperative for an economically and ecologically sound use of manure in sustainable agriculture (Rui et al., 2017). Most of the positive impacts on soil health are likely because the amount of soil organic matter (SOM) is increased via added manure application. SOM plays critical roles in crop growth and productivity by providing higher nutrient contents, improved aggregation, and lower compaction and erodibility (Ozlu, 2016; Babur et al., 2021; Ozlu and Arriaga, 2021). However, non-judicious application of livestock manure may increase greenhouse gas emissions and decrease water quality by increasing nutrient runoff and the concentration of organic compounds in water. Thus, the daily production of massive amounts of manure must be handled under environmentally friendly disposal practices to prevent harmful effects on the agroecosystems.

Livestock manure contains animal excreta (feces and urine) and may include debris. Although manure is typically utilized as an organic fertilizer for crop production, depending on the particular livestock management technique, animal manure can also include fallen feed, scurf, water, and soil. Since the start of human agricultural activities in Neolithic Europe more than 8,000 years ago, the use of manure has been a significant agricultural management practice. In fact, prior to synthetic fertilizer production around the beginning of the 1900s, the majority of out-sourced crop nutrient inputs came from animal manure (Bogaard et al., 2013). At present, there is an increased attention to organic manure usage in modern agriculture as a result of the ever-increasing knowledge regarding the positive influences of manure application on soil quality and environmental sustainability (Peacock et al., 2001).

7.2 MANURE CHARACTERISTICS

The main properties of manure, including compost, green manure, and others, depend on the collection, storage, and handling conditions, type and source of manure, solid content, and particle size, among others (Lorimor, 2000).

Organic manure generally refers to an agricultural by-product, livestock waste, which consists of a variety of fresh or dried plant-derived materials (Green, 2015). Organic manures

DOI: 10.1201/9781003309581-9

(farmyard manure, green manure, compost, etc.) are readily available natural products that can benefit higher soil organic matter and nutrient supply, in contrast to synthetic fertilizers that are industrially produced and are mainly used as a source of nutrients.

Depending on the solid content, manure can be classified as liquid (<4%), slurry (4%–10%), semi-solid (10%–20%), or solid manure (>20% of solid content) (Lorimor, 2000).

Manure characteristics and nutrient contents greatly vary with the animal species utilized, commonly known as the source of manure. Moreover, different animal species also produce a quite dissimilar amount of manure per animal unit, as shown in Figure 7.1. Similarly, manure from different animal species can considerably vary in terms of nutrient concentrations, as depicted in Figure 7.2.

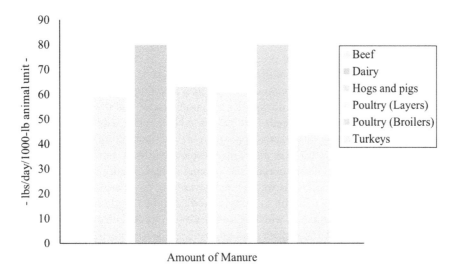

FIGURE 7.1 Manure production per animal unit across different animal species. Adapted from USDA Natural Resources Conservation Service (*Agricultural Waste Management Handbook*, 1999).

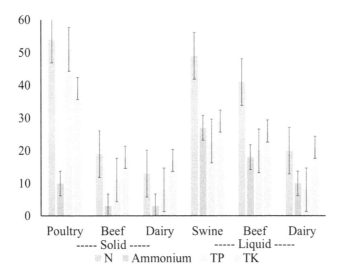

FIGURE 7.2 Nitrogen, ammonium, and total phosphorus (TP) and potassium (TK) contents of manure across different animal species. Adapted from Rosen and Bierman (2005), University of Minnesota Extension Review, 2020.

Compost is another way of using manure. Though composting naturally occurs, several factors must be controlled for successful composting that could minimize pollution and odor problems while maximizing the quality of the final product. Composting is a straight forward process that regulates conditions to separate it from aerobic fermentation. In recent decades, research has focused on mechanisms and dynamic interactions that occur during the composting process between biological, chemical, and physical characteristics. Therefore, composting optimization is an important factor in determining the ideal conditions for organic matter degradation and microbial development. The impacts of management of compost optimization on soil physical, chemical, and biological properties have demonstrated significant contributions to soil health indices (Agnew and Leonard, 2003).

Compost development can be defined as the process by which thermophilic aerobic microorganisms transform organic matter into biostable and hygienic products. A suitable supply of nutrients, oxygen, water, and an atmosphere that can maintain a thermophilic temperature (>40°C) are essential for the growth and normal functioning of microorganisms. Compost temperature, humidity, and air quality are physical properties of themselves, but other physical properties of the composting materials affect both of these requirements (Agnew and Leonard, 2003). In composting, temperature is a significant parameter, both as a result and as an operation determinant. It is generally believed that thermophilic species are more active, and thermophilic temperatures destroy the seeds of pathogens and weeds that may have been contained in the initial mixture. In order to keep microbial communities active, optimum air and humidity levels are also necessary. A constant oxygen supply is required to maintain aerobic conditions. Sufficient water is required for the nutrition and transport of microorganisms. Compost bulk density is also used in construction and transportation calculations, as well as in determining the energy required for operations such as turning and mixing. In addition to compressibility and strength, bulk density can also be attributed to moisture and air quality, which is a very useful physical characteristic. The distribution of particle size determines the surface available to the microorganism and can also affect bulk density and slight compression. The airflow resistance of compost may be related to bulk density and porosity, and mechanical properties facilitate the maintenance and design of compost piles (Agnew and Leonard, 2003).

7.3 HOW TO DETERMINE THE AMOUNT OF MANURE APPLICATION RATE?

Recommended manure application rates are generally calculated according to nutrient contents, nitrogen, and phosphorus (Ozlu, 2016). These calculations consider nutrient content requirements for crop yield expectation, soil nutrient content, and manure nutrient content (Feinerman et al., 2004), where the nutrient requirements of the crops varied depending on nutrient uptake efficiency, sod nutrient supply, and soil nutrient supply. Therefore, the formulation below (1) is a hypothesis that:

Amount of manure to apply = (Crop Nutrient Requirement – Soil Nutrient Content)
/(Manure Nutrient Content)   (7.1)

The nutrients in calculations of manure application rates usually consider nitrogen content; however, some recommendations have also been developed on phosphorus content. Phosphorus-based manure applications requirea lower amount of manure for a particular crop yield demand (Ozlu, 2016), where this rate of manure applications usually leads tolower crop yields, improvements in soil health (Ozlu et al., 2019b), and the production of greenhouse gas emissions (Ozlu and Kumar, 2018b). Similarly, phosphorus-based manure applications do not show salinity issues compared to nitrogen-based manure applications (Ozlu and Kumar, 2018a).

7.4   WHEN SHOULD MANURE APPLICATION TAKE PLACE?

Maximizing the benefits of manure nutrient contents, preventing crop damage, and limiting the risk of environmental pollution can be achieved when the application time of manure is considered. The timing of manure application, which is suitable for land use, crop type, weather, and soil conditions, can reduce nutrient losses and avoid plant quality and yield losses by ensuring nutrient supply when the crop needs it. A study conducted on tomato production evaluated the effects of poultry manure application timing (four different timings before and after transplanting) on leaf nutrient concentrations, above-ground biomass, and yield (Adekiya and Agbede, 2017). This study's results indicated that applying poultry manure 3 weeks before transplantation has higher leaf nutrient content, higher terrestrial biomass, and higher crop yield compared to other application times during or after the transplantation (Adekiya and Agbede, 2017).

In addition to having direct effects on soil nutrient availability, the timing of manure addition can indirectly impact plant growth by altering soil health indices. As manuring approaches planting, root zone salt increases (Chang et al., 1991), soil pH rises, and soil microbial activity is stimulated (Nannipieri et al., 1983). Manure application immediately prior to planting was found to reduce potato yields and tuber quality compared to previously applied fertilizers (Curless et al., 2012). In the same study, it was also reported that common scab and verticillium levels were increased with manure applied directly before planting (Curless et al., 2012). The abovementioned findings recommend that the application of manure take place at least a few months prior to crop planting.

The nutritional requirements of growing plants generally differ during the growing season, with the maximum uptake and maximum intake associated with the fastest growing period. In this case, synchrony comes into prominence and chooses the right time when sufficient nutrients are available from the fertilizer in the soil. Synchronization of soil nutrients available to plants and plant nutrient requirements is essential to achieving best plant performance and better environmental safeguard (Magdoff, 1995). This may also prevent the loss of nutrients that can occur out of the period the plant needs, which can lead to wasted resources in the long run. Optimal application of 20-tons/ha of poultry manure within 60 days after sucker transplantation or planting is optimal for the availability of nutrient release and root uptake from manure (Ndukwe et al., 2011). This was related to the synchronization of nutrient supply from poultry manure in the rhizosphere with plant intake requirements.

Application timing of manure is important for environmental concerns because application time may have a significant impact on nutrient leaching to groundwater, such as nitrate, which is one of the major pollutants in groundwater. It was reported that the timing of fertilization and the type of soil changed the level of nitrate concentration in the wastewater (Van Es et al., 2006). Fertilizer application in late autumn reduced the concentration of nitrate nitrogen compared to application in early autumn of corn. This suggests that the lowest nitrate nitrogen concentration was achieved in the spring application of the study.

Manure application timing also has effects on nitrous oxide (N_2O) emissions. Nitrous oxide, known as a greenhouse gas, is a climate pollutant. On farms in many countries, it is common to apply fertilizer manure to agricultural soils at different times of the year (such as spring and autumn). Applying fertilizer manure to cultivated land can increase N_2O emissions, which may be mitigated by improving fertilizer manure management by choosing the right fertilizer timing (Kulshreshtha et al., 2016). Adding manure to the soil surface can boost N_2O fluxes where high precipitation and temperature conditions exist. According to Ozlu and Kumar (2018b), the variability of N_2O fluxes increases with an increase in soil temperature. In addition, Smith et al. (2019) stated that fall manure application in comparison to spring application may raise these fluxes in cool weather climates because more substrates are available during the spring thaw period when manure is applied in the fall season.

7.5   WEED CONTROL FOR ORGANIC MANAGEMENT

Typically, weeds are described as "plants that grow where they are not wanted". Usually, plants known as weeds are considered undesirable because they decrease yields, increase dockage, host crop diseases or pests, complicate grain storage, make crops harder to harvest, taste or present taint crops, and/or are toxic (Frick, 2005). Manure practices in a field may increase thick and weed populations as manure contains small but mighty weed seeds. The implementation type should be considered as it has a significant impact on weed control. Injection or placement of liquid can be superior to surface application. For instance, Rasmussen (2002) investigated the effects of injection versus surface application of liquid manure on weed density and weed biomass for three growing seasons under barley and oat production. The liquid manure injection or placement improved weed control and reduced the total weed population in barley, suggesting the injection method offers the crop more conservative control by placing minerals near the crop planting (Rasmussen, 2002). Also, manure type may influence weed density in organic cropping systems. Efthimiadou et al. (2012) investigated the effects of different types (cattle manure, poultry manure, and barley as green manure) and rates (half of single, single=10 tons/ha, and double of single) under sweet maize cultivation. They found that a double rate of manure application promoted weed emergence while it was suppressed by poultry manure and green manure under barley. This can be attributed to the different N concentrations and release times of poultry manure compared to cattle manure. As green manure, barley residues may have an allelopathic effect on weed populations.

For organic management, implementing mitigation practices for weed management comes with three important concerns. The first problem is reducing the damage caused by weeds on related crops. Weeds can be harmful by competing for resources, releasing allelochemicals, and physically disturbing the growth and harvest of those crops. The general solution to this obstacle is the removal or suppression of weeds emerging within the crop planting time and for a period of weeks afterwards. The second, longer-term concern is that the production and survival of new weed seeds and vegetative propagules will be reduced, reducing the size of future weed populations. The last concern is inhibiting the introduction of new, more bothersome weed, types into an existing weed flora through tracking, sanitation, and targeted removal efforts. Prevention of all these issues involves comprehensive approaches consisting of both restorative control and system-level style (Anderson, 2007).

Eliminating weeds at the initial phase of seedling by using chemical herbicides is the main focus of conventional weed management. On the other hand, prevention of weeds emerging in organic crop production requires different management strategies, such as direct control. These strategies not only prevent seedling continuity, but also involve more sophisticated methods that impact weed recreation, emerging, survival, and dissemination of seed and vegetative propagule. The physiological and ecological actions associated with the latter group of approaches are closely related to important elements and interactions within organic farming systems, which consist of diverse cultivation systems, soil amendment and disruption systems, and pathogen and seed predator feeding activities (Liebman and Davis, 2000).

Declines in crop yields are due to the larger population of weeds in organic systems than in conventional systems and the absence of effective weed control strategies (Entz et al., 2001). For instance, a study conducted to identify quantities of weeds occurring in manure reported that per 1,000 kg, fresh manure coming from dairy farms comprised an average of 75,000 seeds (Mt and Schlather, 1994). Hence, the advancement of reliable weed control techniques is important to achieve improved crop production in organic farming. The most common and practical cultural methods for weed control are crop rotation, cover cropping, live mulching, and intercropping.

7.5.1   Crop Rotation

Crop rotation is one of the key agricultural practices in organic farming, as crop rotation contributes to soil fertility, soil preservation, and the control of certain insect bugs and pathogens (Seleiman and Hafez, 2021). Also, this agricultural management has been acknowledged as basic to weed control (Leighty, 1938). Weed control strategies are considered the main function of determining rotation period and crop arrangement for lots of organic crop producers (Walz, 1999). Furthermore, the weed life cycle might be disrupted, and becoming too "comfortable" for a weed species might be prevented in the cropping system owing to the diversification of crop attributes within a rotation (Liebman et al., 2001).

7.5.2 Cover Crop and Live Mulching

Besides enhancing soil health, reducing soil erosion, and controlling insects, cover crops and living mulches can be utilized to suppress weeds. As a weed management tool, cover crops and living mulches prevent weed seed production by using multiple tactics, such as blocking light, competition for water, nutrients, and space, thereby resulting in the suppression of weed seed establishment and the lower development of weed seedlings (Teasdale, 1996).

7.5.3 Intercropping

Intercropping is the practice of growing two or more crops together in a way that complements their resource intake patterns. Crops in intercropping systems might make better use of light, water, and nutrients and produce more yields per unit area of land than at least one of the crops in monoculture systems (Willey, 1990). More resource use by intercropping than by monoculture can improve the suppression of weeds through resource competition. Baumann et al. (2000) reported that seed germination, production, and development of common groundsel (*Senecio vulgaris* L.) were reduced by shading. Groundsel (*S. vulgaris* L.) is a weed invading leek cultivation (*Allium porrum* L.), but intercropping of leek and celery (*Apium graveolens* L.) induced a less light-growing season, thereby resulting in a more effectively reduced typical groundsel than did the monoculture. According to Bulson et al. (1997), an intercrop made up of wheat and field bean (*Vicia faba* L.) resulted in less biomass of weed than the bean monoculture, whereas the wheat monoculture produced less weed biomass compared with the wheat and bean intercropping despite growing at the exact same relative density. Patterns of resource use allowed wheat and field beans to be grown at greater densities than usual for monocultures. When this management method was applied, increased density in mixtures consisted of significantly less weed biomass than monocultures of both crops grown at normal density.

7.6 RESPONSES OF CROP YIELD TO ORGANIC MANURE

The application of organic manure to soils can provide additional nutrients that facilitate greater crop growth than those with mineral fertilizer applications due to the greater impacts of manure application on soil health (CAST, 1996). Compost as an organic manure has been considered an excellent soil conditioner that can provide phosphorus content and improve its availability, hence increasing crop yield (Xin et al., 2015). Previous studies have also found greater grain yield values by increasing water holding capacity and improving chemical properties under animal manure treatment (Sattar and Gaur, 1989). For instance, a study was carried out in three different countries where it was reported that the greatest crop yield (14%) was under farmyard manure (10 tons/ha) application in comparison to mineral fertilization (Badaruddin et al., 1999). Besides, Blanchet et al. (2016) documented greater crop yield values by the increasing rate of 3.5% under cattle manure treatment than mineral fertilization alone. However, Cercioglu et al. (2012) determined an increment in lettuce yield of 102.7 tons/ha under 50 tons/ha composted tobacco waste versus those under farmyard manure. In general, previous studies documented that both manure and compost have a significant contribution to maximum crop yield goals and sustain soil health compared to chemical fertilizations (Cercioglu, 2019a, b), since inorganic fertilizations are yield goal-dominated practices and do not perform as well on soil structure and health as manure and compost.

7.7 AGRO-ENVIRONMENTAL CONCERNS OF MANURE APPLICATION

Intensive agricultural practices negatively influence soil structure and functionality and thus contribute to degradation of environmental sustainability. The negative effects of agricultural practices and management, including overdosing organic and chemical fertilization, can be categorized into three different aspects: (i) soil health issues; (ii) water quality issues; and (iii) emissions of greenhouse gases, mainly CO_2, N_2O, and CH_4, from agricultural and integrative livestock.

7.7.1 RESPONSE OF SOIL HEALTH TO MANURE APPLICATIONS

Soil health is a concept that deals with the specific soil characteristics and its ability to maintain ecological processes that are important for a long-term sustainable ecosystem (VeVerka et al., 2019). Healthy soils are important for sustainable agriculture. SOM is a key component for sustainable long-term soil conservation that contributes greatly to improving soil fertility and agricultural productivity by enhancing soil physical, chemical, and biological characteristics (Figure 7.3).

It has been known that organic manures have the ability to develop soil physical, chemical, and biological characteristics by declining acidity and increasing the amount of humus (Ganzhara, 1998). They can increase soil organic carbon (SOC), enhance soil structure (i.e., increase aggregate stability and soil porosity but decrease bulk density), enable the soil to hold water and more nutrients, and thus achieve greater agricultural productivity (Celik et al., 2010). The size distribution and stability of soil aggregates and SOC have recently been linked (Ozlu and Arriaga, 2021). Since manure has a lower bulk density and a higher SOC, the addition of manure can lower bulk density but increase SOM, total porosity, hydraulic conductivity, and aggregate stability compared to chemical fertilizations. Aggregate stability for soil physical quality is a main parameter and can be improved by organic manure application, which can maintain an appropriate soil structure (Ozlu, 2020). Water-stable aggregates greatly impact soil porosity, water holding capacity, infiltration,

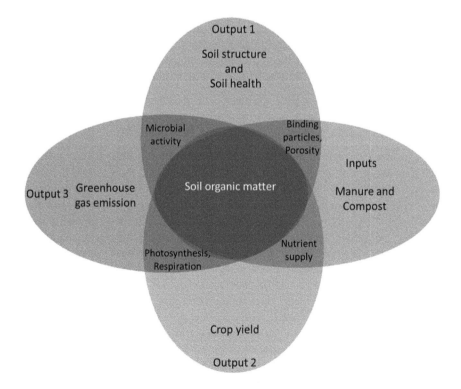

FIGURE 7.3 Improvement in soil health by increasing the soil organic carbon content.

and hence soil structure (Haynes and Naidu, 1998). A decline in soil organic matter negatively affects porosity, water holding capacity, aggregation, compaction, and hence erosion (Ozlu et al., 2019a). Organic manure application is a common and traditional technique to improve soil porosity and quality (Xu et al., 2020). It has also been demonstrated by many researchers that additions of organic manure at increasing rates in long-term studies can improve soil macropores (Lu et al., 2019) due to the increase of stable soil aggregates and SOC (Papadopoulos et al., 2009).

The improvement and maintenance of SOM, poultry manure, plant residuals, urban waste compost, and cotton gin materials have been used, hence providing plant nutrients and reclaiming degraded soils (Tejada et al., 2006). The SOC is a complex group that consists of different divisions (Prietzel et al., 2018), such as hot water-soluble carbon, labile carbon, particulate organic C, and others (Chaudhary et al., 2017). In general, organic manure additions to the soil ensure an increase in SOC (Garcia-Pausas et al., 2017). Numerous studies supported the theory of positive influences on SOC by long-term manure additions. For instance, Blanchet et al. (2016) reported that cattle manure application increased SOC by 6.40% compared to mineral fertilizer alone, whereas others reported the same results for composting (Zhang et al., 2015). Composting also improves the activity of microorganisms (Scotti et al., 2015), available nutrient supply (N, P, K, and Mg), root reinforcement (Goss et al., 2013), and organic matter mineralization process. Weber et al. (2007) applied compost to soil and found an increment in the ratio of humic acid and fulvic acid, which might be partly due to the fact that the humic matter in the compost has an original content, where humic acids are always predominant over fulvic acids. Abu-Zahra and Tahboub (2008) found higher available P contents in soil under manure (cattle, sheep, and poultry) treatments compared to other treatments (conventional, control, and mixture of manure). They also observed greater soil organic matter (1.67%) from the sheep manure treatment compared with other treatments. Liu and Zhou (2017) conducted a long-term field experiment (from 2003 to 2010) in Zhonglianchuan in Gansu Province, China, and reported that the total N, P, and C:N ratios were greater in 2010 than those in 2003 by 112.0%, 225.8%, and 109.2% ($p \leq 0.05$), respectively.

Organic amendments such as manure maintain a soil pH of about 6.9–7. If soil pH is lower, the addition of manure may increase pH (liming effect), but if soil pH is high, manure addition may lower soil pH. Application of organic matter as manure can buffer the soil pH against a decline in pH. Manure that has high ammonium nitrogen and poor organic matter content may lead to a decline in pH due to the acidity produced when the ammonium is oxidized to nitrate in the soil (Ukrainetz et al., 1996). An immediate increment in the pH of two acid soils was analyzed under fresh cattle manure treatment, and the effect of manure on soil pH would depend on the properties of the soil and the origin of manure (Whalen et al., 2000). Previous studies also documented that organic manure and compost applications significantly increased electrical conductivity (Cercioglu, 2019a; Cercioglu et al., 2012).

The enhancement of soil physical properties, particularly porosity and structural stability, controls biological and biochemical activities (Tejada et al., 2006). Microbial community compositions of soil and microbial activities are critical to maintaining soil health; thus, there is a need to consider biological soil properties when the evaluation of impacts of manure application takes place. Applications of dairy manure generally maintain or increase SOC and microbial compositions in comparison to mineral fertilizer treatments (Peacock et al., 2001). For instance, Larkin et al. (2006) found that substrate richness, enzyme activities, bacterial populations, and FAME biomarkers for gram-negative organisms were increased by dairy manure additions in all soils. Like manure, composting also has positive effects on soil biological properties. According to Ferreras et al. (2006), microbial respiration of a silt loam soil significantly increased by 10 tons/ha of poultry manure and vermicompost from household solid waste application as compared with control treatment. However, the highest microbial respiration was found under poultry manure additions. The addition of organic wastes such as poultry manure, cotton gin compost, and beet vinasse composted with crushed cotton gin compost enhanced enzyme activity, microbial biomass carbon, and hence soil respiration (Tejada et al., 2009). Kayikcioglu and Okur (2020) conducted a study focused on the effects of raw tobacco waste, composted tobacco waste, and inorganic fertilizer applications on the soil microbial population and reported that ammonium oxidizer bacteria increased under 40 tons/ha of composed tobacco waste application by 354%, respectively.

Responses of the abovementioned properties of soils to the addition of SOM via manuring showed that manure directly or indirectly modifies soil properties and improves soil health. This theory is well documented by a study of cattle and dairy manure in comparison to inorganic fertilization in eastern South Dakota carried out by Ozlu (2016). Two different experimental areas in eastern South Dakota have been conducted to develop recommended rates of dairy manure, cattle manure, and inorganic fertilizers, considering sustainable soil health and optimum crop yield. As it is shown in Figure 7.3, studies conducted in the same field by Ozlu (2016) showed that the addition of manure, both dairy and cattle manure, increased soil heath, including SOM, soil aggregation, available water content, porosity, soil nutrient supply, microbial activity, crop yield, and GHG emissions. In contrast, studies like Cercioglu (2017), which conducted a 3-year field experiment to test the impacts of composts, showed that poultry manure treatment decreased soil bulk density values by 21.8% and increased soil structure stability index by 20.2%. This specific study also found that the highest field capacity and available water content were found under bio-humus treatment by 16% and composted tobacco waste by 10.7%.

7.7.2 Water Quality Concerns under Manure Applications

The agronomic benefits of organic manures are well documented (Wang et al., 2017). However, the quality of water resources is negatively affected due to continuous and intensive agricultural management and fertility practices (Qian et al., 2018). One of the most important factors reflected in water quality issues is N leaching. Like N, the loss of phosphorus and manure-associated microbial communities by runoff (Qian et al., 2018; Rees et al., 2011) are other problems. The contribution of fertilization, such as manure applications, to human health issues increases awareness of the water quality and site effects of manuring in agriculture.

Manure application rates are usually determined by considering the N or P requirements the crop needs. Studies show that the N:P ratios of most manures (2:1 to 4:1) are smaller than the N:P uptake ratios (6:1 to 8:1) of most crops (Oun et al., 2014). This causes an increase in the P level in the soil. When manure is used continuously or intensively, there is an accumulation of N and P that is greater than sufficient to compensate for the loss of N and P from crop harvest. The higher N and P in soils are then removed by water passing through the soil profile or runoff. While N loss generally occurs as nitrate with rainfall, P is transported to water bodies as soluble P or sediment-bound P by surface runoff (Ahmed et al., 2013). Studies in relation to manure applications indicate that N and P are removed from the soil toward water resources by runoff or percolation. Sherman et al. (2020) reported that application of manure (surface) contributed to the greater concentrations of total N, total P, dissolved N and P, and suspended solids in runoff. In another study, Rees et al. (2011) also found that the flow-weighted yearly runoff concentrations of nitrate, nitrite, total N, P, and other plant nutrients (NO_3, NO_2, N_T, and P) were greatly increased due to manure application. Thus, N and P-induced eutrophication may occur in the water ecosystem.

Another influence of organic manure on water quality is microorganisms. Manure may contain some bacteria and animal pathogens. The addition of manure leads to the interaction of both the native soil species and the introduced species (through manure), which are homogenized once balance is attained. Rainfall events may carry manure-associated microbial communities into the water ecosystem as a pollutant (Rieke et al., 2018). Previous studies also increased awareness of these concerns. Thurston-Enriquez et al. (2005) indicated factors that lead to runoff (heavy rainfall) can trigger high microbial load discharge under field conditions. In addition, Hubbs (2002) reported that fecal coliforms from runoff from plots with manure treatments were above 200 CFU 100/mL. In a related study, Brooks et al. (2012), using poultry litter as treatment, found that microbial discharges were consistently higher than the control.

Furthermore, Miller et al. (2004) found that the samples that were taken from a water body close to a cattle grazing area had high, consistent populations of certain biomes, which include heterotrophs, total coliforms, and *Escherichia coli* bacteria. The greater the manure applied, the more likely it is to reduce water quality by transporting microbial communities to water sources (Goss et al., 1998). These pollutants not only affect the water ecosystem but also human health. Therefore, organic manure in agricultural production should be used appropriately and at the recommended rate, considering its effects on the water ecosystem.

7.7.3 Greenhouse Gas Emissions and Manure Applications

Environmental change has been the subject of concentrated examination. A noticeable increase in GHGs is deduced to be the reason behind these changes, and the Kyoto Protocol was formulated to address this threat to the environment. Considering the trouble of alleviating ecological harm brought about by environmental change, all enterprises should endeavor to lessen GHG discharges, with farming being no exception. As indicated by the Intergovernmental Panel on Climate Change (IPCC) Fourth Assessment Report (2007), agrarian CH_4 and N_2O accounted for close to 15% of all GHG sources. Close to 10% of anthropogenic CO_2 and 37% and 65% of CH_4 and N_2O were associated with animal husbandry, respectively (FAO, 2006). While CO_2-eqv is approximately 18% of absolute anthropogenic GHG discharges (FAO, 2009), it was inferred from the IPCC report that the current GHG outflows may be due to general population development and dietary inclines.

The livestock sector handles a tremendous number of natural resources for feed production while also taking care of the waste resulting from the feeding of the animals. Methane, which is one of the GHG gases, is produced when moist organic matter accumulates and decomposes under anaerobic conditions. N_2O is produced as a result of the nitrification and denitrification of organic matter, such as manure or dissolved organic matter, in wastewater by microorganisms. The moisture content of manure and limiting air supply are key factors in addition to periodic turning of the manure, which control denitrification and nitrification processes. In addition to turning and other routine processes involved in making compost, controlling the moisture content and constraining/limiting the available air decrease CH_4 emissions. With the increase in global demand for animal-based products, such as diary products, meat, and eggs, it is of the utmost importance that strategies be put in place to mitigate/reduce the GHG emissions coming from these industries. Reduction of GHG emissions research is generally focused on composting methods, the application of manure, and the contribution added to compost. Also, climate, soil type, type of manure, and farm size or type affect the amount of GHG emissions directly.

Feedlot manure composting increases the greenhouse effect and reduces the agronomic value of compost. High GHG levels in compost do not equate to an increase in emissions or discharge. Pattey et al. (2005) measured GHG emissions from manure stored as stockpile, slurry, and compost and reported that the largest CO_2 equivalents were associated with stored slurry, stockpiled, and passively aerated compost. Different applications on compost piles could change their GHG emissions. To reduce GHG emissions, manures should be stored in undisturbed piles or should be delayed by the first mixing of compost piles (Ahn et al., 2011). In another emission-reducing study, Maeda et al. (2013) surveyed the effects of blending dried grass into inactively circulated air through manure during the composting procedure. It indicated that CO_2 and NH_3 emissions increased with this method. However, N_2O emissions can be reduced with the addition of dried grass. Zhong et al. (2013) examined the effect of pig manure composting on land application and reported that land application of the manure compost has less GHG emissions than pig manure composting. Moreover, Owen and Silver (2015) reported that the current GHG emission levels do not conform to the emissions from dairy manure compost and feature fluid manure systems as promising objective territories for GHG moderation. The varying properties of compost and ecological conditions require a demonstrating approach for improving appraisals of GHG emissions and anticipating the impacts of executive changes for GHG mitigation (Petersen et al., 2013). To reduce GHG emissions from manure, some dietary works could be partially successful. Especially low crude protein diets have been detected to be effective for reducing GHG emissions in growing pigs' manure (Osada et al., 2011). Therefore, organic manure management and application research projects should involve the development and long-term comparison of recommended rates of different types of organic manures for sustainable agricultural productivity.

7.8 CONCLUSION

The management and application of manure are a perfect example of converting waste into a beneficial material on a nano- to global scale. In order to maximize crop yield, long-term comparisons are needed for critical investigations to improve and update the recommendations on manure applications. Organic fertilizers, such as manure, compost, and others, are among the most important pathways for increasing nutrient supply, SOM, crop yield, and improving soil health. However, non-judicious application of manure may cause higher greenhouse gas emissions and lower water quality. The adaptation to specific application rates of manure can considerably improve the soil's physical, chemical, and biological quality. However, the economic aspects of the application of manure cannot be ignored.

REFERENCES

Abu-Zahra, T. and Tahboub, A. (2008) Effect of organic matter sources on chemical properties of the soil and yield of strawberry under organic farming conditions. *World Applied Sciences Journal* 5, 383–388.

Adekiya, A. and Agbede, T. (2017) Effect of methods and time of poultry manure application on soil and leaf nutrient concentrations, growth and fruit yield of tomato (*Lycopersicon esculentum* Mill). *Journal of the Saudi Society of Agricultural Sciences* 16, 383–388.

Agnew, J. and Leonard, J. (2003) The physical properties of compost. *Compost Science & Utilization* 11, 238–264.

Ahmed, S.I., Mickelson, S.K., Pederson, C.H., Baker, J.L., Kanwar, R.S., Lorimor, J.C. and Webber, D.F. (2013) Swine manure rate, timing, and application method effects on post-harvest soil nutrients, crop yield, and potential water quality implications in a corn-soybean rotation. *Transactions of the ASABE* 56, 395–408.

Ahn, H.K., Mulbry, W., White, J. and Kondrad, S. (2011) Pile mixing increases greenhouse gas emissions during composting of dairy manure. *Bioresource Technology* 102, 2904–2909.

Anderson, R.L. (2007) Managing weeds with a dualistic approach of prevention and control. A review. *Agronomy for Sustainable Development* 27, 13–18.

Babur, E., Kara, O., Fathi, R.A., Susam, Y.E., Riaz, M., Arif, M. and Akhtar, K. (2021) Wattle fencing improved soil aggregate stability, organic carbon stocks and biochemical quality by restoring highly eroded mountain region soil. *Journal of Environmental Management* 288, 112489.

Badaruddin, M., Reynolds, M.P. and Ageeb, O.A. (1999) Wheat management in warm environments: Effect of organic and inorganic fertilizers, irrigation frequency, and mulching. *Agronomy Journal* 91, 975–983.

Baumann, D., Kropff, M. and Bastiaans, L. (2000) Intercropping leeks to suppress weeds. *Weed Research (Oxford)* 40, 359–374.

Blanchet, G., Gavazov, K., Bragazza, L. and Sinaj, S. (2016) Responses of soil properties and crop yields to different inorganic and organic amendments in a Swiss conventional farming system. *Agriculture, Ecosystems & Environment* 230, 116–126.

Bogaard, A., Fraser, R., Heaton, T.H., Wallace, M., Vaiglova, P., Charles, M., Jones, G., Evershed, R.P., Styring, A.K. and Andersen, N.H. (2013) Crop manuring and intensive land management by Europe's first farmers. *Proceedings of the National Academy of Sciences* 110, 12589–12594.

Brooks, J., Adeli, A., McLaughlin, M. and Miles, D. (2012) The effect of poultry manure application rate and AlCl3 treatment on bacterial fecal indicators in runoff. *Journal of Water and Health* 10, 619–628.

Bulson, H., Snaydon, R. and Stopes, C. (1997) Effects of plant density on intercropped wheat and field beans in an organic farming system. *The Journal of Agricultural Science* 128, 59–71.

CAST (1996) Integrated animal waste management. Council for Agricultural Science and Technology, West Lincoln Way, Ames.

Celik, I., Gunal, H., Budak, M. and Akpinar, C. (2010) Effects of long-term organic and mineral fertilizers on bulk density and penetration resistance in semi-arid Mediterranean soil conditions. *Geoderma* 160, 236–243.

Cercioglu, M. (2017) The role of organic soil amendments on soil physical properties and yield of maize (*Zea mays* L.). *Communications in Soil Science and Plant Analysis* 48, 683–691.

Cercioglu, M. (2019a) Compost effects on soil nutritional quality and pepper (*Capsicum annuum* L.) yield. *Journal of Agricultural Sciences* 25, 155–162.

Cercioglu, M. (2019b) The impact of soil conditioners on some chemical properties of soil and grain yield of corn (*Zea mays* L.). *Journal of Agricultural Sciences* 25, 224–231.

Cercioglu, M., Okur, B., Delibacak, S. and Ongun, A. (2012) Effects of tobacco waste and farmyard manure on soil properties and yield of lettuce (*Lactuca sativa* L. var. capitata). *Communications in Soil Science and Plant Analysis* 43, 875–886.

Chang, C., Sommerfeldt, T. and Entz, T. (1991) Soil chemistry after eleven annual applications of cattle feedlot manure. *Journal of Environmental Quality* 20, 475–480.

Chaudhary, S., Dheri, G. and Brar, B. (2017) Long-term effects of NPK fertilizers and organic manures on carbon stabilization and management index under rice-wheat cropping system. *Soil and Tillage Research* 166, 59–66.

Curless, M.A., Kelling, K.A., Speth, P.E., Stevenson, W.R. and James, R.V. (2012) Effect of manure application timing on potato yield, quality, and disease incidence. *American Journal of Potato Research* 89, 363–373.

Efthimiadou, A., Froud, W.R., Eleftherohorinos, I., Karkanis, A. and Bilalis, D. (2012) Effects of organic and inorganic amendments on weed management in sweet maize. International Journal of Plant Production 6(3), 291–308.

Entz, M., Guilford, R. and Gulden, R. (2001) Productivity of organic crop production in the eastern region of the Northern Great Plains: A survey of 14 farms. *Canadian Journal of Plant Science* 81, 351–354.

FAO (2006) *Livestock's Long Shadow: Environmental Issues and Options*. Food and Agriculture Organization of the United Nations, Rome, Italy.

FAO (2009) *The State of Food and Agriculture 2009*. Food and Agriculture Organization of the United Nations, Rome, Italy.

FAOSTAT (2020). FAO Statistics, Food and Agriculture Organization of the United Nations, Rome Accessed 17-May-2020 http://faostat.fao.org/

Feinerman, E., Bosch, D.J. and Pease, J.W. (2004) Manure applications and nutrient standards. *American Journal of Agricultural Economics* 86, 14–25.

Ferreras, L., Gómez, E., Toresani, S., Firpo, I. and Rotondo, R. (2006) Effect of organic amendments on some physical, chemical and biological properties in a horticultural soil. *Bioresource Technology* 97, 635–640.

Frick, B. (2005) Weed control in organic systems. In: J.A. Ivany (ed.) *Weed Management in Transition: Topics in Canadian Weed Science, Volume2*. Canadian Weed Science Society, Quebec, pp. 3–22.

Ganzhara, N. (1998) Humus, soil properties, and yield. *Eurasian Soil Science* 31, 738–745.

Garcia-Pausas, J., Rabissi, A., Rovira, P. and Romanyà, J. (2017) Organic fertilization increases C and N stocks and reduces soil organic matter stability in Mediterranean vegetable gardens. *Land Degradation & Development* 28, 691–698.

Goss, M.J., Barry, D.A.J., and Rudolph, D.L. (1998). Groundwater Contamination in Ontario Farm Wells and its association with Agriculture. 1. Results from Drinking water wells. *Journal of Contaminant Hydrology* 32, 267–293.

Goss, M.J., Tubeileh, A. and Goorahoo, D. (2013) A review of the use of organic amendments and the risk to human health. *Advances in Agronomy* 120, 275–379.

Green, B. (2015) Fertilizers in aquaculture. In D. Allen Davis (ed.).*Feed and Feeding Practices in Aquaculture*. Elsevier, pp. 27–52.

Haynes, R.J. and Naidu, R. (1998) Influence of lime, fertilizer and manure applications on soil organic matter content and soil physical conditions: A review. *Nutrient Cycling in Agroecosystems* 51, 123–137.

Hubbs, A.K.B. (2002) Fecal coliform concentration in surface runoff from pastures with applied dairy manure. LSU Master's Theses. 2223. https://repository.lsu.edu/gradschool_theses/222

Intergovernmental Panel on Climate Change (IPCC) (2007), Climate Change 2007: The Scientific Basis. Contribution of Working Group Ito the Fourth Assessment Report of the Intergovernmental Panel on Climate Change, edited by S. Solomon et al., Cambridge Univ. Press, New York.

Kayikcioglu, H.H. and Okur, N. (2020) Tütün Atığı ve Kompostunun Typic Xerofluvent Bir Toprağın Sağlığı ile Kırmızı Biber (*Capsicum annuum* L.) Verimi Üzerine Etkileri. *ISPEC Journal of Agricultural Sciences* 4, 319–345.

Kulshreshtha, S., Grant, C., Amiro, B., Ominski, K., Legesse, G. and Alemu, A. (2016) Economic and greenhouse gas emission impacts of doubling of forage area in Manitoba, Canada. *Canadian Journal of Soil Science* 97, 487–496.

Larkin, R.P., Honeycutt, C.W. and Griffin, T.S. (2006) Effect of swine and dairy manure amendments on microbial communities in three soils as influenced by environmental conditions. *Biology and Fertility of Soils* 43, 51–61.

Leighty, C.E. (1938) Crop rotation. In: Gove Hambidge (ed.) *Soils and Men: Yearbook of Agriculture*. U.S. Department of Agriculture, Government Printing Office, Washington, DC, pp. 406–430.

Liebman, M. and Davis, A. (2000) Integration of soil, crop and weed management in low-external-input farming systems. Weed Research 40, 27–48.

Liebman, M., Staver, C.P. and Mohler, C. (2001) Crop diversification for weed management. In: M.Liebman and C.P.Staver (eds.) *Ecological Management of Agricultural Needs*. Cambridge University Press, Cambridge, UK, pp. 322–374.

Liu, C.A. and Zhou, L.M. (2017) Soil organic carbon sequestration and fertility response to newly built terraces with organic manure and mineral fertilizer in a semi-arid environment. *Soil and Tillage Research* 172, 39–47.

Lorimor, J. (2000) *Manure Characteristics*. Iowa State University, Iowa.

Lu, S., Yu, X. and Zong, Y. (2019) Nano-microscale porosity and pore size distribution in aggregates of paddy soil as affected by long-term mineral and organic fertilization under rice-wheat cropping system. *Soil and Tillage Research* 186, 191–199.

Maeda, K., Hanajima, D., Morioka, R., Toyoda, S., Yoshida, N. and Osada, T. (2013) Mitigation of greenhouse gas emission from the cattle manure composting process by use of a bulking agent. *Soil Science and Plant Nutrition* 59, 96–106.

Magdoff, F. (1995). Soil quality and management. In: M.A. Altieri (ed.) *Agro-Ecology. The Science* of *Sustainable Agriculture*. CRC Press, Boca Raton, FL, pp. 349–364.

Miller, J.J., Handerek, B.P., Beasley, B.W., Olson, E.C., Yanke, L.J., Larney, F.J., McAllister, T.A., Olson, B.M., Selinger, L.B. and Chanasyk, D.S. (2004) Quantity and quality of runoff from a beef cattle feedlot in southern Alberta. *Journal of Environmental Quality* 33, 1088–1097.

Mt, J. and Schlather, K.J. (1994) Incidence of weed seed in cow (Bos sp.) manure and its importance as a weed source for cropland. Weed Technology 8, 304–310.

Nannipieri, P., Muccini, L. and Ciardi, C. (1983) Microbial biomass and enzyme activities: Production and persistence. *Soil Biology and Biochemistry* 15, 679–685.

Ndukwe, O., Muoneke, C.O. and Baiyeri, K. (2011) Effect of the time of poultry manure application and cultivar on the growth, yield and fruit quality of plantains (*Musa* spp. AAB). *Tropical and Subtropical Agroecosystems* 14, 261–270.

Osada, T., Takada, R. and Shinzato, I. (2011) Potential reduction of greenhouse gas emission from swine manure by using a low-protein diet supplemented with synthetic amino acids. *Animal Feed Science and Technology* 166, 562–574.

Oun, A., Kumar, A., Harrigan, T., Angelakis, A. and Xagoraraki, I. (2014) Effects of biosolids and manure application on microbial water quality in rural areas in the US. *Water* 6, 3701–3723.

Owen, J.J. and Silver, W.L. (2015) Greenhouse gas emissions from dairy manure management: A review of field-based studies. *Global Change Biology* 21, 550–565.

Ozlu, E. (2016) Long-term impacts of annual cattle manure and fertilizer on soil quality under corn-soybean rotation in eastern South Dakota. South Dakota State University. Electronic Theses and Dissertations. 1092. https://openprairie.sdstate.edu/etd/1092

Ozlu, E. (2020) Dynamics of soil aggregate formation in different ecosystems. University of Wisconsin-Madison.

Ozlu, E. and Arriaga, F.J. (2021) The role of carbon stabilization and minerals on soil aggregation in different ecosystems. *Catena* 202, 105303.

Ozlu, E. and Kumar, S. (2018a) Response of soil organic carbon, pH, electrical conductivity, and water stable aggregates to long-term annual manure and inorganic fertilizer. *Soil Science Society of America Journal* 82, 1243–1251.

Ozlu, E. and Kumar, S. (2018b) Response of surface GHG fluxes to long-term manure and inorganic fertilizer application in corn and soybean rotation. *Science of the Total Environment* 626, 817–825.

Ozlu, E., Kumar, S. and Arriaga, F.J. (2019a) Responses of long-term cattle manure on soil physical and hydraulic properties under a corn-soybean rotation at two locations in eastern South Dakota. *Soil Science Society of America Journal* 83, 1459–1467.

Ozlu, E., Sandhu, S.S., Kumar, S. and Arriaga, F.J. (2019b) Soil health indicators impacted by long-term cattle manure and inorganic fertilizer application in a corn-soybean rotation of South Dakota. *Scientific Reports* 9, 1–11.

Papadopoulos, A., Bird, N., Whitmore, A. and Mooney, S. (2009) Investigating the effects of organic and conventional management on soil aggregate stability using X-ray computed tomography. *European Journal of Soil Science* 60, 360–368.

Pattey, E., Trzcinski, M. and Desjardins, R. (2005) Quantifying the reduction of greenhouse gas emissions as a result of composting dairy and beef cattle manure. *Nutrient Cycling in Agroecosystems* 72, 173–187.

Peacock, A.G., Mullen, M., Ringelberg, D., Tyler, D., Hedrick, D., Gale, P. and White, D. (2001) Soil microbial community responses to dairy manure or ammonium nitrate applications. *Soil Biology and Biochemistry* 33, 1011–1019.

Petersen, S.O., Blanchard, M., Chadwick, D., Del Prado, A., Edouard, N., Mosquera, J. and Sommer, S.G. (2013) Manure management for greenhouse gas mitigation. *Animal* 7, 266–282.

Prietzel, J., Müller, S., Kögel-Knabner, I., Thieme, J., Jaye, C. and Fischer, D. (2018) Comparison of soil organic carbon speciation using C NEXAFS and CPMAS ^{13}C NMR spectroscopy. *Science of the Total Environment* 628, 906–918.

Qian, X., Shen, G., Wang, Z., Zhang, X. and Hong, Z. (2018) Effect of swine liquid manure application in paddy field on water quality, soil fertility and crop yields. *Paddy and Water Environment* 16, 15–22.

Rasmussen, K. (2002) Influence of liquid manure application method on weed control in spring cereals. *Weed Research* 42, 287–298.

Rees, H., Chow, T., Zebarth, B., Xing, Z., Toner, P., Lavoie, J. and Daigle, J.L. (2011) Effects of supplemental poultry manure applications on soil erosion and runoff water quality from a loam soil under potato production in northwestern New Brunswick. *Canadian Journal of Soil Science* 91, 595–613.

Rieke, E.L., Soupir, M.L., Moorman, T.B., Yang, F. and Howe, A.C. (2018) Temporal dynamics of bacterial communities in soil and leachate water after swine manure application. *Frontiers in Microbiology* 9, 3197.

Rosen, C.J., and Bierman, P.M. *Nutrient Management for Fruit and Vegetable Crop Production: Using Manure and Compost as Nutrient Sources for Fruit and Vegetable Crops*; University of Minnesota Extension Service: Twin Cities, MN, USA, 2005. http://hdl.handle.net/11299/200639

Rui, M., Han, Y., Ali, A., Tang, X. and Rui, Y. (2017). Impact on yield and heavy metal accumulation of lettuce (var. ramosa Hort.) of different kinds and dosage of organic manure. *Fresenius Environmental Bulletin* 26, 3493–3500.

Sattar, M. and Gaur, A. (1989) Effect of VA-mycorrhiza and phosphate dissolving microorganisms on the yield and phosphorus uptake of wheat (*Triticum vulgare*) [in Bangladesh]. *Bangladesh Journal of Agriculture*, 14(3), 233–239.

Scotti, R., D'ascoli, R., Gonzalez Caceres, M., Bonanomi, G., Sultana, S., Cozzolino, L., Scelza, R., Zoina, A. and Rao, M. (2015) Combined use of compost and wood scraps to increase carbon stock and improve soil quality in intensive farming systems. *European Journal of Soil Science* 66, 463–475.

Seleiman, M.F. and Hafez, E.M. (2021) Optimizing inputs management for sustainable agricultural development. In Hassan Awaad, Mohamed Abu-hashim, Abdelazim Negm (eds.). *Mitigating Environmental Stresses for Agricultural Sustainability in Egypt*. Springer Water; Springer, Cham, Switzerland, pp. 487–507.

Sherman, J.F., Young, E.O., Coblentz, W.K. and Cavadini, J. (2020) Runoff water quality after low-disturbance manure application in an alfalfa-grass hay crop forage system. *Journal of Environmental Quality* 49, 663–674.

Smith, W., Qi, Z., Grant, B., VanderZaag, A. and Desjardins, R. (2019) Comparing hydrological frameworks for simulating crop biomass, water and nitrogen dynamics in a tile drained soybean-corn system: Cascade vs computational approach. *Journal of Hydrology* X2, 100015.

Teasdale, J.R. (1996) Contribution of cover crops to weed management in sustainable agricultural systems. *Journal of Production Agriculture* 9, 475–479.

Tejada, M., Garcia, C., Gonzalez, J. and Hernandez, M. (2006) Use of organic amendment as a strategy for saline soil remediation: Influence on the physical, chemical and biological properties of soil. *Soil Biology and Biochemistry* 38, 1413–1421.

Tejada, M., Hernandez, M. and Garcia, C. (2009) Soil restoration using composted plant residues: Effects on soil properties. *Soil and Tillage Research* 102, 109–117.

Thurston-Enriquez, J.A., Gilley, J.E. and Eghball, B. (2005) Microbial quality of runoff following land application of cattle manure and swine slurry. *Journal of Water and Health* 3, 157–171.

Ukrainetz, H., Campbell, C., Biederbeck, V., Curtin, D. and Bouman, O. (1996) Yield and protein content of cereals and oilseed as influenced by long-term use of urea and anhydrous ammonia. *Canadian Journal of Plant Science* 76, 27–32.

USDA. (1999). Agricultural waste management field handbook, National Engineering Handbook Part 651. US Department of Agriculture, Natural Resource Conservation Service. Washington, DC. www.wsi.nrcs.usda.gov/products/W2Q/AWM/handbk.htm

Van Es, H.M., Sogbedji, J.M. and Schindelbeck, R.R. (2006) Effect of manure application timing, crop, and soil type on nitrate leaching. *Journal of Environmental Quality* 35, 670–679.

VeVerka, J., Udawatta, R. and Kremer, R. (2019) Soil health indicator responses on Missouri claypan soils affected by landscape position, depth, and management practices. *Journal of Soil and Water Conservation* 74, 126–137.

Walz, E. (1999) Third Biennial National Organic Farmers' Survey: Organic Farming Research Foundation. Santa Cruz, CA.

Wang, Y., Dong, H., Zhu, Z., Gerber, P.J., Xin, H., Smith, P., Opio, C., Steinfeld, H. and Chadwick, D. (2017) Mitigating greenhouse gas and ammonia emissions from swine manure management: A system analysis. *Environmental Science & Technology* 51, 4503–4511.

Weber, J., Karczewska, A., Drozd, J., Licznar, M., Licznar, S., Jamroz, E. and Kocowicz, A. (2007) Agricultural and ecological aspects of a sandy soil as affected by the application of municipal solid waste composts. *Soil Biology and Biochemistry* 39, 1294–1302.

Whalen, J.K., Chang, C., Clayton, G.W. and Carefoot, J.P. (2000) Cattle manure amendments can increase the pH of acid soils. *Soil Science Society of America Journal* 64, 962–966.

Willey, R. (1990) Resource use in intercropping systems. *Agricultural Water Management* 17, 215–231.

Xin, X., Qin, S., Zhang, J., Zhu, A. and Zhang, C. (2015) Dynamics of phosphorus in fluvo-aquic soil under long-term fertilization. *Journal of Plant Nutrition and Fertilizer* 21, 1514–1520.

Xu, L., Wang, M., Tian, Y., Shi, X., Shi, Y., Yu, Q., Xu, S., Pan, J., Li, X. and Xie, X. (2020) Relationship between macropores and soil organic carbon fractions under long-term organic manure application. *Land Degradation & Development* 31, 1344–1354.

Zhang, H., Ding, W., Yu, H. and He, X. (2015) Linking organic carbon accumulation to microbial community dynamics in a sandy loam soil: Result of 20 years compost and inorganic fertilizers repeated application experiment. *Biology and Fertility of Soils* 51, 137–150.

Zhong, J., Wei, Y., Wan, H., Wu, Y., Zheng, J., Han, S. and Zheng, B. (2013) Greenhouse gas emission from the total process of swine manure composting and land application of compost. *Atmospheric Environment* 81, 348–355.

8 Efficient Use of Land Resources for Regenerative Agriculture

Surabhi Hota, K.K. Mourya, Arijit Barman,
Gopal Tiwari, Ajay Satpute, Ashok Kumar, R.S. Meena,
Prakash Kumar Jha, Sayantan Sahu, and U.S. Saikia

8.1 INTRODUCTION

Land is a fundamental component of a nation's natural resource base that is required for both agricultural and non-agricultural purposes. Land used in agriculture is a vital resource and condition for human survival and is the ultimate guarantee for realizing people's food security (Viana et al., 2022; Zhou et al., 2021; Liu and Zhou, 2021; Chen et al., 2021). The United Nations Convention to Combat Desertification (UNCCD) defines land as "the terrestrial bio-productive system that comprises soil, vegetation, other biota, and the ecological and hydrological processes that operate within the system". Growing population and consequent growing needs for food, clean water, products from natural resources and the need for rapid socio-economic development are creating increasing pressures on land resources in many countries of the world. Out of the global land area of 13.2 billion ha, 12% of the area is under agriculture. Globally, the per capita cultivated land available is about 0.23 ha. In 1960, it was 0.5 ha (FAO, 2021). This shows that per capita arable land is shrinking. Hence, the need to produce more from limited available land is arising, resulting in the degradation of health and quality of agricultural soils. Hence, the concept of regenerative agriculture (RA) gained importance, which has been defined as 'an approach to farming that uses soil conservation as the entry point to regenerate and contribute to multiple ecosystem services' (Schreefel et al., 2020). Basically, RA is returning more to the soil than extracted, to maintain the soil health for long term. However, this concept is a recent one, and there is a very limited knowledge of its uncertain benefit through practical implementation. Very few research work exists on regenerative agriculture, and its practical implementation in the field is still has a huge gap. Land among all natural resources is obviously an integral part of agriculture, and achieving RA requires efficient use of the available land in a sustainable manner. In this chapter, we have discussed in detail how land resources can be utilized sustainably for RA, with an aim to provide a brief idea about this emerging concept to the readers.

8.2 INVENTORY OF LAND RESOURCES

Soil is the essential component of land in the terrestrial ecosystem and performs a range of ecosystem services, including biomass production, filtering, buffering, storing nutrients, providing habitat for organisms, serving as a repository of cultural heritage, etc. (Sheals, 1969; Wall and Nielsen, 2012). Soils provide more than 90% of food commodities. Hence, the inventory of land resources in terms of agriculture basically includes the inventory of agricultural soils. The capacity of a land parcel to support crop growth is closely associated with the intrinsic properties of soil. The intrinsic properties of soil are the result of complex interactions between various soil formation factors: parent material, relief or topography, climate, organisms and time, or the process called pedogenesis

DOI: 10.1201/9781003309581-10

(Jenny, 1941; Resende et al., 2014). Detailed information about land resources and their distribution is important for countries' sustainable agricultural land use planning and the allocation of lands for other developmental activities (Reddy, 2018). Hence, the study of soil resources is necessary to generate sufficient soil datasets with respect to their morphology, physical, chemical and biological properties and to characterize the soils in terms of their potentials and limitations. The collection of detailed soil information requires intensive sampling and is expensive for developing countries. However, in recent years, with the aid of geo-information technology, geostatistics, remotely sensed imagery and digital elevation models (DEM) that are freely available in the public domain, soil survey procedures have become easier and less time-consuming than conventional soil survey procedures (Garg et al., 2020). For increasing the reliability and quality of data, satellite remote sensing, in conjunction with a geographic information system (GIS), has proved to be an extremely useful tool for generating soil survey information (Thilagam and Sivasamy, 2013). Kalra et al. (2010) stated that integration of remote sensing within a GIS database can decrease the cost, reduce the time, and increase the detailed information generated through soil surveys. The potential utility of remote sensing data has been well recognized in mapping and assessing land attributes such as physiography, soils, land use/land cover, relief and soil erosion pattern (Potdar et al., 2003; Velmurugan and Carlos, 2009; Patil et al., 2010), discussed in detail in the following sections.

8.2.1 Approaches of Land Resource Inventory

Geospatial techniques include the techniques of Remote Sensing (RS), Geographical information system (GIS), Global positioning system (GPS) and Geostatistics that are used for collecting, analysing and interpreting spatial data. Rapid developments in these techniques have opened new approaches to meet the increasing demand for land resources information at large scale for resource planning and studying the various aspects of soils in spatial and temporal domain (Shrestha, 2006; Yeung and Lo, 2002). Timely and steadfast information on nature, extent and spatial distribution of soils is very important for the sustainable utilization of available soil resources. The Geospatial techniques have amplified the efficiency of soil resource studies (Sahu et al., 2015). RS reduces the time required for delineation and visual interpretation of landform and land uses and helps at scales ranging from regional to local levels. GIS along with RS aids to the understanding of the location to be surveyed. GPS helps to record the geographical coordinates and thereby helps to incorporate the soil information into the digital platform. Geostatistics helps in filling the gap of soil resource information for unreachable areas by interpolation techniques. These techniques altogether make the collection, analysis, interpretation and mapping of soil resource information less time-consuming and cost-effective. Many researches have taken the aid of geospatial techniques for the delineation of land use, landform, base map preparation, soil survey and soil mapping (Dwivedi, 2001; Srivastava and Saxena, 2004). Earlier, aerial photos were used for gathering spatial information and mapping. In India, the use of satellite imagery or RS for soil survey and mapping gained appreciation during the early 1980s after the launch of Landsat-1 in 1972 (Velayutham, 1999). During that period, the coarse data of spatial resolution 70 m or more, from IRS LISS-I, AWiFs and LANDSAT-MSS, were used for small-scale mapping (1:250,000 or smaller). During the mid-eighties, high-resolution data of Landsat thematic maps and IRS-LISS II came into use to map soils at 1:50,000 but were limited to soil series or family level (Thilagam and Sivasamy, 2013). The growing necessity of large-scale soil mapping demands a cost and time-effective approach. Large-scale soil mapping by traditional method is expensive and time-consuming as large number of observations are involved (Simon, 2010). The use of satellite imagery can save 60%–80% time compared to manual methods (Liengsakul et al., 1993). The use of high-resolution satellite data like IRS-P6 LISS-III (Velmurugan and Carlos, 2009) and IRS-P6 LISS-IV (Walia et al., 2010; Reddy et al., 2013; Das et al., 2012) has proven to be successful in soil mapping at small, medium and large scales.

In recent years, large-scale soil resource information generation and mapping have been possible by using data from IRS-P6 (LISS-IV In sensor), Cartosat-1, Cartosat-2 and IKONOS. Srivastava and Saxena (2004) prepared Physiography Landuse Units (PLU) maps by using merged IRS-1C PAN (5.8 m) and LISS III (23 m) data for village-level soil mapping (1:12,500 scale) in a basaltic terrain of Nagpur, Maharashtra. Wadodkar and Ravishankar (2011) generated soil resource information at large scale using IRS – Resourcesat-1 LISS-IV and Cartosat-1 merged data in Mohammad village of Nalgonda district of Telangana state and prepared land use plan. Similarly, using IRS Resourcesat-1+Cartosat data, soil resource information and map were generated at 1:10,000 scale (Nagaraju and Gajbhiye, 2014). Jangir et al. (2018) generated detailed soil resource information (1:10,000 scale) for Bharuch district, Gujrat, using IRS-P6 LISS IV and Cartosat-1 images. Bandyopadhyaya et al. (2017) used IRS-P6 LISS IV and Cartosat-1 images for soil resource study at 1:10,000 scale of an upper Brahmaputra valley.IRS-P6 LISS IV and Cartosat-1 images are available on payment basis. However, there are also freely available satellite imageries of Sentinnel-2 and SRTM and ALOS DEM, which have been successfully used for soil resource study and mapping at 1:10,000 scale (Jangir et al., 2020).

Soil map preparation requires the preparation of land use/land cover (LULC) maps and landform maps, which are then superimposed or merged to delineate the Landscape ecological units (LEUs), which serve as base maps, and these units are considered as the basic units of soil survey. Land use/land cover analysis takes into account the elements of visual interpretations like colour, texture and shape of the surface features, and then, these features are classified into the LULC units. Many studies have included the preparation of LULC maps as a pre-requisite of soil map generation (Sahu et al., 2014; Ramteke et al., 2014; Nagaraju et al., 2015) and also to monitor the spatial and temporal changes in LULC (Kotoky et al., 2012).

Bisht and Kothari (2001) delineated land use/land cover classes of a Watershed in Uttaranchal state using visual interpretation of Landsat 5 TM image in GIS software. Kumar et al. (2004) prepared LULC map of Kandi Belt of Jammu using IRS-1C LISS III data. Bose et al. (2008) used IRS P6 LISS-III to prepare major land use land cover map of Sundarban area of West Bengal. IRS-1D LISS-Ill data was used to prepare land use/land cover map of Lendi watershed of Chandrapur district of Maharashtra (Patil et al., 2010).

Kotoky et al. (2012) studied changes in LULC along the Dhansiri River channel, Assam to evaluate the changes in LULC over 33 years from 1975 to 2008 along Dhansiri River channel, Assam. Das et al. (2012) used IRS-P6 LISS-IV and Cartosat-1 merged image to classify LULC of nine villages of Tinsukia districts of Assam. Phukan et al. (2013) determined LULC changes in Golaghat district of Assam over 20 years period, by using multitemporal satellite imagery of LANDSAT ETM of 1989, and IRS LISS III of 2009. Saikia et al. (2019) determined the erosion–deposition of the Brahmaputra River for the period 1973–2014 using Landsat MSS, TM and OLI images using remote sensing software of ERDAS Imagine and ArcGIS 10.1.

Landform analysis is important in understanding the processes of pedogenesis and variations in soil forming factors as well as variations in soil properties. The elevation, slope, aspect, plain curvature, profile curvature, topographic wetness index and drainage or flow direction are the earth surface parameters that are used for visual interpretation and delineation of landform units (Sahu et al., 2014). Conventional approaches of landform delineation include studying of topographical maps, interpretation from aerial photographs and field measurements, which was indeed cumbersome. But nowadays, the earth surface parameters can be obtained from a satellite imagery, by using a digital elevation model (DEM) of various radiometric resolutions, like Cartosat-1 (2.5m) (Bandyopadhyaya et al., 2017), SRTM (30m), ALOS (12.5m) (Jangir et al., 2020). A DEM is an electronic model of the earth's surface that can be stored and manipulated in a computer (Brough, 1986). It has proven to be beneficial in providing greater functional options than the conventional method of delineation and study of topography. DEM enhances the perception of human eye of viewing the land surface features by enabling a 3D view and makes the delineation of landscape units easier (Ziadat, 2010). Reddy et al. (2004) used IRS-P6-LISS III data for systematic analysis of various landform characteristics of a basaltic terrain in central India by taking into account drainage morphometry, soil depth, available water capacity (AWC) and erosion characteristics and found the GIS-based method to be efficient than conventional methods. Vara Prasad Rao et al. (2008) classified the landforms of Ramachandrapuram mandal of Chittoor district of Andhra Pradesh into plain, upland and using GIS.

8.2.2 Characterization of Land Resources

After the preparation of a base map, say LEU or other terms used such terrain mapping units (TMUs), the soil survey is carried out in the field. As per the need of the surveyor, the depth of soil sample collection varies. For example, if the researcher is interested only in shallow rooted or field crops like paddy, they may only consider the properties of the top 15 cm soil layer, and if it is orchard crop, the sampling may be done for the upper 50 cm of soil layer. However, if we are interested in characterizing the entire land for its permanent or intrinsic properties, which serve as a base information dataset for any kind of land use planning, then a soil profile study is carried out. In each LEU, at least one soil profile pit (1.5 m × 1 m and to a depth of underlying rock or 150 cm, whichever is lesser) is dug. The horizon-wise morphological properties such as depth, colour, structure, texture, gravels, consistence and mottles are studied and recorded in field soil survey sheets. The morphological parameters are described according to the United States Department of Agriculture (USDA) soil description guidelines (Soil Survey Staff, 2014). Soil samples are collected from all the horizons from the studied profiles and stored in sterile polythene bags, and again kept in the tagged cloth bags. Soils are then classified up to phase level by following the soil correlation procedure (Reddy, 2006). Classifying a soil as per taxonomy makes the interpretation of the intrinsic properties of soils easier, thereby evaluating the land for viable land use planning.

8.2.3 Evaluation of Land Resources

A sustainable agricultural land use plan requires not only the characterization of soils for their physical and chemical properties but also takes account of climate, the suitability of crops, and the socioeconomic conditions of the farmers (Bindraban et al., 2000). Land evaluation can be defined as the scientific procedure to assess the potential and constraints of a given land parcel for agricultural purposes (Rossiter, 1996). Thus, defining the relationship between crop requirements and soil characteristics is the first step in sustainable land use planning (Bonfante and Bouma, 2015). It becomes important to interpret soil survey information and maps in a user-friendly way so that they can be used for crop planning (Fontes et al., 2009). Land evaluation requires knowledge of soil and landform characteristics, climatic data for the area, and crop requirements. There are both classical and modern concepts of land evaluation that have been used for centuries and evolved over time. The classical concepts include the land capability classification (LCC), land suitability evaluation by the FAO and Storie Index, which have been used commonly. The modern concepts are based mostly on different simulation models, for example, the Automated Land Evaluation System (ALES). These concepts are being discussed in this section.

8.2.3.1 Land Suitability and Capability Assessment

8.2.3.1.1 Land Capability Classification (LCC)

Land capability classification (LCC) is the first method of land evaluation developed by Klingebiel and Montgomery (1966). The system classifies soils into eight classes (represented as I–VIII), based on the degree of limitations of the particular land such as erosion (e), excess wetness (w), rooting depth (s), and climatic limitation (c). This system is still widely used by researchers to classify land based on its capability for regional planning. The land capability classification has three categories, viz., capability unit, capability subclass, and capability class. The objective of capability classification is to group soils based on their capability for growing agricultural field crops and plantation crops while protecting soil health over an extensive time period. Class I–IV are arable lands, and

TABLE 8.1

USDA NRCS Criteria for Land Capability Classification

Characteristics	Class I	Class II	Class III	Class IV	Class V	Class VI	Class VII	Class VIII
Slope (%)	0–1	1–3	3–8	8–15	<3	15–30	30–50	30–50
Erosion	Nil	e0	e1	e2	e3	e0	e1	e2
Texture	l	cl	sl, c	scl	s, c	ls, cl	ls, c, s	ls, c, s
Depth (cm)	>150	150–100	100–50	50–25	50–150+	25–10	<10	NA
Soil pH	5.1–8.0	8.0–8.4, 4.5–5.1	>8.4	NA	NA	<3.6	NA	NA
Permeability	Moderate	Mod, Rapid	Rapid;Slow	Very Rapid	NA	NA	NA	NA

l, loam; cl, clay loam; sl, sandy loam; c, clay; scl, sandy clay loam; s, sand; ls, loamy sand.

class V–VIII are non-arable lands, with no limitations on class I lands and increasing limitations up to class VIII lands. Land capability subclasses are soil groups within one class that are designated by considering the limitations, e.g., IIe (Class II land with major limitations caused by erosion). Land capability units are homogeneous soil mapping units that behave similarly in terms of management practices and have the same degree of constraints. Land capability units are designated by adding an Arabic number (e.g., 1,2,3) to the land capability subclass, e.g., IIe1 or IIe2, etc. (Fenton, 2020) (Table 8.1).

8.2.3.1.2 Land Suitability Evaluation

The land suitability evaluation framework developed by FAO is based on matching land attributes with requirements of land use and includes the factors of climate, soil and vegetation (FAO, 1976). A multiplicative index based on profile development, development of A horizon, texture, soil depth, drainage, and base saturation to evaluate the soils was developed by Riquier et al. (1970). Sys and Frankart (1971) developed a parametric approach for land capability classification. It includes the scoring of all factors on the basis of the degree to which they impact the land use potential. The factors with high impact are scored 1.0 and the factors with lowest impact 0.0., or it ranges between 1.0 and 0.0.

Storie (1978) developed a semi-quantitative method for rating soils mainly for agriculture productions based on crop productivity data. Later on, this approach was revised, and the soil productivity was determined based on the degree of profile development, surface texture, slope, drainage, micro-relief, erosion, alkalinity, acidity, and fertility. The major limitation of Storie ratings is that the scoring options for a particular factor or sub-factor have broad ranges, which creates a great scope for bias among scientists (O'Geen and Southard, 2005). O'Geen (2008) modified the Storie Index (SI), which is calculated by the following equation:

$$SI = [(factor\ A/100) \times (factor\ B/100) \times (factor\ C/100) \times (factor\ X/100)] \times 100$$

where SI is the Storie Index, Factor A is the degree of profile development; factor B is the surface texture; factor C is the slope class, and factor X is the other soil and land scape conditions affecting crop growth. Lands were categorized into five suitability classes based on SI values (Storie, 1978) as presented in Table 8.2.

Naidu et al. (2006) developed a manual for soil site suitability evaluation for major crops across India which includes cereals, pulses, oilseeds, fruit, vegetables and plantation crops. Sehgal (1991) evaluated the soil site suitability of black soils of Nagpur for growing cotton for their suitability to grow cotton based on the FAO method. They concluded that the method is suitable for evaluating soils in semi-arid to sub-humid regions.

TABLE 8.2
Storie Index Rating of Soils (Storie, 1978)

Storie Index (SI) Values	Suitability Class
0.8–1	Excellent
0.6–0.8	Good
0.4–0.6	Fair
0.2–0.4	Poor
0.0–0.2	Very poor

Storie index was used by Sharma and Chaudhary (2008) to evaluate the soils of a watershed in Shiwalik hills of Himachal Pradesh and revealed that land productivity of 4.45%, 8.29% and 15.45% of total area of the watershed were fair, poor and very poor respectively. Verheye (1991) developed an integrative land evaluation approach. This approach was based on the assumption that crop performance is the outcome of the combined effect of physical, human and capital resources of an area.

8.2.3.1.3   Fertility Capability Classification (FCC)

Another system of land evaluation is the fertility capability classification (FCC) system developed by Buol et al. (1975) with the intent to bring together soil classification and soil fertility into a single frame. It is basically grouping the soils according to the fertility constraints they portray, in a quantitative manner for their proper management. FCC was later revised by Sanchez et al. (1982) in the second approximation. The nature of data for soil classification and taxonomic purposes gives more weightage to the subsurface soil properties rather than surface properties because of their more permanent nature, while the interest of the people working in soil fertility is confined to the plough layer and its management. Hence, the FCC system was brought into existence to classify soils into fertility classes using the taxonomic unit data to make technical soil classification more useful for fertility management purposes. The system comprises three levels, viz., type (texture of surface soil), sub-strata type (texture of sub-surface soil) and modifiers with respect to their characteristics in the 50 cm depth of soil. The term "topsoil" refers to the plough layer or the top 20 cm of the soil, whichever is shallower. The term "subsoil" includes the depth interval between the topsoil and 60 cm depth.

In India, Prasad (2000) used the FCC system to convert the taxonomic units into fertility classes for soils of Konheri watershed located in semi-arid tropics (SAT) India. He opined that FCC could give a basic idea of fertility management. Kalaiselvi et al. (2019) have used FCC to classify soils of Palani block in a semi-arid tropical region of Tamil Nadu. They concluded that the FCC was beneficial in identifying the potential constraints of fertility and in suggesting better management options. Hota et al. (2022b) used FCC to categorize soils of lower Assam.

8.2.3.2   Land Quality Assessment

Maintaining land quality requires a better understanding of the multiple functions of soil and a better understanding of the interaction between agricultural activities and soil quality. Traditional measures of land capability and erodibility need to be augmented to better reflect overall land quality. According to Pieri et al. (1995), land quality is the condition and capacity of land, including its soil, weather and biological properties, for purposes of production, conservation and environmental management. Karlen et al. (2013) defined land quality as the capacity of the functions resulting from the nature of the soil within a certain ecosystem and depending on its use under a certain management. FAO (1976) segregated the land qualities into two groups:

TABLE 8.3
Land Quality Classes

Land Quality Classes	Description
Class 1	This is prime land. Soils are highly productive, with few management-related constraints. Soil temperature and moisture conditions are ideal for annual crops. Risk for sustainable crop production is generally less than 20%.
Classes 2 and 3	These soils have few problems for sustainable production. Their productivity is generally very high; however, care must be taken to reduce potential degradation. Risk for sustainable crop production is generally 20%–40%, but risks can be reduced with good conservation practices.
Classes 4, 5 and 6	These soils are not suited for grain crop production without important inputs of conservation management. In fact, no grain production must be contemplated in the absence of a good conservation plan. Lack of plant nutrients is a major constraint. Soil degradation must be continuously monitored. Productivity is not high. Risk for sustainable grain crop production is 40%–60%.
Class 7	These soils are definitely not suitable for low-input crop production. Their low resilience makes them easily prone to degradation. They should be retained as natural forests or range. Risk for sustainable grain crop production is 60%–80%.
Classes 8 and 9	These soils belong to very fragile ecosystems or are very uneconomical to use for crop production. They should be retained in their natural state. Risk for sustainable crop production is greater than 80%.

1. **Internal qualities:** Water holding capacity; oxygen availability; availability of foot hold to roots; tolerance to iron-induced chlorosis; nutrient availability; resistance to structural degradation of top soil; absence of salinity and alkalinity.
2. **External qualities:** Correct temperature regime; resistance against erosion; ability for layout of farm plan and workability.

Based on these groups, the land quality can be classified into nine classes. Class 1 is the class with the most desirable quality and class 9 is the class with the poorest quality. Just about 3% of the global land surface can be regarded as Class I land (Prime), and this is not located in the tropics (Lal, 1994, 2009). An added 8% of land is in Classes II and III. This 11% of land must give food to the 6 billion people today and to 7.6 billion people expected in 2020 (Table 8.3).

Land quality should be assessed for specific types of land use, management and agro-ecological zones (AEZs) in a country. A robust assessment of land quality requires a multi-decision approach that requires the standardization and weighting of the effects of many factors that affect each other, such as physical, chemical, morphological, topographic and climatic soil characteristics, which are interrelated, and differentiated (Mokarram and Mirsoleimani, 2018). Otherwise, trends and performance cannot be sensibly monitored, interpreted and reported. This requires the development and application of spatially located and (normally) geo-referenced temporal databases of the variables to be used to develop the land quality indicators (LQIs).

Assessment of land quality is needed to:

1. Identify the characteristics needed to determine appropriate land use or to address a single resource problem,
2. Monitor the long-term impact of agricultural practices on land properties,
3. Assess the economic impact of management practices,
4. Assess the effectiveness of policies designed to address factors affecting land quality; and improve economic assessments of land by including both economic and environmental values (Granatstein and Bezdicek, 1992).

LQIs play an important role in the assessment of land quality (Pieri et al., 1995). With respect to agriculture, quantitative assessments of the production ability of the land that reflects soil and climatic conditions are useful LQIs. Many methods have been developed for land quality assessment, from qualitative or semi-quantitative visual approaches (Shepherd, 2009) to quantitative methods based on laboratory analysis and calculating land quality index (LQI) using mathematic and statistical methods (Karlen et al., 1998; Imaz et al., 2010; Askari and Holden, 2014).

Unlike SQI, computing a land quality index (LQI) becomes ideally unattainable because the land quality indicators cannot be accurately quantified in an open system as in soil/land. It is possible to attain accuracy through simulation of natural conditions of all the functional factors of land quality. Determining LQI is more challenging because of the contribution of several factors that are responsible towards its development (Ray et al., 2014).

The LQI is commonly developed using the following process:

1. Calculate the climate quality index (CQI) using the following equation

$$CQI = ET_c \times T_Q \times N_S$$

where $ET_C = ET_O/\text{rainfall}$, ET_O is the evapotranspiration for a particular crop during its growth period;
$T_Q = \Delta T/T$ (temperature quotient),

$$\Delta T = T_{max} - T_{Min}$$

T is the average temperature of each month during the cropping season;
$N_s = n/N_0$, n is the number of bright sunshine hours for a particular crop during its growth period; N_0 is the total sunshine hours.
2. To calculate the soil quality index (SQI), soil database is used to identify the minimum datasets (MDS) based on eigen value, by using principal component analysis (PCA).
3. Calculate LQI using the following equation

$$LQI = SQI \times CQI$$

1. Indicator selection: characterize the range of land resources in particular area; identify the important issues (problems); select LQIs relevant to the issues,
2. Indicator standardization and scoring to sub-criteria,
3. Weighting of indicators according to importance level, and
4. Based on LQIs whole area can be delineated into different land units (Figure 8.1).

According to Jenks (1967), agricultural land can be classified into four categories (very low, low, moderate and high) based on their land quality values (Table 8.4).

The indexing methods are most commonly used (Rahmanipour et al., 2014), usually integrating several indicators associated with soil functions appropriate to the intended use into a quantitative factor that can be used for multi-criteria decision-making (Karlen et al., 1998). Thus, Analytical Hierarchy Process (AHP) (Saaty, 1980), which is the Multiple Criteria Decision Analysis, is preferred in the evaluation of multiple - heterogeneous factors (Ceballos and Lopez, 2003; Malczewski, 2006; Dengiz and Sarıoğlu, 2013; Akıncı et al., 2013; Askari and Holden, 2014; Xue et al., 2019; Özkan et al., 2019). AHP is a decision-supported method that divides complex multiple-factor problems into a hierarchical structure (Yang et al., 2008). At the same time, integration of analytical models with geographic information system (GIS) is reliably used by researchers in the production and interpretation of LQI maps (Malczewski, 2006; Yalew et al., 2016).

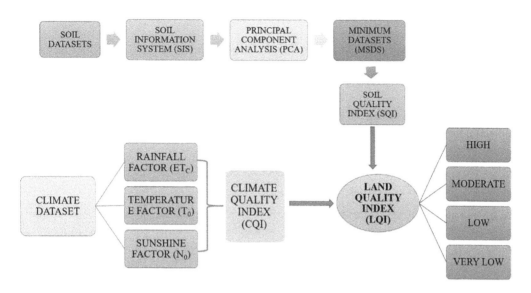

FIGURE 8.1 Schematic diagram for land quality assessment.

TABLE 8.4
Agricultural Land Quality Classes

Land Quality	Classes	Index Values
High	I	>2.850
Moderate	II	2.554–2.849
Low	III	2.061–2.553
Very low	IV	<2.061

8.2.3.3   Application of RS and GIS Technology in Land Evaluation

In the recent years with the advent of RS and GIS, these techniques are also being used in soil site suitability evaluation to expedite the process. Reddy et al. (2004) carried out soil site suitability evaluation for crop production in Nagpur district using IRS – 1D – LISS III data. They opined that landscape data helps to predict soil suitability. The modern land evaluation systems are more of specific approach rather than broad-based approach. Automated Land Evaluation System (ALES) is such a system that uses FAO framework for land evaluation, to build an expert system of land evaluation (Elsheikh et al., 2013). ALES offers a flexible system where evaluator can build their own expert system as per their required characteristics. It takes into account the expert opinion and can be linked to socioeconomic parameters. But, the system is not equipped with GIS functions and is not very easy to handle (Rossiter and Wambeke, 1997). Another model is the Intelligent System for Land Evaluation (ISLE). It takes into account FAO-SYS model for land evaluation. Unlike ALES it includes a map input and GIS system that enables the users to visualize the results in digital map format. But, it is not flexible in terms of a wide range of parameters (Tsoumakas and Vlahavas, 2009).

Using the classical and modern approaches many studies have been conducted on soil site suitability evaluation. Prasad et al. (2009) assessed the suitability for soils of Selsura KVK research farm in Wardha district of Maharashtra and observed that out of nine soil series of Selsura, except soils of Selsura-7 series (very shallow), others are moderately or marginally suitable for one or more commonly grown rain-fed kharif crops, viz. cotton, sorghum, pigeon pea, soybean and groundnut. Vasu et al. (2018) have developed land suitability evaluation using multi-criteria evaluation technique in Thimmajipet area of Telangana at the village level for cotton, maize, rice, pigeon pea and groundnut. They found that integration of soil series data and their distribution, their constraints and potentials, the status of available nutrients, and suitability for cultivated crops can significantly help to generate agricultural land use plan. Integration of geospatial techniques with soil survey data and land evaluation methods proved to be helpful in developing optimal land use planning at the village/ block level for improved crop productivity and maintaining soil health and environment quality.

8.3 MANAGEMENT OF LAND RESOURCES FOR REGENERATIVE AGRICULTURE

The key to manage the agricultural lands under regenerative agriculture is basically regeneration of the soil, which includes conservation of topsoil, adding more soil carbon compared to its losses, and maintaining soil biological diversity for nutrient cycling. In this section, we will briefly discuss the management practices recommended for soil regeneration.

8.3.1 CONSERVATION OF TOPSOIL

The following section represents the soil conservation practices used mainly for soil erosion control from water and wind erosion.

8.3.1.1 Conservation Practices for Water Erosion

8.3.1.1.1 Agronomical or Biological Practices

These measures are also called vegetative measures. It refers to mainly the crop management practices aimed at reducing the erosive potential of the runoff as well as the vulnerability of soil to erosion. These practices ensure a permanent vegetative cover on the soil surface to reduce erosion. The agronomical practices are preferred over the mechanical measures in soils that have gentle to moderate slopes. These measures reduce the impact of raindrops through interception and thus prevent soil erosion. When designed in a site-specific approach, these practices are very effective in controlling erosion and reducing soil loss after proper establishment. Agronomical practices for soil conservation mainly include conservation tillage, residue mulching, contour cropping, strip cropping and cover cropping. Widely used agronomic measures for soil conservation are presented below.

8.3.1.1.2 Conservation Tillage

It has been defined as the tillage practice that maintains at least 30% of residues of the previous crop on the soil surface. This practice encourages the infiltration of rainwater where it falls. The residues on the soil surface facilitate the infiltration. Conservation tillage encompasses many tillage practices which include no-till, minimum tillage, strip tillage, mulch tillage, ridge tillage and vertical tillage. No-till or zero-tillage practice is which involves direct sowing of the crop without seedbed preparation. It maintains nearly constant mulch cover and hence is very successful in reducing soil erosion. Crop residues intercept the raindrops, lower the erosive energy, and consequently eliminate soil particle detachment. This practice is more useful in mitigating splash, sheet, and rill erosion than controlling gully erosion which has concentrated runoff (Rhoton et al., 2002).Similarly, the minimum tillage practice is beneficial as it results in minimum disturbance to the soil surface by limiting the tillage operations (Soni et al., 2020). This results in minimum loosening of the soil and eventually less erosion. The strip tillage separates the rows between the crops in two zones i.e., crop management zone and water management zone. The tillage is limited only to the water management zone and soil near the crop is left undisturbed. Other conservation tillage practices are also more or less similar in practice. In this way, conservation tillage practices are useful in soil conservation (Miner et al., 2013).

8.3.1.1.3 Contour Cropping

It is mainly a farming method in which crops are planted in rows across the slope of the field on the contours. This conservation practice is very effective in controlling soil loss due to water erosion on slopes between 2% and 10%. The contour cultivation checks the erosive velocity of runoff water, induces infiltration, and thereby conserves the topsoil surface. It is useful on sloppy land as it breaks the slope length and reduces the flow velocity.

8.3.1.1.4 Cover Crops

This is another effective soil conservation practice to reduce soil loss. These crops provide permanent covers on the soil surface between the growing period of the main crops. Even after their harvest, their residue continues to protect the soil surface from erosion. Rather than applying it as a sole practice, its effectiveness is enhanced if it is combined with zero tillage or other conservation tillage practice. Apart from erosion control, cover crops also provide other ecosystem services, e.g., soil fertility. Cover crops provide a surface canopy and residue cover to act as a buffer and protect the soil surface against the erosive energy of raindrops, while also aiding the infiltration of rainwater into the soil.

8.3.1.1.5 Mechanical or Structural Measures

Mechanical structures or measures act as a companion to biological or vegetative measures. Agronomical practices keep the soil in place whereas mechanical measures intercept the runoff and cause the deposition of sediment, thereby promoting soil conservation. The mechanical measure comes into the picture when agronomic practices are not capable or inefficient in controlling the soil loss from a particular site. The mechanical measures that are used for controlling water erosion are presented below.

i. **Bunding:**
   A bund is a mechanical measure adapted for the conservation of soil. The bund creates an impediment in the path of the flowing water so that the velocity of the runoff is reduced. It performs a dual function, first, it reduces the velocity of the water and hence prevents soil loss. Secondly, it retains the flowing water and induces its infiltration thereby increasing the water availability in the watershed. These are the embankment-type structures that are constructed across the land slope to break the slope length. Different types of bunds are employed for soil conservation depending upon the suitability for a particular location. The contour bunds are constructed across the slope on the contour lines of the watershed. If the bunds are given a gradient, then they are called graded bunds. The suitability of a bund for a particular location is dependent on the rainfall, soil type, and land slope. The contour bunds are constructed in the area receiving low rainfall (less than 600 mm), having permeable soils and a land slope between 2% and 6%. On the other hand, graded bunds are effective in high rainfall areas (greater than 600 mm) and impervious soils.
   Bunds are very successful for soil conservation on a land slope of less than 10% as they break the slope length and reduce the velocity of the flowing water. This in turn results in soil conservation in the watershed. In India, bunding as a means of soil conservation has been in practice for a long time. But, its large-scale adaptation is limited by ineffectiveness in deep black soils. Also, planting is not possible on bunds. Other bunds such as supplementary bunds, lateral bunds, and side bunds are also constructed along with the contour bunds and graded bunds. Despite their limitations, bunding is still a widely used soil conservation practice.

ii. **Terraces:**
   One of the most effective soil erosion control actions on the slopes is to break up the slope lengths and lower the rate of flowing water. This is achieved by constructing terraces.

Terraces are step-like formations constructed across the slope to protect the soil from erosion. Terracing involves land modification actions for the retention of runoff water followed by safe disposal. It divides the land slope into strips. These strips can be planted depending on the type of terrace. The terraces are mainly categorized into two classes, i.e., broad base terraces and bench terraces. The broad base terraces are primarily constructed to retain or remove water on sloping land which is suitable for cultivation. While the bench terraces are constructed to reduce the land slope. Eventually, both terraces perform the function of soil and water conservation.

A broad base terrace is an embankment or broad surface channel that is constructed across the slope. These are again divided into graded and level terraces. The graded or channel-type terraces have the primary function of removing excess water in such a way that soil loss is minimized. In this terrace system, erosion is controlled by reducing the length of the slope and conveying the runoff to an outlet at a non-erosive velocity. The level terrace is constructed for moisture conservation in the area. Bench terraces are a series of platforms constructed on the contours of the hill by cutting into the hill slope in a step-like formation. These platforms are separated by vertical drops at regular intervals. The bench terraces are used to convert the hilly area into an area that is suitable for agriculture. Depending upon the slope these are again classified as bench terraces sloping inward, bench terraces sloping outward and level bench terraces. Terracing has also proved beneficial in soil conservation in hilly areas.

iii. **Contour trenching:**

It involves the excavation of the trenches along the contours of the hill slope. This measure can be used both on degraded land and hill slopes for soil conservation purposes. The trenches break the continuous length of the land slope, reducing the velocity and scouring capacity of runoff coming from upstream areas. The water retained in the trenches facilitates moisture conservation and at the same time, the sediment deposited in the trenches helps in soil conservation. These trenches are constructed either in a continuous or staggered manner depending upon the hill slope and feasibility of the construction.

iv. **Temporary Gully erosion control structures:**

Very small-sized gullies can be treated with a temporary type of structure. These structures are useful in conserving the soil from such areas. These are made from locally available material and have a short life span. There are various temporary structures used for this purpose. The woven wire dams are constructed in gullies having small to moderate slopes and small catchment areas. They help in the establishment of vegetation for the control of erosion. Brushwood dams are very easy to construct and cheap. These are constructed using straw or mulch which is tightly packed. However, these dams fail to prevent leaks. Loose rock dams are suitable for gullies that have small to a medium size catchment area. If stones of appreciable size are abundant in the area, then this type of dam can be constructed very cheaply. Gabions are constructed by retaining the material against the wired net. Such structures usually form a check dam. It lowers the flow velocity and causes the deposition of sediment. In this way, it helps in soil conservation. Temporary soil conservation structures are limited to small-sized areas. However, their ease of construction and low cost make them the best soil conservation practice for such area. Apart from the above-mentioned structures, other measures such as ripraps, stone walls, stone terracing and compartmental bunding are also useful in soil conservation.

v. **Permanent Gully control structures:**

These types of structures are constructed from concrete and masonry materials. They hold the runoff and reduce the water availability for further erosion, thereby facilitating soil conservation. These structures are mainly constructed in the form of a check dam in the gully area. The permanent structures used for gully erosion control are drop spillways, chute spillways and drop inlet spillways. Each structure has its adaptability and limitations. The drop structure in the gully area helps to check the velocity of runoff. This causes water retention and sediment deposition on the upstream side. The chute spillway is constructed along the steep gradient which is usually present at the gully head. This reduces the erosive energy of the runoff and protects the downstream area from further erosion. The drop inlet spillway has an embankment and hence can store the water on the upstream side. Also, it causes the deposition of the eroded soil that is carried by the runoff. Mechanical erosion control practices reduce flow velocity, store water, and convey runoff to the downstream area at non-erosive velocities. These actions aggregately help in soil conservation. Mechanical practices are very efficient in reducing concentrated flow and gullying at places where biological practices alone are insufficient.

8.3.1.2   Soil Conservation Practices for Wind Erosion

Soil conservation practices adapted to control soil loss due to wind erosion are mainly based on either of two principles. First, to improve the soil surface characteristics and hence wind resistance, and second, to reduce the wind velocity by means of structural measures. The following sections present the soil conservation practices that are implemented for wind erosion control (Baumhardt and Blanco-Canqui, 2014).

8.3.1.2.1   Tillage Practices

Tillage in the soil forms the aggregate or clods which roughens the soil surface. This rough surface creates wind resistance and is very effective in conserving the soil. The aggregates that are formed after the tillage are larger in size, and hence, they cannot be transported by the wind. This results in temporary stabilization of the soil. The Primary and Secondary Tillage operations and use of crop residues are common tillage practices used for wind erosion control. Tillage with the chisel plough, lister plough, disc plough and harrows will produce the desired results. The crop residues on the soil surface retard the wind velocity and conserve the soil. This practice is also known as stubble mulching.

8.3.1.2.2   Strip Cropping

This practice is efficient in controlling wind as well as water erosion. The different types of strips cropping such as contour strip cropping, field strip cropping, wind strip cropping and buffer strip cropping are applied depending upon the circumstances. Wind strip cropping is exclusively used for checking wind erosion. The practice usually involves the planting of erosion-resisting and erosion-susceptible crops in alternate rows or strips. These strips reduce the field width which is susceptible to erosion and also creates resistance to wind. The distance between the crop rows varies depending on the soil erodibility and wind velocity. It can accommodate various crop rotations without affecting production. This practice when combined with the tillage practices can yield very good results in soil conservation (Chepil, 1965; Woodruff et al., 1972).

8.3.1.2.3   Shelterbelts

Shelterbelts are one of the most aesthetically pleasing and efficient permanent wind erosion control and soil conservation practice. It is mainly an agroforestry system. It is constructed by using more than two rows of plants. These rows are usually at the right angle to the direction of the prevailing wind. The rows of the shelterbelt are developed by using trees and shrubs. These rows protect the downstream area from high-velocity wind and prevent soil erosion which consequently results in soil conservation (Brandle et al., 2004; Follett et al., 2012).

8.3.2   Soil Biological Diversity Management

Management of soil biological diversity comprises both flora and fauna, i.e., the diversity of vegetation cover as well as the diversity of the soil macro and micro-organisms, for example, the earthworms, actinomycetes, bacteria and fungi. With the management practices associated with agriculture, both the above-ground and below-ground diversity of soils are affected. The microbial activity below ground is closely associated with the root and canopy characteristics of the land cover type. Hence, in the context of regenerative agriculture, the land use/land cover diversity management is very much important. If the land cover diversity is intensified, it leads to more biomass production (Tilman et al., 1996), which in turn, adds more organic matter to soil and promotes the activity and proliferation of soil fauna. The macro and microfauna help decomposition of these complex organic matter and make more nutrients available to plants and adequate nutrient supply again leads to more biomass production and this cycle of regeneration continues. This is an ideal scenario, but, in actual agricultural field conditions, this ideal scenario does not operate necessarily, due to the choice of cropping system and fertilizer as well as other soil management practices by farmers (Mourya et al., 2022; Hota et al., 2022a). Presently, the cover diversity and fertility both are under decline (Furey and Tilman, 2021).The cropped lands where monocropping is being followed are more prone to this decline because of insufficient biomass contribution to continue the cycle of regeneration. Likewise, the cover intensity and cropping intensity vary for each land parcel and so does the process of regeneration of soil biomass.

The soils are a very heterogenous resource in terms of their intrinsic and dynamic properties, hence, a similar set of management practices can never be applicable in a second land parcel. Hence, for regenerative agricultural crop intensifications, the type of crops has to be decided based on land evaluation and site suitability as mentioned in Section 8.2 of this chapter. Moreover, maintaining the functional diversity of crop species is important. For example, tree crop species can be intercropped with grasses and pastures to provide cover as well as add more biomass; cereal intercropping with legumes; grassland, cereals and legumes in a mixed system. Reports suggest that the more the functional diversity of plants, the more it adds to the fertility regeneration (Furey and Tilman, 2021). Many experiments have been carried out to evaluate the combinations of plant species within and across the functional groups for their yield and biodiversity-enhancing capability (Reich et al., 2005). A functional trait-based approach has been attempted by researchers to evaluate the compatibility of crop species in an agroecosystem (Bolnick et al., 2011; Cadotte et al., 2011; Flombaum et al., 2014; Wood et al., 2015). The evaluation and combinations are based on the ecosystem services provided by a crop species, its niche characteristics, its interaction with environment and its interaction with other crop species (Wood et al., 2015). Introducing a crop species in an agroecosystem should be targeted at providing the service needed to regenerate the particular soil (Naeem and Wright, 2003). For example, if our target is to mitigate water erosion, our target will be to evaluate the suitable cover crop, whereas if our target is to improve fertility, we will evaluate a green manure or a legume compatible with our major cereal. Hence, the trait-based agroecosystem intensification is important for regeneration of soils and management of their biodiversity. Presently, these studies are limited and have been done in small scales. To achieve the target of a net positive soil biomass and nutrient balance, this approach has to be expanded at spatial scale to reach the farmers' field.

8.3.3 Soil Carbon Management

Soil carbon (C) management for regenerative agriculture comprises of C sequestration and maintaining a positive C balance by generating more C than its losses. Soil C is the most crucial component of RA and RA has also been defined as 'practices aimed at encouraging soil health by restoring soil's organic carbon' (WRI, 2020). This can be achieved by reducing tillage, reduce top soil loss, cover crop, organic matter addition through crop intensification and organic amendments. The conservation of top soils through reduced tillage, cover crops and crop intensification has already been discussed in Sections 8.3.1 and 8.3.2 of this chapter. We will discuss them in the context of soil C in this section.

Among many sources of terrestrial C, soil is considered the largest store of C (Batjes, 1996; Mourya et al., 2021), even greater than the C pools of atmosphere and vegetation (Minasny et al., 2013).

But, the conversion of natural vegetation to arable lands has led to a decline in the global C stock. Hence, recent research activities across the globe are focused on increasing soil C sequestration through conservation agriculture, crop intensification and cover management.

Conservation tillage has been reported to increase the soil organic carbon (SOC) in the long term (Smith et al., 1998; West and Post, 2002; Sanden et al., 2018) due to a reduced rate of decomposition of SOC resulting from improved soil aggregation and lowering soil temperature (Huang et al., 2018). Jordon et al.(2022a) reported an increase of SOC by 0.06% over 15 years period by shifting from intensive tillage to no tillage and increase of 0.09% from reduced tillage. The intervention in cropping systems through intensification has also been reported to increase SOC. The inclusion of ley in rotation with the crop was shown to increase the SOC by 0.05% (Jordon et al., 2022a). In another experiment, Jordon et al. (2022b) reported an increase in SOC stock by 6.9%–33.4% depending upon the intensity of rotation with ley, compared to continuous arable cropping. van der Pol et al. (2022) also reported a substantial increase in SOC stock by following a continuous grain-legume cropping system compared to grain-fallow systems.

However, the restoration of SOC is a long-term process and there are very limited studies where the effectiveness of regenerative agriculture has been experimented. Hence, more intensive studies are required to completely understand the cycle of SOC regeneration in agroecosystems.

8.4 LAND USE PLANNING FOR REGENERATIVE AGRICULTURAL PRODUCTIONS

In the past few decades, market-driven land use patterns have led to unsustainable use of natural resources such as land and also threatened the agricultural production and food security. However, in the recent years, a focused discussion on Sustainable Development Goals (SDGs) has raised awareness about the efficient use of land, water and other natural resources. In this context, land use planning (LUP) is considered to be the most apt tool to help policy development, synergize human activities and environment sustainability (Metternich, 2018). The importance of land use planning as a tool to achieve sustainable development, i.e., climate change mitigation and biodiversity protection was highlighted in the agenda 21 of the United Nations Conference on Environment and Development (UNCED), 1992 (GIZ, 2012). According to the FAO (1993):

> land use planning is the systematic assessment of land and water potential, alternatives for land use, and economic and social conditions, with a view to selecting and adopting the best land use options. Its purpose is to select and put into practice land uses that will best meet the needs of the people while safeguarding resources for the future.

LUP is imperative to achieve increased output levels of both land and agricultural productivity and to ensure improved socio-environmental standards.

Global food system reported to have some detrimental impact on the environment through anthropogenic greenhouse gas (GHG) emissions, terrestrial acidification and eutrophication of surface waters (Poore and Nemecek, 2018). However, well-managed agricultural land helps to provide ecosystem services and safeguards the environment (FAO and ITPS, 2021). Regenerative agriculture is gaining currency in many parts of the world as one of the sustainable farming approaches taking soil into consideration as the entry point (Schreefel et al., 2020) and hence, considered relevant to those regions where environmental stresses result in soil degradation or poor soil health (Stolte et al., 2016). Regenerative practices are not equally effective for all farming systems (Giller et al., 2021; Luján Soto et al., 2021); however, to achieve meaningfulness under diverse farming systems, different stakeholders, viz., government agencies, organizations, industries and farmers, need to delve on such methods that can enhance their knowledge to achieve high efficiency of these practices to meet various regenerative objectives within the local sphere (Giller et al., 2021). The feasibility of regenerative practices not only depends on their efficacy to contribute to soil health but also on other sustainability aspects (Schreefel et al., 2022). Therefore, bio-physical and socio-economic

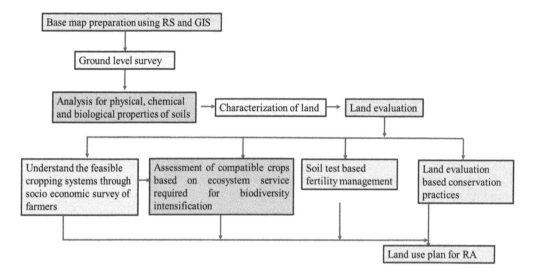

FIGURE 8.2 Schematic presentation of land use planning approach for regenerative agriculture.

aspects need to be considered for the adoption of regenerative agricultural practices in diverse ago-ecological conditions. In this endeavour, sustainable agricultural land use planning seems to be the most feasible solution due to being taken into consideration of bio-physical (soil, climate, crops and cropping systems, livestock), socio-economic (Kumar et al., 2019, 2021a), and environmental aspects such as energy use efficiency and carbon footprint (Kumar et al., 2022b). Moreover, land use planning involves land evaluation which helps to protect the soil resources from degradation processes such as soil erosion, soil salinity and alkalinity and also offers scope to utilize the lands/soils for diversified uses including horticultural crops (Kumar et al., 2021b) and agriculture crops (Kumar et al., 2022a) according to their capability and suitability under various agro-ecological regions and thus, ensure improved land and agricultural productivity.

We have discussed in the previous sections how to evaluate a land parcel for its potential and constraints, how to decide on a suitable crop, and how to follow conservation and regeneration practices. A regenerative agricultural land use planning would be and integrative and hierarchical assessment approach. We are proposing a regenerative agricultural land use planning approach that has been presented in a schematic way in Figure 8.2.

8.5 CONCLUSION

Land resources are an integral part of socio-economic development across the world. Agricultural land use, among other land uses, is directly linked to the food and nutritional security of people. Hence, the management of agricultural land resources has become very much crucial under current circumstances where we witness a shrinking of per capita land holding. In this chapter, we have discussed how regenerative agricultural practices can make the agricultural land resources viable for their long-term productivity with maintained soil health. However, regenerative agriculture is still more of a concept that has not been practically implemented at a large scale. Presently, faulty land use practices such as monocropping, maintaining a single crop for the long term, and leaving the inter-rows of tree crops barren are leading to further degradation of land. Land use planning has remained more of a qualitative approach in the present times, and there is a huge gap among the proposed land use plan and the implementation in farmers' fields. There are only a few cases where land use plans have been successfully implemented in the farmers' field. The large gap between the formulation and implementation of land use plans needs to be addressed in the future. For this, rapid assessment of the land will be necessary, which may be achieved by digital soil mapping, machine learning, and artificial intelligence-based monitoring approaches. These approaches are being successfully used for monitoring the changes in soil properties, and most of the DSM approaches have been taken up for soil C studies. Soil C is the most important component of regenerative agriculture. Hence, monitoring of soil C changes is necessary in this context. The DSM approaches are also limited in terms of monitoring the temporal changes due to scattered legacy dataset availability. Hence, the generation of a network of legacy datasets is also an important task to be carried out in future researches of regenerative agriculture. With an integrated land use planning approach, regenerative agriculture can be achieved successfully, but will need rigorous research to understand the dynamics of the complex agricultural soils.

REFERENCES

Askari, M. S., & Holden, N. M. (2014) Indices for quantitative evaluation of soil quality under grassland management. *Geoderma*, 230(2014), 131–142.

Bandyopadhyay, S., Ray, P., Ramachandran, S., Jena, R.K., Singh, S.K., & Ray, S.K. (2017) Pedogenesis of some hydromorphic soils of upper Brahmaputra Valley Region, Assam, India. *Clay Research*, 36(2), 77–89.

Batjes, N. H. (1996) Total carbon and nitrogen in the soils of the world. *European Journal of Soil Science*, 47(2), 151–163.

Baumhardt, R. L., & Blanco-Canqui, H. (2014) Soil: conservation practices. In Neal K. Van Alfen (ed.) *Encyclopedia of Agriculture and Food Systems*. Elsevier, pp. 153–165. doi: 10.1016/B978-0-444-52512-3.00091-7

Bindraban, P. S., Stoorvogel, J. J., Jansen, D. M., Vlaming, J., & Groot, J. J. R. (2000) Land quality indicators for sustainable land management: proposed method for yield gap and soil nutrient balance. *Agriculture, Ecosystems & Environment*, 81(2), 103–112.

Bisht, B.S., & Kothyari, B.P. (2001) Land-cover change analysis of Garur Ganga watershed using GIS/Remote sensing technique. *Journal of the Indian Society of Remote Sensing*, 29(3), 137–141.

Bolnick, D.I., Amarasekare, P., Araújo, M. S., Bürger, R., Levine, J. M., Novak, M., Rudolf, V. H. W., Schreiber, S. J., Urban, M. C., & Vasseur, D. A. (2011) Why intraspecific trait variation matters in community ecology. *Trends in Ecology & Evolution*, 26, 183–192.

Bonfante, A., & Bouma, J. (2015) The role of soil series in quantitative land evaluation when expressing effects of climate change and crop breeding on future land use. *Geoderma*, 259, 187–195.

Bose, P., Mohapatra, S.N., Behera, M.D., & Padmini, P. (2008) A comparative study of the spectral response curves and the assessment of different land use land cover features in a part of Sundarban area, West Bengal, using Geoinformatics. *International Journal of Information Technology and Knowledge Management*, 1(2), 219–226.

Brandle, J. R., Hodges, L., & Zhou, X. H. (2004) Windbreaks in North American agricultural systems. *Agroforestry Systems*, 61, 65–78. doi:10.2134/agronj1999.916922x

Brough, P.A. (1986) *Principle of Geographical Information Systems for Land Resources Assessment*. Oxford University Press, Oxford, p. 194.

Buol, S.W., Sanchez, P.A., Cate, Jr, R.B., & Granger, M.A. (1975) Soil fertility capability classification. In: *Soil Management in Tropical America*. Proceedings of a seminar held at CIAT, Cali, Columbia (E. Bornemisza & A. Alvarado, editors). North Carolina State University, Raleigh, pp. 126–141.

Cadotte, M.W., Carscadden, K., & Mirotchnick, N. (2011) Beyond species: functional diversity and the maintenance of ecological processes and services. *Journal of Applied Ecology*, 48, 1079–1087.

Ceballos, S. A., & López, B. J. (2003) Delineation of suitable areas for crops using a multi-criteria evaluation approach and land use/cover mapping: a case study in Central Mexico. *Agricultural Systems*, 77(2), 117–136.

Chen, L., Zhao, H., Song, G., & Liu, Y. (2021) Optimization of cultivated land pattern for achieving cultivated land system security: a case study in Heilongjiang Province, China. *Land Use Policy*, 108, 105589.

Chepil, W. S. (1965) Transport of soil and snow by wind. *Meteorological Monographs*, 6, 123–132. doi: 10.1007/978-1-940033-58-7_7

Das, A., Mondal, M., Das, B., & Ghosh, A.R. (2012) Analysis of drainage morphometry and watershed prioritization of Bandu Watershed, Purulia, West Bengal through Remote Sensing and GIS technology– a case study. *International Journal of Geomatics and Geosciences*, 2(4), 995–1013.

Dengiz, O., & Sarıoğlu, F. E. (2013) Parametric approach with linear combination technique in land evaluation studies. *Journal of Agricultural Sciences*, 19(2), 101–112.

Dwivedi, R. S. (2001) Soil resource mapping: a remote sensing perspective. *Remote Sensing Reviews*, 20, 89–122.

Elsheikh, R., Mohamed Shariff, A. R. B., Amiri, F., Ahmad, N. B., Balasundram, S. K., & Soom, M. A. M. (2013). Agriculture Land Suitability Evaluator (ALSE): A decision and planning support tool for tropical and subtropical crops. *Computers and Electronics in Agriculture*, 93, 98–110. doi:10.1016/j.compag.2013.02.003

FAO (1976) *A Framework for Land Evaluation*. Soils Bulletin 32. Food and Agriculture Organization of the United Nations, Rome, Italy.

FAO (1993) *Guidance for Land Use Planning*. FAO Development Series No. 1. FAO, Rome, Italy.

FAO (2021) FAOSTAT: Land use[online]. Available at https://www.fao.org/faostat/en/#data/RL.

FAO and ITPS (2021) *Recarbonizing Global Soils: A Technical Manual of Recommended Sustainable Soil Management*. FAO, Rome, Italy. doi:10.4060/ cb6595en

Fenton, T. E. (2020) Land capability classification. In Yeqiao Wang (ed.).*Landscape and Land Capacity*. CRC Press, pp. 167–171.

Flombaum, P., Sala, O. E., & Rastetter, E. B. (2014) Interactions among resource partitioning, sampling effect, and facilitation on the biodiversity effect: a modeling approach. *Oecologia*, 174, 559–566.

Follett, R. F., Stewart, C. E., Pruessner, E. G., & Kimble, J. M. (2012) Effects of climate change on soil carbon and nitrogen storage in the US Great Plains. *Journal of Soil and Water Conservation*, 67, 331–342. doi: 10.2489/jswc.67.5.331

Fontes, M. P., Fontes, R. M., & Carneiro, P. A. (2009) Land suitability, water balance and agricultural technology as a Geographic-Technological Index to support regional planning and economic studies. *Land Use Policy*, 26(3), 589–598.

Furey, G. N., & Tilman, D. (2021) Plant biodiversity and the regeneration of soil fertility. *Proceedings of the National Academy of Sciences*, 118(49), e2111321118.

Garg, P. K., Garg, R. D., Shukla, G., & Srivastava, H. S. (2020) *Digital Mapping of Soil Landscape Parameters: Geospatial Analyses using Machine Learning and Geomatics*. Studies in Big Data. Springer Verlag, Singapore. doi: 10.1007/978-981-15-3238-2

Giller, K.E., Hijbeek, R., Andersson, J.A., & Sumberg, J. (2021) Regenerative agriculture: an agronomic perspective. *Outlook on Agriculture*, 50, 13–25. doi:10.1177/ 0030727021998063

GIZ(2012) *Land Use Planning: Concept, Tools and Applications*. Deutsche Gesellschaft für Internationale Zusammenarbeit (GIZ), Bonn, 267pp.

Granatstein, D., & Bezdicek, D. F. (1992) The need for a soil quality index: local and regional perspectives. *American Journal of Alternative Agriculture*, 7(1/2), 12–16.

Hota, S., Mishra, V., Mourya, K.K., Giri, K., Kumar, D., Jha, P.K., Saikia, U.S., Prasad, P.V.V., & Ray, S.K. (2022a) Land use, landform, and soil management as determinants of soil physicochemical properties and microbial abundance of lower Brahmaputra Valley, India. *Sustainability*, 14, 2241. doi:10.3390/ su140422

Hota, S., Mishra, V., Mourya, K. K., Saikia, U. S., & Ray, S. K. (2022b) Fertility capability classification (FCC) of soils of a lower Brahmaputra valley area of Assam, India. *Environment Conservation Journal*, 23(3), 192–201. https://doi.org/10.36953/ECJ.10462244

Huang, Y., Ren, W., Wang, L., Hui, D., Grove, J. H., Yang, X., Tao, B., & Goff, B. (2018) Greenhouse gas emissions and crop yield in no-tillage systems: a meta-analysis. *Agriculture, Ecosystems & Environment*, 268, 144–153.

Imaz, M. J., Virto, I., Bescansa, P., Enrique, A., Fernandez, A. O., & Karlen, D. L. (2010) Soil quality indicator response to tillage and residue management on semi-arid Mediterranean cropland. *Soil and Tillage Research*, 107(1), 17–25.

Jangir, A., Sharma, R.P., Tiwari, G., Dash, B., Naitam, R.K., Malav, L.C., Narse, R., Gautam, N., Bhure, S., Chandran, P., & Singh, S.K. (2018) Characterization and classification of soils of Bharuch taluka in Bharuch district of Gujarat. *Agropedology*, 28(2), 86–96.

Jangir, A., Tiwari, G., Sharma, R.P., Dash, B., Paul, R., Vasu, D., Malav, L.C., Tiwary, P., & Chandran, P. (2020) Characterization, classification and evaluation of soils of Kamrej taluka in Surat district, Gujarat for sustainable land use planning. *Journal of Soil and Water Conservation*, 19(4), 347–355.

Jenks, G. F. (1967) The data model concept in statistical mapping. *International Yearbook of Cartography*, 7, 186–190.

Jenny, H. (1941) *Factors of Soil Formation*. McGraw-Hill Book Company Inc., New York.

Jordon, M. W., Smith, P., Long, P. R., Bürkner, P. C., Petrokofsky, G., & Willis, K. J. (2022a) Can regenerative agriculture increase national soil carbon stocks? Simulated country-scale adoption of reduced tillage, cover cropping, and ley-arable integration using RothC. *Science of the Total Environment*, 825, 153955.

Jordon, M. W., Willis, K. J., Bürkner, P. C., Haddaway, N. R., Smith, P., &Petrokofsky, G. (2022b) Temperate regenerative agriculture practices increase soil carbon but not crop yield– a meta-analysis. *Environmental Research Letters*, 17(9), 093001.

Kalaiselvi, B., Lalitha, M., Dharumarajan, S., Srinivasan, R., Hegde, R., Kumar, K. S., & Singh, S. K. (2019) Fertility capability classification of semi-arid upland soils of Palani block, Tamil Nadu for sustainable soil management. *Indian Journal of Soil Conservation*, 47(3), 255–262.

Kalra, N.K., Singh, L., Kachhwah, R., & Joshi, D.C. (2010) Remote sensing and GIS in identification of soil constraints for sustainable development in Bhilwara district, Rajasthan. *Journal of the Indian Society of Remote Sensing*, 38(2), 279–290.

Karlen, D. L., Cambardella, C. A., Kovar, J. L., & Colvin, T. S. (2013) Soil quality response to long-term tillage and crop rotation practices. *Soil and Tillage Research*, 133, 54–64.

Karlen, D. L., Gardner, J. C., & Rosek, M. J. (1998) A soil quality framework for evaluating the impact of CRP. *Journal of Production Agriculture*, 11(1), 56–60.

Klingebiel, A.A., & Montgomery, P.H. (1966) *Land Capability Classification*. Agricultural Hand Book No. 210. USDA, Washington, DC.

Kotoky, P., Dutta, M.K., & Borah, G.C. (2012) Changes in landuse and landcover along the Dhansiri River channel, Assam – a remote sensing and GIS approach. *Journal of the Geological Society of India*, 79, 61–68.

Kumar, A., Lal, S.K., & Meena, R. S. (2021a) Management of natural resources in Indo-Gangetic Plain region of India for sustainable agricultural land use planning – a case study. *Biological Forum – An International Journal*, 13(2), 282–292.

Kumar, A., Mahapatra, S. K., Ramamurthy, V., Meena, R. K., & Singh, T. (2022a) Soil-site suitability evaluation for diversification of rice-wheat cropping system ecology in the Indo-Gangetic Plains of India – a case study. *Annals of Agricultural Research New Series*, 43(4), 396–403.

Kumar, A., Mahapatra, S.K., & Surya, J. N. (2021b) Soil suitability of some major fruit crops for sustainable production in the IGP region of India– a case study. *Biological Forum– An International Journal*, 13(1), 200–210.

Kumar, A., Singh, D., &Mahapatra, S.K. (2019) Study of socio-economic indicators for sustainable agricultural land use planning of Buraka micro-watershed in Mewat Region of Haryana. *Annals of Agricultural Research New Series*, 40(4), 316–321.

Kumar, A., Singh, D., & Mahapatra, S.K. (2022b) Energy and carbon budgeting of the pearl millet-wheat cropping system for environmentally sustainable agricultural land use planning in the rainfed semi-arid agro-ecosystem of Aravalli foothills. *Energy*, 246, 123389. doi:10.1016/j.energy.2022.123389

Kumar, V., Rai, S.P., & Rathore, D.S. (2004) Land use mapping of Kandi belt of Jammu region. *Journal of the Indian Society of Remote Sensing*, 32(4), 323–328.

Lal, R. (1994) Tillage effects on soil degradation, soil resilience, soil quality, and sustainability. *Soil Tillage Research*, 27, 1–8.

Lal, R. (2009) Soils and sustainable agriculture: a review. *Agronomy for Sustainable Development*, 28, 57–64.

Liengsakul, M., Mekpaiboonwatana, S., Pramojanee, P., Bronsveld, K., & Huizing, H. (1993) Use of GIS and remote sensing for soil mapping and for locating new sites for permanent cropland– a case study in the highlands of northern Thailand. *Geoderma*, 60(1–4), 293–307.

Liu, Y., & Zhou, Y. (2021) Reflections on China's food security and land use policy under rapid urbanization. *Land Use Policy*, 109, 105699.

Luján Soto, R., Martínez-Mena, M., Cuéllar Padilla, M., & de Vente, J. (2021) Restoring soil quality of woody agroecosystems in Mediterranean drylands through regenerative agriculture. *Agriculture, Ecosystems & Environment*, 306(8),107–191.

Malczewski, J. (2006) Ordered weighted averaging with fuzzy quantifiers: GIS-based multicriteria evaluation for land-use suitability analysis. *International Journal of Applied Earth Observation and Geoinformation*, 8(4), 270–277.

Metternich, G.I. (2018) *Land Use and Spatial Planning Enabling Sustainable Management of Land Resources*. Springer Nature, Berlin. doi:10.1007/978-3-319-71861-3

Minasny, B., McBratney, A. B., Malone, B. P., & Wheeler, I. (2013) Digital mapping of soil carbon. *Advances in Agronomy*, 118, 1–47.

Miner, G. L., Hansen, N. C., Inman, D., Sherrod, L. A., & Peterson, G. A. (2013) Constraints of no-till dryland agroecosystems as bioenergy production systems. *Agronomy Journal*, 105, 364–376. doi:10.2134/agronj2012.0243

Mokarram, M., & Mirsoleimani, A. (2018) Using Fuzzy-AHP and order weight average (OWA) methods for land suitability determination for citrus cultivation in ArcGIS (Case study: Fars province, Iran). *Physica A: Statistical Mechanics and its Applications*, 508, 506–518.

Mourya, K. K., Jena, R. K., Ray, P., Ramachandran, S., Sharma, G. K., Hota, S., & Ray, S. K. (2021) Profile distribution of soil organic carbon fractions under different landforms in the Meghalaya plateau of India. *Environment Conservation Journal*, 22(3), 9–16. doi:10.36953/ECJ.2021.22302

Mourya, K. K., Saikia, U.S., Hota, S., Ray, P., Jena, R. K., Ramachandran, S., Sharma, G. K., & Ray, S. K. (2022) Effect of landform on some physical and chemical properties of soil under rice cultivation in north east region of India. *Indian Journal of Hill Farming*, 34, 225–229. doi:10.36953/ecj.2021.22302

Naeem, S., & Wright, J.P. (2003) Disentangling biodiversity effects on ecosystem functioning: deriving solutions to a seemingly insurmountable problem. *Ecology Letters*, 6, 567–579.

Nagaraju, M.S.S., & Gajbhiye, K.S. (2014) Characterization and evaluation of soil of Kukadi Command (Minor-25) Ahmednagar district of Maharashtra for land resource management. *Agropedology*, 24(2), 157–165.

Nagaraju, M.S.S., Ganesh, H.B., Srivastava, R., Nasare, R.A., & Barathwal, A.K. (2015) Characterization and evaluation of land resources for management of Saraswati watershed in Buldhana district of Maharashtra. *Indian Journal of Soil Conservation*, 43(1), 102–109.

Naidu, L. G. K., Ramamurthy, V., Challa, O., Hedge, R., & Krishnan, P. K. (2006) *Manual, Soil-Site Suitability Criteria for Major Crops*. NBSS Publications No. 129. NBSS& LUP, Nagpur, p 118.

O'Geen, A. T. (2008) *A Revised Storie Index for Use with Digital Soils Information*. UCANR Publications.

O'Geen, A. T., & Southard, S.B. (2005) A revised Storie Index modelled in NASIS. *Soil Survey Horizons*, 46(3), 98–109.

Özkan, B., Dengiz, O., & Demirağ, T. İ. (2019) Site suitability assessment and mapping for rice cultivation using multi-criteria decision analysis based on fuzzy-AHP and TOPSIS approaches under semihumid ecological condition in delta plain. *Paddy and Water Environment*, 17, 665–676.

Patil, G.B., Nagaraju, M.S.S., Prasad, J., & Srivastava, R. (2010) Characterization, evaluation and mapping of land resources in Lendi watershed, Chandrapur district of Maharashtra using remote sensing and GIS. *Journal of the Indian Society of Soil Science*, 58(4), 442–448.

Phukan, P., Thakuriah, G., & Saikia, R. (2013) Land use land cover change detection using remote sensing and GIS techniques – acase study of Golaghat district of Assam, India. *International Research Journal of Earth Sciences*, 1(1), 11–15.

Pieri, C., Dumanski, J., Hamblin, A. S., & Young, A. (1995) *Land Quality Indicators*. World Bank Discussion Paper 315. World Bank, Washington, DC.

Poore, J., & Nemecek, T. (2018) Reducing food's environmental impacts through producers and consumers. *Science*, 360, 987–992. doi:10.1126/science.aaq0216

Potdar, S.S., Srivastava, R., Nagaraju, M.S.S., Prasad, J., & Saxena, R.K.(2003) Mapping of erosional soil loss in Nanda-Khairi watershed of Nagpur district of Maharashtra using remotely sensed data and GIS techniques. *Agropedology*, 13, 10–18.

Prasad, J. (2000) Application of fertility capability classification system in soils of a watershed in semi-arid tropics. *Journal of the Indian Society of Soil Science*, 48(2), 329–338.

Prasad, J., Ray, S.K., Gajbhiye, K.S., & Singh, S.R. (2009) Soils of Selsura research farm in Wardha district, Maharashtra and their suitability for crops. *Agropedology*, 19, 84–91.

Rahmanipour, F., Marzaioli, R., Bahrami, H. A., Fereidouni, Z., & Bandarabadi, S. R. (2014) Assessment of soil quality indices in agricultural lands of Qazvin Province, Iran. *Ecological Indicators*, 40, 19–26.

Ramteke, I.K., Rajankar, P.B., & Kadu, P. (2014) Land use/land cover appraisal using multi-temporal satellite data in LakhaniTahsil of Bhandara district, Maharashtra. *Journal Soils and Crops*, 24(2), 281–285.

Ray, S. K., Bhattacharyya, T., Reddy, K. R., Pal, D. K., Chandran, P., Tiwary, P., Mandal, D. K., et al. (2014) Soil and land quality indicators of the Indo-Gangetic Plains of India. *Current Science*, 107, 1470–1486.

Reddy, G.P.O. (2018). Geospatial technologies in land resources mapping, monitoring, and management: an overview. In: Reddy, G., Singh, S. (eds). *Geospatial Technologies in Land Resources Mapping, Monitoring and Management. Geotechnologies and the Environment*, vol 21. Springer, Cham. https://doi.org/10.1007/978-3-319-78711-4_1

Reddy, G.P.O., Maji, A.K., & Gajbhiye, K.S. (2004) Drainage morphometry and its influence on landform characteristics in a basaltic terrain, Central India – a remote sensing and GIS approach. *International Journal of Applied Earth Observation and Geoinformation*, 6, 1–16.

Reddy, G.P.O., Nagaraju, M.S.S., Ramteke, I. K., & Sarkar, D. (2013) Terrain characterization for soil resource mapping using IRS-P6 data and GIS –a case study from basaltic terrain of central India. *Journal of the Indian Society of Remote Sensing*, 41(2), 331–343.

Reddy, R.S. (2006) Methodology for correlation of soil series in soil survey and mapping. *Agropedology*, 16(1), 1–11.

Reich, P. B., Oleksyn, J., Modrzynski, J., Mrozinski, P., Hobbie, S. E., Eissenstat, D. M., Chorover, J., Chadwick, O. A., Hale, C. M., & Tjoelker, M. G. (2005) Linking litter calcium, earthworms and soil properties: a common garden test with 14 tree species. *Ecology Letters*, 8(8), 811–818.

Resende, M., Curi, N., Rezende, S.B., & Corrêa, G.F. (2014) *Pedologia: Base para Distinção de Ambientes.* Editora, Lavras, MG.

Rhoton, F. E., Shipitalo, M. J., & Lindbo, D. L. (2002) Runoff and soil loss from midwestern and southeastern US silt loam soils as affected by tillage practice and soil organic matter content. *Soil and Tillage Research,* 66, 1–11. doi:10.1016/S0167-1987(02)00005-3

Riquier, J., Bramao, D.L., & Comet, J.P.(1970) *A New System of Soil Appraisal in Terms of Actual and Potential Productivity.* Soil Resources, Development and Conservation Service, Land and Water Division, FAO, Rome, p. 38.

Rossiter, D. G. (1996). A theoretical framework for land evaluation. *Geoderma, 72,* 165–202.

Rossiter, D.G., & Wambeke, A.R.V. (1997) *Automated Land Evaluation System. ALES Version 4.65 User's Manual.* Cornell University.

Saaty, T. L. (1980) *The Analytical Hierarchy Process, Planning, Priority Setting, Resource Allocation.* RWS Publications, Ithaca, NY.

Sahu, N., Obi Reddy, G.P., Kumar, N., & Nagaraju, M.S.S. (2015) High resolution remote sensing, GPS and GIS in soil resource mapping and characterization –a review. *Agricultural Reviews,* 36(1), 14–25.

Sahu, N., Reddy, G.P.O., Kumar, N., Nagaraju, M.S.S., Srivastava, R., & Singh, S.K. (2014) Characterization of landforms and land use/land cover in basaltic terrain using IRS-P6 LISS-IV and Cartosat-1 DEM data: a case study. *Agropedology,* 24(2), 166–178.

Saikia, L., Mahanta, C., & Mukherjee, A. (2019) Erosion-deposition and land use/land cover of the Brahmaputra River in Assam, India. *Journal of Earth System Science,* 128, 211.

Sanchez, P.A., Water, C., & Buol, S.A. (1982) The fertility capability soil classification system: interpretation, applicability and modification. *Geoderma,* 27, 283–309.

Sandén, T., Spiegel, H., Stüger, H.-P., Schlatter, N., Haslmayr, H.-P., Zavattaro, L., Grignani, C., Bechini, L., D'Hose, T., Molendijk, L., Pecio, A., Jarosz, Z., Guzmán, G., Vanderlinden, K., Giráldez, J. V., Mallast, J., & tenBerge, H. (2018) European long-term field experiments: knowledge gained about alternative management practices. *Soil Use and Management,* 34, 167–176.

Schreefel, L., de Boer, I.J.M., Timler, C.J., Groot, J.C.J., Zwetsloot, M.J., Creamer, R.E., Schrijver, A.P., van Zanten, H.H.E., & Schulte, R.P.O. (2022) How to make regenerative practices work on the farm: a modelling framework. *Agricultural Systems,* 198, 103371. doi: 10.1016/j.agsy.2022.103371

Schreefel, L., Schulte, R. P. O., de Boer, I. J. M., Schrijver, A. P., & van Zanten, H. H. E. (2020) Regenerative agriculture– the soil is the base. *Global Food Security,* 26, 100404.

Sehgal, J.L. (1991) Soil-site suitability evaluation for cotton. *Agropedology,* 1, 49–63.

Sharma, J.C., & Chaudhary, S.K. (2008) Land productivity and site-suitability assessment for crop diversification using remotely sensed data and GIS technique. *Agropedology,* 18(1), 1–11.

Sheals, J. G. (1969) *The Soil Ecosystem: Systematic Aspects of the Environment, Organisms and Communities.* The Systematics Association, Publication No. 8. Staples Printers Ltd, London.

Shepherd, T. G. (2009) *Visual Soil Assessment: Field Guide for Pastoral Grazing and Cropping on Flat to Rolling Country.* Horizons Regional Council, Palmerston North, New Zealand.

Shrestha, H. L. (2006) Using GPS and GIS in participatory mapping of community forest in Nepal. *The Electronic Journal of Information Systems in Developing Countries,* 25(5), 1–11.

Simon, P. (2010). *Remote Sensing in Geomorphology.* Jaipur: Oxford Book Company.

Smith, P., Powlson, D. S., Glendining, M. J., & Smith, J. U. (1998) Preliminary estimates of the potential for carbon mitigation in European soils through no-till farming *Global Change Biology,* 4,679–685.

Soil Survey Staff (2014) *Keys to Soil Taxonomy* (12th ed.) United States Department of Agriculture, Natural Resources Conservation Service, Washington, DC.

Soni, J. K., Choudhary, V. K., Singh, P. K., & Hota, S. (2020) Weed management in conservation agriculture, its issues and adoption: a review. *Journal of Crop and Weed,* 16(1), 9–19.

Srivastava, R., & Saxena, R.K. (2004) Techniques of large scale soil mapping in basaltic terrain using satellite remote sensing data. *International Journal of Remote Sensing,* 25(4), 679–688.

Stolte, J., Tesfai, M., Øygarden, L., Kværnø, S., Keizer, J., Verheijen, F., Panagos, P., Ballabio, C., & Hessel, R. (2016) Soil threats in Europe; EUR 27607 EN. doi:10.2788/488054

Storie, R. (1978) *Storie Index Soil Rating.* Special Publication 3203. University of California Division of Agricultural Sciences, Oakland.

Sys, C., & Frankart, R. (1971) Evaluation de l'Aptitude des Sols dans les Tropiques Humides. *Sols Africains/ African Soils,* 16(3), 177–200.

Thilagam, V.K., & Sivasamy, R. (2013) Role of remote sensing and GIS in land resource inventory. *Agricultural Reviews,* 34(3), 223–229.

Tilman, D., Wedin, D., &Knops, J. (1996) Productivity and sustainability influenced by biodiversity in grassland ecosystems. *Nature*, 379, 718–720.

Tsoumakas, G., Katakis, I., Vlahavas, I. (2009). Mining multi-label data. In: Maimon, O., Rokach, L. (eds) *Data Mining and Knowledge Discovery Handbook*. Springer, Boston, MA. https://doi.org/10.1007/978-0-387-09823-4_34

UNCED. (1992). United Nations Conference on Environment & Development Rio de Janeiro, Brazil, 3 to 14 June 1992, AGENDA 21. Retrieved from https://sustainabledevelopment.un.org/content/documents/Agenda21.pdf (chrome-extension://efaidnbmnnnibpcajpcglclefindmkaj/https://sustainabledevelopment.un.org/content/documents/Agenda21.pdf)

van der Pol, L. K., Robertson, A., Schipanski, M., Calderon, F. J., Wallenstein, M. D., & Cotrufo, M. F. (2022) Addressing the soil carbon dilemma: legumes in intensified rotations regenerate soil carbon while maintaining yields in semi-arid dryland wheat farms. *Agriculture, Ecosystems & Environment*, 330, 107906.

Vara Prasad Rao, A.P., Naidu, M.V.S., Ramavatharam, N., & Rama Rao, G.(2008) Characterisation, classification and evaluation of soils on different landforms in Ramachandrapuram mandal of Chittoor district in Andhra Pradesh for sustainable land use planning. *Journal of the Indian Society of Soil Science*, 56(1), 23–33.

Vasu, D., Srivastava, R., Patil, N. G., Tiwary, P., Chandran, P., & Kumar Singh, S. (2018) A comparative assessment of land suitability evaluation methods for agricultural land use planning at village level. *Land Use Policy*, 79, 146–163.

Velayutham, M. (1999) *National Soil Resources Mapping*. National Bureau of Soil Survey and Land Use Planning, Nagpur, India.

Velmurugan, A., & Carlos, G.G.(2009) Soil resource assessment and mapping using remote sensing and GIS. *Journal of the Indian Society of Remote Sensing*, 37, 511–525.

Verheye, W.V. (1991) Soil survey interpretation, land evaluation and land resource management. *Agropedology*, 1, 17–32.

Viana, C.M., Freire, D., Abrantes, P., Rocha, J., &Pereira, P.(2022) Agricultural land systems importance for supporting food security and sustainable development goals: a systematic review. *Science of the Total Environment*, 806, 150718.

Wadodkar, M., & Ravishankar, T. (2011) Soil resource database at village level for developmental planning. *Journal of the Indian Society of Remote Sensing*, 39(4), 529–536.

Walia, C. S., Singh, S. P., Dhankar, R. P., Ram, J., Kamble, K. H., & Katiyar, D. K.(2010) Watershed characterization and soil resource mapping for land use planning of Moolbari Watershed, Shimla District, Himachal Pradesh in Lesser Himalayas. *Current Science*, 98(2), 176–182.

Wall, D. H., & Nielsen, U. N. (2012) Biodiversity and ecosystem services: is it the same below ground. *Nature Education Knowledge*, 3(12), 8.

Water Research Institute (WRI) (2020) Regenerative agriculture: good for soil health, but limited potential to mitigate climate change. https://www.wri.org/insights/regenerative-agriculture-good-soil-health-limited-potential-mitigate-climate-change

West, T. O., & Post, W. M. (2002) Soil organic carbon sequestration rates by tillage and crop rotation: a global data analysis. *Soil Science Society of America Journal*, 66,1930–1946.

Wood, S. A., Karp, D. S., DeClerck, F., Kremen, C., Naeem, S., & Palm, C. A. (2015) Functional traits in agriculture: agrobiodiversity and ecosystem services. *Trends in Ecology &Evolution*, 30(9), 531–539.

Woodruff, N. P., Lyles, L., Siddoway, F. H., & Fryrear, D. W. (1972) *How to Control Wind Erosion*. US Department of Agriculture Bulletin 354. Government Print Office, Washington, DC.

Xue, R., Wang, C., Liu, M., Zhang, D., Li, K., & Li, N. (2019) A new method for soil health assessment based on analytic hierarchy process and meta-analysis. *Science of the Total Environment*, 650, 2771–2777.

Yalew, S. G., van Griensven, A., Mul, M. L., & van der Zaag, P. (2016) Land suitability analysis for agriculture in the Abbay basin using remote sensing, GIS and AHP techniques. *Modeling Earth Systems and Environment* 2, 1–14.

Yang, F., Zeng, G., Du, C., Tang, L., Zhou, J., & Li, Z. (2008) Spatial analyzing system for urban land-use management based on GIS and multi-criteria assessment modeling. *Progress in Natural Science*, 18(10), 1279–1284.

Yeung, A. K. W., & Lo, C. P. (2002) Concepts and techniques of geographic information systems. *International Journal of Geographical Information Science*, 17(8), 819–820.

Zhou, Y., Li, X., & Liu, Y. (2021) Cultivated land protection and rational use in China. *Land Use Policy*, 106, 105454.

Ziadat, F.M. (2010) Prediction of soil depth from digital terrain data by integrating statistical and visual approaches. *Pedosphere*, 20, 361–367.

9 New Trends and Criteria for Responsible Plant Nutrition

Rakesh S, Bodiga Divya, Dewali Roy, Jogarao Poiba,
Dinesha S, Arun Kumar, Kishore Nalabolu,
Raghupathi Balasani, Manju Bhargavi,
Saritha JD, Sana Rafi, and Himadri Saha

9.1 ROLE OF NUTRIENTS IN GLOBAL FOOD SECURITY AND CHALLENGES FOR FUTURE PLANT NUTRITION

Global agricultural output has grown by 2.2% per annum during the past 60 years (Dobermann et al., 2022). Food production growth is entirely dependent on land expansion under cultivation and fertilizer consumption. Green Revolution in the past decades enabled the prevailing mode of agriculture through efficient input use and enhanced yields (Fuglie, 2018), including land expansion in response to global market opportunities and food security concerns. Globally, in the last two decades, there has been an increment of 63 million ha of cropland area (FAO, 2021). However, on one hand, increased crop yields and prominent animal production have saved billions of hungry people (Stevenson et al., 2013). On the other hand, intense crop production to fulfill the demands of food security has caused externalities that are now highly difficult to manage. Major crop nutrients such as nitrogen and phosphorus are highly reactive and prone to various types of losses impacting the soil, air, and water quality, as well as micronutrient-related deficiencies. Enhanced crop yields are certainly important for ensuring the food security of 9.5 billion people in 2050 (Vollset et al., 2020). As per the projections of the UN (2015), Asia and Africa would be crossing 4 billion populations each (*i.e.*, >8 billion) by 2100 (Figure 9.1). Upcoming years are more challenging and difficult to transform the global food system in which we sustainably produce and consume food (Herrero et al., 2020), while also ensuring the hidden health of $12 trillion and the environmental and socio-economic costs of it (FOLU, 2019).

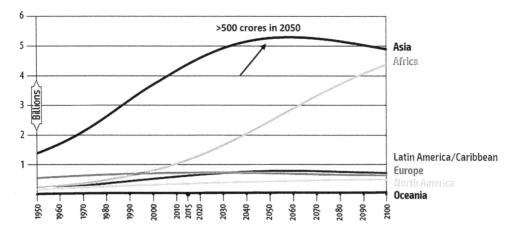

FIGURE 9.1 Projection showing the human population growth by 2100 in different continents. Adapted from UN2015.

DOI: 10.1201/9781003309581-11

There are about 118 elements on this planet, but only 20 mineral elements [carbon (C), hydrogen (H), oxygen (O), nitrogen (N), phosphorus (P), potassium (K), calcium (Ca), magnesium (Mg), sulfur (S), boron (B), chlorine (Cl), iron (Fe), manganese (Mn), zinc (Zn), copper (Cu), molybdenum (Mo), nickel (Ni), silicon (Si), cobalt (Co) and sodium (Na)] are actually playing a significant role in plant, animal and/or human health (Brown et al., 2021). Many of these nutrients are entering food systems from the soil, fertilizers, organic manures, biological N fixation, etc. through crops and grasslands. Therefore, responsible plant nutrient management is critically necessary to ensure food security and protect the natural ecosystem.

9.2 RECENT INNOVATIONS FOR RESPONSIBLE PLANT NUTRITION

9.2.1 GENOMICS AND IONOMICS

Recently, advances in genomics have been recognized as an innovation for plant nutrition, called plant nutritional genomics. Ionomics is used to simultaneously measure the concentration of multiple minerals in plants (Salt, 2004). These are widely helpful in understanding plant nutrition and its underlying genetic basis. Currently, there are new biotechnological crop 'input traits' on the market that have hybrid vigour, virus resistance, insect resistance, herbicide resistance, and delayed fruit ripening traits that would help in enhancing agricultural productivity and saving external inputs. Such improvements in yields have an indirect positive effect on fertilizer consumption. The application of micronutrient fertilizers will be significantly increased due to the continuous uptake of micronutrients from the soil for higher yields of these traits.

9.2.2 NUTRIENT-EFFICIENT CROP GENOTYPES

The ability of a system to minimize the waste of inputs is referred to as nutrient efficiency. The nutrient-efficient genotypes can convert the nutrient inputs into the desired outputs. Usually, in acidic and alkaline soils, mineral stresses are highly dominant. In such cases, plant scientists should screen out the genotypes that are highly resistant/tolerant to the low concentrations of P, K, Ca, Mg, and Fe/Al toxicity in acid soils and low P, S, and Fe in calcareous soils. An experiment conducted in the ICAR Research Complex in the North East Hill (NEH) region helped in developing acid-tolerant and Al toxicity-tolerant groundnut genotypes after screening 600 groundnut genotypes (Singh et al., 2015). At DGR, Junagadh, efforts were made to identify the groundnut genotypes/cultivars having a tolerance for lime-induced iron chlorosis in calcareous soils (Singh et al., 2004). Similar efforts are also needed for many such crops grown in calcareous soils. Keeping in view of increasing problems in crop nutrition, time-bound efforts are critical to developing crop-specific genotypes/cultivars in order to bring about another green revolution.

9.2.3 LIQUID BIO-FERTILIZERS

Usually, solid bio-fertilizers have a lower shelf life of microbes (valid up to 6 months), less tolerance to UV rays and a temperature of >30°C, and a population density of 10^8 cfu/mL. However, liquid bio-fertilizers have an average shelf life of two years, and they are tolerant to higher temperatures (up to 55°C), and UV radiation with a population density of 10^9 cfu/mL (Verma et al., 2018). They have the potential to counteract the adverse effects of chemical fertilizers. As these are eco-friendly and cost-effective, every farmer can be able to afford and use them feasibly effectively. Liquid bio-fertilizers act on rhizospheric zones in plants or the interior of plants and modulate the effects of both biotic and abiotic stresses that ultimately help in enhancing plant growth. These fertilizers also play a significant role in enhancing soil moisture retention capacity, nitrogenase activity, soil organic carbon (SOC), and microbial biomass carbon (MBC).

TABLE 9.1

Different Groups of Microbes Available in the Form of Liquid Bio-Fertilizer

Type	Microbial Group	Example
Nitrogen (N_2) fixing	Symbiotic	*Rhizobium, Frankia*
	Free-living	*Azotobacter*
	Associative Symbiotic	*Azospirillum*
P-mobilizing	Arbuscular mycorrhiza	*Glomus* sp., *Gigaspora* sp., *Acaulospora* sp.
P-solubilizing	Fungi	*Penicillium* sp., *Aspergillus awamori*
	Bacteria	*Bacillus megaterium* var. *phosphaticum*, *Bacillus circulans, Pseudomonas striata*
Plant growth promoting rhizobacteria	Pseudomonas	*Pseudomonas fluorescens*

Liquid bio-fertilizers can be applied as a seed treatment, soil application, or plant root treatment. For seed treatment, mix the bio-fertilizer solution with 100% jaggery solution, and then spread the slurry over the seeds under the shade and dry them overnight before sowing. Seedlings' roots can be dipped in the solution for half an hour. For this, about 2–2.5 L of inoculant solution is required. For soil application, about 20 mL of inoculant solution may be mixed with well-decomposed compost and then applied at the planting stage. As a precautionary measure, it should not be mixed with any nitrogenous fertilizers or fungicides. Liquid bio-fertilizers are always to be prepared as a fresh solution for spraying, and store them at a temperature of 0°C–30°C. Generally, the application of 1 mL of liquid bio-fertilizer is equal to 1 kg of solid career bio-fertilizer; hence, their dosage is ten times less than any other traditional bio-fertilizer. They should always be mixed with bone meal, wood ash, or any other naturally occurring manure to maximize their potential.

A National Project on Development and Use of Bio-fertilizers (NPDB) was implemented under the Ministry of Agriculture, Government of India, during the ninth Five-Year Plan. During 2016–2017, the production status of liquid bio-fertilizer production was 7,526.33 kL (Ministry of Agriculture). The Indian Farmers Fertilizer Cooperative (IFFCO) Limited- MLN Farmers' Training Institute produces all strains of bio-fertilizers and has distributed them in different states other than the home state, *i.e.* Uttar Pradesh (Mazid and Khan, 2014). Some of the liquid bio-fertilizers of different groups of microbes have been presented in Table 9.1.

9.2.4 PLANT BIOFORTIFICATION

Plant biofortification is the process of enhancing specific nutrient compounds and vitamins that help enhance plant yields and improve biological quality (Khush et al., 2012). Due to unawareness, less market access, and the low purchasing power of small farmers, such nutrient supplements are not reaching the majority. This technique for different crop varieties provides a sustainable and long-term solution for producing micronutrient-rich crops. Agronomic biofortification can be achieved through foliar spraying and/or soil application of micronutrient fertilizers that supply iodine (I), Zn, Mo, selenium (Se), etc.

9.2.5 NANO-FERTILIZERS

These are highly synthesized forms of traditional fertilizers manufactured by extracting the elements from different parts of the plant through various physical, chemical, and biological methods with the help of nanotechnology. Nano-fertilizers play a greater role in improving soil fertility, productivity, and the quality of agricultural produce. About 100 nm-sized nanoparticles (NPs) are used

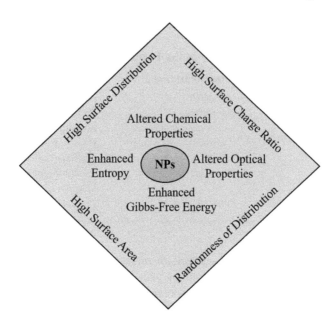

FIGURE 9.2   Important physicochemical properties of nanoparticles.

as fertilizer, which potentially enhances the nutrient use efficiency (NUE). Any substance in this size (10^{-9}) in all three dimensions is always called a nanoparticle (NP)/material (NM) (Ball, 2002; Klaine et al., 2008). They are highly effective for precise nutrient management and also protect the plant from various biotic and abiotic stresses. Some of the unique properties of NPs have been illustrated in Figure 9.2.

9.2.5.1   Carbon-Based NPs

Carbon-based NMs, including fullerols, C60/70 fullerenes, both single-walled carbon nanotubes (SWCNTs) and multiwalled carbon nanotubes (MWCNTs), possess the potential to enhance plant growth (Khot et al., 2012). Both SWCNTs and MWCNTs have been detected in the fruits, leaves, and roots of treated tomato plants, where they significantly improved the plant biomass (Khodakovskaya et al., 2013). In another experiment, the MWCNTs enhanced the growth of cultured tobacco cells by 55%–64% over controls (Khodakovskaya et al., 2013). Similarly, citric acid-coated CNTs (Khodakovskaya et al., 2013) and water-soluble carbon nano-onions (wsCNOs) (Sonkar et al., 2012; Tripathi and Sarkar, 2014) were reported to be more effective in enhancing the growth of different crop species.

9.2.5.2   Titanium Dioxide NPs

The application of titanium oxide (TiO_2) was found to be involved in the fixation of atmospheric nitrogen (N_2), thereby providing more nitrogen to the plants. It also helps in improving enzymatic activities and is involved in photosynthesis (Su et al., 2009). Application of 2.5% rutile TiO_2 NPs solution in spinach (*Spinacea oleracea*) crop showed increments in RubisCO activity, photosynthetic rate, and chlorophyll formation (by 23%) and overall growth (by 63%–76%) (Zheng et al., 2005).

9.2.5.3   SiO₂ NPs

SiO_2 NPs are observed to be highly effective for enhancing plant growth and improving chlorophyll fluorescence parameters. Directly, it increases the effective and actual photochemical efficiency, photosystem (PS) II potential activity, rate of transpiration and electron transport, photochemical quench, and stomatal conductance (Xie et al., 2011; Siddiqui et al., 2015).

9.2.5.4 Zinc Oxide NPs

Application of ZnO NPs at 1,000 mg/L increased the growth and germination of peanuts, as well as chlorophyll content and pod yield, in comparison to bulk zinc sulphate. Biosynthesized ZnO NPs extracted from *Aspergillus fumigates* applied to cluster bean leaves (*Cyamopsis tetragonoloba* L.) showed a significant increase in total protein content by 17.2% and rhizospheric microbial population by 13.6% (Raliya and Tarafdar, 2013).

9.2.5.5 Iron NPs

Application of iron (III) oxide (Fe_2O_3) NP in soybean crops effectively increased root length and photosynthesis. However, the foliar spray was observed to be more effective when compared with soil application, which might be due to the extensive precipitation of Fe ions in soil (Alidoust and Isoda, 2013). The use of phosphate-sorbed zero-valent Fe NPs increased the plant growth and biomass of hydroponically grown spinach crops four-fold (Almeelbi and Bezbaruah, 2014).

9.2.5.6 Manganese (Mn) NPs

When the hydroponically grown mung bean (*Vigna radiata*) was treated with Manganese (Mn) NP at 1 mg/L, there was about a 10%–100% increase in growth parameters such as bean shoot, root, fresh weight, dry weight, etc. In excess doses, it results in toxicity in plants (Pradhan et al., 2013, 2014).

9.2.5.7 Nano-Hydroxyapatite

Nano-hydroxyapatite (nHA) is a rich source of phosphorus (P). Its application in the soybean (*Glycine max*) crop increased growth rate by 32.6% and seed yield by 20.4% over the use of soluble phosphorous fertilizers [$Ca(H_2PO_4)_2$] (Liu and Lal, 2014).

9.2.6 BIOFILMED BIO-FERTILIZERS

Biofilms are associated with single or multiple species (microorganisms) adhering to the biotic or abiotic surfaces in a self-produced matrix of extracellular polymeric substances (EPS) (Rana et al., 2020). In recent years, biofilmed bio-fertilizers (BFBFs) have emerged as a novel approach to improving biofertilizer efficiency that potentially helps in sustaining soil fertility (Parween et al., 2017). Biofilm formation in the BFBFs helps in competing with the resident organisms and coping with the heterogeneity of biotic and abiotic factors in the soil (Ünal Turhan et al., 2019). Many studies have reported that BFBFs have significantly increased P-solubilization (Swarnalakshmi et al., 2013), Zn solubilization (Triveni and Jhansi, 2017), and N_2-fixation (Wang et al., 2017).

9.2.7 METAL–ORGANIC FRAMEWORKS (MOFs)

MOFs are emerging hybrid inorganic-organic porous materials that have greater potential in sustainable agriculture. These frameworks are produced by lining the metal ions with organic ligands. MOFs exhibit distinctive properties such as exceptionally high surface area, adjustable pores, and excellent functionalities (Begum et al., 2019). MOFs constructed from Ca^{2+} ions can encapsulate an agriculturally important fumigant, cis-1,3-dichloropropene, which showed a release rate 100 times lower than that of liquid cis-1,3-dichloropropene (Yang et al., 2017). To manage the ripening of climacteric banana and avocado fruits, Zhang et al. (2016) prepared Cu^{2+}-based MOFs for the encapsulation of the plant hormone ethylene. Iron-based MOFs (Fe-MOFs) have been applied as an iron fertilizer that promotes crop growth rate (Anstoetz et al., 2016; Abdelhameed et al., 2019). A pot experiment conducted by Shan et al. (2020) revealed that the application of FeMOFs built from trimers of iron octahedra linked by 1,3,5-benzenetricarboxylate (Fe-MIL-100) at 50 and 300 mg/L concentrations increased the wheat plant height by 9.6% and 16.4%, respectively, when compared with the control. This indicated that Fe-MIL-100 would be an effective Fe micronutrient and also act as the safest pesticide carrier for wheat growth.

9.2.8   STCR, DRIS, AND SSNM

Soil Test Crop Response (STCR) technology uses the targeted yield approach. It develops the correlation between crop yields, soil test estimates, and fertilizer inputs. This approach is used to balance fertilizing the crop with soil fertility levels. It integrates the use of organic (renewable) and inorganic (non-renewable) sources for sustainable plant nutrition. The Diagnosis and Recommendation Integrated System (DRIS) focuses on increasing net incomes through efficient plant nutrient management. For this approach, we need to initially determine the yield-limiting impact of a given nutrient. Nutrient concentrations above or below critical levels drastically reduce vegetative growth, yield, and quality. The DRIS can detect yield-limiting nutrients even when none of the nutrients are below the critical level, and finally, it allows the diagnosis of the total plant nutritional balance (Baldock and Schulte, 1996). The site-specific nutrient management (SSNM) approach effectively involves its principles in the new decision support tools such as nutrient experts, green seekers, remote sensing, real-time nutrient management, etc. that help in developing the recommended dose of fertilizers in the presence or absence of soil test data. This method effectively replaces the blanket fertilizer nutrient recommendations.

9.3   CRITERIA FOR RESPONSIBLE PLANT NUTRITION

Future plant nutrition should involve multiple objectives to achieve responsible plant nutrition and potentially contribute to sustainable development goals (SDGs) (Ladha et al., 2020) and land degradation neutrality (LDN). The new criterion for responsible plant nutrition encompasses a scientific understanding of needs, technologies, business models, and policies that directly or indirectly affect agricultural production. A new criterion aims to achieve high income from the farming sector, enhanced nutrient use efficiency, high crop productivity, recycling of nutrients, soil health maintenance, human food and nutrition security, and environmental protection by minimizing nutrient losses. There are six key action points to be implemented worldwide to attain responsible plant nutrition in the agricultural system. A framework of action for responsible plant nutrition has been illustrated in Figure 9.3.

9.3.1   ACTION 1: PRECISE NUTRIENT MANAGEMENT

Digital technological solutions enable modifying nutrient applications in a precise manner. The application of digital tools supported by precise crop nutrition in India helped in enhancing nutrient use efficiency (Sharma et al., 2019) and maximizing crop yields (Sapkota et al., 2021), while improving soil health (Parihar et al., 2020) and reducing fertilizer inputs (Sapkota et al., 2014, 2021).

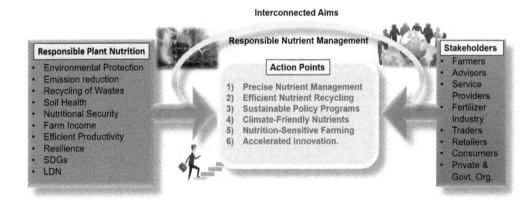

FIGURE 9.3   Illustration showing a framework of action for responsible plant nutrition.

Integration of such digital tools in agriculture, supported by the advisory system, helps benefit the farmer community while ensuring food security. Sustainability-driven nutrient policies and road-maps are to be implemented in every developing country to attain the ambitious goal of increased nutrient use efficiency.

9.3.2 Action 2: Efficient Nutrient Recycling

Generally, soil nutrients are highly susceptible to several losses and accumulate in various living or non-living species as they flow in many ways in animals, humans, and the environment. We need to monitor the nutrient flow and conduct life-cycle analysis to provide benchmarking solutions. Nevertheless, the novel technologies supported by political incentives will enable greater nutrient recycling from multiple waste streams. Additionally, the integration of crops and livestock, efficient utilization of by-products, and minimizing the wastage of food significantly enhance nutrient recovery and recycling.

9.3.3 Action 3: Sustainable Policy Programs

No doubt, the nutrient roadmaps, in combination with innovative technologies and sustainability-driven policies in the agribusiness models, will optimize the NUE in the next two decades. We are still lacking the integration of these components, or they have not existed in recent times. These must be linked with the SDGs to achieve high productivity and reduce nutrient losses. Nutrient steward-ship principles (International Plant Nutrition Institute, 2016) will increasingly guide policy-making and business innovations. However, the targets and priorities vary with the countries, agricultural practices, and nutrient use history. The point of focus here is how to develop and install roadmaps for achieving responsible nutrient use in the country. Participatory back-casting approaches play a pivotal role in meeting such a purpose (Kanter et al., 2016).

9.3.4 Action 4: Climate-Friendly Nutrients

Fertilizers manufactured in an environmentally friendly manner have a greater potential for releasing nutrients to the plant. Production of low-carbon fertilizer nutrients would be a possible solution to cope with pre-farm greenhouse gas emissions, specifically CO_2 and N_2O (nitrous oxide). New approaches in fertilizer formulations or inhibitors, precise nutrient application, and agronomic field management would effectively deal with GHG emissions (van Loon et al., 2019; Maaz et al., 2021). Innovations in fertilizer production such as bio-based coatings (Chen et al., 2018), smart fertilizers (Zhang et al., 2013), NMs, etc. are highly efficient in tailoring nutrient release and maintaining synchrony with plant demand.

9.3.5 Action 5: Nutrition-Sensitive Farming

To address issues such as under nutrition, malnutrition, obesity, and noncommunicable diseases, it is paramount to consider the whole nutritional contribution of food crops (Poole et al., 2020). The choice of consumers would also create market demand for growing different nutritional value crops. In consideration of local preference, nutrition-sensitive crop production would provide a way to diversify crop rotations and effective nutrient management (Singh et al., 2018; Zhang et al., 2021).

9.3.6 Action 6: Accelerated Innovation

Future innovations and research in plant nutrition should be rapid in the progress of the development and dissemination of new technologies and knowledge on a wider scale, as there is a huge gap between innovators, researchers, and end users in developing the right nutrient roadmaps and solutions. Setting benchmarks in major cropping systems at the global level is important to identify the priorities and possible solutions for bringing drastic yield increments and nutrient use efficiency. Sharing of knowledge, resources, and coordination among the public and private sectors could accelerate innovations in the agriculture sector (Berthet et al., 2018). Stakeholders and end users should be involved in focusing on the problems; learning science approaches, collaborations, entrepreneurship, and agribusiness activities with farmers are critical (Herrero et al., 2020).

9.4   ROLE OF STAKEHOLDERS FOR RESPONSIBLE PLANT NUTRITION

Consumers are the ultimate end users who have a significant change in plant nutrition as there is a drastic change in healthy food patterns and there is a high demand for food that is produced in a more sustainable manner. Changes in food behavior are partly compensated by growing food consumption, a burgeoning population, and income growth. *Farmers*, *Farm Advisers*, and *Service Providers* hold the primary responsibility for responsible plant nutrition and promoting soil health on larger scales. All should be aware of new technologies, services, etc., and they must adapt and share the innovations in farming. *Fertilizer Industries* need to provide integrated plant nutrition solutions based on the requirements and new business models, including transparent monitoring and reporting that helps in transforming industry strategies. *Food Traders* and *Retailers* have a great deal of power to influence the producers, as they have a strong focus on the consumers' eating patterns. More transparent, data-driven, and vertically integrated supply chains, including direct sourcing from farmers, would reduce production losses. Both *Private* and *Government organizations* should collaborate and invest in technologies and businesses that support key elements of the new criteria. *Policymakers* can drive changes in food consumption. They must set out a clear vision for national or regional roadmaps through the dynamic policies that incentivize innovation in technologies. They should ensure that farmers have worldwide access to the internet and digital services at affordable prices. *Scientists* should focus on applications, reality checks, and discoveries and achieve faster translation into practice.

9.5   CONCLUSION

Acceleration in research and development by private and government bodies will support the expansion of responsible crop nutrition worldwide in the upcoming decades. Technological advancements would certainly increase the fertilizer formulations and application methods; as a result, there would be high nutrient use efficiency. The implication is that society should change its mindset in view of achieving and sharing the outcomes. A new nutrient economy can be achieved in two decades if we set ambitious targets through suitable policies and investments that stimulate stakeholders towards tailored plant nutrition solutions. With this new criterion, the following outcomes can be achieved:

- We can increase nutrient use efficiency by 70%.
- Nutrient waste can be halved through responsible consumption and effective crop management practices.
- Excess carbon loss and soil nutrient depletion can be halted.
- Attractive policies can trigger a farming system that drastically increases soil health.
- Millions of hectares of degraded land can be restored.
- Malnutrition can be eradicated through the use of micronutrient-enriched fertilizers and nutrient-biofortified crops.
- GHG emissions from fertilizers can be reduced by 30% through novel approaches.
- Ultimately, the globe will be free from hunger.

REFERENCES

Abdelhameed, R.M., Abdelhameed, R.E., & Kamel, H. A. (2019) Iron-based metal-organic-frameworks as fertilizers for hydroponically grown *Phaseolus vulgaris*. *Materials Letters*, 237, 72–79.

Alidoust, D., & Isoda, A. (2013) Effect of γFe_2O_3 nanoparticles on photosynthetic characteristic of soybean (*Glycine max* (L.) Merr.): foliar spray versus soil amendment. *Acta Physiologiae Plantarum*, 35(12), 3365–3375.

Almeelbi, T., & Bezbaruah, A. (2014) Nanoparticle-sorbed phosphate: iron and phosphate bioavailability studies with *Spinacia oleracea* and *Selenastrum capricornutum*. *ACS Sustainable Chemistry & Engineering*, 2(7), 1625–1632.

Anstoetz, M., Sharma, N., Clark, M., & Yee, L. H. (2016) Characterization of an oxalate-phosphate-amine metal-organic framework (OPA-MOF) exhibiting properties suited for innovative applications in agriculture. *Journal of Materials Science*, 51, 9239–9252.

Baldock, J.O., & Schulte, E. E. (1996) Plant analysis with standardized scores combines DRIS and sufficiency range approaches for corn. *Agronomy Journal*, 88, 448–456.

Ball, P. (2002) Natural strategies for the molecular engineer. *Nanotechnology*, 13, R15.

Begum, S., Hassan, Z., Brase, S., Wöll, C., & Tsotsalas, M. (2019) Metal-organic framework-templated biomaterials: recent progress in synthesis, functionalization, and applications. *Accounts of Chemical Research*, 52, 1598–1610.

Berthet, E.T., Hickey, G.M., & Klerkx, L. (2018) Opening design and innovation processes in agriculture: insights from design and management sciences and future directions. *Agricultural Systems*, 165, 111–115.

Brown, P.H., Zhao, F.-J., & Dobermann, A. (2021) What is a plant nutrient? Changing definitions to advance science and innovation in plant nutrition. *Plant and Soil*, 476, 11–23. doi:10.1007/s11104-021-05171-w

Chen, J., Lü, S., Zhang, Z., Zhao, X., Li, X., Ning, P., & Liu, M. (2018) Environmentally friendly fertilizers: a review of materials used and their effects on the environment. *Science of the Total Environment*, 613–614, 829–839.

Dobermann, A., Bruulsema, T., Cakmak, I., Gerard, B., Majumdar, K., McLaughlin, M., …Zhang, X. (2022) Responsible plant nutrition: a new paradigm to support food system transformation. *Global Food Security*, 33, 100636.

FAO (2021) *The State of the World's Land and Water Resources for Food and Agriculture – Systems at Breaking Point (SOLAW 2021): Synthesis Report*. FAO, Rome.

FOLU (2019) Growing better: ten critical transitions to transform food and land use. https://www.foodandlandusecoalition.org/globa l-report/.

Fuglie, K.O. (2018) Is agricultural productivity slowing? *Global Food Security*, 17, 73–83.

Herrero, M., Thornton, P.K., Mason-D'Croz, D., Palmer, J., Benton, T.G., Bodirsky, B.L., …West, P.C. (2020) Innovation can accelerate the transition towards a sustainable food system. *Nature Food*, 1, 266–272.

International Plant Nutrition Institute (2016) *4R Plant Nutrition Manual: A Manual for Improving the Management of Plant Nutrition, Metric Version*. IPNI, Norcross, GA.

Kanter, D.R., Schwoob, M.H., Baethgen, W.E., Bessembinder, J., Carriquiry, M., Dobermann, A., …de Lima, J.M.S. (2016) Translating the Sustainable Development Goals into action: a participatory backcasting approach for developing national agricultural transformation pathways. *Global Food Security*, 10, 71–79.

Khodakovskaya, M.V., Kim, B.S., Kim, J.N., Alimohammadi, M., Dervishi, E., Mustafa, T., & Cernigla, C. E. (2013) Carbon nanotubes as plant growth regulators: effects on tomato growth, reproductive system, and soil microbial community. *Small*, 9(1), 115–123.

Khot, L.R., Sankaran, S., Maja, J.M., Ehsani, R., & Schuster, E. W. (2012) Applications of nanomaterials in agricultural production and crop protection: a review. *Crop Protection*, 35, 64–70. doi: 10.1016/j.cropro.2012.01.007

Khush, G. S., Lee, S., Cho, J. I., & Jeon, J. S. (2012) Biofortification of crops for reducing malnutrition. *Plant Biotechnology Reports*, 6(3), 195–202.

Klaine, S.J., Alvarez, P.J.J., Batley, G.E., Fernandes, T. F., Handy, R. D., Lyon, D. Y., …Lead, J. R. (2008) Nanomaterials in the environment: behavior, fate, bioavailability, and effects. *Environmental Toxicology and Chemistry*, 27, 1825–1851. doi: 10.1897/08-090.1

Ladha, J.K., Jat, M.L., Stirling, C.M., Chakraborty, D., Pradhan, P., Krupnik, T.J., …Gerard, B. (2020) Achieving the sustainable development goals in agriculture: the crucial role of nitrogen in cereal-based systems. *Advances in Agronomy*, 163, 39–116.

Liu, R., & Lal, R. (2014) Synthetic apatite nanoparticles as a phosphorus fertilizer for soybean (*Glycine max*). *Scientific Reports*, 4(5686), 1–6.

Maaz, T.M., Sapkota, T.B., Eagle, A.J., Kantar, M.B., Bruulsema, T.W., & Majumdar, K. (2021) Meta-analysis of yield and nitrous oxide outcomes for nitrogen management in agriculture. *Global Change Biology*, 27, 2343–2360.

Mazid, M., & Khan, T. A. (2014) Future of bio-fertilizers in Indian agriculture: an overview. *International Journal of Agricultural and Food Research*, 3, 10–23.

Parihar, C.M., Singh, A.K., Jat, S.L., Dey, A., Nayak, H. S., Mandal, B. N., …Yadav, O. P. (2020) Soil quality and carbon sequestration under conservation agriculture with balanced nutrition in intensive cereal-based system. *Soil and Tillage Research*, 202, 104653. doi: 10.1016/j.still.2020.104653

Parween, T., Bhandari, P., Siddiqui, Z. H., Jan, S., Fatma, T., & Patanjali, P. K. (2017) Biofilm: a next-generation biofertilizer. In *Mycoremediation and Environmental Sustainability*. Fungal Biology, edited by R. Prasad (Cham: Springer), 39–51. doi: 10.1007/978-3-319-68957-9_3

Poole, N., Donovan, J., & Erenstein, O. (2020) Agri-nutrition research: revisiting the contribution of maize and wheat to human nutrition and health. *Food Policy*, 100, 101976.

Pradhan, S., Patra, P., Das, S., Mitra, S., Dey, K. K., Akbar, S., … Goswami, A. (2013) Photochemical modulation of biosafe manganese nanoparticles on *Vigna radiata*: a detailed molecular, biochemical, and biophysical study. *Environmental Science & Technology*, 47(22), 13122–13131.

Pradhan, S., Patra, P., Mitra, S., Dey, K. K., Jain, S., Sarkar, S., … Goswami, A. (2014) Manganese nanoparticles: impact on non-modulated plant as a potent enhancer in nitrogen metabolism and toxicity study both in vivo and in vitro. *Journal of Agricultural and Food Chemistry*, 62(35), 8777–8785.

Raliya, R., & Tarafdar, J.C. (2013) ZnO nanoparticle biosynthesis and its effect on phosphorous-mobilizing enzyme secretion and gum contents in clusterbean (Cyamopsis tetragonoloba L.). *Agricultural Research*, 2, 48–57.

Rana, K. L., Kour, D., Yadav, A. N., Yadav, N., & Saxena, A. K. (2020). Agriculturally important microbial biofilms: biodiversity, ecological significances, and biotechnological applications. In *New and Future Developments in Microbial Biotechnology and Bioengineering: Microbial Biofilms*, edited by M. K. Yadav and B. P. Singh (Amsterdam: Elsevier), 221–265. doi: 10.1016/B978-0-444-64279-0.00016-5

Salt, D. E. (2004) Update on plant ionomics. *Plant Physiology*, 136, 2451–2456.

Sapkota, T. B., Jat, M. L., Rana, D. S., & KhatriChhetri, A. (2021) Crop nutrient management using nutrient expert improves yield, increases farmers' income and reduces greenhouse gas emissions. *Scientific Reports*, 11, 1564. doi: 10.1038/s41598-020-79883-x

Sapkota, T. B., Majumdar, K., Jat, M.L., Kumar, A., Bishnoi, D. K., McDonald, A. J., & Pampolino, M. (2014) Precision nutrient management in conservation agriculture-based wheat production of Northwest India: profitability, nutrient use efficiency and environmental footprint. *Field Crops Research*, 155, 233–244.

Shan, Y., Cao, L., Muhammad, B., Xu, B., Zhao, P., Cao, C., & Huang, Q. (2020) Iron-based porous metal-organic frameworks with crop nutritional function as carriers for controlled fungicide release. *Journal of Colloid and Interface Science*, 566, 383–393.

Sharma, S., Panneerselvam, P., Castillo, R., Manohar, S., Raj, R., Ravi, V., & Buresh, R. J. (2019) Web-based tool for calculating field specific nutrient management for rice in India. *Nutrient Cycling in Agroecosystems*, 113, 21–33.

Siddiqui, M.H., Al-Whaibi, M.H., Firoz, M., & Al-Khaishany, M. Y. (2015) Role of nanoparticles in plants. In *Nanotechnology and Plant Sciences*, edited by M. Siddiqui, M. Al-Whaibi and F. Mohammad (Cham: Springer), 19–35. doi: 10.1007/978-3-319-14502-0_2

Singh, A.L., Basu, M. S., & Singh, N. B. (2004) *Mineral Disorders of Groundnut*. National Research Center for Groundnut (ICAR), Junagadh, India, p85.

Singh, A. L., Chaudhari, V., & Ajay, B. C. (2015). Screening of groundnut genotypes for phosphorus efficiency under field conditions. Indian Journal of Genetics, 75(3), 363–371. doi: 10.5958/0975-6906.2015.00057.7

Singh, B.R., Timsina, Y.N., Lind, O.C., Cagno, S., & Janssens, K. (2018) Zinc and iron concentration as affected by nitrogen fertilization and their localization in wheat grain. *Frontiers in Plant Science*, 9, 307.

Sonkar, S.K., Roy, M., Babar, D.G., & Sarkar, S. (2012) Water soluble carbon nano-onions from wood wool as growth promoters for gram plants. *Nanoscale*, 4(24), 7670–7767.

Stevenson, J.R., Villoria, N., Byerlee, D., Kelley, T., & Maredia, M. (2013) Green Revolution research saved an estimated 18 to 27 million hectares from being brought into agricultural production. *Proceedings of the National Academy of Sciences of the United States of America*, 110, 8363–8368.

Su, M., Liu, H., Liu, C., Qu, C., Zheng, L., & Hong, F. (2009) Promotion of nano-anatase TiO_2 on the spectral responses and photochemical activities of D1/D2/Cyt b559 complex of spinach. *Spectrochimica Acta. Part A, Molecular and Biomolecular Spectroscopy*, 72, 1112–1116.

Swarnalakshmi, K., Prasanna, R., Kumar, A., Pattnaik, S., Chakravarty, K., Shivay, Y. S., & Saxena, A.K. (2013) Evaluating the influence of novel cyanobacterial biofilmed biofertilizers on soil fertility and plant nutrition in wheat. *European Journal of Soil Biology*, 55, 107–116. doi: 10.1016/j.ejsobi.2012.12.008

Tripathi, S., & Sarkar, S. (2014) Influence of water-soluble carbon dots on the growth of wheat plant. *Applied Nanoscience*, 5, 609–616. doi: 10.1007/s13204-014-0355-9

Triveni, Y. N. P., & Jhansi, R. S. (2017) Biofilm formation of zinc solubilizing, potassium releasing bacteria on the surface of fungi. *International Journal of Current Microbiology and Applied Sciences*, 6, 2037–2047. doi: 10.20546/ijcmas.2017.604.241

Ünal Turhan, E., Erginkaya, Z., Korkluoglu, M., & Konuray, G. (2019) Beneficial biofilm applications in food and agricultural industry. In *Health and Safety Aspects of Food Processing Technologies*, edited by A. Malik, Z. Erginkaya and H. Erten (Cham: Springer International Publishing), 445–469. doi: 10.1007/978-3-030-24903-8_15

United Nations (UN) (2015) World Population Prospects: the 2015 Revision [Online]. Available at: https://esa.un.org/unpd/wpp. Accessed November 2016.

van Loon, M.P., Hijbeek, R., ten Berge, H.F.M., De Sy, V., ten Broeke, G.A., Solomon, D., & van Ittersum, M.K. (2019) Impacts of intensifying or expanding cereal cropping in sub-Saharan Africa on greenhouse gas emissions and food security. *Global Change Biology*, 25, 3720–3730.

Verma, N.P., Kuldeep, U.K., & Yadav, N. (2018) Study of liquid biofertilizer as an innovative agronomic input for sustainable agriculture. *International Journal of Pure & Applied Bioscience*, 6(1), 190–194.

Vollset, S.E., Goren, E., Yuan, C.-W., Cao, J., Smith, A.E., Hsiao, T., …Murray, C.J.L. (2020) Fertility, mortality, migration, and population scenarios for 195 countries and territories from 2017 to 2100: a forecasting analysis for the Global Burden of Disease Study. *The Lancet*, 396, 1285–1306. doi:10.1016/S0140-6736(20)30677-2

Wang, D., Xu, A., Elmerich, C., & Ma, L. Z. (2017) Biofilm formation enables free-living nitrogen-fixing rhizobacteria to fix nitrogen under aerobic conditions. *The ISME Journal*, 11, 1602–1613. doi: 10.1038/ismej.2017.30

Xie, Y., He, Y., Irwin, P.L., Jin, T., & Shi, X. (2011) Antibacterial activity and mechanism of action of zinc oxide nanoparticles against *Campylobacter jejuni*. *Applied and Environmental Microbiology*, 77, 325–331.

Yang, J., Trickett, C. A., Alahmadi, S. B., Alshammari, A.S., & Yaghi, O.M. (2017) Calcium l-lactate frameworks as naturally degradable carriers for pesticides. *Journal of the American Chemical Society*, 139, 8118–8121.

Zhang, B., Luo, Y., Kanyuck, K., Bauchan, G., Mowery, J., & Zavalij, P. (2016) Development of metal-organic framework for gaseous plant hormone encapsulation to manage ripening of climacteric produce. *Journal of Agricultural and Food Chemistry*, 64, 5164–5170.

Zhang, W., Zhang, W., Wang, X., Liu, D., Zou, C., & Chen, X. (2021) Quantitative evaluation of the grain zinc in cereal crops caused by phosphorus fertilization. A meta-analysis. *Agronomy for Sustainable Development*, 41, 6.

Zhang, X., Chabot, D., Sultan, Y., Monreal, C., & DeRosa, M.C. (2013) Target-molecule-triggered rupture of aptamer-encapsulated polyelectrolyte microcapsules. *ACS Applied Materials & Interfaces*, 5, 5500–5507.

Zheng, L., Hong, F., Lu, S., & Liu, C. (2005) Effects of nano-TiO_2 on strength of naturally aged seeds and growth of spinach. *Biological Trace Element Research*, 104, 83–92.

10 Watershed as a Potential Site for Regenerative Agricultural Practices

Subhadip Paul, Prabhakar Prasad Barnwal,
Anirban Sil, and Amitava Rakshit

10.1 INTRODUCTION

With the steep growth in the world population, demand for food has swelled up. Thus, intensive agricultural practices have left a significant footprint on climate change and land-use systems, pushing soil emissions to an extortionate level along with land degradation. To maintain the productivity of land, the soil needs to be exploited in such a way that it can achieve higher output without losing quality. Today, topsoil is being treated with organic manures, produced by both onsite and offsite farmlands, to maintain the organic carbon in the soil at the desired level. There are also other in situ resources, i.e., vegetation, water, nutrients, and soil microbes, that need to be maintained at the desired level to sustain crop production besides maintaining a healthy ecosystem. However, most of these natural resources might not be renewed as quickly as needed under intensive cultivation practices. So, the question lies in whether topsoil can be cured with the existing resources or not.

Recently, the regeneration of soil resources has received profound appreciation from international communities for its ability to sustain crop production. Though regenerative agriculture is somewhat considered vogue, some have claimed that regenerative agriculture can reverse climate change and land degradation without loss of vegetation, water, and land qualities (Kastner, 2016; Rhodes, 2017; White, 2020). Pioneer of regenerative agriculture, Gabe Brown, a farmer, highlighted the need for soil recharge in degraded lands to sustain the functions of an ecosystem in the long run (White, 2020). Given the defeatist impact of synthetic agri-inputs, alternate approaches have become an urgent need for sustaining soil productivity. The regenerative approach seeks a stable input-output relationship between the living and non-living components of an ecosystem. However, not one single agronomic approach can reshape ecosystem functions alone. For example, simple crop rotation and manuring cannot control soil erosion, but with the adoption of conservation practices, they can minimize the effect, while contour farming has no effect on leveled flat lands. Hence, regenerative development should be holistic, i.e., the integration of different management practices, either known or to be included soon, for different environments. The whole context has the farm as its baseline for adoption, while watersheds can have different types of lands such as croplands, pasturelands, forestlands, and water channels. Therefore, watersheds can adopt such integration. This is also synonymous with the restoration of degraded land. Given the concept, the identification of resources in regenerative agricultural practices is quite comprehensive.

10.2 RESOURCE RECYCLING IN REGENERATIVE CULTIVATION PRACTICES

Regenerative agriculture is the plausible answer for aiding the reuse and recycling of natural resources in a well-defined ecosystem, apart from the restoration of degraded agricultural lands. The main baseline lies within the soil. Soil health improvement is considered a primary target to achieve resource regeneration in agriculture. Overexploitation of natural resources has transformed

DOI: 10.1201/9781003309581-12

the atmosphere into a major carbon sink, while making soil more decarbonized and less diverse in terms of microbial population and fertility. Apart from the soil and above-ground biosphere, water quality also needs to be furnished properly for restoring sustained activities. Soil biology is the prime concern for all agricultural activities. Soil organic carbon and soil microbiology are also used interchangeably from a soil health standpoint. Jones et al. (2011) has pointed out the keys to enriching soils with organic carbon, as mentioned by White (2020):

i. Storage of solar energy within simple carbon compounds via photosynthesis
ii. Conversion of the simple carbon compounds into diverse components that serve as "fuel" for life
iii. Creating a hotspot for microbial proliferation within the rhizosphere through the secretion of easily mineralizable exudates
iv. Formation of biochemically stable humus from litter falls with the help of soil-active microbiota
v. Physical conditioning of soil through mycorrhiza-mediated glomalin, generating aggregates by binding the loose soil materials

Without the soil microbiome, the conversion of the sun's energy within chlorophytes becomes impossible. On a broader scale, the flow of solar energy should be optimized and maintained for all activities within an ecosystem. Thus, both upper- and below-ground biota play an important role in sustaining soil health. The following are the key dramas played by the microbes within a soil (Anderson, 2003; Bending et al., 2004):

i. Mineralization of soil, an unavailable form of plant nutrients
ii. Production of various growth factors for plants, such as growth hormones, vitamins, organic acids, etc.
iii. Catalysis of important biochemical reactions via the synthesis of enzymes
iv. Bioremediation of pollutant elements
v. Profuse development of the desired soil structure through aggregate formation
vi. Water filtration as well as retention through escalating soil pores
vii. Gas exchange between two adjoining spheres

Among all the soil resources, microbial proliferation in the rhizosphere can be changed abruptly, but the result will always be short-term. Apart from these, macro- and meso-biomes (mites, collembolans, ants, earthworms, enchytraeids, and other soil-inhabiting insects) also accelerate these biogeochemical cycles through routine changes in soil morphology (Coleman et al. and Wall, 2015; Nielsen et al., 2015). Soil exchange capacity, clay content, type of reaction, base saturation, nutrient content, and most importantly, buffering capacity, have a tremendous influence on the overlying biological parameters. The type of soil reaction, base saturation, and nutrient contents are also heavily affected by climate, parent material, and mineralogy (Dahlgren et al., 1997; Kraus, 1999; Pincus et al., 2017). Changes in mineralogy and clay content can only be achieved over centuries (Pincus et al., 2017). Thus, control over pedogenesis is out of the question; however, soil exchange capacity, nutrient concentration, and base saturation need a few decades to change (Ulery et al., 1995; Richter and Markewitz, 2001). The higher the clay content in a particular soil, the greater the exchange capacity, resulting in higher nutrient retention and buffering capacity in that soil. The presence of higher organic carbon can also mask the lower soil exchange capacity in degraded lands, as organic matter itself carries sufficient negative charges. Soil biological and chemical parameters, together, also incorporate desired soil physical conditions for water infiltration and plant growth. Lands receiving continuous agri-inputs, i.e., synthetic fertilizers and plant protection chemicals, have been reported to lose their microbial diversity (Hartmann et al., 2015). This has resulted in a loss of soil fertility over time. Exclusion of synthetic plant protection chemicals should be the first thing in mind while performing regenerative agriculture because these also knock down agriculturally important microbes and insects. Nevertheless, abstained use of synthetic chemicals can also lead to low land productivity. Recharging these unfertile lands is at risk as the biological products are not patentable. Therefore, market interest in the commercialization of these products is not at par as compared to synthetic agri-products. All that remains is the use of on-and off-farm resources.

When we see degraded land, all that comes to mind is how much fertile soil has been eroded since time immemorial. However, the regeneration of natural resources also comes from regenerative thinking as well. Instead of focusing on the severity of the loss, our objective should be to improve the existing soil. Effective agronomic management practices can still conserve the existing soil resources. Improvement of land productivity and sustainable health can go hand in hand through reducing soil disturbances, improved crop diversification, and integrated nutrient management practices. The principles behind this were elaborated by Brown (2018) as follows:

i. Limiting mechanical disturbances on topsoil as plowing destroys soil structure, exposing underground to an open atmosphere
ii. Keeping the bare soil covered to control rainfall impact, runoff flow, erosion, gaseous losses of nutrients, and fluctuations in soil temperature and moisture
iii. Maintenance of upper-and below-ground biodiversity through the cultivation of differentially rooted plants (i.e., grasses, legumes, shrubs, trees, etc.) in proper succession
iv. Retention of living roots in the soil as a hotspot for microbial activities and carbon recycling
v. Integration of animals (livestock, annelids, and arthropods)

Regenerative agriculture itself carries a broader definition. Any activities that fall under soil conservation and sustenance can also be considered to have regeneration capability. Thus, in pursuit of resource rehabilitation, different potent agronomic activities are emerging. Important among them are natural farming, carbon farming, mixed farming, permaculture, integrated farming systems, climate-smart agriculture, circular agriculture, biodynamic agriculture, organic agriculture, conservation agriculture, and agroforestry (Mollison, 1988; Devendra and Thomas, 2002; Udawatta et al., 2002; Howard, 2006; Hobbs et al., 2008; Fukuoka, 2009; Gill et al., 2009; Turinek et al., 2009; Lipper et al., 2014; Toensmeier, 2016; Toopet al., 2017; Paul et al., 2019).

Hydrologic cycles in any area are also affected by these management practices. As agriculture is considered a potential non-point source of water pollution, the quality of water will always be a concern before input applications. Being a geohydrological unit, water quality enhancement in a watershed is one of the prime goals covered by all watershed planners. Heavy doses of nitrogenous and phosphate fertilization must be avoided during groundwater recharge, as the leaching of NO_3^- and phosphate into groundwater can pose serious health consequences (Böhlke and Denver, 1995). Nevertheless, nutrient runoff through streams also causes eutrophication (Wan et al., 2014). Instead of indiscriminate use of nitrogenous fertilizers, rotation with legume crops in succession or within mixed cropping, followed by its incorporation within the soil, can recover an appreciable amount of soil nitrogen (Paul et al., 2019). Sediment loads can also be cut down from tributaries via grassed waterways along the slope (Fiener and Auerswald, 2003). Growing erosion-resisting crops in alternate rows with erosion-permitting crops across the slope of the watershed can somehow retard the mudflow (Gray and Sotir, 1996). Agroforestry has also been found to be promising to enhance water quality and plant water use efficiency with respect to crop rotation and soil conservation points of view (Udawatta et al., 2002; Chaturvedi et al., 2014; Bajigo et al., 2015; Suprayogo et al., 2020).

Repeatedly, it has been observed that the community development approach is neglected from being included in this resource category. The whole of regenerative agriculture lies in the innovative thoughts, skills, and energized attitude of the farmers. Scientific findings in the research laboratories and their subsequent introduction in the farmers' field can be manifested as a game-changer concerning the regeneration of ecosystem services. The farmer-centered approach will enable farmers to think rationally about themselves as well as their farming ecosystems, so that they can co-evolve with their farming practices. This co-evolving mutualism between farmers and their farming ecosystems can only take place with the help of technology transfer. Hence, community- and capacity-building initiatives must be formulated through different extension programs and policy strengthening. As per Sherwood and Uphoff (2000), the basic training of farmers for regenerative agricultural practices must convey the following messages:

  i. Soil is a living body
  ii. Farming practices can affect the biodiversity of living soil organisms
  iii. An organic approach, in association with integrated and need-based external fertilization, can favor sustained soil functioning
  iv. One has to be there in charge of developing local communities to take small but necessary steps at each cycle

However, without fostering institutional collaboration and proper policy assistance, this communication system will soon become systematically unstable.

10.3   POTENT SITES WITHIN A WATERSHED FOR RESOURCE MANAGEMENT

A watershed is a topographically delineated geohydrological unit drained by streamlines into a common outlet. It is also a biophysical unit, as the biosphere strongly interacts with its physical surroundings. The management of this unit carries potent socioeconomic and political impacts. Guiding streams of water through land can serve the desired ecosystem functions, mitigating land deterioration. The characteristics of the watershed are of utmost importance for its suitable management. Throughout the decades, remote sensing and GIS (geographic information system) techniques have been operated with salient decision support systems to draw management-based specific areas within a watershed. Important models among them such as watershed characterization and modeling system (WCMS), systemic dynamic (SD) modeling, multiple criteria decision-making (MCDM) system, technique for order of preference by similarity to ideal solution (TOPSIS), simple additive weighting (SAW), analytic hierarchy process (AHP), watershed analysis risk management framework (WARMF), generalized watershed loading function (GWLF), watershed management decision support system (WAMADSS), elevation derivatives for natural applications (EDNA), etc. are used for delineating, mapping, and prioritizing the dynamic storage behavior and recharge zone in watershed, potentially inundated area, agriculturally productive area, and urban planning (Haith and Shoemaker, 1987; Fulcher, 1996; Chen et al., 2005, 2011; Strager et al., 2010; Pourghasemi et al., 2012; Kotir et al., 2016; Meshram et al., 2020).

Generally, flat slopes (0%–8%) within a watershed are used for cultivation because an increase in slope steepness under simultaneous land disturbances can cause accelerated soil erosion (Ziadat and Taimeh, 2013). Furthermore, runoff losses of nutrients and the loading of sediments within tributaries and stream channels can reduce the quality of water and the carrying capacity of streams. Care should be taken not to apply land perturbation before water recharging time in undulating catchment areas. Water recharge zones must be bestowed with enough soil coverage, preferentially vegetative ones. Besides the development of different engineered structures, agroforestry is considered the best management practice across the transition zone between catchment and command areas (Chaturvedi et al., 2014; Bajigo et al., 2015; Suprayogo et al., 2020). Perennial trees and shrubs in strips also perform buffer action in pastures against erosion. If not naturally present within a defined ecosystem, pastures should not be expanded artificially at the expense of the native forest cover. Also, the maintenance of pastures by livestock grazing should be in a rotational order rather than a continuous one, as grass growth is also an essential factor for sustaining soil health (Teague et al., 2016; Teague and Barnes, 2017). Grassed waterways are to be promoted along the streamlines. Grasses have profuse rooting habits that bind loose soil materials tightly, reducing mudflow and sedimentation along the channels and minimizing stream bank erosion (Schultz et al., 2004). Crop diversification can be achieved near the outlet point of a watershed under well-managed command facilities. Uncovering soil texture, structure, underlying rocks, and potential capacity of underground aquifers should be prioritized first for performing resource regeneration activities in watersheds (Pintoet al., 2017; Arulbalaji et al., 2019). Rainwater harvesting techniques should be applied at different points distant from rainfall-receiving zones (Walsh et al., 2014). If needed, suitable reservoirs can be made along the primary and secondary stream channels for the supply of irrigation water during off-season cultivations. The capacities of the reservoirs should be planned according to the rainfall intensity. Not to mention, runoffs in micro- and small-watersheds are more concentrated. Thus, knowledge of slope, texture, vegetative barrier, and flow direction should be kept in mind before the construction of a rainwater harvesting facility. Whether in macro-watersheds, enough time is given for runoff water to infiltrate the soil, recharging the groundwater at the same time due to its expanded area. Appropriate contour management and vegetative barriers can aid rainwater harvesting in the macro-watershed without promoting soil erosion (Glendenning et al., 2012). Therefore, agroforestry in relatively undulating areas of the watershed would be considered the prime practice to be prioritized for regenerative agricultural management.

10.4   AGROFORESTRY: KEY TO SOIL RESOURCE REGENERATION IN WATERSHEDS

According to Nair et al. (2021), "Agroforestry is the collective term for land-use systems and technologies in which woody perennials (trees, shrubs, palms, bamboos, etc.) are used deliberately on the same land-management units as crops and/or animals in some form of spatial arrangement or temporal sequence. In agroforestry systems, there are both ecological and economic interactions between the different components". It is a holistic approach marking socioeconomic and ecological benefits. For the conservation of natural resources, especially soil, agroforestry has a vital role. Adopting agroforestry systems not only enhances productivity but also provides different services or functions. Productive functions include fuel wood, fodder, fruits, gums, resins, medicines, and fibers, whereas service functions include shade, reduction in wind seed, control of erosion, and improvement of soil fertility.

Benefits of forest cover to the watershed:

i. **Reduction in stormwater runoff and flooding**

   With the assistance of their canopy, trees reduce the amount and intensity of precipitation on the ground, resulting in lower runoff. The infiltration rate has significantly increased due to the slowdown of runoff. The addition of litter increases the storage of water in the soil.

ii. **Reduction in stream channel erosion**

   Trees grown along the banks of watershed areas prevent erosion by stabilizing the soil with root systems and by substantially dispersing raindrop energy. This also adds organic matter to the soil.

iii. **Improve soil and water quality**

   Trees take up storm water pollutants such as nitrogen from soil and groundwater. Forested areas can filter sediment and associated pollutants from runoff. Certain tree species break down pollutants commonly found in urban soils, groundwater, and runoff, such as metals, pesticides, and solvents.

iv. **Provide habitat for terrestrial and aquatic wildlife**

   Forests provide habitat for wildlife in the form of food supplies, interior breeding areas, and migratory corridors. Streamside forests provide habitat in the form of leaf litter and large woody debris for fish and other aquatic species. Forest litter, such as branches, leaves, fruits, and flowers, forms the basis of the food web for stream organisms.

v. Provide food

Perennials with differentially fruiting habits are best known for their contribution to hunger management. Indigenous plants like mango, banana, sapota, apple, jackfruit, guava, litchi, orange, etc. can also mitigate hunger in a short period of time and generate income through marketing.

The term agroforestry is elaborated with different synonymous practices, i.e., forest farming, silvopastoral culture, riparian forest buffer, multi-storeyed cropping, alley cropping, windbreak, etc., to address natural resource conservation. Core practices for watersheds must follow the different aspects of land cover utilization (Table 10.1).

TABLE 10.1
Three Perspectives on the Relationship between Forest Cover and Watershed Functions (Van Noordwijk 2003)

Aspect	Forests as Sponge Theory (Heringa, 1939)	Infiltration Theory (Roessel, 1939)	Synthesis and Quantification (Coster, 1938)
1. Dry season river flow	Depends on the forest cover	Depends on the geological formation	Vegetation determines soil permeability
2. Required forest area for hydrological functions	A minimum required fraction can be calculated from the area of rice fields to be irrigated with dry season flow	There is no minimum forest cover	The discharge of springs depends on the amount of water that percolates into the soil minus the loss of water because of evaporation.
3. What to do if the forest target is not met?	Farmland of farmers and agricultural estates has to be purchased and reforested	Reforestation is only carried out if certain soil types expose susceptibility to erosion, but then after other measures, such as terracing, catching holes, and soil cover have proved insufficient	Depends on elevation. Lysimeter measurements indicated that the evaporation of a free soil surface of 1,200, 900, and 600 mm/year at locations with an elevation of 250, 1,500, and 1,750 m above mean sea level, respectively
4. Forests or ground cover?	All soil types are equal; afforestation with industrial wood species has the same hydrological effect as natural forest and is (always) better than agricultural estates	An agricultural estate that succeeds to ban superficial runoff by terracing etc. or soil cover is hydrologically more valuable than an industrial timber plantation, where surface runoff can still take place, for example, because of steep slopes, poor undergrowth or poor humus formation	Measurements by the Forest Research Institute showed that well-maintained tea, coffee, rubber, and kina plantations are from a hydrological point of view nearly the same as forests (planted or natural) but superior to agricultural fields. Fires in the grass wilderness in the mountains stimulate water runoff and erosion.
5. Scope of reforestation	All problems with 'watershed functions' can be cured with reforestation	Recovery by reforestation can only be expected in cases where superficial runoff and erosion can be controlled with good forests. Forests without undergrowth and good humus formation are usually not sufficient. A soil cover with grass, dense herbaceous, or shrubby vegetation, however, will do.	Afforestation in low lands may probably decrease the discharge (including that in the dry season), because of the high evaporation rate from the forest; in the mountains the increased infiltration of abundant rain into the soil more than offsets the increased water use by trees.

Forests make excellent watersheds, chiefly because their soils usually have a high infiltration capacity—they are capable of quickly absorbing large amounts of water (Dhyani et al., 2006). Therefore, rainstorms or melting snow in woodlands produce relatively little surface runoff with the associated problems of erosion (detachment and movement of soil) and sedimentation (the deposition of soil) (Udawatta et al., 2002; Suprayogo et al., 2020). The forest vegetation also protects the soil's infiltration capacity. Raindrops falling on exposed soil may have enough energy to break up soil aggregates. Individual soil particles are then easily eroded and washed into soil pores, clogging them and preventing rainwater absorption.

Turbidity is the term applied to water that has reduced clarity due to suspended sediments (Sitaram, 2012). Turbid water looks cloudy. Generally, the water flowing through streams in stable forests has very low turbidity (Shanwal and Dahiya, 2002). Trees contribute to the high infiltration capacity of forest soils. The litter layer, which consists of leaves and bits of wood in various stages of decay on the forest floor, helps maintain healthy populations of soil organisms. By shielding the soil from the elements, the litter layer provides soil organisms with a less hostile, more stable environment (Markart et al., 2021). The forest vegetation also protects the soil's infiltration capacity. Raindrops falling on exposed soil may have enough energy to break up soil aggregates. Individual soil particles are then easily eroded and washed into soil pores, clogging them and preventing rainwater absorption (Dhyani et al., 2006). As one approach for agroforestry over longer periods, numerous benefits can be obtained (Table 10.2).

The proper certification process can be guided by third-party assurance organizations such as the International Standards Organization, based on the sound guidelines of the USDA Natural Resources Conservation Service (NRCS) for adopting core agroforestry systems in desired watersheds (Elevitch et al., 2018). Due to the diverse components of agroforestry, identification of interrelated characteristics can be achieved with intricate standardization for adopting resource regeneration in different farmlands or environments. The quantification of criteria must yield a certain threshold value to meet those standards.

10.5 IMPACT OF GRAZING ON REGENERATIVE SOIL MANAGEMENT

The landscape around water catchments requires a proper understanding of grazing management and its impact on resource regeneration. Grazing land or rangeland stewardship must enhance its productivity for providing different ecosystem services, but most of the inappropriately managed grazing lands have lost their productivity and biodiversity, resulting in land degradation and, to some extent, desertification of lands. Rangelands are one of the key land features in a watershed, protecting soil from getting eroded by the runoff flow from the recharge zone (Park et al., 2017). By doing so, grazing lands also control the nutrient and sediment loads in the tributaries. Thus, soil health needs to be maintained for the productive outcome of these lands. Research has revealed that improper management of ranches via grazing deteriorates different physio-chemical and biological properties of soil (Krzic et al., 2006; Lehman et al., 2015; Teague et al., 2016). Different types of grazing, i.e., continuous grazing, rotational grazing, deferred rotational grazing, management-intensive grazing, rotational rest grazing, mob grazing, strip grazing, multi-paddock grazing, creep grazing, and light continuous grazing, have been performed over the ages to sustain rangeland productivity and improve animal husbandry (Teague et al., 2016; Park et al., 2017; Teague and Barnes, 2017). The negative impact of continuous grazing can result in impaired soil health. Reports have enlightened that continuous grazing showed low productivity and less ground cover, which caused higher runoff coefficients over rotational grazing (Sanjari et al., 2009; Teague et al., 2011). Therefore, sufficient time should be given for pasture recovery after encroachment by animals. Rotational grazing and multi-paddock grazing are being supported as better management for rangelands with respect to the optimum stocking rate (Teague et al., 2011, 2016; Teague and Barnes, 2017). The popularity of these management methods is focused on adequate canopy covering, short-duration grazing, and stock number adjustment concerning forage biomass (Teague et al., 2011, 2016; Teague and Barnes, 2017). However, diversity within a stock should also be considered because, for a particular stock,

TABLE 10.2

Benefits of Agroforestry on Different Watersheds

Sl. No.	Location	Tree Components	Benefits	Reference
1.	Missouri, USA	*Agrostis gigantea, Quercus palustris, Q. bicolor, Q. macrocarpa*	• Agroforestry incorporation helped in reduction of runoff by 1%. • Reduction in total phosphorus loss was found to be 17%. • It was also concluded that buffer trips can be used to control degradation of stream water quality from agricultural nonpoint source pollution.	Udawatta et al. (2002)
2.	Sukhomajri watershed, Haryana	*Acacia catechu, Dalbergia sissoo, Ipomoea carnea, Agave americana*	• *Agave americana* was planted in critical areas to protect soil against erosion. • Here, mechanical measures were supported by vegetative measures. • This is aimed at containing surplus rainwater and sediment in situ.	Shanwal and Dahiya (2002)
3.	Permafrost-dominated watersheds, Northern Boreal Plain, Alberta, Canada	*Populus balsamifera, Picea glauca, Populus tremuloides, Larix laricina, Betula papyrifera`Populus tremuloides*	• Forestry management improved water quality indicators such as total nitrogen, total phosphorus, and dissolved organic carbon. • Disturbances of boreal forests have increased due to anthropogenic activities, which was controlled with the inclusion of forest. • The extent of disturbed watershed area relative to lake volume is the first determinant of the degree of impact of watershed disturbances. Hence, forest components are worth considering for the maintenance of watershed.	Pinel-Alloul et al. (2002)
4.	Watersheds of Doon Valley	*Eucalyptus camaldulensis, E. grandis, E. globulus, Acacia mearnsii*	• Runoff was reduced by 28% and the reduction in peak rate of discharge was noted to be 73% compared to natural vegetation. • Total soil nitrogen, organic carbon, and exchangeable K, Ca, and Mg contents increased which in turn helped in more infiltration of rainwater, hence low runoff and erosion.	Dhyani et al. (2006)
5.	Horticulture and Agroforestry Research Center (HARC), New Franklin, MO	*Schedonorus phoenix, Trifolium pretense, Lespedeza* sp., *Populus deltoides*	• Agroforestry approach reduced non-point source pollution losses from gazed and row cropped sites. • Runoff, sediment, nitrogen, and phosphorus losses were significantly reduced by establishment of agroforestry system.	Udawatta et al. (2011)
6.	Bunga watershed, Siwalik foothills	*Acacia catechu, Eulatiopsis bianata, Dalbergia sissoo, Eucalyptus* sp.	• For stabilization and to provide fodder, *Acacia* was planted. • *Dalbergia sissoo* was planted to strengthen the mechanical measure of watershed. • With the help of vegetation, there was a sharp decline in the sedimentation rate from 768 tonnes/ha/year to 240 tonnes/ha/year.	Sitaram (2012)

(Continued)

TABLE 10.2 (Continued)
Benefits of Agroforestry on Different Watersheds

Sl. No.	Location	Tree Components	Benefits	Reference
7.	Gununo watershed, Wolayitta zone, Ethiopia	*Enset ventricosum, Musa accuminata, Moringa oleifera, Brassica oleracea, Croton macrostachyu,* and *Acacia* sp.	• The study has shown that the dominant agroforestry practices in Gununo watershed are differently important in storing carbon in the system. • The total tree biomass carbon and above-ground tree carbon was highest in lower elevation suggesting that more tree plantations are needed in upper and middle elevation for better carbon storage of the area. • Therefore, promotion of agroforestry practices and technologies in Gununo watershed can be potential activity in carbon storage.	Bajigo et al. (2015)
8.	Garhkundar-Dabar watershed, Bundelkhand	*Tectona grandis, Acacia senegal, Emblica officinalis*	• According to NRCAF, Garhkundar-Dabar watershed as a model is replicable to 56% red soils of Bundelkhand region, Vindhyanchal, Satpura, and Aravali ranges. • Successful adoption and replication of these water conservation techniques and agroforestry can help overcome the problems of soil erosion and water crisis for drinking as well as for irrigation in the entire region of Bundelkhand. • Cropping intensity increased to 116% and soil loss and runoff reduced by 34%.	Singh et al. (2016)
9.	Rejoso watershed, Indonesia	*Pinus merkusii, Casuarina junghuniana, Swieteniamacrophylla, Duriozibethinus, Albiziasaman, Mangiferaindica*	• Forest and tree cover can influence various steps in the chain from rainfall to streamflow and erosion. • Agroforestry helped in maintenance of both upstream and midstream watersheds. • This also provided profitable yields for several crops.	Suprayogo et al. (2020)
10.	Alpine watersheds, Austria	*Nardus stricta, Festuca* sp., *Fagus sylvatica, Quercus* sp., *Picea abies, Abis alba, Larix decidua, Pinus cembra*	• There was a significant reduction in runoff. • Forests also influence erosion, transport, and deposition. • Root system contributes significantly to the stabilization of slopes, preventing shallow, landslides and potentially reducing material supply for bedload transport.	Markart et al. (2021)
11.	Indonesia	*Rhizophora* sp., *Aegiceras corniculatus, Ficus retuse*	• Rehabilitation of degraded watersheds was done through forests with the help of various government policies. • Flood control is an essential concern in watershed restoration programs in Indonesia, which can be accomplished by agroforestry measures. • It was concluded that degraded watershed rehabilitation was only possible with the inclusion of agroforestry.	Narendra et al. (2021)

there will always be some plants or forage patches preferred for exploitation over other plant types. These can bring about undesirable changes in plant community structures as well as soil microbial diversity, resulting in the progressive degradation of rangelands. Reports suggested that grasslands of mid- and tall-grass ecosystems get deteriorated over time if the perturbation is not given periodically (Knapp, 1985; Teague and Barnes, 2017). Hence, zero grazing is also not desirable to sustain the ecosystem functioning of rangelands in watersheds. A better grazing land also depends on the amount of water infiltration and percolation through soil, not just the amount of precipitation received in a watershed (Teague and Barnes, 2017). Therefore, adequate plant cover is necessary besides litter addition as a soil cover. Some tree covers should also be in pastures, but not at full canopy coverage, as this may prevent sunlight from reaching the ground, consequently lowering photosynthesis in small grasses, which again can change the below-ground biodiversity. Patches of forests can reshape the soil's physical, chemical, and biological properties and lower soil erosion under stream flow (Udawatta et al., 2002; Suprayogo et al., 2020). Litter addition by these trees can enhance the soil's organic carbon and nitrogen contents, along with higher fungal and bacterial community development. Therefore, patches of trees are to be maintained for excellent rangeland productivity in watersheds.

A potent ecological service can only be achieved when all the above- and below-ground biota can influence various soil functions together and minimize negative consequences. In most research, biota from the above ground was considered only, while biota from nearly 90% below ground was responsible for major ecosystem services in grazing lands (Lehman et al., 2015). Improvements in nutrient transformation and recycling, nutrient delivery in plant systems, regulation of important soil biogeochemical cycles, maintenance of soil structure, water conductivity, and retentivity, exchange of gases between soil and atmosphere, bioremediation, and control of soil-borne diseases are some of the major contributions of these soil biota to ecosystem functioning (Wall et al., 2004). Soil ecosystem engineers such as earthworms, ants, and dung beetles also have a strong positive influence on achieving desired soil properties for the better functioning of rangelands (Lehman et al., 2015). That is the reason why pasturelands should include the identification of potent soil function drivers for further studies.

10.6   PROSPECT LIES FOR FARMING COMMUNITIES

Regenerative agriculture seeks crucial elements that can assign farming activity to the uninterrupted evolution of the in situ landscape. One sustained system must fulfill the needs of the status quo. As residing in the same territory, farmers must support the constant regeneration of soil resources, as all living systems are considered to be interacting and self-organizing. While regenerative agriculture seeks continuous interactions between farmers and landscapes, for effective rural development in watersheds, the praxeology of farmers should be prioritized (Sherwood and Uphoff, 2000):

i. Adoption of innovative technology, transferred from different institutions
ii. Participation in non-formal learning
iii. Stating subsidy-based farmer-friendly policies that provide sufficient incentives for farm renovation
iv. Collaboration with multiple organizations
v. Integrated community development
vi. Local initiatives along with leadership

Participatory watershed management has been adopted in tribal areas of different countries, enabling farming communities to achieve more control over their livelihoods and natural resources (Wani et al., 2003). Benefits lie in the management of natural resources by land owners and the overall development of rural livelihoods, mitigating poverty in rural areas. The approach entails farmers' income from their spontaneous participation. Crop diversification, livestock growing, biomass management, and restoration of farmlands through government policies can generate per capita income in farming households, thereby influencing farmers' participation. The participating attitude of farmers can be quantifiable with certain indexing. Daru and Tips (1985) assessed such indexing and found that farmer income and participation were strongly correlated (coefficient value+0.844). Care should be taken to override the immediate outcomes of soil health management in the long term.

10.7 CONCLUSION

Soil is a living body, diversified with the functions of various organisms. From the management point of view, crop yield and soil function are somehow interdependent with respect to the fertility status of the farming landscape. Regeneration of in situ land resources can repair the damage caused by improper land management in agriculture. Regenerative agriculture looks for ways to restore the existing land assets with the help of innovative cultural practices. Among different cultural practices, agroforestry is now considered helpful in the restoration of degraded farmlands in watersheds. Researchers have proven that integrated nutrient management, soil carbon sequestration, crop rotation, crop diversification, manuring, pasture management, livestock management, soil conservation management, and residue incorporation over some time can augment soil health, land restoration, and reduce soil emissions. However, communication gaps between research and technology adaptation have already had an impact on transforming conventional agriculture into a regenerative one. As watersheds have the potential to mitigate environmental impact, our approach toward the farming community should be holistic. Without alleviating poverty, farmers' participation cannot be guaranteed. Therefore, governments, research institutions, and non-governmental organizations should leap to formulate suitable policies.

REFERENCES

Anderson, T. H. 2003. Microbial eco-physiological indicators to asses soil quality. *Agriculture, Ecosystems and Environment* 98, no. 1–3: 285–293.

Arulbalaji, P., D. Padmalal, and K. Sreelash. 2019. GIS and AHP techniques based delineation of groundwater potential zones: a case study from southern Western Ghats, India. *Scientific Reports* 9, no. 1: 1–17.

Bajigo, A., M. Tadesse, Y. Moges, and A. Anjulo. 2015. Estimation of carbon stored in agroforestry practices in Gununo watershed, Wolayitta zone, Ethiopia. *Journal of Ecosystem & Ecography* 5, no. 1: 1.

Bending, G. D., M. K. Turner, F. Rayns, M. C. Marx, and M. Wood. 2004. Microbial and biochemical soil quality indicators and their potential for differentiating areas under contrasting agricultural management regimes. *Soil Biology and Biochemistry* 36, no. 11: 1785–1792.

Böhlke, J. K., and J. M. Denver. 1995. Combined use of groundwater dating, chemical, and isotopic analyses to resolve the history and fate of nitrate contamination in two agricultural watersheds, Atlantic coastal plain, Maryland. *Water Resources Research* 31, no. 9: 2319–2339.

Brown, G. 2018. Dirt to Soil: One Family's Journey into Regenerative Agriculture. Vermont: Chelsea Green Publishing.

Chaturvedi, O. P., R. Kaushal, J. M. S. Tomar, A. K. Prandiyal, and P. Panwar. 2014. Agroforestry for wasteland rehabilitation: mined, ravine, and degraded watershed areas. In *Agroforestry Systems in India: Livelihood Security & Ecosystem Services*, edited by J. C. Dagar, A. K. Singh, and A. Arunachalam, 233–271. New Delhi: Springer.

Chen, C. W., J. W. Herr, R. A. Goldstein, G. Ice, and T. Cundy. 2005. Retrospective comparison of watershed analysis risk management framework and hydrologic simulation program Fortran applications to Mica Creek watershed. *Journal of Environmental Engineering* 131, no. 9: 1277–1284.

Chen, V. Y. C., H. P. Lien, C. H. Liu, J. J. Liou, H. G. Tzeng, and L. S. Yang. 2011. Fuzzy MCDM approach for selecting the best environment-watershed plan. *Applied Soft Computing* 11, no. 1: 265–275.

Coleman, D. C., and D. H. Wall. 2015. Soil fauna: occurrence, biodiversity, and roles in ecosystem function. In *Soil Microbiology, Ecology and Biochemistry* (4th ed.), edited by Eldor A. Paul, 111–149. Academic Press.

Coster, C. 1938. Naschrift: herbebossching op Java (Postscript: reforestation on Java). *Tectona* 32: 602–605.

Dahlgren, R. A., J. L. Boettinger, G. L. Huntington, and R. G. Amundson. 1997. Soil development along an elevational transect in the western Sierra Nevada, California. *Geoderma* 78, no. 3–4: 207–236.

Daru, R. D., and W. E. J. Tips. 1985. Farmers participation and socio-economic effects of a watershed management programme in Central Java (Solo river basin, Wiroko watershed). *Agroforestry Systems* 3, no. 2: 159–180.

Devendra, C., and D. Thomas. 2002. Crop-animal interactions in mixed farming systems in Asia. *Agricultural Systems* 71, no. 1–2: 27–40.

Dhyani, B. L., A. Raizada, and P. Dogra. 2006. Impact of watershed development and land use dynamics on agricultural productivity and socio-economic status of farmers in Central Himalayas. *Indian Journal of Soil Conservation* 34, no. 2: 129–133.

Elevitch, C. R., D. N. Mazaroli, and D. Ragone. 2018. Agroforestry standards for regenerative agriculture. *Sustainability* 10, no. 9: 3337.

Fiener, P., and K. Auerswald. 2003. Effectiveness of grassed waterways in reducing runoff and sediment delivery from agricultural watersheds. *Journal of Environmental Quality* 32, no. 3: 927–936.

Fukuoka, M. 2009. *The One-Straw Revolution: An Introduction to Natural Farming*. New York: Review of Books.

Fulcher, C. L. 1996. A watershed management decision support system (WAMADSS): economic and environmental impacts of land use activities for reducing nonpoint source pollution. Columbia: University of Missouri.

Gill, M. S., J. P. Singh, and K. S. Gangwar. 2009. Integrated farming system and agriculture sustainability. *Indian Journal of Agronomy* 54, no. 2: 128–139.

Glendenning, C. J., F. F. Van Ogtrop, A. K. Mishra, and R. W. Vervoort. 2012. Balancing watershed and local scale impacts of rain water harvesting in India – a review. *Agricultural Water Management* 107: 1–13.

Gray, D. H., and R. B. Sotir. 1996. *Biotechnical and Soil Bioengineering Slope Stabilization: A Practical Guide for Erosion Control*. New York: Wiley-Interscience, John Wiley and Sons.

Haith, D. A., and L. L. Shoemaker. 1987. Generalized watershed loading functions for stream flow nutrients. *Journal of the American Water Resources Association* 23, no. 3: 471–478.

Hartmann, M., B. Frey, J. Mayer, P. Mäder, and F. Widmer. 2015. Distinct soil microbial diversity under long-term organic and conventional farming. *The ISME Journal* 9, no. 5: 1177–1194.

Heringa, P. K. 1939. De Boschspons Theory? (The Forest Sponge Theory?) *Tectona* 32: 239–246.

Hobbs, P. R., K. Sayre, and R. Gupta. 2008. The role of conservation agriculture in sustainable agriculture. *Philosophical Transactions of the Royal Society B: Biological Sciences* 363, no. 1491: 543–555.

Howard, A. 2006. *The Soil and Health: A Study of Organic Agriculture*. United States: University Press of Kentucky.

Jones, D. L., Edwards-Jones, G., Murphy, D. V. 2011. Biochar mediated alterations in herbicide breakdown and leaching in soil. *Soil Biology & Biochemistry* 43, 804–813.

Kraus, M. J. 1999. Paleosols in clastic sedimentary rocks: their geologic applications. *Earth-Science Reviews* 47, no. 1–2: 41–70.

Krzic, M., R. F. Newman, C. Trethewey, C. E. Bulmer, and B. K. Chapman. 2006. Cattle grazing effects on plant species composition and soil compaction on rehabilitated forest landings in central interior British Columbia. *Journal of Soil and Water Conservation* 61, no. 3: 137–144.

Lehman, R. M., C. A. Cambardella, D. E. Stott, V. A. Martinez, D. K. Manter, J. S. Buyer, J. E. Maul et al. 2015. Understanding and enhancing soil biological health: the solution for reversing soil degradation. *Sustainability* 7, no. 1: 988–1027.

Lipper, L., P. Thornton, B. M. Campbell, T. Baedeker, A. Braimoh, M. Bwalya, P. Caron et al. 2014. Climate-smart agriculture for food security. *Nature Climate Change* 4, no. 12: 1068–1072.

Markart, G., M. Teich, C. Scheidl, and B. Kohl. 2021. Flood protection by forests in Alpine watersheds: lessons learned from Austrian case studies. In Teich, Michaela, Cristian Accastello, Frank Perzl, and Karl Kleemayr (eds.). *Protective Forests as Ecosystem-Based Solution for Disaster Risk Reduction (Eco-DRR)*. IntechOpen. doi:10.5772/intechopen.95014.

Meshram, S. G., E. Alvandi, C. Meshram, E. Kahya, and A. M. F. Al-Quraishi. 2020. Application of SAW and TOPSIS in prioritizing watersheds. *Water Resources Management* 34, no. 2: 715–732.

Mollison, B. 1988. *Permaculture: A Designer's Manual*. New South Wales: Tagari Publications.

Nair, P. K. R., Kumar, B. M., Nair, V. D. 2021. Definition and concepts of agroforestry. In: *An Introduction to Agroforestry*. Springer, Cham. https://doi.org/10.1007/978-3-030-75358-0_2

Narendra, B. H., C. A. Siregar, I. W. S. Dharmawan, A. Sukmana, I. B. Pramono, T. M. Basuki, H. Y. S. H. Nugroho et al. 2021. A review on sustainability of watershed management in Indonesia. *Sustainability* 13, no. 19: 11125.

Nielsen, U. N., D. H. Wall, and J. Six. 2015. Soil biodiversity and the environment. *Annual Review of Environment and Resources*, 40: 63–90.

Park, J. Y., S. Ale, W. R. Teague, and S. L. Dowhower. 2017. Simulating hydrologic responses to alternate grazing management practices at the ranch and watershed scales. *Journal of Soil and Water Conservation* 72, no. 2: 102–121.

Paul, S., N. Chatterjee, J. S. Bohra, S. P. Singh, D. Dutta, R. K. Singh, and A. Rakshit. 2019. Soil health in cropping systems: an overview. In *Agronomic Crops, Volume 1: Production Technologies*, edited by M. Hasanuzzaman, 45–66. Springer Singapore.

Pincus, L. N., P. C. Ryan, F. J. Huertas, and G. E. Alvarado. 2017. The influence of soil age and regional climate on clay mineralogy and cation exchange capacity of moist tropical soils: a case study from Late Quaternary chronosequences in Costa Rica. *Geoderma* 308: 130–148.

Pinel-Alloul, B., E. Prepas, D. Planas, R. Steedman, and T. Charette. 2002. Watershed impacts of logging and wildfire: case studies in Canada. *Lake and Reservoir Management* 18, no. 4: 307–318.

Pinto, D., S. Shrestha, M. S. Babel, and S. Ninsawat. 2017. Delineation of groundwater potential zones in the Comoro watershed, Timor Leste using GIS, remote sensing and analytic hierarchy process (AHP) technique. *Applied Water Science* 7, no. 1: 503–519.

Pourghasemi, H. R., B. Pradhan, and C. Gokceoglu. 2012. Application of fuzzy logic and analytical hierarchy process (AHP) to landslide susceptibility mapping at Haraz watershed, Iran. *Natural Hazards* 63, no. 2: 965–996.

Rhodes, C. J. 2017. The imperative for regenerative agriculture. *Science Progress* 100, no. 1: 80–129.

Richter Jr, D. D., and D. Markewitz. 2001. *Understanding Soil Change: Soil Sustainability over Millennia, Centuries, and Decades*. Cambridge University Press, New York.

Roessel, B. W. P. 1939. Herbebossching op Java (Reforestation on Java). *Tectona* 32: 230–238.

Sanjari, G., B. Yu, H. Ghadiri, C. A. A. Ciesiolka, and C. W. Rose. 2009. Effects of time-controlled grazing on runoff and sediment loss. *Soil Research* 47, no. 8: 796–808.

Schultz, R. C., T. M. Isenhart, W. W. Simpkins, and J. P. Colletti. 2004. Riparian forest buffers in agroecosystems-lessons learned from the Bear Creek Watershed, central Iowa, USA. *Agroforestry Systems* 61, no. 1: 35–50.

Shanwal, A. V., and S. S. Dahiya. 2002. Strategies for soil conservation and watershed management in Siwaliks, India. In *12th ISCO Conference*, Beijing.

Sherwood, S., and N. Uphoff. 2000. Soil health: research, practice and policy for a more regenerative agriculture. *Applied Soil Ecology* 15, no. 1: 85–97.

Singh, R., O. P. Chaturvedi, R. K. Tewari, R. P. Dwivedi, and R. H. Rizvi. 2016. Drought proofing and rural livelihood security through watershed and agroforestry interventions in Bundelkhand region. ICAR-Central Agroforestry Research Institute. https://bundelkhand.in/sites/default/files/research-icar-drought-proofing-and-rural-livelihood-security-bundelkhand.pdf (accessed September 2, 2022).

Sitaram, S. S. 2012. Role of agroforestry in watershed management. https://www.researchgate.net/profile/S-Sarvade/publication/284023409_Role_of_Agroforestry_in_Watershed_Management/links/564b061408ae127ff987ab5b/Role-of-Agroforestry-in-Watershed-Management.pdf (accessed August 22, 2022).

Strager, M. P., J. J. Fletcher, J. M. Strager, C. B. Yuill, R. N. Eli, J. T. Petty, and S. J. Lamont. 2010. Watershed analysis with GIS: the watershed characterization and modeling system software application. *Computers and Geosciences* 36, no. 7: 970–976.

Suprayogo, D., M. V. Noordwijk, K. Hairiah, N. Meilasari, A. L. Rabbani, R. M. Ishaq, and W. Widianto. 2020. Infiltration-friendly agroforestry land uses on volcanic slopes in the Rejoso watershed, East Java, Indonesia. *Land* 9, no. 8: 240.

Teague, R., and M. Barnes. 2017. Grazing management that regenerates ecosystem function and grazingland livelihoods. *African Journal of Range and Forage Science* 34, no. 2: 77–86.

Teague, W. R., S. Apfelbaum, R. Lal, U. P. Kreuter, J. Rowntree, C. A. Davies, R. Conser et al. 2016. The role of ruminants in reducing agriculture's carbon footprint in North America. *Journal of Soil and Water Conservation* 71, no. 2: 156–164.

Teague, W. R., S. L. Dowhower, S. A. Baker, N. Haile, P. B. DeLaune, and D. M. Conover. 2011. Grazing management impacts on vegetation, soil biota and soil chemical, physical and hydrological properties in tall grass prairie. *Agriculture, Ecosystems and Environment* 141, no. 3–4: 310–322.

Toensmeier, E. 2016. *The Carbon Farming Solution: A Global Toolkit of Perennial Crops and Regenerative Agriculture Practices for Climate Change Mitigation and Food Security*. London: Chelsea Green Publishing.

Toop, T. A., S. Ward, T. Oldfield, M. Hull, M. E. Kirby, and M. K. Theodorou. 2017. AgroCycle – developing a circular economy in agriculture. *Energy Procedia* 123: 76–80.

Turinek, M., S. G. Mlakar, M. Bavec, and F. Bavec. 2009. Biodynamic agriculture research progress and priorities. *Renewable Agriculture and Food Systems* 24, no. 2: 146–154.

Udawatta, R. P., J. J. Krstansky, G. S. Henderson, and H. E. Garrett. 2002. Agroforestry practices, runoff, and nutrient loss: a paired watershed comparison. *Journal of Environmental Quality* 31, no. 4: 1214–1225.

Ulery, A. L., R. C. Graham, O. A. Chadwick, and H. B. Wood. 1995. Decade-scale changes of soil carbon, nitrogen and exchangeable cations under chaparral and pine. *Geoderma* 65, no. 1–2: 121–134.

Van Noordwijk, M., Farida, A., Suyamto, D., Lusiana, B., and Khasanah, N. 2003. Spatial variability of rainfall governs river flow and reduces effects of land use change at landscape scale: GenRiver and SpatRain simulations. In MODSIM Proceedings, Townsville (Australia), July 2003.

Wall, D. H., R. D. Bardgett, A. P. Covich, and P. V. R. Snelgrove. 2004. The need for understanding how biodiversity and ecosystem functioning affect ecosystem services in soils and sediments. In *Sustaining Biodiversity and Ecosystem Services in Soils and Sediments*, edited by D. H. Wall, 1–12. Washington, DC: Island Press.

Walsh, T. C., C. A. Pomeroy, and S. J. Burian. 2014. Hydrologic modeling analysis of a passive, residential rainwater harvesting program in an urbanized, semi-arid watershed. *Journal of Hydrology* 508: 240–253.

Wan, R., S. Cai, H. Li, G. Yang, Z. Li, and X. Nie. 2014. Inferring land use and land cover impact on stream water quality using a Bayesian hierarchical modeling approach in the Xitiaoxi river watershed, China. *Journal of Environmental Management* 133: 1–11.

Wani, S. P., H. P. Singh, T. K. Sreedevi, P. Pathak, T. J. Rego, B. Shiferaw, and S. R. Iyer. 2003. Farmer-participatory integrated watershed management: Adarsha watershed, Kothapally India. *Case* 7: 123–147. https://oar.icrisat.org/3678/1/161-2004.pdf (accessed August 25, 2022).

White, C. 2020. Why regenerative agriculture? *American Journal of Economics and Sociology* 79, no. 3: 799–812.

Ziadat, F. M., and A. Y. Taimeh. 2013. Effect of rainfall intensity, slope, land use and antecedent soil moisture on soil erosion in an arid environment. *Land Degradation & Development* 24, no. 6: 582–590.

11 Combating the Effects of Climate Change through Regenerative Organic Agriculture

Ankita Begam, Bappa Paramanik, Susanta Dutta,
Gopal Dutta, and Sayantan Bhattacharjee

11.1 INTRODUCTION

The dependence on synthetic agrochemicals has been reflected in the attainment of food security. The Green Revolution in India concentrated on ensuring food security by introducing fertilizer-responsive cultivars, using synthetic inorganic chemicals as external inputs, and improving water management. These enhanced actions contributed to the "Green Revolution" of the 1960s and turned the nation into a food exporter. However, a negative and competitive mindset has also developed among farmers, who now seek high yields while neglecting the fertility condition of the soil. As a result, they involve the indiscriminate use of inorganic fertilizer and pesticide, as well as significant groundwater use. These specific actions are primarily to blame for groundwater pollution and depletion, which created a number of health risks. As an illustration, nitrate leaching from the overuse of nitrogenous fertilizers contaminated groundwater. In terms of soil security approach, a significant decline in soil fertility and productivity potential poses enormous issues for modern agriculture. In addition, the loss of arable land became a significant national concern. In addition, the lack of arable land created a significant national problem for supplying the enormous amount of production. Urbanization, which is also a necessary evil, is most likely to blame. Because of this, horizontal agricultural expansion is essentially impossible. In this case, monocropping has declared that the alarming problem caused by that production strategy has been restricted. Additionally, the indiscriminate use of external inputs in conventional farming systems significantly decreased input use efficiency. For instance, the difficult situation in agriculture was pushed by input use efficiency (IUE), water usage efficiency (WUE), or another input. In order to get greater input usage efficiency, it is the area of agriculture in which we may effectively manage the various practices. Due to excessive groundwater consumption, blind use of external inputs, and insufficient or nonexistent use of organic manure, respectively, these serious problems have arisen. These methods stop the least investment for maximum productivity approach, which threatens both soil security and the agricultural industry's financial potential. Not only has climate change caused these alarming problems, but it has also made it more difficult for agriculture to develop due to (i) increasing temperatures, (ii) changing precipitation patterns, (iii) more frequent extreme weather events, (iv) a loss of ecosystem services, and (v) declining biodiversity. The depletion of natural resources, including (i) the erosion of the most fertile soil, (ii) the extensive use of groundwater, (iii) the mining of carbon, (iv) the burning of carbon storage such as fossil fuels, etc., have simultaneously occurred, creating difficult agricultural circumstances. However, the scenario of a changing climate has various negative effects on the ecosystem that were divided into two categories, namely, anthropogenic and natural causes. Achieving sustainable growth was hampered by anthropogenic factors such as

 DOI: 10.1201/9781003309581-13

industrial pollution, burning fossil fuels, deforestation, and agriculture itself, as well as natural factors such as continental drift, volcanoes, the earth's tilt, and ocean currents. Regenerative organic agriculture is one of the most important options for addressing the many difficulties.

11.2 REGENERATIVE ORGANIC AGRICULTURE

Instead of destroying or depleting the resources it uses, regenerative organic agriculture improves them. It is a comprehensive systems approach to agriculture that promotes ongoing innovation on farms for the benefit of the environment, society, economy, and religion. Regenerative organic agriculture is a term that Robert Rodale created to describe a type of farming that goes beyond simply being sustainable. Organic regenerative farming makes use of ecosystems' innate capacity to heal after being disturbed. It stands out from other forms of agriculture in that respect since they either reject or disregard the importance of such natural tendencies. Regenerative organic farming is characterized by a tendency toward closed nutrient loops, increased biological community variety, fewer annuals and more perennials, and a greater dependence on internal resources as opposed to external ones. In order for the earth to produce the finest quality crops possible, it is important to support the planet's natural processes. Long-term agricultural health and productivity are ensured by these procedures. Organic farming that is regenerative gives back as much as it takes, if not more.

Soil health and cooperation with nature form the basis of regenerative organic agriculture. The five guiding elements of regenerative agriculture are highlighted: Avoid tillage to reduce soil disturbance, reduce chemical inputs such as fertilizer and pesticides, increase plant and microbial biodiversity, use cover crops all year to maintain a functioning root system, and utilize grazing livestock (where possible) to replicate natural, regenerative processes (LaCanne and Lundgren 2018). English agronomist Sir Albert Howard laid the intellectual groundwork for organic, regenerative farming. Howard was strongly opposed to the industrial system's reductionist approach, which included the development of synthetic fertilizers such as "NPK" (nitrogen, phosphorus and potassium). For instance, mycorrhizal fungi improve the roots' accessibility to minerals and trace elements such as phosphorus and nitrogen and receive any sugar (carbon) through photosynthesis (Kaiser et al. 2015). This symbiotic relationship is disrupted when synthetic fertilizers are supplied to plants, which decreases the number of beneficial bacteria and, ultimately, the health of the plant (Yarwood 2018). It has been discovered that plants grown in soils with synthetic fertilizers are less nourishing and disease-resistant than plants grown in soils with compost (Saxena et al. 2020). Numerous studies have also shown that introducing cover crops can help narrow the initial production difference between conventional and organic systems (Wittwer et al. 2017). Regenerative organic systems are more effective the longer they are in place because they improve water retention, naturally resist pathogens, and increase the availability of nitrogen and carbon in the soil (Cavigelli et al. 2008). The farmers who practice regenerative agriculture respect nature and the future by treating their land as one big ecosystem, with the soil as its base, while still placing a high priority on productivity and profitability.

11.3 SIGNIFICANT FEATURES OF REGENERATIVE ORGANIC AGRICULTURE

- A sustainable or regenerative agricultural method depends more on the farm's own resources than it does on outside ones.
- The emphasis is on a variety of agricultural enterprises or activities (as opposed to a single enterprise or monocrop).
- The amount of chemical input used, such as fertilizers, is lowered (the transition to reduced levels of use is gradual, not abrupt).
- The selection of crop/tree species and seeds can frequently have an impact on long-term security and stability.
- Harvesting water and preserving it.

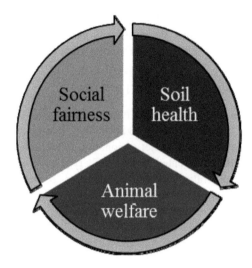

FIGURE 11.1   Three principal pillars of regenerative organic agriculture.

- The energy security and efficiency of a household or farm.
- In the revitalization and regeneration of small farms, trees play a specific role.
- Integration is a crucial quality (Figure 11.1).

11.4   REGENERATIVE ORGANIC FARMING PRACTICES (ON CLIMATE CHANGE VIEW)

11.4.1   ORGANIC FARMING

The life in the soil is suppressed by synthetic fertilizers, herbicides, pesticides, and fungicides, which reduce soil fertility. The symbiotic interactions between fungi, bacteria, and plant roots are destroyed by external input application such as agro-chemicals. To address the issues, organic farming or organic agriculture is introduced, where the use of inorganic pesticides, fertilizers, genetically modified organisms (GMOs), antibiotics, or growth hormones is totally restricted. Organic soils are capable of producing a full suite of ecosystem services, among them soil carbon sequestration and improved soil water retention. Most climate-smart practices have to do with leveraging ecosystem processes to increase soil organic matter and soil biodiversity, which serves the dual purpose of fostering forage growth without chemicals and increasing water holding capacity in order to reduce vulnerability to droughts and floods. Managing soil carbon is a major focus and is accomplished through a number of techniques, including reducing or eliminating tillage, increasing soil organic matter through spreading compost, planting cover crops to reduce bare ground (and tolerating weeds);and diversifying crops to reduce vulnerability to disease and pests (Toensmeier 2016; Montgomery 2017; Brown 2018). Transitioning to regenerative agriculture involves giving up conventional agricultural chemicals and learning how to cultivate fertility through strategic land management and natural inputs, such as organic compost.

11.4.2   COVER CROPS

Cover crops are a strong contingent from a protective or conservative standpoint. It can cover the maximum area of land feasible, which inhibits weed growth and stores soil moisture for later use. The inclusion of cover crops in the crop rotation significantly decreased N leaching compared to the control treatments. Non-legume cover crops reduced soil NO_3 content, which is vulnerable to N leaching during autumn and winter (Thorup-Kristensen and Magid 2003), and made additional soil N available for the primary crop following mineralization of their residues (Kaspar and Singer 2011). It depletes the soil NO_3 pool, which is the major substrate for denitrification (Liebig et al. 2015), reducing N leaching and consequently decreasing the contribution of indirect N_2O emissions to the NGHGB. Cover crops (i.e., both legume and non-legume) increase SOC, and so they can enhance C sequestration in soils (Ding et al. 2006). Here, the decomposition of dead roots and biomass from cover crops results in improved SOM quantity and quality (Villamil et al. 2006). This could help improve food security, reduce the net greenhouse gas balance (NGHGB) and mitigate climate change. However, it is quite common that the inclusion of cover crops interferes with the grain yield production of an objective crop due to interspecies competition. The legume cover crops significantly increased N content in the grain of the primary crop (Wortman et al. 2012; Tribouillois et al. 2018).

11.4.3 Compost Application

Another important input in the global fight against climate change is compost. Compost helps the environment in a number of ways, including by lowering greenhouse gas emissions at landfills, encouraging flora to absorb carbon dioxide, and increasing adaptability to the effects of climate change. Despite these significant advantages, other necessities have also evolved, such as:

- Landfills produce methane, a strong greenhouse gas, from organic waste. Composting waste food and other organic materials considerably lowers methane emissions.
- Compost decreases, and in some cases, completely replaces, the requirement for synthetic fertilizers.
- Increased crop yields are enhanced by compost.
- By enhancing contaminated, compacted, and marginal soils, compost can benefit reforestation, wetlands restoration, and habitat revitalization projects.
- Hazardous waste-contaminated soils can be remedied using compost in an economical way.
- The appropriate application of compost can reduce the cost of standard soil, water, and air pollution treatment methods.
- Soil water retention is improved by compost.
- Carbon dioxide is absorbed by compost.
- Farm waste is transformed into compost, a natural fertilizer, and mulch that help the soil retain moisture and controls weed growth.

11.4.4 Crop Rotation

Increases in harsh weather have brought about a number of issues, drastically decreased crop yields, and led to a decline in agricultural cultivation in the context of climate change. Crop rotation is a crucial tool for enhancing the agricultural production system's resiliency to climate change and for successfully addressing the drawbacks of the continuous crop technology now in use. Crop rotation entails growing several crops on the same property throughout successive growth and sowing cycles (Arriaga et al. 2017).

- Crop rotation is essential to many national initiatives, such as food security, environmental protection, and rural redevelopment.
- Numerous studies have shown that crop rotation can significantly increase the resistance of crops to climate change by enhancing water dynamics, soil health, and biological conditions in planting systems.
- Bowles et al. (2020) confirmed the concept that varied crop rotation can successfully enhance soil health and interrupt the cycle of herbivores, weeds, and diseases, enhancing crop yields and bringing about significant economic advantages.

- By ensuring that maize and other crops can withstand extreme weather, diverse crop rotation can even help decrease the effects of droughts and heat waves when they occur.
- Li et al. (2019a) made note of the fact that diverse crop rotation can enhance the stability of the planting system and that, in the event of harsh weather, a strong agricultural ecosystem can lessen stress and withstand unpredictable weather and organisms.
- Crop rotation can boost farmers' revenue while maintaining the quality of their land and protecting them from the consequences of climate change.
- Crop rotation lessens the impact that extreme weather can have on the planting system and lessens how vulnerable the agricultural system is.

11.4.5 Multiple Cropping

Multiple cropping is characterized as the growing of a number of crops to obtain the primary objective, such as subsistence, as well as a commercialized goal. This cropping system is categorized into mixed cropping, intercropping, multistoried cropping, double cropping, etc. In other words, these have the potential to fulfill the requirements of a livelihood, like their own consumption and earning of money. Besides that, these have a great opportunity to address the concerning climate change situation through several mechanisms.

- There are many synergies and trade-offs in food production and climate adaptation and mitigation (FAO 2010b). Most intercropping research have demonstrated that forage-legume intercropping can help farmers somewhat buffer the effects of climate change. The addition of legumes to cattle feed enhances digestibility by supplying fibrous feedstuffs (FAO 2010a). As a result of more effective feed use, the resultant increase in digestibility is anticipated to boost intake and animal efficiency while lowering methane emissions per unit of animal product. As most CH_4 emissions are produced by intestinal fermentation, increasing dietary digestibility is the best mitigation strategy (Verge et al. 2007). Gurian-Sherman (2011) observed in earlier experiments that increased digestibility resulted in a 15%–30% reduction in CH_4 emissions.
- Legume crops can thrive on little to no nitrogen fertilizer. Because of this, it can be shown that intercropping with legumes has a strong mitigation potential because nitrous oxide (N_2O) emissions are predicted to be lower in a legume crop than in a fertilized cereal crop (Bryan et al. 2011; Birteeb et al. 2011). Similar to this, the addition of legumes to grass-based forage production systems is anticipated to further reduce N_2O emissions since the intercropped grass will absorb less nitrate from the soil, which will lower soil nitrate levels.
- Soil carbon sequestration has the technical ability to reduce greenhouse gas emissions by 89%, according to Fischlin et al. (2007). The balance between carbon inputs and losses determines how much carbon can be stored in soil (Jensen et al. 2012). In a multi-year experiment, Cong et al. (2015) found that an intercropped system had up to 4% more soil organic carbon in the top 20 cm than a single crop system, indicating the possibility of intercropping as a climate change mitigation strategy.

11.4.6 Agroforestry

The sector of the economy most susceptible to climate change is agriculture. Although agroforestry has the potential to significantly reduce the atmospheric buildup of greenhouse gases (GHG), it also has the potential to aid smallholder farmers in their efforts to adapt to climate change. Options for agroforestry may offer a way to increase the sustainability of smallholder farming systems by diversifying production methods. Agroforestry offers the potential to create synergies between initiatives to reduce climate change and those to assist vulnerable groups in making adaptations to its unfavorable effects. From the perspective of smallholder farmers, the increased interannual variability in rainfall and temperature is the most concerning aspect of climate change. Tree-based systems have some obvious advantages for maintaining production during wetter and drier years.

- Initially, during droughts, their deep root systems' ability to explore a larger area of soil for water and nutrients will be helpful.
- Second, greater soil porosity, decreased runoff, and greater soil cover result in greater water uptake and retention in the soil profile, which might lessen moisture stress during years with little precipitation.
- Third, tree-based systems can maintain aerated soil conditions by pumping surplus water out of the soil profile more quickly than other production systems because they have higher evapotranspiration rates than pastures or row crops.
- Finally, crops produced by tree-based agricultural systems are frequently more valuable than those from row crops.

In order to mitigate revenue risks brought on by climatic fluctuation, the production system may be diversified to incorporate a substantial tree component.

11.4.7 Low- to No-Tilling

By replacing conventional tillage with no-till methods in agriculture, organic carbon is accumulated in the soil, preventing climate change through carbon sequestration. One of the numerous sustainable agricultural methods that can assist farmers in reducing the effects of the climate problem and adjusting to it is no-till farming. A no-till approach involves planting seeds directly into undisturbed soil, which has several positive effects on the ecosystem and the climate. Additionally, the advantages are increased when no-till is used with other environmentally friendly techniques, such as cover crops. No-till farming reduces greenhouse gas emissions in two ways: it uses less machinery that is driven by fossil fuels, and it helps soil hold on to carbon, limiting the release of greenhouse gas emissions during tillage. No-till farming reduces emissions by using less fuel because a tractor is not needed to draw a plough. In the farming method of crop residue-returned, no-till enhances soil organic carbon storage and lowers carbon dioxide emissions. It also assists the soil in retaining water and accumulating organic materials. A quantitative measure of soil health based on a combination of biotic and abiotic soil factors is known as soil stability. The microbial community regulates the impact of physical and chemical properties on soil resilience and resistance (Griffiths and Philippot 2013).

11.4.8 Restorative Grazing

Reduced root mass, elevated soil temperature, and runoff are all effects of overgrazing, a type of biological disturbance. If correctly managed, grazing animals may revitalize meadows, boosting biodiversity both below and above ground. Numerous researchers have looked closely at the process of revegetating "Bare Land" using cultivated grasslands. The study found that cultivating grasslands could enhance "Bare Land's" ecological and economic values (Xu et al. 2019). Human interventions, such as fertilization and the management of dangerous weeds, are suggested after 3–5 years of cultivation to encourage the self-recovery of damaged grasslands after revegetation (Dong et al. 2013; Zhang et al. 2015). By combining many researchers' perspectives on what the degradation of the grassland is related to

- Overgrazing was the primary cause (Shang and Long 2005; Li et al. 2019b),
- Causes dominated by climate change (Yang 2004),
- Uncertain causes (Harris 2010),

- Multiple causes (Wang et al. 2015; Liu et al. 2018)
- Dissociation between human and natural systems (Dong et al. 2012)

In order to restore degraded grasslands, we should consider implementing a number of strategies, including:

- Selection of native plant species for restoration
- Mixed-grass sowing
- Fertilization and irrigation
- Rotational grazing

11.4.9 SEED OR SOIL INOCULATION WITH BIOFERTILIZER

Because of the serious effects it has on many aspects of life, climate change has become more critical. The productivity of agricultural and natural ecosystems, as well as human health, are all directly or indirectly impacted by rising temperatures, drought, and greenhouse gases. While the soil's ability to deliver nutrients is deteriorating, the demand for food as a result of population growth is rising. The continued use of agrochemicals has a negative impact on the food chain and environmental processes. More than ever, there is a need to use ecologically friendly methods to lessen the impact of agricultural activities on climate change. There is growing research on the potential significance of plant-beneficial microbes in addressing this global issue. Due to their capacity to serve as biofertilizers and encourage plant growth, the employment of functional microbial guilds constitutes an alternative or even complementary approach to traditional agricultural approaches. When compared to chemical inputs, the use of microbial inoculum has a far smaller environmental impact, yet the agricultural industry will profit and customers will have access to high-quality products. Microbial inoculants may be crucial in managing agricultural stress and reducing the harmful effects of climate change. The development of synthetic microbial consortia with specialized functions that can assist plants in responding to environmental circumstances that affect agricultural yields is required in order to introduce microorganisms to combat the negative effects of climate change. In fact, according to Wallenstein (2017), a plant's rhizosphere can be engineered through inoculation, which ultimately helps plants by reducing abiotic and/or biotic stress conditions. Synthetic microbial communities that are habitat-specific and functionally appropriate will be important for climate-smart agriculture since they can be used to tailor a crop's drought, salt, or heat tolerance, according to Saad et al. (2020). Recognizing that each plant harbors a community of bacteria or fungi that collaborates with its roots, it becomes evident that plants with symbiotic relationships with specific bacteria and fungi tend to exhibit superior functionality compared to those relying on a diverse, wild population of microorganisms (Harman et al. 2021). Both the cover crop and the primary crop need to be vaccinated. In order to develop healthy plants, the cover crop must contain a variety of seeds that can be inoculated with bacteria that fix nitrogen, such as legume seeds. If seeds are infected with these kinds of bacteria, there is no need to treat the soil with nitrogen (Mao et al. 1997; Bressan 2003). Mycorrhizal fungi that form an arbuscular network are crucial to plant growth. In particular, in conditions of low or medium available phosphorus, corn inoculated with arbuscular mycorrhizal has greater phosphorus absorption, improves vegetative biomass, and enhances grain production (Stoffel et al. 2020) (Figure 11.2).

11.5   ADAPTATION OF CULTURAL MANAGEMENT

- Nutrient enrichment of soil: Provide organic sources of nutrients to rejuvenate the soil, which is severely affected by chemical use.
- Management of temperature: Regarding the management of soil temperature, mulching is found to be a beneficial alternative.

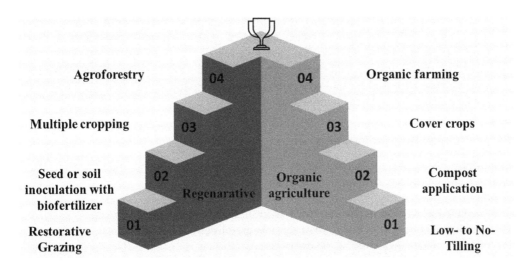

FIGURE 11.2   Different regenerative organic agricultural practices.

- Conservation of soil and rainwater: Mulching and particularly offseason tillage are quite significant practices for these kinds of issues.
- Harvesting of sun energy: Green stands, afforestation, or planting of tree saplings are effective for harvesting radiant energy, which thereby transforms into chemical energy.
- Self-resilience in inputs: Integrated approach to inputs enhances input use efficiency (IUE) and builds the self-perpetuating ability of these inputs, such as manuring, botanical extracts, etc.
- Maintenance of live forms: Biological entity creates a self-sustaining ecosystem with the development of large biodiversity around them.
- Integration of animals: Animal–plant interaction has evolved into beneficial terms such as farmyard manure (FYM) for organic supplementation.
- Use of renewable energy: Energy dissipation in different interventions is a challenging issue in modern agriculture. Therefore, most focus is on the utilization of renewable energy.

11.6 CHALLENGES TO SUCCESS

The technology, techniques, and practices of regenerative organic agriculture are proven. Research provides a sound basis for a national phasing out of environmentally harmful agricultural methods and a phasing in of regenerative organic systems. Widespread implementation will dramatically benefit from additional support for research and development.

11.6.1 SOIL CARBON MANAGEMENT

- The minimum and no application of organic nutrient sources, as well as the acceleration of carbon burning by intensive tillage practices, have reflected the most significant constraints for today's agriculture. However, carbon mining and the ignition of fossil fuels substantially reduce the soil carbon content, which is actually important for enhancing input use efficiencies (IUE), leading to sustainable development.
- Further research is needed on the function of mycorrhizae and glomalin in the maintenance of soil carbon, as well as on other basic biology that increases soil's potential to effectively absorb carbon and optimize its physical attributes.

- Knowledge of carbon sequestration through afforestation, development of grazing areas, etc. is particularly important in order to obtain a global terrestrial perspective on how much carbon may be stored to prevent global warming.
- For regenerative purposes and more precise in-field soil-carbon measurement, it is necessary to use improved technologies, environmentally sound approaches, and integrated management of several nutrition sources.

11.6.2 MODERN FARMING PRACTICES

Despite being responsible for meeting the growing population's demand for food, modern farming techniques simultaneously damage the ecosystem through

- The nutrient overload in our waterways is due to the use of synthetic nitrogen.
- Loss of energy reserves due to the excessive use of petrochemicals (which increases the financial burden on farmers as oil prices rise).
- Degradation of soil health: a probable reason may be the practice of monocropping with the supplementation of synthetic fertilizers, which gradually reduces the soil fertility.
- Concerns about the health issues of human beings and the welfare of animals.
- Reduced soil carbon content has caused soil erosion, loss of water and nutrient retention capacity, draught susceptibility, and soil structure disintegration.

11.6.3 SIGNIFICANT YIELD REDUCTION

Initially, a significant yield reduction was observed when we transformed our cultivation practices from conventional to organic farming. That consequence is very difficult for farmers to accept. This is the probable reason why farmers did not come into organic farming.

- Most of the improved high-yielding varieties are responsive to fertilizer, and as a result, they produce lower yield.
- Transforming from synthetic cultivation to organic cultivation required a transition period of upto 5 years. Thus, farmers do not prefer to invest their time in this type of transformation.
- Changing climate scenarios, such as the uneven distribution of rainfall, greatly affect the production system by reducing yield. Here is an alternative option to boost production by providing nutrient-rich synthetic fertilizer instead of low-nutrient organic manure.
- Infestation by insect pests substantially damages the crop, resulting in a lower yield and creating a challenging situation for livelihood. Improved high-yielding varieties (HYVs) are less resistant to insect pests than the traditional variety used in organic farming.

11.7 CONCLUSIVE APPROACH

More importantly, public policies and research should concentrate on how organic agriculture practices might be adapted. An increase in uncertainty, both for meteorological events and global food markets, is one of the primary implications of climate change. In the face of climate change, organic agriculture has a great potential for increasing resilience. A market-based incentive for environmental care is provided by certified organic products, which also provide growers with higher earning options. Globally, the expansion of organic agriculture would encourage and support farming methods that are beneficial to the environment. To better realize its potential and expand its use, organic agriculture requires investments in research and development. Organic farming's potential for mitigating climate change is discussed in Table 11.1.

TABLE 11.1

Mitigation Potential of Organic Agriculture

GHG Source	Effect of Improved Organic Management	Remarks
	Direct Emissions from Agriculture	
N_2O from soils	Decreased	Efficient utilization of nitrogen
CH_4 from enteric fermentation	Adverse effects	Increased by lower performance but reduced by lower replacement rate and domestication of multi-use breeds
Biomass burning	Decreased	Increasing the residue load on the field and facilitate of increasing organic matter
Paddy field	Adverse effects	Increased by organic amendments but lowered by drainage and aquatic weeds
Manure handling	Equal	Reduced methane emissions
	Indirect Emissions	
Mineral fertilizers	Totally avoided	Use of mineral fertilizers is restricted
	Carbon Sequestration	
Arable lands	Improved	Carbon sequestrated
Grasslands	Improved	Carbon sequestrated

BOX 11.1   RECENT TRENDS IN ORGANIC AQUACULTURE

The term "organic aquaculture" has gained popularity as a result of diminishing fisheries harvests, questions about the safety of wild fish as food, environmental concerns, rising fish consumption, and an increasing market share for organic products. Consumer demand may, in the next 10 years, force organic fish, shellfish, and other aquatic species production into the mainstream. The study of organic aquaculture has drawn the attention of academics from a range of disciplines, environmentalists, and business people.

One of the current issues with aquaculture is the use of wild fish as farmed fish feed, which wastes protein resources and has a negative impact on ocean fisheries. Aquaculture, however, can also inadvertently deplete native fisheries by altering habitats, gathering wild seed stock, altering the ocean food web, introducing alien fish species, and spreading diseases that impact wild fish populations. Organic aquaculture is a sustainable method of food production and farming that protects the biological and ecological aspects of the environment. The principles of organic aquaculture are as follows: (i) using natural breeding methods without the use of hormones or antibiotics, (ii) avoiding artificial fertilizers, (iii) incorporating native plant communities into farm management, (iv) avoiding synthetic pesticides and herbicides are just a few examples, (v) purchasing feed and fertilizer from fisheries and certified organic agriculture, (vi) organic sustainability standards for sources of fishmeal, (vii) limitations on stocking density, and (viii) no GMOs (genetically modified organisms) in feed and stocks.

REFERENCES

Arriaga, Francisco J., Jose Guzman, and Birl Lowery. "Conventional agricultural production systems and soil functions." In M. M. Al-Kaisi and B. Lowery (eds.), *Soil Health and Intensification of Agro-Ecosystems*, Academic Press, 2017: 109–125. doi: 10.1016/B978-0-12-805317-1.00005-1

Birteeb, Peter T., Weseh Addah, Jakper Naandam, and A. Addo-Kwafo. "Effects of intercropping cereal-legume on biomass and grain yield in the savannah zone." *Livestock Research for Rural Development* 23, no. 9 (2011): 1–4.

Bowles, Timothy M., Maria Mooshammer, Yvonne Socolar, Francisco Calderón, Michel A. Cavigelli, Steve W. Culman, William Deen et al. "Long-term evidence shows that crop-rotation diversification increases agricultural resilience to adverse growing conditions in North America." *One Earth* 2, no. 3 (2020): 284–293. doi: 10.1016/j.oneear.2020.02.007

Bressan, Wellington. "Biological control of maize seed pathogenic fungi by use of actinomycetes." *BioControl* 48, no. 2 (2003): 233–240. doi: 10.1023/A:1022673226324

Brown, Gabe. *Dirt to Soil: One Family's Journey into Regenerative Agriculture.* Chelsea Green Publishing, 2018.

Bryan, Elisabeth, Claudia Ringler, Barrack Okoba, Jawoo Koo, Mario T. Herrero, and Silvia Silvestri. Agricultural land management: capturing synergies among climate change adaptation, greenhouse gas mitigation and agricultural productivity. IFPRI, Washington, DC, 2011.

Cavigelli, M. A., Teasdale, J. R., and Conklin, A. E. Long-term agronomic performance of organic and conventional field crops in the mid-atlantic region. *Agronomy Journal*, 100, no. 3 (2008): 725–731. https://doi.org/10.2134/agronj2006.0373

Cong, Wen-Feng, Ellis Hoffland, Long Li, Johan Six, Jian-Hao Sun, Xing-Guo Bao, Fu-Suo Zhang, and Wopke Van Der Werf. "Intercropping enhances soil carbon and nitrogen." *Global Change Biology* 21, no. 4 (2015): 1715–1726. doi: 10.1111/gcb.12738

Ding, Guangwei, Xiaobing Liu, Stephen Herbert, Jeffrey Novak, Dula Amarasiriwardena, and Baoshan Xing. "Effect of cover crop management on soil organic matter." *Geoderma* 130, no. 3–4 (2006): 229–239. doi: 10.1016/j.geoderma.2005.01.019

Dong, Quan-Min, Xin-Quan Zhao, Gao-Lin Wu, Jian-Jun Shi, and Guo-Hua Ren. "A review of formation mechanism and restoration measures of "black-soil-type" degraded grassland in the Qinghai-Tibetan plateau." *Environmental Earth Sciences* 70, no. 5 (2013): 2359–2370. doi: 10.1007/s12665-013-2338-7

Dong, S. K., L. Wen, Y. Y. Li, X. X. Wang, L. Zhu, and X. Y. Li. "Soil-quality effects of grassland degradation and restoration on the Qinghai-Tibetan plateau." *Soil Science Society of America Journal* 76, no. 6 (2012): 2256–2264. doi: 10.2136/sssaj2012.0092

FAO. Challenges and opportunities for carbon sequestration in grassland systems. A technical report on grassland management and climate change mitigation. *Integrated Crop Management*. Food and Agriculture Organization, Rome, 2010a.

FAO. "Climate-smart" agriculture: policies, practices and financing for food security, adaptation and mitigation. Food and Agriculture Organization, Rome, 2010b.

Fischlin, A., Midgley, G. F., Price, J. T., Leemans, R., Gopal, B., Turley, C., Rounsevell, M. D. A., Dube, O. P., Tarazona, J., Velichko, A. A. Ecosystems, their properties, goods, and services. Climate Change 2007: Impacts, Adaptation and Vulnerability. Contribution of Working Group II to the Fourth Assessment Report of the Intergovernmental Panel on Climate Change, M. L. Parry, O. F. Canziani, J. P. Palutikof, P. J. van der Linden and C. E. Hanson, Eds., Cambridge University Press, Cambridge, UK (2007), 211–272.

Griffiths, Bryan S., and Laurent Philippot. "Insights into the resistance and resilience of the soil microbial community." *FEMS Microbiology Reviews* 37, no. 2 (2013): 112–129. doi: 10.1111/j.1574-6976.2012.00343.x

Gurian-Sherman, Doug. Raising the steaks: global warming and pasture-raised beef production in the United States, Vol. 3. Union of Concerned Scientists, Cambridge, MA, 2011.

Harman, Gary, Ram Khadka, Febri Doni, and Norman Uphoff. "Benefits to plant health and productivity from enhancing plant microbial symbionts." *Frontiers in Plant Science* 11 (2021): 610065. doi: 10.3389/fpls.2020.610065

Harris, Richard B. "Rangeland degradation on the Qinghai-Tibetan plateau: a review of the evidence of its magnitude and causes." *Journal of Arid Environments* 74, no. 1 (2010): 1–12. doi: 10.1016/j.jaridenv.2009.06.014

Jensen, Erik Steen, Mark B. Peoples, Robert M. Boddey, Peter M. Gresshoff, Henrik Hauggaard-Nielsen, Bruno J. R. Alves, and Malcolm J. Morrison. "Legumes for mitigation of climate change and the provision of feedstock for biofuels and biorefineries. A review." *Agronomy for Sustainable Development* 32, no. 2 (2012): 329–364. doi: 10.1007/s13593-011-0056-7

Kaiser, Christina, Matt R. Kilburn, Peta L. Clode, Lucia Fuchslueger, Marianne Koranda, John B. Cliff, Zakaria M. Solaiman, and Daniel V. Murphy. "Exploring the transfer of recent plant photosynthates to soil microbes: mycorrhizal pathway vs direct root exudation." *New Phytologist* 205, no. 4 (2015): 1537–1551. doi: 10.1111/nph.13138

Kaspar, T. C., and J. W. Singer. "The use of cover crops to manage soil." In Jerry L. Hatfield and Thomas J. Sauer (eds.) *Soil Management: Building a Stable Base for Agriculture*, American Society of Agronomy and Soil Science Society of America, 2011: 321–337. doi: 10.2136/2011.soilmanagement.c21

LaCanne, Claire E., and Jonathan G. Lundgren. "Regenerative agriculture: merging farming and natural resource conservation profitably." *PeerJ* 6 (2018): e4428. doi: 10.7717/peerj.4428

Li, Junxian, Lidong Huang, Jun Zhang, Jeffrey A. Coulter, Lingling Li, and Yantai Gan. "Diversifying crop rotation improves system robustness." *Agronomy for Sustainable Development* 39, no. 4 (2019a): 1–13. doi: 10.1007/s13593-019-0584-0

Li, Yong, Junjie Li, Kayode Steven Are, Zhigang Huang, Hanqing Yu, and Qingwen Zhang. "Livestock grazing significantly accelerates soil erosion more than climate change in Qinghai-Tibet plateau: evidenced from ^{137}Cs and ^{210}Pbex measurements." *Agriculture, Ecosystems & Environment* 285 (2019b): 106643. doi: 10.1016/j.agee.2019.106643

Liebig, M. A., J. R. Hendrickson, D. W. Archer, M. A. Schmer, K. A. Nichols, and D. L. Tanaka. "Short-term soil responses to late-seeded cover crops in a semi-arid environment." *Agronomy Journal* 107, no. 6 (2015): 2011–2019. doi: 10.2134/agronj15.0146

Liu, Shibin, Kazem Zamanian, Per-Marten Schleuss, Mohsen Zarebanadkouki, and Yakov Kuzyakov. "Degradation of Tibetan grasslands: consequences for carbon and nutrient cycles." *Agriculture, Ecosystems & Environment* 252 (2018): 93–104. doi: 10.1016/j.agee.2017.10.011

Mao, Weili, J. A. Lewis, P. K. Hebbar, and R. D. Lumsden. "Seed treatment with a fungal or a bacterial antagonist for reducing corn damping-off caused by species of *Pythium* and *Fusarium*." *Plant Disease* 81, no. 5 (1997): 450–454. doi: 10.1094/PDIS.1997.81.5.450

Montgomery, David R. *Growing a Revolution: Bringing our Soil Back to Life*. WW Norton & Company, Washington, 2017.

Saad, Maged M., Abdul Aziz Eida, and Heribert Hirt. "Tailoring plant-associated microbial inoculants in agriculture: a roadmap for successful application." *Journal of Experimental Botany* 71, no. 13 (2020): 3878–3901. doi: 10.1093/jxb/eraa111

Saxena, Beenam, Asha Rani, R. Z. Sayyed, and Hesham Ali El-Enshasy. "Analysis of nutrients, heavy metals and microbial content in organic and non-organic agriculture fields of Bareilly Region-Western Uttar Pradesh, India." *Biosciences Biotechnology Research Asia* 17, no. 2 (2020): 399–406. doi: 10.13005/bbra/2843

Shang, Z. H., and R. J. Long. "Formation reason and recovering problem of the "black soil type" degraded alpine grassland in Qinghai-Tibetan plateau." *Chinese Journal of Ecology* 24, no. 6 (2005): 652–656.

Stoffel, Shantau Camargo Gomes, Cláudio Roberto Fonsêca Sousa Soares, Edenilson Meyer, Paulo Emílio Lovato, Admir José Giachini. "Yield increase of corn inoculated with a commercial arbuscular mycorrhizal inoculant in Brazil." *Ciência Rural* 50, no. 7 (2020). doi: 10.1590/0103-8478cr20200109

Thorup-Kristensen, Kristian, and Jacob Magid. "Biological tools in nitrogen management in temperate zones." *Advances in Agronomy* 79 (2003): 233.

Toensmeier, Eric. *The Carbon Farming Solution: A Global Toolkit of Perennial Crops and Regenerative Agriculture Practices for Climate Change Mitigation and Food Security*. Chelsea Green Publishing, 2016.

Tribouillois, Hélène, Julie Constantin, and Eric Justes. "Cover crops mitigate direct greenhouse gases balance but reduce drainage under climate change scenarios in temperate climate with dry summers." *Global Change Biology* 24, no. 6 (2018): 2513–2529. doi: 10.1111/gcb.14091

Verge, X. P. C., C. De Kimpe, and R. L. Desjardins. "Agricultural production, greenhouse gas emissions and mitigation potential." *Agricultural and Forest Meteorology* 142, no. 2–4 (2007): 255–269. doi: 10.1016/j.agrformet.2006.06.011

Villamil, M. B., G. A. Bollero, R. G. Darmody, F. W. Simmons, and D. G. Bullock. "No-till corn/soybean systems including winter cover crops: effects on soil properties." *Soil Science Society of America Journal* 70, no. 6 (2006): 1936–1944. doi: 10.2136/sssaj2005.0350

Wallenstein, Matthew D. "Managing and manipulating the rhizosphere microbiome for plant health: a systems approach." *Rhizosphere* 3 (2017): 230–232. doi: 10.1016/j.rhisph.2017.04.004

Wang, Jingsheng, Zhikai Wang, Xianzhou Zhang, Yangjian Zhang, Congqian Ran, Junlong Zhang, Baoxiong Chen, and Bingsong Zhang. "Response of *Kobresia pygmaea* and *Stipa purpurea* grassland communities in northern Tibet to nitrogen and phosphate addition." *Mountain Research and Development* 35, no. 1 (2015): 78–86. doi: 10.1659/MRD-JOURNAL-D-11-00104.1

Wittwer, Raphaël A., Brigitte Dorn, Werner Jossi, and Marcel G.A. Van der Heijden. "Cover crops support ecological intensification of arable cropping systems." *Scientific Reports* 7, no. 1 (2017): 1–12. doi: 10.1038/srep41911

Wortman, Sam E., Charles A. Francis, Mark L. Bernards, Rhae A. Drijber, and John L. Lindquist. "Optimizing cover crop benefits with diverse mixtures and an alternative termination method." *Agronomy Journal* 104, no. 5 (2012): 1425–1435. doi: 10.2134/agronj2012.0185

Xu, Yudan, Shikui Dong, Xiaoxia Gao, Mingyue Yang, Shuai Li, Hao Shen, Jiannan Xiao, et al. "Trade-offs and cost-benefit of ecosystem services of revegetated degraded alpine meadows over time on the Qinghai-Tibetan plateau." *Agriculture, Ecosystems & Environment* 279 (2019): 130–138. doi: 10.1016/j.agee.2019.04.015

Yang, Jian-Ping. "Climatic features of eco-environmental change in the source regions of the Yangtze and Yellow rivers in recent 40 years." *Journal of Glaciology and Geocryology* 26 (2004): 7–16.

Yarwood, Stephanie A. "The role of wetland microorganisms in plant-litter decomposition and soil organic matter formation: a critical review." *FEMS Microbiology Ecology* 94, no. 11 (2018): fiy175. doi: 10.1093/femsec/fiy175

Zhang, Wenjiang, Yonghong Yi, John S. Kimball, Youngwook Kim, and Kechao Song. "Climatic controls on spring onset of the Tibetan Plateau grasslands from 1982 to 2008." *Remote Sensing* 7, no. 12 (2015): 16607–16622. doi: 10.3390/rs71215847

Section III

Converging Science to Action in Different Continents

Practice and Performance

12 Meeting the Challenges of the Developing World with Regenerative Agriculture
Asian Perspective

Jayesh Singh and Amitava Rakshit

12.1 GRAVITY OF PROBLEM

Agriculture on a global scale has reached a tipping point. Unprecedented technologies have altered the agricultural environment over the previous few decades, raising agricultural output to new heights in order to satisfy expanding global demands. These advancements, however, have come at the expense of significant environmental and societal consequences such as land degradation, biodiversity loss, water and soil contamination, and increased greenhouse gas emissions. There is huge pressure on the global ecosystem, putting the world's natural resources' productive capacity at risk and jeopardizing the planet's future fertility (FAO, 2022a; FAO, 2022b). All South Asian countries (Nepal, Bangladesh, Bhutan, Maldives, Afghanistan, Pakistan, Sri Lanka and India) have become a global epicentre for climate change due to the exhaustive utilization of water resources, land and soil for feeding the exponentially growing population. It is estimated that about 83 million people per year are increasing globally, which is calculated to reach up to 9.7 billion in 2050 with a major share of developing countries and will put additional stress on our arable land to provide sufficient food (United Nations, 2019). Besides this, on the one hand, the human population is increasing but on the other hand, the share of plants and animals' population is declining. According to the report of IPBES (2019a), 1,000,000 species of plants and animals are on the verge of being extinct as well as biodiversity is also declining at an unprecedented rate. At the global level, over half of the land excluding glacier agriculture is practiced (McCue and Durkin, 2021) thus making 'agriculture' as the primary driver of biodiversity loss (IPBES, 2019). Land is one of the key components for maintaining the biodiversity of the ecosystem, but due to intensive agricultural practices at marginal lands, overgrazing, exploitation of land and water resources, and failures of resource management policies have made Asia to have the world's largest area under dryland (Land Desertification 2005; White, 2020). The ease and development of irrigation system has significantly improved the total production and has exponentially increased the water resource consumption. In 2019, the total area under irrigated agricultural land was calculated to be 342 million ha out of which 70% of the irrigated land area comes under Asian countries, particularly China has a share of 75 million ha followed by India with 70 million ha of area equipped with irrigation, whereas America and Europe have a share of 16% and 8%, respectively, out of the total area. Irrigation-intensive rice cultivation prevalence in the majority of Asian countries is one of the rationales behind higher irrigated areas than in other countries. However, irrigated agriculture practices regions had to compete with other uses of water. In order to supply irrigation, a huge amount of groundwater is abstracted. It has been reported that most African and Asian countries have the highest share of agricultural water withdrawal in total withdrawals share. Agricultural water withdrawal in total withdrawals indicates the relative weight of water used for agricultural practices in comparison to municipal or industrial uses. Somalia has the highest percentage (99.7%) of water withdrawals in Africa, whereas Afghanistan is the second

DOI: 10.1201/9781003309581-15

TABLE 12.1

Percentage of Water Withdrawal by Agriculture Sector of Top 20 Countries (Year 2000–2018)

Continents/ Regions	Country	Water Withdrawal (%) (Year 2000–2018)				
		2000	2005	2010	2015	2018
Asia	Afghanistan	98.6	98.2	98.2	98.2	98.2
	Nepal	97.5	98.1	98.1	98.1	98.1
	LPDR	—	91.4	94.8	96.2	95.9
	Vietnam	94.0	94.8	94.8	94.8	94.8
	Turkmenistan	96.5	94.3	94.3	94.3	94.3
	Bhutan	—	—	94.1	94.1	94.1
	Cambodia	94.0	94.0	94.0	94.0	94.0
	Pakistan	94.3	94.3	94.0	94.0	94.0
	Kyrgyzstan	93.8	93.2	92.8	92.7	92.6
	Azerbaijan	58.0	66.5	72.2	91.1	92.4
Africa	Somalia	99.7	99.5	99.5	99.5	99.5
	Mali	98.2	97.9	97.9	97.9	97.9
	Sudan	—	—	—	87.4	87.4
	Madagascar	97.2	96.6	95.9	95.9	95.9
	Eritrea	70.1	94.5	94.5	94.5	94.5
	Eswatini	96.5	94.2	94.2	94.2	94.2
	Senegal	89.9	93.0	93.0	93.0	93.0
	Cabo Verde	—	92.6	92.6	92.6	92.6
Americas	Guyana	97.6	94.8	94.3	94.3	94.3
	Peru	—	—	86.6	82.1	91.8

Source: Adapted and modified from https://www.fao.org/documents/card/en/c/cb4477en/

highest agricultural water withdrawing country with its share of 98.6% out of total withdrawals, thus badly exploiting the water resources (Table 12.1) (FAO, 2021b).

In the present scenario, the main emphasis of modern agriculture is production oriented and extractive from the nature earth. In the race of achieving higher produce, modern agriculture depends on synthetic fertilizers, herbicides and pesticides (Gordon et al., 2021). Hence, agriculture with this aim became intensive in nature. Consequently, the intensive agricultural system has a share of 30% in global greenhouse gas emission and is also responsible for eroding 24 billion tonnes of topsoil per year. If the trend continues, it will only take 60% of the harvest until our ecosystem can no longer support external anthropogenic intervention (Bosma et al., 2022; EIT Food, 2021). Intensive agriculture not merely affects land/soil but also results in biodiversity loss, due to the blind use of artificial nitrogenous fertilizer. As a repercussion, the quality of air, water and soil is badly affected which is further responsible for changes in ecosystem, vegetation and eutrophication and mainly depletes stratospheric ozone. In fact, several researches and studies reported that chemical inputs in the agriculture sector of developing countries are majorly responsible for environmental pollution. Specifically, the volume of pesticides and fertilizer used in China is the highest, which is estimated to be more than 1.8 and 59 million tonnes, respectively (National Bureau of Statistics of China, 2014; Zhang et al., 2018), in the world. As a consequence of these, huge additions lead to climate change and biodiversity loss (Erisman et al., 2015). Exploitation of natural resources and degradation of environments are major causes of food insecurity because degraded and exhausted land cannot give qualitative and quantitative produce. Although more than 55% of the world's crop production is directly consumed by the global population (Muller et al., 2017), it is

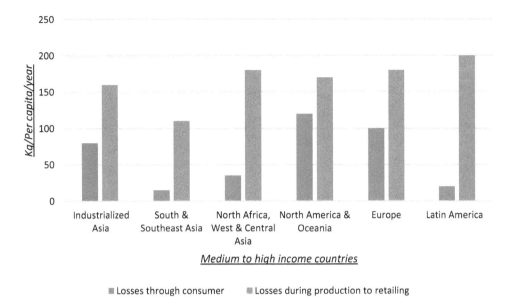

FIGURE 12.1 Food losses in the world's medium- to high-income countries per capita per kg per year. Adapted and modified from https://www.fao.org/3/ca6396en/ca6396en.pdf.

very unfortunate that about 40% of the total global yield gets wasted per year including postharvest losses (Figure 12.1) (Alexander et al., 2017). Simultaneously, the burgeoning population put huge pressure on the agricultural production system to meet their requirements (Harvey, 2019). However, development agronomist reported across tropical regions for more than 50 years that regenerative agriculture is the best-suited means for enhancing yield with minimum additional input.

Moreover, the need of more land area for farming is also a driver of clearing forests, which leads to the destruction of the ecosystem as well as people's habitats (WWF, 2022). Particularly, India, the heartland of the Asian green revolution, still has the scares of exhausted soil nutrients. To accomplish the increase in crop production demand, crops were grown repeatedly, and the very practice also reduced crop failure. The entire soil nutrient cycle was exploited, thus resulting in a decline in soil fertility (Srivastava et al., 2020). New dwarf varieties and seeds were developed, in order to meet the newly developed varieties and seed's demand for nutrients, and farmers warranted excessive application of inorganic inputs. In that short time, wrong agronomic practices caused the soil to deteriorate, and there was insufficient natural potential of the soil to meet the demand for a variety of high-yielding crops. Consequently, the blind use of fertilizers and pesticides led to overall soil health degradation and contaminated soil ecosystem with hazardous heavy metals like cadmium, arsenic and lead. The impact of these fertilizers was not only on the soil but also on the water quality. Leaching, runoff and additional biodiversity losses caused the water quality to decline, which had an adverse effect on human health (Sharma and Singhvi, 2017).

The agricultural production system of Asian countries is reaching its peak, and its major challenge is meeting the exponentially rising global requirement for food, fibre and energy in order to achieve sustainability and food-nutritional security. The agricultural production system in South Asian countries is mainly dominated by subsistence farmers as most of the farmers have small/ fragmented land holdings, i.e., marginal, and practice farming in an intensive manner with the prime objective of higher economic profit ignoring the soil health status (FAO, 2020; FAO, 2021a; FAO, 2022b). Surge in the climate change occurring mainly in tropical region repercussion of which agricultural production in Asia is being adversely affected (Chew and Soccio, 2016). Moreover, rapid change in climate in the past five decades has affected the length of growing seasons, increase

TABLE 12.2

Intensification in Use of Inputs of Asian Crop Production System during Green Revolution Era

Inputs	Year Duration		Input Increase % per Year
	1977–1979	1994–1996	
Use of fertilizer (kg/ha arable land)	60.18	133.55	8.3
Imported pesticides ($/ha arable land)[a]	1.669	3.628	7.5
Irrigation (% arable land)	30.50	35.75	1.0
Use of agricultural machinery (units/1,000 ha arable land)			
Tractors	6.361	13.471	7.1
Harvesters/threshers	1.788	3.699	6.3
All machines	8.481	17.576	6.7

Source: Adopted and modified from FAOSTAT database.

[a] From 1979 onward.

in evapotranspiration, of various crops as well as water stress (Table 12.2) and heat stress period in agricultural production system (Aryal et al., 2020; Lasco et al., 2011).

12.2 REGENERATIVE AGRICULTURE: AMALGAMATION OF FARMING AND PROFITABLY MANAGING NATURAL RESOURCES

Before moving ahead, it is important to understand what the term 'regenerative' means in the context of agriculture. Regenerative is composed of prefix 're' which literally means 'again'; hence, when added before generative, it means the ability to exist again or to get generated again. Therefore, if the set of practices are called regenerative, then it clearly means that the set of practices are capable enough to bring itself into existence once again. A best example of regenerative capability is 'forest' where the entire ecosystem heals and regenerates itself without leaving any waste behind. The regenerative agriculture is the set of such practices that have the potential to restore, rejuvenate and reenergize the entire resource bases with the core objective to achieve better soil health augmenting to mitigate climate change and nurturing the Mother Nature (Rhodes, 2017). It comprises of techniques and practices that are generally followed in organic agriculture, biodynamic farming and natural farming with the prime intention to enhance the SOC content as well as to check the oxidation of SOC (Ranganathan et al., 2020) with minimum interference to nature, including composting, minimum or no tillage, green manuring, crop rotation, mulching and growing cover crops. The use of synthetic inputs, for instance, herbicides, fertilizers and pesticides, is also restricted as these inputs are significantly responsible for destroying the soil microbial ecosystem as well as responsible for biodiversity losses. In addition, regenerative organic agriculture proposed by Robert Rodale has also been reported to sequester organic carbon in soil resulting in reduced carbon percentage in the atmosphere by natural means (Rodale Institute, 2014). Regenerative farming approaches become ecologically intensive practices instead of capital or yield intensive since their primary goal is to enhance the rate at which organic carbon is sequestered, hence restoring soil health (Rodale Institute, 2014).

Regenerative agricultural practices ensure that all the by-products (wastes) produced during crop production should get utilized as input for following season crops, but if the input for the next crop is not from the farm resources, then the system can't be regenerative or even not sustainable. However, it is often misunderstood that sustainability is merely about the 'ability to last' or 'the potential to endure' but sustainable agriculture simply means self-sustaining not intrinsically regenerative

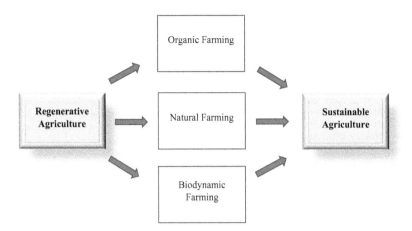

FIGURE 12.2 Orchestration of various agricultural practices with regenerative potential to attain sustainability.

(Rhodes, 2015, 2017). Therefore, in the longer term, all sustainable ways become unsustainable if they lack the capability to generate again or bring into existence again.

Figure 12.2 explains that the regenerative approach of the agricultural production system is the core of sustainability. Organic farming, natural farming and biodynamic farming systems are the subset of regenerative agriculture and should be the practicing way with the inherent nature of regeneration resource base to achieve sustainability in agricultural production system, and hence, the entire set of practices comes under the regenerative approach of agricultural production system. For instance, excluding regenerative concept and capability from natural farming, organic farming and biodynamic farming then, just think would we be able to carry out organic farming as organic and natural farming as natural? The answer is 'no' because the organic or natural input resource base will no longer sufficiently exist as all are exhaustible resource bases, and a regenerative approach will be required to sustain the practice.

However, regenerative agriculture is defined exclusively by many researchers more or less having the same concept of orchestration of best organic, conventional and biological farming practices into such a system which has the potential to enhance production via rejuvenating the ecosystem. According to McCue and Durkin (2021),'Regenerative farming is a system producing food and biomass that focuses on building functional diversity and soil health to produce consistent yields without relying on synthetic inputs (herbicides, pesticides, and chemical fertilizers)' (Rhodes, 2017).

Furthermore, it had envisaged that practices of regenerative agriculture are capable of sequestering 100% of the total annual CO_2 emission as well as keeping the annual carbon emissions within the proposed lower range of 41–47 Gt CO_2e. Unfortunately, our current conventional agricultural practices are the part of problem instead of being the solution; conventional practices are the net emitter of GHGs and are responsible for the oxidation of soil organic carbon resulting in depleted soil carbon stocks and leading to increased concentration of CO_2 into the atmosphere and poor soil health (Rodale Institute, 2014). The recent data from pasture trials and farming system reported by Rodale Institute indicated that regenerative practices have huge potential to enhance organic carbon content in soil and climate change mitigation (Figure 12.3).

12.3 UNIFYING PRINCIPLES FOR A CONSISTENT REGENERATIVE FARMING

12.3.1 TILLAGE

Conventional tillage practice greatly contributes to SOC losses through mineralization and simultaneously it exposes the soil to water erosion and wind which leads to degraded soil health around

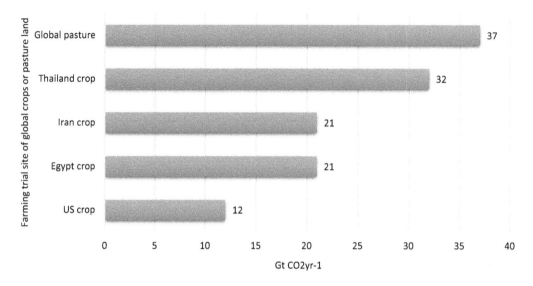

FIGURE 12.3   Adapted and modified from Rodale Institute (2014).

the globe (Lal, 1991). Urgency to tackle the issue led to the concept of conservation tillage practice. *'Conservation tillage'* has been proved to improve soil structure, check the oxidation of SOC
and play a crucial role in increasing SOC, improving soil moisture content and maintaining soil
temperature (Abdalla et al., 2013). In addition, no-till practice is a boon when it is performed com-
binedly with organic management. It has been reported that no-till practice increased the SOC by
nine after 2 years and 21% of increment in 6 years when conventional no-till is replaced with organic
no till (Carr et al., 2013). There are several studies and researches which clearly mentioned that
glomalin-related soil protein or AMF colonization is significantly increased in the soil where no
tillage is practised, whereas conventional tillage disrupts hyphae network responsible for glomalin
production (Datta and Meena, 2021; Curaqueo et al., 2010; Castro Filho et al., 2002). Therefore, it
concludes that instead of conventional no till, the organic no till has huge potential to reciprocate
the organic carbon losses in agriculture.

12.3.2   Crop Rotation and Cover Crops

Crop rotation is not a new concept. It had been followed since the ancient period (BC centuries)
but in the blind race of maximum profit, monocropping and lack of awareness, the practice lags
somewhat in this regard. It has been found that crop rotation without fallow or polyculture with
no fallow significantly increases SOC stock and improves soil biodiversity as well (West and Post,
2002). For instance, rotation of wheat–sunflower or wheat–legume is beneficial instead of practicing wheat–fallow rotation. In addition, growing cover crops (e.g. seeded grass species) bushy
perennials (Conant et al., 2001; West and Post, 2002) along with intensive crop rotation facilitates
the soil with continuous cover, thereby increasing soil microbial biomass carbon as it avails the
microbes with energy and root as host shelter (Rodale Institute, 2014; Álvaro-Fuentes and Paustian,
2011). However, orchestration of cover cropping and crop rotation with no tillage practice have been
reported to significantly reduce the yield gaps with improvement in soil fertility (García-Torres
et al., 2013). In order to get better crop yield and accomplish plant nutrient requirements, legumes,
for instance, millet, sesbania and mucuna, are better options as these are rich in nutrients like N and
C (Thierfelder et al., 2013; Nascente and Crusciol, 2012). These legumes (particularly millets) start

decomposing prior to rice transplantation and hence facilitate the nutrient to the growing sapling in ample amount (Nascente et al., 2011; Singh et al., 2018), and macuna, in addition to cover crop, has significant termite suppression potential because of the presence of several alkaloids like L-Dopa (Thierfelder et al., 2013).

12.3.3 Crop Residue Retention, Recycling and Mulching

Improvement in the soil health and mitigating crop residue burning through residue recycling is the core objective of crop residue retention and mulching in order to transit conventional agricultural practice to regenerative and sustainable agriculture. Residue recycling has been found to potentially enhance organic matter formation leading to improved soil physico-chemical and biological properties. Furthermore, it has been found in many researches and studies that fresh organic matter is preserved in the soil through crop residue retention and hence improves soil health (Wezel et al., 2014). Crop residue retention along with no tillage practice significantly regulates the soil aggregates' stability, reduces the crust formation, bulk density and runoff, and increases water infiltration and hydraulic conductivity. Additionally, the soils having alkalinity problems can also be amended by retention of crop residue having a lower C/N ratio (e.g. oilseeds and pulses), whereas acidic soil can be also amended with crop residues having higher C/N ratio (e.g. cereals) as residues of cereals release hydroxyls at the time of decomposition (Singh et al., 2018). Besides, crop residue retention has been found to play a crucial role in sequestering soil organic carbon in relation to mitigating climate change (Tivet et al., 2013).

12.3.4 Arbuscular Mycorrhizae: 'Glomalin' Super Glue

The link between fungal biomass abundance and soil carbon is now pervasively known. Recent findings of carbon sequestration in boreal forests reveal that root-associated, or mycorrhizal, fungi have huge potential for fixing soil carbon over extended time periods, to such a degree that it has an impact on the global carbon cycle. Arbuscular mycorrhizal fungi are root-symbiotic fungi that release a glycoprotein named glomalin (Datta and Meena, 2021; Rodale Institute, 2014). However, experimental findings of studies found glomalin in those samples only where plant roots were colonized with AMF (Smith and Read, 2008). Glomalin is hydrophobic, insoluble, recalcitrant and sticky in nature, hence called super glue for the soil particle augmenting the soil aggregate formation, which checks the oxidation of soil organic carbon as CO_2. Furthermore, glomalin-related soil protein also improves soil structure and soil pore space and provides resistance against water and wind erosion (Wuest et al., 2005). However, Wright and Anderson (2000) reported that glomalin content in the soil and stability of soil aggregates are significantly modulated by crop rotation patterns (Tables 12.3 and 12.4).

12.3.5 Agroforestry System

There is a huge potential for SOC sequestration through multispecies agroforestry system as tree species in this system have good interaction with roots and deep below the soil, but yet experimental evidences are not limpid (Ong et al., 2004; Rao et al., 2004). Emphasis should be made for the selection of those tree species that penetrate deep into the soil and have extensive\broad rhizosphere augmenting the addition of more carbon input into the soil and can lead to increased sequestration of SOC in agroforestry system (Kell, 2012; Lorenz and Lal, 2010). Instead of coniferous tree species, the selection of such tree species having broadleaf would complement to generate more SOC inputs as the roots of very trees have more root biomass and well-adhered root system (Laganiere et al., 2010). The adoption of conservation-effective strategies that minimize the water and nutrient losses contributes to retarding the decomposition rate of biomass and enhances the rate of biomass carbon input into the soil of agroforestry system, as well as increases the chemical,

TABLE 12.3

Water Stress Percentage of Asian Countries during 2000–2017

Asian Countries		Water Stress Percentage (2000–2017)								
		2000	2005	2010	2012	2013	2014	2015	2016	2017
Western Asia	Israel	139.2	121.3	115.6	108.9	105.5	102.1	98.9	102.8	103.4
	Turkey	31.2	29.9	34.9	37.5	38.1	38.6	39.9	44.3	44.6
	UAE	1,556.0	1,490.0	1,612.4	1,661.4	1,685.9	1,710.4	1,734.8	1,759.3	1,708.0
	Lebanon	41.1	35.6	47.2	51.8	54.1	56.5	58.8	58.8	58.8
	Oman	91.8	91.1	107.1	113.3	116.7	116.7	116.7	116.7	116.7
	Kuwait	1,911.8	2,075.0	2,075.0	–	–	–	–	–	–
	Iraq	92.7	79.6	66.6	61.4	58.8	56.2	49.0	54.1	54.1
	Georgia	6.2	5.9	5.9	5.9	5.9	5.9	5.9	5.9	5.9
	Saudi Arabia	819.8	894.8	914.5	900.1	894.2	894.7	948.9	906.9	883.3
	Yemen	161.1	169.8	169.8	169.8	169.8	169.8	–	–	–
	Qatar	282.6	374.1	409.9	424.2	431.4	434.7	431.0	432.4	432.4
	Syria	134.2	126.0	126.0	126.0	126.0	126.0	–	–	–
	Jordan	82.6	95.9	98.9	94.0	99.8	107.4	96.2	100.1	100.1
	Azerbaijan	49.1	53.2	51.1	52.9	55.2	53.5	54.3	55.2	56.4
	Cyprus	22.0	22.8	27.5	34.9	28.3	29.7	31.7	29.8	29.5
	Bahrain	248.9	196.4	173.1	163.7	159.1	154.4	137.2	133.7	133.7
	Armenia	37.7	55.9	42.9	59.3	59.6	57.7	66.0	64.2	57.8
Central Asia	Tajikistan	74.9	74.0	71.6	70.4	69.9	69.3	68.7	68.7	68.7
	Kyrgyzstan	65.4	52.6	50.0	50.0	50.0	50.0			
	Turkmenistan	127.9	143.6	143.6	143.6	143.6	–	–	–	–
	Uzbekistan	153.1	141.0	143.1	143.9	144.3	144.7	158.1	156.4	168.9
	Kazakhstan	29.1	34.4	33.0	29.7	31.2	32.0	30.0	30.0	31.1
Southern Asia	India	62.7	70.4	66.5	66.5	66.5	66.5	66.5	66.5	66.5
	Bangladesh		5.7	5.7	5.7	5.7	5.7	5.7	5.7	5.7
	Iran	77.4	81.3	81.3	81.3	81.3	–	–	–	–
	Pakistan	105.9	109.8	113.7	115.3	112.6	119.5	120.8	122.5	122.7
	SriLanka	91.2	90.8	90.8	90.8	90.8	90.8	–	–	–
	Nepal	8.4	8.3	8.3	8.3	8.3	8.3	8.3	–	–
	Maldives	17.7	16.3	15.7	15.7	15.7	15.7	15.7	15.7	15.7
	Bhutan			1.4	1.4	1.4	1.4	1.4	1.4	1.4
	Afghanistan	54.8	54.8	–	–	–	–	–	–	–
Eastern Asia	Mongolia	3.6	3.8	3.9	3.6	3.5	3.3	3.2	3.4	3.4
	North Korea	–	–	–	–	–	–	–	–	–
	South Korea	–	–	–	–	–	–	–	–	–
	Japan	41.6	38.4	37.3	37.3	37.3	37.3	37.3	37.3	37.3
	China	40.2	40.5	42.9	43.7	44.0	43.3	43.2	43.2	43.2

Source: Adapted and modified from FAO Statistics (2021).

biological and physical stabilization mechanism for the protection of soil organic carbon losses (Lal and Follet, 2009).

It has been reported that to achieve higher SOC pool in agroforestry system, demands for higher biomass carbon return to soil must be fulfilled; also, there is a need for strengthening the stabilization of organic matter or reducing the biomass decomposition (Lal, 2005; Sollins et al., 2007). Agroforestry system is more capable of utilizing the available resources for biomass production

TABLE 12.4

Impact of Crop Rotation over Glomalin Content and Aggregate Stability of Soil (Wright and Anderson, 2000; Dutta and Meena, 2021)

Sample	Stability of 1–2 mm Soil Aggregates	Total Glomalin (mg/g)	Immunoreactive Total Glomalin (mg/g)
W-F	11.6 (4.11)	2.3 (0.7)	0.57 (0.08)
W-C-M	12.6 (3.4)	2.9 (0.3)	0.56 (0.16)
W-C-M-F	12.0 (5.9)	2.5 (0.5)	0.61 (0.16)
W-C-F	11.5 (6.0)	2.4 (0.4)	0.62 (0.12)
W-S-F	7.4 (3.5)	2.3 (0.4)	0.52 (0.08)
Crested wheatgrass	59.9 (19.9)	3.0 (0.3)	1.70 (1.34)
Triticale	7.3 (3.3)	1.5 (0.3)	0.41 (0.08)

Mean value and standard deviation are in parentheses.
Rotation includes: W, wheat; C, corn; M, proso millet; S, sunflower; F, fallow.

(compared to Monoculture), and thus, more biomass production leads to higher carbon return into the soil. There are some agroforestry practices through which we can directly add carbon to the soil. Those are:

- Leaving the pruned-off parts or material of the woody species at the site's soil, so that it can act as mulch and in situ decomposition of tree litter.
- Promoting livestock grazing and addition of dung to the soil
- Let woody species grow and contribute litters at surface and beneath the ground during the fallow phases of crops.
- For the animal production system, integrate trees and their litter.
- Let the litter of shade-tolerant species be added into the soil that grows under canopy shade of the tree.
- Deliberate growing of agricultural crops during the establishment period of forestry plantation so that soil can be benefited with soil carbon input by agricultural crops (Lorenz and Lal, 2005).

12.3.6 STABILIZATION OF SOIL ORGANIC CARBON THROUGH SOIL MINERALS TO ACHIEVE NET ZERO CARBON OXIDATION LOSSES

In order to stabilize SOC via soil minerals, physical, chemical and biochemical/biological stabilization are the three proposed mechanisms. Protection or stabilization of SOC through physical mechanism involves the aggregate formation which acts as a layer and separates SOC from microbial enzymes; hence, it modulates the food web interaction as well as the rate of microbial turnover (Figure 12.4) (Sufian, 2021; Singh et al., 2018; Edwards and Bremner, 1967; Elliott, 1986; Coleman and Elliot, 1988; Jastrow, 1996; Six et al., 2000). Moreover, in the chemical mechanism for stabilization of SOC, physiochemical or chemical bonding of soil minerals with organic carbon takes place. Subsequently, organo-mineral complexes are formed, which play a significant role in protecting SOC from microbial attack. Biological protection of SOC takes place through the formation of complexes for instance, condensation reactions and recalcitrant as the consequence of chemical composition of the compound itself (e.g. lignin and polyphenols) (Sufian, 2021; Singh et al., 2018) (Figures 12.5 and 12.6).

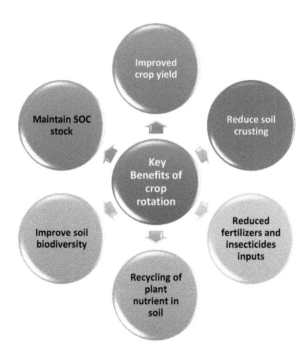

FIGURE 12.4 Key benefits of crop rotation in order to improve soil health and rejuvenate the agricultural system.

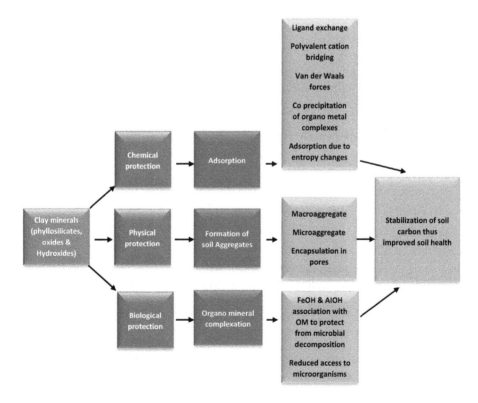

FIGURE 12.5 Chemical, physical and biological protection mechanism for SOC stabilization through clay minerals (Singh et al., 2018).

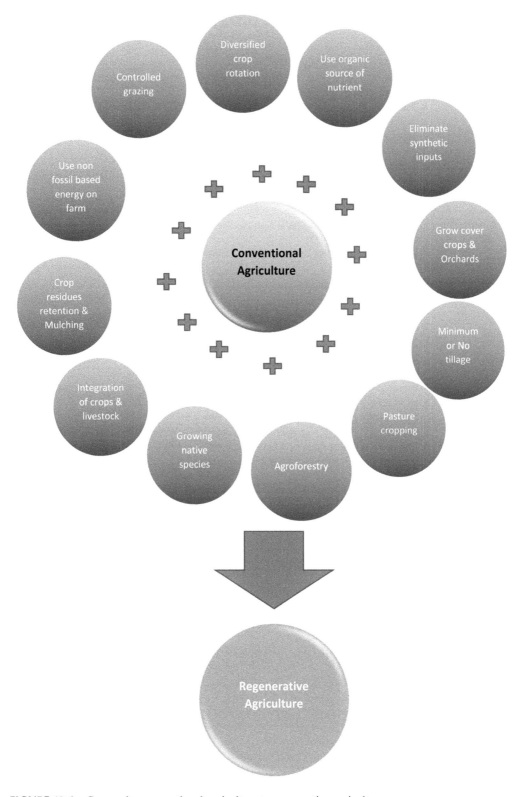

FIGURE 12.6   Converging conventional agriculture to regenerative agriculture.

12.4   ORGANIZATIONAL AND POLICY INTERVENTIONS

Countries	Policies Interventions	References
India	• National Mission for Sustainable Agriculture (2014–2015) • The Paramparagat Krishi Vikas Yojana (2015) • Rashtriya Vikas Yojana (2007) • National Programme for Organic Production (2001) • The mission for Integrated Development of Horticulture (2014) • Organic Value Chain Development in North Eastern Region Scheme (2015)	https://www.agrifarming.in/ government-schemes-for-organic-farming-in-india; Yadav (2017)
Bangladesh	• New Agricultural Extension Policy (NAEP) 1996 • NGOs like PROSHIKA (1976), Hunger Free World (2001), CARITAS • Naya Krishi Andolan (New Agriculture Movement) (1990)	
China	• Establishment of Organic Food Development and Certification Center (1994) • Establishment of Certification and Accreditation Administration (2003) • Establishment of COFCC (2003) • China instituted 'Chinese National Organic Product Standard' (2005)	Chen (2015); https://en.wikipedia.org/ wiki/Organic_Food_Development_ Center; https://certifications. controlunion.com/en/certification-programs/certification-programs/ china-national-organic-standard; Dhiman (2020)
Thailand	• Formation of Royal Project Foundation (1969) • Launched Organic Farm Village Project • Program for growing organic tea at Chiang Rai Province	Hsieh (2005); Organic News Line No. 2 (2001)
Japan	• Establishment of Agriculture and Forestry Regulation for Organic Product, Accreditation Standard for Agricultural Production, Japanese Standard of Processing Organic Products and Standard for Organic Product and Specially Produced Agricultural Products (2000) • Establishment of Organic Agriculture Management Office • Enacted an Act for Promotion of Organic Agriculture (2006) • Japan Agriculture Standard for Organic Food (2001)	https://www.elibrary.imf.org/display/ book/9781451943818/ch04.xml; Miyake and Kohsaka (2020)
Republic of Korea	• Act of Sustainable Agriculture (1997) • Provision of subsidized loan to organic growers (1994) • Initiation of labelling program by Ministry of Agriculture	Hsieh (2005); https://www.fftc.org.tw/ en/publications/main/1287
Indonesia	• Establishment of Board of Indonesian Organic Certification by nongovernment organization • Organic farming project by NGO in Bogor • Establishment of Saluyu Organic Vegetable Farmer Group (2007)	Hsieh (2005); https://hal.archives-ouvertes.fr/hal-00521832/document
Taiwan	• stablishment of Taiwan Mokichi Okada International Association (MOA) International Foundation of Natural Ecology (1990) in cooperation with MOA of Japan • Establishment of Taiwan Organic Production Association • Formed Organic Standard Law (2003) • Accreditation to NGOs as organic certification organizations	Hsieh (2005)

12.5 CONCLUSION

Agriculture in the developing world needs to be transformed into more sustainable agricultural practices in order to mitigate all negative effects. Regenerative agriculture is indispensable in addressing the challenges of developing Asian countries with its unified regenerative potential approaches through the integration of organic and natural farming practices. In order to get maximized monetary output, regenerative agriculture gives emphasis to integration of livestock and agroforestry system of agriculture. However, there is a need to mitigate the ethical issues pertaining to livestock integration so that marginal farmers fetch the aim of doubled income. Regenerative agriculture employs farming practices that are intended to imitate nature, a variety of techniques, including agroforestry and properly managed grazing, are combined to create healthy soils and productive, thriving agro-ecosystems. Thus Richer soil, cleaner water systems, enhanced biodiversity, resiliency to climate change, and stronger farming communities are all advantages of regenerative agriculture.

REFERENCES

Abdalla, M., Osborne, B., Lanigan, G., Forristal, D., Williams, M., Smith, P., & Jones, M. B. (2013). Conservation tillage systems: a review of its consequences for greenhouse gas emissions. *Soil Use and Management*, *29*(2), 199–209.

Alexander, P., Brown, C., Arneth, A., Finnigan, J., Moran, D., & Rounsevell, M. D. (2017). Losses, inefficiencies and waste in the global food system. *Agricultural Systems*, *153*, 190–200.

Álvaro-Fuentes, J., & Paustian, K. (2011). Potential soil carbon sequestration in a semiarid Mediterranean agroecosystem under climate change: quantifying management and climate effects. *Plant and Soil*, *338*(1), 261–272.

Aryal, J. P., Sapkota, T. B., Khurana, R., Khatri-Chhetri, A., Rahut, D. B., & Jat, M. L. (2020). Climate change and agriculture in South Asia: adaptation options in smallholder production systems. *Environment, Development and Sustainability*, *22*, 5045–5075.

Bosma, D., Hendriks, M., & Appel, M. (2022). Financing regenerative agriculture

Carr, P. M., Gramig, G. G., & Liebig, M. A. (2013). Impacts of organic zero tillage systems on crops, weeds, and soil quality. *Sustainability*, *5*(7), 3172–3201.

Castro Filho, C. D., Lourenço, A., Guimarães, M. D. F., & Fonseca, I. C. B. (2002). Aggregate stability under different soil management systems in a red latosol in the state of Parana, Brazil. *Soil and Tillage Research*, *65*(1), 45–51.

Chen, A. (2015). China's path in developing organic agriculture: opportunities and implications for small-scale farmers and rural development. https://en.wikipedia.org/wiki/Organic_Food_Development_Center

Chew, P., & Soccio, M. (2016). Asia-Pacific: agricultural perspectives. https://www.fao.org/family-farming/detail/en/c/396943/#:~:text=Asia's%20position%20in%20the%20global,population%20and%20limited%20agricultural%20resources

Coleman, D. C., & Elliot, E. T. (1988). Let the soil work for us. *Ecological Bulletin*, *39*, 23–32.

Conant, R. T., Paustian, K., & Elliott, E. T. (2001). Grassland management and conversion into grassland: effects on soil carbon. *Ecological Applications*, *11*(2), 343–355.

Curaqueo, G., Acevedo, E., Cornejo, P., Seguel, A., Rubio, R., & Borie, F. (2010). Tillage effect on soil organic matter, mycorrhizal hyphae and aggregates in a Mediterranean agroecosystem. *Revista de la ciencia del suelo y nutrición vegetal*, *10*(1), 12–21.

Datta, R., & Meena, R. S. (eds.) (2021). Soil Carbon Stabilization to Mitigate Climate Change. https://doi.org/10.1007/978-981-33-6765-4

Dhiman, V. (2020). Organic farming for sustainable environment: review of existed policies and suggestions for improvement. *International Journal of Research and Review*, *7*(2), 22–31.

Edwards, A. P., & Bremner, J. (1967). Microaggregates in soils. *Journal of Soil Science*, *18*(1), 64–73.

EIT Food (2021). What is regenerative agriculture? *EIT Food*. https://www.youtube.com/watch?v=uCZFwivd2Vg

Elliott, E. T. (1986). Aggregate structure and carbon, nitrogen, and phosphorus in native and cultivated soils. *Soil Science Society of America Journal*, *50*(3), 627–633.

Erisman, J. W., Galloway, J. N., Dise, N. B., Sutton, M. A., Bleeker, A., Grizzetti, B., Leach, A. M., & de Vries, W. (2015). *Nitrogen: too much of a vital resource: Science Brief*. (WWF science brief NL). WWF Netherlands. http://www.louisbolk.org/downloads/3005.

FAO (2020). Climate change: Unpacking the burden on food safety. Rome. https://doi.org/10.4060/ca8185en

FAO (2021a). *World Food and Agriculture – Statistical Yearbook 2021*. FAO, Rome. https://www.fao.org/documents/card/en/c/cb4477en/

FAO (2021b). The State of the World's Land and Water Resources for Food and Agriculture – Systems at breaking point. Synthesis report 2021. Rome. https://doi.org/10.4060/cb7654en

FAO (2022a). Thinking about the future of food safety – A foresight report. Rome. https://doi.org/10.4060/cb8667en

FAO (2022b). Soils for nutrition: State of the art. Rome. https://doi.org/10.4060/cc0900en

García-Torres, L., Benites, J., Martínez-Vilela, A., & Holgado-Cabrera, A. (eds.) (2013). *Conservation Agriculture: Environment, Farmers Experiences, Innovations, Socio-Economy, Policy*. Springer Science & Business Media, Dordrecht.

Gordon, E., Davila, F., & Riedy, C. (2021). Transforming landscapes and mindscapes through regenerative agriculture. *Agriculture and Human Values*, *39*, 809–826. doi: 10.1007/s10460-021-10276-0

Harvey, F. (2019). Can we ditch intensive farming-and still feed the world? *The Guardian*.

Hsieh, S. C. (2005). Organic farming for sustainable agriculture in Asia with special reference to Taiwan experience. Research Institute of Tropical Agriculture and International Cooperation, National Pingtung University of Science and Technology, Pingtung, Taiwan, 65pp.

IPBES (2019). Summary for policymakers of the global assessment report on biodiversity and ecosystem services of the Intergovernmental Science-Policy Platform on Biodiversity and Ecosystem Services. S. Díaz, J. Settele, E. S. Brondízio E. S., H. T. Ngo, M. Guèze, J. Agard, A. Arneth, P. Balvanera, K. A. Brauman, S. H. M. Butchart, K. M. A. Chan, L. A. Garibaldi, K. Ichii, J. Liu, S. M. Subramanian, G. F. Midgley, P. Miloslavich, Z. Molnár, D. Obura, A. Pfaff, S. Polasky, A. Purvis, J. Razzaque, B. Reyers, R. Roy Chowdhury, Y. J. Shin, I. J. Visseren-Hamakers, K. J. Willis, & C. N. Zayas (eds.). IPBES Secretariat, Bonn, Germany, 56 pp.

Jastrow, J. D. (1996). Soil aggregate formation and the accrual of particulate and mineral-associated organic matter. *Soil Biology and Biochemistry*, *28*(4–5), 665–676.

Kell, D. B. (2012) Large-scale sequestration of atmospheric carbon via plant roots in natural and agricultural ecosystems: why and how. *Philosophical Transactions of the Royal Society B* 367: 1589–1597. doi: 10.1098/rstb.2011.0244

Laganière, J., Angers, D., & Paré D. (2010) Carbon accumulation in agricultural soils after afforestation: a meta-analysis. *Global Change Biology* 16, 439–453. doi:10.1111/j.1365-2486.2009.01930.x

Lal, R. (1991). Tillage and agricultural sustainability. *Soil and Tillage Research*, *20*(2–4), 133–146.

Lal, R. (2005). Forest soils and carbon sequestration. *Forest Ecology and Management*, *220*(1–3), 242–258.

Lal, R., & Follett, R. F. (2009) Soils and climate change. In: Lal R, Follett RF (eds) *Soil Carbon Sequestration and the Greenhouse Effect*. SSSA Special Publication 57, 2nd edn. Madison, WI, xxi-xxviii

Lasco, R. D., Habito, C. M. D., Delfno, R. J. P., Pulhin, F. B., & Concepcion, R. N. (2011). Climate change adaptation for smallholder farmers in Southeast Asia. World Agroforestry Centre, Philippines, 65 pp.

Lorenz, K., & Lal, R. (2005). The depth distribution of soil organic carbon in relation to land use and management and the potential of carbon sequestration in subsoil horizons. *Advances in Agronomy*, *88*, 35–66.

Lorenz K., & Lal, R. (2010). *Carbon Sequestration in Forest Ecosystems*. Springer, Dordrecht.

McCue, L., & Durkin, A. (2021). Regenerative agriculture: Farming in nature's form. *Metabolic*. https://www.metabolic.nl/news/regenerative-agriculture-farming-in-natures-form/

Miyake, Y., & Kohsaka, R. (2020). History, ethnicity, and policy analysis of organic farming in Japan: when "nature" was detached from organic. *Journal of Ethnic Foods*, *7*(1), 1–8.

Muller, A., Schader, C., El-Hage Scialabba, N., Brüggemann, J., Isensee, A., Erb, K. H., … Niggli, U. (2017). Strategies for feeding the world more sustainably with organic agriculture. *Nature Communications*, *8*(1), 1–13.

Nascente, A. S., & Crusciol, C. A. C. (2012). Cover crops and herbicide timing management on soybean yield under no-tillage system. *Pesquisa Agropecuária Brasileira*, *47*, 187–192.

Nascente, A. S., Kluthcouski, J., Rabelo, R. R., de Oliveira, P., Cobucci, T., & Crusciol, C. A. C. (2011). Upland rice yield under different soil management systems and nitrogen application times. *Pesquisa Agropecuária Tropical*, *41*(1), 186–192.

National Bureau of Statistics of China (2014) *China Statistical Yearbook 2013*. China Statistics Press.

Ong, C. K., Kho, R. M., & Radersma, S (2004) Ecological interactions in multispecies agroecosystems: concepts and rules. In: Ong CK, Huxely P (eds) *Tree-crop Interactions, a Physiological Approach*. CAB International, Wallingford, pp. 1–15.

Ranganathan, J., Waite, R., Searchinger, T., & Zionts, J. (2020). Regenerative agriculture: good for soil health, but limited potential to mitigate climate change. https://www.wri.org/blog/2020/05/regenerative-agriculture-climate-change

Rao, M. R., Schroth, G., Williams, S. E., Namirembe, S., Schaller, M., & Wilson, J. (2004) Managing bewlo-ground interactions in agroecosystems. In: Ong CK, Huxely P (eds) *Tree-crop Interactions, a Physiological Approach*. CAB International, Wallingford, UK, pp 309–328

Rhodes, C. J. (2015). Permaculture: regenerative – not merely sustainable. *Science Progress*, *98*(4), 403–412.

Rhodes, C. J. (2017). The imperative for regenerative agriculture. *Science Progress*, *100*(1), 80–129.

Rodale Institute (2014). Regenerative organic agriculture and climate change: a down-to-earth solution to global warming. http://rodaleinstitute.org/assets/RegenOrgAgricultureAndClimateChange_20140418.pdf

Sharma, N., & Singhvi, R. (2017). Effects of chemical fertilizers and pesticides on human health and environment: a review. *International Journal of Agriculture Environment and Biotechnology*, *10*, 675–680.

Singh, M., Sarkar, B., Sarkar, S., Churchman, J., Bolan, N., Mandal, S., Menon, M., Purakayastha, T. J., & Beerling, D. J. (2018). Stabilization of soil organic carbon as influenced by clay mineralogy. *Advances in Agronomy*, *148*, 33–84.

Singh, S., Singh, R., Mishra, A. K., Upadhyay, S., Singh, H., & Raghubanshi, A. S. (2018). Ecological perspectives of crop residue retention under the conservation agriculture systems. *Tropical Ecology*, *59*(4), 589–604.

Six, J., Paustian, K., Elliott, E. T., & Combrink, C. (2000). Soil structure and organic matter I. Distribution of aggregate-size classes and aggregate-associated carbon. *Soil Science Society of America Journal*, *64*(2), 681–689.

Smith, S. E., & Read, D. J. (2008). *Mycorrhizal Symbiosis*. 3rd edn. Academic Press, Amsterdam. DOI: https://doi.org/10.1016/B978-0-12-370526-6.X5001-6.

Sollins, P., Swanston, C., & Kramer, M. (2007). Stabilization and destabilization of soil organic matter—a new focus. *Biogeochemistry*, *85*(1), 1–7.

Srivastava, P., Balhara, M., & Giri, B. (2020). Soil health in India: past history and future perspective. In: B. Giri & A. Varma (eds.) *Soil Health* (pp. 1–19). Springer, Cham.

Sufian, O. (2021). Adsorption: an important phenomenon in controlling soil properties and carbon stabilization. In: *Soil Carbon Stabilization to Mitigate Climate Change* (pp. 205–241). Springer, Singapore.

Thierfelder, C., Cheesman, S., & Rusinamhodzi, L. (2013). Benefits and challenges of crop rotations in maize-based conservation agriculture (CA) cropping systems of southern Africa. *International Journal of Agricultural Sustainability*, *11*(2), 108–124.

Tivet, F., de Moraes Sa, J. C., Lal, R., Briedis, C., Borszowskei, P. R., dos Santos, J. B., … Séguy, L. (2013). Aggregate C depletion by plowing and its restoration by diverse biomass-C inputs under no-till in sub-tropical and tropical regions of Brazil. *Soil and Tillage Research*, *126*, 203–218.

United Nations. (2019). *World Population Prospects 2019*. Department of Economic and Social Affairs, Population Division

West, T. O., & Post, W. M. (2002). Soil organic carbon sequestration rates by tillage and crop rotation: a global data analysis. *Soil Science Society of America Journal*, *66*(6), 1930–1946.

Wezel, A., Casagrande, M., Celette, F., Vian, J. F., Ferrer, A., & Peigné, J. (2014). Agroecological practices for sustainable agriculture. A review. *Agronomy for Sustainable Development*, *34*(1), 1–20.

White, C. (2020). Why regenerative agriculture? *American Journal of Economics and Sociology*, *79*(3), 799–812.

World Wildlife Fund (WWF) (2022). *Impact of Sustainable Agriculture and Farming Practices*. World Wildlife Fund. https://www.worldwildlife.org/industries/sustainable-agriculture

Wright, S. F., & Anderson, R. L. (2000). Aggregate stability and glomalin in alternative crop rotations for the central Great Plains. *Biology and Fertility of Soils*, *31*(3), 249–253.

Wuest, S. B., Caesar-TonThat, T. C., Wright, S. F., & Williams, J. D. (2005). Organic matter addition, N, and residue burning effects on infiltration, biological, and physical properties of an intensively tilled silt-loam soil. *Soil and Tillage Research*, *84*(2), 154–167.

Yadav, M. (2017). Towards a healthier nation: organic farming and government policies in India. *International Journal for Advance Research and Development*, *2*(5), 153–159.

Zhang, L., Yan, C., Guo, Q., Zhang, J., & Ruiz-Menjivar, J. (2018) The impact of agricultural chemical inputs on environment: global evidence from informetrics analysis and visualization. *International Journal of Low-Carbon Technologies*, *13*(4), 338–352.

13 Regenerative Agriculture Practices for Rice-Based Systems in South Asia

Ajay Kumar Mishra, Malay K. Bhowmick,
Panneerselvam Peramaiyan, Sheetal Sharma,
and Sudhanshu Singh

13.1 INTRODUCTION

South Asia comprises low-middle-income countries where depletion of groundwater and land resources, climate change, and population growth are the most severe challenges and concerns for long-term development. The most significant problem for farmers, scientists, and policymakers is feeding South Asia's increasing population using finite resources (Gough, 2017). Economic development in the region is progressing at a different level than population growth; rapid urbanization, changing food consumption patterns, and using nonrenewable inputs like water, fertilizers, and pesticides to achieve high yields need effective use of natural resources. Current land-use practices in South Asia disrupt environmental integrity by depleting groundwater supplies and soil organic carbon (SOC) and harming soil physicochemical qualities (Qadri and Bhat, 2020).

Since rice is the primary staple food in South Asia, increasing rice production to meet the growing population's demand is a core component of the new agenda for sustainable development. Hence, transforming agri-food systems in the coming decades must be achieved through building resilience and mitigating environmental impacts, with at least 30%–50% increases in the efficiency of limited resources used while ensuring the accessibility of healthy and nutritious food for all individuals and significantly reducing many negative environmental impacts associated with modern food systems (Dobermann et al., 2013).

The perception and knowledge of current intensive land use, especially in the rice-wheat cropping system (RWCS), suggests immediate attention and rigorous initiative for addressing the adverse effects on soil, water, and overall ecosystems. To achieve the overall sustainability of this critical rice-based cropping system (RBCS) in the region, it is necessary to adjust the tillage and crop establishment methods in conventional RWCS by replacing intensive tillage practices in wheat and avoiding puddling operation for rice production (Bhatt et al., 2021). In the RBCS, rice is primarily grown using traditional wet tillage (puddling) and transplanting methods. Besides, agricultural wastes in rice and wheat continue to be burnt or removed (Bhatt et al., 2016).

Institutions, researchers, and NGOs have been promoting different conservation techniques for controlling the intense effects on soil and ecosystems. Since the late 2000s conservation agriculture (CA) has started being adopted by farmers as an alternative to conventional agricultural practices to minimize the ill impacts (Erenstein et al., 2012). Although CA practices already evidenced a positive result, the research efforts were directed toward developing new technologies for the betterment of the ecosystem. Later, sustainable agriculture (SA) and organic agriculture (OA) came into existence, and all these practices displayed a positive impact by using naturally available resources (Somasundaram et al., 2020). Anticipating the dearth of these resources, researchers have developed the evolution of regenerative agriculture (Rodale, 1983). The name says regenerative

DOI: 10.1201/9781003309581-16

technologies for restoring depleting resources to enhance agricultural productivity. Regenerative agriculture (RA) is a holistic approach of all good means and possible ways from CA and SA practices. The RA practices mainly focus on improving soil health, increasing carbon sequestration, promoting crop residue management, producing nutritious food, reducing greenhouse gases (GHGs) emissions, controlling soil erosion, and raising the socioeconomic and living standards throughout the value chain (Giller et al., 2021). The present chapter intends to illustrate the RA practices useful for RBCS in South Asia.

13.2 RESOURCE-EXHAUSTIVE CONVENTIONAL FARMING SYSTEMS

In South Asia, conventional farming was adopted immensely for achieving higher crop yields without considering any appropriate practices for restoring soil health and climate mitigation. Heavy reliance on synthetic chemical fertilizers and pesticides has seriously impacted public health and the environment (Pimentel et al., 2005). Besides, the injudicious use of irrigation water leads to water scarcity, and of course, this method cannot give good yields in arid and semi-arid regions. Intensive tillage practices lead to leaching out of most of the nutrients available in the soil and disturb the soil's physical properties and soil biomass (Mwiti et al., 2022). Farmers do not follow any proper SOC restoration practices that lead to the release of carbon dioxide (CO_2) and the exhaustion of carbon in the soil. Continuous monocropping of rice leads to reduced soil fertility and the loss of the capability to maintain the soil ecosystem (Nair, 2019).

In response to the apparent difference between sustaining livelihoods through agricultural production and maintaining the ecosystem functions on which humanity and production rely, conventional agriculture has been bombarded by alternative production methods and practices since 1970–1980 (Beus and Dunlap, 1990). Emerging alternatives to conventional farming are CA, RA, agroecology, precision agriculture, permaculture, OA, and biodynamic agriculture. Some date back to the early 20th century, but their promotion as alternatives is firmly tied to sustainability. Whereas conventional agriculture is referred to as the dominant production system in an area, RA is the most recent trend to gain worldwide traction as an alternative to conventional farming methods.

13.3 STATUS OF SOIL DEGRADATION AND EROSION

Soil degradation is described as a change in soil health conditions that reduces the ecosystem's ability to provide consumer resources and services (FAO, 2018). Crop growth and production are affected as a result of soil degradation, which shows a negative impact on crop production. Around 140 million hectares (m ha) of agricultural land in South Asia are majorly affected by soil erosion through water and wind (Figure 13.1) and waterlogging (Jahan and Gurung, 2017) as well as diverse processes (Flores et al., 2020), including physical (excess tillage operations, usage of heavy machinery, soil compaction), chemical (salinity, injudicious use of agrochemicals, nutrient deficiency/toxicity) and biological (loss of biodiversity, reduction in soil organic matter).

The soil degradation indicators react differently based on agricultural practices (Walmsley and Sklenička, 2017). The soil's physical properties are the primary indicators of soil degradation, and each property of the soil is interlinked. For example, declining soil porosity leads to the compaction of soil layers which may be due to the usage of heavy equipment on highly saturated soils (Défossez et al., 2014). Capowiez et al. (2012) state that soil compaction works inversely to soil organic matter (SOM). SOM, cation exchange capacity (CEC), and clay practices in soil are interlinked. If soil organic matter is reduced, then CEC is also reduced, and thereby the soil's clay particles are reduced, leading to erosion at the time of imposition of agricultural practices or during changes in climatic conditions (Goldberg et al., 2020). Soil acidification is the secondary indicator of soil degradation. Routine application of chemical fertilizers and pesticides leads to soil acidity. Copper is the primary chemical in pesticides in higher concentrations, negatively affecting soil biodiversity

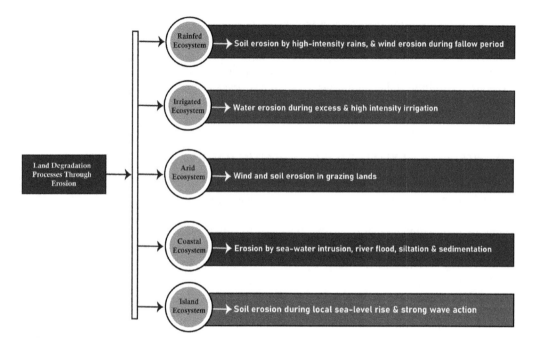

FIGURE 13.1 Soil degradation based on soil erosion in different ecosystems. Adapted from Srinivasarao et al., 2021.

(Micó et al., 2006; Ciarkowska et al., 2014). Soil degradation status always depends on the type of degradation, location, and indicators.

In South Asia, soil erosion occurs because of natural and man-made factors such as deforestation, intensive rainfall, unstable soils that are naturally eroded, and inappropriate agricultural practices like an inefficient use of inorganic fertilizers, burning of crop residues, overgrazing, continuous monocropping, and shifting cultivation (Panagos and Katsoyiannis, 2019). About 42.4 m ha of agricultural land is highly deficient in SOM (Lal et al., 2011). Soil erosion significantly impacts mountainous and semi-arid regions where wind and water are prominent erosion sources (Iqbal and Khan, 2014). It occurs mainly in the Himalayan areas of Nepal due to heavy rainfall and landslides, often leading to soil erosion.

Moreover, these regions exhibit an annual loss of SOC up to about 256 kg/ha (Shrestha et al., 2004). Because of soil erosion, all the macronutrients and micronutrients, including zinc, iron, selenium, and boron, get depleted along with soil, resulting in nutritional deficiencies in food production, causing malnutrition, particularly in children (Blaylock, 2017). Erosion also causes reservoir siltation, which reduces the ability of dams to hold water, raising the risk and danger at the time of flooding during the rainy season (Ghosh and Mistri, 2015), which negatively impacts the cultivated crops. Thus, increasing soil erosion severely harms the overall food security in South Asia.

Tillage operations, mulching, contour grass strips, and contour farming can help check soil erosion in South Asia (Figure 13.2). However, no-tillage is the most popular operation farmers adopt for soil erosion management. No-tillage practices help preserve and maintain soil health, like physical and biological properties to promote infiltration and water holding capacity (Ahnand Kim, 2016). Himalayan regions are more prone to soil erosion. Intercropping between the crops helps to control erosion and runoff. The use of organic matter, along with contour tillage and straw mulching strategies, can reduce soil erosion (Zhang et al., 2016). Soil erosion management based on land type and interlinking two or more management practices can exhibit a significant impact.

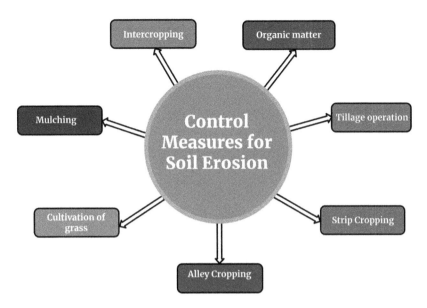

FIGURE 13.2   Agricultural practices to control soil erosion in South Asia (Ahmad et al., 2020).

13.4   TRANSITIONING FROM CONVENTIONAL TO CONSERVATION AGRICULTURE

Although conventional agriculture practices were targeted to achieve higher yields as compared to organic practices (Tal, 2018), there are concerns due to high input use (synthetic fertilizers, pesticides, and herbicides), causing environmental pollution and deterioration in soil health, which ultimately dismisses the target of attaining higher yields in the long run. There is no standard protocol for conventional agriculture which is a major drawback. In the late 1980s, much research was conducted in Pakistan, India (Punjab state), Bangladesh, and Nepal (Rehman et al., 2015; Legoupil, 2011). Compared with the conventional agriculture (Erenstein et al., 2012), farmers have started adopting no-tillage and CA practices due to the reduced cost of cultivation in the RWCS of the Indo-Gangetic Plains (IGPs) of India and other countries of South Asia since 2000. A few areas of Bangladesh and other southern and eastern parts of India have also reported no-tillage in rice-rice monocropping (Kassam et al., 2019).

The main advantage of CA practices is having a standard protocol for management practices based on crop, area, and climatic factors, aiming to reduce the environmental impact and mitigate climatic changes. Reduced tillage and cover cropping in CA practices help improve the soil's physical and biological health and the SOC (Das et al., 2018). After rice cultivation, the crop residues are burnt in conventional practice, whereas the residues are incorporated into the soil in CA practices (Turmel et al., 2015).Reduced tillage practices along with the incorporation of crop residues into the soil checks soil erosion, reduces the chance of crop failure, increases the SOC, influences the soil chemical parameters, and improves the diversity of soil microbial biomass as compared to the conventional agriculture practices (Somasundaram et al., 2020). Even though the CA practices are helpful in improving SOC, they do not improve the SOC stock (Dey et al., 2016). Integrated nutrient management (INM) helps reduce the application of high doses of synthetic fertilizers (Wu and Ma, 2015), thereby curtailing the cost of cultivation and improving the soil health. Loss of water and nutrients is reduced, and thereby their use efficiency is improved. Whereas the rice crop yields have become almost stable in conventional agriculture (Somasundaram et al., 2020) with ill impacts on soil health and climate change, the CA practices display higher crop yields along with soil health improvement and climate change mitigation.

13.5   ESCALATING FROM CONSERVATION TO REGENERATIVE AGRICULTURE PRACTICES

Whereas the CA practices are used to mitigate the environmental impact and help in soil conservation, the RA, being the mixer of a few good practices from CA and SA, exhibits more positive impact on crop, soil, and environment as compared to the CA. In South Asia, farmers generally practice RWCS in major fertile lands of IGPs, some parts of Khyber Pakhtunkhwa, Sindh region, Brahmaputra floodplains, and the Terai region of Nepal (Nawaz et al., 2019), whereas mostly continuous mono-cropping of rice is in the southern parts of India and eastern India (Krishna, 2010; Das et al., 2015). Continuous practice of RWCS has expanded the cultivation area, water requirements, and use of fertilizers, pesticides, and herbicides (Ladha et al., 2003). Although the yields of rice and wheat were earlier increasing, it got stagnated in the past decade (Bhatt et al., 2016) due to water scarcity, improper irrigation practices, degrading soil health, low organic matter content in soil, burning of crop residues, and poor management of pesticides and herbicides (Ladha et al., 2007; Bhattacharyya et al., 2015; Bhatt et al., 2016). Because of the high decomposition rate, the soils in dry and semi-arid areas of the IGPs lack organic carbon. The adverse weather conditions cause an increase in $CaCO_3$ precipitation, depleting the soils of Ca^{2+} ions on the soil exchange complex and forming sodicity in the subsoils. Rice seedlings are traditionally transplanted into puddled soil after harvesting. After the puddled soil is broken down by tillage practices, wheat crop is sown. Puddling operation in rice cultivation becomes only beneficial to inhibit water percolation and reduce the weed population (Gopal et al., 2019). Hand weeding also becomes easier after puddling (Hobbs et al., 2002). Still, the puddled soil physically destroys the soil structure, resulting in the creation of a hardpan at 15–18 cm depth, causing crop establishment challenges for the subsequent *rabi* crops like wheat and others due to soil aeration constraints (Nawaz et al., 2016).

Puddling influences pore-size distribution, altering moisture-retention qualities during the wheat crop (McDonald et al., 2006). It also raises the soil bulk density (Farooq and Nawaz, 2014) and inhibits root and shoot development of the following wheat crop (McDonald et al., 2006). The extent to which these physical modifications occur in puddled fields is determined by soil type, the prevalence of rice cropping within the area, and the intensity and kind of tillage (Singh and Ladha, 2004). Puddling-induced hardpan formation induces subsurface compaction in soil (Saharawat et al., 2010), creating a barrier to root growth in winter wheat (Aggarwal et al., 1995; Ray and Gupta, 2001).

Intensive mono-cropping practices in rice farming in eastern and southern parts of India and a few regions of Bangladesh have been leading to the exhaustion of available nutrients in the soil, increasing soil acidity, formation of hard pan, destruction of soil structure, pore size distribution, etc. Thus, it comes to the level of exhausting the naturally available nutrients from the soil, climate impacts and loss of SOC. There is a need to regenerate the resources for obtaining good yields and improve soil quality sustainably through the promotion and adoption of RA practices. The RA practices have been reported by Rodale (1983). Research accomplishments since 1983 on RA and noticed that it influences soil biodiversity and improvement in SOC with different combinations of practices.

13.6   PRINCIPLES AND PRACTICES OF REGENERATIVE AGRICULTURE

RA is completely organic or entirely conventional. While the main principles of OA are to keep the cultivation as natural as possible by avoiding the use of pesticides and genetically modified crops, and the emphasis of conventional agriculture is to achieve maximum yield through the use of synthetic fertilizers and input-intensive technologies, the focus of RA is on the soil and environment together, working collaboratively with nature. The objective is to build a profitable agricultural farm and healthy ecology simultaneously. Robert Rodale was the first person who gave the definition in 1983, and later on Hardwood worked further on RA and summarized the following essential points (Harwood, 1983):

- Agriculture should provide high-yielding, nutritionally pure food without any biocides.
- Agriculture should boost up soil productivity rather than diminishing it by improving the higher soil layers' depth, fertility, and physical qualities.
- Nutrient-flow systems incorporating soil fauna and flora into the system are more efficient, less environmentally hazardous, and provide crop nutrition. Such systems offer a renewed upward movement of nutrients in the soil profile, which reduces adverse environmental effects.
- For crop sustainability, crop production should be based on biological interactions by avoiding the need of synthetic biocides.
- Substances that alter the biological structure of agricultural practices should be avoided.
- RA necessitates, in its biological structure, an important part of the network between system managers/participants and the system itself.
- Integrated systems are mostly nitrogen self-sufficient due to biological nitrogen fixation.
- Agricultural production should enhance job levels and opportunities.
- RA involves national-level planning but a high degree of local and regional self-reliance to stop nutrient-flow loops.

RA principles (Figure 13.3) and practices work interlinked to each other, and these play the most important role in maintaining the ecosystem and mitigating agricultural land. Recent studies (McGuire, 2018; Merfield, 2019; Burgess et al., 2019) stated the principles with their interlinked

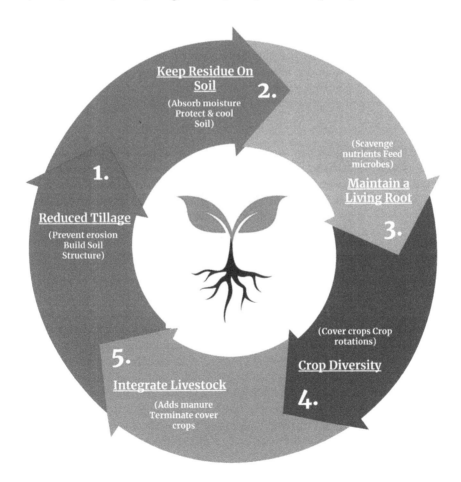

FIGURE 13.3 Principles of regenerative agriculture.

practices. The minimum tillage principle works on ZT, reduced tillage, and CA practices. Maintaining soil cover principle works with mulching, permaculture, and cover cropping practices, crop rotation. Improving soil carbon content is possible through the application of biochar, compost, animal or green manures, and organic fertilizer practices. Carbon sequestration principles work on agroforestry, plantation, and silvopasture practices. Relying more on biological nutrient cycle principles works on animal manures, compost, compost tea, green manures, and cover crops, maintaining living roots in the soil, inoculation of soils and composts, reducing reliance on mineral fertilizers, organic agriculture, and permaculture practices. Plant diversity principles work on diverse crop rotations, multi-species cover crops, and agroforestry. The principle of integrating livestock works on rotational grazing, holistic grazing, pasture cropping, and silvopasture practices. The principle of avoiding pesticide use works on diverse crop rotations, multi-species cover crops, and agroforestry practices. Improvement in water quality and quantity principles works on biochar, compost, green manures, animal manures, holistic practices, and grazing.

Based on the RA principles, the promising practices in RBCS are as follows:

1. Improved crop establishment methods to enhance soil aggregation, water infiltration and retention, and carbon sequestration. *e.g.* direct-seeded rice (DSR), un-puddled transplanted rice (UPTR), mechanical transplanting of rice (MTR), and zero tillage (ZT)-DSR
2. Site-specific INM including more of organics like FYM, biochar, green manuring, residue mulch, etc., for boosting soil fertility.
3. Bio-intensive IPM including IWM for building biological ecosystem
4. Improved water management through alternate wetting and drying (AWD), drip irrigation, laser land leveling, etc.
5. Integrated farming system like rice-cum-fish culture, rice farming with livestock integration
6. Introduction of legumes in rice-fallows for restoring or improving soil fertility and health
7. Straw management and well-managed grazing practices to stimulate plant growth, and increased soil carbon deposits, soil fertility, insect and plant biodiversity, and soil carbon sequestration.

All the principles and practices have shown an improvement in soil structure, biodiversity, and water holding capacity, field capacity, and nutrient availability in soil. This also improves the maintenance of soil temperature, which helps mitigate the carbon and incorporate it into the soil, leading to improved SOC. These practices control soil erosion and also re-habitat the degraded soil. The application of manures helps provide the soil's micronutrients in the available form to plants.

13.7 CONTEXTUALIZING REGENERATIVE AGRICULTURE

South Asia's uplands and mountain areas provide enormous prospects for economic growth on other fronts such as sources of water, electricity, biological diversity, rich minerals, and a diverse range of forest and agricultural products. Investment opportunities include forestry and silviculture, medicinal plant harvesting, and the environmentally friendly manufacturing of high-value items such as organic foods, morels, and fine wool. Similarly, these locations feature some of the most magnificent natural environments in the world, making them ideal for eco-tourism (Thapa, 2005).

Around 26.9% of the world's population belong to South Asia (World Meters, 2020), and a rapid increase in population growth creates an enormous challenge year by year to meet the growing demand for food, and it is more so since people have been expanding their agricultural areas through deforestation (Barker, 2004) and currently converting their agricultural lands for residential and non-agricultural uses. Healthy food is critical since many kinds of malnutrition persist to a greater extent. In 2019, 31.7% of children under the age of 5 years were stunted in South Asia, compared to other continents (UNICEF, WHO, & WB, 2020). Hence, the researchers at IRRI, CIMMYT, and other institutions worked together to meet the demand and came up with the "Green Revolution"

(Eliazer Nelson et al., 2019). It was a great initiative, but this revolution focused on high-yielding varieties, resistant varieties, chemical fertilizers, and pesticides (Gollin et al., 2021). With the progress of time, these practices gave good yields, but soils started degrading and losing their quality.

Along with soil degradation, GHG emissions have been noticed at high levels in the RWCS. Generally, poor management practices and crop residue burning are the causes of worries due to the loss of SOM and nutrients, air pollution, and increased GHG emissions (Jat et al., 2004). Recycling crop residues and adopting mulching practices can reduce GHG emissions. Mainly the puddled transplanted rice (PTR) emits more methane (CH_4), nitrous oxide (N_2O), and CO_2 as compared to the DSR (Gupta et al., 2016; Liu et al., 2014) and UPTR as well. Flooded rice cultivation practices show more CH_4 release than the DSR, whereas N_2O releases are more in DSR than the flooded rice (Pathak et al., 2014; Nawaz et al., 2019). DSR shows no hard pan formation and reduces the soil bulk density and earlier crop maturity (enabling timely sowing of wheat or other rabi crops), and reduces GHG emissions (Kumar et al., 2018). In wheat crop, ZT practices improve the input-use efficiency, enhances crop yield, boosts farmers' livelihoods (Erenstein et al., 2008), and decreases GHG emissions (Sapkota et al., 2015).

Carbon sequestration is improved with RA practices as it reverses CO_2 emission and increases SOC. GHG emissions and carbon sequestration work in an inverse proportion which means if GHG emission is reduced, it shows an increase in SOC. Carbon sequestration by the plantation of deep-rooted trees tends to increase SOC content (Crossman et al., 2010). RA practices like reduced tillage, inclusion of livestock, intercropping, cover cropping, inclusion of crop residues, crop rotation, and adoption of different crops including legumes and vegetables show positive effects on carbon sequestration (Kataki et al., 2001). Different cropping systems like rice-wheat-mungbean/cowpea, soybean-wheat, and diversified crop rotations show increased carbon sequestration (Somasundaram et al., 2020) with an increase in SOC content which has a positive influence on soil aggregations, soil nutrient use efficiency, soil porosity, and soil biodiversity.

ZT in wheat shows an improvement in soil biological activities, soil microbial biomass carbon, soil respiration, and soil enzyme activities in ZT as compared to the plough tillage crop (Alam et al., 2018; Nawaz et al., 2017; Sharma et al., 2011; Lupwayi et al., 2007). The healthy soil is a home to diverse species of microorganisms, vertebrate animals, and earthworms. Incorporating the crop residues in the soil increases SOC and soil microbial biomass carbon in the surface soil by 45% and 83% respectively (Balota et al., 2004).Long-term studies on RA practices for mitigating the changes in climate, and improvement in soil health have shown positive benefits in agronomic aspects as well as soil parameters that can control GHG emissions (Figure 13.4). The socio-economic parameters like the cost of cultivation are reduced, and it gives a scope for labor and women empowerment and improving financial stability.

13.8 EVIDENCE ON THE IMPACT OF REGENERATIVE SYSTEMS IN SOUTH ASIA

A brief study on RA practices on crop productivity, sustainability, and profitability (Table 13.1) in the South Asia region shows that the RA promotes soil health and quality through good agricultural practices (GAPs) like diversification of RBCS over the years (Lorenz and Lal, 2023). The reduced tillage along with the retention of crop residues on the surface layers shows favorable effects on other soil properties (Dalal et al., 2011) and results in the accumulation of soil nutrients (Kumar et al., 2008). All the parameters are interlinked with each other. Recycling of crop residues also enhances microbial activity as compared to conventional agriculture practices.

Soil erosion is a major global problem due to intensive practices and the loss of productive soils (Pal and Chakrabortty, 2022). Deep-rooted perennial grasses, such as intermediate wheatgrass, cereals, millets, or legumes, have the benefit of providing numerous products, such as feed and grain, as well as continuous soil cover, which helps prevent soil erosion and minimize the volatilization

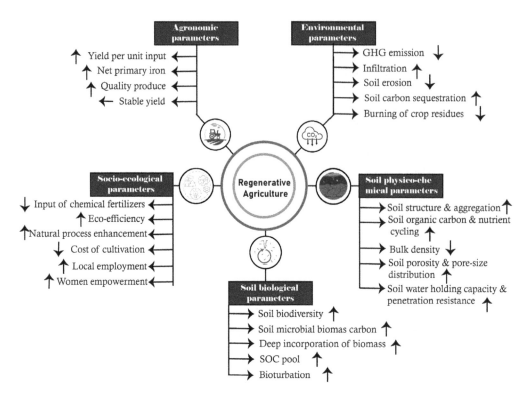

FIGURE 13.4 Benefits delivered through regenerative agriculture.

TABLE 13.1

The Impact of Reduced Tillage and Conservation Tillage in South Asia

Soil Properties	Cropping Systems	Reduced Tillage (RT)	Conventional Tillage (CT)	RT *vs.* CT
Soil moisture (%)	Rice-wheat-maize	18.6	7.4	11.2
Infiltration rate (mm/h)	Rice-wheat	6.19	6.15	0.04
	Rice-wheat (mungbean and daincha)	17.30	15.55	1.75
Soil aggregate (%)	Rice-wheat	77.63	66.01	11.62
	Rice-maize	89.18	86.38	2.8
Soil organic carbon (g/kg)	Rice-wheat	7.86	5.81	2.05
	Rice-maize	5.38	4.74	0.64
	Rice-wheat/chickpea-mungbean	5.21	3.73	1.48
SMBC (μg C per dry soil)	Rice-wheat-mungbean	160.66	119.93	40.73
Rice yield (t/ha)	Rice-wheat	6.14	5.97	0.17

and leaching of nutrients (Glover et al., 2010). Even though the SOM gets improved due to GAPs, the annual rate of increase in SOC is transient. Controlling deforestation for agricultural needs is important to protect SOC stocks. Agroforestry highly contributes to mitigating climate change by capturing carbon in the soil (Feliciano et al., 2018; Loboguerrero et al., 2019).

RA shows a major healing effect on the soil and helps restore soil health by improving its properties. Rice-rice monocropping system in southern and eastern parts of India and Bangladesh shows severe problems in the soil and the yield levels stagnate. Hence, instead of going with monocropping patterns, farmers must go with cover cropping, crop rotation with pulses and vegetables.

Agroforestry shows a major effect in yield as well as socio-economic standards of the farmers (Naik et al., 2023; Pingali, 2023; Yifan et al., 2023).

South Asia is frequently affected by natural calamities like floods, drought, landslides, and erosion (Aggarwal and Sivakumar, 2010), and this region always carries high temperatures (Jat et al., 2018) which rapidly decomposes the SOM. In RA practices, incorporating organic matter into the soil is helpful for plants to intake nutrients after decomposition. Soil microbial biomass carbon has been found to increase in the reduced tillage and cover cropping systems as compared to the conventional tillage practices. Instead of routine RWCS, crop rotation with legumes and maize shows positive impacts like increased infiltration capacity of the soil along with improvement in soil aggregates, soil biodiversity, and soil microbial biomass.

13.9 ENABLING AND PROMOTING SOIL HEALTH AND ECOSYSTEM SERVICES THROUGH REGENERATIVE AGRICULTURE

RA practices generally protect the soil from soil erosion and other hazards. There is a chain of interlinks between soil, crop and ecosystem services to maintain a healthy atmosphere (Soto et al., 2021). Reduced tillage practices improve soil parameters like an increase in soil aggregate stability and SOM on the surface layer, leading to improved soil strength and yield quality. Improving soil structure and biological activities helps maintain the soil ecosystem (Soane et al., 2012). As evidenced from the agro-environmental ratings for various agricultural systems based on ecosystem services and soil functions, the conservation systems display the highest score. Hence, the soil's ecosystem services are essential indirect linkages to the soil (Stavi et al., 2016).

The SOC is an essential indicator of soil quality and a promoter of agricultural sustainability. Along with its quantity, additional SOC criteria include its integrity or qualities (physical, chemical, biological) and churn rate or mean residence duration. The amount and stability of aggregates, susceptibility to crusting and compaction; porosity, infiltration rate, and retention as plant-available water capacity; aeration and gaseous exchange; adequate rooting depth; soil thermal expansion and temperature regimes are all relevant indicators of soil physical quality. Similarly, suitable markers of soil chemical quality include pH, CEC, nutrient availability, elemental balance, and the absence of toxicity or deficiency. Microbial biomass carbon, activity and variety of soil flora and fauna, and the lack of diseases and pests, as evidenced by a soil's disease-suppressive properties, are all significant indicators of soil microbial quality. An appropriate mix of these qualities influences agronomic production, water, nutrient, and other input efficiency, and management system sustainability. Soil quality indicators fluctuate depending on soil type, climate, and land use. For example, soil quality indices for intensively managed soils in the IGPs (Ray et al., 2014) diverge from those calculated for the tropical Alfisols soils (Sharma et al., 2008).

To measure the changes in soil health under different landscapes, we propose to determine different soil properties including chemical changes (SOC content, macronutrient, and critical micronutrient), physical changes (bulk density, penetration resistance, water holding capacity, and aggregate stability) and biological attributes (phosphatase activity, nitrogenase activity, dehydrogenase activity, soil microbial biomass carbon, and soil respiration), using standard soil testing protocols and methods. The soil properties to be captured and reported include (but are not limited to) (i) pH, (ii) electrical conductivity, (iii) organic carbon, (iv) soil compaction, (v) available P, and (vi) available K, (vii) available N, (viii) soil porosity, (ix) soil microbial biomass carbon and enzyme analysis, and (x) soil respiration rate.

Soil health can be promoted by GAPs like reduced tillage operations, mulching, cover cropping, livestock inclusion, conserving soil microbes, using nature-based nutrient management for agriculture like vermicompost, biochar, vermiwash, *Azolla* in rice, residue recycling, etc., which also helps in increasing soil available nitrogen while decomposing (Schreefel et al., 2020; Giller et al., 2021; Dai et al., 2019). Retaining crop residues favors soil quality, SOM and carbon storage, soil moisture retention, improved nutrient cycling, and reduced soil loss, among other environmental and soil health advantages. The effect of surface retention *versus* integration on various soil parameters vary, suggesting the need to consider ecological parameters such as climate, soil texture, and agronomic practices (Turmel et al., 2015).

13.10 STRATEGIES AND FRAMEWORK FOR ADOPTION AND SCALING REGENERATIVE AGRICULTURE IN SOUTH ASIA

Generally, farmers take a lot of time to adopt new methods and GAPs due to a lack of awareness. The major limiting factors to adopting RA are farmers. It requires new skills for management. The major concern to adopt any alternatives to conventional farming is reduced yield along with socio-economic factors. These negative perceptions and knowledge gaps in regenerative farming limit the farmers. The main objectives to adopt RA are soil quality improvement, enhancing the ecosystem, carbon sequestration, water percolation, and maintaining soil biodiversity.

The farmers should be aware of RA principles and practices. What is it? Why practice RA? Income sources of RA? Are the cropping systems that are suitable in their field, based on location, and climatic factors? The farmers and researchers when they start adopting RA practices need to know how to utilize their farm with 100%potential by deploying proper management practices. For example, if a farmer adopts RWCS on a farm, he/she can divide and interlink different crops along with the inclusion of livestock, and utilize the bunds by growing flowering plants, and agroforestry (orchards or timber plants with intercropping of legumes), which helps in fulfilling the aim of RA (Figure 13.5).

Carbon payments are important for restoring the carbon stock in the soil. In Western countries, institutions, private organizations, and companies provide a lot of scope to the farmers, and research scholars can learn and earn certificate course credits for carbon farming practices (Newton et al., 2020). Researchers should be exposed to different certificate courses and training to have an in-depth knowledge of RA in South Asia, especially in developing countries. The certification programs by private companies and institutions may also start a chain among them to produce quality yield. The yield and quality of grain and by-products of RA are good in terms of being sustainable and chemical-free, which fetch a huge demand in the markets. These products need recognition and standard market prices as compared to the crop produced by chemical fertilizers and pesticides. Proper pricing and recognition of the RA produce can help younger and future generations to gain much interest in it. South Asia contributes major employment in the agriculture sector, which also takes a place in increasing the income and impacts the GDP.

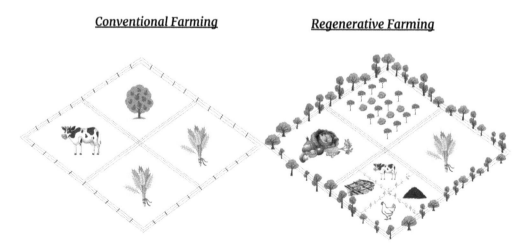

FIGURE 13.5 Framework for regenerative agriculture.

13.11 PUBLIC-PRIVATE PARTNERSHIPS AND INDUSTRIAL NETWORKING IN THE DISSEMINATION OF RA PRACTICES

Misunderstanding or confusion regarding what a farmer or organization understands when they use the word "regenerative agriculture" can lead to various complications. Without a clear and defined definition of RA, researchers may find it challenging or impractical to evaluate a specific statement regarding the advantages or results of RA. Specific aspects may be an essential component of efficient communication and collaboration between researchers and practitioners (White and Andrew, 2019). Furthermore, consumers may be misled or confused about the relevance or factual foundation of a claim regarding food produced utilizing RA if they do not have a reasonable knowledge of what it is or is not. Uncertainty regarding eco-labels, in turn, can lead to customer mistrust. Some of these issues are discussed further below in connection with the creation of certification systems and carbon subsidies for RA. Consequences for certification program sustainability standards, which have gained support internationally, can clarify criteria and expectations for certain types of agricultural practices (Tayleur et al., 2017). Process-oriented certification programs are widespread and may even be the standard. It is up to the customer to decide whether to buy and support the label, and they may decide whether to believe claims or make assumptions about the causal relationships between processes and results. However, at least one outcome-based certification scheme relating to RA is in the works (Savory Institute, 2019), which may be more strong and cause fewer uncertainties.

One suggested technique for motivating farmers and ranchers to practice RA is to compensate them financially for the ecological service of carbon sequestration in soil and plants on their property (Lal, 2020). Such a method would basically be a sort of payment for environmental services programs (Wunder, 2005), and it has also been suggested as "carbon farming." Some organizations have highlighted agricultural ideas and practices associated with carbon farming (Carbon Cycle Institute, 2020). Donors, investors, or taxpayers who would support a carbon farming project might legitimately expect it to be connected with a Monitoring, Reporting, and Verification (MRV) system to quantify and show the carbon sequestered by a particular farmer, project, or area. Carbon trading provides an investment infrastructure for carbon sequestration via new plantings and the conservation of established plantations (Crossman et al., 2010). Burning or removal of crop residues which increases GHG emissions can be incorporated into the soil that increases the SOC stocks. Carbon sequestration is the main center of the whole concept of RA which shows a greater impact on socioeconomic conditions.

13.12 CONCLUSION

In South Asia, the rice production area is higher in comparison to other crops. Implying RA practices in the degraded soils of South Asia have been noticed to restore their properties to increase yield, grain quality, and SOC. The GHG emissions are decreased as compared to the others. Further developments are required from different institutions, and NGOs to create more awareness sessions and campaigns related to RA principles, practices, and carbon credits, which would have a huge impact on women empowerment and rural livelihoods in the agricultural and small-scale industries.

REFERENCES

Aggarwal, G., Sidhu, A. S., Sekhon, N. K., Sandhu, K. S., & Sur, H. S. (1995) Puddling and N management effects on crop response in a rice-wheat cropping system. *Soil and Tillage Research*, 36, 129–139. doi: 10.1016/0167-1987(95)00504-8

Aggarwal, P. K., & Sivakumar, M. V. (2010) Global climate change and food security in South Asia: an adaptation and mitigation framework. In Lal, R., Sivakumar, M., Faiz, S., Mustafizur Rahman, A., Islam, K. (eds) *Climate Change and Food Security in South Asia* (pp. 253–275). Springer, Dordrecht.

Ahmad, N. S. B. N., Mustafa, F. B., & Didams, G. (2020) A systematic review of soil erosion control practices on the agricultural land in Asia. *International Soil and Water Conservation Research*, 8(2), 103–115.

Ahn, S. R., & Kim, S. J. (2016) The effect of rice straw mulching and no-tillage practice in upland crop areas on nonpoint-source pollution loads based on HSPF. *Water*, 8(3), 106.

Alam, M. J., Humphreys, E., & Sarkar, M. A. (2018) Comparison of dry seeded and puddled transplanted rainy season rice on the High Ganges River Floodplain of Bangladesh. *European Journal of Agronomy*, 96, 120–130. doi: 10.1016/j.eja.2018.03.006

Balota, E. L., Colozzi Filho, A., Andrade, D. S., & Dick, R. P. (2004) Long-term tillage and crop rotation effects on microbial biomass and C and N mineralization in a Brazilian Oxisol. *Soil and Tillage Research*, 77, 137–145. doi: 10.1016/j.still.2003.12.003

Barker, R. (2004) Evolution of Irrigation in South and Southeast Asia (Vol. 5). International Water Management Institute, Colombo.

Beus, C.E., & Dunlap, R.E. (1990) Conventional versus alternative agriculture: the paradigmatic roots of the debate. *Rural Sociology*, 55, 590–616.

Bhatt, R., Kukal, S. S., Busari, M. A., Arora, S., & Yadav, M. (2016) Sustainability issues on rice-wheat cropping system. *International Soil and Water Conservation Research*, 4, 64–74. doi: 10.1016/j.iswcr.2015.12.001

Bhatt, R., Singh, P., Hossain, A., & Timsina, J. (2021) Rice-wheat system in the northwest Indo-Gangetic plains of South Asia: issues and technological interventions for increasing productivity and sustainability. *Paddy and Water Environment*, 19(3), 345–365.

Bhattacharyya, R., Ghosh, B., Mishra, P., Mandal, B., Rao, C., Sarkar, D., … Franzluebbers, A. J. (2015) Soil degradation in India: challenges and potential solutions. *Sustainability*, 7, 3528–3570. doi: 10.3390/su7043528

Blaylock, A. (2017) Managing secondary nutrients and micronutrients. In W.M. (Mike) Stewart and W.B. Gordon (eds.). *Fertilizing for Irrigated Corn: Guide to Best Management Practices*. The International Plant Nutrition Institute. http://www.ipni.net/ipniweb/portal.nsf/0/9bbc50427c6469ae852574f20016279 6/$FILE/ATT4QHV2/Irrigated_%20Corn.pdf

Burgess, P. J., Harris, J., Graves, A. R., & Deeks, L.K. (2019) Regenerative agriculture: identifying the impact; enabling the potential. Report for SYSTEMIQ. Cranfield University, Cranfield.

Capowiez, Y., Samartino, S., Cadoux, S., Bouchant, P., Richard, G., & Boizard, H. (2012) Role of earthworms in regenerating soil structure after compaction in reduced tillage systems. *Soil Biology and Biochemistry*, 55, 93–103. doi: 10.1016/j.soilbio.2012.06.013

Carbon Cycle Institute (2020) Carbon farming. Available online at: https://www. carboncycle.org/carbon-farming/ (accessed June 26, 2020).

Ciarkowska, K., Sołek-Podwika, K., & Wieczorek, J. (2014) Enzyme activity as an indicator of soil-rehabilitation processes at a zinc and lead ore mining and processing area. *Journal of Environmental Management*, 132, 250–256. doi: 10.1016/j.jenvman.2013.10.022.

Crossman, N. D., Connor, J. D., Bryan, B. A., Summers, D. M., & Ginnivan, J. (2010) Reconfiguring an irrigation landscape to improve provision of ecosystem services. *Ecological Economics*, 69, 1031–1042. doi: 10.1016/j.ecolecon.2009.11.020

Dai, Y., Zhang, N., Xing, C., Cui, Q., & Sun, Q. (2019) The adsorption, regeneration and engineering applications of biochar for removal organic pollutants: a review. *Chemosphere*, 223, 12–27.

Dalal, R. C., Allen, D. E., Wang, W. J., Reeves, S., & Gibson, I. (2011) Organic carbon and total nitrogen stocks in a Vertisol following 40 years of no-tillage, crop residue retention and nitrogen fertilisation. *Soil and Tillage Research*, 112, 133–139. doi: 10.1016/j.still.2010.12.006

Das, A., Layek, J., Ramkrushna, G. I., Patel, D. P., Choudhury, B. U., Chowdhury, S., & Ngachan, S. V. (2015) Raised and sunken bed land configuration for crop diversification and crop and water productivity enhancement in rice paddies of the north eastern region of India. Paddy and *Water* Environment, 13(4), 571–580.

Das, A., Mohapatra, K. P., & Ngachan, S. (2018) Conservation agriculture for restoration of degraded land and advancing food security. In: A. Das, K. P. Mohapatra, S. Ngachan, A. S. Panwar & D. J. Rajkhowa (eds.) *Conservation Agriculture for Advancing Food Security in Changing Climate* (pp. 1–35). Today and Tomorrow's Printers and Publishers, New Delhi.

Défossez, P., Richard, G., Keller, T., Adamiade, V., Govind, A., & Mary, B. (2014) Modelling the impact of declining soil organic carbon on soil compaction: application to a cultivated Eutric Cambisol with massive straw exportation for energy production in northern France. *Soil and Tillage Research*, 141, 44–54.

Dey, A., Dwivedi, B. S., Bhattacharyya, R., Datta, S. P., Meena, M. C., Das, T. K., & Singh, V. K. (2016) Conservation agriculture in a rice-wheat cropping system on an alluvial soil of north-western Indo-Gangetic plains: effect on soil carbon and nitrogen pools. *Journal of the Indian Society of Soil Science*, 64, 246–254. doi:10.5958/0974-0228.2016.00034.7

Dobermann, A., Nelson, R., Beever, D., Bergvinson, D., Denning G, Jahn M, Masters W, Naylor R, Neath G., Onyido I, Remington T, Wright I. (2013) Solutions for sustainable agriculture and food systems. Technical report for the post-2015 development agenda (pp. 1–99). Sustainable Development Solutions Network, New York. Available online at: www.unsdsn.org.

Eliazer Nelson, A. R. L., Ravichandran, K., & Antony, U. (2019) The impact of the Green Revolution on indigenous crops of India. *Journal of Ethnic Foods*, 6(1), 1–10.

Erenstein, O., Farooq, U., Malik, R. K., & Sharif, M. (2008) On-farm impacts of zero tillage wheat in South Asia's rice-wheat systems. *Field Crops Research*, 105, 240–252. doi: 10.1016/j.fcr.2007.10.010

Erenstein, O., Sayre, K., Wall, P., Hellin, J., & Dixon, J. (2012) Conservation agriculture in maize- and wheat-based systems in the (sub)tropics: lessons from adaptation initiatives in South Asia, Mexico, and Southern Africa. *Journal of Sustainable Agriculture*, 36, 180–206. doi: 10.1080/10440046.2011.620230

FAO (2018) Soils portal. Available online at: https://www.fao.org/soils-portal/en/.

Farooq, M., & Nawaz, A. (2014) Weed dynamics and productivity of wheat in conventional and conservation rice-based cropping systems. *Soil and Tillage Research*, 141, 1–9. doi: 10.1016/j.still.2014.03.012

Feliciano, D., Ledo, A., Hillier, J., & Nayak, D. R. (2018) Which agroforestry options give the greatest soil and above ground carbon benefits in different world regions? *Agriculture, Ecosystems & Environment*, 254, 117–129.

Flores, B. M., Staal, A., Jakovac, C. C., Hirota, M., Holmgren, M., & Oliveira, R. S. (2020) Soil erosion as a resilience drain in disturbed tropical forests. *Plant and Soil*, 450(1), 11–25.

Ghosh, S., & Mistri, B. (2015) Geographic concerns on flood climate and flood hydrology in monsoon-dominated Damodar river basin, Eastern India. *The Geographical Journal*, 2015, 486740. doi: 10.1155/2015/486740

Giller, K. E., Hijbeek, R., Andersson, J. A., & Sumberg, J. (2021) Regenerative agriculture: an agronomic perspective. *Outlook on Agriculture*, 50(1), 13–25.

Glover, J.D., Culman, S.W., DuPont, S.T., Broussard, W., Young, L., Mangan, M.E., …Wyse, D.L. (2010) Harvested perennial grasslands provide ecological benchmarks for agricultural sustainability. *Agriculture, Ecosystems & Environment*, 137, 3–12.

Goldberg, N., Nachshon, U., Argaman, E., & Ben-Hur, M. (2020) Short term effects of livestock manures on soil structure stability, runoff and soil erosion in semi-arid soils under simulated rainfall. *Geosciences*, 10(6), 213.

Gollin, D., Hansen, C. W., & Wingender, A. M. (2021) Two blades of grass: the impact of the Green Revolution. *Journal of Political Economy*, 129(8), 2344–2384.

Gopal, R., Jat, R. K., Malik, R. K., Kumar, V., Alam, M. M., Jat, M. L., … Gupta, R. (2019) Direct dry seeded rice production technology and weed management in rice based systems. Technical Bulletin (p.28). International Maize and Wheat Improvement Center, New Delhi, India.

Gough, I. (2017) *Heat, Greed and Human Need: Climate Change, Capitalism and Sustainable Wellbeing.* Edward Elgar Publishing. https://onlinelibrary.wiley.com/topic/browse/000018

Gupta, D.K., Bhatia, A., Kumar, A., Das, T.K., Jain, N., Tomer, R., …Pathak, H. (2016) Mitigation of greenhouse gas emission from rice-wheat system of the Indo-Gangetic plains: through tillage, irrigation and fertilizer management. *Agriculture, Ecosystems & Environment*, 230, 1–9.

Harwood, R. R. (1983) International overview of regenerative agriculture. In: *Proceedings of Workshop on Resource-efficient Farming Methods for Tanzania*, Morogoro, Tanzania, 16–20 May 1983, Faculty of Agriculture, Forestry, and Veterinary Science, University of Dares Salaam. Rodale Press, Morogoro, Tanzania.

Hobbs, P. R., Singh, Y., Giri, G. S., Lauren, J. G., & Duxbury, J. M. (2002) Direct seeding and reduced tillage options in the rice-wheat systems of the Indo-Gangetic Plains of South Asia. In: S. Pandey, M. Mortimer, L. Wade, T. P. Tuong, K. Lopez & B. Hardy (eds.) *Direct Seeding: Research Issues and Opportunities* (pp. 201–215). IRRI, Los Baños.

Iqbal, M. F., & Khan, I. A. (2014) Spatiotemporal land use land cover change analysis and erosion risk mapping of Azad Jammu and Kashmir, Pakistan. *The Egyptian Journal of Remote Sensing & Space Sciences*, 17, 209–229.

Jahan, F. N., & Gurung, T. R. (2017) *Best Practices of Integrated Plant Nutrition System in SAARC Countries* (1st edn, p.172). The South Asian Association for Regional Cooperation Agriculture Centre, Dhaka.

Jat, M. L., Pal, S. S., Shukla, L., Mathur, J. M. S., & Singh, M. (2004) Rice residue management using cellulolytic fungi and its effect on wheat yield and soil health in rice-wheat cropping system. *Indian Journal of Agricultural Sciences*, 74, 117–120.

Jat, M. L., Stirling, C. M., Jat, H. S., Tetarwal, J. P., Jat, R. K., Singh, R., … Shirsath, P. B. (2018) Soil processes and wheat cropping under emerging climate change scenarios in South Asia. *Advances in Agronomy*, 148, 111–171.

Kassam, A., Friedrich, T., & Derpsch, R. (2019) Global spread of conservation agriculture. *International Journal of Environmental Studies*, 76(1), 29–51.

Kataki, P. K., Hobbs, P., & Adhikary, B. (2001) The rice-wheat cropping system of South Asia: trends, constraints and productivity – a prologue. *Journal of Crop Production*, 3(2), 1–26.

Krishna, K. R. (2010) *Agroecosystems of South India: Nutrient Dynamics, Ecology and Productivity*. Universal-Publishers, Chennai, India.

Kumar, B., Gupta, R. K., & Bhandari, A. L. (2008) Soil fertility changes after long-term application of organic manures and crop residues under rice-wheat system. *Journal of the Indian Society of Soil Science*, 56(1), 80–85.

Kumar, V., Jat, H. S., Sharma, P. C., Gathala, M. K., Malik, R. K., Kamboj, B. R., ...McDonald, A. (2018) Can productivity and profitability be enhanced in intensively managed cereal systems while reducing the environmental footprint of production? Assessing sustainable intensification options in the breadbasket of India. Agriculture, *Ecosystems & Environment*, 252, 132–147.

Ladha, J. K., Dawe, D., Pathak, H., Padre, A. T., Yadav, R. L., Singh, B., ...Hobbs, P. R. (2003) How extensive are yield declines in long-term rice-wheat experiments in Asia? *Field Crops Research*, 81, 159–180. doi:10.1016/S0378-4290(02)00219-8

Ladha, J. K., Pathak, H., & Gupta, R. K. (2007) Sustainability of the rice-wheat cropping system: issues, constraints, and remedial options. *Journal of Crop Improvement*, 19, 125–136. doi:10.1300/J411v19n01_06

Lal, R. (2020) Regenerative agriculture for food and climate. *Journal of Soil and Water Conservation*, 75, 123A–124A. doi: 10.2489/jswc.2020.0620A

Lal, R., Delgado, J. A., Groffman, P. M., Millar, N., Dell, C., & Rotz, A. (2011) Management to mitigate and adapt to climate change. *Journal of Soil and Water Conservation*, 66(4), 276–285.

Legoupil, J. C. (2011) The Conservation Agriculture Network for South East Asia (CANSEA) an initiative to develop and disseminate CA in South East Asia. In: 5th World Congress on Conservation Agriculture, Brisbane, Australia, 26–29 September 2011. ACIAR, Canberra.

Liu, S., Zhang, Y., Lin, F., Zhang, L., & Zou, J. (2014) Methane and nitrous oxide emissions from direct-seeded and seedling-transplanted rice paddies in southeast China. *Plant and Soil*, 374, 285–297

Loboguerrero, A. M., Campbell, B. M., Cooper, P. J., Hansen, J. W., Rosenstock, T., & Wollenberg, E. (2019) Food and earth systems: priorities for climate change adaptation and mitigation for agriculture and food systems. *Sustainability*, 11(5), 1372.

Lorenz, K., & Lal, R. (2023) Combining conventional and organic practices to reduce climate impacts of agriculture. In Klaus Lorenz, Rattan Lal (eds.). *Organic Agriculture and Climate Change* (pp. 201–218). Springer, Cham.

Lupwayi, N., Hanson, K., Harker, K., Clayton, G., Blackshaw, R., O'Donovan, J., ...Monreal, M. (2007) Soil microbial biomass, functional diversity and enzyme activity in glyphosate-resistant wheat-canola rotations under low-disturbance direct seeding and conventional tillage. *Soil Biology & Biochemistry*, 39, 1418–1427. doi: 10.1016/j.soilbio.2006.12.038

McDonald, A. J., Riha, S. J., Duxbury, J. M., Steenhuis, T. S., & Lauren, J. G. (2006) Soil physical responses to novel rice cultural practices in the rice-wheat system: comparative evidence from a swelling soil in Nepal. *Soil and Tillage Research*, 86, 163–175. doi: 10.1016/j.still.2005.02.005

McGuire, A. (2018) Regenerative agriculture: solid principles, extraordinary claims. Available online at: https://csanr.wsu.edu/regen-ag-solid-principles-extraordinary-claims/ (accessed February 1, 2021).

Merfield, C. N. (2019) Integrated weed management in organic farming. In: *Organic Farming* (pp. 117–180). Woodhead publishing. https://doi.org/10.1016/C2016-0-04227-4

Micó, C., Recatalá, L., Peris, M., & Sánchez, J. (2006) Assessing heavy metal sources in agricultural soils of an European Mediterranean area by multivariate analysis. *Chemosphere*, 65, 863–872. doi: 10.1016/j.chemosphere.2006.03.016.

Mwiti, F. M., Gitau, A. N., & Mbuge, D. O. (2022) Edaphic response and behavior of agricultural soils to mechanical perturbation in tillage. *AgriEngineering*, 4(2), 335–355.

Naik, S. K., Mali, S. S., Jha, B. K., Kumar, R., Mondal, S., Mishra, J. S., ...Chaudhari, S. K. (2023) Intensification of rice-fallow agroecosystem of South Asia with oilseeds and pulses: impacts on system productivity, soil carbon dynamics and energetics. Sustainability, 15(2), 1054.

Nair, K. P. (2019) Soil fertility and nutrient management. In: *Intelligent Soil Management for Sustainable Agriculture* (pp. 165–189). Springer, Cham.

Nawaz, A., Farooq, M., Ahmad, R., Basra, S. M. A., & Lal, R. (2016) Seed priming improves stand establishment and productivity of no till wheat grown after direct seeded aerobic and transplanted flooded rice. *European Journal of Agronomy*, 76, 130–137. doi:10.1016/j.cja.2016.02.012

Nawaz, A., Farooq, M., Lal, R., & Rehman, A. (2017) Comparison of conventional and conservation rice-wheat systems in Punjab, Pakistan. *Soil and Tillage Research*, 169, 35–43. doi:10.1016/j.still.2017.01.012

Nawaz, A., Farooq, M., Nadeem, F., Siddique, K. H., & Lal, R. (2019) Rice-wheat cropping systems in South Asia: issues, options and opportunities. *Crop and Pasture Science*, 70(5), 395–427.

Newton, P., Civita, N., Frankel-Goldwater, L., Bartel, K., & Johns, C. (2020) What is regenerative agriculture? A review of scholar and practitioner definitions based on processes and outcomes. *Frontiers in Sustainable Food Systems*, 194.

Pal, S. C., & Chakrabortty, R. (2022) Introduction to soil erosion study. In: *Climate Change Impact on Soil Erosion in Sub-Tropical Environment* (pp. 1–14). Springer, Cham.

Panagos, P., & Katsoyiannis, A. (2019) Soil erosion modelling: the new challenges as the result of policy developments in Europe. *Environmental Research*, 172, 470–474. doi: 10.1016/j.envres.2019.02.043

Pathak, H., Bhatia, A., & Jain, N. (2014) *Greenhouse Gas Emission from Indian Agriculture: Trends, Mitigation and Policy Needs*. Indian Agricultural Research Institute, New Delhi.

Pimentel, D., Hepperly, P., Hanson, J., Siedel, R., & Douds, D. (2005) Organic and conventional farming systems: Environmental and economic issues. Environmental Biology. Forthcoming.

Pingali, P. (2023) Are the lessons from the Green Revolution relevant for agricultural growth and food security in the twenty-first century? In Jonna P. Estudillo, Yoko Kijima, Tetsushi Sonobe (eds.). *Agricultural Development in Asia and Africa* (pp. 21–32). Springer, Singapore.

Qadri, H., & Bhat, R. A. (2020) The concerns for global sustainability of freshwater ecosystems. In Humaira Qadri, Rouf Ahmad Bhat, Mohammad Aneesul Mehmood, Gowhar Hamid Dar (eds.). *Fresh Water Pollution Dynamics and Remediation* (pp. 1–13). Springer, Singapore.

Ray, S., Bhattacharyya, T., Reddy, K., Pal, D., Chandran, P., Tiwary, P., ... Gautam, N. (2014) Soil and land quality indicators of the Indo-Gangetic Plains of India. *Current Science*, 107, 1470–1486.

Ray, S. S., & Gupta, R. P. (2001) Effect of green manuring and tillage practices on physical properties of puddled loam soil under rice-wheat cropping system. *Journal of the Indian Society of Soil Science*, 49, 670–678.

Rehman, Hu., Nawaz, A., Wakeel, A., Saharawat, Y. S., & Farooq, M. (2015) Conservation agriculture in South Asia. In: M. Farooq & K. H. M. Siddique (eds.) *Conservation Agriculture*. Springer Publishing House, Cham.

Rodale, R. (1983) Breaking new ground: the search for a sustainable agriculture. *The Futurist*, 1, 15–20.

Saharawat, Y. S., Singh, B., Malik, R. K., Ladha, J. K., Gathala, M., & Jat, M. L. (2010) Evaluation of alternative tillage and crop establishment methods in a rice-wheat rotation in north-western IGP. *Field Crops Research*, 116, 260–267. doi: 10.1016/j.fcr.2010.01.003

Sapkota, T. B., Jat, M. L., Aryal, J. P., Jat, R. K., & Khatri-Chhetri, A. (2015) Climate change adaptation, greenhouse gas mitigation and economic profitability of conservation agriculture: some examples from cereal systems of Indo-Gangetic Plains. *Journal of Integrative Agriculture*, 14, 1524–1533. doi:10.1016/S2095-3119(15)61093-0

Savory Institute (2019) Ecological Outcome Verified (EOV) Version 2.0.

Schreefel, L., Schulte, R. P. O., De Boer, I. J. M., Schrijver, A. P., & Van Zanten, H. H. E. (2020) Regenerative agriculture– the soil is the base. *Global Food Security*, 26, 100404.

Sharma, K., Grace, J., Mandal, U., Gajbhiye, P., Srinivas, K., Korwar, G., ...Yadav, S. (2008) Evaluation of long-term soil management practices using key indicators and soil quality indices in a semi-arid tropical Alfisol. *Australian Journal of Soil Research*, 46, 368–377.

Sharma, P., Singh, G., & Singh, R. P. (2011) Conservation tillage, optimal water and organic nutrient supply enhance soil microbial activities during wheat (*Triticum aestivum* L.) cultivation. *Brazilian Journal of Microbiology*, 42, 531–542. doi: 10.1590/S1517-83822011000200018

Shrestha, B. M., Sitaula, B. K., Singh, B. R., & Bajracharya, R. M. (2004) Soil organic carbon stocks in soil aggregates under different land use systems in Nepal. Nutrient Cycling in Agroecosystems, 70(2), 201–213.

Singh, Y., & Ladha, J. K. (2004) Principles and practices of tillage system in rice-wheat cropping system in Indo-Gangetic plains of India. In: R. Lal, P. R. Hobbs, N. Uphoff & D. O. Hansen (eds.) *Sustainable Agriculture and the International Rice-Wheat System* (pp. 167–207). Marcel Dekker, New York.

Soane, B.D., Ball, B. C., Arvidsson, J., Basch, G., Moreno, F., & RogerEstrade, J. (2012) No-till in northern, western and south-western Europe: a review of problems and opportunities for crop production and the environment. *Soil and Tillage Research*, 118, 66–87.

Somasundaram, J., Sinha, N. K., Dalal, R. C., Lal, R., Mohanty, M., Naorem, A. K., ... Chaudhari, S. K. (2020) No-till farming and conservation agriculture in South Asia– issues, challenges, prospects and benefits. *Critical Reviews in Plant Sciences*, 39(3), 236–279.

Soto, R. L., de Vente, J., & Padilla, M. C. (2021) Learning from farmers' experiences with participatory monitoring and evaluation of regenerative agriculture based on visual soil assessment. *Journal of Rural Studies*, 88, 192–204.

Srinivasarao, C., Rakesh, S., Kumar, G. R., Manasa, R., Somashekar, G., Lakshmi, C. S., & Kundu, S. (2021) Soil degradation challenges for sustainable agriculture in tropical India. *Current Science*, 120(3), 492.

Stavi, I., Bel, G., & Zaady, E. (2016) Soil functions and ecosystem services in conventional, conservation, and integrated agricultural systems. A review. *Agronomy for Sustainable Development*, 36, 32.

Tal, A. (2018) Making conventional agriculture environmentally friendly: moving beyond the glorification of organic agriculture and the demonization of conventional agriculture. *Sustainability*, 10(4), 1078.

Tayleur, C., Balmford, A., Buchanan, G. M., Butchart, S. H. M., Ducharme, H., Green, R. E., … Phalan, B. (2017) Global coverage of agricultural sustainability standards, and their role in conserving biodiversity. *Conservation Letters*, 10, 610–618. doi: 10.1111/conl.12314

Thapa, G. (2005) Rural poverty reduction strategy for South Asia. In Raghbendra Jha (ed.). *Economic Growth, Economic Performance and Welfare in South Asia* (pp. 384–401). Palgrave Macmillan, London.

Turmel, M. S., Speratti, A., Baudron, F., Verhulst, N., & Govaerts, B. (2015) Crop residue management and soil health: a systems analysis. *Agricultural Systems*, 134, 6–16.

United Nations Children's Fund (UNICEF), World Health Organization, & The World Bank Group Joint Child Malnutrition Estimates (2020) Levels and trends in child malnutrition: key findings of the 2020 edition. World Health Organization, Geneva.

Walmsley, A., & Sklenička, P. (2017) Various effects of land tenure on soil biochemical parameters under organic and conventional farming – implications for soil quality restoration. *Ecological Engineering*, 107, 137–143. doi:10.1016/j.ecoleng.2017.07.006

White, R. E., & Andrew, M. (2019) Orthodox soil science versus alternative philosophies: a clash of cultures in a modern context. *Sustainability*, 11, 2919. doi: 10.3390/su11102919

World Meters (2020) https://www.worldometers.info/world-population/southern-asia-population/#:~:text=Countries%20in%20Southern%20Asia&text=Southern%20Asia%20population%20is%20equivalent, among%20subregions%20ranked%20by%20Population.

Wu, W., & Ma, B. (2015) Integrated nutrient management (INM) for sustaining crop productivity and reducing environmental impact: a review. *Science of the Total Environment*, 512, 415–427.

Wunder, S. (2005) Payment for environmental services: some nuts and bolts. Center for International Forestry Research, Bogor, Indonesia.

Yifan, L., Tiaoyan, W., Shaodong, W., Xucan, K., Zhaoman, Z., Hongyan, L., & Jiaolong, L. (2023) Developing integrated rice-animal farming based on climate and farmers choices. *Agricultural Systems*, 204, 103554.

Zhang, Q., Liu, D., Cheng, S., & Huang, X. (2016) Combined effects of runoff and soil erodibility on available nitrogen losses from sloping farmland affected by agricultural practices. *Agricultural Water Management*, 176, 1–8.

14 Conservation Agriculture in North Africa
From Concept to Sustainability

R. Mrabet, R. Aboutayeb, R. Moussadek, and M. Benicha

14.1 INTRODUCTION: WHAT NEEDS TO CHANGE?

North African region includes six countries namely Morocco, Algeria, Tunisia, Libya, Egypt, and Sudan. Its land area reaches about 7.9 million km^2 constituting around 6% and 3% of the world's total land area and the world's population, respectively (Mrabet et al., 2022). The region is at a strategic crossroad: reform and prosper or keep in risks of vulnerability, marginalization and of falling back into poverty. The region is facing different challenges related mainly to high population growth rates and youth unemployment, increasing food needs, variable income levels, and fragile and threatened natural resources. Though cereals originated in the Mediterranean basin and produced since Neolithic times, ironically countries of North Africa are unable to produce them in sufficient quantities for their burgeoning populations.

According to MedECC (2020), the region is at the confluence of numerous bio-geographical landscapes and is home to a large diversity of ecosystems. The highly diverse agro-ecological systems are a complex mixture of pastoral, irrigated and rainfed systems. Of the 36.8 million hectares of total agricultural land, 77% is rainfed. However, the agricultural expansion opportunities are either not possible or very limited. The expansion of irrigation is also limited with the exception of the Nile Valley of Egypt and Sudan (Mrabet et al., 2022). In Egypt and Algeria, agriculture occupies 3.4% of the total national land area, while Libya's land does not exceed 1.2% (Zdruli, 2012).

Surprising agricultural lands are still degrading even though United Nations treaties and programs have been signed and approved by all North African countries. Under the existing situation, the productive landscape does not measurably contribute to the achievement of global environmental benefits. The region is the hot spot for climate change (Ibrahim and Lal, 2013; Tuel and Eltahir, 2020) and is pushed to exceed planetary boundaries (Campbell et al., 2017). Water scarcity and drought are the common denominators for problems affecting farmers in North African countries (Bazza et al., 2018; World Bank, 2017). In addition, weather-related degradation and drought events are growing in intensity and frequency and are weakening economic growth (Jedd et al., 2020; World Bank, 2017). According to these authors, the North African region faces difficult socioeconomic and political consequences during dry seasons and risk to experience harsher conditions based on future climate change projections. For instance, in Morocco, long dry seasons lead to soil degradation and erosion affecting nearly half of the lands receiving less than 400 mm (Sustainable Food Trust, 2015). This caused both Morocco and Tunisia to increase their food import mainly cereals to meet their growing population demands (FAO, 2018).

Land degradation disturbs the ecosystem functions mainly water retention, nutrient cycling, food and feed provision and habitat (FAO and ITPS, 2015). Among the main processes leading to soil deterioration, soil erosion and mining are considered the most important. Soil erosion affects significantly topsoil fertility. This latter plays a key role in agricultural productivity and thus contributes directly to enhance food security (Montanarella, 2015; Raclot et al., 2018). Land use change and reduced vegetation and forest cover have further promoted gully erosion and runoff generation

DOI: 10.1201/9781003309581-17

(Winkler et al., 2021). Besides, wind erosion has been considered as a challenging problem, in large parts of North African countries, exacerbated due to limited vegetation cover and restricted rainfall, mainly in arid and semiarid and oasis zones. The following countries are the most affected by wind erosion, arranged in order of surface area affected: Sudan, Libya, Algeria, Tunisia, and Egypt (FAO and ITPS, 2015). Currently, the forested area in these countries remains relatively low; it covers only 6.9%, 8.4% and 12% of the total area of Tunisia, Algeria and Morocco respectively (Sabir et al., 2022).

According to Abahussain et al. (2002) and later by FAO and ITPS (2015), North Africa has been considered as highly affected by water erosion. From a study by Montanarella (2007), the economic costs of both land degradation and desertification are about up to €1.2 and €1.5 billion per year or 3.7% and 3.6% GDP in Morocco and Algeria respectively while it ranges between €2.7 and €5.1 billion per year or 3.2%–6.4% GDP in Egypt. In some countries, several policies and programs were launched and devoted to limit negative impacts and the extent of natural resource degradation (Sabir et al., 2022). However, soil erosion and sedimentation are still at high rates and putting farmers in marginality due to aggressive climate extremes and human pressure.

Nitrogen (N) and phosphorous (P) are critical to crop growth and development as well seed/fruit quality and, after water, are often the most limiting factors due to low fertility of North African soils (Zdruli, 2014). All North African countries are the net larger importer of fertilizers (Sanz-Cobena et al., 2017; Lassaletta et al., 2014) and dependence will increase with time (FAO, 2017) in order to meet crop nutritional requirements.

As it is well known, in North Africa, tillage operations were imported from Europe to serve to enhance plant nutrition through soil organic matter mineralization and control weeds. Contour ploughing and strip cropping techniques are used for erosion control on all lands exceeding 5% in slopes. However, due to the increased fragility of soils, conventional systems based on tilling and seed preparation became a regional concern.

Worldwide and in North Africa, tillage-based agriculture has been demonstrated to be responsible for soil organic matter (SOM) depletion and soil erosion (Lal, 2015; Kassam and Kassam, 2020b; Mrabet et al., 2021; Rouabhi et al., 2018; Eekhout and de Vente, 2022). According to Reicosky (2011), tillage practices have depleted from 30% to 50% of SOM within the last two decades of the 20th century.

In North Africa, tillage erosion during soil ploughing varied from 1 to 60 tons/ha/year (Sabir et al., 2022). Considered as a non-renewable resource, any soil loss of more than 1 ton/ha/year could be considered as irreversible. According to MedECC (2020), Morocco and northern Algeria are hotspots of active erosion with rates predicted to increase further. This fact was exacerbated by the degradation of soil physico-chemical properties and led to nutrient loss over time. Amongst the main causes of soil degradation and reduced productivity, we count soil erosion, and dust storms induced by soil tillage, overgrazing and low land cover (Mrabet et al., 2021). Such phenomena are widespread and more expressed in water-stressed production basins where soils are weak and unstable, the temperature is relatively high and precipitations are low and irregular (Lagacherie et al., 2017; Devkota et al., 2021). This fact is worsened by livestock activities leading to grazing almost all plant residues and stubble left on the field post-harvesting crops (El-Shater and Yiegezu, 2021).

In the Mediterranean basin, studies showed that sustainable land management (SLM) could potentially enhance crop productivity by 30%–170%, contribute to mitigating climate change through sequestrating up to 3% of organic carbon in soils, and improve water use efficiency, especially during dry seasons, by up to 100% (WOCAT, 2007).

Societal and land challenges are increasing in magnitude and scales (Kassam and Kassam, 2020b). The adoption of a sustainable development as a regional strategic direction implies that North African governments should spur agricultural strategies that protect the environment, use natural resources efficiently and safeguard the interests of future generations (i.e., Morocco's Green Generation 2020–2030). The vision of conventional farming based on separating increasing crop yields, livestock performances, and food quantity from food chain externalities (soil erosion, water, and air) should be revisited. This entails a need for a paradigm shift to address apprehensions related to food security, health and diet quality, and resource use efficiency.

In this new redesign, conservation agriculture (CA) was launched in the early 1980s as an SLM-based on three pillars, namely, minimal soil disturbance, and mulching associated with crop rotations (Mrabet et al., 2012; Aboutayeb et al., 2020; Giller et al., 2015). In this context, enhancing food security while preserving soil resources had been set as a cornerstone of the CA approach as defined by the Food Agriculture Organization (FAO, 2010; Kassam et al., 2022). Several projects and initiatives were implemented to mainstream CA since the 1980s by governments with the support from farmers and international organizations and the results and impacts are discussed herein. Recently, an upsurge of studies has focused on conservation agriculture in order to analyse, explain and quantify the various benefits and impacts in terms of food security, climate change mitigation and environmental quality, as well as its ability to provide multiple functions and/or services. These efforts have generated a set of influential reports and frameworks that have brought new perspectives and shaped shifts in development agenda and international programmes. These items are also addressed in this chapter. However, explicit collaboration to ensure the transitions to sustainability through CA systems requires a challenge-driven, crosscutting, multi-actor and multilevel policy and strong engagements from all stakeholders, especially policymakers and financial actors. Hence, the current work aims to complement existing literature reviews and put the current state of knowledge into the context of sustainability.

14.2 CONSERVATION AGRICULTURE: CONCEPT AND APPROACH

Conventional tillage (CT) practices involve soil disruption and mixing to promote seed germination and crop establishment. The purpose is to control weeds, incorporate crop residues and stubble into deeper soil layers and homogenize the seedbed for even crop growth. Conservation agriculture includes three interlinked components or pillars: (i) Continuous no or minimum anthropogenic soil perturbation, (ii) crop rotation/diversification of cropping systems and (iii) permanent maintenance of crop cover and/or residue mulch. No-tillage systems were first adopted in the 1960s in the USA and in the 1970s in Brazil.

The term "Conservation Agriculture" was first used in 1997 and adopted by FAO (Kassam et al., 2020). Reicosky (2015) expressed concerns with the use of the term "conservation tillage" as there is no "soil conservation" with any type of tillage, which has led to the modern-day CA systems (Table 14.1).

According to the FAO, CA is defined as an ecosystem approach to regenerative sustainable agriculture based on the practical application of the three principles depending on the specificities of

TABLE 14.1
CA Principles Explained

CA Principle	Explanation
Continuous no or minimum anthropogenic soil perturbation	Zero tillage is ideal, or a minimum disturbance of no more than 20%–25% of the soil surface or it must be less than 15 cm wide.
	Direct placement of seeds into untilled soil either manually, animal drawn or using mechanical seeders. Avoiding soil disturbance during cultural and harvest operations and farm traffic. Terms generally used are No-Tillage, Direct Seeding, Planting Green, No-till Weeding
Permanent maintenance of crop cover and/or residue mulch	Retaining rootstocks and stubbles and crop biomass from cropping systems on/in the soil. No removal, overgrazing or burning of crop residues.
Crop rotation/diversification of cropping systems	Adopting local adapted cropping systems involving annual, pasture, shrubs, forage and perennial crops, legumes and non-legume crops.

locations, social conditions and societal contexts (Kassam et al., 2020). In other words, the three core principles of CA are universal, but the solutions are local.

Conservation agriculture's origins, developments, and trends have been extensively discussed and debated in several reviews (i.e. Kassam and Kassam, 2020a, b). CA is a way of managing agro-ecosystems that combine productivity improvements with higher intensity of knowledge, resilience and sustainability.

According to several authors, it becomes evident that when CA is not applied properly, crop yields are compromised and extra costs are generated than expected (Rosenstock et al., 2014; Brown et al., 2017; Su et al., 2021a, b; Yigezu et al., 2021). In other terms, while each principle can be used separately, the fluid integration of all three principles is key for successfully delivering the full benefits of CA systems. CA is considered to be accurately practised only when its three pillars are applied altogether (Reicosky, 2015).

When complemented, in a timely and efficient manner, with additional best practices related to integrated management of soil, crop, water, pest, and energy, CA systems are considered as the basis for sustainable and regenerative agriculture (Kassam et al., 2019). In other terms, shifting to CA systems means optimization of the need and utilization of production inputs of seeds, agrochemicals, water, energy, time and labour. CA systems open and favor options for the integration of livestock, pastures and trees in order to expand adoption, reduce risks and respond to local contexts and priorities (Mutua et al., 2014; Martin et al., 2016; Guesmi et al., 2019; Lal, 2020a) seeking to strengthen the interactions among system components (crops, grasslands, trees and animals). Livestock constitutes one of the most important challenges facing CA spread in the region besides soil organic matter depletion, water scarcity, climate changes, social assets and resource limitations (Mrabet, 2017; Fouzai et al., 2018). Hence, still designing agroecological pathways and policy incentives for these integrations is needed (Fouzia et al., 2018).

14.3 CONSERVATION AGRICULTURE ADOPTION IN NORTH AFRICA: DISMANTLING BARRIERS AND PAVING THE WAY TO DRIVERS

In North Africa, land challenges required a strategic reappraisal of how agri-food systems are designed and managed (Benlhabib et al., 2014). Henceforward, a major research on CA has been mainly conducted in early 1980s in Morocco, followed by Algeria and Tunisia while Egypt embarked CA research fairly recently (Mrabet et al., 2022; Sharkawy et al., 2022). CA systems are still poorly documented in Sudan, Libya and Egypt compared to Algeria, Tunisia and Morocco. In fact, yet, agricultural science and innovation continue to deal with tillage agriculture. There is not yet a great intention to change the input-intensive Green Revolution mindset.

Over the last decades, there have been ambitious national and international projects and initiatives to develop and share knowledge and technologies related to CA systems (AAAID, 2018; FERT, 2018; Degrande and Benoudji, 2017; El-Areed, 2019; El Gharras et al., 2017). The knowledge, tools and experience with the adoption and spread of conservation agriculture have expanded noticeably since 2000, especially with support from FAO, AFD, World Bank, GIZ and ICARDA and many other international organizations. Mrabet et al. (2022) presented a detailed list of such projects and initiatives and recommended further development and intensification of networking and collaboration to spread CA among farmers. The number of publications on various subjects and aspects of CA is growing, and the number of local successes of CA is also increasing. The expanding knowledge and successful field experiences provide the required basis for the massive scaling of CA systems in the region (Bahri et al., 2019).

Conservation agriculture has been adopted worldwide on about 205.4 million hectares for various reasons and challenges (Kassam et al., 2022). An exponential adoption of CA systems has been recorded since the 1990s reaching about 14.7% of global croplands. CA systems are adopted in a wide range of farming systems and in all continents. Overall, this gaining momentum has continued since 2008/2009 at a rate of about 10 million hectares per year. The number of countries has increased significantly to reach 102 compared to only 36 countries in 2008/2009 adopting CA.

In many countries, the prevalent implementation of CA systems was activated by community-led and farmer's initiatives intensely sustained by research and development organizations rather than as a result of usual technology transfer system struggles. In this path, countries with Mediterranean type of climate, (e.g. Australia, Argentina, USA, Spain, and South Africa) are increasingly adopting CA systems on diverse farm types, soils and cropping systems (Kassam et al., 2022).

Unfortunately, the adoption of CA remains very low and fragmented in North Africa. So far, most of the CA areas have been recorded in rainfed annual cropping systems and research is starting for perennial crops in Morocco and for irrigated crops in Morocco and Egypt (Shaalan et al., 2022).

For instance, within three decades of CA introduction in Algeria, the adoption of CA remains very limited. The CA cropland has reached only 5,600 ha by 2016 despite all the efforts made during this period; this fact could be explained by the lack of information among farmers and probably low educational level of practitioners (Djouadi et al., 2021). In Tunisia, CA adoption was relatively better and CA areas switched from 52 to 14,000 ha in 1999 and 2015, respectively, and is stagnating at this adoption level (Bahri et al., 2019). The most concerning issue are the competitive uses for agricultural residues and stubbles as well as the problematic of weed control. There is a need to address the competitive uses for agricultural residues and stubbles as well as the challenges associated with weed control. There are still a high rivalry between CA systems and livestock feeding. This poses a significant hindrance to the elevation of CA areas in rainfed environments.

In terms of weed abundance, CA pillars seem to have different effects, on the one hand, tillage reduction tends to offer favorable conditions for weed infestation; on the other hand, crop diversification and mulch cover seem to deal with it effectively to decrease it. Weed research has been carried out to understand weed infestation and shifts in CA systems (Hajjaj and Mrabet, 2022; Labad et al., 2018a, 2019).

In Morocco, CA systems are increasing in acceptance due to new programs such Al Moutmir initiative by OCP Group. The recently launched CA Road Map to reach 1 million hectares by 2030 is providing policy support at the provincial and national levels to farmers to accelerate the adoption and development of CA. This initiative, impulsed by the Green Generation Plan, is mobilizing institutional support in terms of extension, research, education, and private sector service provisioning. The unique North African initiative of mainstreaming CA is aiming at realigning all relevant institutions and stakeholders towards the provisioning of a full range of the required support to CA farmers and their associations. However, additional and durable financial and non-financial incentives and motivations should be intensified and guaranteed to farmers and their acquaintances for voluntary adoption of CA.

According to Mrabet et al. (2022), the total CA in the region is approximate 54,600 ha. In the region, CA has been considered as a potential alternative to conventional system, to ensure yield stability and to protect natural resources mainly soil and water from degradation and evapotranspiration in bioclimatic areas where limited rainfall is prevalent and erratic as well (Zaghouane et al., 2006; Ben-Salem et al., 2006). In this region, cereal crops and derived products play a key role in food security of the national economy and diversification through crop rotations and sequences were found to address these issues under CA systems. CA based on NT systems is practised in major crops (i.e. cereals, pulses, forage and oil seed crops). In Egypt recent study by El-Areed (2019) concluded that CA system under sandy soil conditions can improve yellow corn yields under both normal and water deficit stress compared to conventional system. This finding assumes the feasibility of CA in irrigated systems.

In fact, a number of studies have discussed the impacts and future of CA in the region while discoursing drivers, trends and opportunities (Boulal et al., 2014; El Gharras et al., 2017; Devkota et al., 2021; Mrabet et al., 2021, 2022). Fortunately, scientific research and investment in CA are growing steadily. Soil health or quality is optimized under CA systems because minimal mechanical disturbance allows soil to maintain its structure, moisture and mineral composition. It should be noted that in the North African experience in CA, residue retention is often neglected due to livestock competition while this component is very important for the success of CA (Bahri et al., 2018;

Moujahed et al., 2015; Souissi et al., 2018; Cheikh M'hamed et al., 2014; Mrabet et al., 2012; Hajer et al., 2020). Farmers generally seed bare no-till fields which may negatively impact crop productivity and soil functions. Unregulated movement of herds and uncontrolled grazing are limiting the appropriate implementation of CA principles. North African farmers need to develop a different mindset towards crop and soil management under CA systems and adapt CA principles to local conditions without compromising any of them (Souissi et al., 2018; Yigezu et al., 2021).

Long-term strategies and historical dynamics adopted by farmers are generally not sufficiently analysed and documented before shifting to CA systems. Hence, CA adoption process is facing constant socioeconomic and technical constraints as shown by Rouabhi et al. (2016, 2018, 2019) in Algeria and by Bahri et al. (2018) and FERT (2016, 2018) in Tunisia. CA adoption has reached a plateau in Tunisia but deep and upscaling is needed to increase CA acreage (Cheikh M'hamed et al., 2016).

The high price of imported direct seeders and low level of the subsidy ceiling for all types of no-till seeders do not encourage private providers to invest in this type of equipment and hence reduce their availability and access to farmers. However, research institutions in the Maghreb countries invested in developing local seeders for CA systems (El Gharras and Idrissi, 2006; Cheikh M'hamed et al., 2018).

According to Idoudi et al. (2020), CA systems are likely to increase in Algeria through the development of low-cost no-till called "Boudour" ZT seeder, incentives from the Government through subsidy to farmers and their associations, and support and guidance from Technical and Research Institutions and ICARDA. It is also extremely important to encourage local entrepreneurship, retailers and after-sales services to advertise and commercialize CA tools and equipment.

Successful decisions in CA adoption under context uncertainty require consideration of multiple plausible futures and being prepared for diverse scenarios. Countries should also learn more on international initiatives and policies. According to Bahri et al. (2019), the suitable land area for CA systems is estimated to be 260,000 hectares which represents one-third of the total area under cereal production in Tunisia. For the case of Central Morocco, the study carried out by Moussadek et al. (2016) has highlighted that 63% of cereal-producing bassins are suitable for CA systems (or 3.8 million ha). However, Bonzanigo et al. (2016) estimated that 40% of farmers in the Central Morocco region could adopt CA systems.

Multidimensional assessment considering stakeholders' concerns should be performed to adapt the integration of CA systems to every specific context. Most CA studies recognized the need to change the attitudes and mindsets of farmers and that it is vital for decision-makers, technicians, extensionists, and researchers to shift their thinking away from soil-degrading tillage practices towards CA systems. Hence, mainstreaming CA requires improved scientific capacity and systemic approach to be able to bring in close collaboration between farmers and other stakeholders (agricultural leaders, extension agents).

Transition to CA is a knowledge-intensive process and hence imposes to narrow the science-policy gap and strengthen public-private partnership. In the same sense, the financial side should be considered, through budget allocations, while establishing national strategies aiming to protect natural resources and ensure sustainable development. Sustainable land management through the adoption of CA systems does require a holistic long-term approach. Such implementation requires both sizeable commitments of resources and a methodical approach based on a continuous assessment plan able to overcome faced challenges.

14.4   CROP PRODUCTIVITY AND FOOD SECURITY

Agriculture and livestock are key sectors in the North African economy and to its future. The growing population has become a real concern inducing issues of food security and malnutrition. The region witnessed an increase in the prevalence of undernourishment during the last few decades (FAO et al., 2019).

It implies a need to generate a greater resource for increasing food production to meet people's daily needs and ensure food security (Giller et al., 2015; Smith et al., 2021; Mrabet and Moussadek, 2022). This fact is exacerbated due to different economic and environmental facts including low productivity, price volatility, and food availability (Mrabet et al., 2022).

In North Africa, fragile and low-fertility soils and lack of rainfall limit the opportunity for investing in crop production and diversification. Despite being food producers, many of the farmers and herders are themselves food insecure. The region has slipped to become a net food importer, spending yearly on food importation (Ziadat et al., 2022). Taking actions against soil-erosion-induced nutrient depletion, combating climate change, eliminating the inefficiencies along the entire agro-value chain, and unlocking socioeconomic opportunities are fundamental for reversing trends while ensuring food security and economic growth in North Africa (MedECC, 2020; Benlhabib et al., 2014).

When shifting to CA systems, the soil-crop continuum undergoes immediate and long-term significant changes. However, in general, it takes time to transform from a tillage system to CA, and it is often not possible to show yield advantages based on short-term experiments. In other terms, crop performances under CA systems are dependent on (i) initial soil quality conditions, (ii) the experience of farmers, and (iii) the dynamics of changes in soil health (i.e., SOM) improvements that can continue for a long time before a new equilibrium status is established (Kassam and Kassam, 2020c). In fact, several studies have found that a fully implemented CA system enhances crop productivity and improves resilience to climate change (Table 14.2).

CA was found by several authors effective in mitigating crop yield loss in dry north African environments prone to variable weather patterns and hence narrowing yield gaps vis-à-vis drought severity (Cheikh M'hamed et al., 2014; Mrabet, 2011a; Djouadi et al., 2021; El Mekkaoui et al., 2021; Shaalan et al., 2022). CA system has been proven to have the potential for closing the yield gap, especially in wheat, in the Mediterranean rainfed production system (Devkota and Yigezu, 2020). In a very recent publication, Devkova et al. (2022) concluded that CA can close cereals (wheat, barley) and legumes (lentil, and chickpea) yield gaps in a semiarid region of Morocco. The authors found that over the five contrasting rainfall years, in comparison to CT, CA had greater grain yield stability and increased yield by 43%, 8%, 11%, and 19% for wheat, barley, lentil, and chickpea, respectively.

Under semi-arid conditions of Northern Algeria, Djouadi et al. (2021) found that tillage systems had a significant effect on the average wheat yield of 2 years, with CA being 28% and 35% higher

TABLE 14.2
Wheat Grain Yields (Mg/ha) under Conservation Agriculture (CA) and Conventional Tillage (CT) Systems from Experiments with a Duration Exceeding 5 Years in North Africa

Country	Soil Type/Site Name	Duration (years)	CA	CT	Percent Change (%)	References
Morocco	Vertisol	19	3.1	2.4	29	Mrabet et al. (2012)
		10	3.7	2.6	42	
		10	1.9	1.4	35	
	Mollisol	9	2.21	1.9	16	
	Rendzine	9	2.53	1.47	72	
	Vertisol	5	2.31	1.62	42	Devkota et al. (2022)
Algeria	Clay loam	5	2.78	2.78	0	Abdellaoui et al. (2010)
Tunisia	Mateur	8	4.18	3.52	19	Angar et al. (2011)
	Krib	8	2.41	2.04	18	
	Clay	5	2.8	2.71	3	Mouelhi et al. (2016)
		5	2.73	2.61	5	
		5	3.76	3.43	10	

than CT and minimum tillage systems, respectively. However, grain quality and yield components were mostly affected by climatic conditions. However, the authors stated that a stable and good grain quality, under CA system, is tightly associated with the right nitrogen fertilization.

Other authors reported that for higher crop yields under CA systems, the three pillars are mandatory and that residue cover of at least 60% may be needed (Souissi et al., 2018; Amara et al., 2015; Fellahi et al., 2013). A dataset containing 4,403 paired (CA vs. CT) yield observations collected between 1980 and 2017 for eight major staple crops in 50 countries presented by Su et al. (2021a) also confirmed that crop residue maintenance has the largest positive impact on crop productivity under CA.

In Morocco, the first work on CA system which began in 1982 in the semi-arid areas of Chaouia and Abda showed that grain yields of cereals are higher than those obtained under tilled soils (Mrabet 2000; Mrabet et al., 2012). Other experiments took place in the same area and have consolidated the superiority of wheat production under CA systems (Laghrour et al., 2016). In another site near Rabat (Morocco), wheat grain yields under CA were equal to or greater than those under CT regardless of rainfall conditions during the 7-year study (Figure 14.1). This figure shows that wheat yields in semi-arid areas are affected more by the distribution of rainfall during the growing season than by its total quantity. This is to reflect that the wheat crop can be properly managed under CA in Mediterranean conditions marked by important climatic variability and allow stable production ensuring food security. Hence, CA system has been proved to potentially mitigate yield loss in harsh and risky environmental conditions, which was also concluded by Michler et al. (2019).

Maintaining a soil cover and zero tillage alleviates water and wind erosion severity, which helps enhance resource use efficiency and consequently set higher yield goals (Devkota et al., 2021; Belloum, 2008). Fellahi et al. (2013) concluded that CA systems with bare soil surface are detrimental to wheat growth and development.

CA can reduce drought effects through better water storage and availability during crop growing season, which was found in early 1990 by Bouzza (1990) in wheat-based systems. Another important operational benefit from CA is the flexibility for the implementation of field crop management in terms of planting time and crop input application, despite unfavourable field conditions that do prevent such operations in conventional agriculture such as wet soil at sowing time (Mrabet, 2011a;

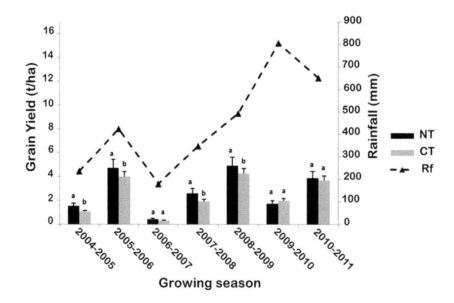

FIGURE 14.1 Tillage effect on wheat grain yield in relation to total rainfall received during the growing season (November–May) in semiarid Morocco (Moussadek, 2012).

Nefzaoui et al., 2012). The extra water stored in soil profile under CA is an important insurance to reduce yield gaps due to extreme, delayed, and variable rainfall events (Benkherbache et al., 2012; Mrabet, 2008).

The yield goal is the key objective of CA systems and should integrate a more efficient use of resources towards economic-environmental sustainability. Though, food security is more than just increasing production. It seems that a good application of CA can produce both sufficient food quantity and good quality (Ziervogel and Ericksen, 2010). Especially, under CA systems dual-purpose legumes play a significant role in nutritional diversity at the farm level (Rusinamhodzi, 2020). However, limited landholdings and access to seeds and other inputs prevent the widespread adoption of cereal-legume rotations (Al Balghiti et al., 2020).

CA principles, mainly crop rotations using legumes, have been shown as a key factor to get access to pulse meals rich in vegetable proteins and micronutrients mainly iron and selenium (Rusinamhodzi, 2020). When crops are rotated in a sequence, water use and soil fertility are optimized, because the different crop species complement each other in their mode of absorbing and conserving soil water and nutrients. Further, crop rotations including legumes contribute to increasing nitrogen availability which generates two major benefits: crop yield improvement and chemical nitrogen fertilizers' use reduction (Harb et al., 2015; Yigezu et al.; 2019; Aboutayeb et al., 2020; Devkova et al., 2022). In fact, inclusion of legumes in the rotation crops induces atmospheric N fixation leading to reduced synthetic N fertilizers and would also optimizethe use of P and K via mycorrhizal fungi and bacteria and improve carbon capture.

Crop diversification is an essential component of CA and it was reported that several crops can be successfully grown without tillage in North Africa. Among such crops, cereals (wheat, barley, sorghum, oat and corn), food legumes (chickpea, lentil, faba bean, and soybean), oilseed crops (sunflower and sesame), and forage crops (vetch) were included (M'hedhbi et al., 2004; Aboudrare et al., 2006; Ben-Hammouda et al., 2007; Abdalla et al., 2007; Mrabet, 2011a, b; Rezgui et al., 2014; Harb et al., 2015; Abou El-Enin and Abo-Remalia, 2015; El-Areed, 2019; Devkova et al., 2022; Sharkawy et al., 2022).

In the Setif province (northeast of Algeria), the study by Bouguendouz (2010) indicated that CA improved barley grain yield by 31% and reduced the costs by 28.3%, compared to the CT technique. Harb et al. (2016) reported equal yields of corn and broad bean between CA and CT while Harb et al. (2015) reported that wheat and soybean yields were higher under CA in Egypt. Wheat yields were improved under CA in irrigated fields of Middle Egypt as reported by El-Areed (2019). Sharkawy et al. (2022) found a 5% increase in rainfed wheat grain yields under CA compared to traditional tillage in Wadi El Raml area (Northwest Coastal Zone of Egypt). Due to reduced early growth and plant density using inappropriate direct seeder, Elsoury et al. (2015) found higher wheat yield under reduced tillage than CT or CA. Therefore, reduced tillage systems were favored by farmers due to increased wheat production compared to CT.

Crop mixtures, like triticale vetch and oats-vetch, and forage crops such as vetch, and triticale were included for improved integration of livestock within cereal-based CA systems and were identified as highly suitable options for the marginal wheat systems (Mrabet et al., 2012; Cheikh M'hamed et al., 2016; Abidi et al., 2021).

According to the French Association for International Cooperation for Agricultural Development in Developing and Emerging Countries (FERT, 2018), yield increases of 8%–20% were observed by CA farmers in the Maghreb compared to conventional practices. Mrabet et al. (2021) reported that crop productivity under CA systems increases over time with a range of 0.2%–146% compared to that under the conventional tillage (CT) systems in Maghreb region. It was also observed that soil conditions under CA systems favor more vigorous and healthier plants that are resilient to a range of biotic or edaphic stresses (Mrabet, 1997). This later author also observed that the CA system improved seedling establishment and growth of corn and wheat. Corn yields under CA increased by 8%–22% compared to that under CT systems depending on the soil moisture regimes. Correspondingly, Benkherbache et al. (2012) reported enhanced physiological parameters (low stomata resistance and higher relative water content) of wheat, higher grain yields and better morphological features under CA than under CT even during the first year of conversion. However, Angar et al. (2011) observed that wheat grain yield gradually increased under CA in semi-arid and sub-humid areas of Tunisia. In the sub-humid regions, yield of durum wheat under CA was on average higher by 800 kg/ha compared to that under CT. In the lower semi-arid zone, the difference was 350 kg/ha, and reaching up to 700 kg/ha in the higher semi-arid zone. In another study carried in the semi-arid conditions of the El Kef (Tunisia), Rezgui et al. (2014) found that the yield of grains under NT conditions increased by 20% in durum wheat and nearly tripled in fababean in years of rainfall deficit. Mouelhi et al. (2016) found higher durum wheat yields over 5 years under CA compared to that under CT and reported the highest yields under wheat-fababean compared to wheat-barley and wheat-oat rotations for both CA and CT systems.

A survey by Labad and Tarik (2016) showed that farmer's fields under CA permitted simultaneously higher wheat yields, improved soil quality parameters (SOM, moisture retention and biological activity), and reduced erosion rates. Additionally, a farmers' survey of 1,901 households in the major wheat-growing region in Morocco revealed that adoption of CApractice helped to minimize attainable yield and profit gaps under farmers' management practices in rainfed systems (Devkota and Yigezu, 2020).

A yield stability analysis carried out by Mrabet (2011b) found that wheat yields under CA system were less influenced by adverse growing conditions compared to CT system, particularly during dry seasons. These trends in yield improvements were also confirmed by Chennafi et al. (2011), Jemai et al. (2013), Fellahi et al. (2013) and Mrabet (2002a).

In Tunisian semi-arid areas, Chaieb et al. (2020) did not find significant differences between CA and CT systems in terms of durum wheat yields, yield components, and grain quality parameters.

Early seeding is an important management benefit associated with CA systems and helps the crops to benefit from the most available rain (Bouzza, 1990; Mrabet et al., 2012; Labbaci et al., 2015). However, appropriate weed control is required to avoid difficult infestation (Labad et al., 2018b, 2019; Labbaci et al., 2015; Raunet et al., 1998). Generally, early seeding is associated witha lower seeding rate due to the use of direct seeding which places seeds at a suitable and uniform depth resulting in good seed germination and crop growth (Mrabet, 2008).

According to Brouziyne et al. (2018), both CA systems and the 10 days early wheat sowing strategies have been proved to be the best adaptation strategies among the management policies in North-western Morocco. Using the SWAT model, these authors concluded that the CA provided the best solution compromising between water use efficiency and food securities.

In North Africa, crop residues are limited due to overgrazing and biomass removal and cover crops are difficult to promote and apply under field conditions. The typical dry weather from spring to fall, and competition for water during the rest of the year, strongly limit the use of cover crops by farmers practising CA. Cover crops were successfully applied in north of Tunisia under CA (Bahri et al., 2018). However, additional research on cover crop is needed in terms of cultivars, sowing rates, and times to find the most suitable combinations for CA systems. Using judicious cereal-based rotations including cover crops, farmers could both produce grains and forage for livestock (FERT, 2018) and reduce the pressure on land and crop residues.

Regarding soil properties, SOM is considered as powerful soil quality indicator; it induces-physico-chemical soil properties enhancement (Aboutayeb et al., 2021; Abou-Tammame et al., 2022; El-mrini et al., 2022; Sharkawy et al., 2022) while N, P, and K are critically needed nutrients for crop production and to a large extent, hold the land productivity and crop yields. Several authors have highlighted the importance of SOM content increase to advancing food security either in dry and tropical areas (Lal, 2020b; Devkota and Yigezu, 2020; Mrabet et al., 2021). The relationship between SOM and plant productivity, especially agricultural yields, has been studied for over a century (Oldfield et al., 2019). Recently, Kane et al. (2021) found that SOM stocks were positively correlated with yield, and the positive relationship strengthened when drought conditions were more severe. In others, increased soil fertility is necessary for the improvement of crop yields in long-term

CA systems and productivity continues to increase as the natural capital of the system is enhanced over time. Carbon rich and structured soils under CA systems helped to both increase crop yields and input factor productivity through higher utilization efficiency of water, nutrients, energy, and labor. CA also contributes to the increased stability of food supplies due to the greater resilience of crops in the face of drought.

Climate change threatens to disrupt annual rainfall patterns by reducing the duration, inducing prolonged dry periods, and increasing the intensity of rainfall. From CA studies, yield benefits of CA are more pronounced in climate-stressed production basins, especially in the drier climates of North Africa, where climate-proofing yields are crucial to enhance food security given a highly variable climate in the region. These findings were also claimed by Michler et al. (2019).

Under Tunisia conditions, Bahri et al. (2019) using the APSIM model found that CA is more effective than CT (under semi-arid and sub-humid environments) in enhancing wheat yield by 15% and water use efficiency by 18% and 13% for both regions, respectively. Devkota et al. (2022) found that the long-term simulated average yield was significantly higher for the CA than the CT system by 24%, 32%, 38%, and 48%, for wheat, lentil, barley, and chickpea, respectively. This shows clearly that CA systems help to capture and utilize the maximum possible available water, which is crucial to sustaining crop production in arid and semi-arid regions.

14.5 UNLOCKING THE SOIL SECRETS AND MITIGATING CLIMATE CHANGE UNDER CA SYSTEMS

According to Desa (2016), soils are critically important in achieving SDGs. However, in North Africa, soils are still forgotten aspects and concerns in many discussions about food security and sustainability. In other terms, the reduced capacity of land to support soil functions or services required for sustainable intensification results in immense gaps between actual and potential yields in farmers' fields. Sustainable and healthy feeding of the population should be a priority of any policy-maker's agenda which implies rethinking agricultural intensification in a way allowing minimizing harming natural resources (The Montpellier Panel, 2013; Mrabet et al., 2021). SOM dynamics and buildup are the most striking and critical processes to be developed and enhanced for regenerating already degraded soils of North Africa (Belloum, 2008; Schjønning et al., 2018). They are determinants for crop productivity and food security. It is important to note and consider that attributes and functional benefits of CA systems may take several years to consistently and fully affect yields, profits, soil health and function and environmental outcomes (Cusser et al., 2020). This suggests that management and policy recommendations based on short-term CA studies can be not appropriately expressive and may be misleading.

14.5.1 Carbon Storage and Sequestration in Soils

At present, atmospheric C sequestration in agricultural soils and hence their recarbonization are considered the most promising negative emission technologies (Bossio et al., 2020; Lembaid et al., 2021). Soil organic matter (SOM) includes all of the organic material in soils, including decaying plant material, soil microbes and humified substances. Its conservation and buildup are vital to sustain food production and sidestep an irreversible climate crisis (Rumpel et al., 2022; Bahri et al., 2022). For sequestration of C and formation of new SOM in agricultural soils, positive and durable interaction between tillage management, SOM dynamics and composition, and biota of soil is necessary. In addition, initial soil conditions and climate features strongly affect carbon storage and dynamics in semiarid environments as reported by recent work by Lembaid et al. (2022).

Due to minimal mechanical disturbance of the soil, residue maintenance, and diversified cropping systems, CA systems play a key role to increase soil capacity as a carbon sink (Mrabet et al., 2021; Moussadek et al., 2011b; Mouelhi et al., 2016; Laghrour et al., 2019; Aboutayeb et al., 2020;

TABLE 14.3

SOC Contents under Conservation Agriculture (CA) and Conventional Tillage (CT) Systems in Selected Sites from North Africa

Country	Rainfall Regim	Soil Type/ Site Name	Horizon (mm)	Duration (years)	CA (%)	CT (%)	Change (%)	References
Morocco	Semi-arid	Calcixeroll	0–25	11	3.98	1.64	142.7	Mrabet et al. (2001b)
	Arid	Vertisol	0–25	32	1.91	1.30	46.1	Laghrour et al. (2019)
	Sub-humid		0–100	11	2.22	1.71	29.8	Moussadek (2012)
Tunisia	Semi-arid	Kef	0–100	9	1.55	0.95	63.1	Chibani et al. (2018)
	Sub-humid	Mateur	0–100	7	2.31	1.93	19.7	Angar et al. (2011)
	Semi-arid	Krib	0–100	7	2.17	1.50	44.7	
	Semi-arid	Borj Elifa	0–100	7	2.31	1.93	19.7	

Devkota et al., 2022). In fact, among the most affected soil properties, Nitrogen and SOM are significantly improved over time under the CA systems, while soil acidity slightly increased through a pH reduction in calcareous soils which implies nutrient availability enhancement.

There is a general consensus among authors from North Africa about the positive effects of CA with regard to SOM increase in the topsoil layers, which in global warming terms means greater carbon sequestration in soils (Table 14.3) (Mrabet et al., 2001a, b, 2021, 2022; Ben-Hammouda et al., 2004; Angar et al., 2011; Moussadek, 2012; Chibani et al., 2018; Aboutayeb et al., 2020; Devkota et al., 2021, 2022). In fact, CA systems redistribute organic matter to the soil surface (called stratification, Mrabet, 2002) with either decreasing or maintaining SOM levels in the subsurface depending on climate, soil type, cropping systems, and residue management and level (Brahim et al., 2009; Bouzrara et al., 2011; Angar et al., 2011; Jemai et al., 2012).

In three contrasting bioclimatic regions of Tunisia, Angar et al. (2011) found an increase in SOM content of 0–40 cm depth after 10 years of CA and CT. They did not observe any decline in SOM levels in sub-soil layers under CA in comparison to that under CT over the entire duration of the study.

Field studies in Morocco (Mrabet et al., 2001b) and Tunisia (Jemai et al., 2012) showed 14% and 28% rises in the SOC from the surface soil layer after 11 and 7 years of converting from conventional tillage to conservation agriculture practices, respectively (Table 14.3). Mrabet et al. (2004) reported that SOM content under CA improved respectively by 0.036% and 0.015% of each Mg/ha of crop residues added at 0–5 cm and 5–10 cm depths. Moussadek et al. (2011b) reported a significant difference among bare no-till, partially covered, and tilled treatments in terms of SOM (1.79%, 2.05%, and 1.47%, respectively). These authors concluded that although CA systems improve SOM compared with the CT system, returning 50% of crop residues at the soil surface is compulsory under CA to protect these Vertisols against water erosion. Later, Belmekki et al. (2014) stated that carbon content under the CA system increased by 10% (from 3.08% to 3.36%) by doubling crop residue cover from 50% to 100%.

Rotating and diversifying crops help to accumulate further organic carbon in soils, this fact is more evident when legume crops are cultivated (Devkota et al., 2022; Mouelhi et al., 2016). Legumes ensure crop diversification and thus enhance soil biology and resilience. In Egypt, Harb et al. (2015) showed significant improvement in soil fertility parameters under CA systems in maize-wheat-soybean-wheat-soybean rotation. According to a recent study by Devkota et al. (2022), the CA system helped to increase SOM by 7%, available phosphorus by 3%, and exchangeable potassium by 15% compared to CT after 5 years of experimentation in a semiarid region of Morocco. In Egypt, Sharkawy et al. (2022) found a 51% increase in SOM when comparing CA with traditional tillage systems due to maintenance of residue cover.

In northern Tunisia, conversion to CA system sequestered SOM at the rate of up to 0.9 Mg C/ha/year even with most rates of residue maintenance (Brahim et al., 2009). These same authors found that carbon storage after 7 years of CA systems with wheat-corn rotation was 18.1 Mg/ha compared to only 11.7 Mg/ha under CT in the top 10 cm, an increase of 35%. In a recent study, Brahim et al. (2022) found an increase of 12.6% in SOC under CA after 3 years only compared to CT in a slopping vertisol. For the authors, the total amount of carbon stored in the 0–30 cm horizon of the soil was equal to 103.14 and 91.59 Mg/ha under CA and conventional tillage, respectively.

In the same region, Ben Moussa-Machraoui et al. (2010) observed a minor buildup of SOM after 4 years of CA as compared to CT systems. In Tunisia, Bahri et al. (2017) did not observe an increase in SOM under CA even after 17 years of adoption due to excessive removal of crop residues, either for direct livestock feeding or collected and sold off the farm for cash income.

In a simulation study using the DNDC soil organic model, Lembaid et al. (2021) concluded that combining no-tillage system with C additions through manure amendment and crop residues are the optimized management practices to improve the SOC stock over time, especially in semi-arid areas.

Lal (2020b) suggested the nominal threshold level of SOC required for optimum yields to approximately 2% in temperate soils and 1% in tropical soils. However, research is still urgently needed to define such critical ranges or thresholds of SOM for securing crop production and mitigating climate risks across soil types and climates in North Africa. Determining such target values for ensuring sustainable soil functions is valuable for farmers as well as other stakeholders involved in soil security and policy.

14.5.2 GHG Emissions: Although the Path is Proven, Significant Challenges Remain

Conservation agriculture has been endorsed for its potential to mitigate climate change (Smith et al., 2019) and hence as Climate Smart Agriculture (Michler et al., 2019). In other terms, CA can simultaneously sequestercarbon in agricultural soils and reduce greenhouse gas (GHG) emissions (Sanz-Cobena et al., 2017).

Moussadek et al. (2011a) measured CO_2 emissions from fields under different tillage operations, providing an interesting and unique example of the carbon dynamics with and without tillage in North Africa. They reported a significant reduction in CO_2 emission with conversion to no-tillage systems. Sharp and continuous reduction in CO_2 emissions was reported under the CA system compared to that under the CT system in the semi-arid areas of Morocco by Moussadek et al. (2011a). Chiselling, stubble ploughing, and disk ploughing induced rapid oxidation of organic matter and CO_2 loss to the atmosphere. The authors reported that accumulated CO_2 flux over a period of 96 hours was three times higher under conventional tillage systems compared to CA. This process leads to concomitant loss of SOM, soil health and functions, and crop productivity as explained in previous sections.

Optimization and smart management of fertilizers are essential. In other terms, optimized nitrogen fertilizer application (in terms of input rate and time of application), as well as the careful selection of the type of fertilizer used are crucial to improve crop productivity under CA systems mainly in the early years of adoption while reducing the ecological footprint. The estimated N_2O mitigation potential, through optimized fertilization (rate and timing) in Mediterranean agro-ecosystems ranges between 30% and 50% compared to non-adjusted fertilizer practices (Mrabet et al., 2020). It is obvious that the more carbon-input soils get, the more soil microbial mass and activity increase which leads to improved nutrient cycling (Verhulst et al., 2010; Reicosky, 2020). Even though, other studies claimed higher

O emission under CA due to higher N fertilizer application (Palm et al., 2014).

14.5.3 Soil Quality and Health

Soil health is the capacity of soil to function as a vital living system while soil quality describes the soil's capability to sustain crop productivity, maintain environmental quality, support good plant, animal, and human health, and hence deliver ecosystem services (Creamer et al., 2022). They are effective tools for monitoring soil changes or alterations under varying cropping systems, land management, and climate settings (Bünemann et al., 2018). Soil quality and health improvement is the foundation on which sustainable agriculture is based.

14.5.3.1 Soil Physical Properties

SOM dynamics is a pulsating indicator of the state of soil quality and health under tillage management (Reicosky, 2020). Tillage disrupts soil structure, exacerbates soil compaction, and compromises soil aggregation leading to destroying the physical properties of the soil and making it vulnerable to sealing and crusting as well as to water runoff and erosion (Montgomery, 2007). Conventional tillage has contributed to soil quality deterioration due mainly to SOM depletion and soil aggregate breakdown. However, through its three components, the CA system has a significant impact on soil physical quality (Bohoussou et al., 2022; Laghrour et al., 2016; Devkota et al., 2021).

It is generally agreed that the change from CT to CA marked an early increase in bulk density and hence a reduction in soil porosity, likely due to the instability of transient macropores and dispersion of unstable soil fragments created by intensive cultivation practices (Abdellaoui et al., 2011; Lahlou et al., 2005; Moussadek et al., 2011a, b; Mouelhi et al., 2016). Such changes occurred only within the first years of CA management with bulk density much lesser in CA after 8 years as explained by Lahlou et al. (2005). These authors reported that bulk density evolution under CA systems over time was accompanied by an associated modification in pore volume and an increase in pore size distribution as compared to those in soil under a CT system. Jemai et al. (2013) reported lower soil bulk density under CA vs CT which was due to improved SOM over time.

Based on a study on a sub-humid site in central Algeria, Abdellaoui et al. (2011) found an improvement in soil properties in the 0–30 cm layer under CA compared to that under CT with regard to an increase in water-holding capacity and soil porosity and decrease in soil bulk density. In semiarid Morocco, Moussadek et al. (2011b) found that CA systems enhanced bulk density compared to CT systems but no-till plots with residue cover have significantly lower bulk density than bare no-tilled plots.

In other terms, a biologically formed structure helped recover and enhance porosity beyond the values observed in CT. According to Mrabet et al. (2012), CA favors properties related to soil structure, such as aggregate size distribution and aggregation index, among others (Mrabet et al., 2004, 2012; Bouzrara et al., 2011; Rezgui et al., 2014; Belmekki et al., 2014; Chibani et al., 2018).

14.5.3.2 Soil Fertility

Particulate organic matter (POM) is closely related to nutrient cycling and availability, quality of SOM, and the development of the soil structure. POM is easily destroyed by tillage operations and accumulated by CA systems as indicated by Bessam and Mrabet (2003) and Mrabet et al. (2001b) in semi-arid Morocco. The same authors reported that minimum soil disturbance in CA leads to greater efficiency of the phosphate and potassium fertilizer, increasing the concentration and availability of P and K, due to the stratification of SOM in the surface horizon. Further, several long-term studies showed an increase in nitrogen (N) content in soil under CA compared to CT (Ben Moussa-Machraoui et al., 2010; Chibani et al., 2018; Laghrour et al., 2015, 2016, 2019). Ben Moussa-Machraoui et al. (2010) reported that conversion to CA significantly enriched the soil of N, K_2O, and P_2O_5 in northwest Tunisia after 4 years. The same P_2O_5 results were found after 5 years in Tunisia by Mouelhi et al. (2016). Souissi et al. (2020) reported that even though water use efficiency was not affected by tillage systems, nitrogen use efficiency was higher under CA compared to that under CT systems.

Slow decomposition of crop residues and plant roots gives rise to a superficial layer rich in humus, which, through its mineralization, makes available to the crops and microbial community the nutrients contained therein (Mrabet et al., 2001a; Devkota et al., 2021). Stratification of nutrients improves crop vigour and growth and increases the availability of plant nutrients which may alleviate any nutrient deficiency or fertilizer misapplication. However, in case of prolonged drought, confinement of roots to the nutrient-rich surface layer may adversely affect crop growth aggravating the effects of water deficit (Mrabet et al., 2021).

Suitably managed SOM increases nutrient availability to crops, which allows farmers to reduce and optimize fertilizer use (Mrabet et al., 2001a). In other terms, with the increasing price of fertilizers, enhanced availability of plant nutrients under CA systems could contribute to fertilizer management and optimization. In the Egypt, Harb et al. (2015) instituted that CA reduced by half NPK requirements of wheat compared to CT systems in a wheat-soybean rotation.

Moussadek et al. (2014) found that soils under CA exhibited higher humic acids and humin contents compared to those under CT. The authors also reported significantly lower fulvic acid concentrations under NT than CT in Vertisol. Such changes in SOM quality through increased humic acids and lowered fulvic acid are particularly important in the stabilization of structural aggregates according to Moussadek et al. (2011b). According to Mrabet et al. (2012) and Aboutayeb et al. (2020), the tillage system did not significantly affect exchangeable cation contents in semiarid soils.

14.5.3.3 Soil Biology and Biodiversity

Tillage impacts take many forms and range in scale and complexity when related to soil biota or microbiome. Avoiding tillage and soil manipulation preserves the SOM and habitat of insects, earthworms, and millions of fungi, bacteria, and other microorganisms essential to the proper functioning of agri-ecosystems. The residue mulch maintained on the soil surface in CA buffers temperature and moisture fluctuations and provides energy and nutrients essential for soil microorganisms including bacteria, mycorrhiza, and earthworms (Bouzrara et al., 2011; Errouissi et al., 2011; Hamim et al., 2012; Taibi etal., 2020). Recently, Taibi et al. (2020) underlined the importance of CA systems in re-establishing the soil microbiome disturbed by tillage in semi-arid regions of Algeria. Oulbachir et al. (2014) recommended assessing the soil microbial activity and diversity over time in order to understand the biochemical processes involved.

According to Hamim et al. (2012) in Morocco and Taibi et al. (2020) and Mouelhi et al. (2016) in Tunisia, CA systems are associated with an improvement in the diversity of fungal populations in soils.

After 4 years, Bouzrara et al. (2011) reported an increase in earthworm activity despite compaction of the topsoil under CA compared with that under CT practices in Setif (Algeria). Errouissi et al. (2011) also observed enriched fauna and earthworms under CA compared to CT in some soils of northern Tunisia.

In Egypt, El-Areed (2019) found enhanced soil biological activity and aggregation under CA in irrigated corn fields compared to traditional systems. These findings were also confirmed by Elsoury et al. (2015) who showed significantly higher levels of soil microbial biomass and soil enzyme activities under CA than CT in wheat fields in Burg Elarab region of Egypt. In other terms, with CA systems, soil biodiversity is preserved and enriched, which translates into improved ecosystem services.

14.6 WATER BALANCE AND DYNAMICS: DROUGHT BUFFERING

CA healthy soils offer both in-situ and ex-situ services and benefits. It is well documented that CA systems positively affect the water balance at the farm and the watershed. Regardless of farm size, Nyanga et al. (2020) reported lessened erosion and run-off processes and hence lower risks of downstream sedimentation and flood damage to infrastructure. Improved soil structure and accumulated SOM with CA decrease soil erodibility (Dimanche, 1997) and increase infiltration and water retention on smaller scales (Angar et al., 2011; Mrabet et al., 2012; Jemai et al., 2013). Consequently, the risk of flooding is slighter at the watershed level (Moussadek et al., 2011b; Chibani et al., 2018).

A rainfall simulation was carried out by Moussadek et al. (2011b) to study the impacts of CA, residue cover, and tillage system on runoff and sediment dynamics. The results showed that under the rainfall intensity from 36 to 60 mm/ha, CA delayed run-off starting time and run-off rates were two to three times higher under bare untilled soil and CT. Moussadek et al. (2011b) also reported a reduction of 50% in soil losses with partial residue cover under CA compared to that under CT. Sharkawy et al. (2022) confirmed also that CA reduced runoff by 12%–28% and soil loss by 40%–68% depending on the season as compared to traditional tillage systems in Wadi El Raml area (Egypt).

Devkota et al. (2022) found that rainfall use efficiency and available soil moisture increased by 13% and 14% respectively under CA compared to CT in a 5-year experiment of semiarid Morocco. Increases in the rate of water infiltration and reduced runoff rates under CA are due to better aggregate stability and bioporosity. Compared to the conventional system, SOM accumulation could be due partially to soil erosion mitigation (Giller et al., 2015).

In CA systems, SOM buildup over time enhances the soil's ability to retain water while it reduces water runoff. In two contrasting regions of Tunisia, Bahri et al. (2019) reported that CA systems are more effective in enhancing soil resilience and minimizing risks of water erosion (1.7 and 4.6 Mg/ha/year of soil loss under CA and CT correspondingly). Earlier, the same team, reported that after 5 years, higher soil aggregate stability under CA systems minimized risks of soil erosion compared to that under CT systems (Bahri et al., 2016).

In other hydrological studies of Tunisia, despite low residue cover under CA systems average annual soil losses were 30%–40% lower compared to CT (2–4 tons/ha/year under CA vs 3–7 tons/ha/year under CT). Water infiltration rates were 45% higher under CA (65 versus 45 mm/ha under CA and conventional tillage, respectively (Raunet et al., 2004).

In a sub-humid site in central Algeria, increased SOM content was reflected in a higher aggregation and better resistance of CA soil to erosion and rapid wetting compared to that under CT and reduced tillage practices (Abdellaoui et al., 2011). Research showed that CA systems improve soil's available water capacity, water-stable aggregation, and hydraulic conductivity through the accumulation of organic matter and formation of biopores (Mrabet et al., 2012; Abdellaoui et al., 2011).

In Tunisia, Angar et al. (2011) reported that, over a period of 8 consecutive years, infiltration rates under CA increased from 41 to 73 L/ha in sub-humid areas, from 32 to 40 L/ha in lower semi-arid, and from 19 to 43 L/ha in higher semi-arid areas. In contrast, infiltration rates under CT were lower approaching 20 L/ha and stayed constant in soil of the semi-arid sites and increased slightly in the sub-humid site (18–29 L/ha at the end of the experiment). The authors also reported that the water dynamics under CA systems could be improved further if the pressure exerted by sheep flocks on crop residues was minimized and surface soil compaction alleviated. Such benefits in water balance are achieved and even enhanced with the maintenance of crop residues and stubble at/near the soil surface.

Mrabet (1997) and Moussadek (2012) reported higher soil water potentials under CA compared to CT and hence lower soil water losses as vapor due to the elimination of soil mechanical disturbance and maintenance of crop residues as barriers at the soil surface.

Upgraded soil porosity and pore systems in CA improved the holding and infiltration of rainfall and irrigation water in several North African sites (Mrabet, 2008; Jemai et al., 2013; Rezgui et al., 2014; Oulbachir et al., 2014). Such amelioration in water dynamics allows better groundwater recharge and regular-stream flow during the year. Over time community water supply and quality will be improved and sustained.

Jemai et al. (2013), under sub-humid bioclimate of Tunisia, found that CA systems generated a noticeable improvement in the surface SOM and a decrease in dry bulk density, reflecting an amelioration of the porous system which positively affected the soil moisture recharge in the profile. However, according toother authors (Abdellaoui et al., 2011; Moussadek, 2012; Mekhlouf et al., 2013; Belagrouz et al., 2016), water dynamics and especially water entry in soils is restricted under CA (lower sorptivity). Such results were linked to soil consolidation, residue removal, and grazing of CA fields. In these experiments, soils under CA did not yet recover from the initial state of degradation, which requires more time and more judicious management in order to improve water balance and dynamics.

If well managed, CA systems increase water uptake, conservation, and use by mitigating evaporation and runoff processes, improving water distribution in soil profile, and restoring water-holding capacity of soils. These hydrological improvements allow higher soil resilience to shocks and extreme events.

14.7 ENERGY SAVINGS AND ECONOMICS OF CONSERVATION AGRICULTURE

In North Africa, rising prices of fuel, seeds, fertilizers, pesticides, and machinery are discouraging farmers to invest in rainfed agriculture due to uncertainty and high risks. In addition, farmers favour annual cropping systems due to rapid incomes and small time-lag on earnings. However, instant benefits should not come at the expense of continuing sustainability. Uncertainty is not a good excuse for inaction.

Undoubtedly, the environmental cost of tillage systems is mind-boggling making conventional agriculture practices non-sustainable. On the opposite, the CA system has been perceived as a smart and cost-efficient solution implying integrated management of natural resources at the farm and reduced off-farm externalities. Many wondrous scientific advances agreed that CA systems are cost-effective and energy-efficient and allow farmers higher and more stable incomes and profits (Boughlala et al., 2011; Sharkawy et al., 2022).

Authors reported that conventional tillage operations consume substantial amounts of energy and upsurge equipment and labor needs, so there may be numerous economic benefits and savings to convert to conservation agriculture (Chouen et al., 2004; Ben-Salem et al., 2006; Boughlala et al., 2011; Magnan et al., 2011; Fenni, 2013; El Gharras et al., 2017; Labbaci et al., 2015; Labad and Hartani, 2016; Bahri et al., 2018; Rouabhi et al., 2019; Sharkawy et al., 2022). These authors have shown that CA systems reduce the number of operations, and thus labour costs and fuel consumption. However, Fouzai et al. (2018) found that increased off-farm incomes were correlated with lower CA adoption levels in the Siliana Governate of Tunisia.

Above all, in mechanized farming systems, the conversion of plow-based tillage to no-tillage-based CA systems leads to immediate energy savings and reduced labor. According to El Gharras et al. (2004), CA systems can lead to eight times the saving in energy needed to perform primary and secondary tillage operations. For an experiment running for 5 years, CA increased system yield by 20% and total benefits by 40% with production costs reduced by 14.5% (Devkota et al., 2022). Sharkawy et al. (2022) also found higher net profits under CA than traditional tillage in rainfed wheat systems of Egypt.

Labbaci et al. (2015) found that farmers by opting for the CA save an average of 80 US dollars/ha for planting wheat compared to the conventional system, which is equivalent to the value of 0.37 tonnes of wheat. The fuel saving is also consequent (from 22 to 33 L/ha according to the slope and type of soil) due to the reduction by two of the number of operations. CA systems also allowed reduced indirect energy consumption from more efficient use of all inputs (e.g., seeds, fertilizers, pesticides, and machinery) and timelier sowing as shown by Labbaci et al. (2015). These benefits were also incentives to farmers.

Under CA systems, crop diversification enhances nutrient cycling and accumulation and breaks pest and disease cycles, leading to reduced use of inorganic fertilizer and pesticide. Such reduced dependence on external inputs makes CA systems less costly and more affordable for farmers over time.

Such profit-driven advantages should consent farmers to gain confidence in CA systems. However, long-term social, financial, and economic benefits of CA are still difficult to expect and ex-ante assessments are desirable. In addition, to overcoming past mindset, farmers and policy makers often find it challenging to make precise estimates about long-term returns on investments in

CA systems, due to system intricacy and lengthened planning horizons. Expert knowledge, decision analysis, and models to forecast CA performances and associated risks are enormously needed to explore prime management options and best ways to nurture CA uptake and adoption rates.

It is also imperative for CA farmers to get adequate recognition for the off-farm benefits of CA, principally those related to ecosystem services, soil functionalities, and security (Wall et al., 2020; Reicosky, 2020). However, payments for these services require metrics to allocate cost/benefit, validate impact, and the ability to monitor participation.

14.8 HARNESSING THE POTENTIAL OF CONSERVATION OF AGRICULTURE FOR SUSTAINABLE DEVELOPMENT

Innovation and technological growth in CA systems have played a fundamental part in economic and social development for a range of countries mainly in the USA, Canada, Latin America, and Australia (Kassam et al., 2022). CA systems when associated with biotechnology, precision agriculture, agricultural mechanization, and renewable energy technologies can improve yields and farmers' livelihoods challenged by adverse climatic conditions (Mrabet and Moussadek, 2021). For wide adoption of these innovations, economic, social, or environmental trade-offs should be identified, evaluated, and addressed (mitigated) (Dang et al., 2020). In this regard, explicit national policies sustained by ample national and international investments and effective mechanisms are needed to guarantee the acceleration of the transfer of technology.

CA benefits cannot be established overnight. Current instruments and policies may not be appropriate for up/deep scaling CA systems. Hence, North African institutions should grow their capacities to acquire, adopt, and diffuse CA knowledge and technologies to promote sustainable and inclusive agriculture development. Tapping into the potential of CA systems requires an environment that enables and nurtures learning and strengthens innovation. To obtain additional benefits from CA systems, North African countries should make available incentives and dedicate funds, time, resources, and strenuous efforts to build and manage road maps for CA implementation and mainstreaming at a large scale.

CA system is emerging as a prime inclusive and knowledge-based solution for sustainable agriculture and soil security (Pretty and Bharucha, 2014; Giller et al., 2015; Mugandani et al., 2021). To take fuller advantage of the potential of CA systems for addressing SDGs, end-to-end strategies based upon systemic and comprehensive inclusion of stakeholders, actors, and partnerships at different scales and levels are necessary if not mandatory. In this sense, stakeholders need to develop and evolve their capability to ascertain, approve, assimilate, and diffuse existing and emerging CA knowledge and technologies and to invest in while expanding networks and linkages. Flow and assimilation of CA knowledge either local or foreign should be embedded in a strong and durable innovation system that allows and supports critical thinking, problem-solving as well as policy learning and creative decision making.

For CA systems, science–push linear model for technology transfer is no longer suitable and needed. The conception and development of successful CA networks is a long-term process based on a common vision, shared goals, and trust. Hence, functional networks and clusters need technology brokers and intermediaries that should facilitate knowledge exchange and communication which help deliver results and impacts to strengthen the endogenous potential of communities and the country as a whole within a designed time-frame.

The competency and creativity of actors in research and academia should be upgraded and enforced to generate and apply CA knowledge and develop expertise and skills to improve learning and communication capabilities and absorptive capacity of scholars, extension agents, researchers, technicians, firms, and farmers.

Policymakers can deploy diversified instruments to benefits society and farmers from CA systems. Tackling systemic failures and barriers that inhibit the performance and uptake of CA by farmers is a critical issue and should be a primacy. Aligning CA potentials with the challenges addressed by actors in agriculture is another relevant priority for policymakers. Developing incentives and motivation schemes are of paramount importance for CA systems to develop and up/deep scale. Policies should afford other stakeholders an established and liable environment to enable both short and long-term planning and monitoring of CA systems.

Human capital development is essential in benefiting from CA systems. It allows a country to fully and sustainably engage and help in the adoption and upscaling CA processes. Education, vocational training, technical, and managerial skills are of paramount importance and essential in communication, dialogue, problem-solving, teamwork, creativity, co-design, systemic thinking, and learning to shear.

Civil society and consumers are among the key actors in shifting to healthy and sustainable food systems through regenerative agriculture (i.e., conservation agriculture, organic farming, agroforestry, nature-based solutions). NGOs, grass-roots movements, social enterprises, and engaged citizens have crucial role in directing public policy on meeting societal challenges, acquiring and assimilating new technologies and knowledge and eliciting technological and institutional transformations. Hence, civil society, NGOs, and farmer organizations can be both influential and contributors in testing, supporting, and disseminating CA systems designed to benefit large and diverse groups. In this respect, robust and evolving linkages among and within actors and stakeholders as well as the development of collaboration capacities enable breakthroughs in CA system diffusion. Integration and diversification of strong and dedicated actors guaranty consistent appropriation and flow of key resources (i.e. finance, logistics and human capital) which also mitigate barriers and limit trade-offs.

14.9   CONCLUSION AND DIRECTIONS FOR A BRIGHT FUTURE AHEAD

The SDG process incorporates an ambition of social, economic, and environmental transformation that is improbable to be realized unless North African countries board on fresh and innovative agricultural development trajectories that break with the historical pattern of environmental degradation or increased scarcity and inequality. In this regard, it is vital to narrow the gaps in human, technological, and innovative capabilities as well as in the performances and efficiencies of the agriculture sector. Hence, policies should be supported to empower and motivate technological development, diffusion and transfer of regenerative agriculture and sustainable and healthy food systems. In this sense, soils should be granted the same level of protection as water and air.

To substitute current unsustainable practices and systems requires a more profound understanding of conservation agriculture (CA) metrics and guidelines (FAO and ITPS, 2017). Our goal with this review was to make an assessment of the various benefits and impacts of CA systems and shed light on the three dimensions of sustainability.

An over-arching need is a greater understanding of and trust in science behind CA systems. In a series of papers, scholars and scientists from the region analysed the region's most pressing challenges, alerted of the serious impacts of conventional and industrial farming and warned on the exceeding of multiple-planet boundaries. At the same time, they claimed that the vital central point for achieving food security in the face of age-old issues such as climate change and soil deterioration is at the farm level and with farmers.

CA systems constitute a major departure from past and traditional ways of managing resources and farming. From the present review, CA systems have huge potential to deliver multiple benefits in coherence with the values of sustainability. Introduced as a soil regenerative practice, the CA is able to ensure agricultural production while enhancing soil properties through decarbonization coupled with soil degradation prevention (Ogle et al., 2019; Mrabet et al., 2021). Considered eco-friendly and socioeconomically very promising, CA tries to balance between agricultural production targets and land resources protection.

CA systems offer a prodigious and distinctive opportunity to all North African nations to transform their out-of-date degrading agriculture into regenerative and sustainable agriculture.

Studies both in research stations and farmer fields showed that CA systems provide a wide range of soil multiple functions and yield optimization and benefits. CA systems have demonstrated soil quality and fertility improvements, soil conservation, and carbon sequestration, thus leading to an overall enhancement of soil resilience and crop productivity. In other terms, with CA farming; soil, water, and atmospheric health can be optimized.

CA systems can play a double role in mitigating climate change (carbon sequestration and CO_2 emission abatement) and in enhancing food systems resilience to droughts and extreme events (better water conservation, higher water and nutrient use efficiency and improved functioning of soils).

Soils are central to achieving 8 of the 17 SDGs (Hou, 2020; Hou et al., 2020). Kassam and Kassam (2020b) synthesized all SDGs that may benefit from large-scale adoption and meanstreaming of CA systems. For attaining soil-linked SDGs (Keesstra et al., 2016), CA systems should be applied and implemented across wide and continuous spectrum, from basic science to farming practices, and from political perceptions and economic foresights to consumer conduct. All stakeholders should be prepared and hard headed to make some strong common decisions and even irreversible choices to address CA issues and challenges along the 21st century.

CA should be regarded as "cohesive and blended", pairing and harmonizing the economic, social, and environmental dimensions of sustainability. Hence, CA shifts in archi types request for an innovation system perspective to deal with diverse and context-specific needs of resources, practices and technologies and their management. An innovation system (IS) should include all factors that influence development, diffusion, and use of CA systems. The IS should also include risk analysis, learning across diversity, understanding of organizations and individuals responsible for creation, generation, diffusion, adaptation, and use of knowledge and institutional context that governs the way these interactions and processes take place and spillover. For strong innovation systems, it is vital to enquire high mobility of human resources and capital in order to strengthen the relationships between research sphere and CA users.

CA systems are at a timely moment and should be well aligned with multiple international contexts. CA, as climate smart agriculture, has a fundamental role to play in terms of facilitating soil recarbonization and accomplishing climate action targets. CA should be used in carbon offset trading schemes and in low-carbon programs. It is crucial that the roles of CA in climate change mitigation and adaptability be further recognized in national policies and institutional land use strategies in response to international agreements (i.e. Nationally Determined Contributions (NDCs); Land Degradation Neutrality (LDN) mechanisms) (Mrabet et al., 2022; Ziadat et al., 2022).

While the present appraisal showed that CA has considerable potential to contribute to sustainability, however, still more advanced and applied research, scenario analysis, and modelling are required to further improve our understanding of the benefits of CA in terms of sustainability, where CA adoption is heavily constrained by a set of socioeconomic and institutional challenges (Mrabet et al., 2022). Even though economic benefits have been and continue to be the main drivers of CA adoption, but the economic rational and theory behind farmers' behavior are often overlooked and hence need to be addressed. Strong research linking different disciplines (i.e. finance, sociology, supply chain and environmental sustainability) is strongly required to identify efficient incentives and financial opportunities and accompanying policies for rapid and sustained development of CA systems.

There is no one size that fits all. Recently, FAO Global Soil Partnership and The Intergovernmental Technical Panel on Soils (ITPS) released a protocol for the assessment of sustainability of soil management practices and identification of actions to improve their sustainability (FAO and ITPS, 2020). Such protocol should be adopted and used by countries of North Africa for CA systems.

Transformative innovation like CA systems may create tensions and rigidities among advocates and promoters of change and incumbents. Hence, constructing a shared comprehension and visualization of how CA systems can help meet SDGs and related societal challenges is fundamental for mustering strategic corporations and confirming stakeholders' rights of and commitments to CA priorities and resolutions. Strong influencers and knowledge spillovers are needed to raise awareness and adoption of CA across scales and contexts and to mitigate barriers while creating bridges.

Reorienting or shifting agricultural systems towards sustainable and inclusive outcomes embroils modifications in the priority-setting process. Still, in some North African countries, there is a circular trap of real integration of CA systems in agricultural development strategy. Countries need to be able to guarantee knowledge and institutional resources that remain weak and unstable. Without these resources, it would be difficult to convey the paradigm shift and policy stimulus to convert to and develop CA systems.

Political commitment and leadership are vital for CA emergence and development and in anticipating and managing potential conflicts. Civil society groups, consumers, social entrepreneurs and grass-root organizations that are active actors in the informal economy should be strongly engaged in the adoption process and chains of CA systems. Ethnic, gender, and generational groups should be encouraged and their roles enforced for higher impacts and fair transition to CA systems.

Finally, the bottom-up approach putting humans and especially farmers at the center of policies should be further developed and bound in North Africa. In other terms, CA adoption should be maintained by proper and context-specific tailored policies, but also supported by inclusive governance and financial/investment mechanisms that enable and facilitate the enhancement of performances, prosperity, and decent livings.

REFERENCES

AAAID 2018. Annual report 2018. Available at: https://www.aaaid.org/wp-content/uploads/2019/11/annual_report_2018_E_compressed.pdf

Abahussain, A. A., Abdu, A. Sh., Al-Zubari, W. K., El-Deen, N. A. and Abdul Raheem, M. 2002. Desertification in the Arab region: Analysis of current status and trends. *Journal of Arid Environments* 51: 521–545. doi: 10.1006/jare.2002.0975

Abdalla, M. A., Mohamed, A. E. and Makki, E. K. 2007. The response of two-sorghum cultivars to conventional and conservation tillage systems in central Sudan. *AMA, Agricultural Mechanization in Asia, Africa and Latin America* 38: 67–71.

Abdellaoui, Z., Teskrat, H., Belhadj, A. and Zaghouane, O. 2011. Étude comparative de l'effet du travail conventionnel, semis direct et travail minimum sur le comportement d'une culture de blé dur dans la zone subhumide. *Options Méditerranéennes: Série A* 96: 71–87.

Abidi, S., Benyoussef, S. and Salem, H. B. 2021. Foraging behaviour, digestion and growth performance of sheep grazing on dried vetch pasture cropped under conservation agriculture. *Journal of Animal Physiology and Animal Nutrition* 105: 51–58. doi: 10.1111/JPN.13456

Abou El-Enin, M. M. and Abo-Remalia, S. H. 2015. Effect of conservation agriculture on broad bean and maize productivity in Egypt. *International Journal of Innovative Research and Creative Technology* 1: 447–452.

Aboudrare, A., Debaeke, P., Bouaziz, A. and Chekli, H. 2006. Effects of soil tillage and fallow management on soil water storage and sunflower production in a semi-arid Mediterranean climate. *Agricultural Water Management* 83(3): 183–196.

Abou-Tammame, D., Zouhri, A., Boutarfa, A., Fathi, J. and Aboutayeb, R. 2022. The effect of purified wastewater on the physicochemical properties of agricultural soils in Chaouia in Morocco. *Journal of Ecological Engineering* 23(1): 34–42.

Aboutayeb, R., El Yousfi, B. and El Gharras, O. 2020. Impact of no-till on physicochemical properties of Vertisols in Chaouia region of Morocco. *Eurasian Journal of Soil Science* 9(2): 119–125.

Aboutayeb, R., El-mrini, S., Zouhri, A., Idrissi, O. and Azim, K. 2021. Hygienization assessment during heap co-composting of Turkey manure and olive mill pomace. *Eurasian Journal of Soil Science* 10(4): 332–342.

Al Balghiti, A., Dahan, R. and Kradi, C. 2020. *Analyse de la chaîne de valeur des légumineuses alimentaires.* INRA - Editions. 172 pp. ISBN: 978-9920-35-593-3

Amara, M., Feddal, M. A. and Hamani, A. 2015. Analyse du comportement du sol sous l'action de trois techniques de mise en place d'un blé dur (*Triticum durum*). Effet sur le développement des racines et conséquences sur le rendement. *Nature & Technologie* A–C(12): 130–141.

Angar, H., Ben Haj Salah, H. and Ben Hammouda, M. 2011. Semis direct et semis conventionnel en Tunisie: Les résultats agronomiques de 10 ans de comparaison. *Options Mediterranéennes: Série, A.* 96: 53–59.

Bahri, H., Annabi, M., Cheikh M'Hamed, H., Chibani, R., Chtourou, M., Riahi, N. and Ben Becher, L. 2018. Evaluation de l'impact agro-environnemental et de la durabilité de l'adoption du semis direct au Nord de la Tunisie. *Annales de l'INRAT* 91: 98–111.

Bahri, H., Annabi, M., Cheikh M'Hamed, H. and Frija, A. 2019. Assessing the long-term impact of conservation agriculture on wheat-based systems in Tunisia using APSIM simulations under a climate change context. *Science of the Total Environment* 692: 1223–1233.

Bahri, H., Annabi, M., Chibani, R., Cheikh M'Hamed, H. and Hermessi, T. 2016. Can conservation agriculture reduce the impact of soil erosion in northern Tunisia? *Geophysical Research Abstracts* 18: EGU2016-12234.

Bahri, H., Annabi, M., Saoueb, A., Cheikh M'Hamed, H., Souissi, A., Chibani, R. andBahri, B. A. 2017. Can conservation agriculture sequester soil carbon in the long term in northern Tunisia? In: *Recent Advances in Environmental Science from the Euro-Mediterranean and Surrounding Regions. Euro-Mediterranean Conference for Environment Integration*, 22–25 November, Sousse, Tunisia, pp. 69–71. https://www.cabidigitallibrary.org/doi/full/10.1079/9781789245745.0007

Bahri, H., Raclot, D., Barbouchi, M., Lagacherie, P. and Annabi, M. 2022. Mapping soil organic carbon stocks in Tunisian topsoils. *Geoderma Regional* 30: e00561. doi: 10.1016/j.geodrs.2022.e00561.

Bazza, M., Kay, M. and Knuston, C. 2018. Drought characteristics and management in North Africa and the Near East. FAO Water Reports 45. FAO, Italy. Available at: https://www.fao. org/3/CA0034EN/ca0034en.pdf

Belagrouz, A., Chennafi, H., Hakimi, M., Soualili, N., Razem, R., Boutalbi, W. and Ferras, K. 2016. Conductivité hydraulique et densité apparente sous labours de conservation du sol. *Revue Agriculture Numéro Spécial* 1: 100–105.

Belloum, A. 2008. Conservation agriculture (CA) in the Arab region between concept and application. In: Stewart, B. A., Asfary, A. F., Belloum, A., Steiner, K. and Friedrich, T. (eds.) *The Proceedings of the International Workshop on Conservation Agriculture for Sustainable Land Management to Improve the Livelihood of People in Dry Areas*, 7–9 May, ACSAD & GTZ, Damascus, Syria, pp. 13–24.

Belmekki, M., El Gharous, M., El Gharras, O., Boughlala, M., Iben Halima, O. and Bencharki, B. 2014. Tillage effects on basic properties of a calcareous soil under Moroccan semi-arid climate. *International Journal of Advanced Research in Engineering and Technology* 5(3): 130–146.

Ben Moussa-Machraoui, S., Errouissi, F., Ben-Hammouda, M. and Nouira, S. 2010. Comparative effects of conventional and no-tillage management on some soil properties under Mediterranean semi-arid conditions in northwestern Tunisia. *Soil and Tillage Research* 106(2): 247–253.

Ben-Hammouda, M., Guesmi, M., Nasr, K. and Kammassi, M. 2004. Evolution de la matière organique en semis direct et conventionnel. In Par Raouf Seddik (ed.) *Deuxièmes rencontres méditerranéennes sur le semis direct*. Tabarka, Tunisia, pp. 104–107.

Ben-Hammouda, M., M'Hedhbi, K., Kammassi, M. and Gouili, H. 2007. Direct drilling: an agro-environmental approach to prevent land degradation and sustain production. In: Stewart, B., Fares Asfary, A., Belloum, A., Steiner, K. and Friedrich, T. (eds.) *Proceedings of the International Workshop on Conservation Agriculture for Sustainable Land Management to Improve the Livelihood of People in Dry Areas*, 7–9 May, ACSAD & GTZ, Damascus, Syria, pp. 37–48.

Benkherbache, N., Benniou, R., Merat, M., Mekhalfia, T. and Makhlouf, M. 2012. From minimum tillage to no tillage, reaction of Waha, variety of durum wheat in Algerian semi-arid region. *The Online Journal of Science and Technology* 2(3): 17–22.

Benlhabib, O., Yazar, A., Qadir, M., Lourenço, E. and Jacobsen, S. E. 2014. How can we improve Mediterranean cropping systems? *Journal of Agronomy and Crop Science* 200: 325–332. doi: 10.1111/jac.12066

Ben-Salem, H., Zaibet, L. and Ben-Hammouda, M. 2006. Perspectives de l'adoption du semis direct en Tunisie: Une approche économique. *Options Méditerranéennes, Série A* 69: 69–75.

Bessam, F. and Mrabet, R. 2003. Long-term changes in soil organic matter under conventional and no-tillage systems in semiarid Morocco. *Soil Use and Management* 19(2): 139–143.

Bohoussou, Y. N. D., Kou, Y.-H., Yu, W.-B., Lin, B. J., Virk, A. L., Zhao, X., Dang, Y. P. andZhang, H. L. 2022. Impacts of the components of conservation agriculture on soil organic carbon and total nitrogen storage: a global meta-analysis. *Science of the Total Environment* 842, 156822. doi: 10.1016/j.scitotenv.2022.156822

Bonzanigo, L., Giupponi, C. and Moussadek, R. 2016. Conditions for the adoption of conservation agriculture in Central Morocco: an approach based on Bayesian network modeling. *Italian Journal of Agronomy* 11(1s): 665. doi: 10.4081/ija.2016.665

Bossio, D. A., Cook-Patton, S. C., Ellis, P. W., Fargione, J., Sanderman, J., Smith, P., Wood, S., Zomer, R. J., von Unger, M., Emmer, I. M. and Griscom, B. W. 2020. The role of soil carbon in natural climate solutions. *Nature Sustainability* 3(5): 391–398. doi: 10.1038/s41893-020-0491-z

Boughlala, M., El Gharras, O. and Dahan, R. 2011. Economic comparison between conventional and no-tillage farming systems in Morocco. *Hommes: Terre et Eaux* 149–150: 35–39.

Bouguendouz, A. 2010. Effet de trois itinéraires techniques sur l'élaboration du rendement de l'orge (*Hordeum vulgare* L.) sous conditions semi-arides des hautes plaines Sétifiennes. *Options Méditerranéennes* 96: 83–89.

Boulal, H., El Mourid, M., Ketata, H. and Nefzaoui, A. 2014. Conservation agriculture in North Africa: past and the future. In: Jat, R. A., Sahrawat, K. L. and Kassam, A. H. (eds.) *Conservation Agriculture: Global Prospects and Challenges*. CABI Publishing, Boston, MA, pp. 293–310.

Bouzrara, S., Ould Ferroukh, M. E. H. and Bouguendouz, A. 2011. Influence du semis direct et des techniques culturales simplifiées sur les propriétés d'un sol de la ferme pilote Sersour (Sétif). *Options Méditerranéennes : Série A* 96: 123–129.

Brahim, N., Gallali, T. and Bernoux, M. 2009. Effects of agronomic practices on the soil carbon storage potential in northern Tunisia. *Asian Journal of Agricultural Research* 3(3): 55–66.

Brahim, N., Ibrahim, H. and Gallali, T. 2022. Organic carbon stocks evaluation after three years of no-tillage practice in a Vertisol, northern Tunisia. In: Çiner, A., Grab, S., Jaillard, E., Doronzo, D., Michard, A., Rabineau, M. and Chaminé, H. I. (eds.) *Recent Research on Geomorphology, Sedimentology, Marine Geosciences and Geochemistry*. Advances in Science, Technology & Innovation. Springer, Cham, pp. 31–33. doi: 10.1007/978-3-030-72547-1_7

Brouziyne, Y., Abouabdillah, A., Hirich, A., Bouabid, R., Zaaboul, R. and Benaabidate, L. 2018. Modeling sustainable adaptation strategies toward a climate-smart agriculture in a Mediterranean watershed under projected climate change scenarios. *Agricultural Systems* 162: 154–163.

Brown, B., Nuberg, I. and Llewellyn, R. 2017. Stepwise frameworks for understanding the utilisation of conservation agriculture in Africa. *Agricultural Systems* 153: 11–22.

Bünemann, E., Bongiorno, G., Bai, Z., Creamer, R., De Deyn, G., de Goede, R., Fleskens, L., Geissen, V., Kuyper, T. W., Mader, P., Pulleman, M., Sukkel, W., van Groenigen, J. W. and Brussaard, L. 2018. Soil quality –a critical review. *Soil Biology and Biochemistry* 120: 105–125.

Campbell, B. M., Beare, D. J., Bennett, E. M., Hall-Spencer, J. M., Ingram, J. S. I., Jaramillo, F., Ortiz, R., Ramankutty, N., Sayer, J. A. and Shindell, D. 2017. Agriculture production as a major driver of the Earth system exceeding planetary boundaries. *Ecology and Society* 22(4): 8. doi: 10.5751/ES-09595-220408

Chaieb, N., Rezgui, M., Ayed, S., Bahri, H., Cheikh M'hamed, H., Rezgui, M. and Annabi, M. 2020. Effects of tillage and crop rotation on yield and quality parameters of durum wheat in Tunisia. *Journal of Animal and Plant Sciences* 44(2): 7654–7676.

Cheikh M'hamed, H., Angar, H. and Annabi, M. 2014. Conservation agriculture as alternative to reduce impact of climate change for smallholder in North Africa: Tunisian case. In: *6ème Congrès mondial sur l'agriculture de conservation*, 22–25 June, Winnipeg, Canada.

Cheikh M'hamed, H., Annabi, M., Ben Youssef, S. and Bahri, H. 2016. L'agriculture de conservation est un système de production permettant d'améliorer l'efficience de l'utilisation de l'eau et de la fertilité du sol. *Annales de l'INRAT* 89: 68–71.

Cheikh M'hamed, H., Bahri, H. and Annabi, M. 2018. Conservation agriculture in Tunisia: historical, current status and future perspectives for rapid adoption by smallholder farmers. In: *Second African Congress on Conservation Agriculture*, 9–12 October, Johannesburg, South Africa, pp. 57–60.

Chennafi, H., Hannachi, A., Touahria, O., El Abidine Fellahi, Z., Makhlouf, M. and Bouzerzour, H. 2011. Tillage and residue management effect on durum wheat [*Triticum turgidum* (L.) thell. ssp. turgidum conv. durum (Desf.) MacKey] growth and yield under semi-arid climate. *Advances in Environmental Biology* 5(10): 3231–3240.

Chibani, R., Bahri, H., Annabi, M. and Cheikh M'hamed, H. 2018. L'agriculture de conservation comme alternative pour améliorer la résistance des sols à l'érosion hydrique dans le Nord de la Tunisie. *Annales de l'INRAT* 91: 86–97.

Chouen, S., Quillet, J. C. and Rojat, D. 2004. Semis direct et techniques conventionnelles en Tunisie: comparison des couts de production sur des exploitations types et éléments d'analyse économique. In: *AFD/ CIRAD/CTC/ESAK/ICARDA, Deuxièmes rencontres méditerranéennes sur le semis direct*. Tabarka, Tunisia, pp. 116–120.

Creamer, R. E., Barel, J. M., Bongiorno, G. and Zwetsloot, M. J. 2022. The life of soils: integrating the who and how of multifunctionality. *Soil Biology and Biochemistry* 166: 108561. doi: 10.1016/j. soilbio.2022.108561

Cusser, S., Bahlai, C., Swinton, S. M., Robertson, G. P. and Haddad, N. M. 2020. Long-term research avoids spurious and misleading trends in sustainability attributes of no-till. *Global Change Biology* 26(6): 3715–3725.

Dang, Y. P., Page, K. L., Dalal, R. C. and Menzies, N. W. (2020). No-till farming systems for sustainable agriculture: an overview. In: Dang, Y., Dalal, R. and Menzies, N. (eds) *No-Till Farming Systems for Sustainable Agriculture: Challenges and Opportunities*. Springer, Cham, pp. 533–565. https://doi. org/10.1007/978-3-030-46409-7_1

Degrande, A. and Benoudji, C. 2017. L'agriculture de Conservation Repensée: contextualiser l'innovation pour la Résilience au Tchad et au Soudan. BRACED Innovation for Resilience Case Studies. Available at: https://www.researchgate.net/publication/323799498_Rethinking_Conservation_Agriculture_ Contextualisation_of_Innovation_for_Resilience_in_Chad_and_Sudan

Desa, U. N. 2016. Transforming our world: the 2030 agenda for sustainable development. United Nations, New York, NY.

Devkota, M., Devkota, K. P. and Kumar, S. 2022. Conservation agriculture improves agronomic, economic, and soil fertility indicators for a clay soil in a rainfed Mediterranean climate in Morocco. *Agricultural Systems* 201: 103470. doi: 10.1016/jgsy.2022.103470

Devkota, M., Singh, Y., Yigezu, Y. A., Bashour, I., Mussadek, R. and Mrabet, R. 2021. Conservation agriculture in the drylands of the Middle East and North Africa (MENA) region: past trend, current opportunities, challenges, and future outlook. *Advances in Agronomy* 172: 253–305. doi: 10.1016/bs.agron.2021.11.001

Devkota, M. and Yigezu, Y. A. 2020. Explaining yield and gross margin gaps for sustainable intensification of the wheat-based systems in a Mediterranean climate. *Agricultural Systems* 185: 102946. doi: 10.1016/j. agsy.2020.102946

Dimanche, P. H. 1997. Impacts des différents itinéraires techniques de travail du sol sur la dégradation des sols argileux dans la région de Meknès, Maroc. PhD Thesis. Louvain-La-Neuve, Belgique, 268 p.

Djouadi, K., Mekliche, A., Dahmani, S., Ladjiar, N. I., Abid, Y., Silarbi, Z., Hamadache, A. and Pisante, M. 2021. Durum wheat yield and grain quality in early transition from conventional to conservation tillage in semi-arid Mediterranean conditions. *Agriculture* 11: 711. doi: 10.3390/agriculture11080711

Eekhout, J. P. C. and de Vente, J. 2022. Global impact of climate change on soil erosion and potential for adaptation through soil conservation. *Earth-Science Reviews* 226: 103921. doi: 10.1016/j.earscirev. 2022.103921

El Gharras, O., Ait Lhaj, A. and Idrissi, M. 2004. Développement d'un semoir non-labour industriel. In: *2èmes rencontres méditerranéennes sur le semis direct*. Tabarka, Tunisia.

El Gharras, O., El Mourid, M. and Boulal, H. 2017. Conservation agriculture in North Africa: experiences, achievements and challenges. In: Kassam, A. H., Mkomwa, S. and Friedrich, T. (eds.) *Conservation Agriculture for Africa: Building Resilient Farming Systems in a Changing Climate*. CAB International, Wallingford, UK, pp. 127–138.

El Gharras, O. and Idrissi, M. 2006. Contraintes technologiques au développement du semis direct au Maroc. Troisièmes rencontres méditerranéennes du semis direct (Zaragoza): CIHEAM. *Options méditerranéennes: série A. Séminaires Méditerranéens* 69: 121–124.

El Mekkaoui, A., Moussadek, R., Mrabet, R., Chakiri, S., Douaik, A., Ghanimi, A. and Zouahri, A. 2021. The conservation agriculture in northwest of Morocco (Merchouch area): the impact of no-till systems on physical properties of soils in semi-arid climate. *E3S Web of conferences* 234: 00037. doi: 10.1051/ e3sconf/202123400037

El-Areed, S. R. H. 2019. Improvement of yellow corn productivity under water deficit stress using conservation agriculture system. *Egyptian Journal of Plant Breeding* 23(1): 11–27.

El-mrini, S., Aboutayeb, R. and Zouhri, A. 2022. Effect of initial C/N ratio and turning frequency on quality of final compost of turkey manure and olive pomace. *Journal of Engineering and Applied Science*, 69(1): 1–20.

El-Shater, T. and Yigezu, Y. A. 2021. Can retention of crop residues on the field be justified on socio-economic grounds in mixed crop-livestock production systems of the drylands? *Agronomy* 11(8): 1465.

Elsoury, H. A., Shouman, A. E., Abdelrazek, S. and Elkony, H. M. 2015. Soil enzymes and microbial activity as influenced by tillage and fertilization in wheat production. *Egyptian Journal of Soil Science* 55: 53–65.

Errouissi, F., Ben Moussa-Machraoui, S., Ben-Hammouda, M. and Nouiraab, S. 2011. Soil invertebrates in durum wheat (*Triticum durum* L.) cropping system under Mediterranean semi arid conditions: a comparison between conventional and no-tillage management. *Soil and Tillage Research* 112(2): 122–132.

FAO 2010. Conservation agriculture and sustainable crop intensification in Lesotho. Integrated Crop Management (Vol. 10). FAO, Rome, Italy.

FAO 2017. Strategic work of FAO for sustainable food and agriculture. FAO, Rome, Italy, p. 28.

FAO 2018. Regional analyses of the nationally determined contributions of countries in southern-eastern Europe and Central Asia: gaps and opportunities in the agriculture sectors. Available at: https://www.fao.org/3/CA2518EN/ca2518en.pdf

FAO, IFAD, UNICEF, WFP and WHO 2019. The state of food security and nutrition in the world 2019. Safeguarding against economic slowdowns and downturns. FAO, Rome.

FAO and ITPS 2015. Status of the world's soil resources. Available at: https://www.fao.org/3/a-i5199e.pdf

FAO and ITPS 2017. Voluntary guidelines for sustainable soil management. Available at: https://www.fao.org/3/a-bl813e.pdf

FAO and ITPS 2020. Protocol for the assessment of sustainable soil management. FAO, Rome. Available at: https://www.fao.org/fileadmin/user_upload//GSP/SSM/SSM_Protocol_EN_006.pdf

Fellahi, Z., Hannachi, A., Chennafi, H., Makhlouf, M. and Bouzerzour, H. 2013. Effets des résidus et du travail du sol sur la production de la biomasse et le rendement du blé dur (*Triticum durum* Desf., variété MBB) en lien avec l'utilisation de l'eau dans les conditions semi-arides des Hautes Plaines Sétifiennes. *Revue de l'Agriculture* 06: 03–11.

Fenni, M. 2013. Socio-economic and environmental benefits of direct seeding of wheat in Sétif high plains (north east of Algeria). In: *WEI International Academic Conference*, Istanbul, Turkey. West East Institute (WEI), Westchester, PA, p. 47.

FERT 2016. Le semis direct en Tunisie: situation actuelle et perspectives. Fert-APAD-ATAE-INGC. 66 pp.

FERT 2018. L'agriculture de conservation au Maghreb: les agriculteurs font évoluer leurs pratiques. Available at: https://www.agricord.org/sites/default/files/2018_med_c api_ac_maghreb_fr.pdf.

Fouzai, A., Smaoui, M., Frija, A. and Dhehibi, B. 2018. Adoption of conservation agriculture technologies by smallholder farmers in the semiarid region of Tunisia: resource constraints and partial adoption. *Journal of New Sciences, Sustainable Livestock Management* 6(1): 105–114.

Giller, K. E., Andersson, J. A., Corbeels, M., Kirkegaard, J., Mortensen, D., Erenstein, O. and Vanlauwe, B. 2015. Beyond conservation agriculture. *Frontiers in Plant Science* 6: 870.

Guesmi, H., Ben Salem, H. and Moujahed, N. 2019. Integration crop-livestock under conservation agriculture system. *Journal of New Sciences, Agriculture and Biotechnology* 65(1): 4061–4065.

Hajer, G., Cyrine, D., Salah, B. Y., Mohamed, C., Sourour, A., Hichem, B. S. and Nizar, M. 2020. Wheat stubble from conventional or conservation agriculture grazed by ewes: biomass dynamics and animal performances. *Animal Nutrition and Feed Technology* 20(2): 187–200.

Hajjaj, B. and Mrabet, R. 2022. Gestion des adventices en agriculture de conservation. In: Bouhache, M. and Taleb, A. (eds.) *Gestion des Adventices des Principales Cultures au Maroc*. Association Marocaine de Protection des Plantes, pp. 219–240.

Hamim, A., Essahat, A., El Othmani, S., Douiek, A., Mrabet, R., Duponnois, R. and Hafidi, M. 2012. Etude de l'effet de la rotation et du travail du sol sur la densité spécifique des champignons mycorhiziens arbusculaires. International Congress: Microbial Biotechnology for Development (MICROBIOD 2), Marrakech, Morocco.

Harb, O. M., Abd El-Hay, G. H., Hager, M. A. and Abou El-Enin, M. M. 2015. Studies on conservation agriculture in Egypt. *Annals of Agricultural Sciences* 60: 105–112.

Harb, O. M., Abd El-Hay, G. H., Hager, M. A. andAbou El-Enin, M. M. 2016. Calibration and validation of DSSAT V.4.6.1, CERES and CROPGRO Models for simulating no-tillage in Central Delta, Egypt. *Agrotechnology* 5: 143. doi: 10.4172/2168-9881.1000143

Hou, D. 2020. Knowledge sharing and adoption behaviour: an imperative to promote sustainable soil use and management. *Soil Use and Management* 36(4): 557–560. doi: 10.1111/sum.12648

Hou, D., Bolan, N. S., Tsang, D. C. W., Kirkham, M. B. and O'Connor, D. 2020. Sustainable soil use and management: an interdisciplinary and systematic approach. *Science of the Total Environment* 729: 138961. doi: 10.1016/j.scitotenv.2020.138961

Ibrahim, M. and Lal, R. 2013. Climate change and land use in the WANA region with a specific reference to Morocco. In: Sivakumar, M. V. K., Lal, R., Selvaraju, R. and Hamdan, I. (eds.) *Climate Change and Food Security in West Asia and North Africa*. Springer, New York, pp. 89–113.

Idoudi, Z., Louahdi, N., Devkota, M., Djender, Z., Frija, A. and Rekik, M. 2020. Public-private partnership for enhanced conservation agriculture practices: the case of Boudour zero-till seeder in Algeria. International Center for Agricultural Research in the Dry Areas (ICARDA), Lebanon.

Jedd, T., Fragaszy, S. R., Knutson, C., Hayes, M. J., Fraj, M. B., Wall, N., Svoboda, M. and McDonnell, R. 2020. Drought management norms: is the Middle East and North Africa region managing risks or crises? *Journal of Environment & Development* 30(1): 3–40. doi: 10.1177/1070496520960204

Jemai, I., Ben Aissa, N., Ben Guirat, S. and Gallali, T. 2012. On-farm assessment of tillage impact on the vertical distribution of soil organic carbon and structural soil properties in a semiarid region in Tunisia. *Journal of Environmental Management* 113: 488–494.

Jemai, I., Ben Aissa, N., Ben Guirat, S., Ben-Hammouda, M. and Gallali, T. 2013. Impact of three and seven years of no-tillage on the soil water storage, in the plant root zone, under a dry subhumid Tunisian climate. *Soil and Tillage Research* 126: 26–33.

Kane, D. A., Bradford, M. A., Fuller, E., Oldfield, E. E. and Woo, S. A. 2021. Soil organic matter protects US maize yields andlowers crop insurance payouts under drought. *Environmental Research Letters* 16: 044018.

Kassam, A., Derpsch, R., and Friedrich, T. 2020. Development of conservation agriculture systems globally. In *Advances in Conservation Agriculture*, Volume 1—Systems and Science; Kassam, A., Ed.; Burleigh Dodds: Cambridge, UK, Chapter 2; pp. 31–86

Kassam, A., Friedrich, T., and Derpsch, R. 2022. Successful experiences and lessons from conservation agriculture worldwide. *Agronomy*, 12: 769. https://doi.org/10.3390/agronomy12040769

Kassam, A., Friedrich, T., and Derpsch, R. 2019. Global spread of conservation agriculture. *International Journal of Environmental Studies*, 76: 29–51.

Kassam, A. and Kassam, L. 2020a. The need for conservation agriculture. In: Kassam, A. (ed.) *Advances in Conservation Agriculture. Volume 1: Systems and Science*. Burleigh Dodds, Cambridge, UK, pp. 1–30.

Kassam, A. and Kassam, L. 2020b. Paradigms of agriculture. In: Kassam, A. and Kassam, L. (eds.) *Rethinking Food and Agriculture. New Ways Forward*. Elsevier, Amsterdam, pp. 181–218.

Kassam, A. and Kassam, L. 2020c. Practice and benefits of conservation agriculture. In: Kassam, A. (ed.) *Advances in Conservation Agriculture. Volume 2: Systems and Science*. Burleigh Dodds, Cambridge, UK, pp. 1–36.

Keesstra, S. D., Bouma, J., Wallinga, J., Tittonell, P., Smith, P., Cerdà, A., Montanarella, L., Quinton, J. N., Pachepsky, Y. and van der Putten, W. H. 2016. The significance of soils and soil science towards realization of the United Nations Sustainable Development Goals. *Soil* 2: 111–128.

Labad, R. and Hartani, T. 2016. Analyse des performances de quelques exploitations agricoles céréalières en semis direct dans la wilaya de Sétif. *Revue de l'Agriculture* 1: 78–81.

Labad, R., Hartani, T., Belguet, H., Bendada, H., Louahdi, N. and Taibi, M. 2018b. Evaluation de la biologie du sol sous l'effet du traitement chimique en semis direct dans une zone semi-aride de l'Algérie. *Agriculture Journal* 9(1): 46–55.

Labad, R., Hartani, T. and Shinde, G. U. 2018a. Optimum herbicide dose management in direct seeding for cereals production: case of semi-arid area of Algeria. *Journal of Agronomy* 17: 99–105.

Labad, R., Hartani, T. and Shinde, G. U. 2019. Effect of weed treatment on cereal yield in direct seeding: achallenge between soil pollution and seeds quality. *Indian Journal of Agricultural Research* 54: 101–106. doi: 10.18805/IJARe.A-304

Labbaci, T., Dugué, P., Kemoun, H. and Rollin, D. 2015. Innovation et action collective: le semis direct des cultures pluviales Au Moyen Sébou (Maroc). *Cahiers Agricultures* 24(2): 76–83.

Lagacherie, P., Álvaro-Fuentes, J., Annabi, M., Bernoux, M., Bouarfa, S., Douaoui, A., Grünberger, O., Mekki, I., Montanarella, L., Mrabet, R., Sabir, M. and Raclot, D. 2017. Managing Mediterranean soil resources under global change: expected trends and mitigation strategies. *Regional Environmental Change* 18: 663. doi: 10.1007/s10113-017-1239-9

Laghrour, M., Moussadek, R., Mekkaoui, M., Zouahri, A., Dahan, R. and El Mourid, M. 2015. Impact of no-tillage on physical proprieties of a clay soil in Central Morocco. *Journal of Material and Environmental Science* 6: 391–396.

Laghrour, M., Moussadek, R., Mrabet, R., Dahan, R., El Mourid, M., Zouahri, A. and Mekkaoui, M. 2016. Long and midterm effect of conservation agriculture on soil properties in dry areas of Morocco. *Applied and Environmental Soil Science* 2016: 1–9. doi: 10.1155/2016/6345765

Laghrour, M., Moussadek, R., Mrabet, R. and Mekkou, M. 2019. Effet à moyen et à long terme du semis direct sur la matière organique, la stabilité structurale et la compaction des sols argileux au Maroc. *Revue Marocaine des Sciences Agronomiques et Vétérinaires* 7(2): 356–362.

Lahlou, S., Ouadia, M., Malam Issa, O., Le Bissonnais, O. Y. and Mrabet, R. 2005. Modification de la porosité du sol sous les techniques culturales de conservation en zone semi-aride Marocaine. *Etude et Gestion des sols* 12(1): 69–76.

Lal, R. 2015. Sequesteri ng carbon and increasing productivity by conservation agriculture. *Journal of Soil and Water Conservation* 70(3): 55A–62A. doi: 10.2489/jswc.70.3.55A

Lal, R. 2020a. Integrating animal husbandry with crops and trees. *Frontiers in Sustainable Food Systems* 4: 113. doi: 10.3389/fsufs.2020.00113

Lal, R. 2020b. Soil organic matter content and crop yield. *Journal of Soil and Water Conservation* 75(2): 27A–32A. doi: 10.2489/jswc.75.2.27A

Lassaletta, L., Billen, G., Grizzetti, B., Garnier, J., Leach, A. M. and Galloway, J. N. 2014. Food and feed trade as a driver in the global nitrogen cycle: 50-year trends. *Biogeochemistry* 118: 225–241. doi: 10.1007/s10533-013-9923-4

Lembaid, I., Moussadek, R., Mrabet, R. and Bouhaouss, A. 2022. Modeling soil organic carbon changes under alternative climatic scenarios and soil properties using DNDC model at a semi-arid Mediterranean environment. *Climate* 10(2): 23. doi: 10.3390/cli10020023

Lembaid, I., Moussadek, R., Mrabet, R., Douaik, A. and Bouhaouss, A. 2021. Modeling the effects of farming management practices on soil organic carbon stock under two tillage practices in a semi-arid region, Morocco. *Heliyon* 7(1): e05889. https://doi.org/10.1016/j.heliyon.2020.e05889

Magnan, N., Lybbert, T. J., Mrabet, R. and Fadlaoui, A. 2011. The quasi-option value of delayed input use under catastrophic drought risk: the case of no-till in Morocco. *American Journal of Agricultural Economics* 93(2): 498–504.

Martin, G., Moraine, M., Ryschawy, J., Magne, M. A., Asai, M., Sarthou, J. P., Duru, M. and Therond, O. 2016. Crop-livestock integration beyond the farm level: a review of prospects and issues. *Agronomy for Sustainable Development* 36: 53. doi: 10.1007/s13593-016-0390-x

MedECC 2020. *Climate and Environmental Change in the Mediterranean Basin – Current Situation and Risks for the Future. First Mediterranean Assessment Report* [Cramer, W., Guiot, J. and Marini, K. (eds.)]Union for the Mediterranean, Plan Bleu, UNEP/MAP, Marseille, France, 632 pp. ISBN: 978-2-9577416-0-1. doi: 10.5281/zenodo.4768833

M'hedhbi, K., Ben-Hammouda, M., Letoumy, P., Nasr, K., Ali Hannachi, M., Chouen, S., Mahouachi, M. A., Jarrahi, T., Nasraoui, R., Zaouani, R. and Fakhfakh, M. M. 2004. Résultats agronomiques de production pour les semis directs et conventionnels. In: *Deuxièmes rencontres méditerranéennes sur le semis direct.* Tabarka, Tunisia, pp. 87–89.

Michler, J. D., Baylis, K., Arends-Kuenning, M. and Mazvimavi, K.2019. Conservation agriculture and climate resilience. *Journal of Environmental Economics and Management* 93: 148–169.

Montanarella, L. 2007. The EU thematic strategy for soil protection and its implications in the Mediterranean. In: Zdruli, P. and Trisorio Liuzzi, G. (eds.) *Status of Mediterranean Soil Resources: Actions Needed to Support their Sustainable Use. Mediterranean Conference*, Tunis, Tunisia, 26–31 May. MEDCOASTLAND Publications, Bari.

Montanarella, L. 2015. Govern our soils. *Nature.* 528: 32–33.

Montgomery, D. R. 2007. *Dirt: The Erosion of Civilizations.* University of California Press, Berkeley and Los Angeles, 285 pp.

Mouelhi, B., Slim, S., Arfaoui, S., Boussalmi, A. and Ben Jeddi, F. 2016. Effet du mode de semis et de la rotation culturale sur les paramètres de croissance et les composantes de rendement du blé dur (*Triticum durum* Desf.) variété "Karim ". *Journal of New Sciences, Agriculture and Biotechnology* 28(11): 1638–1648.

Moujahed, N., Abidi, S., Ben Youssef, S., Darej, C., Chakroun, M. and Ben Salem, H. 2015. Effect of stocking rate on biomass variation and lamb performances for barley stubble in Tunisian semi arid region and under conservation agriculture conditions. *African Journal of Agricultural Research* 10(50): 4584–4590.

Moussadek, R. 2012. Impacts de l'agriculture de conservation sur les propriétés et la productivité des vertisols du Maroc Central. PhD Dissertation. Ghent University, Belgium.

Moussadek, R., Iaaich, H., Mrabet, R., Dahan, R. and El Mourid, M. 2016. Land suitability to conservation agriculture in Central Morocco. Morocco Collaborative Grant Program report. INRA-ICARDA, 157 pp.

Moussadek, R., Mrabet, R., Dahan, R., Douaik, A., Verdoodt, A., Van Ranst, E. and Corbeels, M. 2011a. Effect of tillage practices on the soil carbon dioxide flux during fall and spring seasons in a Mediterranean Vertisol. *Journal of Soil Science and Environmental Management* 2: 362–369.

Moussadek, R., Mrabet, R., Dahan, R., Zouahri, A., El Mourid, M. and Van Ranst, E. 2014. Tillage system affects soil organic carbon storage and quality in Central Morocco. *Applied and Environmental Soil Science* 2014: 1–8. doi: 10.1155/2014/654796

Moussadek, R., Mrabet, R., Zante, P., Lamachere, J. M., Pepin, Y., Le Bissonnais, Y., Ye, L., Verdoodt, A. and Van Ranst, E. 2011b. Impact of tillage and residue management on the soil properties and water erosion of a Mediterranean Vertisol. *Canadian Journal of Soil Science* 91: 627–635.

Mrabet, R. 1997. Crop residue management and tillage systems for water conservation in a semiarid area of Morocco. PhD Dissertation. Colorado State University, Fort Collins, CO. 220 pp.

Mrabet, R., 2000. Long-term no-tillage influence on soil quality and wheat production in semiarid Morocco. In: *Proceedings of the 15th ISTRO Conference Tillage at the Threshold of the 21st Century: Looking Ahead, Fort Worth, TX, USA*, 2–7 July 2000

Mrabet, R. 2002. Stratification of soil aggregation and organic matter under conservation tillage systems in Africa. *Soil and Tillage Research* 66: 119–128.

Mrabet, R. 2011a. Effects of residue management and cropping systems on wheat yield stability in a semiarid Mediterranean clay soil. *American Journal of Plant Sciences* 2(2): 202–216.

Mrabet, R. 2011b. No-tillage agriculture in West Asia and North Africa, In: Tow, P. G., Cooper, I. M., Partridge, I. and Birch, C. J. (eds.) *Rainfed Farming Systems*. Springer, Dordrecht, Netherlands, pp. 1015–1042.

Mrabet, R., Ibno-Namr, K., Bessam, F. and Saber, N. 2001a. Soil chemical quality changes and implications for fertilizer management after 11 years of no-tillage wheat production systems in semiarid Morocco. *Land Degradation & Development* 12(6): 505–517.

Mrabet, R., Lahlou, S., Le Bissonnais, Y. and Duval, O. 2004. Estimation de la stabilité structurale des sols semiarides marocains: influence des techniques culturales simplifiées. *Bull. du Réseau Erosion* 23: 405–415.

Mrabet, R., Moussadek, R., Fadlaoui, A., & van Ranst, E. (2012). Conservation agriculture in dry areas of Morocco. *Field Crops Research*, 132: 84–94. doi: 10.1016/j.fcr.2011.11.017

Mrabet, R. and Moussadek, R. 2022. Climate smart agriculture development in Africa. In: Mkomwa, S.and Kassam, A. (eds.) *Conservation Agriculture in Africa: Climate Smart Agricultural Development*. CABI, pp. 17–65. ISBN: 9781789245745. doi: 10.1079/9781789245745.0002. Available at: https://www.cabi.org/bookshop/book/9781789245769/

Mrabet, R., Moussadek, R., Devkota, M. and Lal, R. 2021. No-till farming in Maghreb Region: enhancing agricultural productivity and sequestrating carbon in soils. In Lal, R. (ed.) *Advances in Soil Science: Soil Organic Matter and Feeding the Future: Environmental and Agronomic Impacts*. CRC Press, Taylor and Francis Group, pp. 339–364. doi: 10.1201/9781003102762-14

Mrabet, R., Saber, N., El-Brahli, A., Lahlou, S. and Bessam, F. 2001b. Total, particulate organic matter and structural stability of a Calcixeroll soil under different wheat rotations and tillage systems in a semiarid area of Morocco. *Soil and Tillage Research* 57(4): 225–235.

Mrabet, R., Savé, R., Toreti, A., Caiola, N., Chentouf, M., Llasat, M. C., Mohamed, A. A. A., Santeramo, F. G., Sanz-Cobena, A. andTsikliras, A. 2020. Food. In: Cramer, W., Guiot, J. and Marini, K. (eds.) *Climate and Environmental Change in the Mediterranean Basin – Current Situation and Risks for the Future. First Mediterranean Assessment Report*. Union for the Mediterranean, Plan Bleu, UNEP/MAP, Marseille, France, pp. 237–264.

Mugandani, R., Mwadzingeni, L. and Mafongoya, P. 2021. Contribution of conservation agriculture to soil security. *Sustainability* 13: 9857. doi: 10.3390/su13179857

Mutua, J., Muriuki, J., Gachie, P., Bourne, M. and Capis, J. 2014. *Conservation Agriculture with Trees: Principles and Practice. A Simplified Guide for Extension Staff and Farmers*. ICRAF, Nairobi.

Nefzaoui A., Ketata H. and El Mourid M. 2012. Agricultural Technological and Institutional Innovations for Enhanced Adaptation to Environmental Change in North Africa. In: Stephen S. Young and Dr. Steven E. Silvern (eds), *International Perspectives on Global Environmental Change*. ISBN 978-953-307-815-1, p. 57-84

Nyanga, P. H., Umar, B. B., Chibamba, D., Mubanga, K. H., Kunda-Wamuwi, C. F. and Mushili, B. M. 2020. Reinforcing ecosystem services through conservation agriculture in sustainable food systems. In: Rusinamhodzi, L. (ed.) *The Role of Ecosystem Services in Sustainable Food Systems*. Academic Press, San Diego, CA, pp. 119–133.

Ogle, S. M., Alsaker, C., Baldock, J., Bernoux, M., Breidt, F. J., McConkey, B., Regina, K. and Vazquez-Amabile, G. G. 2019. Climate and soil characteristics determine where no-till management can store carbon in soils and mitigate greenhouse gas emissions. *Scientific Reports* 9(1): 11665. doi: 10.1038/s41598-019-47861-7

Oldfield, E. E., Bradford, M. A. and Wood, S. A. 2019. Global meta-analysis of the relationship between soil organic matter and crop yields. *Soil* 5: 15–32.

Palm, C., Blanco-Canqui, H., DeClerck, F., Gatere, L. and Grace, P. 2014. Conservation agriculture and ecosystem services: an overview. *Agriculture, Ecosystems & Environment* 187: 87–105.

Pretty, J. and Bharucha, Z. P. 2014. Sustainable intensification in agricultural systems. *Annals of Botany* 114: 1571–1596. doi: 10.1093/aob/mcu205

Raclot, D., Le Bissonnais, Y., Annabi, M., Sabir, M. and Smetanova, A. 2018. Main issues for preserving Mediterranean soil resources from water erosion under global change. *Land Degradation & Development* 29(3): 789–799.

Raunet, M., Richard, J. F. and Rojat, D. 2004. Premiers résultats d'introduction du semis direct sous couvert et lutte antiérosive en Tunisie. In Roose, E., De Noni, G., Prat, C., Ganry, F. and Bourgeon, G. (eds.) *Gestion de la biomasse, érosion et séquestration du carbone. Séquestration du carbone et érosion des sols*. Institut de recherche pour le développement, Paris, France, pp. 388–404.

Raunet, M., Seguy, L. and Rabots Fovet, C. 1998. Semis direct sur couverture vegétale permanente du sol: de la technique au concept. Available at: http://agroecologie.cirad.fr

Reicosky, D.C. 2011. Conservation agriculture: global environmental benefits of soil carbon management. In: *Fifth World Congress on Conservation Agriculture*, Brisbane, Australia. Vol. 1. ACIAR, Canberra, ACT, pp. 3–12.

Reicosky, D. C. 2015. Conservation tillage is not conservation agriculture. *Journal of Soil and Water Conservation* 70(5): 103A–108A.

Reicosky, D.C. 2020. Conservation agriculture systems: soil health and landscape management. In: Kassam, A. (ed.) *Advances in Conservation Agriculture. Volume 1: Science and Systems*. Burleigh Dodds, Cambridge, UK, pp. 87–154.

Rezgui, M., Mechri, M. and Gharbi, A. 2014. Effet du travail du sol sur les propriétés physiques du sol et sur le rendement de la fèverole et du blé dur cultivés sous les conditions semi-arides du Kef. *Annales de l'INRAT* 87: 1–10.

Rosenstock, T. S., Mpanda, M., Rioux, J., Aynekulua, E., Kimaro, A. A., Neufeldt, H., Shepherd, K. D. and Luedeling, E. 2014. Targeting conservation agriculture in the context of livelihoods and landscapes. *Agriculture, Ecosystems &Environment* 187: 47–51.

Rouabhi, A., Dhehibi, B., Laouar, A., Houmoura, M. and Sebaoune, F. 2016. Adoption perspectives of direct seeding in the high plains of Sétif-Algeria. *Journal of Agriculture and Environmental Sciences* 5: 53–64.

Rouabhi, A., Laouar, A., Mekhlouf, A. and Dhehibi, B. 2018. What are the factors affecting no-till adoption in the farming system of Sétif Province in Algeria?*Turkish Journal of Agriculture - Food Science and Technology* 6(6): 636–641.

Rouabhi, A., Laouar, A., Mekhlouk, A. and Dhehibi, B. 2019. Socioeconomic assessment of no-till in wheat cropping system: a case study in Algeria. *New Medit* 18(1): 53–64.

Rumpel, C., Amiraslani, F., Bossio, D., Chenu, C., Henry, B., Espinoza, A. F., Koutika, L., Ladha, J., Madari, B., Minasny, B., Olaleye, A. O., Shirato, Y., Sall, S. N., Soussana, J.-F. and Varela-Ortega, C. 2022. The role of soil carbon sequestration in enhancing human resilience in tackling global crises including pandemics. Soil Security 8: 100069. doi: 10.1016/j.soisec.2022.100069

Rusinamhodzi, L. 2020. Managing crop rotations in no-till farming systems. In: Dang, Y., Dalal, R. and Menzies, N. (eds.) *No-Till Farming Systems for Sustainable Agriculture: Challenges and Opportunities*. Springer, Cham, pp. 21–32. doi: 10.1007/978-3-030-46409-7_2

Sabir, M., Laouina, A., Morsli, B. and Annabi, M. 2022. Institutional and technical efforts for the soil and water conservation in North Africa. In: Li, R., Napier, T. L., El-Swaify, S. A., Sabir, M. and Rienzi, E. (eds.) *Global Degradation of Soil and Water Resources*. Springer, Singapore, pp. 49–59. doi: 10.1007/978-981-16-7916-2_5

Sanz-Cobena, A., Lassaletta, L., Aguilera, E., del Prado, A., Garnier, J., Billen, G., Iglesias, A., Sánchez, B., Guardia, G., Abalos, D., Plaza-Bonilla, D., Puigdueta-Bartolomé, I., Moral, R., Galán, E., Arriaga, H., Merino, P., Infante-Amate, J., Meijide, A., Pardo, G., Álvaro-Fuentes, J., Gilsanz, C., Báez, D., Doltra, J., González-Ubierna, S., Cayuela, M. L., Menéndez, S., Díaz-Pinés, E., Le-Noë, J., Quemada, M., Estellés, F., Calvet, S., van Grinsven, H. J. M., Westhoek, H., Sanz, M. J., Gimeno, B. S., Vallejo, A. andSmith, P. 2017. Strategies for greenhouse gas emissions mitigation in Mediterranean agriculture: a review. *Agriculture, Ecosystems & Environment* 38: 5–24. doi: 10.1016/j.agee.2016.09.038

Schjønning, P., Jensen, J. L., Bruun, S., Jensen, L. S., Christensen, B., Munkholm, L., Oelofse, M., Baby, S. and Knudsen, L. 2018. The role of soil organic matter for maintaining crop yields: evidence for a renewed conceptual basis. In: Sparks, D. L. (ed.) *Advances in Agronomy*. Vol.150. Academic Press, San Diego, CA, pp. 35–79.

Shaalan, A. H., Amer, S. and Khalil, H. E. 2022. Enhancement of wheat productivity under different levels of tillage, seeding rate and nitrogen sources in an arid region. *Alexandria Science Exchange Journal* 43(2): 271–287.

Sharkawy, S. F. T., Ali, A. A., Wassif, O. M. and Meselhy, A. A. 2022. Impact of conservation agriculture system on combating water erosion hazards at Wadi El-Raml, northwestern coast of Egypt. *Haya: The Saudi Journal of Life Sciences* 7(7): 210–219.

Smith, H. J., Trytsman, G., Nel, A. A., Strauss, J. A., Kruger, E., Mampholo, R. K., Van Coller, J. N., Otto, H., Steyn, J. G., Dreyer, I. D., et al. 2021. From theory to practice—key lessons in the adoption of Conservation Agriculture in South Africa. In Advances in Conservation Agriculture, Volume 3— Adoption and Spread; Kassam, A., Ed.; Burleigh Dodds: Cambridge, UK.

Souissi, A., Bahri, H., Cheikh M'hamed, H. and Annabi, M. 2018. Une méta-analyse sur les effets de la fertilisation azotée sur le rendement et l'efficience de l'utilisation de l'azote chez le blé dur en Tunisie. *Annales de l'INRAT* 91: 62–85.

Souissi, A., Bahri, H., Cheikh M'hamed, H., Chakroun, M., Benyoussef, S., Frija, A. and Annabi, M. 2020. Effect of tillage, previous crop and N fertilization on agronomic and economic performances of durum wheat (*Triticum durum* Desf.) under rainfed semi-arid environment. *Agronomy* 10: 1161. doi: 10.3390/agronomy10081161

Su, Y., Gabrielle, B., Beillouin, D. and Makowski, D. 2021b. High probability of yield gain through conservation agriculture in dry regions for major staple crops. *Scientific Reports* 11: 3344. doi: 10.1038/s41598-021-82375-1

Su, Y., Gabrielle, B. and Makowski, D. 2021a. A global dataset for crop production under conventional tillage and no tillage systems. *Scientific Data* 8: 33. doi: 10.1038/s41597-021-00817-x

Sustainable Food Trust 2015. Moroccan agriculture: facing the challenges of a divided system. Available at: https://sustainablefoodtrust.org/articles/moroccan-agriculture-facing-challenges-divided-system/

Taibi, H. H. Y., Smail-Saadoun, N., Labidi, S., Abdellaoui, K., Makhlouf, M., Laouar, A., Benouaret, C., Rezki-Sekhi, L., Boukais, A. B. and Sahraoui, A. L. 2020. The influence of no-till farming on durum wheat mycorrhization in a semi-arid region: a long-term field experiment. *Journal of Agricultural Science* 12(4): 77–96.

The Montpellier Panel 2013. Sustainable intensification: a new paradigm for African agriculture. Agriculture for Impact, London. Available at: https://ag4impact.org/wp-content/uploads/2014/07/Montpellier-Panel-Report-2013-Sustainable-Intensification-A-New-Paradigm-for-African-Agriculture-1.pdf

Tuel, A. and Eltahir, A. B. 2020. Why is the Mediterranean a climate change hot spot? *Journal of Climate* 33(14): 5829–5843. doi: 10.1175/JCLI-D-19-0910.1

Verhulst, N., Govaerts, B., Verachtert, E., Castellanos-Navarrete, A., Mezzalama, M., Wall, P., Decker, J. and Sayre, K. D. 2010. Conservation agriculture, improving soil quality for sustainable production systems? In: Lal, R. and Stewart, B. A. (eds.) *Advances in Soil Science: Food Security and Soil Quality*. CRC Press, Boca Raton, FL, pp. 137–208.

Wall, P., Thierfelder, C., Hobbs, P., Hellin, J. and Govaerts, B. 2020. Benefits of conservation agriculture. In: Kassam, A. (ed.) *Advances in Conservation Agriculture. Volume 2: Practice and Benefits*. Burleigh Dodds and Publishing Science, London, UK, p. 40.

Winkler, K., Fuchs, R., Rounsevell, M. and Herold, M. 2021. Global land use changes are four times greater than previously estimated. *Nature Communications* 12(1): 2501. doi: 10.1038/s41467-021-22702-2

WOCAT 2007. *Where the Land is Greener: Case Studies and Analyses of Soil and Water Conservation Initiatives Worldwide* [Liniger, H. and Critchley, W. (eds.)]CTA, FAO, UNEP, CDE, Stampfli, Bern.

World Bank 2017. Beyond scarcity: water security in the Middle East and North Africa [MENA Development Series].

Yigezu, Y. A., El-Shater, T., Boughlala, M., Bishaw, Z., Niane, A. A., Maalouf, F., Degu, W. T., Wery, J., Boutfiras, M. and Aw-Hassan, A. 2019. Legume-based rotations have clear economic advantages over cereal monocropping in dry areas. *Agronomy for Sustainable Development* 39: 58.

Yigezu, Y. A., El-Shater, T., Boughlala, M., Devkota, M., Mrabet, R. and Moussadek, R. 2021. Can an incremental approach be a better option in the dissemination of conservation agriculture? Some socioeconomic justifications from the drylands of Morocco. *Soil and Tillage Research* 212: 105067. doi: 10.1016/j.still.2021.105067

Zaghouane, O., Abdellaoui, Z. and Houassine, D. 2006. Quelles perspectives pour l'agriculture de conservation dans les zones céréalières en conditions algériennes? *Options Méditerranéennes. Série A* 69: 183–187.

Zdruli, P. 2012. Land resources of the Mediterranean: status, pressures, trends and impacts on future regional development. Land Degradation & Development 25: 373–384. doi: 10.1002/ldr.2150

Ziadat, F. M., Zdruli, P., Christiansen, S., Caon, L., Abdel Monem, M. and Fetsi, T. 2022. An overview of land degradation and sustainable land management in the Near East and North Africa. *Sustainable Agriculture Research* 11(1): 11–24.

Ziervogel, G. and Ericksen, P. J. 2010. Adapting to climate change to sustain food security. *Wiley Interdisciplinary Reviews: Climate Change* 1(4): 525–540.

15 A Case Study of Natural Farming in Mizoram, North-East India

Rahul Sadhukhan, L. Devarishi Sharma, Lalhmingsanga, Rojeet Thangjam, and Chingtham Chanbisana

15.1 INTRODUCTION

The north-eastern region, especially Mizoram, has tremendous potential for adaptation and popularization of natural farming. The north-eastern region (NER) of India comprises eight states, namely, Arunachal Pradesh, Assam, Manipur, Meghalaya, Mizoram, Nagaland, Tripura, and Sikkim, which range between 22°05′ and 29°30′N latitudes, 87°55′ and 97°24′E longitudes, and 500–1,500 m above mean sea level. The total geographical area of the region is 2.62 lakh (1 lakh=0.1 million) km², which occupies about 8% of the total area and 3.4% of the total cultivable area of India. The net sown area in this region is 4.13 million hectares (m ha), out of which approximately 1.3 m ha suffer from serious soil erosion problems (Yadav et al. 2020). Approximately 84% of the total soil of the north-eastern region is acidic and low in available P and Zn, but the total soil is medium to high in available nitrogen and potassium. The total geographical area of Mizoram is 21,081 sq. km. The studies using Remote Sensing and Geographical Information System (GIS) techniques confirmed that there are 74,644 ha of area with a slope of 0%–25% for potential cultivable area. The net cultivated area (WRC areas) is only 15,620 ha and the remaining areas are 59,024 ha. The farmers of Mizoram are totally dependent on organic manures rather than synthetic fertilizers. As we know, the use of synthetic/chemical fertilizer in the north-eastern region is usually 10–12 kg/ha (Singh et al. 2021).Natural farming, also referred to as "the Fukuoka Method", "the natural way of farming" or "do-nothing farming", is an ecological farming approach established by Masanobu Fukuoka (1913–2008). Fukuoka, a Japanese farmer and philosopher, introduced the term in his 1975 book, "The One-Straw Revolution". The title refers not to lack of effort but to the avoidance of manufactured inputs and equipment. Natural farming is related to fertility farming, organic farming, sustainable agriculture, agro-ecology, agro-forestry, eco-agriculture, and permaculture, but should be distinguished from biodynamic agriculture. In principle, practitioners of natural farming maintain that it is not a technique but a view, or a way of seeing ourselves as a part of nature, rather than separate from or above it. Accordingly, the methods themselves vary widely depending on culture and local conditions. Rather than offering a structured method, Fukuoka distilled the natural farming mindset into five principles: (i) no tillage, (ii) no fertilizer, (iii) no pesticides or herbicides, (iv) no weeding, and (v) no pruning. A young man helps harvest rice by hand at a natural farm in a production still from the film "Final Straw: Food, Earth, Happiness".

Before going to the adoption of natural farming in the north-eastern region, the strengths and challenges of natural farming should be surveyed.

DOI: 10.1201/9781003309581-18

15.2 STRENGTHS OF NORTH-EASTERN REGION ESPECIALLY IN MIZORAM FOR NATURAL FARMING

1. The jhum is the main pattern of cultivation. Maize and rice are the main food crops. Cash crops are sugarcane, tapioca, ginger, and cotton. Pigs and fowl are reared by many farmers. Exotic varieties and breeds of pigs and fowl have been introduced and have become popular among the villagers. The state has a considerable cultivation of fruit. Orange, lemon, kagzi lime, passion fruits, hatkora, jamir, pineapple, and papaya are the main horticulture crops (indiawris.gov.in).
2. The north-eastern hill region accounts for 45% of total pineapple production in India. The total pineapple production area in Mizoram is 432 ha and production is 2,390 tonnes which is produced organically.
3. As the AgriExport Zone is already set up in Tripura for organic pineapple cultivation and in Sikkim for organic ginger cultivation, there are several opportunities for development of AgriExport Zone in Mizoram for the cultivation of maize, rice, bird's eye chilli, dragon fruits, and several vegetables organically following the principles of natural farming.
4. The north-eastern region is the fourth largest producer of orange, but Mizoram is also not lagging behind.
5. As we know, the north-eastern hill region is a thinly populated area (13–340 person/km^2, so there is a high potential for the cultivation of large acreages of land following organic/natural farming principles.
6. There are timely tested indigenous farming systems and indigenous technical knowledge in agriculture in north-eastern India, especially in Mizoram.
7. Approximately 18 lakhs of hectares of land in the north-eastern region is under 'Organic by Default'. So, it is easier to adopt natural farming in NER, especially in Mizoram.
8. North-eastern states have mega-biodiversity in different species that receive annual rainfall ranging from 2,000 to 11,000 mm, which helps in the widespread proliferation of plant biomass (shrubs, weeds, and other herbs). Those plant species may be used for mulching materials, fuels, and compost preparation.

15.3 CHALLENGES FOR NATURAL FARMING IN NORTH-EASTERN INDIA, ESPECIALLY IN MIZORAM

1. The basic need for natural farming is to identify the potential zones for its adoption.
2. There is an urgent need for research, development and extension for the promotion of natural farming in the north-eastern region, especially in Mizoram.
3. There is a lack of human resource development in the production and maintenance of bio-fertilizers, Jeevamrut, Panchagavya, vermicompost, and 'botanicals for pest control' etc.
4. Lack of proper infrastructure and the marketing chain of the products for natural farming.
5. Lack of high technical knowledge for post-harvest handling, processing, and value addition.

For the building up of soil fertility, natural farming requires an interim time period called conversion period. The conversion period is the time period when the whole farm, including livestock, becomes organic from the conventional farming system.

The duration of the conversion period may take 1–3 years based on the number of years the land has been put under conventional agriculture, cultivation type, and inputs used in the farm. As in Mizoram, shifting cultivation is very common, so the conversion period may be 5 years.

For natural farming, well-defined norms, procedures and packages of practices for the land preparation, application of natural inputs (e.g., seeds and organic manures), and other bio-inputs should conform to rigorous production guidelines in Mizoram, north-eastern India.

15.4   STANDARDS AND PROTOCOLS FOR CROP HUSBANDRY

1. Crop production under natural farming using on-farm input (based on choice of crops and varieties)
2. Maintenance of organic input management under natural farming
3. Landscaping under natural farming (including grassland, orchards, hedge rows, bushes, and forest land)
4. Conversion period of natural farming (based on the past 10 years of the land and existing ecological situation)
5. Diversity in crop production (including crop diversification and crop rotation).

15.5   STANDARDS AND PROTOCOLS FOR SOIL HEALTH MANAGEMENT

1. Soil health management policy under natural farming uses local bio-degradable microbial, plant, and animal-origin materials.
2. Fertilization Policy (including organic manure application of microbial, plant, and animal origin (compost, vermicompost, and FYM), green manure, compost, legume rotation, vermiwash, brahmaastra, jeevamruta, PSB, VAM and ITK based bio-fertilizer, viz., Azolla and BGA and cover crop.

15.6   STANDARDS AND PROTOCOLS FOR AGRONOMIC MANAGEMENT

Agronomic management of crop production under natural farming (maintaining cultural methods of crop production, organic inputs application for fertilization of crop, allelopathy, minimum tillage, zero tillage, land preparation by maintaining natural micro-climate, trap crop, catch crop in crop husbandry).

15.7   STANDARDS AND PROTOCOLS FOR PEST, DISEASE, AND WEED MANAGEMENT

Pest, disease and weed management (by using trap crop, catch crop, allelopathic effect, crop rotation and cultural method of pest control, Neemastra, Panchagavya, Herbal Kunapajala, smother crop, intercropping, push and pull theory, bioherbicide and ITK-based microbial bio-formulation and botanical pesticide, use of bio-agents (including insects, plants, and micro-organisms, viz., *Zygogramma bicolorata*, etc.) (Figures 15.1 and 15.2)

In Mizoram, the total population is 10.91 lakhs (2011 Census), which makes it the second least populated state in India. So, there is a good opportunity to adopt organic/natural farming in this state. Another opportunity for Mizoram is that every household has its own homestead garden for vegetable consumption as well as livestock consumption. The tribal communities of Mizoram are using local compost using the roughages. Nowadays, the local farmers show keen interest in the production of vermicompost from cow dung, pig manure, and poultry manure (Table 15.1).

So, in Mizoram, there is a knowledge gap for the adoption of organic farming as well as natural farming in the prevailing situation, but there is greater potential for adopting natural farming in Mizoram, NE India (Tables 15.2 and 15.3).

So, there is a good potential for the production of organic manures for the adoption of natural farming in Mizoram.

At Tuichhuahen village (Kolasib district), the existing cultivation of local *jhum*mimban (maize) lines was replaced by sweet corn under the project of the NEH region. Smt. Zonunsangi, Principal Investigator, successfully cultivated sweet corn (sole crop) replacing local mimban (corn) under slash and burn agriculture in the steep hill slopes without any fertilizer application or use of plant protection chemicals during the pre-Kharif season. Inspired by her success, the farmers in the

FIGURE 15.1 Intercropping of cowpea in the dragon fruit crop following natural farming in Thenzawl, Mizoram.

FIGURE 15.2 Growing of various landraces of maize organically by the tribal communities of Mizoram, north-eastern India.

TABLE 15.1
Knowledge Gap of Farmers on the Basis of the Organic Farming Practices (Chaudhary et al. 2013)

S. No.	Organic Farming Practices	Maximum Obtained Knowledge (Score)	Total Obtained Knowledge (Score)	Percentage of Knowledge Gap	Rank
1	Knowledge about concept of organic farming	180	152	15.56	IX
2	Use of bio-pesticides	180	110	38.88	III
3	Use of organic manure and crop residues	180	132	26.66	VII
4	Use of mechanical cultivation	180	122	32.22	VI
5	Use of vermicompost	180	148	17.77	VIII
6	Use of bio-fertilizers	180	116	35.55	V
7	Use of HaNPV	180	102	43.34	I
8	Use of NADEP compost	180	112	37.77	IV
9	Use of trichocards	180	106	41.12	II
	Overall knowledge gap	1,620	1,100	32.10	VI

Knowledge = $100 \times$ (Total obtained knowledge score)/(Maximum obtained knowledge score)

TABLE 15.2
Cultivation of Different Crops Organically in Mizoram

Name of the Districts of Mizoram	Crops/Items Grown	Potential Crops for Natural Farming
Champhai	Corn, grape, bamboo, ginger, chilli, honey, amla, pineapple	Corn, grape, bamboo, ginger, chilli, honey, amla, pineapple
Khawzawl	Ginger, maize, chilli, tumbu	Ginger, maize, chilli, tumbu
Aizawl West	Ginger, citrus, elephant foot yam, turmeric, sugarcane	Ginger, citrus, elephant foot yam, turmeric, sugarcane
Aizawl East	Banana, rosella, turmeric, hill broom grass, bamboo shoot, chilli, ginger, pineapple	Banana, rosella, turmeric, hill broom grass, bamboo shoot, chilli, ginger
Lunglei	Sesame, perilla, chilli, bamboo shoot, hill broom, passion fruit, maize	Sesame, perilla, chilli, bamboo shoot, hill broom, passion fruit, maize
Mamit	Turmeric, chilli, arecanut, ginger, sesame, bamboo	Turmeric, chilli, arecanut, ginger, sesame, bamboo
Kolasib	Amla, chilli, turmeric, hill broom, chilli, maize, ginger, arecanut	Amla, chilli, turmeric, hill broom, chilli, maize, ginger, arecanut
Serchhip	Amla, hill broom grass, ginger, chilli, sugarcane, banana, dragon fruit, honey	Amla, hill broom grass, ginger, chilli, sugarcane, banana, dragon fruit, honey
Siaha	Pineapple, hill broom grass, chilli, ginger, elephant foot yam, mango, anchiri, turmeric	Pineapple, hill broom grass, chilli, ginger, elephant foot yam, mango, anchiri, turmeric

nearby low-lying valley areas of Tuichhuahen village also adapted the standardized package of practices for growing the *Rabi* sweet corn in the rice fallows (September to February) as developed by the ICAR-Research Complex for NEH Region, Mizoram Centre.

The introduction of sweet corn cultivation during early 2018 resulted in a gradual expansion in the maize area, particularly under the *Rabi* sweet corn cultivation in the nearby streambed areas of Tuichhuahen village (29.3% increase over the past 2 years). Many of the regular large-scale sweet

TABLE 15.3

Livestock Population, Excreta Produced per Head and Dung Production per Animal per Year of Mizoram, 2002 (Parmar et al. 2018)

Animals	Animal Population (in thousands)	Dung Production per Animal per Year (Dry Weight Basis)	
		Range (tonne/year)	Average (tonne/year)
Cattle	33	0.4–1.8	1.10
Buffalo	5	0.8–1.9	1.35
Pigs	163	0.2–0.3	0.25
Sheep	1	0.1–0.2	0.15
Goat	16	0.1–0.2	0.15
Horses	2	0.4–0.6	0.5
Total poultry	1,307	0.14	0.14

corn growers (mostly October sown) harvested their produce (green tender cobs) periodically from the fourth week of January to the second fortnight of February in Tuichhuahen village.

Shri Vanlalruaii, one of the first farmers to adapt the sweet corn cultivation (replacing *Rabi* culti-vation of the local French bean– rajmah) became a model sweet corn grower in his village. He grows sweet corn crops in a large area on a commercial scale with a single sowing window (mid-October) to meet the huge market demand. He followed the nutrient management practices with a source of nutrients (FYM @ 5–10 t/ha) for growing *Rabi* sweet corn (Figures 15.3–15.11).

FIGURE 15.3   Sub-soil compaction leads to the anti-geotropic movement of radish in Mizoram. Natural farming may correct these graviences.

FIGURE 15.4 Growing of onions under natural farming in Thenzawl, Mizoram.

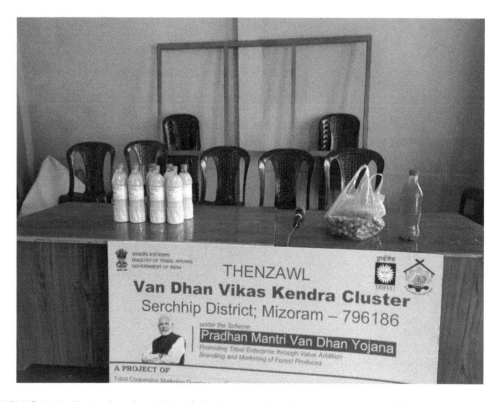

FIGURE 15.5 Production of amla juice following organic cultivation techniques in Mizoram.

FIGURE 15.6 Preparation of amla candy organically from the amla tree (gooseberry) under the natural farming of Thenzawl.

FIGURE 15.7 Amla candy preparation and sale for the market of Thenzawl.

FIGURE 15.8 Preparation and demonstration of vermicompost from goat manure in the Thenzawl village under the Serchhip district of Mizoram.

FIGURE 15.9 Production of honey organically from both stinged and stingless honey bees from Serchhip districts of Mizoram.

FIGURE 15.10 Poultry rearing organically using the locally available resources of Thenzawl, Mizoram.

FIGURE 15.11 Manually produced water harvesting structure for harvesting of rain water for natural farming.

In this modern world, the cost of agricultural inputs is skyrocketing, so it is the right time to convert all the agricultural waste into wealth. Agricultural waste like weeds, harvested crop residues, etc., or kitchen waste can be used to prepare vermicompost, which is a portion of good food for the earthworm. Before vermicomposting, a fine-tooth comb analysis should be done for the general requirements of the earthworms, substrates, benefit-cost ratio, appraisal of quality, pros and cons, etc.

A thorough study of vermicompost is crucial, as it will help the farmers as it is eco-friendly and will help keep the environment greener. The prices of chemical fertilizers and pesticides are soaring, which has become a burden for farmers. So using vermicompost can be an excellent, cost-effective option because it can replace chemical fertilizers in crop production. Above this, farmers can earn handsome money by selling organic products on the market. Organic agriculture products are in high demand as people worldwide have realized the gruesome effect of chemical fertilizers on human health. As a result, organic products have become essential for our existence.

Using agricultural waste to make compost is a better waste management method. In this aspect, a study was conducted to use agricultural waste as a useful product that could benefit agriculture. The experiment on vermicomposting using various agricultural wastes was performed to improve the quality of vermicompost.

On the contrary, the disposal of agro-waste is a constraint for most farmers. Most farmers burn the agro-waste in the field after harvest to save money; the smoke emanating from this burning makes our air quality inferior, which we consider gruesome for our environment. So to avert this situation, making compost or vermicompost from agro-waste is the best way to manage the waste efficiently. Based on the facts in the preceding paragraph, an experiment was carried out to convert agro-waste into a valuable product that can be useful for agriculture and farmers.

In Mizoram, agriculture depends mainly on imported agrochemical inputs, i.e., chemical fertilizers and pesticides, with high costs. Substituting these chemical fertilizers with organic inputs, such as vermicompost, can provide an impulse for organic farming systems. Therefore, a study was conducted to produce quality vermicompost from locally available organic waste materials using composting earthworms.

The treatment details are T_1=cow manure and fresh rice straw, T_2=cow dung and dry grass, T_3=cow manure and paddy residue from the mushroom unit, T_4=cow manure and chopped banana pseudostem, T_5=cow manure and a combination of fresh rice straw and dry grass, T_6=cow manure and a combination of paddy residue from the mushroom unit and chopped banana pseudostem, and T_7=cow manure and a combination of fresh rice straw, dry grass, paddy residue from the mushroom unit and chopped banana pseudostem.

In Mizoram conditions, vermicompost preparation from wild banana pseudostems is cost-effective and less laborious. The wild banana pseudostem is available extensively at the foothills and is wasted without being utilized properly (Figure 15.12).

15.8   COMPACTION

Cultivation of fruits and vegetables in the north-eastern hilly regions of India frequently faces myriad constraints, especially physical, chemical, and biological properties. The associated constraints are soil compaction (Patterson 1977; Craul 1992), transplant stress (Waring and Schlesinger 1985), water stress, elevated soil temperature, etc. (Craul 1992). Hence, many horticulturists from NE India face many confrontations in establishing fruits and vegetables owing to unfavorable conditions for plant growth. Therefore, planting crops in this area requires a thorough understanding of the soil's physical, chemical, and biological properties.

Compaction elevates the bulk density and plummets the total porosity among the soil's physical constraints (Patterson 1977). Not only this, but compaction also decreases oxygen and water levels, which in turn affect drainage (Chiapperini and Donnelly 1978). Compaction is one of the most common physical constraints in urban areas due to the construction of buildings, highways, railways,

A. Vermicompost Preparation from goat manure

B. Vermicompost preparation from mushroom straw residue

C. Farmers harvesting vermicompost

D. Harvesting of vermicompost Farmers

FIGURE 15.12 (a) Vermicompost preparation from goat manure. (b) Vermicompost preparation from mushroom straw residue. (c) Farmers harvesting vermicompost. (d) Harvesting of vermicompost farmers.

etc. In fields, use of heavy machinery like tractors and the tillering machine also helps increase compaction levels.

A study was conducted at the College of Horticulture, Thenzawl, Mizoram, in 2020–2021. The average annual temperature was 25°C, with little monthly variation. The annual average precipitation was 3,200 mm, with a dry season from December to April (monthly average rainfall of 68 mm) and a rainy season from July to September. The objective of this study was to evaluate the compaction indicator plant by growing radish in Mizoram conditions.

Due to the formation of a hard pan or impervious layer in the sub-soil, the radish moved anti-geotropically, a scan be observed from the plate number. The possible solutions to overcome these constraints are the application of vermicompost, FYM, cowdung, poultry manure, pig manure, and goat manure for Mizoram conditions under natural farming. Application of a disc plough to break the hard pan of the sub-soil is not suitable for Mizoram since it is a sloppy region (Figure 15.13).

15.9 CONCLUSION

There is a lot of potential thrust for natural farming in the hilly region, especially in Mizoram, NE India. As Mizoram is the biodiversity hub of NE India, the use of chemical fertilizer and pesticides leads to environmental degradation. It is evident that mizo-farmers, in particular, have anapathy towards using inorganic inputs. So, these regions are highly effective for the adoption of natural farming among the farming communities. In Mizoram, there is also an added advantage that, besides producing vegetables in their own homestead gardens, each and every household rears livestock. The livestock (pigs, poultry, cattle, and goats) produce a lot of organic manure, which can be easily utilized for agriculture under natural farming. As Mizoram receives ~3,500 mm of rainfall annually, profuse vegetative growth of shrubs, herbs, and weeds leads to the organic production of compost. This can also be used for mulching materials. Organic manure can also help reduce the

FIGURE 15.13 Sub-soil compaction creates upward movement of radish (anti-geotropism) in Mizoram.

sub-soil compaction problem. So, there is an urgent need to adopt natural farming over Mizoram. As we know, sugarcane, cowpea, and paddy are grown in Mizoram, so it is very easy to adopt those crops following natural farming. Organic maize and honey cultivation have become common day by day in Mizoram. Application of vermicompost in vegetable crops encouraged the Mizofarmers for agriculture.

REFERENCES

Chaudhary, K. P., Prasad, A. and Ram, D. 2013. Organic farming practices by farmers of Mizoram. *Agriways* **1**(1):12–14.

Chiapperini, G. and Donnelly, J. R. 1978. Growth of sugar maple seedlings in compacted soil. Fifth North American Forest Biology Workshop. pp. 196–200.

Craul, P. 1992. *Urban Soil Landscape Design*. John Wiley and Sons, New York, NY.

Parmar, B., Vishwakarma, A. K., Pathak, K. A. and Singson, L. 2018. Organic farming in Mizoram – a prospective review. *International Journal of Current Microbiology and Applied Sciences* **7**(1):3049–3055.

Patterson, J. 1977. Soil compaction – effects on urban vegetation. *Journal of Arboriculture* **3**:161–167.

Singh, R., Babu, S., Avasthe, R. K., Das, A., Praharaj, C. S., Layek, J., Kumar, A., Rathore, S. S., Kancheti, M., Kumar, S., Yadav, S. K. and Pashte, V. 2021. Organic farming in North-East India: status and strategies. *Indian Journal of Agronomy* **66**(5):163–179.

Waring, R. H., and Schlesinger, W. H. 1985. *Forest Ecosystems: Concepts and Management*. Academic Press, Inc., Orlando, FL.

Yadav, G. S., Babu, S., Das, A., Mohapatra, K. P., Singh, R., Avasthe, R. K. and Roy, S. 2020. No-till and mulching enhance energy use efficiency and reduce carbon footprint of a direct-seeded upland rice production system. *Journal of Cleaner Production* **271**: 122700. https://doi.org/10.1016/j.jclepro.2020.122700

16 Reviewing Regenerative Agriculture through an Economic Lens

Anwesha Dey, Shiwani Bhadwal, Sonali Katoch, H. P. Singh, and Rakesh Singh

16.1 BACKGROUND

In this twenty-first century, the biggest challenge is of providing food to an estimated 9–11 billion people by 2050 (Fróna et al., 2019; Grelet et al., 2021), as well as reducing the environmental footprint of agriculture. The growing food demands are anticipated as a consequence of the increasing population (Bodirsky et al., 2015; Newton et al., 2020). The global food production system currently emits 25% of the total annual anthropogenic greenhouse gases (Schreefel et al., 2022). Agriculture is responsible for 80% of total global deforestation; each year, 1.2 billion tonnes of food worth $370 million get wasted on farms, which produce 2.2 giga tonnes of carbon dioxide, which is approximately 4% of total anthropogenic greenhouse gas emissions (WWF-UK, 2021). Agriculture is identified as the primary driver for accelerating biodiversity losses, such as putting 24,000 species (nearly 86%) at risk of extinction (Benton et al., 2021). Modern agriculture is dominated by high-intensity industrial agricultural practices (Gliessman, 2016), with heavy dependence on fossil fuels, chemical inputs, subsidies and highly mechanized conventional practices such as tillage (Foley et al., 2011). Currently, one-third of the world's soils fall under the degraded soils category (Montanarella et al., 2015; Wilson et al., 2022), losing the productive top soil almost by one inch per decade (Montgomery, 2012). The world economy has already suffered a huge loss of about 18–20 trillion USD annually due to land degradation (Albaladejo et al., 2021) and is threatened to lose nearly half of the global GDP (44 trillion USD) (Mohan, 2022). According to the United Nations, in the next 50–60 years, there will be no soil left for agriculture purposes due to declining organic content (Vasudev, 2022). There is an urgent need to view modern agriculture through the prism of transformation and build a regenerative agro-ecosystem through sustainable intensification to meet the gap between the amount of food required to feed and the amount of food currently produced (Suparak Gibson, 2022).

16.2 INTRODUCTION

Of the total habitable land on this planet, 49% is occupied by agriculture (51 million sq.km) (Ritchie, 2019). To reduce the soil degradation losses resulting from the current intensive agriculture system, an alternate food-producing system with a higher net positive environmental and social impact, such as regenerative agriculture, is needed (Rhodes, 2017). Regenerative agriculture is a dynamic and holistic approach comprising farmland management practices to rejuvenate soil health, improve agro-ecosystems, combat climate change, support biodiversity and recapture carbon (Milinchuk, 2020; Singh, 2022), along with improvements in farm profitability (Bennett, 2021). In simple terms, regenerative agriculture grows food the way nature does. Regenerative agriculture is a possible solution to regenerate our four billion acres of cultivated farmland, eight billion acres of pasture land and ten billion acres of forest land so we can feed the future global population, reduce biodiversity

DOI: 10.1201/9781003309581-19

271

loss and control global farming below 20°C (Diwan et al., 2021). The main pillars of regenerative agriculture are to minimize soil disturbance, maximize crop diversity, keep the soil covered, maintain living root systems year-round and integrate livestock (CBF, 2022). Regenerative agriculture is a movement to revive our indigenous approach to farming in order to restore ecosystems, combat climate change and spark economic development by bringing producer and consumer on the same plate. In the future, to abate the financial risk arising due to altered agriculture systems resulting from the cultivation of crops in extreme temperatures, regenerative agriculture has the potential to bridge the gap between natural and industrial agriculture (Schrama et al., 2018).

16.3   WHY WE NEED REGENERATIVE AGRICULTURE

Regenerative agriculture is an effective way to enhance soil quality and productivity by continuously trapping carbon beneath it, helping the farmers enhance their livelihood by raising the resistance of their farm's soil against the ongoing environmental disruptions, and offering several benefits, some of which are well represented in Figure 16.1. At present, regenerative agriculture is gaining quite a bit of popularity, yet the term has no official definition or one that is widely accepted in common usage (Newton et al., 2020).

16.4   GLOBAL SCENARIO

Currently, the global market for regenerative agriculture is USD 7.4 billion in year 2022 and is projected to grow at an annual rate of 14.4% and become a USD 23.84 billion market by 2030; it is anticipated that North America will play a crucial role in dominating the global market during this period, followed by Europe and Asia (Research and Markets, 2022). The economic impact of regenerative agriculture has been assessed at different farm levels across the globe, but significant macro evidence of the same is lacking. Following an extensive review, various scenarios were assembled to provide an insightful review of the work done on this aspect of regenerative agriculture. There has been no critical evaluation of the studies because there is very little validity in extrapolating

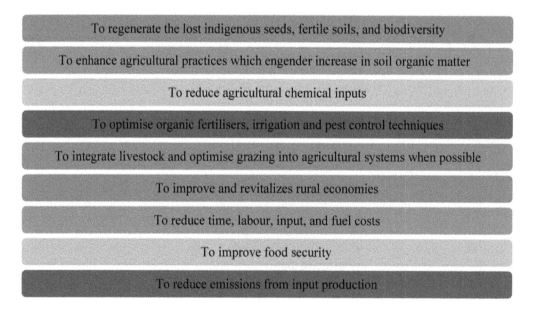

FIGURE 16.1 Benefits of regenerative agriculture.

economic results from these studies. The ill effect of climate change on biodiversity and natural resources is ultimately going to affect farm incomes, leading to a low capacity for farmers to invest in various environmental projects (McRobert et al., 2020). As a regenerative agriculture system is both cost-effective and environmentally sustainable, it can be used to conserve resources and combat climate change in order to meet future needs. Table 16.1 represents a conclusive view of various regenerative measures adopted in various countries and their impact.

16.5   INDIAN SCENARIO

Agriculture in India provides a livelihood to two-thirds of its population (Nkonya et al., 2016). 96.4 million hectares (29.3%) of the total country's geographical area are degraded, raising the issues of food and nutritional security, water scarcity, poverty and social insecurity, migration and rapid climate change (Mohan, 2022). The country is the seventh most vulnerable nation to harsh climatic fluctuations (Eckstein et al., 2020). In 2014–2015, India is estimated to lose 2.5% of its economic output due to land degradation (Inani and Jazeera, 2019). In such a situation, rebuilding the ecosystem is necessary in addition to adjusting to the threats. In this light, India has pledged to be a neutral land degraded nation by 2030 by restoring 26 million hectares of degraded land (Economic Diplomacy Division, 2022). Policymakers and organizations in the United States, Brazil and India are already seeking innovations that would assure sustainable food supplies (Michail, 2019; Tripathi, 2018). They intend to use regeneration techniques on millions of acres (General Mills, 2021). To combat land degradation and restore 26 million hectares of degraded land by 2030, India is all scaled up to establish the center of excellence in the nation. The restoration of land will start a virtuous cycle of good soil health, better productivity, food security and improved livelihoods. Several Indian states are prominently practicing regenerative/nature-based farming to reverse the damage to land caused by mankind (Figure 16.2).

16.6   SOME INITIATIVES BY INDIA TO PROMOTE REGENERATIVE/NATURE-BASED FARMING

- India's proposal to the United Nations for declaring 2023 as the International Year of Millets mainstreams the idea of diversifying the current agriculture system. Millets have high efficiency in absorbing and utilizing carbon dioxide. They provide food/livelihood security to millions of households, contributing to the economic efficiency of the country. Millets stand as the best integrated cropping system for sustainable farming. According to ICAR-IIMR Millets for Health, millets are themselves insurances in climate change scenarios.
- Bharatiya Prakritik Krishi Paddhati Programme (BPKP), under the centrally sponsored scheme - Paramparagat Krishi Vikas Yojana (PKVY), is aimed at promoting traditional indigenous practices that reduce externally purchased inputs. It is largely based on on-farm biomass recycling, with a major emphasis on biomass mulching, the use of on-farm cow dung-urine formulations, periodic soil aeration and the exclusion of all synthetic chemical inputs.
- Promotion of organic farming under the dedicated scheme of Paramparagat Krishi Vikas Yojana (PKVY), which encourages all kinds of chemical-free farming systems, including Zero Budget Natural Farming.
- Establishment of centers to develop scientific approaches to combat land degradation and restore millions of hectares land through nature-based solutions such as conservation of forests, practicing organic agriculture, utilizing land as per land use delineation and conservation of water bodies by 2030.

TABLE 16.1

Case Studies of Regenerative Agriculture

Country	Study Area	Parameters	Major Findings	References
Australia	Canberra	Comparison of 16 regenerative agriculture sheep farm finances to industry benchmark data (conventional agriculture). Earnings before interest and tax per dry sheep equivalent (EBIT/DSE) were used for comparison.	i. 60% of regenerative agriculture (RA) farmers earned moderate to higher profit in comparison to 32% conventional agriculture farmers. ii. Financial stress was claimed by 21% of regenerative agriculture farmers against 14% of conventional agriculture farmers.	Ogilvy et al. (2018)
	Marra region of New South Wales (Salisbury case study)	Rearing of self-replacing merino flocks (5,000 ewes and 2,500 ewe lambs each year)	i. Of the total income earned 58% was from livestock and rest 42% was from sale of wool. ii. The sheep gross margin per hectare per 100 mm rainfall was higher than the average from 2009 to 2017. iii. Higher farm business profit was maintained above average level during the low rainfall period from 2011 to 2015.	Bennett (2021)
	Grampians(Collingwood case study)	Black Angus cattle was reared	i. A 36% increase in average annual profits in 2019 was observed as compared to 1996. ii. Significant reduction in cost of inputs.	
	Mungallala, Queensland (Glenelg case study)	Rearing of around 4,100 sheep, 180 breeding cattle and 60–100 feral goats	i. Most significant RA practice on this farm was conservative stocking, which ensured steady income even during poorer rainfall years. ii. Higher profits than Meat and Livestock Australia (MLA) industry benchmarks (average New South Wales farm)	

(Continued)

TABLE 16.1 (*Continued*)
Case Studies of Regenerative Agriculture

Country	Study Area	Parameters	Major Findings	References
United States of America		Comparative study of regenerative agriculture and conventional agriculture	i. The economic advantages of RA are most noticeable on smallholder farms where higher yields and less labour is required for preparing the land and weeding (9 and 19 d/ha, respectively). ii. A greater RA return to labour compared with CONVA suggested that it can be an efficient low-input farming approach that requires less energy and reduces waste while sustaining productivity and perhaps increasing profitability within a semi-closed system.	Al-Kaisi and Lal (2020)
	Northern Plains of the United States	Relative effects of regenerative and conventional corn production systems on soil conservation, farmer profitability and productivity	i. The regenerative systems achieved 70% higher profit than conventional cornfields. ii. The variation in profitability in both the systems was attributed to: a. high seed and fertilizer costs that conventional farms incurred (32% of the gross income spent on these inputs on conventional fields, whereas only 12% in regenerative fields), b. higher revenue obtained from grain and other products produced (e.g., meat production) on the regenerative corn fields.	LaCanne and Lundgren (2018)
	South Dakota (US)	32 RA farmers were surveyed	i. 67% of the sample farmers reported RA to be more profitable than CvnA farming. ii. Major reasons reported were: a. lower input costs, b. improved market prices for RA output, c. lower production and price risk.	Taylor and Dobbs (1988)
Africa	Sub-Saharan Africa	Forecasting of outcomes of adopting RA up to 50% by 2040	i. Increase in yields by 13% in 2040 and this could be as high as 40% in the future. ii. Creation of as many as five million new full time jobs by 2040 in farming, processing and allied industries. iii. Projected to increase food security through reduction of prices and easy accessibility of increased caloric intake. iv. Addition of gross value of 70 billion USD across Sub-Saharan Africa.	Africa Regenerative Agriculture Study Group (2021)

Benchmarks are useful when comparing regenerative agriculture to conventional agriculture. The usefulness of the benchmark as a comparison will depend on the scope of the benchmark and how closely it corresponds to the case study farm.

FIGURE 16.2   Indian states practicing nature-based farming (NITI Aayog).

16.7   WAYS FORWARD FOR PROMOTION

1. Spreading awareness to farmers through training programs on regenerative agriculture
2. Educating the future generation about the traditional ways of farming
3. Providing incentives for practicing nature-based farming
4. Encouraging the development of local food systems
5. Investing in research and development to enhance the adoption
6. Improvising and sustaining the local food value chains

16.8   CONCLUSION

Regenerative agriculture has come under more attention as global stakeholders step up their efforts to achieve sustainable development goals. The profitability of regenerative agriculture compared with conventional agriculture is not only limited to cost but has many dimensions, such as improved soil fertility, sustainable productivity and the well-being of farmers. As agriculture stakeholders, we should use our expertise in indigenous agriculture knowledge and skills practiced by our forefathers since ages and redefine regenerative agriculture for ourselves by sharing our local practices with the world (local to global), thus promoting sustainable production. Global markets without regulations and environmental externalities have the potential to overshadow the positive effects of regenerative agriculture. The old-age farming practices are imperative to regenerate the soil and maintain a healthy ecosystem. It is our collective duty to reverse the damages done to date in order to provide food and natural resources to our future generation. Also, there is a need for regression research as most of the economic findings are based on small samples, case studies, or models. Thus, it restrains the extrapolation of the information available to represent regenerative agriculture performance more generally.

REFERENCES

Africa Regenerative Agriculture Study Group (2021). Regenerative agriculture: an opportunity for businesses and society to restore degraded land in Africa. 62pp.

Albaladejo, J., Díaz-Pereira, E., & de Vente, J. (2021). Eco-holistic soil conservation to support land degradation neutrality and the sustainable development goals. *CATENA*, *196*, 104823.

Al-Kaisi, M. M., & Lal, R. (2020). Aligning science and policy of regenerative agriculture. *Soil Science Society of American Journal*, *84*(6), 1808–1820.

Bennett, A. (2021). A review of the economics of regenerative agriculture in Western Australia. Department of Primary Industries and Regional Development, Western Australian Government.

Benton, T. G., Bieg, C., Harwatt, H., Pudasaini, R., & Wellesley, L. (2021). Food system impacts on biodiversity loss. Three levers for food system transformation in support of nature. Chatham House, London. https://www.ciwf.com/media/7443948/food-system-impacts-on-biodiversity-loss-feb-2021.pdf

Bodirsky, B. L., Rolinski, S., Biewald, A., Weindl, I., Popp, A., & Lotze-Campen, H. (2015). Global food demand scenarios for the 21st century. *PloS One*, *10*(11), e0139201.

CBF (2022). Regenerative agriculture. https://www.cbf.org/issues/agriculture/regenerative-agriculture.html

Diwan, A. D., Harke, S. N., Pande, B. N., & Panche, A. (2021). Regenerative agriculture farming. *Indian Farming*, *71*(12), 3–8.

Eckstein, D., Künzel, V., Schäfer, L., & Winges, M. (2020). Global Climate Risk Index 2020. Germanwatch.

Economic Diplomacy Division, 2022. https://indbiz.gov.in/

Foley, J. A., Ramankutty, N., Brauman, K. A., Cassidy, E. S., Gerber, J. S., Johnston, M., ... Zaks, D. P. (2011). Solutions for a cultivated planet. *Nature*, *478*(7369), 337–342. https://doi.org/10.1038/nature10452

Fróna, D., Szenderák, J., & Harangi-Rákos, M. (2019). The challenge of feeding the world. *Sustainability*, *11*(20), 5816.

Gliessman, S. (2016). Transforming food systems with agroecology. *Agroecology and Sustainable Food Systems*, *40*(3), 187–189.

Grelet, G., Lang, S., Merfield, C., Calhoun, N., Robson-Williams, M., Horrocks, A., ... Kerner, W. (2021). Regenerative agriculture in Aotearoa New Zealand – research pathways to build science-based evidence and national narratives. White paper prepared for Our Land and Water National Science Challenge and the NEXT Foundation. p59. Manaaki Whenua Landcare Research, Lincoln, New Zealand. https://www.landcareresearch.co.nz/publications/regenag/regenerative-agriculture-white-paper-sets-out-pressing-research-priorities/

Inani, R., & Jazeera, A. L. (2019). As Land Degrades, India Struggles to Save Its Farms. https://www.scientificamerican.com/article/as-land-degrades-india-struggles-to-save-its-farms/

LaCanne, C. E., & Lundgren, J. G. (2018). Regenerative agriculture: merging farming and natural resource conservation profitably. *PeerJ*, *6*, e4428. doi: 10.7717/peerj.4428

McRobert, K., Fox, T., Heath, R., Dempster, F., & Goucher, G. (2020). Recognising on-farm biodiversity management. Research report. Australian Farm Institute, New South Wales.

Michail, N. (2019). Large scale regenerative agriculture is possible and profitable, Rizoma. Available at: https://www.foodnavigator-latam.com/Article/2019/04/08/Regenerative-agriculture-on-large-scale-is-profitable-in-Brazil

Milinchuk, A. (2020, January 30). Is regenerative agriculture profitable? Forbes. https://www.forbes.com/sites/forbesfinancecouncil/2020/01/30/is-regenerative-agriculture-profitable

Mohan, V. (2022, December 05). Over-exploitation over centuries has degraded 96m hectares of India's land. The Times of India. https://timesofindia.indiatimes.com/india/over-exploitation-over-centuries-has-degraded-96m-hectares-of-indias-land/

Montanarella, L., Badraoui, M., Chude, V., Baptista Costa, I. D. S., Mamo, T., Yemefack, M., & McKenzie, N. (2015). Status of the world's soil resources. Main report. Food and Agriculture Organization of the United Nations [FAO], Rome, Italy.

Montgomery, D. C. (2012). *Design and Analysis of Experiments*. 8th Edition, John Wiley & Sons, New York.

Newton, P., Civita, N., Frankel-Goldwater, L., Bartel, K., & Johns, C. (2020). What is regenerative agriculture? A review of scholar and practitioner definitions based on processes and outcomes. *Frontiers in Sustainable Food Systems*, *4*, 1–11. https://dx.doi.org/10.3389/fsufs.2020.577723

Nkonya, E., Mirzabaev, A., & Von Braun, J. (2016). *Economics of Land Degradation and Improvement – A Global Assessment for Sustainable Development*. 686pp. Springer Nature, Springer Cham.

Ogilvy, S., Gardner, M., Mallawaarachichi, T., Schirmer, J., Brown, K., & Heagney, E. (2018). Report: Graziers with better profitability, biodiversity and wellbeing. Canberra, Australia, p. 89.

Research and Markets (2022, June). Regenerative agriculture market share, size, trends, industry analysis report, by practice, by application, by region, segment forecast, 2022–2030. https://www.researchand-markets.com/reports/5626410/regenerative-agriculture-market-sharesize

Rhodes, C. J. (2017). The imperative for regenerative agriculture. *Science Progress*, *100*(1), 80–129. https://doi.org/10.3184/003685017X14876775256165

Ritchie, H. (2019, November 11). Half of the world's habitable land is used for agriculture. Our World in Data. https://ourworldindata.org/global-land-for-agriculture

Schrama, M., De Haan, J. J., Kroonen, M., Verstegen, H., & Van der Putten, W. H. (2018). Crop yield gap and stability in organic and conventional farming systems. *Agriculture, Ecosystems & Environment*, *256*, 123–130.

Schreefel, L., de Boer, I. J. M., Timler, C. J., Groot, J. C. J., Zwetsloot, M. J., Creamer, R. E., Schrijver, A. P., van Zanten, H. H. E., & Schulte, R. P. O. (2022). How to make regenerative practices work on the farm: a modelling framework. *Agricultural Systems*, *198*, 103371.

Singh, A. K. (2022, December 02). Here is why world needs regenerative agriculture. *Down to Earth*. https://www.downtoearth.org.in/blog/agriculture/here-is-why-the-world-needs-regenerative-agriculture

Suparak Gibson, A. (2022). The underground economy: regenerative farming's hidden economic, ecological, and social value. Master's Thesis, Harvard University Division of Continuing Education.

Taylor, D. C., & Dobbs, T. L. (1988). South Dakota's sustainable agriculture farmers. Economics Commentator, Paper 260. South Dakota State University.

Tripathi, S. (2018). Investing in regenerative agriculture and food. Available at: https://www.ceew.in/sites/default/files/CEEW_ZBNF_Issue_Brief_2nd_Edition_19Sep18.pdf

Vasudev, S. J. (2022, July 21). Incentivize world's farmers to improve soil health. Mint. https://www.livemint.com/opinion/online-views/incentivize-the-world-s-farmers-to-improve-soil-health-11658421618297.html

Wilson, K. R., Myers, R. L., Hendrickson, M. K., & Heaton, E. A. (2022). Different stakeholders' conceptualizations and perspectives of regenerative agriculture reveals more consensus than discord. *Sustainability*, *14*(22), 15261.

WWF-UK (2021). Driven to waste: the global impact of food loss and waste on farms.

Index

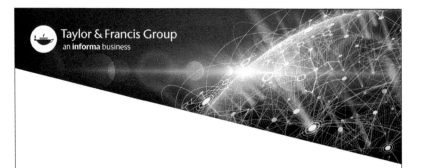

Taylor & Francis eBooks

www.taylorfrancis.com

A single destination for eBooks from Taylor & Francis
with increased functionality and an improved user
experience to meet the needs of our customers.

90,000+ eBooks of award-winning academic content in
Humanities, Social Science, Science, Technology, Engineering,
and Medical written by a global network of editors and authors.

TAYLOR & FRANCIS EBOOKS OFFERS:

A streamlined
experience for
our library
customers

A single point
of discovery
for all of our
eBook content

Improved
search and
discovery of
content at both
book and
chapter level

REQUEST A FREE TRIAL
support@taylorfrancis.com